PEASANTS AND LANDLORDS
IN LATER MEDIEVAL ENGLAND

An allegorical view of women harvesting, from Der Jungfrauenspiegel; *the top panel shows the exalted state of widowhood; the centre panel shows the married woman; and the bottom panel shows the lowly state of maidenhood (Rheinisches Landesmuseum, Bonn: no. 15326)*

PEASANTS
AND LANDLORDS
IN LATER
MEDIEVAL
ENGLAND
C. 1380–C. 1525

E.B. FRYDE

ALAN SUTTON PUBLISHING · STROUD

ST. MARTIN'S PRESS · NEW YORK

First published in the United Kingdom in 1996
Alan Sutton Publishing Limited
Phoenix Mill, Far Thrupp, Stroud, Gloucestershire

First published in the United States of America in 1996
St. Martin's Press · Scholarly and Reference Division
175 Fifth Avenue · New York · N.Y. 10010

Copyright © E.B. Fryde, 1996

All rights reserved. No part of this publication may be reproduced, stored in a retrieval system, or transmitted, in any form, or by any means, electronic, mechanical, photocopying, recording or otherwise, without the prior permission of the publishers and copyright holder.

British Library Cataloguing-in-Publication Data

Fryde, E. B.
  Peasants and Landlords in Later Medieval England
  I. Title
  305.50942

ISBN 0-86299-866-2 ✓

WITHDRAWN

Class 942.03 FRY

Typeset in 10/13pt Bembo.
Typesetting and origination by
Alan Sutton Publishing Limited.
Printed in Great Britain by
Butler & Tanner, Frome, Somerset.

CONTENTS

LIST OF ILLUSTRATIONS

PREFACE

This is a book about the relationships between English landowners and their peasants in the late Middle Ages. Because of the limitations of our evidence much more is known about landlords than about peasants, and about a minority of richer peasants than about the great mass of small landholders and landless men. Only much further research in unpublished records could alter this somewhat, but I have been able to use only a few collections of unpublished sources and I have had to rely chiefly on what is already in print. I have not tried to discuss farming practices, though some of my illustrations give glimpses of them. Nor have I discussed the life of peasant communities. This is not a history of English agriculture or of peasant societies, but only a set of explorations into the present state of knowledge about some problems facing the historians of the English countryside.

I have received an immense amount of help over many years from a large number of friends, too many to enumerate them here adequately. The late Professor V.H. Galbraith and the late Professor Edouard Perroy particularly encouraged me to write about this subject. Dr Edward Miller and Dr Clive Knowles gave me opportunities to publish earlier studies of some of its aspects. In recent years Professor Maldwyn Mills gave me much help with literary evidence. Elin Fitzpatrick designed the map of the south-western Midlands. Professor Colin Richmond and Dr Isobel Harvey provided me with valuable materials and they have scrutinized critically parts of this book, though I alone bear responsibility for its shortcomings.

CHAPTER 1

INTRODUCTION

I

This book has originated out of a chapter contributed by me to volume III of *The Agrarian History of England and Wales, 1348–1500* (ed. E. Miller, Cambridge, 1991). I completed writing it in 1976 and a more up-to-date version of some of its contents is obviously overdue. Its subject was 'Peasant rebellion and peasant discontents'.[1] While I do not intend to provide a fresh account of the various popular risings, another look is needed at some of their causes and consequences. That applies particularly to the Great Revolt of 1381.

There still survives an immense amount of unpublished and unused materials from which the medieval English countryside can be studied. Every time one looks at some fresh series of unpublished records there are unsuspected surprises. There was also a very great diversity not only between different regions but within the same districts. My study can only be a very provisional report, summarizing some of the information that can be reconstructed at present.

I am not prefacing this book by an extensive general survey of all the more important changes in the rural society and economy in the period studied here. In the introduction to that volume III, its editor, Dr Edward Miller, has provided just such a survey.[2] It is a wise summary of the present state of our knowledge, very well-balanced, as well as very lucid, and eminently readable. Anything similar that I could have written would have largely repeated what he has said.

However, some of the most important developments must be outlined. The arrival of the first epidemic of plague in 1348/9 was a decisive turning-point in the history of England during the last two centuries of the Middle Ages. That first epidemic was the most devastating of a series of outbreaks that followed at intervals during the second half of the fourteenth century and recurrently in the fifteenth century. Perpetual centres of infection appear to have become established, especially in London and some other towns. The same was true of western Europe in general and recurrent re-infection from that region is probable. There were also epidemics of other diseases, though the shrunken population suffered much less from famines (the worst in 1370 and 1438/9).

The more prosperous parts of England seem to have been overpopulated in 1348. I shall return to this when discussing some tentative demographic statistics. It is probably the main explanation for the puzzling situation that down to the 1370s there was no substantial breakdown in the functioning of the earlier system of large manorial estates, consisting of demesnes exploited directly by the owners of these properties through extensive use of the labour of their tenants, many of whom were legally their serfs. Prices for foodstuffs remained high in the 1350s and 1360s, so that Dr Miller can speak of 'something like an Indian summer of demesne farming'.[3] For this reason I have chosen to start my detailed studies mostly with the Great Revolt of 1381 and its aftermath, rather than in 1348.

The one major departure from this chonological framework is to be found in chapter 2 and the first part of chapter 3. In chapter 2 I will trace the evolution of the Common Law of serfdom from the late twelfth century onwards, as my account of what happened in the last quarter of the fourteenth century would be scarcely intelligible without such an introduction. The first part of chapter 3 charts the increasing friction between landlords and their peasants and the causes of it in the three decades between the Black Death of 1348/9 and the revolts of 1381. Chapter 4 likewise partly antedates the main limits of this book. As the evidence from the estates of the Bishops of Worcester constitutes one of my major sources, it is essential to review the conditions on the principal Worcester manors between 1348 and *c.* 1380 as an introduction to their later history.

The last thirty years of the fourteenth century appear to have been a period of further continuous decline in population. Prices of foodstuffs started on a fairly permanent lower trend in the 1390s, though there were inevitably some fluctuations.[4] This is, probably, one of the chief reasons why most landlords gave up direct management of the bulk of their demesnes between *c.* 1390 and *c.* 1420. The agrarian depression continued fairly uninterruptedly down to the last decades of the fifteenth century, with the most marked slump in the 1450s and the 1460s. This long-term trend is 'virtually incapable of explanation' without recourse to continuing population decline.[5] In the third quarter of the fifteenth century it may have been 'reduced to a level barely if at all higher than that of Domesday England' in 1085.[6]

People in a reasonably good state of health can survive plague in its normal, bubonic form and can acquire a good, though not complete, measure of immunity from subsequent infection.[7] The second plague epidemic of 1361 was remembered as 'the mortality of children', as a large proportion of victims were children born since the first Black Death of 1348/9 and lacking such immunity. 'A like description may have applied to that of 1369 and perhaps to some later outbreaks' (the next in 1375).[8] This pattern of mortality, added to the immense normal death rate of medieval infants, was an exceptional menace to replacement rates of the English population and may help to explain the declining trend which lasted over a century.

The average mortality from the first plague of 1348/9 can be reasonably estimated at between 30 per cent and 45 per cent of the population of the afflicted localities.[9] The one important and uncertain factor is the incidence of the pulmonary variety, which unlike the bubonic form, is extremely contagious from person to person and which, until the advent of modern antibiotics, hardly anybody has ever survived. After the first plague, the inhabitants of England and Wales may have amounted to not more than half the population of *c.* 1300, when it reached its medieval peak. Contemporaries were overwhelmed by a sense of an immense decline. In the parliament of 1376 the Commons asserted that 'there is not a third part of the people or of other things that there used to be'.[10] The only overall statistic from the second half of the fourteenth century that deserves serious attention arises out of the first Poll Tax of 1377. Unlike the third Poll Tax of 1380/1, which provoked the Great Revolt, this first experiment in universal taxation was levied at a very moderate rate of 4*d* per person. Probably there was, therefore, much less evasion than in 1381, though some concealment of taxpayers may have occurred. The largest element of uncertainty surrounding it arises out of the stipulation that children below fourteen were exempted. We have no means of judging the size of this group, especially as there had been recent epidemics of plague in 1369 and 1375 as well as a serious famine in 1370. In 1377 the total of assessed lay taxpayers amounted to 1,355,201 persons in England (not including the clergy, destitute beggars and inhabitants of the palatinates of Durham and Chester).[11] That could mean that the total English population may have amounted to at least 2.5 million. The comparable figures for the middle of the fifteenth century may have ranged between 2 and 2.5

million and perhaps between 2.5 and 2.75 million around 1520. Those tentative figures of Edward Miller are higher than the conjectures of Julian Cornwall in 1970. Dr Miller does mention them and they are worth citing, as Cornwall's methods are cautious and sensible. For 1377 he suggested around 2 million, for *c.* 1430 as little as 2.1 million and for 1522–5 (using military musters and subsidy assessments) around 2.3 million.[12]

II

This book consists of a selection of studies where I can offer much fresh evidence (such as in chapter 6 on the wool of the Cotswolds) or can look at problems in a way personal to me. Much of the existing literature seems unduly optimistic about the improvements in the condition of the peasantry in the period between *c.* 1380 and 1500. One can ignore extreme attempts, like A.R. Bridbury's writings,[13] to prove that in the late Middle Ages England experienced widespread economic growth. However, various features of this period can create an impression of it being a better time for the bulk of the peasantry than any previous period of the Middle Ages. I shall be enumerating some of these features. But if one scrutinizes each of them critically, the picture of substantial betterment of the peasants' lot partly fades away, though not entirely. Landlords were generally abandoning the direct exploitation of their estates, handing them over as leases to farmers drawn predominantly from the ranks of the peasantry. This was happening because prices of agricultural products were low and costs of large-scale farming threatened to eat up much of the income. But the same slump in the profits of farming was also affecting the lesser producers, though admittedly their costs were lower. Dr Miller wisely warns that 'it is going much too far to regard that period as a "golden age" for the peasant farmer, for the balance between coping and failing to cope in the changing circumstances was inevitably a fine one'.[14]

Enough has already been said about the shrinking population and its continuing decline until, perhaps, the 1470s.[15] The high death rate made it easier for the survivors to get enough food and Dr Miller is right to remark that 'for many it may have seemed enough that they had more to eat for more of the time than had always been the case in times past',[16] but even that was far from assured. Poor harvests were always to be dreaded. Besides, an age which relies on the maintenance of higher living standards than was normal previously because of excessive high death rates from plague and other epidemics 'is somewhat less than golden, with a large number of its members dying at an early age and suffering the frequent losses of spouses, children, relatives, friends and colleagues'.[17] Wages of labourers were high and the low cost of basic foodstuffs raised the real wages to a level not attained again until the late nineteenth century.[18] But the high level of wages deterred employers from using more labour than they absolutely needed and landless men or smallholders, who depended on wages for all or much of their sustenance, may have often suffered from chronic under-employment. This, as much as good prospects of work away from their homes, may account for the unwonted mobility of labourers during this period.

Dr Barbara Harvey has rightly stressed that the peasantry could have never felt any 'goodwill' towards their landlords, and P.R. Hyams has reminded us that 'peasant discontent was endemic'.[19] In the late fourteenth and the fifteenth centuries the sense of 'relative deprivation',[20] always experienced by the medieval peasantry, found more active outlets, as they could bargain with their landlords on somewhat less uneven terms. Rents that landowners could effectively exact were falling, because empty cultivable land was more abundant than ever before and landlords were forced to forgo some income in order to retain tenants.[21] Because many landlords were now anxious to pay some attention to the demands of their tenantry, the servile part of the peasantry could now effectively question some of their more glaring disabilities.[22] 'Servile tenure' largely disappeared. But there is a danger of exaggerating the extent to which the disabilities of peasant tenants (and not just serfs 'by blood') ceased to affect their lives. Thorold Rogers was showing curious blindness to the testimony of the manorial court rolls from every part of England when he wrote that 'by the fifteenth century villeinage was only a legal fiction'.[23] I shall have much to say about the abundance of evidence disproving this. In this introduction I want only to touch upon the distressing consequences of the lords' exaction of 'heriots', the right to demand the surrender of the best beast by the heir, widow or other relatives of a deceased tenant in order to secure the reversion of his tenement. The range of people liable to this went beyond the servile tenantry, but only they were without any legal remedies if they failed to deliver the required heriots. For the poorer peasants (and the vast majority continued to be poor, or very poor) heriots represented a distressing burden. Thus, on 28 April 1483, at Henbury Saltmarsh, an estate of the Bishop of Worcester near Bristol, Helen Ludlow claimed half a messuage and half a virgate of her deceased husband. She had to give as heriot one cow, worth 10s. However, by the next court, held on 27 July, she had given up this tenement and another tenant took it while Helen could retain her cow. The new tenant compounded with 30s both for Helen's heriot and his own fine. He was to make some provision for Helen, including an enclosed pasture, presumably for her cow and any other animals she may have had.[24]

Throughout the fifteenth century enough remnants of serfdom persisted to aggravate endemic peasant discontent. Some of the major lay magnates continued to enforce their rights over their serfs with particular harshness, because they had exceptional power to coerce their dependants.

Some recent students of the desertion during the later Middle Ages of previously inhabited localities have tried to minimize the element of wilful destruction of settlements by their lords. I am particularly critical of the views expressed recently on this subject by Professor Christopher Dyer and one of the studies in this volume is specially devoted to this problem (chapter 12).

Nobody would dispute Professor Dyer's contention that many settlements disappeared after a prolonged period of gradual decline, through a variety of demographic and economic misfortunes.[25] But he tries to fit most disappearances of villages and hamlets into this pattern, disregarding the evidence that some villages were brutally 'murdered' by their owners and that this might happen quite suddenly. It should be noted that deliberate mass evictions of tenants repeatedly took place in the autumn or early winter, after the last harvest had been cleared, and in good time to prepare the conversion to pasture, in utter disregard of the dangers threatening the hapless victims during the most inhospitable part of the year.[26] Professor Dyer chooses to profess that the inquiry of 1517 into depopulating enclosures 'recorded accusations rather than proven cases',[27] though in a number of cases Cardinal Wolsey, who instigated this inquiry, clearly did not share Professor Dyer's scepticism. It is disturbing to find a present-day historian questioning the reality of social evils that seriously worried Sir Thomas More in the preface to his *Utopia* and perturbed hard-headed chiefs of government like Wolsey and Thomas Cromwell.

III

There has been a tendency in the past to minimize the long-term consequences of the Great Revolt of 1381. One of the most forcible protests against this misconception was penned by the late V.H. Galbraith in one of his last publications.[28]

Stacking sheaves (By permission of The British Library: Add. MS. 42130, f.173)

The revolts were precipitated by the wholly ineffective, but excessively costly, war policies of young Richard II's uncles. The Commons in the first parliament of Richard II, in the autumn of 1377, complained that the resistance by servile peasants was impoverishing many landowners, and warned that England might become the scene of troubles comparable to the rebellion of French serfs against their lords (a reference to the *Jacquerie* of 1358).[29] Members of Parliament failed to foresee, however, that this dreaded uprising would be precipitated by the taxes for war that they were themselves piling upon the English people.

The revolts of 1381 put an abrupt stop to all that and proved a turning-point in the war. Parliaments became terrified that further taxes might provoke more risings. For a time they refused to grant any more direct taxes. This happened in the first parliament after the Great Revolt, held in November 1381. The Commons said that they dared not grant a direct tax of any kind. Parliaments of May 1382 and February 1383 likewise refused grants 'in spite of considerable pressure from the lords and the council'. The internal turmoil in France during the early years of the minority of King Charles VI was creating exceptional opportunities for successful English expeditions into France, but parliaments would not provide money for any further warlike adventures. There was a drastic curtailment in the expenditure on the defence of French territories still under English control.[30] The first part of the Hundred Years War effectively came to an end. Its revival by Henry V was due to quite different circumstances. No medieval government ever dared to impose again general poll taxes.

V.H. Galbraith's protest against underestimating the long-term consequences of the revolt of 1381 was concerned with something even more fundamental than the political, military and financial aftermath of the risings. He stressed rightly that English society could never be the same again after the events of May, June and July 1381. Even he did not spell out one of the most astonishing features of this upheaval. The rebels from Essex and Hertfordshire, and possibly also from Kent, secured briefly from Richard II fundamental changes in the laws of England and the social structure that the law bolstered up. The idea that this could be done was breathtaking in its revolutionary boldness and was quite unprecedented. One has to wait until the revolutionary changes after 1640 to find anything comparable.

The rebels from Essex and Hertfordshire procured on 14 June at Mile End royal charters abolishing serfdom. A more complete demand for the abolition of serfdom throughout England seems to have been put forward by Wat Tyler at Smithfield.[31] The draft of a charter which the men of Somerset presented (or were intending to present) as part of a petition to the king stipulated the freeing of the men of that county from all bondage ('*ab omni bondagio*').[32]

When in November 1381, in the first parliament held after the revolt, the king asked the Lords and Commons whether they approved his revocation of the charters granted to the rebels abolishing serfdom, they answered 'with one voice that this repeal was well done', because the enfranchisement of serfs would have abrogated their property rights and could not be valid without their assent. 'And they had never agreed to it . . . nor would they ever do so, even if it were their dying day.'[33]

The men of Essex and Hertfordshire also secured another promise of a fundamental restriction on the laws of property: in future *servile* land[34] (without crops on it) was not to be rented at more than 4*d* an acre. At that date it was not an unreasonable demand in those two counties. Some of the holdings confiscated subsequently from the Essex rebels were valued at precisely this sum.[35]

One other promise exacted from the king at Mile End could have had staggeringly ruinous consequences for all the towns of the kingdom. The king was made to promise that all his subjects should be allowed to sell freely in all cities, boroughs and market-places, and everywhere in the kingdom. The main trading privileges of towns would have been cut out and one of their main sources of income, from tolls, destroyed.

Among Wat Tyler's demands at Smithfield the *Anonimalle Chronicle* mentions his insistence on the abolition of outlawry. After 1349 outlawry had frequently been applied to fugitive labourers and servants who failed to stand trial for violations of the labour legislation of 1349–51. According to Henry Knighton's well-informed chronicle, Tyler also demanded that 'all warrens as well as in fisheries as in parks and woods should be common to all; so that throughout the realm . . . poor as well as rich might take the venison and hunt the hare in the fields'. The achievement of freedom to fish and hunt would have fulfilled one of the most cherished dreams of the English peasantry.[36]

Henceforth the upper classes of English society lived in dread of another general upheaval and saw its coming in every manifestation throughout the 1380s and long beyond them. In Kent, rebellion continued to smoulder through the summer and early autumn of 1381. There were conspiracies of peasants, or rumours of conspiracies, in Norfolk in 1382 and 1384, and in Sussex in 1383. There was an outbreak of risings in Kent and other southern counties in April and May 1388. Fear of a more generalized revolt in Kent appears to have been one of the important reasons for the execution, during the Merciless Parliament, of Sir Simon Burley, deputy king's chamberlain (sentenced to death on 5 May).[37] He was detested in Kent, where he held extensive estates. A chronicler recording a rising in Cheshire early in 1393 remarked that 'men all over England were sure another general insurrection was at hand'.[38]

The extraordinary bid by the rebels of 1381 for the outright abolition of serfdom by the king's order was never forgotten. Henceforth the servile villeins refused with ever increasing persistence to accept the implications of serfdom, and all the burdens that specifically arose out of servile tenure and status met with resistance for that very reason. In this atmosphere of frequent local disorder and of continuous tension between lords and tenants the direct exploitation of domanial estates largely disappeared from England in the fifty years after the Great Revolt. Once that happened villeinage became an oppressive anachronism and it, too, largely faded away, though not entirely. In V.H. Galbraith's words this was one 'astonishing' and 'significant' long-term consequence of 1381 and 'the complicated process by which this happened owed much . . . to that Revolt'.[39] P.R. Hyams, the author of the most important recent book on English serfdom,[40] expressed the same view more cautiously when he remarked 'that 1381 had greater influence on long-term trends in lord–peasant relations than is sometimes allowed'.[41]

One final general comment is needed. The Norman landlords, who took over the estates of their Anglo-Saxon predecessors after 1066, found in England an unusually well-developed economy and a large population of peasants in a state of fairly complete subordination to their lords, much more so than was the case in Normandy.[42] The new feudal nobility, thus introduced into England, increased the numbers of dependent peasants and managed to exploit even more harshly the potential prosperity of its new colony. A second age of agrarian expansion occurred in the late twelfth and over much of the thirteenth centuries. There was a return to direct exploitation of demesnes by landlords, or its intensification where it had already existed previously. The burdens of the servile part of the peasantry were increased still further. When from the late fourteenth century onwards the expansion of the English economy was temporarily checked, and later reversed for nearly a century, that servile part of the peasantry, though allowed to commute the services owed to landlords for increased money rents, found themselves saddled with an excessively heavy burden of payments. This was the legacy of previous ages of agrarian prosperity. The economy of fifteenth-century England could ill sustain that legacy. This helps to explain a wave of peasant resistances that occurred on many estates, manifesting themselves especially through flights of tenants and refusals to pay some of the customary renders, especially the distinctly servile ones. The origins and increase of these troubles will form one of the chief subjects of this book.

CHAPTER 2

Social and Economic Background to the Great Revolt of 1381, I: Serfdom and the Economic Condition of Servile Peasants

I

This chapter is intended as a secondary introduction to some of the most important developments discussed in this book. It has, therefore, to transcend the chronological limits observed in the bulk of this study.

The treatment by the royal courts of a large proportion of the peasantry as servile, thereby denying them the protection of royal justice, except in serious criminal cases, was one of the salient features of the royal Common Law as it emerged in the late twelfth century. Two hundred years later, on the eve of the Great Revolt of 1381, some peasant communities, especially in south-eastern and southern England, could not understand what the origins of the serfdom of their members were. Their puzzlement and their deep sense of injustice enhanced the widespread peasant discontent that was one of the major causes of that rising. It is essential to explain the main features of this economic and legal development. In order to do so, I shall have to go back to the emergence of the Common Law under Henry II and his sons.

Some educated English laymen regarded certain aspects of the law of serfdom as wrongful. Andrew Horn, the Chamberlain of the City of London between 1320 and 1328, was a learned antiquarian and not a practising lawyer. His *Mirror of Justices* is a bizarre book; many of the opinions voiced there seem eccentric. But what he had to say about serfdom is worth pondering. He denies that ordinary villagers ('villeins') should be equated with people of slave origin. He treats as wrongful what had happened after the Norman Conquest, when many 'villeins were driven by tortious distresses to do their lords the service of blood ransom [?liability to "merchet"] and many other arbitrary customs to bring them into servage and the power of their lords'.[1] Later, I shall be citing Geoffrey Chaucer's condemnation of some features of the lords' treatment of their serfs.

As is amply explained in the previous chapter, and discussed further in chapter 3, hostility to serfdom was a very important feature of the rising of 1381 and it continued to underline much of the peasant discontent during the next century. The violent evictions of peasants in the later fifteenth and the sixteenth centuries, on which I commented briefly in my introduction, were made legally possible because their victims were descendants of men who held their holdings by servile tenure. In the eyes of landlords, and the lawyers who advised them, these peasants were tenants 'at the will of the lord'.[2] As the court book of the Abbey of Ramsey put it in 1397, their holdings 'were servile tenements, held in bondage, at the will of the lord for customary services and obligations'.[3] The clerk of Earl Robert of Oxford, who after the rising of 1381 wrote the record of 'the first court . . . after the burning of all the court rolls' at the earl's manor of Wivenhoe in Essex, went on to state that the tenants claimed to hold land 'at their own will for ever, freely, and not at the will of the lord', in 'disinheritance of the lord', as the clerk put it.[4]

II

In the Netherlands, parts of France and the Christian realms of northern Spain the subjection of the bulk of the peasantry and of their land-holdings to a very oppressive lordship of the feudal nobility was mainly a development of the later tenth and the eleventh centuries.[5] It affected the majority of the rural population irrespective of their previous status (a minority of former slaves, the majority legally freemen, often holding previously their land in 'allodial' free ownership). This 'new servitude' has been described by Georges Duby in 1953 as subjection to the *seigneurie banale* of feudal lords, a jurisdictional or castral lordship exercised by notables who controlled castles (with dungeons inside them).[6]

The evidence for Normandy in the eleventh century is much more scanty than for many other regions of France. There had been a savage peasant rising there shortly after 996.[7] In the first half of the eleventh century there are mentions of some rural serfdom in parts of the Duchy. But the Norman peasantry seems to have remained unusually free, perhaps because Normandy had been badly devastated before the Normans finally conquered it in the late ninth century and they had to attract new settlers on favourable terms.[8] After 1066 they found in parts of Anglo-Saxon England large peasant populations reduced to a considerable degree of subjection by the Anglo-Saxon nobles and great churches. In the words of Sir Frank Stenton, 'in the south and west the French aristocracy of the eleventh century could ask for little more than Old English custom gave them'. The new Norman lords consolidated these landed lordships. To quote Stenton again, 'in this village or that we may trace under its new rulers a tightening of seignorial control, a depression of the local peasantry'. Repeatedly some free peasants were depressed into a much more burdensome position.[9] Many Anglo-Saxon churches and lay notables were holding private courts from at least the ninth century 'by virtue of custom reinforced' by royal grants,[10] but the new Norman lords extended this, subjecting the population of the villages under their control to a regime of private justice akin to French 'banal lordship'. The legal reforms of Henry II and his sons, by excluding a large part of the peasantry from the protection of the 'new' Common Law, legally defined and expanded this 'new servile class'. In the words of Pierre Bonnassie, using the researches of Paul Hyams, if all English peasants 'were not born *servi*, all had a vocation to be so, and ought, so far as was possible, and for the common good, to be treated as such'.[11]

It is not the purpose of this book to give a detailed, technical account of the doctrines of the Common Law on serfdom. But certain basic features of its origins and development must be explained, as an introduction to the history of the servile part of the peasantry in the second half of the fourteenth century.[12] It was an artificial body of law, fertile in creating anomalies and injustices. The peasants who suffered from the disabilities of their servile tenure and status were intermixed in the same communities with men and women who were deemed to be free. This constant reminder of their disadvantages intensified the chronic discontent of the servile peasants. Furthermore, there existed one group of estates, the manors of the crown's Ancient Demesne, which produced the same exasperating contrast. These were estates which had belonged to the king after the Norman Conquest and were recorded as his in Domesday Book. Many of them were subsequently alienated to private owners (especially to religious houses), but in the thirteenth century their tenants continued to enjoy the special protection of the king's court against any aggravation of their charges. The main reason for this appears to have been fiscal. The king did not wish to allow any impoverishment of the estates of the Ancient Demesne, as he periodically exacted from them special seignorial taxes, the royal tallage.[13] As events in the years immediately before 1381 clearly showed, the rest of the peasantry did not understand why they should not enjoy the same legal, privileged position as the tenantry of the manors of the Ancient Demesne, especially if they, too, lived on properties that had at some stage belonged to the English kings, or were believed to have done so.[14]

At the core of the Common Law of serfdom, as it began to evolve in the second half of the twelfth century, lay a distinction between hereditary, personal servile *status* and servile *tenure*. Both traced their roots to a much more archaic, earlier, real slavery. Servile tenure was perpetuating the hold of the lord on his dependent tenants and their inability to leave the lord's land without his permission.

When the judges of Henry II began to dispense new legal remedies to the king's subjects the practical problem arose of how far they could allow the great mass of humble peasants to be included in these new legal benefits. The only possible answer was not at all. The judges of the king's court were a small group of men. They neither wished nor could cope with most of the civil litigation of the king's subjects. The problem was where to draw the line and which cases to exclude. In John Hatcher's words, 'It was never for a moment intended that the crown courts should be open to all lowly folk and to the petty disputes they had with their lords; such an intention would have not only been completely unworkable in practice, it would have appeared absurd to contemporaries.'[15] The outlook and interests of the upper class of society, the feudal landowners of England, precluded anything else. The attitude of these men to their humble, peasant dependants was one of contempt. To the author of the 'Laws of Henry I' (c. 1115), probably a judge of the king's court, the *villani* were 'lowly people and lacking in substance' (*viles et inopes personae*').[16] Contempt for the peasant certainly remained the dominant sentiment in the seigneurial world[17] for the rest of the Middle Ages. The judges of Henry II and his sons did not wish to interfere in the relations between English landlords and their lowly dependants.

A legal case between 1165 and 1168 brings out the social attitudes that lay behind this exclusion. Bishop Gilbert Foliot of London, a member of an aristocratic Norman family, received a royal writ summoning him to face a suit about half a virgate of land (roughly 15 acres) in his lordship, held for an annual rent of 12*d*. He returned it to his close acquaintance, the king's chief justiciar, with a covering letter which explained that the matter was too trivial and the complainant a mere rustic ('*fere rusticus*'), a term implying that the man was a serf. He was returning the writ, as he did not think he could be expected to treat it seriously.[18]

Thus it became necessary to decide who could and who could not get the protection of his rights and property in the king's court. This was not easy. Some men were well known in their villages as descendants of former real slaves. Large numbers of peasants had been unable for many generations to leave their lords' lands and attempts would have been made to recapture them had they tried to do so. Such peasants obviously could not be regarded as deserving the protection of the king's court. But there were many people in the countryside who were neither traditionally personal serfs nor part of the customary labour force of their lords. These individuals were, therefore, dispensable dependants whose departure could be permitted. They were in many cases quite prosperous compared with their servile neighbours, holding their land only for fixed rents. Commutation of the services for fixed money payments had been quite frequent in the twelfth century, and men who had been in that condition, often for many decades, would have been regarded as freer than the more obviously servile tenants. Were they to be treated as freemen and allowed to litigate against their lords? And what criteria were to be applied in defining their status and tenure if they tried to avail themselves of the emerging Common Law's new remedies? 'The lawyers were striving in the face of great difficulties to reduce the whole population into the simple classification, free or serf. Ultimately they were successful in degrading most of the peasants into the position of serfdom.'[19]

That does not mean that the position of the majority of the peasants had legally deteriorated because the new Common Law did not protect them. Before Henry II's time there had been no arrangements by which such humble men could have got any legal hearing outside the courts of their own lords and they would have been given brutal, short shrift if they had tried to challenge these lords. The emergence of the Common Law did not worsen their position; it merely did not allow them to improve it. The exclusion of the peasants deemed to be servile from the protection of the Common Law was likely to have an adverse effect on the chances that their descendants might prosper.

A brief summary of the resultant legal situation of the servile peasants might read as follows. The royal courts came to treat them as owning nothing. All that they possessed was deemed to belong to their lords. If a villein tried to litigate in the king's court against his lord, and was successfully challenged as being his serf, that at once ended the case in the lord's favour.

The servile villeins and their tenements were left in practice to the arbitrary will of their lords. This was the great *legal* difference between serfs and freemen, customary servile tenants and freeholders. As we shall see later, in real life the differences were less obvious, because humble freemen were often virtually helpless when dealing with powerful and unscrupulous lords. But this was a fact of medieval life, not a matter of law.

III

There are 'unmistakable signs of economic expansion in thirteenth-century England', or, 'perhaps more accurately, during the period stretching from the last quarter of the twelfth century to the end of the first quarter of the fourteenth'.[20] The emergence of the Common Law of serfdom can only be properly understood within this framework of expanding population, increasing competition for land among the peasantry and the enhanced opportunities for profit from agriculture for the landlords.

John Hatcher has estimated that in the last quarter of the thirteenth century, when the medieval English population had reached its maximum size, 'probably not more than three-fifths of the English tenantry were unfree'.[21] Proportions of servile populations varied greatly from one region to another and even between adjoining localities. 'None of [even] the big medieval English estates was completely homogenous in character' and they were all likely to have some 'scattered possessions of a non-manorial type'.[22]

As one would expect, there were greatest numbers of serfs on very old English estates, going back to the earlier centuries of the Anglo-Saxon period. Many of these estates belonged to bishoprics and Benedictine religious houses, which had been to a large extent originally endowed by the Old English rulers or their aristocracies. Those donors probably handed over groups of slaves or of dependent peasants tied hereditarily to these properties. The estates of the Bishops of Worcester, much discussed in this book, were of this kind.[23] The estates of the Bishops of Winchester in the later thirteenth and the first half of the fourteenth centuries provide an extreme example: the overall proportion of free tenants on them amounted to only 5 per cent of the total tenantry.[24]

Another type of manorial estate which was likely to be inhabited largely, or even entirely, by servile peasantry was the property of minor landowners, who possessed only a single manor or very few estates, which they exploited intensively. Locally these people could be influential, as they particularly needed, and often secured, the support of important lay and ecclesiastical patrons.

Before 1348, and even more so before the famine of 1315/16, cultivable land or good meadows and pastures were scarce. Peasants competed fiercely with each other for such additional customary holdings, for contractual leases of tenements or for leases of demesne lands as lords were willing to concede to them. Unfree tenants with holdings would not in these circumstances lightly disobey their landlords and there was little danger of many servile peasants trying to migrate elsewhere. These were the social and economic constraints behind the persistence of serfdom.

Already in Domesday Book we find considerable differences of economic condition between men described there as *villani*.[25] A small minority of peasants did prosper during the prolonged period of economic expansion in the thirteenth century. The only large body of statistical evidence is available in the records of a royal inquiry into land tenure conducted in 1279. They are known as the Hundred Rolls and survive for parts of Bedfordshire, Buckinghamshire, Cambridgeshire, Huntingdonshire, Leicestershire, Oxfordshire and Warwickshire. In this area, as E.A. Kosminsky has shown, the amount of land held for money rent alone (both by free tenants and villeins) was much greater than the extent of tenements burdened with labour services. Some two-fifths of the recorded tenantry were free, though more than half of these were smallholders. Only 8 per cent of the free tenants possessed more than a virgate (*c.* 30 acres), but only about 1 per cent of the servile villeins did so.[26]

In any large and prosperous village the servile villeins collectively might hold considerable possessions which were deemed, of course, to belong legally to their lords. At Michaelmas 1340 the goods held by the villeins of William de la Pole in the great lordship of Burstwick in the East Riding of Yorkshire were being valued by the royal commissioners. The estate had been sold by the king to William, the principal English royal banker, and the possessions of the villeins formed part of the assets of the estate, just like the animals in his domanial flocks and herds. The East Riding of Yorkshire was one of the most prosperous regions of northern England. In 1341 Burstwick produced an annual income of £989, out of which £851 was available in ready cash. It was one of the most valuable blocks of property in the country, yet the collective value of its villeins, distributed between at least fourteen different villages and hamlets, assessed at £2561, was three times larger than the net yearly income from Burstwick.[27]

A small group of prosperous villeins accounted for a large proportion of this wealth. But there was also in the countryside a vast crowd of smallholders and landless men earning a precarious living by working for others, while owing only very limited labour services to their lords (often one day in each week, except during harvest time). It was an ancient state of affairs. Domesday Book mentioned 82,000 bordars and cottars as opposed to 108,000 or 109,000 *villani*.[28] In the later Middle Ages many of the people with little or no land may have been free personally, but their precise legal status was often a matter of indifference and it was their wretched poverty and precarious survival that men noted. In a famine it was they who died off in largest numbers, as did the peasants who were nearly landless. This is well documented for the famine of 1315–17, 'the worst agrarian crisis since manorial records began [in England] at the start of the thirteenth century'.[29]

Historians have tended to be too optimistic about the economic condition of the middling group of servile peasants, the holders of the average standard customary tenements. Professor R.H. Hilton and Professor Christopher Dyer are welcome exceptions. They both tried to evaluate from a survey·in 1299 of the estates of the bishopric of Worcester[30] the economic position of such tenants. They derived their evidence from the manor of Kempsey to the south-east of the city of Worcester.[31] Its medieval layout can be satisfactorily reconstructed.[32] The people whose resources they tried to assess were not dying of hunger in normal years, though they were likely to be undernourished (especially their womenfolk), because they had to sell as much of their crops and other produce as they could spare.

A typical customary tenant at Kempsey held half a virgate, sixteen acres in all. As it was a two-field village, half of his arable land lay fallow each year. One can estimate roughly how much wheat, rye and barley he was likely to raise each year (an average of three to four times the amount of seed). One can also calculate what the surplus of corn that he could spare for sale could fetch at the average prices then prevailing (c. 12s to 13s each year). His yearly money rent for his holding was 5s and on top of that there were various seignorial renders. Professor Dyer has estimated the total size of his yearly obligations (including the money value of his labour services) at 17s 10½d. He certainly could not afford to commute for money the regular labour services owed by him, nor could he have afforded to hire labourers to render them, as richer peasants were able to do. If he had to pay all his obligations in cash, as he was obliged to do during the vacancy of the see of Worcester in 1302–3, 'his grain sales would be insufficient to cover him'.[33] Kempsey was regarded by the bishops as having poor soils,[34] though it was a good place for keeping sheep.[35] But it had a ford over the River Severn and the village was near enough to Worcester to offer opportunities of casual employment in the city and of transporting supplies to it. With its numerous dependent hamlets it was in 1334 one of the more highly assessed villages in Worcestershire, as were many of the other episcopal manors.[36] Our half-virgater and his family may have increased their chances of survival by practising some crafts. 'But if we assume, as we are entitled to do, that the main marketable asset was his grain, he must usually have been on the edge of destitution and must often have reduced his family's subsistence in order to sell more of his product for the money needed to pay to the lord and others.'[37] There existed at Kempsey in around 1300 a large number of smallholders and other even more miserable men: 68 per cent of tenants with some land had less than half a virgate.[38]

Professor Dyer attempted a more elaborate estimate of the income of a similar half-virgater (with some 15 acres) on another of the Bishop of Worcester's estates, Bishop's Cleeve, to the south-east of Kempsey. Here the land was more fertile (heavy clays, difficult to exploit, but suitable for growing various corns). Dyer again reaches fairly pessimistic conclusions about such a man's resources. Below him there were twenty-seven cotlanders with less land (each with 12 acres), 'who would have only broken even in normal years'.[39]

IV

Any fruitful discussion of the organization and functioning of manorial estates must be prefaced by the examination of one central problem: how far were the relations of landlords with their unfree tenants governed in practice by the custom of each manor? There is no agreement among historians about this.

'In practice, most tenants in villeinage enjoyed a large measure of security even in the thirteenth century. What really mattered in practice were the comparative bargaining powers of lord and tenants in the manorial court.'[40] The custom of each manor was the outcome of practical compromises gradually established. It would have been unwise for landlords to live permanently in a state of open conflict with the majority of their villein tenants, though this did happen on some estates.[41] There was a contrast between what the Common Law lawyers were asserting about the lords' sole and complete ownership of the land and other possessions of their servile tenants, and the latter's consequent complete lack of rights in their relations with their lords, and the situation in real life where lords needed the rents, labour and other services of their tenantry and expected to exact them without undue friction.

However, my own researches in manorial accounts and court rolls of many estates in different parts of England have made me sceptical about the effectiveness of manorial custom in protecting the servile peasantry against the arbitrary will of determined and unscrupulous lords. When servile holdings lapsed into the lords' hands through deaths of tenants or surrender by them of their lands, medieval lords felt entitled to decide who were to be their next tenants, even if the choice made by them might disregard the manorial custom by excluding the next of kin. If they finally did accept new tenants who were not initially chosen by them, they often did so only on payments of exorbitantly large fines.[42]

G.C. Homans in 1941, and John Hatcher forty years later,[43] in what are otherwise very interesting discussions of the application of these local customs *in normal conditions*, seem to me to have been over-optimistic in estimating the effectiveness of custom in protecting the servile peasantry when conditions ceased to be stable and normal. Even Dr Hatcher admits that in the course of the later twelfth and thirteenth centuries 'many, perhaps most, lords succeeded in burdening their unfree tenants with increased and additional obligations of one sort or another', but he nevertheless concludes that 'it is not the breaching of custom which is most striking, but the observing of it'.[44]

In dissenting from this over-optimistic view of the binding force of custom, it is wise to start with R.M. Smith's observation 'that in England a "customary law" in any locality did not exist in an absolute sense'.[45] Even really radical alterations of manorial custom were possible, if a lord insisted on them. Thus, at some date before 1287, on the Stuteville estate of Gressenhall in Norfolk, the rule of impartible inheritance of servile tenements was altered to partible inheritance because 'the lord wishes to have numerous tenants' ('*vellet habere plures tenentes*').[46] It must also be remembered that in the manorial courts 'the presenting jury and trial jury were [normally] staffed by men who came disproportionately from the wealthiest levels of village society'.[47] Estate officials were mostly recruited from the same class of rich servile tenants. All these men had much to lose from a lord's displeasure and in normal circumstances were likely to do his bidding.

Beneath the surface of apparent stability there was endemic mutual distrust between lords and their servile tenantry, and often much tension. When on occasions it erupted into violent confrontations the strength of the accumulated hatred against manorial lords was revealed. The events of 1381 are particularly instructive. The widespread burning of the manorial accounts and court rolls was one of its most striking features[48] and they were singled out for destruction because they were, among other things, records of serfdom. The fact that they were also a record of the application of the local manorial customs obviously aroused only the hostility of the peasants, who clearly did not regard these manorial customs as an effective protection against excessive exploitation and much arbitrary injustice.

Servile tenants formed a reserve of labour for the cultivation of the lord's demesne. Where they were numerous, only a part of their labour was needed on a regular basis, while the rest was commuted for money payments. But on certain special occasions, like harvesting, or in emergencies, all the servile peasants might be called out by the lord's officials.

By the later thirteenth century, even on estates with large seignorial demesnes, the regular week-work provided by the servile tenants was less important in quantity than the labour of permanent servants and hired labourers. By then it seldom amounted to more than a third of the man-hours required by the lords. The lord's full-time servants (the *famuli*) were normally the most important part of his labour force,[49] supplemented temporarily by hired labourers, whenever this might be necessary. In the over-populated countryside of England in the later thirteenth century there was a plentiful supply of landless men who depended entirely, or almost entirely, on working for others for very low wages.

However, the services rendered by the holders of the more substantial servile tenements (half-virgates or virgates) were of a special sort. They provided plough teams, carts and other more expensive agricultural equipment. This dispensed their lords from much costly investment in such things.

As has been already mentioned, the reeves and other manorial officials were chiefly drawn from among the minority of prosperous servile villeins and these offices were therefore likely to become quasi-hereditary in an élite of leading village families. Adam Jop at the Suffolk manor of Redgrave, belonging to the Abbey of Bury St Edmunds, acted as reeve during at least fifteen years between 1260 and 1309. By 1289 he held some 50 acres (at least 39 of servile land and 9 of freehold land). By the time of his death in 1309 he had acquired another 14 acres of servile land. His accumulation of property had been built up by piecemeal purchases. Within his lifetime his sons purchased an additional 45 acres.[50] Reeves and other manorial officials were normally excused rents during their time of office and had many opportunities for licit, and illicit, profits.

Regular labour services through most of the year, two or three times a week, were regarded in the thirteenth century as among the main legal tests of servile tenure. Servile smallholders owed usually at least one day a week. As time went on, much of this regular week-work was increasingly commuted for money payments but this was done at the will of the lord (or his officials) and arrangements would vary from year to year. Landlords attached special value to additional, seasonal labour services on particularly important occasions, like the harvest and the tasks that followed it. These were known as 'boon works' and free as well as servile tenants might owe them. As one studies a long series of estate accounts, it becomes clear that what lords particularly valued was the possession of a reserve of dependable labour that could be used in an emergency. Thus, in 1375/6, the manorial officials on the Bishop of Worcester's huge estate of Henbury Saltmarsh, with a vast number of tenants,[51] specified during a spell of bad weather at the time of the harvest that the sons and daughters of twenty-four customary tenants should join the others normally liable to perform this boon work.[52]

Servile tenants did derive some advantages from their condition. While they could litigate about their servile holdings only in the lord's manorial court, in cases where the lord had no reason to take sides they could get cheaper justice than freeholders litigating in the royal courts. Tenants on the estates of powerful lords enjoyed a considerable degree of security from attacks by brigands and malefactors. They were likewise more secure from the activities of some kinds of particularly oppressive royal officials. Thus, I have never found during the earliest phase of the Hundred Years War (1336–40) any evidence of the royal purveyors of supplies for the army and navy venturing to act within villages owned by earls or barons. They also as a rule avoided estates of knights, though they did dare purvey within villages held by ladies of the knightly class.

On the majority of estates the servile peasantry enjoyed normally a reasonable fixity of rents and services. The limits of how far the lord could change them were, however, purely practical (fear of resistance), not legal. Hence peasants might seek to buy special promises of greater security. In 1378, on the estate of the Nunnery of Barking at Ingatestone in Essex, after a dispute, the servile tenantry offered a fine of £2 so that their rents and services could be made 'certain'.[53]

On the majority of estates the one important exception to the customary fixity of dues paid by servile tenements was the lord's right to fix according to his arbitrary wishes the 'fines' demanded from new tenants as a condition of admitting them to these servile tenements. Often there was no obvious close correlation between the size of the holdings and the amount of such 'fines'. The agrarian value of particular holdings must have formed one important consideration. This is something about which a modern historian is almost always in the dark, though everybody in the village must have been familiar with the value of every bit of soil. The expectation of what a new tenant could pay and the consideration of whether he or she was the next heir, as opposed to strangers, were normally taken into account in fixing the amount of the fine.

On the estates of the Abbey of Crowland, in eastern England, a widow could retain her dead husband's holding as long as she did not remarry. If she took a new husband, she was only allowed to do so by paying a large fine. In the first half of the fourteenth century these fines became quite exorbitant on Crowland's manor of Cottenham, some five miles north of Cambridge. R.M. Smith, who has studied this evidence and the comparable information from manors in East Anglia, speaks of lords taking 'excessively high non-customary dues with regard to widow remarriage'. They were exploiting the avid competition for land in that densely populated countryside.[54]

Changes in profitability of agriculture, but also in the fortunes of particular landlords, shaped the evaluation of the 'fines for entry'. Around 1250, on the estates of the Abbey of Ramsey in Huntingdonshire, the new tenant of a standard virgate usually paid a mark (13s 4d) or a pound as his fine, but in the first decade of the fourteenth century it rose to as much as 66s 8d, with half-virgaters paying proportionately even more (40s).[55] At Redgrave in Suffolk, an estate of the Abbey of Bury St Edmunds, average fines for entry doubled between the late thirteenth century and the second decade of the fourteenth century.[56]

Economic necessity, greed or simply indifference to people whom they despised as their social inferiors, often led lords into innovations at the expense of their serfs. They could, and did, impose on their villeins new and unusual obligations. Thus, in 1346 Thomas Beauchamp, Earl of Warwick, the Earl Marshal of England, was rebuilding Elmley Castle, his principal fortified residence in Worcestershire. Judging by the castle mound, which alone survives, it must have been a huge structure. He hired skilled craftsmen but put under their direction his servile tenants, to be used for various unskilled tasks. The agricultural services of his tenantry at Elmley had been commuted for money at some earlier date, but they were now demanded for this novel purpose as well as for further repairs to the manorial buildings.[57]

Another example of the reserve powers retained by lords over their serfs being put to novel uses comes from the Cathedral Priory of Durham. After the priory had leased some of its demesnes around 1370, it tried to compensate for the loss of corn from these properties by prohibiting its tenants to sell their surplus corn to anybody except the priory. They could sell it to others only by permission of the priory's officials.[58]

Servile villeins hated their condition because it put them at a disadvantage in competing with others in a struggle for subsistence.[59] They were usually burdened with higher rents and heavier labour services than the free tenants. They had to devote part of their time and equipment to the cultivation of their lord's land. If they were fairly prosperous, they could hire other men to do this work for them, but this cost money. The lords collected special imposts from them. They needed the lord's licence to live outside his lands, to send their children to school, to marry off their womenfolk.

Free tenants often also owed some labour to their lords, but they were obliged, normally, to perform only occasional boon works and were free from regular week-work. The latter became in the eyes of the lawyers one characteristic feature of servile tenure. Above all, the dues and services of free tenants were fixed and, if these had been arbitrarily increased, they could seek legal redress in the king's court, though, if they were poor and their lords were rich and influential, their chances of success were admittedly doubtful.

V

It is time to trace in more detail the development of the law of serfdom from the reign of Henry II onwards. I shall be more concerned with what actually happened in royal and manorial courts than with theoretical treatises. If one reads the royal jurists writing between *c.* 1220 and *c.* 1250, it becomes apparent that the jurists deliberately treated villeins as slaves of their masters in the ancient Roman sense of slavery. 'It was even by reference to the status of the slave, as defined in [Justinian's] Institutes, that the status of villeinage was defined.'[60]

Fortunately for the peasantry, in everyday relations between lords and their peasants, much more flexible and less legalistic usages often prevailed. Hence the name of Henry de Bracton, to whom the most important of these treatises has been attributed in the past,[61] will never be mentioned again. Nor shall I try to cite other older treatments by modern historians, though I will refer occasionally to F.W. Maitland.[62] My account is totally based on the distinguished and authoritative writings of Paul Hyams.[63] My intention is to make more accessible the main conclusions of his fascinating but technical publications.

Sheep farming and weaving in the twelfth century, from the Eadwine Psalter, Canterbury (Reproduced by permission of the Master and Fellows of Trinity College, Cambridge: MS. R.17.1, f. 263)

It was a very artificial and complex body of law: a fertile source of anomalies and abuses. At the core of its legal doctrines lay a distinction between personal, hereditary, servile status and servile tenure. In real life the two influenced each other and it was often very difficult to separate them.

As each new lord succeeded to his inheritance all his tenants were required to swear fealty to him. There is a record of this at the first court of Thomas Mowbray, Earl of Norfolk, held at Forncett (Norfolk) on 13 December 1400. It starts with a list of his free tenants. Then follow men described as '*native tenentes*'. These were freemen, either by birth or through previous emancipation of themselves or their ancestors, who held tenements reputed servile and burdened with rents and services customarily due from such tenements. Both these groups are described as swearing fealty ('*fecerunt domino fidelitatem*'). Lastly come tenants described as 'the Lord's serfs by blood' ('*nativi domini de sanguine*'). These rendered *servile* fealty ('*fecerunt domino fidelitatem servilem*').[64] Other comparable records maintain the same distinction between status and tenure and enumerate the same three categories of dependent peasants.

One special category of land at Forncett deserves separate comment. This was freehold land acquired by the earl's servile villeins. This was treated as the earl's property, was required to be surrendered into his hands and was then redelivered to the villein purchasers to hold as servile land at the earl's will. It was known as '*terra soliata*' (or '*terra solidata*'). At Forncett, between 1358 and 1376, as many as '10½ messuages and some 50 acres were degraded to the lower tenure'.[65] Intelligent contemporaries, like Geoffrey Chaucer, regarded this as an abuse. In the *Parson's Tale* he condemns the taking away from bondmen of possessions that had never been given to them by their lords. Chaucer was no radical and he was presumably voicing here an opinion shared by some other contemporaries.[66]

Particularly detailed information about this type of land is preserved in a unique record compiled by the Abbey of Peterborough early in the reign of Edward III. It contains copies of charters confiscated by the abbey from its villeins, by which they had purchased land, very often free land. Most of these transactions occurred in the reign of Edward I. The abbey regarded as particularly reprehensible the wording of the charters by which freehold properties were conveyed to the villeins 'and their heirs'. According to the legal doctrines of the Common Law, serfs could not, of course, have heirs. The possessions thus sequestered were regranted to the villein purchasers, to be held henceforth at the will of the abbey and for payments of augmented rents.[67]

Servile status meant that a serf could not leave a lord's property without his licence, while a freeman holding land deemed to be a servile tenement was supposed to be free to depart, though in practice the lord might try to prevent this (see below, section VII, for an example from 1356).

The distinction between serfs tied to the lordship and freemen, theoretically at least, free to depart, had very ancient history behind it, which went back to the time long before the Norman Conquest. In that distant past, as for centuries afterwards, one of the chief preoccupations of landowners had been the retention of a maximum number of dependent men obliged to pay rents and till their demesnes.

Servile tenure ensured that nobody else had any right to interfere with the lord's exaction of rents and labour on terms that suited him. To ensure that these servile tenements remained under the lord's undisputed control, they could not be alienated without the lord's licence and the royal courts refused to interfere with what was regarded as the lord's exclusive property. In practice it was often very difficult to separate in particular cases the evidence about the status of the men occupying tenements deemed to be servile from the evidence about the true nature of their tenure of these holdings. Much of the uncertainty of legal actions about serfdom arose from conflicts of facts about status and tenure.

Status was normally proved by producing the kinsmen of the alleged villein, preferably on his father's side, though if the case arose out of a man holding an allegedly servile tenement because he had married a woman who had inherited it, her kinsmen would need to be produced. Testimony about more than one kinsman had to be adduced. Tenure was normally proved by a variety of tests about the liability to renders reputed servile and about the services performed by the alleged villein.

Initially a major cause of confusion was the attempt by lawyers to impose a body of legal distinctions on a peasant society that had evolved hitherto unaware that such distinctions would be forced upon them. Mixed marriages between people of servile and free status were a fertile source of legal puzzles, or, as was often the case, complications were caused by women succeeding to servile holdings but marrying freemen. Lastly, freemen often took up servile holdings in order to have something to live on. Offspring of mixed marriages, or of freemen holding servile tenements, could be a source of intractable legal complications.

Except in cases concerning estates that had belonged to the crown in the time of William the Conqueror (and came to be defined as the royal Ancient Demesne) the legal actions available to servile peasants were very few. I shall start with a list of them. While the writ of Naifty ('*de nativo habendo*') was developed primarily to suit the needs of lords,[68] down to *c.* 1230 it was occasionally procured by peasants in order to start an action establishing their free status. Thereafter this ceased to be possible.[69] Only a free tenant aggrieved by new oppressive demands of his lord could start an action by a writ of *Ne vexes*.[70] Only two types of actions in the royal courts remained permanently open to men treated as servile by their lords, but claiming to be free. An action initiated by a lord using a writ of Naifty could be countered by the alleged serf with a writ *De libertate probanda*. The form of it, as cited by Glanvill in his treatise of *c.* 1187–9,[71] was modified subsequently in its wording and came to be known from the initial word of its later (thirteenth-century) form as *Monstravit*.[72] The required proof would normally be confined to facts about status.

Lastly, anybody could start an action under Henry II's 'possessory assizes'. These were actions under which litigants claimed that they had been deprived violently and without judgement of some free property or some free property of their ancestors whose lawful heirs they claimed to be. A challenge that the plaintiff was unfree or that the land in question was held in unfree tenure would defeat such an action, but until this 'exception of unfreedom' was raised the litigant and his land were presumed to be free. A peasant who wanted to establish his freedom securely could do so by starting a possessory assize against his lord, provoking him into an exception of serfdom and relying on his good case for rebutting this.[73]

If the exception of unfreedom was alleged, the assize jury would then be asked to pronounce on this exception. Often in such cases the royal judges might adjourn the case and a new jury would be summoned to pronounce on the relevant facts that might turn on either status or tenure.

The origins and the historical evolution of these actions must be briefly outlined to make their development more intelligible. The writ of Naifty appears to have originated as an action brought by a landlord to recover a serf who had been appropriated by another lord.[74] Its use to recover a fugitive serf may have been a secondary development. In this variant of the situation

Assize of Northampton (1176) of Henry II from Roger of Howden Chronica *(By permission of The British Library: Royal MS. 14.C.II, f. 158)* the lord would have been well advised to secure a writ of *Pone de nativis* which would have transferred the action to the king's court, but would have assured considerable advantages of a speedy procedure. If the lord failed to do this rapidly, the alleged serf could instead procure a *Monstravit* that gave him, and not the lord, notable procedural advantages. The peasant who had secured it placed himself thereby, with his holding and all his chattels, under the king's protection. The lord had henceforth no right to arrest him or seize his tenement and goods until the issue came for trial before the royal justices.[75] In the thirteenth century such a case was normally deferred until the next visitation of the county by the king's itinerant justices, which could mean a delay of several years.[76] The writ of *Monstravit* was usually decided by tests of status and became the favourite defensive weapon of peasants claimed as serfs by their lords. Its one drawback was that if the peasant plaintiff lost and was adjudged a serf, this was an irrevocable verdict and he could never bring in another writ of *Monstravit*.[77]

The usefulness of *Monstravit* to men trying to vindicate their freedom was drastically curtailed by legislation enacted in 1351. The petition of the Commons which lay behind it complained that fugitive villeins had abused the use of *Monstravit* to the detriment of their lords.[78] There was some justification for this complaint, but the enactment of the resultant statute should probably be viewed as a symptom of a seignorial reaction against the peasantry during the period of agrarian upheaval after the Black Death of 1348/9. The upshot of the statute was to deprive the writ of *De libertate probanda (Monstravit)* of much of its practical usefulness, so that it virtually fell into disuse. Hitherto, a man claimed by a lord as his bondman could secure a temporary respite from all danger of arrest by procuring this writ. Under the regime created by the new statute a lord would not be hindered by a *Monstravit* and could recapture a fugitive villein and detain him until the time of the trial. The practical consequences were important as after 1348/9 there was an increase in illegal withdrawals of unfree tenants in most parts of the country and instances of this greatly multiplied from the late 1360s onwards.[79]

I have briefly explained earlier how possessory assizes could be used to vindicate a peasant's freedom. As in the case of the writ of Naifty there was a change from the original effect of these actions. These assizes of *Novel Disseisin* (since 1166[80]) and *Mort d'Ancestor*[81] (since 1176) were very expeditious actions and deservedly became very popular. Peasant litigants who at an early date initiated such actions might find themselves challenged, often quite unexpectedly, about the freedom of their status or tenure. An early such case lies behind the fine of 1 mark imposed by the royal judges on the Abbot of Peterborough's men of Quadring, who in 1170 were amerced 'for seeking an assize as freemen when they were rustics'.[82]

However, the possessory assizes could be turned to their advantage by peasants who thought that they had a good case for being accepted as freeholders. The one additional superiority of possessory assizes over a *Monstravit* was that the peasant plaintiff, if successful, would also secure damages.[83] Besides, while a *Monstravit* was an action about status, to be settled by the quality of the peasant's relatives (and liable to produce uncertain results in court), an exception of servile status or tenure under a possessory assize would be tested by a wider range of proofs, especially tenurial ones, which might be more suitable for some peasant litigants.

Who could bring in an exception of serfdom in proceedings under a possessory assize? The plea rolls seldom tell us that it was the lord of the villein who was doing this, because the justices' clerks, who wrote them, assumed that this would be normally the case. But could a defendant who was not the lord bring in an equally decisive exception of bondage? At first he could, but as acquisitions by villeins of free land from third parties became increasingly common, royal justices became hesitant. The Bedfordshire visitation of the itinerant justices in 1285, as recorded in the *Annales de Dunstaplia*, included a case 'which may imply that a villein could at this time succeed in a *Novel Disseisin* against one who was not his lord'.[84]

Behind many of the actions about status there lay, undoubtedly, attempts by lords to increase the burdens of their dependent peasants. 'Pleas of service were certainly behind a number. . . . Study of the cases conveys the strong impression that land tenure and the struggle for villein customs and services were major factors.'[85]

The uncertainties of the law of personal status sprang from an attempt to impose the lawyers' simple alternative 'either free or servile' on a complex rural society. 'Real rustics and yokels caused the courts few problems. Royal guarantees of their rights would have appeared patently absurd, but this was not true of all villagers. The crux for the law was around the borderline cases whose status might have gone either way. . . . Such arbitrary distinctions turned perhaps on some special or temporary circumstance, or occasionally on a suit in a royal court', where failure might be interpreted as proof of villein status. 'Success or failure in early civil actions at Common Law had consequences beyond the mere allotment of seisin in the disputed land.' Failure 'in any of the early real actions . . . must have condemned some families to classification as villein, and perhaps social decline'.[86]

As stressed by me before, mixed marriages between servile and free peasants produced one type of complication. Before the rules of the new Common Law were elaborated in the second half of the twelfth century, peasant families had been intermarrying without any idea that one day they might be classified by royal courts on opposing sides of the barrier which separated freemen from serfs.[87] Mixed marriages remained frequent even after peasants became aware of the new doctrines of the Common Law. This was particularly the case when freemen married servile women with claims on succession to the servile holdings of their families. English villagers were much more concerned with accumulating land, which might be acquired through such marriages, than with legal differences of personal status.[88] The offspring of these mixed marriages occasioned prolonged arguments in the royal courts about their status.[89] Legal doctrines on this subject fluctuated for the rest of the thirteenth century and beyond. Finally, the rule prevailed that the status of these children was determined by the status of their fathers.[90] One of the logical, but absurd, consequences of this doctrine emerged as accepted law only in the first half of the fourteenth century, when illegitimate children came to be regarded as being always free, because their fathers were unknown. This rule emerged only quite late: 'the earliest statement of it in the Year Books dates from as late as 1326, but it seems to have become the accepted law by 1345'.[91]

Poor freemen, who were numerous (especially the younger sons of peasant freeholders), often took up servile holdings in order to have something to live on.[92] The royal courts fairly uniformly enforced the doctrine that the tenure of these men was not protected by the Common Law, though such judgements were sometimes arrived at only after protracted arguments about the true facts.[93] There was, perhaps, one moment of hesitation. The original Magna Carta of 1215 guaranteed tenure to all freemen, without making any reservations as to the kind of tenure. We do not know why this was done. However, the normal rules were soon restored in the reissue of the charter in 1217.[94] Later in the thirteenth century 'many lawyers were prepared to allege villein status' of men whose free origin is known to us, because they held servile tenements. 'Thus for many free peasant families the acquisition of customary holdings was a stage in their loss of freedom.' A case in 1270 concerned 'John le Coke, a smallholder who once held half an acre and a rod of land freely . . . He took up a virgate of villeinage land in the same village' for rent *per servilem condicionem* and later, *necessitate compulsus*, sold his free holding. John's status was undoubtedly 'in danger by this stage'.[95] Occasionally some lords even insisted that such freemen, holding in villeinage, should also publicly acknowledge servile status. The descendants of freemen holding servile tenements were at risk of being regarded as serfs in status.[96] While a freeman holding a servile tenement was supposed to be free to leave the manor (while abandoning his tenement), there was a danger that lords might want to retain them and even more so their descendants.[97]

The more prosperous villeins often came to combine their original servile tenements with a collection of parcels of free land. These freehold acquisitions might be used to endow their younger children. This is amply documented for some Suffolk villages of the Abbey of Bury St Edmunds in the late thirteenth century and likewise in a register drawn up at the Abbey of Peterborough recording the acquisitions by its tenants, mainly in the reign of Edward I.[98]

An interesting example of an accumulation of free and villein land in possession of a family which had been originally servile is to be found among the Bursary Muniments of Balliol College at Oxford.[99] This is a collection of over fifty deeds concerning parcels of land in and near the village of Northmoor, south of Oxford, which were gradually combined into a single estate. Its starting point was two acres of arable land held in servile tenure (probably in the first half of the thirteenth century) by Germanus, son of Walkelin of Northmoor. A man with the same unusual name (but called son of Richard) was married to Emma, sister of Robert de Leya of Northmoor, who freed from serfdom Germanus, son of Walkelin, probably a near relative. The collection of deeds includes two charters of Robert de Leya freeing Germanus and his offspring from personal serfdom (for a payment of half a mark of silver) and freeing his messuage and two acres of arable for a further 48*s* 1*d*.[100] Gradually, during a period stretching in the surviving deeds to 1428, this erstwhile servile holding became joined to an accumulation of other, mostly small, parcels of arable and meadow changing hands through all manner of transactions (outright sales, simple leases, leases in mortgage). Judging by the tiny rents, most of these holdings may have been freeholds, but a few, burdened with much heavier rents, may have been former servile tenements.[101]

VI

Under Henry II and his sons no conclusive tests of villein tenure were available, as yet, to royal judges. Attempts to establish easily recognizable distinctions between free and servile tenures were hampered by the complexity of social and economic divisions in the English villages. 'The recent artificial creation of Common Law ensured that peasant customs did not obligingly divide into free and villein items. . . . The degree of dependence on the lord shaded off almost imperceptibly from one group of tenants to another.'[102]

Recognition by the royal courts of more assured tests of servile tenure was furthered by the preference of lords for using legal actions based on tenure rather than status. 'The procedure by which [lords] had to attempt proof of villein status was full of legal pitfalls. In any event many actions of Naifty arose from tenurial disputes, for all the most valuable rights of lords over their villeins could be put into tenurial terms. Thus lords simply preferred to litigate . . . on tenure and the customs and services due from their villeinage holdings. Once lords had established their right to these, the Common Law would give them all the assistance they could desire.'[103] Besides, while a lord's victory in an action about status merely settled the position of a single family adjudged to be servile, by securing a favourable verdict on tenure, a lord would thereby assume that all his other dependent peasants holding their tenements on similar terms could also be treated as his servile tenants. 'When once it has been established that a tenement is unfree, that tenement will not become free, at least in the eyes of the lawyers, even though the services are modified or transformed.'[104] A change to tenure for rents alone, without the exaction of any labour services, would henceforth make no difference.

The recognition by the royal courts of fairly conclusive tests of villein tenure was a gradual process, stretching over much of the thirteenth century, but the available evidence about marginal cases 'should not suggest that villein tenure was anywhere as hard to establish as villein status'.[105] In the early thirteenth century 'no precise tests of villein tenure existed'.[106] At that stage 'the justices . . . frequently proceeded by a rule of thumb that compared alleged villeins with their neighbours: they would find him free if he were less burdened than the villeinage tenants around him'.[107] Two tests of serfdom came gradually to be recognized as most useful for proving the lord's claims. The most conclusive was 'merchet', an arbitrary payment exacted from a tenant for the permission to marry off his daughter, and sometimes his sister.[108] The other was 'tallage', the liability to arbitrary taxation at the lord's will. Neither test was conclusive in all cases beyond reasonable doubt, but in a majority of instances they were likely to procure for lords the verdicts that they sought. The liability of tenants to heavy and regular labour services, the regular 'week-work', was another likely criterion of serfdom, but as many disputes were precisely about the imposition, or the increase, of such services that test was often not applicable in practice. Merchet was a tenurial liability: a freeman holding a servile tenement would be liable to it.[109] Tallage was a species of financial aid to the lord. But while free tenants might be asked to consent to paying aid occasionally in difficult moments of a lord's life, tallage on serfs was an annual impost, not 'as of grace but by custom'.[110]

'The increasing precision of pleading seen in villeinage cases of the 1230s and 1240s about kinship links, tallage and merchet' points to a clearer recognition of increasingly accepted legal rules.[111] 'In consequence fuller records of existing "custom" for lords became essential to avoid costly mistakes.'[112] This need was partly met by the introduction of regular records of seignorial courts normally held on manors several times during each year. The resultant records were the manorial court rolls. They came to contain the evidence of tenure by which various tenements were held. Once such a record of tenure was established, it could be treated as immutable (unless the lord wished to change it).

Our earliest evidence about the keeping by English landlords of rolls of proceedings in their private manorial courts goes back to the second quarter of the thirteenth century.[113] Lords began to demand that their tenants should bring the charters or other evidences of their tenure to the officials holding their courts, so that they could be copied on the manorial rolls or special registers kept for this purpose.[114] The manorial court rolls came to contain a record of transfers of servile tenements from one tenant to another. Each time this happened, such tenements were required to be surrendered into the lord's hands and regranted on either customary or new conditions specified in the court rolls.

In addition to customary rents and labour services, servile tenements were burdened with several supplementary renders peculiar to particular manors and often of very ancient origin. These customary payments could likewise be used as proofs of servile tenure. On the older estates of the Bishops of Worcester, besides annual tallage, servile tenements were liable to a 'spinning fee', a 'fish fee' (for licence to fish within the bishop's woods) and an annual 'common fine'. By 1300 the rates of all these payments were mostly fixed according to the size of the tenements. Even servile 'tallage', which probably originated later than these other renders, was by then not arbitrary but fixed in the same manner.

These renders are well documented on two of the bishopric's easterly estates, Bishop's Cleeve and Bredon. According to the vacancy account for the bishop in 1302/3, they were expected to yield at Bishop's Cleeve (Gloucestershire) £6 19s 1d, as compared with the customary villein rents assessed at £14 4s 4d per year.[115] Some of the renders were scaled down during the second half of the fourteenth century. At Cleeve, in 1393/4, a virgate was liable to 1s 6d of seignorial tallage, while the annual rent of a virgate amounted to 6s.[116]

At Bredon (eastern Worcestershire), in 1302/3, tallage and other supplementary renders amounted to £4 3s, as compared with customary servile rents assessed at £10 15s 6d. Here, too, the rates of payment were diminished by 1375/6. While earlier in the fourteenth century a virgate contributed 1s 10d to the yearly tallage and 2d to the spinning fee, in the manorial account for 1375/6 tallage and 'spinning fee' amounted together to only 6d per virgate. The fish fee was now levied at the rate of 1d per virgate.[117]

Merchet emerged earliest as a decisive test 'where a clear liability to a servile form of marriage custom could be established'. But this did not happen generally until about the middle of the thirteenth century.[118] 'No other English custom (apart perhaps from merchet) was conclusive proof of villeinage before the end of the thirteenth century.[119] But a combination of what seemed servile customs would tend to convince justices and juries that the lord's claim about the villeinage of his tenant was justified.

By the end of the thirteenth century doctrine about serfdom 'was more or less settled and accepted'. This is to be related 'to the Edwardian judicature's increasingly formalistic and equity-less atmosphere'. 'But that did not prevent men from struggling for advantage in the courts' in what was a species of 'a handicap race'. 'Error, or an imaginative dodge dreamed up by a legal adviser, determined how an alleged villein was handicapped for the future.'[120]

VII

The agrarian expansion of the thirteenth century encouraged many landlords, especially the wealthier ones, to intensify production from their demesnes.[121] This not only led to increased demands for labour from the tenants usually regarded as servile, but also to attempts to convert into serfs men who considered themselves to be free and had been hitherto accepted as such.[122]

The advent of a new lord might be a particularly dangerous time for the tenants of a manor. In 1242 King Henry III gave the manor of North Ashby (now Mears Ashby, Northamptonshire) to a favoured follower, Robert de Mares. He tried to reduce free sokemen, holding between them twelve virgates, to servile status by 'demanding the payment of merchet and the right to tallage them as he pleased'. The tenants won a case against him in the king's court, but after 1256 his widow resumed the new demands on them. A series of legal actions followed, with six villagers acting 'for themselves and for the other men of North Ashby in common'. In June 1261 they agreed to pay 4½ marks in return for a concession that all further claims should be suspended until Robert's son grew of age. This proved a definitive settlement, as the holders of the twelve virgates were still recognized as free at the time of the son's death in 1282.[123]

While freeholders could seek redress in the royal courts if their free tenure and status were challenged, this was a costly exercise. Also there was always the risk of defeat in actions against important and wealthy lords. In a brutal society, where powerful lords were apt to use violent and unscrupulous methods to get their way, the position of humble free tenants could be in practice far more precarious than it was in law.

Two outrageous cases in manorial courts can be instanced from the third quarter of the fourteenth century. The first comes from the estates of Countess Margaret of Norfolk (countess 1338–99), a mean, harsh and grasping woman.[124] In 1373, at the countess's manor of Earl's Soham (Suffolk), Alice Comyn was challenged in the manorial court about her claim to hold in free tenure. She and her sister had married without the countess's licence. She produced a charter of manumission from serfdom granted to her father in 1337 by Earl Thomas, the countess's father. But the manorial court of Earl's Soham discovered a loophole in her claim to be free. Earl Thomas had held the manor under an entail by the terms of which he could not alienate property except in his lifetime. Countess Margaret's court ruled that the earl's death in 1338 had nullified the charter of manumission. In strict law this ruling was apparently wrong. But Alice and her sister were each required to pay marriage fines at the punitively high rates of 13s 4d.[125]

My second example describes what looks like another flagrant denial of justice. The manorial court of Thomas, Earl of Warwick, at Elmley Castle (Worcestershire), held on 6 May 1356, was ordered to summon Adam le Bedel, who was accused of having withdrawn from the earl's lordship without his licence. Adam answered that he was a freeman, as his father had been, though he did hold a servile tenement. A jury of tenants confirmed this. This was the second time that he had been tried, as a jury of tenants had likewise upheld his personal freedom on an earlier occasion. However, the earl's officials were not going to accept such a verdict this time. A special jury of twenty-eight members made a presentment that he was a serf ('*ipsum esse nativum*'). The earlier jury, which had testified that he was a freeman, was fined the enormous sum of £20.[126]

While the thirteenth century was on many estates a time of intensified exploitation of seignorial demesnes, achieved, in part, through the increased use of the labour services of servile tenants, there was also a parallel current of trying to increase lords' incomes through the leasing of peasant land for money rents alone. A good deal of this land was newly reclaimed, free from all customary restrictions, or else some portion of the lord's demesnes. For example, on the lands of the Abbey of Westminster, previous to the Black Death of 1348/9, new contractual tenancies were created predominantly out of the monks' demesnes.[127]

Some of the takers of leases were hitherto landless freemen. But there was also on many estates a significant number of purely contractual leases to villeins. In many instances, hitherto labour-yielding servile tenements were changed into wholly, or largely, rent-paying ones. This sometimes occurred very simply where holdings had lapsed into a lord's hands through the failure of legitimate successors to servile tenements. But it occurred also by persuading, or in some cases forcing, the villein tenants into such a change. As a rule there was no intention of altering the personal status of such tenants, who continued to be the lord's serfs. This type of change anticipated what would become a widely generalized transformation in the late fourteenth and the fifteenth centuries.

A well-documented example of the increase in the proportion of seignorial income derived from contractual rents is provided by comparing two extents, in 1251 and 1299, of the properties of the Bishops of Ely. The customary assized rents increased between these two surveys by only 10 per cent, but in the same period the volume of contractual rents of one sort and another increased threefold.[128] 'The gradual increase in the proportion of manorial income accounted for by contractual payments . . . may be illustrated from the episcopal manor of Somersham in Huntingdonshire. In 1299 half of the bishop's rent income from the manor was already made up of contractual rents, leaving only half for customary rents and the sale of labour services at the customary rate. In 1342 the share of contractual rents had risen to 57 per cent' and it amounted to over 75 per cent by 1381.[129]

The archives of the Abbey of Gloucester contain a series of deeds recording contractual leases on its estates in the second half of the thirteenth and early fourteenth centuries.[130] Some are copies in one of its registers, while others are originals, with their seals still attached to them, some clearly seals of undoubted villeins. R.H. Hilton discovered deeds concerning forty-nine leases, of which over half dated from the time of Abbot Reginald de Homme (1263–84). This abbot had to cope with an abbey debt of 1500 marks inherited on his accession and some of the leases may have been prompted by substantial premiums which some of the takers of these leases were willing to pay to the abbey.

Each lease resulted from an individual bargain and the rents and premiums cannot be fitted into any pattern. The leases of villein holdings were usually for three lives, of the tenant, his wife and a son. After their expiry they were to revert automatically to the abbey. The premiums and rents were usually fairly high, certainly higher than the comparable charges (assized rents and fines for entry) exacted from customary servile holdings. In the conditions of land shortage prevalent at that time richer villeins were obviously willing to compete for these tenements, as additions to the holdings already exploited by them.

In the case of the leases of servile holdings the various rights reserved to the Abbey of Gloucester clearly implied that the tenants continued to be regarded as serfs. The most explicit statement to that effect appears in a deed of lease in 1289 at Coln Rogers in south-eastern Gloucestershire.[131] Perhaps the need for a particularly clear stipulation of continued servile status arose out of a relatively high importance of that particular tenant. The lease was granted to William, the abbey's reeve, and his wife for their two lives. They took on lease 'two thirds of the virgate which may have been free and half a virgate of land stated to be servile for money rents of 10s and 8s respectively'. Their personal status 'was in no way to change, but they and their heirs were to remain of servile condition'.[132]

An instance of a temporary freeing from serfdom is revealed by a deed of Hugh Hwyt, a holder of a servile virgate at Brailes in Warwickshire, an estate of Earl William Mauduit of Warwick (1263–8). Hugh was to hold land freely of the earl, and to render free homage for it, as long as he served as his lord's bailiff. Hugh's administrative skills were obviously valued highly by the earl. Should he cease to act as bailiff, he agreed that he should forthwith revert to serfdom and his virgate should again be regarded as servile, notwithstanding any charter of the earl granted to him, while he had ranked as a free bailiff. The deed seems to fall outside all normal expectations of the royal Common Law, but it shows that, in practice, a vast variety of temporary arrangements was possible between lords and their servile tenants.[133] 'The absence of any right of appeal beyond the seignorial court no doubt helps to explain how it was that lords in thirteenth-century England could, if they so wished, put an end to customary arrangements on villein holdings and substitute new arrangements giving them a much higher income from the land in question.'[134]

In some cases there is a justified suspicion that the change was forced upon the tenantry of a manor. This probably happened at Langenhoe in Essex, some four miles south of Colchester.[135]

Its lord, still a minor in 1325, but of age by 1338, and still holding it as late as 1370, was Lionel de Bradenham. This was his only manor. He was an unscrupulous gangster and on 3 July 1362 a special commission was appointed to inquire into his misdoings at the behest of the town of Colchester associated with twelve coastal villages. Three days later his presence on the Essex Commission of Labourers (to which he had been appointed intermittently since 1355) was terminated. As justice of labourers he had abused his authority and extorted money from his neighbours. By 1348 Lionel had been able nearly to double his seignorial annual income by changing the customary tenements of his servile peasantry from customary tenure to contractual leases (from £8 9s 11d p.a. to £14 18s 5½d p.a.). How he achieved this we do not know, but in view of his record of violence one has a right to suspect that he imposed these changes by brutal pressure. He cultivated his demesne intensively (250 acres of arable and much pasture), using entirely hired labour.

CHAPTER 3

Social and Economic Background to the Great Revolt of 1381, II: 1349–81

I

The developments surveyed in this chapter have been studied by me in the early sections of my chapter in volume III of the Cambridge *Agrarian History*. This new account is an extended and emended version. I completed the original chapter in 1976, though the volume itself was not published until 1991, and a number of subsequent studies have added considerably to our knowledge. Various details in my original chapter need altering or supplementing. On some points deeper understanding of what was happening has become possible.

In 1981 the Past and Present Society commemorated the risings of 1381 by a special conference. Its proceedings were published, but were also reprinted later with additions.[1] For my present purpose I found particularly important the papers by Rosamund Faith on 'The *Great Rumour* of 1377 and peasant ideology'[2], by Christopher Dyer on 'The social and economic background to the rural revolt of 1381'[3], by Alan Harding on 'The revolt against the justices' and by J.A. Tuck on 'Nobles, Commons and the Great Revolt of 1381'. In 1985 was published the remarkable paper by Nicholas Brooks on 'The organization and achievements of the peasants of Kent and Essex in 1381',[4] providing a critical re-examination of the origins and progress of the risings there until the rebels of those two counties reached the outskirts of London on 12 June. The wisest and most penetrating study of a particular estate is Barbara Harvey's *Westminster Abbey and its Estates in the Middle Ages* (Oxford, 1977). With it should be mentioned R.H. Britnell's 'Feudal reaction after the Black Death in the Palatinate of Durham', *Past and Present*, 128 (1990), pp. 28–47.

As I have explained in my introductory chapter, this book is not concerned with the details of how individual landlords reacted to the plague epidemics between 1348 and 1375 and the social and economic upheavals caused by them. The one exception is chapter 4, on the properties of the Bishops of Worcester, which provides a preface to subsequent discussions of the history of those estates. But certain main features of the relations between landlords and their peasants in these years need stressing (section II). The assistance provided by the royal government to landlords in trying to keep down wages of labourers and the exceptionally zealous enforcement of this legislation was a major cause of the hostility to the legal system (section III), which found such terrible expression in the murders of several people connected with legal administration, including Sir John Cavendish, Chief Justice of the King's Bench. The rebels of south-eastern counties destroyed royal legal records in large quantities, depriving modern historians of the bulk of the information about the enforcement of labour legislation up to 1381. It is clear, as the contemporary chroniclers supposed, 'that the insurgents regarded the law as an instrument of social repression, as the means by which the landed gentry maintained the economic and social dependence of the bulk of the rural populace'.[5] It is equally clear that between 6 and 12 June the rebels in Kent and Essex deliberately organized and achieved a shattering blow to the financial and judicial organization of these two counties.[6]

The decade preceding the revolts of 1381 was a period of increasing economic disruption and social unrest (section IV). The renewal of the war with France led from 1371 onwards to the return of heavy taxation. The famine of 1370 was the second most destructive such disaster of the century (surpassed only by the more lethal famine of 1315–17). There were two further generalized outbreaks of plague in 1369 and 1374/5. The last of these was followed by an exceptional slump in grain prices, which finally undermined the value of land. The years after 1375 were a time of intensified economic dislocation and of unprecedented peasant unrest.[7]

As I noted in section III of chapter 1, members of the propertied class voiced fears of a forthcoming social upheaval. The Kentish squire and poet, John Gower, in his *Mirrour de l'Omme*, written in the last years of Edward III's reign, urged '*la seignourie*' to face up to the growing insubordination and assertiveness of the villeins and warned of the danger of a sudden popular uprising. The same fear was voiced in a Commons petition in the autumn of 1377, in the first parliament of Richard II.[8] But Members of Parliament failed to anticipate that this dreaded rising was going to be precipitated by the taxes that they themselves were piling upon the English people.

It is certain that without experiments in new types of direct taxation, culminating in the disastrous third Poll Tax of 1*s* on each person from the age of fifteen upwards, granted by parliament in December 1380, there would have been no general popular uprisings in May–July 1381. I have discussed extensively those financial experiments elsewhere[9] and only a summary will be needed here (section V). This will be followed by an account of some of the main features of the risings and their aftermath, of what they revealed of the revendications of the peasantry and the reactions to them of their landlord masters (section VI).

II

In the immediate aftermath of the plague epidemic of 1348/9 most landlords had to make some concessions to their peasant tenants. Vacant land was much more plentiful and labourers scarcer than at any time that men could remember. The concessions made then are well summarized by the chronicler of Leicester Abbey, Henry Knighton, though he was looking back at events some forty years earlier, as this section of his chronicle could not have been composed before 1389.[10] He wrote that 'the great men of the land, and other lesser lords who had tenants, remitted the payment of their rents, lest their tenants should go away on account of the scarcity of servants and the high price of all things – some half their rents, some more, some less, some for one, two or three years, according as they could come to an agreement with them'.[11] Knighton was correct in describing *temporary* relaxations of demands which most landlords were hoping soon to reverse. Several major landlords did this successfully, like, for example, the Abbot of Battle at Hutton in Essex, and, more speedily, on his most efficiently exploited estate of Alciston in Sussex.[12] Thomas Hatfield, Bishop of Durham, likewise had considerable success in regaining after a while some lost revenues.[13] On the Black Prince's properties in the Duchy of Cornwall a large proportion of the revenue came from contractual seven-year leases, which could be flexibly modified and the prince's council sensibly ordered considerable remissions of payments until 1356, because 'the surviving tenants were so impoverished that they would relinquish their holdings if the fines and tallages were not remitted'.[14]

Knighton goes on to list other types of concessions by landlords. 'Similarly, those who had let lands on yearly labour-services to tenants, as is the custom in the case of villeins, were obliged to

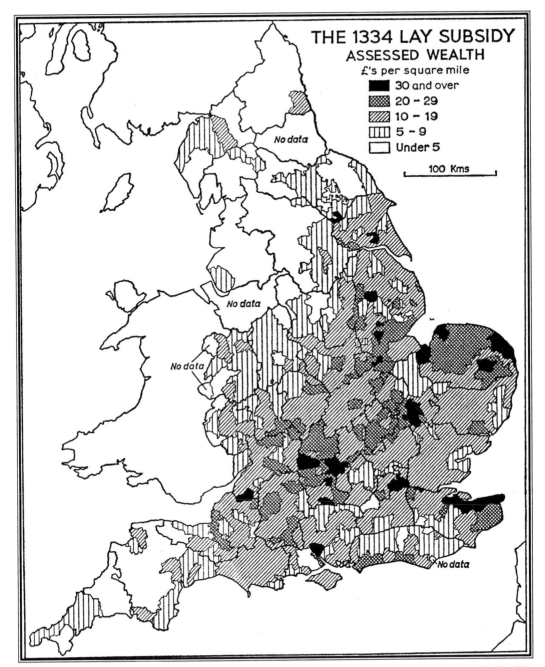

THE 1334 LAY SUBSIDY
ASSESSED WEALTH
£'s per square mile
- 30 and over
- 20 - 29
- 10 - 19
- 5 - 9
- Under 5

100 Kms

Map showing the distribution in England of movable wealth in 1334, from R.E. Glasscock (ed.) The Lay Subsidy of
1334 *(London, 1975), p. xxvii (Reproduced by permission of the British Academy)*

relieve and remit these services, either excusing them entirely, or taking them on easier terms, in the form of a small rent, lest their houses should be irreparably ruined and the land should remain completely uncultivated.'[15] He does not treat these kinds of concessions as irrevocable, but, in fact, they were more likely to be irreversible. It would have been very difficult to revive labour services, if they had been entirely suspended.

One widespread change was the fall in the value of peasant land, as it was now much more widely available. The traditional rents charged for it, as a combination of money renders and labour services, came to be regarded as excessive by many peasants. Hence they were increasingly not prepared to take the vacant holdings offered to them unless the charges on them were drastically lightened. This happened, for example, on the estates of the Bishops of Coventry and Lichfield.[16] Where peasants ceased competing desperately against each other to acquire land on any terms, the whole basis of the hold that landlords had over them was undermined.

The other great change was the end, for many years, of chronic under-employment, with spells of total unemployment, which had kept landless men or peasants with smallholdings in dread of starvation. Now, this dramatically altered into assurance of as much work for wages as they chose to seek. For a mass of the poorest peasants this was a permanent improvement and there were more diverse employment opportunities than hitherto. This possibility of choosing work and of bargaining about its terms bewildered and infuriated the employers of rural labour, and the labour laws that were enacted to check this in 1349–51 (see section III) were only marginally effective.[17]

Following the initial shock of the first few years after 1348/9, came a second stage, which some historians have described as a 'seigneurial (or feudal) reaction', as landlords had recourse to new methods with the help of which they might maintain the profitability of their estates. If they were successful, as some major landlords were, the phrase is an appropriate one. Dr Britnell is, for example, quite justified to use it about Thomas Hatfield, Bishop of Durham (1345–81).[18] But it would be inappropriate to speak of 'an age of seigneurial reaction', which would suggest a picture of concerted seigneurial pressure in the country as a whole. This would obscure the great diversity of problems facing different landlords and the corresponding variety of responses to this disturbing situation.

Local conditions determined in each case what bargains it was possible to strike. These great divergences were in itself a very disorganizing feature of the years after 1348. Different solutions might be forced on neighbouring lords and even the same landowner might be compelled to treat differently estates within easy reach of each other. My study in chapter 4 of the properties of the two neighbouring bishoprics of Worcester and of Coventry and Lichfield will provide some illustrations of this. Peasants everywhere came to learn that changes were occurring all around them and this was the most potent knowledge, weakening the power of the landlords to deal with their dependent men.

At this stage, as indeed at all subsequent stages, the gradual undermining of the manorial type of estates, and sometimes even their total collapse, was mostly brought about not by organized violence but through an accumulation of petty acts of obstruction and insubordination on the part of the peasantry. They were refusing to take up vacant holdings, except on their own terms. They were managing to make less use of various services provided by their lords and constituting seigneurial monopolies, such as the compulsory use of the seigneurial mill or the pasturing of animals on the lord's meadows. There was a sharp rise in the number of minor delinquencies in the performance of such labour services as still remained. On the estates of the Abbey of Ramsey 'the court rolls reveal fines for such wholesale non-performance of certain work over the two decades after the Black Death, that it may be logical to consider the lord's acceptance of these fines as another form of commutation'.[19] There was much piecemeal withholding of rents and of other customary payments, and, especially, of any amercements that might be imposed by the lords' courts. Fear of desertion by tenants, as Knighton pointed out, formed the ultimate sanction that persuaded many landowners into prudent compromises, though flights of villeins were, apparently, less common at first than they were destined to become after the two further plagues of 1361/2 and 1369 and the famine of 1370.

III

On 18 June 1349, while the plague was still raging and no parliament could be convened safely, the royal council issued an ordinance 'considering the grievous incommodities which of the lack especially of Ploughmen and such Labourers may hereafter come'.[20] It forbade the payment of wages higher than those of 1346/7.[21] The choice of this normative date is no accident, because this was a time of economic recession when wages had been depressed.[22]

This Ordinance of Labourers remained in force, with some alterations, until November 1378, when it was, at long last, re-enacted as a parliamentary statute. It was this ordinance, and not a number of supplementary statutes enacted between 1351 and 1378, that was enforced henceforth in the courts.[23] Contemporaries regarded the ordinance, and the supplementary statute of 1351 as the most important legislation of their time. Bishop Thomas Hatfield of Durham immediately, in June 1349, appointed a commission to enforce the Ordinance of Labourers in his Palatinate of Durham. The Statute of Labourers of 1351 was copied into his chancery roll, 'the only statute to appear there'.[24]

The first parliament held after the plague, in February 1351, enacted a Statute of Labourers. It included a specific schedule of maximum wages for various occupations.[25] It clarified and amended some of the provisions of the conciliar ordinance. During the next twenty-five years there was a number of further alterations, brought about mostly by the petitions of the landowning interests in the House of Commons.

The Ordinance of Labourers, and the supplementary statutes, sought to regulate on a national scale matters which in a much less uniform way were the subject of local restrictions on numerous manors. Long before 1349 inhabitants of English villages were used to elaborate regulation of agricultural practices. This was particularly essential in villages with open-field agriculture.[26] Over and above this, landlords, as a matter of course, minutely regulated the conduct of their villein tenants and other servile dependants. It was the essence of servile tenure and status that anything that suited the lord's interests might be demanded of his bondmen and anything that hurt the lord was sure to be prohibited. The study of any long series of manorial court rolls brings out the oppressive interference of the lords with the lives and conduct of their servile dependants. As long as land was scarce, and peasants competed fiercely with each other for such tenements as lords were willing to concede to them, men with holdings would not lightly disobey and there was little danger that many of them would flee. While labourers were plentiful, under-employment the common lot of many, and wages correspondingly low, wage-earning smallholders and landless men could be kept on the manors of their birth by fear that there might be even less employment for wandering strangers outside them.

It was a symptom of the new situation created by the plague that in 1349 landowners needed royal intervention over a much wider range of conflicts with their dependants. Their grip over servile tenants and other labouring employees was clearly loosening and the royal government had to help them over matters that had hitherto been fairly adequately regulated by the manorial courts and the councils of individual landlords. Thus, some of the provisions of the legislation of 1349 and 1351 tried to apply uniformly to the whole country regulations that many manorial lords had been in the habit of enforcing on their own manors. On the estates of the Abbey of Ramsey, since at least 1299, a succession of manorial ordinances had tried to keep down the price of ale.[27] This subject looms large in 1352 in the earliest surviving roll of the justices enforcing the ordinance of 1349 in Wiltshire.[28] To come to graver matters, landlords were trying to stop labourers from leaving their native villages during harvest. This was a fairly common manorial regulation. It reappears in the Statute of Labourers of 1351. An example of such a rule being enforced can be cited in 1368 on the manor of Aldham in Suffolk, belonging to Humphrey Bohun, Earl of Hereford, where a servile peasant was allowed to reside outside the manor most of the time, but was given such a licence only on condition that he would return each year to help the lord with the harvest.[29]

The chief aim of the new royal legislation was to freeze wages and prices at a low, pre–plague level, though the records of its enforcement show, above all, preoccupation with wages. Only local squires could enforce effectively this kind of legislation. Hitherto men drawn from this class were appointed as keepers of the peace, responsible for keeping records of breaches of law and order, but not empowered to try them. There had been brief departures from this restriction on their powers during periods of emergency, but, as a matter of general royal policy, the trying of offences was reserved for judges of the central royal courts or for special commissions appointed to deal with particular cases. The enforcement of the labour legislation was the first quasi-permanent breach with this older system. From December 1352 to November 1359 there were two sets of commissions for each county. There were keepers of the peace, as in the past. But for dealing with the labour legislation men were commissioned to be 'justices', not 'keepers'. The total number of men appointed between 1349 and 1359 to enforce the labour legislation was 664.[30] The same men often sat on both commissions, as there was only a limited number of suitable local gentry that could be entrusted with such functions. The way was prepared for the merging in 1361 of both groups into single commissions of 'justices of the peace' and 'justices of labourers', though special circumstances (to be explained later) may have accounted for the taking of this final step.[31]

In the third quarter of the fourteenth century a large part of the English landowning class still exploited their demesnes directly. Since the disaster of the plague the demands of their servants, and of agricultural labourers in general, for higher wages and other benefits threatened to curtail drastically the profits of large-scale farming. The incomes of moderately wealthy and especially of the lesser landowners were particularly menaced. As a parliamentary petition of 1368 reminds us, they included people who were not lords of manors and did not possess any villeins of their own, but farmed substantial properties using only personal servants and hired labourers. Hence the fierce demand by this group of petitioners that fines imposed on delinquent labourers should be doubled.[32]

From this class of moderately wealthy landowners were recruited the men who ran the local government for the king, including service on the commissions of peace and labourers. Some of them had taken part in the royal wars as men-at-arms in magnate retinues. They represented their shires in the House of Commons. Their need for cheaper labour demanded, and of course received, a speedy recognition.

Lionel Bradenham, owner of the single village of Langenhoe, four miles south of Colchester, which he supplied with food, provides a good example of a local squire who would be sure to enforce zealously labour legislation, as he himself relied entirely on hired labour. He acted as a justice of labourers from 1355 to 1359 and, again in 1361–2, abused his authority and extorted money from his neighbours. The town of Colchester, which he had been terrorizing with armed gangs, procured a commission of inquiry against him on 3 July 1362 and he was dismissed from being a justice three days later.[33]

Unlike most medieval English enactments, lacking any machinery for effective enforcement, the labour legislation of 1349–51 continued to be enthusiastically applied. Its provisions about wages and contracts of servants were, perhaps, the most zealously enforced enactments in medieval English history. This was particularly true of the 1350s. In Essex in 1351 the justices took fines for labour offences from over 7,500 persons. This was, possibly, about one-sixth of the adult population. Fines totalling £719 were imposed on these offenders. Essex would continue for nearly forty years to attract a maximum number of such prosecutions.[34]

Throughout England the receipt of excessive wages was the offence most frequently mentioned in indictments and most of the accused were members of the labouring classes. These cases were relatively uncomplicated, except for the computation of the exact amounts received in excess of the permitted wages, which caused the resultant fines to fluctuate erratically. Many of the employers were among the worst culprits, but there is no evidence that people of higher social rank were prosecuted for paying excessive rates. The labour legislation remained fairly ineffective, especially in the more developed areas of the country, because many employers found it to their advantage to ignore it and could safely do so. In section V of chapter 4 I provide conclusive illustrations of this from the estates of the Bishops of Worcester. While, as a class, landowners supported the enactment of labour legislation, they lacked the solidarity necessary to ensure its successful enforcement. Each employer's own best interests were served by securing enough labour and this involved competing with other employers by offering higher wages and other attractive benefits.[35]

An important clause of the Ordinance of Labourers insisted that servants should remain in the employment of the same master for at least a year. They could be prosecuted for an earlier withdrawal from service, though the employers could dismiss them at any time. In practice the justices found these cases of alleged breaches of contracts very troublesome and frequently adjourned them. The ordinance also gave the lords the first claim on the labour of their bondmen. The need for such a provision illustrates strikingly the weakening of the lords' grip over their serfs. The existence of such a regulation may explain a case in 1372/3, at Ikham in Suffolk, belonging to John of Brittany, Earl of Richmond, where the parson paid a fine in order to obtain the services of the earl's bondwoman.[36] The enforcement of this rule produced some complex and very awkward cases, where lords claimed the labour of serfs who had entered into regular yearly contracts with other employers. An oft-quoted, though clearly exceptional, case concerned the claim of the Cistercian Abbot of Meaux in Holderness (in the East Riding of Yorkshire) that a family of particularly wealthy villeins of his abbey had suborned some of his other serfs into contracts of annual service. The abbot won.[37] Most such cases were decided, similarly, in favour of the lords.

A widely resented provision of the ordinance gave to the justices the power of compelling able-bodied persons without property of their own or regular employment to enter into the service of employers chosen for them.[38] This was specifically intended to increase the supply of agricultural labour. Prosecutions under this clause produced some very interesting instances of the drift of former agricultural workers into a great variety of other jobs.

The fiscal preoccupations of Sir William Shareshull, Chief Justice of the King's Bench from 1350 to 1361, were an important force behind the vigorous enforcement of the labour legislation. In order to finance the war with France, the direct taxes on the laity (fifteenths and tenths) went on being collected during most of the decade after 1348. It was probably Shareshull's idea that the revenue from fines imposed for breaches of labour laws might be used to reduce the burden of ordinary direct taxation. The economic disarray after the Black Death made it very desirable that this should be attempted and Shareshull was a great believer in using the judicial machinery to raise revenue.[39]

This new scheme was put into operation in connection with the three fifteenths and tenths levied in 1352–4. In each county the revenue from fines was to be used to alleviate the tax burden of localities most impoverished by the plague.[40] In order to stimulate still further the zeal of the special justices of labourers, their salaries were to be paid out of the proceeds, only the residue being allotted to lessen the tax burden of localities most hit by the plague.

It is impossible to calculate exactly the revenue from fines and the resultant deductions from taxes, but in 1352–4 the latter came to at least £8,371 or 7⅓ per cent of the total assessment of the lay-taxes levied in those three years. In a few shires the proportion of tax remitted on account of fines was very high. One is not surprised to find it rising in 1352 in Essex to 58 per cent. The proportion in Buckinghamshire was about 50 per cent and it amounted to around 33 per cent in Berkshire, Cambridgeshire and the Lindsey division of Lincolnshire.[41]

Writing of the first decade after the Black Death, B.H. Putnam was convinced that 'regulations as efficiently carried out as these were' for a short period were bound to have some effect. D.L. Farmer's researches on wages confirm that by 1354/5 wage levels were often lower than in the previous years, though Farmer fails to take into account other benefits of labourers, and especially of permanent agricultural servants, which it is impossible to estimate precisely. Putnam concluded that 'wages were not kept at the statutory level but they were kept for ten years at a lower level than would have resulted from a régime of free competition'.[42] This may have been true in some cases, to be examined presently, but Dr John Hatcher seems to be nearer the truth when he estimates that a large proportion of agricultural wages rose beyond the permitted legal limits. It is nice to have the example he cites from Professor Farmer that on one occasion, at Knightsbridge, 'even the carpenter who made the stocks with which to imprison those workers who refused to swear obedience to the Statute of Labourers was paid at the illegal rate of 5½d per day'.[43]

Above all, the labour legislation strengthened the hands of those employers who, because they managed to preserve control reasonably well over their bondmen, or were able for local reasons to secure sufficient hired labour, remained in any case in a strong position. On the manor of Alciston in coastal Sussex, an exceptionally rewarding and well-managed estate of the Abbey of Battle, wages soared in 1349/50. But in the following year the wages of its permanent agricultural servants (famuli) were reduced again to the level of 1347, in accordance with the ordinance of 1349, and stayed there for some years, while the wages of temporarily hired labour also declined. In this, as in most other respects, at Alciston 'the plague caused only a slight and temporary dislocation'. But there was local discontent and its villein tenants withheld labour services during the crisis of 1381, though their 'strike' did not last long.[44]

The enforcement of labour legislation was reformed by a statute in a parliament held from 24 January to 18 February 1361. The end of the war with France meant that direct taxation was discontinued (until 1371) but Edward III was determined to retain higher wartime rates of duty on exported wool when the previous grant of them was due to expire in 1362. Unfortunately

Men digging the lord's land (Bodleian Library, Oxford: Bodl. MS. 264, f. 69r)

the roll for this parliament is lost and we do not know whether the concessions on the other matters made to the Commons were related in any way to the king's desire to procure the renewal of the higher rate of duties. One of the concessions made to the Commons in 1361 satisfied the strong desire of the more important landowners in each county to tighten their grip on the administration of justice. The commission of the peace restored the powers of its members as justices, not keepers, and those commissions included henceforth the power to try offences against labour legislation.

Hitherto the leading magnates, together with royal judges, had opposed the entrusting of judicial powers to the county commissions. But the paying of annual royal fees to some of the magnates was secured on the customs. In the early 1360s these payments have been estimated to range between £6,300 and £6,900 and they could only be comfortably continued if the higher rates of duty were retained. This is the reason for my conjecture that some assurances about the eventual renewal, in 1362, of the wartime rates of duties, may have played some part in the consent of the magnates to appeasing the Commons over the restoration of judicial powers to the justices of the peace. Be that as it may, Edward III and the magnates did secure the renewal, in 1362, of the wartime rate of subsidy on exported wool. In 1363/4 the fees and annuities paid out of the customs amounted to £5,818, and between 1362 and 1368 the customs yielded an average annual income of about £47,000, about two-thirds of the king's yearly revenue in those years.[45]

The combined commission of justices of the peace and of labourers had emerged at long last. It was again suspended in 1364 but was revived in 1368 and endured this time until the revolts of 1381, which the operations of its members helped to provoke.[46]

Because of the absence of the parliament roll for 1361 we cannot be sure about the origin of another statutory enactment in the same assembly. But it is probable that its exceptionally vicious provisions derived from a Commons petition and represent another concession to county pressures. It was enacted that labourers who had escaped from their masters and had been outlawed for not standing trial, if recaptured and convicted, were to be branded on the forehead with the letter 'F', signifying falsehood, if their accusers insisted. The final section of this clause of the statute included various regulations which were likely in practice to diminish the number of occasions on which this barbarous penalty would be applied. They read like practical safeguards tacked on to the original petition by the royal judges.[47]

A serious new challenge to the effectiveness of labour laws came with the return of plague in the summer of 1361. Again lords of manors had to bid against each other to attract workers. Even the estate officials of the very authoritarian Bishop William Edington of Winchester, who was royal treasurer and chancellor for nineteen years (1344–63), had to break custom by giving bribes and presents. Average harvesting costs came to 2½d per acre more in 1362 than in 1360. Henceforth, in general, the justices' efforts to control wages in the 1360s seem to have been less successful than in the previous decade.[48] Things got no better later, despite numerous prosecutions of alleged offenders. I shall pursue this story further when speaking in the next section about the exceptionally turbulent 1370s.

IV

Professor Christopher Dyer has greatly expanded our knowledge of the revolts of 1381 and their background by undertaking a wide-ranging inquiry into the manorial records, especially the court-rolls, of the four counties particularly involved: Suffolk, Hertfordshire, Essex and Kent.[49] His is only a partial sample, as the estates of the Abbey of St Albans, for example, are not included in his survey.[50] But he did study the records of over a hundred manors and compiled a list of about 440 rebels coming from 330 villages.[51] This body of material certainly justifies, in part, one of the traditional descriptions of the risings as a Peasants' Revolt.

The evidence assembled by Dyer, together with other records, like the rolls of the justices enforcing labour legislation, confirms the picture of the 1370s as a period of mounting social tension and quickening economic changes in this corner of south-eastern England. It was one of the regions of exceptional economic vitality, stimulated by the proximity to London. As will be documented more fully later (section V), it was particularly hit by experiments with new types of taxation. Above all, if the men from Hertfordshire, Essex and Kent took the lead in the march on London, it was because they knew that they could get there quickly, especially if they moved on horseback, as they certainly did.[52] They could confidently expect to be able to confront the king in person and obtain from him the satisfaction of their demands. Rural unrest of increasing intensity existed, of course, in other more distant counties, like the area stretching from Sussex and Surrey through Hampshire, into Wiltshire and Devon, where a wave of agrarian troubles occurred in 1376–8; this has been illuminated by the researches of Dr Rosamund Faith.[53]

'Many lines of continuity can be seen between the events of the pre-revolt period and the 1381 outbreak. . . . The protests made before the revolt concerned issues that figured' very prominently in the rebel demands to the king – 'the abolition of serfdom and servile tenure, the removal of service beyond a simple cash rent', and the curtailing of the judicial powers of the landlords in their manorial and franchisal courts.[54]

In granting, in November 1381, a pardon to nobles and others who had taken the law into their own hands in suppressing the revolts, the government described the rebels as 'villeins and other malefactors'.[55] The rebellion was clearly regarded as, above all, a rising of the servile villeins. This is also what John Gower thought of it: in his terrifying description of the rising, which for a few days perhaps drove him into hiding in forests, he speaks of it as a rebellion of 'servile peasants against nobles and gentlefolk'.[56] In Professor Dyer's sample of 79 rebels from Suffolk, Hertfordshire and Essex whose holdings of land can be identified, 38 were customary tenants. At least eight were 'serfs by blood' ('*nativi de sanguine*').[57]

The eyewitness account of the irruption of the rebels into London in the so-called *Anonimalle Chronicle*, written by someone very close to the young Richard II, assumes that the '*supreme* [my italics] and overriding purpose of the revolt was the abolition of villeinage and all that went with it. This was the heart of the matter.'[58] 'Nede they free be most' is the summing up of the anonymous writer of the poem 'The Rebellion of Jack Straw', very hostile to the rebels,[59] and it was the keynote of the rising to most contemporary chroniclers. The demand for freedom from serfdom was certainly 'the one most persistently presented when the rebels were directly negotiating with the king and his advisers'.[60]

Villeins hated their servile tenure and status because they were left without any rights in their relations with their lords. Any concessions that the lord had made to his villeins could be revoked as long as they remained his bondmen or held their lands by servile tenure. Though demesnes might be leased and labour services commuted, servile tenants had every reason to remain insecure in their new way of life. We know now that most of the leases of manorial demesnes and commutations of labour services became permanent, but contemporaries had no such certainty. Many of them were turning to industrial employment or were taking advantage of the diminution of their seigneurial burdens to develop and increase their holdings. They dreaded the reversal of those new opportunities. This helps to explain why the demand for the abolition of serfdom was very widespread and vociferous in regions like East Anglia and Essex, where servile tenure was being commuted rapidly and rural industries were growing most prosperously.

Thaxted in Essex, held in 1381 by Edmund Mortimer, Earl of March,[61] provides a model example of a village in this situation.[62] Its net value in 1377/8 was £109 7s. Its demesnes had been gradually leased during the twenty years before the revolt and a remnant of labour services was demanded only in emergencies. It was the most important centre of metalwork in Essex. The Poll Tax return of 1381 shows that 96 men, or a third of its adult male population, were engaged in metalwork, mostly as cutlers. If other craftsmen are included, about half the inhabitants of Thaxted earned their living from various crafts. 'On the face of it there would appear less reason for the revolt of 1381 to have spread to Thaxted than to many other Essex manors.'[63] Yet it did. Resentment at the restrictions threatened by the labour legislation may have been one cause. As some of the men of Thaxted took part in the attack on Duke John of Lancaster's castle of Hertford, they obviously shared in the widespread hatred of his political influence, which was a major feature of the revolts. Some of them joined later in the march of other Essex men on London.[64]

What must interest a student of agrarian discontent most are the events at Thaxted itself. Some of the tenants broke into the manor-house there. Though they removed and destroyed the manorial custumal recording the servile charges and disabilities, some sort of copy of it was made and henceforth secretly preserved by certain of the tenants. When in 1393 a new seigneurial survey was being drawn up by the earl's council, as members of it came to know of this copy, they sought to secure it. The tenantry refused to divulge it.[65] They clearly wanted to keep their lord in the dark about his traditional claims and dreaded, presumably, that he might restore these older arrangements.

Defaults in performance of labour services multiplied in the 1370s. The evidence from the Ramsey manor of Holywell-cum-Needingworth (Huntingdonshire) is instructive. While such defaults appear to have been infrequent before the Black Death, there were 32 occurrences of them in 1372 and 24 in 1378.[66]

During the thirteenth century the Premonstratensian Abbey of Halesowen (Staffordshire) had a long series of bitter conflicts with the tenants of a large manor around it, consisting of 12 different rural settlements. Chronic troubles revived again after the Black Death, as the abbey tried to reverse the decline of its revenues. 'The Abbey's servants and officials were assaulted and abused, and there was a widespread plundering of the Abbey property. . . . Never in the recorded history of the manor had so many peasants trespassed so openly on the Abbey crops, pastures, fishponds and warrens.' Troubles came to a head in 1380. 'We do not know exactly what happened, but in the court held in September 1380 all the tenants in the manor, free as well as bond, were declared to be in mercy, except a small number of villagers who had bought their peace.'[67]

One of the best documented examples of an outbreak of anti-seigneurial agitation in more purely rural districts comes from 1376–8, involving some forty villages from Sussex to Devon.[68] All except one belonged to ecclesiastical landlords. Thus, the records of the west Berkshire village of Coleshill, belonging to Edington Priory in Wiltshire, preserve the information that 'all the tenants who [should] work at harvest-time did not work on account of the great rumour ('*prout magnum rumorem*') among various other tenants'.[69] That 'rumour' was that Colleshill, and other villages aroused by it, had once been royal manors and that, therefore, their peasants should enjoy a privileged tenure of the estates of the royal Ancient Demesne. They believed that they were entitled, therefore, to personal freedom, disappearance of all labour services and security of tenure as long as they rendered fixed rents. The rebellious villages were advised by some 'councellors' that they could vindicate their claims by securing copies of statements about them in Domesday Book. At least forty villages procured such copies from the royal chancery.

Many of the tenants on Ancient Demesne estates which were still held by the crown did really enjoy a privileged position of a secure tenure for fixed rents.[70] One of the advantages of such manors, like for example Havering in Essex, was that they did not normally fall within the jurisdiction of the justices of the peace and of labourers. Hence there is virtually no evidence at Havering of any attempt to enforce the labour laws, except for one isolated case where a jury from outside Havering's privileged liberty presented in 1389 to the visiting central royal court of the King's Bench one such offender.[71]

The southern and south-western villages which were aroused by the 'rumour' of their right to share in Ancient Demesne's privileges were quite mistaken in this. A long series of adverse judgements of the royal central courts had denied the claims to any privileged treatment for the tenants of former royal estates alienated by kings to other owners.[72] Besides, many of the villagers were appealing to Domesday Book quite mistakenly, for they were not numbered among royal estates there in 1086.[73] Some of them had, indeed, belonged to Anglo-Saxon kings at various remote dates before the Norman Conquest and it is interesting that traditions of this were still preserved. But this was of no use legally in 1376–8.

If we are to believe the wording of a few special commissions of inquiry and of some petitions from aggrieved ecclesiastics, fairly serious disturbances occurred in a number of localities.[74] Such records should be used with caution as they habitually abound in extreme statements. But they do identify places where some troubles had occurred. These included the tenants of Ottery St

Mary in Devon, belonging to a collegiate church founded by a Bishop of Exeter, the 'bond men and bond tenants' of the Bishop of Winchester at Farnham in Surrey, the men of the Abbey of Chertsey at Chobham, Thorpe, Frimley and Egham in the same county, the tenants of the Nunnery of Shaftesbury on eight of its manors in Wiltshire and Dorset and the Prior of Bath's tenants on two Somerset estates. The most alarming was the petition from the Abbot of Chertsey, that his tenants on the four above-mentioned manors in Surrey had purchased an exemplification of entries in Domesday Book, in their view, justified their claim that they only owed payments of rent and suit to the abbot's court. When the abbot's officials had tried to distrain them, they had allegedly resisted with armed force and had threatened to burn down the abbey with the monks in it. When the men of the Sheriff of Surrey intervened, the rioters are reported to have nearly killed them.[75] These tenants of Chertsey could in fact prove nothing from Domesday Book, but they believed that their villages had been given to the abbey in the tenth century by King Edgar.[76]

These incidents lay behind the frequently cited petition of the Commons in the first parliament of Richard II's reign. I have quoted in section I its alarmist warnings of a possible general peasant uprising. After reciting the attempts to seek exemplification out of Domesday Book, it alleged that the tenantries who had procured them 'have withdrawn and still withdraw the customs and services due to their lords . . . and they threaten to kill their lord's servants if these make distraint upon them for services . . . Accordingly the said lords lose much profit from their lordships. . . . Moreover, in many parts of the realm the corn lies unharvested for this reason and is lost for all time. . . . To sustain their errors and rebellions they have collected large sums of money among themselves.' It was answered on the king's behalf that exemplifications of Domesday Book could not alter the relationship of these men to their lords and that they 'neither can nor ought to have any value or relevance to the question of personal freedom'. Furthermore, any lords who so wished could secure the appointment of special commissions of inquiry.[77]

No returns from any such commissions can be traced[78] and it looks as if the aggrieved landowners soon realized that they could end these troubles through their own courts. Nor is there any record of further exemplifications from Domesday Book being sought after February 1378. All this suggests that one must not erect the Commons petition into a witness to a desperate crisis, though it certainly points to considerable peasant discontents.

That petition included the gratuitous charge that 'the villeins and tenants will, to avenge themselves on their lords, adhere to foreign enemies in the event of a sudden invasion'. This shows that the landowners who dominated the Commons completely misunderstood their humbler countrymen and grossly misrepresented the real state of mind of the population of southern England. In reality the rebels of 1381 expressly prohibited the inhabitants of the coastal districts from joining their march on London, lest this should weaken the coastal defences against the French.

Another petition of the Commons in the same parliament demanded desperate remedies to ensure a satisfactory supply of agricultural labour at statutory wages. This included a demand that no labourer should be excused from being compelled to work for employers designated for him by the justices on the ground that he had some smallholding of his own or practised a craft. The royal ministers wisely refused in this case to add any further to the existing laws.[79] On the eve of 1381 a section of the landed class was clearly displaying a truculence that matched the violence of the discontented peasantry.

In the 1370s many parts of the country saw vigorous action by the justices enforcing labour legislation. In 1373–5 Lincolnshire justices tried 152 violations of the labour laws. Most common among the charges were refusals to take employment when directed to do so and the giving or receiving of excessive wages.[80] In 1377–9, in Essex, 200 out of 280 extant indictments before the justices of the peace involved labour offences, mostly of the same sort as the ones tried by the Lincolnshire justices.[81] More than half the cases tried by Norfolk justices in 1375–9 dealt with breaches of labour laws.[82]

Some 'middlemen' appear to have acted habitually as agents for making labourers available to employers, who paid them for this service. At the Suffolk judicial sessions of 1361 a man described as a weaver was accused of being a 'common procurator of agricultural *famuli* for taking them outside their vill in the autumn', clearly for employment during harvesting. Similarly, at the Norfolk manor of Forncett, belonging to Margaret, Countess of Norfolk, a man was indicted for leading each autumn six or eight others to work at higher wages. This is not surprising, as Countess Margaret was a harsh landlord with a large tenantry of disgruntled servile smallholders. Another Norfolk man was indicted in 1378 for suborning labourers of various people and then hiring them out to others.[83]

The labour legislation stirred popular hatred out of all proportion to any economic effectiveness it might have achieved. It led to numerous outlawries of people who failed to face trial. A petition of the Commons in the parliament of 1376 claimed that this was no hardship for people who had no intention of returning to their native counties and were never likely to be tracked down in other parts of the country.[84] This might have been true as far as the chances of finding new employment was concerned, but meant painful losses of contact with relatives and friends.

The enforcement of the Ordinance of Labourers and the Statute of Labourers, with their various subsequent 'enlargements', greatly increased the perennial popular hostility towards the local agents of the king. The justices of labourers became the special target of popular hatred and in the last part of this chapter (section VI) I shall describe what happened to some of them. Their activities constituted one of the most important causes of the revolts of 1381. It is no accident that 'the area of the greatest intensity of the revolt coincides with the area for which there is definite evidence of the greatest efforts at the enforcements of the labour laws'.[85] William Langland, in a version of his poem *Piers the Plowman* dating from around 1377, makes labourers curse 'the kynge and al his conseille after, Suche lawes to loke laborers to greve'.[86]

V

Generalized peasant discontent and conflicts between numerous landlords and their tenantries created a countryside where a widespread popular uprising could occur. But it was the backing provided by royal judicial administration for the authority of the landlords, as manifested especially in the enforcement of the labour laws, that sharpened to the point of exasperation popular hostility against the royal government. It was a government that seemed unable to check widespread official corruptions and perversions of the judicial system. The poet John Gower was speaking of his native Kent at the end of the reign of Edward III when he described 'a regularly established class of men whose occupation it was to arrange for the packing and bribery of juries' and the terrible abuses that had been caused by their activities.[87] The systematic attack by the rebels on most Kentish royal officials and justices was a thoroughly intelligible reaction against a peculiarly sophisticated body of abuses and corruption in local government and justice in that county.

There was plenty of inflammable matter around, but the final spark that set fire to it was excessive fiscal pressure. Here the princes of the royal family bore heavy responsibility, especially John of Gaunt, the oldest and most powerful of the surviving sons of Edward III. Duke John was an extremely haughty and arrogant man, hot-tempered but very devious, with a long history of feuds with leading prelates and magnates. We have no evidence that he entertained sinister designs for taking over his young nephew's kingdom, as was widely believed in 1380/1, but he certainly behaved throughout his career as though the realm existed mainly to provide members of the ruling dynasty with all conceivable military and financial help for their private schemes. In 1380–1 he intended to use the resources of England to conquer the kingdom of Castile, to which he had a claim by right of his wife. An ineffective but well-meaning group of royal ministers was committed to financing this scheme and other enterprises of John's two younger brothers. In pursuance of these plans the royal government blundered into disaster as a result of tragic illusions and misconceptions about what was financially practicable. Simon Sudbury, Lord Chancellor and Archbishop of Canterbury, who had been the official head of the royal administration since January 1380, was an experienced statesman, moderate and sensible, who tried to stand above magnate factions, but he could not avoid deferring to the wishes of the royal princes. His murder in London by the rebels as a traitor to king and country highlights the grotesque misjudgement and misrepresentation of the king's leading ministers in the country at large. But the revolts did achieve something that nothing else could have assured. They terrified parliaments for a long time into refusing to grant new taxes for fear of provoking further uprisings. This put an abrupt halt to most warlike enterprises.[88]

No account of the risings of 1381 is intelligible without a discussion of the financial mess caused by the ambitious schemes of John of Gaunt and his brothers. I have devoted to this subject a number of earlier studies, but another, somewhat improved version is desirable.[89] Between 1369 and the summer of 1381 the English government incurred extraordinary expenditures on war with France and Scotland amounting to at least £1,100,000. Just over half of this sum was met out of direct taxation, the share of the laity alone amounting to just over a third (£382,000), assessed through eight separate parliamentary grants (1371–80).[90] The traditional type of lay direct taxes, the fifteenths and tenths as they were called, had been levied from 1334 onwards using the same fixed assessment each time. The heavy mortality from the plagues between 1348 and 1369 had made the charges demanded from each locality seriously obsolescent, but it was deemed politically unthinkable to reform this tax or reassess it. When particularly heavy taxes were needed in December 1380 the Lords believed, justifiably enough, that another fifteenth and tenth would be 'very grievous' to the taxpayers. Hence the alternative of the Poll Tax, which led to the revolts of May–July 1381.

After the Anglo-French war restarted in 1369, the government began experimenting with new taxes which were assessed not on property, but on people. There were four such attempts, the fatal Poll Tax of 1380 being the last. These new taxes were bound to fall most heavily on the more densely populated counties. We can compare them with the old assessments to the fifteenths and tenths. In the first of these experiments, the Parish Tax of 1371, the assessment of Norfolk was increased by a third and that of Essex by four-fifths, while the charge for Suffolk was almost doubled. All these shires were in the forefront of revolt in 1381. The most fatal of the new financial experiments, the third lay Poll Tax, imposed in December 1380, was expected to yield £66,666 13s 4d (100,000 marks), almost twice as much as a traditional fifteenth and tenth. Its effect on the more densely populated counties would have been even more crushing than the burdens imposed by the Parish Tax of 1371 if widespread evasion had not occurred in the early months of 1381. The commissions of inquiry into this evasion precipitated the armed revolts.

In the case of the fifteenths and tenths the government knew how much each locality was supposed to contribute. In any place that failed to produce its quota the missing amounts could be raised through the seizure and sale of a proportion of the goods of the entire population. Such a threat was quite sufficient to prevent serious evasion: multiple fifteenths and tenths were collected in the years immediately before 1381 without much trouble. By contrast, in the case of the Poll Taxes, the government could not know beforehand how much it could expect from any particular locality. The first Poll Tax, imposed in 1377, was levied at a fairly light rate of 4d per person. But this still would equal two days' wages of an ordinary carpenter, as prescribed in the statute of 1351.[91] That first Poll Tax seems to have been collected reasonably successfully, yielding about £22,000. The second Poll Tax, granted in 1379, was an exceptionally fair, graduated tax, but it yielded only some £18,600. In granting the third Poll Tax in December 1380 parliament inevitably returned to the first model of 1377, with a single basic rate. Because it wanted three times as much money, compared with the yield of the 1377 tax, it trebled the rate per person to 12d. If we go back to the wage schedule of the 1351 statute, this was equivalent to the wages of a master mason for four days or the pay for harvesting for four days.[92] The charge of 12d per person contrasted sharply with the rate of 4d demanded jointly from the poorest married couples in the graduated tax of 1379. In the case of such a couple there was in 1380 a sixfold increase.

The experience of 1377 gave some idea of how much money could be raised from each locality. No exact comparisons were possible, because in 1377 children below the age of fourteen were exempted, and in 1380 children below the age of fifteen. As the government expected to finance two armies in the spring and summer of 1381 (possibly even three), in addition to covering the needs of defending the Scottish border and protecting England from French naval attacks, it was essential that the levying of the Poll Tax should proceed smoothly and quickly. By late February 1381 the exchequer officials knew for certain that the levy was a failure in both these respects.

Colossal evasion was being discovered when in the course of February the exchequer conducted the preliminary 'viewing' of the accounts of the collectors of the Poll Tax. The size of the original evasion was even greater than the amount ultimately 'lost', after counter-measures ordered in the last days of February and in March produced some results. The final loss still amounted to a third of the total number of taxpayers in 1377. Obviously the raising of the age limit by one year from fourteen to fifteen could not explain the 'disappearance' by 1381 of 458,356 taxpayers since 1377, when the intervening period had been free from any serious disasters.

Evasion of such heroic proportions amounted to an initial act of rebellion, albeit a passive one, much more universal than the armed risings of May–July 1381. Some 102,500 taxpayers were finally 'missing' in London and the nine shires of the south-east, where the subsequent armed risings were concentrated. The still higher rates of evasion occurred, however, in the less developed areas of England. Some 115,000 taxpayers were finally 'concealed' in the six south-western counties, amounting to 43 per cent of the contributors of 1377. This proportion rose to 47 per cent in the particularly poor northern region of Cumberland, Westmorland and the North and West Ridings of Yorkshire. This passive resistance to financial exactions might be described as the first of the two Great Revolts in 1381, though a bloodless one, unlike the wave of armed risings that followed later.[93]

After discovering in February 1381 the immense amount of evasion, the government had two choices. It could either modify its military plans or speed up the levy and take measures to overcome evasion. The former course of action was unthinkable; the government panicked and chose the latter. To the last, nobody in power seems to have feared any serious armed resistance. Oral instructions must have been given at the exchequer to ordinary collectors to improve their performance. In almost all the cases where comparison is possible, the final returns of the collectors, dating mostly from late April or May 1381, were larger than the provisional figures that they had originally produced at their 'views of account' in February or March. If nothing more had been done, most probably there would have been no armed rising. But, as a supplement to the inquiries by the ordinary collectors, the government took the further, fatal step of appointing between 16 March and 20 May additional commissioners in fifteen counties and the town of Canterbury. They appear to have included some high-handed and notoriously unpopular notables. These men were given additional powers to arrest anybody obstructing them and this appears to have added to the hostility that they aroused. Their task was to discover and collect the 'concealed' arrears of the Poll Tax.

The unpopularity of the special commissioners is strikingly confirmed by the fact that, even after the armed risings were put down, the ordinary collectors in Suffolk still did not risk to collect some of the money 'rediscovered' by the new commission of inquiry. This additional sum amounted to £184 7s. The ordinary collectors had managed to collect £128 6s 4d, but the outstanding balance of £56 8d they dared not collect for 'fear of death'.[94]

The author of the *Anonimalle Chronicle* blamed much of the loss of revenue from the Poll Tax on the corrupt practices of the collectors and he was probably right in part. The various supplementary measures to check on evasion did lead to the 'rediscovery' between February and May 1381 of 47,161 further 'concealed taxpayers', but this was only the tip of the iceberg. The final net yield of the tax fell short of the government's target of 100,000 marks by some £22,700. At least 83 per cent of this net yield had reached the exchequer by the end of May, before the rebellion started. The military operations that were meant to be financed by that tax failed miserably, though for other reasons than lack of money.[95]

It should be stressed that contemporary chroniclers, with three exceptions, do not discuss the importance of the Poll Tax in causing the risings. Thomas Walsingham, at the Abbey of St Albans, for instance, did not do so.[96] Two of the exceptions are the Evesham chronicler, perhaps Nicholas Herford, prior of that abbey, and Henry Knighton of Leicester Abbey. The latter's highly dramatic and anecdotal account of what allegedly happened in Kent may not be credible.[97] Only the *Anonimalle Chronicle* provides a well-informed and detailed treatment, though it may be confused about some details.[98]

The inquiries of the supplementary commissioners finally convinced people that there was no end to squeezing more money out of them. Their previous payments to the ordinary collectors should have discharged them, or so they thought. The *Anonimalle Chronicle* says this explicitly. It describes the encounter between John Bampton, one of the commissioners, and the men of Fobbing and the neighbouring Essex villages. The men of Fobbing said that they would pay nothing more as they already had an acquittance for their share of the tax. When Bampton tried to arrest them, they drove him out, starting the rising.[99]

Thus, the new commissions to levy the unpaid Poll Tax, following on from the first collections and the supplementary inquiries by the ordinary collectors, can be seen to have triggered off the earliest uprisings in Essex and Kent.

VI

The main area of armed revolts consisted of Kent and the districts of Sussex nearest to it, parts of Surrey and Middlesex nearest to London, most of Essex, Hertfordshire, Cambridgeshire and some of Huntingdonshire, Norfolk and Sussex. Throughout this area (though largely not in Kent and Sussex) religious houses were at risk. Nobles and gentry were given a bad fright, though the risings were threatening their properties and especially their estate records more than their persons. Any killing of people by the rebels that took place occurred in London and a few other towns. One outstanding feature of events in the countryside was the rarity of murders and the absence of lethal class animosities. In contrast to the peasant risings around Paris in 1358, in which numerous nobles of both sexes and all ages were indiscriminately murdered, almost nobody was killed in England in 1381 merely because he was a substantial landowner. There is no evidence of womenfolk or children of landowners being killed and very little evidence of them being even insulted or molested.[100]

In almost all cases it is possible to explain why particular English notables were singled out for attack. John of Gaunt, Duke of Lancaster, headed the list of 'traitors' whose execution was demanded by the Essex and Kentish rebels and anybody connected with him was in great peril throughout the area of the revolt. Thus Thomas Haselden, a top household official of John of Gaunt, had his properties ravaged both in Kent and in Cambridgeshire and escaped death only

John of Gaunt, Duke of Lancaster, feasting with the King of Portugal, 1386 (By permission of The British Library: Royal MS. 14.E.iv, f. 244v)

because he had fled with his master to Scotland. Central and local government officials, some judges of the central royal courts, justices of the peace and of labourers, financial officials, and especially people associated with the levy of the Poll Tax, made up the great majority of the men who were murdered or violently pursued and whose houses and properties were ravaged or destroyed.

Professor N. Brooks has ably reconstructed the organization of the risings in Essex and Kent during their early days before the rebels reached London on 12 June. He has shown that they systematically attacked all notables connected with the administration of their counties and destroyed the entire fiscal and judicial establishments. They discovered where those people kept government records and set about methodically seizing and burning them. In Essex, on 10 June, the insurgents captured Sir John Sewale, the sheriff, in his house at Great Coggeshall, seized all the records connected with the exchequer as well as his other official muniments and burnt them. On the same day they killed at Coggeshall the Essex escheator, John Clerk of Ewell, and then went to his country house in order to destroy all his muniments there. Sir John Gildesburgh had been the Speaker for the Commons in the parliament of December 1380 which had granted the Poll Tax and was a leading councillor of Thomas, Earl of Buckingham, whose expedition to France was financed out of that tax. Gildesburgh was also a leading member of the Essex commission of the peace and had presided over the session of the inquiring commission at Brentwood that had triggered off the rising. His three Essex manors were sacked in simultaneous attacks by three detachments of rebels and all his records were likewise destroyed. Other acting or recent justices of the peace who were victims of attacks on their houses and lost records were Walter Fitz Walter, a peer, and six other men besides Gildesburgh. John Bampton, whose altercation with the men of Fobbing on 30 May started the rising, was one of these victims; he may have been killed later, as he was dead by early August. As Sir Robert Hales, who had been the royal treasurer since 1 February 1381, was the Prior of the Hospitallers of St John in England, their Essex preceptory at Cressing Temple was destroyed on 10 June, while Hales was executed in London four days later.[101] In subsequent risings in East Anglia and adjoining counties the house of Hugh Fastolf, collector of the Poll Tax in Norfolk, was ransacked at Yarmouth and houses of some Poll Tax collectors in Cambridgeshire were likewise sacked. Edmund Walsingham, a Cambridgeshire justice of the peace in 1375, and again in 1380, was murdered at Ely on 17 June.[102]

It was the same in Kent, except that here only local officials were attacked and there was no attempt to do any damage to the properties of the chancellor and the Archbishop of Canterbury, Simon Sudbury, who was later murdered in London at the same time as Treasurer Hales. The Sheriff of Kent, Sir William Septvans, was captured on 10 June in Canterbury Castle. He was taken to his rural manor of Milton, where 'fifty rolls of the pleas of the county and of the crown' were seized, together with all the royal writs in his custody. All this was later burnt at Canterbury. The next day two parties of rebels proceeded to the manor-house of Mersham, in the south of the county, belonging to John Brode, who had been escheator from 1377 to 1380, and had then acted as one of the collectors of the Poll Tax. They destroyed the escheat roll for his period in office and also the 'roll of the receipt' of the Poll Tax. The records of his successor as escheator, Elias Reyner, had already been destroyed two days earlier. Sir Nicholas Heryng, a leading Kentish justice, had his town house in Rochester and his two manors plundered. Of the three members of the special commissions inquiring into the Poll Tax at Canterbury, two had their houses ransacked and one was killed by a party of rebels returning from London on 15 June. Even though the rebellion was clearly defeated by then, Kentishmen were still venting their vengeance on men connected with enforcing the Poll Tax. Between 6 and 12 June were also destroyed the records of the sub-sheriff, of two former coroners and of two commissioners for inquiring into the Poll Tax.[103]

It is interesting to note that very few of the chroniclers give adequate details of what the Essex and Kentish rebels demanded of King Richard II at the two meetings with him in London, at Mile End and Smithfield (14–15 June). Only the *Anonimalle Chronicle* gives a detailed list of their demands, and even this is not exhaustive. The only other chronicler, valuable for the rebel demands of Smithfield on 15 June, is Henry Knighton.[104] In my introductory chapter I have set out some of the most important agrarian and 'libertarian' demands, but they should be discussed in more detail. They must be pieced together from various sources, which should be critically examined.

A royal proclamation of 2 July 1381[105] abrogated the concessions granted by the king on 14 June to the men of Essex and Hertfordshire at the meeting with them at Mile End. Complete abolition of serfdom had been the most important promise, followed up by charters to the county communities of Essex and Hertfordshire conceding this. The king had also granted a general pardon for all felonies and trespasses arising out of the revolts and the abrogation of all subsequent outlawries.

The royal proclamation of 2 July, besides cancelling these concessions, also revoked two other promises extorted from Richard II at Mile End. One concerned the renting of peasant land. The *Anonimalle Chronicle* mentions the demand that land should not be rented at more than 4*d* an acre. The proclamation of 2 July makes it clear that this was meant to apply only to servile land.[106] Comparisons with valuations of property in Hertfordshire and Middlesex show that this could only refer to arable without crops on it.[107]

The other royal promises abrogated on 2 July concerned restrictions on internal trade. At Mile End the rebels had been promised that all the king's subjects should be allowed to buy and sell freely in all the cities, boroughs and market-places and everywhere else in the kingdom. Interpreted strictly, this would have meant that the abrogation of all internal tolls, depriving towns of one of the main sources of their revenues, as well as the destruction of their trading monopolies and privileges. This had been a live issue in East Anglia, where, for example, Yarmouth had a recent royal charter giving it a monopoly of trading within the radius of seven miles, which enabled its merchants to monopolize the trade in herrings and raise the price of fish. On 18 June men of lesser towns of Suffolk had joined a rebel force marching on Yarmouth and, on its capture, the hated charter was torn up and the houses of the offending Yarmouth merchant oligarchy were sacked.[108]

The *Anonimalle Chronicle* mentions some other royal concessions at Mile End which do not reappear in their revocation of 2 July, possibly because the repeal of the promise to end serfdom could have been regarded as covering these further articles. They included a pledge that nobody should render any service to a lord or should be obliged to work for others except of his own free will, and then by contract.[109] This would have meant the end of all seigneurial claims to the obligatory labour of their tenants and would have also consigned to oblivion some of the core provisions of the labour legislation.

Taken together, the demands put forward at Mile End (partly repeated by Wat Tyler at Smithfield) came from rebels who generally had some property and who had hopes of improving their condition still further. The peasants among them appear to have been predominantly not

The Peasants' Revolt, 15 June 1381: two successive events at Smithfield (the killing of Wat Tyler and Richard II facing the now leaderless rebels) (By permission of The British Library: Royal MS. 18.E.i, f. 41v)

landless men but rather tenants wishing to be rid of the irksome burdens of villeinage. They were moved by rising expectations. There was an element of truth in the Netherlandish chronicler Froissart's subsequent comment attributing the risings in south-eastern England to 'the ease and riches that the common people were of'.[110]

The *Anonimalle Chronicle* attributed to Wat Tyler at his meeting with the king at Smithfield some absurd demands, but perhaps they were put forward merely in order to kill off all further negotiations. The men of Essex and Hertfordshire had gone home after securing all the desired promises at Mile End and Tyler was possibly terrified that any further agreement would lead also to the disbanding of his Kentish followers. His offensive behaviour towards the king at Smithfield would confirm this suggestion. These enormities included the demands 'that there was to be no law in future save that of Winchester [the statute of 8 October 1285], that all lordship should be abolished except that of the king, that the goods of the church should be given to the parishioners and that there was to be no bishop except one'.[111]

Mixed with these fantastic articles some other, more realistic, demands were apparently put forward at Smithfield, more akin to the practical concessions wrested from the king at Mile End. The demand for the abolition of serfdom was reiterated. Outlawry was to be abolished. Its frequent use against delinquent labourers absconding from trial must have added to the detestation with which it was regarded. According to Henry Knighton's chronicle, Tyler also demanded that 'all warrens, as well as in fisheries as in parks and woods, should be common to all; so that throughout the realm, in the waters, ponds, fisheries, woods and forests, poor as well as rich might take venison and hunt the hare in the field'.[112] As I have remarked in my introductory chapter, the achievement of the freedom to fish and hunt would have fulfilled one of the most cherished dreams of the English peasantry.

While the risings in the countryside were not directed against the persons (as opposed to the properties) of nobles and gentry as a class, it is not surprising that the landowners of the south-eastern counties were petrified. Their familiar, everyday world was suddenly turned upside down. Most of them were too bewildered and too helpless to offer any resistance and this helped to minimize bloodshed. Many fled or went into hiding. In an addition inserted some time later (probably in 1382) into his *Vox Clamantis* the poet John Gower gave a terrifying glimpse of their fears and tribulations. He had a vision of the rebels changing into beasts, mostly familiar domestic animals, asses, oxen, pigs, dogs, even frogs and flies, but all suddenly turned savage and dangerous to men.[113] He described how his fellow Kentish landowners hid in forests, scarcely daring to emerge except when dire necessity compelled them. The friends on whom they had relied deserted them and hardly anyone could be trusted. Thomas Walsingham, the St Albans chronicler, described how one of the leading East Anglian magnates, William Ufford, Earl of Suffolk, fled in disguise and how in Norfolk and West Suffolk 'the knights and men of gentleblood . . . who had hid themselves for fear of the Commons', during the middle part of June, emerged from their places of refuge only when Bishop Henry le Despenser, one of the most ruthless repressors of the revolt, returned to his diocese with a small armed force.[114]

Professor Dyer has noted 107 cases of the burning of manorial records by the rebels in the four counties surveyed by him (Essex, Hertfordshire, Suffolk and Kent).[115] Destruction of manorial archives even took place on several manors belonging to the king's mother in Essex, and on at least one royal manor, at Kennington in Surrey, on 14 June, an outrage for which Richard ordered the arrest of all his tenants at Kennington a month later.[116] Michael de la Pole, Earl of Suffolk since 1385, claimed that he lost many of his family's muniments stored at Wingfield in Suffolk.[117]

Landlords whose records were destroyed could not normally afford to punish their tenants like the king had done at Kennington. They needed them too much. For example, a court roll of the manor of Moze in Essex bears the heading 'The first court held after the rebellion and the burning of the court rolls'. This is mentioned as the sole crime of the manor's servile tenants and their associates. For this outrage all the servile tenements were resumed into the hands of the lady of the manor, either the wife of Sir John Plays, or her daughter, wife of Sir John Howard. But all the sequestered holdings were regranted to their former tenants in return for fines of 20s or 10s. It should be noted that these servile holdings were surrendered back to these *nativi* and to 'their heirs and assigns', which shows that at Moze the customary tenants already enjoyed in practice a virtually hereditary tenure, though this had not restrained them from violence.[118]

On the manors where manorial records were destroyed, there were often also temporary refusals on the part of the tenants to render customary services (though not at Moze). Strikes by tenants spread to areas outside the main centres of revolt.

Some of the attacks on monasteries are among the best documented incidents of the revolt, because of the special interests of the monastic chroniclers. Monasteries tended to be particularly conservative in the treatment of their tenantries and stubbornly tenacious in enforcing their rights, though with this often went much inefficiency.

The Abbey of St Albans in Hertfordshire had a long history of troubles with the town which had grown around it, because it persisted in treating its townsmen as if they were rightless manorial tenants. The townsmen were the ringleaders, but they boasted that they were allied with men of thirty-two localities in the Abbey's liberty. The most unpopular monks fled in time, including the prior, John Mote, who, as a former cellarer between 1353 and 1374, had aroused much hostility in organizing a 'seigneurial reaction' after the Black Death, vigorously attempting to recover arrears and enforcing his house's domanial claims. The rebellion on the estates of St Albans was not 'an outburst born of economic misery' but a rising 'against the inescapable seigneurial pressure of the abbey's administration'. The tenants did not suffer from particularly galling labour services, but they objected to their unfree status, their compulsory suit to the lord's mills, to the strictness with which the abbey had been preserving its rabbit warrens and hunting and fishing rights. Their 'discontent was enhanced by the proximity to London and by the sharpened demand for wealth'. There was a steady drain of villeins from its villages 'with or without permission'. Many went to London. As early as 1275 the abbey had tried to prohibit the introduction by the tenantry of 'skilled pleaders' from London into its local courts, presumably representing the tenants against its officials![119]

The rising against the Abbey of Bury St Edmunds had similar causes, but was a much more savage affair. It was the fifteenth most populous town in England, the centre of a thriving area of woollen textile industries. The denial of any autonomous government to it was particularly anomalous. Its townsmen took the lead in the rising and in the execution of the prior, John Cambridge, and of John Lakenheath, the *Custos Baroniae*, who was in charge of the abbey's estate administration. The peasant rebels of the surrounding region supported the townsmen.[120]

At Peterborough only the surprise arrival of Bishop Henry le Despenser of Norwich saved the abbey from being sacked. The rebels consisted mainly of peasants, though the townsmen supported them.[121] In Norfolk several prosperous monastic houses, including St Benet Hulme, Binham and Bromholm suffered the destruction of their estate records.[122]

In East Anglia, Essex and the central Weald of Kent the revolts were as much a movement of rural industrial workers as of mere peasants, with textile workers being particularly prominent. This was notably so around North Walsham, in north-eastern Norfolk, which formed the 'cradle' of the revolt in that county on 16 June and where weavers, fullers and other textile craftsmen greatly outnumbered men who lived mainly by agriculture. The leader there was a dyer, Geoffrey Lister. Ten days later the village was the site of the last desperate stand of the Norfolk rebels against Bishop Henry le Despenser of Norwich, who defeated them there.[123]

In an England where lawlessness was growing and the royal government was increasingly ineffective in stemming the tide of corruption and oppression by the local notables and the officials associated with them, the humbler part of the population sought security in acting collectively against all outsiders as well as against the more notoriously oppressive landowners in their midst. Strong feelings of local solidarity promoted the speedy spread of the risings in June 1381 and some of the local officials assumed the lead in their native villages. In all the main areas of the revolt several of the local organizers were men of some substance, fairly prosperous or even rich peasants or craftsmen, who presumably owed their position to being the accepted leaders of their communities in expressing their discontents.

Professor Dyer has identified several such people in records of the last years before 1381. Leading villagers were spokesmen in 1379 for the rest of their community at Ingatestone in Essex, belonging to the Abbey of Barking. This was an oppressive monastic owner. Its chief steward was John Bampton, who had been Sheriff of Essex in 1372/3, was on the commission of the peace, caused the initial revolt at Fobbing and seems to have been murdered during the rising. In 1379 the leading tenants at Ingatestone tried to negotiate a new arrangement by which their rents and services would be made 'certain' and offered £2 to secure this.

The tenants of Fingrith in Essex collectively refused in 1375 to elect a rent collector and the Earl of Oxford, their lord, reacted sharply with threats of high penalties and evictions from holdings. In June 1376, the chief pledges of Fingrith sabotaged the view of frankpledge at which various local offences would normally be presented and its business had to be abandoned until next December. At East Hanningfield in Essex, an estate belonging to the Earl of Pembroke, the chief pledges annoyed the lord's steward by prolonging the business of the view for a whole day. Village notables were refusing to serve as seignorial officials. A radical dissatisfaction with royal justice in Essex in 1378 is apparent from the refusal of the constables of Dunmow Hundred to make any attempt to enforce the labour laws.[124]

We encounter similar men leading their neighbours during the rising. The royal bailiff of the Hundred of Tendring in Essex was accused of organizing a march on Colchester and of being assisted by the constable of the village of Manningtree, whose men subsequently killed a Fleming. In Kent an official of the Hundred of Wye made a proclamation that all men should assemble in arms to assist the rebels.[125] 'It is tempting to see the involvement of so many local officials in the revolt' as an attempt to reject their ambiguous position 'and an unequivocal siding with their neighbours against the constant demands of lords.'[126]

The risings were much more than just a reaction against local economic grievances and against exactions of manorial lords. They were also a tremendous demonstration against absence of good governance. The Speaker for the Commons in the first parliament after the revolts, assembled in November 1381, was Sir Richard Waldegrave from Suffolk, a king's household knight and a very experienced soldier.[127] He made a remarkable speech in which he recognized that the 'outrages . . . which have lately been done to the poor commons, made the said poor commons feel so hardly oppressed that they caused the said lesser commons to rise'. He expressed the general exasperation at the lack of effective defence against the French raids on the coastal districts of southern England, despite the 'great treasure' that had been granted to the government for this purpose. He complained of the perennial abuses of the royal purveyors, 'who pay nothing to the commons for the victuals and carriage taken from them', of the heavy taxes levied by the king and of 'other grievous and outrageious oppressions done . . . by various servants of our lord the king and other lords of the realm'. He particularly blamed the lords for the perversions of justice, complaining that their men 'act like kings in the country, so that justice and law are scarcely administered to anybody'.[128]

A similarly realistic, though more limited, analysis of the causes of the rebellion is to be found in the opening speech to the parliament of October 1383 by the Lord Chancellor, Michael de la Pole. He was the heir of Sir William, the richest English financier of the mid-century and his own career was not free from corrupt financial dealings.[129] He had himself suffered losses in 1381 as a landlord, but he was an intelligent man and he was prepared to recognize publicly that exasperation against the lesser royal officials was the most immediate cause of the rising. As he put it, 'The acts of disobedience and rebellion which men have recently committed . . . towards the lesser servants of the king, such as the sheriffs, escheators, collectors of the subsidies and others of the same type, were the source and the chief cause of the treasonable insurrection recently made by the commune of England. . . . This insurrection . . . was firstly a rebellion against the said lesser servants, then against the great officers of the kingdom and finally against the king himself.'[130]

At the conclusion of his speech in November 1381, Waldegrave warned parliament that still worse troubles were to be feared 'if good and proper remedy is not provided in time for the above-mentioned outrageous oppressions and mischiefs'.[131] He was not isolated in his fears. The poet Gower, writing perhaps in 1382, dreaded the resentment of the defeated peasantry and warned of the continuous danger of further troubles.[132] Henceforth the upper classes lived in dread of another general upheaval and saw its coming in every more serious manifestation of local unrest. The writer of the *Annales Ricardi Secundi* (Thomas Walsingham), in recording the troubles in Cheshire early in 1393, remarked that 'men all over England were sure another general insurrection was at hand'.[133] In this atmosphere of frequent local disorders, and of continuing tension between lords and tenants, the domanial type of estate all but disappeared from England in the fifty years after the Great Revolt and, as part of this change, serfdom largely ceased to matter economically.

CHAPTER 4

The West Midlands before the Peasants' Revolt: the Estates of the Bishops of Worcester and of Coventry and Lichfield

I

I have been studying the largely unpublished estate records of the Bishops of Worcester for over a quarter of a century. It is one of the most voluminous collections of its kind. My own researches have been mostly independent of the work of Professor Christopher Dyer on these estates.[1] A combination of his many valuable publications with the materials assembled by me constitutes one of the main sources for parts of this book. Whenever possible, I shall try to make comparisons with the estates of the Bishops of Winchester, the best documented of all the episcopal estates, and with other ecclesiastical properties.

Apart from the richness of the Worcester materials there are several special reasons for using the estates of that bishopric as one of the examples for the wider study of peasants and landlords in later medieval England which this book attempts. Its properties were confined almost entirely to a fairly homogenous area comprising southern Warwickshire, Worcestershire and Gloucestershire. Almost all were within the medieval diocese of Worcester. Most of the bishop's income came from seventeen estate units, though some of these consisted of a pair of connected manors or contained several outlying properties.

Most of the bishop's estates were acquired between the seventh and eleventh centuries. Before 1066 it was, indeed, the third richest English bishopric, surpassed only by Canterbury and Winchester, though it lost a part of its lands either through the wholesale usurpation of entire manors by Norman magnates, or through the need to create after 1066 extensive military tenancies. But the value of the properties retained by the bishops still remained at more than double the value of the subinfeudated lands.[2]

Some of the episcopal lands came from direct grants of the members of the family of the kings of the Hwicce. The Bishopric of Worcester was the diocese of their kingdom. Later the bishops gradually appropriated the properties of many monastic houses, minster churches and other ecclesiastical establishments within their diocese. A number of those other estates likewise derived originally from gifts by the dynasty of the Hwicce or their overlords, the Kings of Mercia.[3] This might provide a partial explanation why the peasantry on them were burdened very heavily with rents and services. Professor Dyer has also rightly stressed that 'power applied continuously over many generations, enabled wealthy and ancient churches to make greater demands on their tenants than did the gentry'.[4]

The estates of some of the religious houses of this region, like the Abbey of Gloucester, had largely a similar origin,[5] and yet their tenantry was burdened more lightly. On many Gloucester estates there existed in the thirteenth century heavy labour services, but the rents paid by the customary tenants were not high.[6] By contrast the survey of the Worcester properties in *c.* 1299,

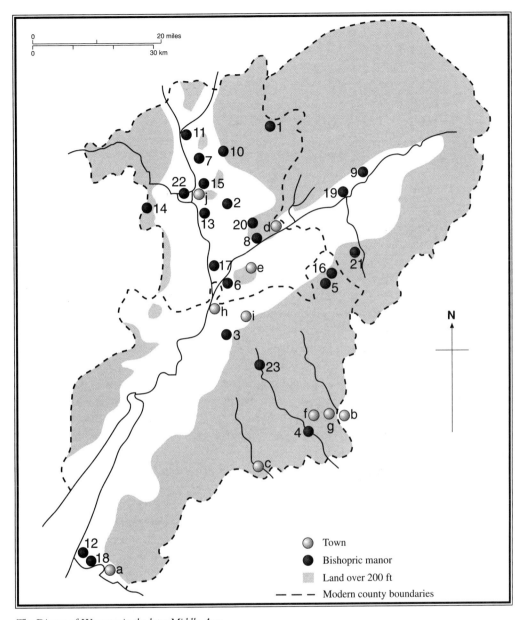

The Diocese of Worcester in the later Middle Ages

Manors
1. Alvechurch
2. Aston
3. Cleeve
4. Bibury
5. Blockley
6. Bredon
7. Droitwich
8. Fladbury
9. Hampton
10. Hanbury
11. Hartlebury
12. Henbury
13. Kempsey
14. Knightwick
15. Northwick (and Whitstones)
16. Paxford
17. Ripple
18. Stoke
19. Stratford
20. Throckmorton
21. Tredington
22. Wick
23. Withington

Towns
a. Bristol
b. Burford
c. Cirencester
d. Evesham
e. Elmley Castle
f. Northleach
g. Sherborne
h. Tewkesbury
i. Winchcombe
j. Worcester

preserved in the *Red Book of Worcester*,[7] reveals a combination on many estates of both considerable labour services and heavy money rents.

Around 1300 the customary tenants of these Worcester properties were among the most heavily burdened servile peasants in England. This was probably the legacy of the exceptional wealth and power of the Bishops of Worcester in the late Anglo-Saxon period. The dues and services exacted from their tenants seem to have increased still further in the course of the thirteenth century.

When in the second half of the fourteenth century and the early years of the fifteenth all the demesnes of the bishops were farmed out and the labour services of their customary tenants were permanently commuted for rents charged over and above the old 'assized rents', the peasantry of the bishopric found itself saddled with exceptionally heavy money charges. One can estimate the size of this new burden of additional rents on nine episcopal estates in the accounting year ending at Michaelmas 1419. Four were Gloucestershire properties and five were in Worcestershire. Commuted labour services accounted there for just under one-fifth of the bishop's revenue.[8] Hence there developed very persistent friction between the bishops and some of their tenantry, leading in 1433 on some manors (especially the eastern Cotswold group) to the refusal by the customary tenants to render some of their servile dues. These Worcester villages will provide one of the clearest examples from the middle decades of the fifteenth century of the resistance of a section of the English peasantry to seignorial demands (cf. Chapters 8 and 11).

In 1299 there were some 1,600 rent-paying tenants on the estates of the Bishops of Worcester.[9] The Black Death of 1348/9 caused a catastrophic decline that persisted for nearly half a century. Professor Dyer mentions the disappearance by Michaelmas 1349 of 42 per cent of the tenants on fifteen estates (781 out of 1,346). His figures include many, though not all, free tenants.[10] My own figure for fourteen manors (omitting Dyer's small estate at Aston), covering only customary tenants and small-holders, but omitting free tenants, amounts to a fall of 36 per cent (681 out of *c.* 1160).[11]

The rest of this chapter will survey the gradual adjustment to this disaster during the second half of the fourteenth century, bringing the story to the point when the bulk of the bishop's demesne began to be leased permanently (c. 1392–5).[12] This will provide an introduction to an account of their estates in the fifteenth century and to the tale of prolonged friction between the bishops and their servile tenants.[13]

II

The principal sources used in this chapter require discussion. The disastrous loss of tenants and revenues in the plague epidemic of 1348/9 is revealed by the records of the two episcopal vacancies at Worcester from 6 August 1349 to 10 January 1350 and in 1353. The inquiries held on these two occasions by the custodian of the vacant bishopric, Leo de Perton, reveal similar figures of losses which were accepted by the royal exchequer.[14]

The evidence about the bishopric's estates in Worcestershire that were particularly impoverished is indirectly confirmed by another record covering the whole of that county. The grant of a triennial fifteenth and tenth conceded to the king in the parliament of January–February 1352 included a stipulation that fines imposed for breaches of the Ordinance of Labourers should be distributed between the localities recently impoverished by the plague or by other causes.[15] Medieval abatements of taxation are justifiably distrusted by historians as likely to reflect political pressures. But the records of abatements in Worcestershire in 1353 (actually apportioned in January 1355)[16] can be treated with more confidence. They reveal a credible pattern, with the greatest decline in parts of the valleys of the Avon and the Severn and of some of their tributaries, where one would expect a higher proportion of plague-carrying rats. Furthermore, there is a substantial correspondence between the estates of the bishopric particularly damaged by the plague in 1349/50 and the abatements granted to these localities in 1355.[17]

There were four episcopal vacancies at Worcester between 1361 and 1375. The records of the keepers of the vacant bishopric and of the inquiries into its value[18] are particularly important for revealing further losses of tenants and of revenues, as the result of further outbreaks of plague. That of 1361 was particularly disastrous.[19]

It is instructive to compare the effects of the plague of 1348/9 on the estates of the Bishops of Worcester with the effects on the properties of the adjoining bishopric of Coventry and Lichfield, further to the north. A few of these estates lay in the same region of south-eastern Warwickshire (the Feldon region) as the Bishops of Worcester's properties in the same county. But the most important ones were to be found further to the north, in the western Midlands. I have studied detailed evidence for the estates of the see of Coventry and Lichfield in Staffordshire, Shropshire and Derbyshire, in regions with very different patterns of settlement from the episcopal Worcester properties in Gloucestershire and Worcestershire. The records of the episcopal vacancy at Coventry and Lichfield in 1358–60 provide detailed evidence for such a comparison and reveal important contrasts with what happened on Worcester estates.[20]

A series of estate accounts and court rolls starts in the 1360s for the eastern and southern groups of the Bishopric of Worcester's properties in Gloucestershire. This widens in the 1370s to include more estates in that county and also at Bredon in Worcestershire and Hampton Lucy in Warwickshire.[21] The series of records continues, with various gaps, to the end of the fifteenth century and beyond.[22]

In the spring of 1394 the auditors of the bishopric were compiling 'a new roll of the annual revenues and farms for the estates of the bishopric'.[23] They were only concerned with regular income, to the exclusion of casual items.[24] The resultant record, covering most of the estates, except for Alvechurch in Worcestershire, was based on the accounts for 1392/3[25] and is preserved in a miscellaneous register of evidences covering the late fourteenth and the first quarter of the fifteenth centuries.[26] These figures provide a useful summary of the bishop's income from properties on the eve of the leasing of most of the episcopal demesnes, though the exclusion of casual revenues makes the totals lower than the figures surviving in the accounts of a few estates available from the adjoining years.[27]

III

The plague epidemic of 1348/9 affected unevenly the localities where Bishops of Worcester had properties.[28] But most of the episcopal estates remained viable agricultural units and for over a decade the bishops avoided any radical reforms in their methods of estate management. As will be described later, this was in marked contrast to what happened on the properties of the Bishop of Coventry and Lichfield, to the north of the diocese of Worcester.[29]

Only on two properties where the Bishops of Worcester controlled the entire manors were the effects of the plague utterly devastating.[30] Bibury in south-eastern Gloucestershire had never been an important manor econonically, except that it was a good place for raising sheep. Of the twenty-four tenants mentioned in the survey of 1299 only five remained after the disaster of the Black Death, though a quarter of a century later the first surviving account (for 1372/3) reveals a return to the pre-plague tenant numbers.[31]

Hanbury by Droitwich, in north-eastern Worcestershire, may have lost nearly half its population in 1349 'and two thirds of the holdings of the bishop's manor lay vacant in the autumn of that year'.[32] This total included tenements of freeholders. The picture was particularly catastrophic for the customary tenants and small-holders. Of the sixty-one in the survey of 1299, only four remained at the end of 1349. Recovery was slow and Hanbury was one of the earliest substantial manors to be leased to farmers. The resultant saving on costs must have been considerable. In one of the earliest extant accounts (for 1377/8) the lessee, who farmed most of the revenues (except for the servile taxes and the profits of the manorial court), paid £34 in cash in the year after October 1377.[33] That was slightly more than the revenue of £32 received in 1302/3 during a year's vacancy of the bishopric. But the earliest surviving court rolls (1375/6) show that several tenants at Hanbury were refusing to render the services due from them. Three had been resisting doing this since 1361 and two more started defaulting in the early 1370s. Obviously the bishops found it difficult to control tenants in a locality where depopulation had made vacant land abundant.[34]

Hanbury lay within an area in northern Worcestershire where, judging by the remissions of the royal tax of 1353, the ravages of the plague had been particularly grave. Droitwich, where the bishop owned some of the town's saltworks, lies further to the west. It received one of the highest remissions in the county amounting to a third of its total assessment (£3 6s 4d out of the normal assessment of £10 13s 4d).[35] Hanbury's remission of 13s 4d, constituting a fifth of its normal assessment, was slightly lower than that of the richer village of Alvechurch where 14s was remitted (c. 18 per cent of its normal assessment). After the city of Worcester (remission of £5) and Droitwich, the remission at Alvechurch was the third highest abatement of tax in any locality where the bishops owned property. The bishop's loss of tenants was, however, much smaller here than at Hanbury (forty-five remained in 1349 out of sixty-one customary tenants and small-holders in the 1299 survey), but it must be remembered that in sizeable villages, like Alvechurch, there were other inhabitants, besides the episcopal tenants. Throckmorton, to the south-east of Hanbury, a much smaller place, did have a remission of 10s (22 per cent of its normal tax).

If one looks at localities not connected with the Bishops of Worcester, there is a similar picture of severe impoverishment in some localities in this area. The second highest remission in the whole county after the city of Worcester itself was at Churchill and Bredicot, lying east of Worcester and south-west of Hanbury. These two villages had a remission of £4 2s 6d, wiping out their tax liability for nearly two years. Churchill remained henceforth a much shrunken village.[36]

Another area of sizeable abatements of taxation was the valley of the lower Avon and the adjoining countryside. Here Bredon on Avon, and its two southerly members of Hardwick and Mitton, very near that river, received an abatement of 18 per cent of their normal tax. The vacancy survey of the Worcestershire escheator confirms that this group of estates had suffered severely. Out of the fifty-eight customary tenants and small-holders recorded in 1299, only fifteen remained at the end of 1349. The bishop's revenue from Bredon largely recovered within the next quarter of the century, though not quite to the level of the income during the vacancy of 1302/3.[37]

Aerial photograph of Worcester Cathedral from the west (By permission of the Cambridge University Committee for Aerial Photography)

At Ripple, in the valley of the Severn, not far to the west of Bredon, the tenant figures at the end of 1349 amounted to half the figure for 1299 (forty-two out of eighty-five). The absence of accounts for this manor in the second half of the fourteenth century makes it difficult to discuss its later history, but the evidence of later extents and surveys shows that ultimately it, too, became again a prosperous estate.

Disturbances in the diocese of Worcester contributed to the impoverishment of the bishop's estates. In, or before, November 1348 there had been a violent riot in the city of Worcester against the cathedral priory. Some of its servants were seriously injured and there was allegedly an attempt to burn down the cathedral. The attack was led by the two bailiffs of the city of Worcester. There was also plundering on two of the priory's manors. One has an impression of strong anti-clerical feelings.[38]

The plague produced considerable demoralization within the diocese of Worcester, involving exceptionally extensive pilfering of the episcopal estates during the vacancy after the death of Bishop Wolstan on 6 August 1349. We are told that the looting occurred during 'the time of the late pestilence'. It revealed the undercurrent of hostility to the bishops among the population. Wolstan's executors requested the new bishop, John Thoresby, to issue a mandate ordering a solemn proclamation after Mass in all the parish churches that anyone who detained anything due to the executors should restore it. The offenders were described as 'certain sons of perdition, whose names we do not know'. It does not look as if this had much effect, as the executors had ultimately to pay Thoresby £766 13s 4d in compensation for his losses.[39]

Three members of larger episcopal estates became wholly deserted in the second half of the fourteenth century. At Hatton, adjoining Hampton Lucy in Warwickshire, this only happened after 1375 and the special reasons for its depopulation will be considered later. Upton, one of the dependent hamlets of the large and very valuable manor of Blockley (north-eastern Gloucestershire), had disappeared altogether by 1383. In 1299 the bishop had here sixteen tenants, holding between them thirteen virgates, but there is no reference to any tenants at Upton in the earliest surviving manorial account of Blockley dating from 1383/4. Furthermore, the bishop paid that year Upton's quota of royal tax, which confirms that it must have been wholly depopulated by then.[40] Wontley, an outlying member of Bishop's Cleeve, was wholly depopulated by 1372 and used only for pasture, for which it was eminently suited.[41]

IV

As manorial accounts and court rolls begin to survive for several episcopal estates in some quantity only from the 1370s onwards, it is difficult to speak with any assurance about what was happening on the properties of the bishops of Worcester during the two decades after 1348/9. Professor Dyer has said comparatively little about these years in his important book of 1980. However, it is possible to make some general comments.[42] The records connected with the episcopal vacancies of 1361/2 and 1364 show that the bishops attempted no general reorganization of their methods before the second epidemic of plague in 1361, and even that was not followed by any really radical changes. The bishops still exploited directly considerable areas of demesne arable, though they were doing so on a somewhat more reduced scale than had been practicable around 1300. They were not able to maintain their old methods on the impressive scale of the Bishops of Winchester, who in the 1370s 'were still cultivating about 85% of their pre-Black Death area of arable'; furthermore, by 1382/3 the Bishops of Winchester were able to compensate for income lost in assized rents from holdings no more occupied on customary terms by raising slightly more money through other temporary arrangements.[43] The estate accounts of the Bishops of Worcester show that in the years 1370–5 the direct exploitation of their demesnes was still profitable and, on more populous manors, there was impressive recovery of income from rents.

When Henry Wakefield became bishop in October 1375, and had to decide whether he should restock his estates after their moveable assets had been appropriated by the executors of his deceased predecessor, he decided to continue direct exploitation. This is all the more significant, as he was an experienced administrator and had acted as Keeper of the King's Wardrobe from 1369 to 1375. Had he become bishop a few years later, possibly he would have become more pessimistic about the long-term prospects of profitable exploitation of the episcopal estates.

Profits from direct farming were more precarious after 1375 because of the volatility of agricultural prices and, probably, also because of more peasant resistance to seignorial demands.[44]

Even in the 1350s the Bishops of Worcester had been forced into some piecemeal adjustments by the distressed condition of the tenants on some of their properties. There is only one known case of violent trouble. Significantly, it was on the populous manor of Henbury just outside Bristol, where the nearby presence of that rich city may have had an unsettling effect. Here, and at the adjoining manor of Stoke, the demand of peasants for land was so considerable that in 1353 the actual number of servile virgates in cultivation was nearly the same as it had been in 1299. In February 1352 a special commission had been issued to Chief Justice Sir William Shareshull on complaint of Bishop Thoresby that a number of men had entered Henbury and had carried away his goods. They had also seriously injured one of the bishop's servants. Furthermore, 'by conspiracy [they] procured his bondmen and other tenants . . . to refuse to do their services due to him and so he had to expend a great sum before he could compel them by law to do the said services'.[45] Thoresby was Lord Chancellor, which makes this act of defiance all the more significant.

Certain concessions by Bishop Thoresby can be reconstructed from the records of the vacancy after his translation to York in 1353. On a number of estates he had remitted some of the labour services due during Lent, presumably because the depleted peasantry needed all their time and equipment to prepare for the sowing of the spring crops. At Fladbury the bishop's surviving tenants were freed from the duty of ploughing and harrowing their lord's demesne in Lent 'because their tenure has been changed into a different service',[46] which implies a permanent concession. At Ripple, similarly, the tenants were exempted from having to plough and harrow 18 acres of demesne during Lent, while at Kempsey all the servile tenants were excused these same labour services during Lent. It should be noted that all these three estates in eastern Worcestershire continued to decline during the 1350s.

The one enduring casualty of the epidemic of 1348/9 was the yield of various customary servile renders, which went into permanent decline. The renders varied in rate from one episcopal estate to another, but were related to either the number of customary tenants or the total number of servile virgates they held between them. The disappearance of many tenants and the large number of vacant virgates meant a drastic cut in this source of revenue. In the immediate aftermath of the plague it was quite catastrophic. Each new lord of the estates of the bishopric (including the royal custodians during the episcopal vacancies) was entitled to collect a 'recognition'. Humphrey de Walden, the keeper of the bishopric during the vacancy of 1302/3, had collected £40 7s 4d. During the vacancy of 1349 the royal keepers collected a mere £1 8s 8d from the episcopal properties in Worcestershire and Warwickshire. This increased to £3 during the vacancy of 1353, levied from most of the bishop's estates. By the vacancy of 1364 the total increased somewhat, as the prosperous twin estates of Henbury and Stoke by Bristol refilled with tenants more rapidly than the other manors of the bishop. In 1302–3 these two had paid £10. Only 13s 4d were levied there during the vacancy of 1353. This rose to £2 in the vacancy of 1364 and this increase was the principal reason why the overall total from the bishopric rose on this occasion to £5 8d.[47]

On some estates the levy of some other renders was given up completely after the plague. Thus at Northwick, outside the walls of the city of Worcester, Bishop Thoresby remitted permanently the render of 'fishfee', paid by servile tenants on the first day of Lent in return for their right to fish.[48] On most estates the annual customary renders lingered on, but much reduced. At Henbury and Stoke, where the decline was ultimately less marked than elsewhere, they had produced in 1302/3 during a year's vacancy £14 17s 7¾d. In a year's account for 1375/6 they yielded a total of £8 12s 11d.[49] Not only did the number of contributors decline, but there were also reductions in the rates demanded, though this varied from estate to estate. At Bredon, in eastern Worcestershire, tallage used to be levied in the early fourteenth century at 1s 10d per virgate and 'fishfee' at 2d per virgate. By 1375/6 the combined rate for these two renders fell to 6d per virgate.[50] The survey of permanent sources of income in 1392/3[51] shows that annual receipts from customary renders on thirteen estates had fallen by nearly two thirds from the amount they were yielding in 1299.[52] When opposition to all servile dues increased on Worcester properties in the second quarter of the fifteenth century, these renders were among the main casualties.[53]

In contrast to the Bishopric of Worcester, the estates of the see of Coventry and Lichfield were in 1349 the scene for far-reaching immediate concessions to the bishop's tenants.[54] Bishop Roger Northburgh had been Keeper of the King's Wardrobe in 1321/2 during the civil war fought by Edward II on a financial shoestring but ending with his terrible vengeance on his magnate opponents. Northburgh was the king's treasurer in a period of exceptional financial stringency in the second half of 1340. It is unlikely that such a man would have been easily induced to make concessions to his tenants unless he had become convinced that he had no other choice.

Several of the bishop's most important properties lay in Staffordshire. This was a county where manorial demesnes tended to be fairly small, but the estates of the bishops contained a number of the larger demesnes. In 1298 there were 849 acres at Eccleshall, 488½ at Haywood and 406 at Brewood. But they did not have good soils, as is shown by the fact that in the middle of the thirteenth century only oats were grown at Haywood, Baswich, Brewood and Eccleshall. Late in the century some other crops were also cultivated, but the cereal production for the market was of only limited importance on these episcopal properties. 'On the bishop's manors much of the harvest was consumed on the estate in the form of liveries to servants, fodder for stock and seed-corn.'[55]

Staffordshire was not a prosperous agrarian county in the Middle Ages and conditions worsened in the first half of the fourteenth century. This helps to explain why its peasantry was not involved in a brisk competitive demand for land and why Bishop Northburgh found it difficult to get new tenants from 1349 onwards and had to make important concessions to retain such peasants as he still had. Labour services, though nothing like as oppressive as on Worcester episcopal estates, tended to form a relatively heavy burden on these Staffordshire properties. That, too, helps to explain why these services had to be partly abandoned or relaxed after the plague of 1348/9.[56]

Faced with the deaths of ninety-one unfree tenants on his Staffordshire, Shorpshire and Derbyshire properties, Bishop Northburgh wass forced to regrant their holdings to new tenants on condition that they were released from all servile burdens. Presumably it was impossible to find fresh tenants on any other terms.

The bulk of the bishop's Staffordshire properties lay in the south-eastern corner of the county. Several of them adjoined Cannock Forest. The presence of ample woodland pastures and extensive meadows, the scattering of some of the tenants through small hamlets, the abundant possibilities of reclaiming new land within the forest area:[57] all these were factors encouraging the bishop's tenants to procure a measure of greater independence in the years after 1348.

At Baswich one-third of the servile tallage had to be permanently remitted to the remaining tenants. At Rugeley, Brewood, Haywood and Longdon in Staffordshire and at Prees in Shropshire, the bishop was able to find new tenants for 26½ vacant virgates and two other holdings. At Sawley in Derbyshire he managed to replace the deceased eleven tenants of either twenty-seven or twenty-nine bovates by freeholders. But in all these cases, while the money rents remained unchanged, the customary annual servile tallage ('stuth') had to be abandoned, together with all the labour services due from these holdings.[58] Bishop Northburgh lost more than half his annual income from 'stuth' (£14 4s 2d out of £25 10s 10d).

On the Staffordshire estates generous offers of better terms of tenure failed in part to attract new tenants. At Rugeley the bishop could not replace any of the five smallholders who had died. Of nineteen holdings that became vacant in 1349 at Haywood, thirteen were still vacant in 1358 when Bishop Northburgh died. The six which were filled (comprising 6 half-virgates) were taken up by strangers ('*adventiti*'), who were immigrants from other localities. Brewood was one of the most important episcopal manors. In 1377 280 persons were assessed there to the Poll Tax, so that it is reasonable to suppose that there remained quite a large population at Brewood in the 1350s. Yet in place of twenty holders of servile half-virgates who had died there in 1349, only ten new tenants could be found and the new holders were all only paying rents. The bishop, who held here as late as 1358 four carucates of demesne arable, was compelled to suspend all commutation of the labour services of the remaining twenty-nine unfree tenants, as he needed again all the labour that could still be exacted. Longdon was another populous village. Twenty tenants had died of plague; 7 virgates and 3 half-virgates still remained in the bishop's hands in 1358 for lack of new holders.

In 1349 12½ virgates fell into the bishop's hands on his four manors in Warwickshire. None of these was ever reoccupied in Bishop Northburgh's lifetime, because nobody else wanted 'to perform the services which the previous tenants had been accustomed to render before the pestilence'.[59] Only at Bishop's Tachbrook can severe economic decline be suggested as a possible reason for Northburgh's inability to find new tenants. Of the eighteen listed in a vacancy survey of 1321 only nine remained in 1358. The remaining three Warwickshire episcopal manors remained fairly well populated in the 1350s, but 4 virgates had remained vacant at Chadshunt and Gaydon and 3¾ virgates at Bishop's Itchington. However, except at Tachbrook, the bishop still retained an adequate number of tenants.

The vacancy account for the Bishopric of Coventry (22 November 1358 to 19 September 1360) deals with the period just before the second onset of plague in 1361/2. Some estates were certainly again further impoverished. Manorial courts held in the last two months of 1361 revealed fourteen deaths of tenants at Chadshunt, Gaydon and Bishop's Tachbrook. The disappearance of six of them at Tachbrook was particularly damaging as there was already a lack of sufficient tenants there.[60] Arrears of £12 in a part of the manor of Longdon near Lichfield in Staffordshire were said to date from 1365. 'It is possible that the effects of the crisis and population decline [in Staffordshire] were more marked in the more populous manors in the south and centre of the county'[61] where lay some of the episcopal properties.

The properties of the Bishops of Worcester were badly hit again, especially in the eastern group of estates.[62] Bishop Reginald Brian himself died on 10 December 1361 at Alvechurch[63] within that especially afflicted region. The largest losses of tenants are recorded at Kempsey on the Severn, just below Worcester, where all the different categories of tenants declined in number. If the figures of the 1353 vacancy survey are compared with those of the 1361/2 vacancy, it seems that as many as twenty tenants may have disappeared there. On five estates

(Alvechurch, Fladbury, Blockley, Ripple and Kempsey) as many as 29½ virgates became vacant, and £3 was paid as recognition in 1353 by the servile tenants on all the estates, though this fell even lower in the vacancy of 1361/2 (to £2 6s 6d). At Alvechurch the assized rents slumped from £1 2s at each of the quarterly terms of payment to 6s 6d per term. But some other episcopal properties appear to have been affected only very slightly, or not at all.

The extent drawn up on 2 April 1364 by the Worcestershire escheator Leo de Perton, the author of all the surveys during the successive vacancies since 1349, reveals one important recent change in the sources of the bishop's income. Bishop John Barnet (1362/3) increased the revenue from the assized rents on Worcestershire estates from £23 7s 6d to £32 16s 5d. It is to be assumed that, after the setback caused by plague in 1361/2, Bishop Barnet decided to commute some of the labour services and servile renders of unfree tenants into fixed rent charges and that he was filling some of the vacant holdings by offering purely financial charges to new tenants. Such a partial commutation of servile renders is revealed by the manorial accounts for some of the estates, which survive from the later 1360s, onwards. This series of accounts (and court rolls) opens up a new phase for a more effective study of the economic and seignorial policies of the Bishops of Worcester.

V

The early 1370s were the last years of fairly confident large-scale demesne farming on the estates of the Bishops of Worcester.[64] Out of slightly over twenty estates only about seven were probably leased. But several of these – Aston, Throckmorton, Knightswick – were small places. Hanbury by Droitwich (as explained earlier) had been crippled by the plague. Wick, just outside the city of Worcester, offered unusually profitable opportunities for leasing. The other farmed manors were Paxford, a dependency of Blockley; Hartlebury (northern Worcestershire) which had suffered much from the plague; lastly Tredington in Warwickshire. This left fourteen manors out of twenty in direct management. Some of these estates had been leased temporarily, but were soon returned to direct exploitation. Thus, the rural manor of Stratford was brought back into direct management in 1373.[65]

The three estates for which there survives particularly early evidence from accounts were in Gloucestershire: Bibury, Bishop's Cleeve and Stoke Bishop. There is also early information for Hampton Lucy in Warwickshire. At both Bibury and Hampton wholesale commutation of the labour services had already occurred earlier in the fourteenth century, but demesnes continued to be exploited through the use of *famuli* supplemented by much hired labour.[66] Thus, at Hampton, where slightly over 161 domanial acres were under crops in 1371/2, there is no mention of any labour services in the account for that year.[67] At Bibury, where 96 acres of demesne were cultivated in the same year, labour services were still recorded, but the servile population of twenty-four customary tenants was too slight to count as an adequate labour force, except for providing boon works.[68]

The manorial officials at Hampton and Bibury, having to employ much hired labour, ignored the regulations about wages imposed by the Ordinance of Labourers[69] and appear to have done so with complete impunity. The example of their conduct at Hampton Lucy in Warwickshire is particularly instructive.[70] For comparison we have a Warwickshire roll of proceedings before the justices of labourers. Some of these took place at Stratford upon Avon, very near Hampton Lucy. In 1357 a number of people were prosecuted for receiving excessive wages for reaping corn. On this occasion 3*d* was described as the lawful daily wage of a reaper and several labourers were indicted for receiving 6*d* a day for such work. But in August 1372 the reeve of Hampton was paying labourers employed in gathering the harvest as much as 6½*d* a day. Thirty men were employed in this fashion for three-and-a-half days in the second week of August and thirty-four more during most of the following week. That autumn the harvesting of corn on the 172 acres of the bishop's demesne worked out at 12½*d* an acre, much beyond the permitted legal rate. Even more (around 13*d* an acre) was paid in 1377 to get the harvest in and in the autumn of 1378 payments were again made at the rate of 12½*d* an acre (8*d* per acre appears to have been the more normal rate).

At Bibury the bishop's auditors appear to have regarded the annual hiring of labour as inevitable. The charge for this appears in virtually every account between 1372 and 1382, the one exception being the account for 1375/6.[71] The auditors seem to have accepted 8*d* an acre as the normal rate. Extraordinary measures had to be taken in the autumn of 1372.[72] The reeve had to take the drastic step of hiring for one day as many as 127 labourers, at 5*d* each, to gather and bind the lord's corn. Presumably bad weather threatened to destroy the harvest. In addition to the hired people, who must have been specially brought in from outside, he also used forty-seven tenants of the bishop. The latter probably represented the entire labour force available locally at Bibury, including women, as nine years later the royal Poll Tax was collected here from forty-seven persons.[73] That single day cost the reeve 53*s*.

Despite the special problems caused by the need to hire numerous labourers at high cost, direct exploitation of demesnes seems to have continued to be worthwhile on the majority of estates far into the 1370s. Thereafter difficulties mutlitplied, as will be shown in the last two sections of this chapter.

To return to the period until 1375, Bishop's Cleeve lay east of the River Severn and on the edge of the Cotswolds. Its outlying member of Wontley on the Cotswold escarpment, south-east of the main village, was badly hit by the plague and was abandoned by 1372/3, when its site was rented as pasture.[74] Cleeve itself continued to prosper. It was sited on so called 'Cheltenham Sands', permeable gravel soils, avoiding the surrounding heavy clays. Its site provided dry, light, easily worked soil, still greatly appreciated today for market gardening. There was plenty of water reachable through shallow wells.[75] In 1299 the bishop had here fifty-eight unfree tenants; forty-four were still left after the plague of 1349. By 1372/3 the number of servile tenants rose again to fifty-five. The disappearance of the settlement at Wontley was one of the reasons for some permanent loss of revenue. Assized rents, which had amounted to £18 14*s* 6¾*d* in 1299, yielded now only £4 14*s* and the reeve ascribed half the loss to the disappearance of the tenants at Wontley.[76] In 1372/3 79 acres of the demesne were leased at 2*s* per acre, but 215¼ acres were still under crops that year and the manor yielded a net revenue of £28 15*s* 10*d*,[77] which surpassed by some £10 the net revenue during the vacancy of 1302/3.[78]

The manor of Bibury lies in the south-eastern corner of Gloucestershire. It was never a well-populated property. There were twenty-four servile tenants in 1299, reduced to five in 1349. By 1372/3 there were again twenty-four customary tenants. But in 1371/2 the cultivated demesne (96 acres) was only half the size of that of 1299.[79] I have mentioned a moment ago the heavy expense of hiring outside labour. In the account for 1371–2 the exceptional cost of wages was only offset by the sale of 239 sheep.[80] In the following year expenses, chiefly on the permanent *famuli* and hired labour, absorbed more than half the receipts, but the reeve was still able to deliver £10 17*s* to the bishop's receiver,[81] exceeding by over £3 the net revenue in 1302/3.

Arlington Mill, Bibury, Glos., was an estate, in part, of the Bishops of Worcester (By permission of the Corinium Museum, Cirencester)

Bibury's value for the bishops lay, above all, in its sheep farming. But only some profits from it (for example, the proceeds of the sales of sheep) appeared in its reeves' accounts. The wool, though shorn at Bibury, was forwarded to Blockley to swell the bulk sale of the bishopric's wool and the proceeds figure in the accounts for that manor.[82] Bibury lies on the edge of the Cotswolds and of abundant good pastures there. The River Coln and numerous springs made it an excellent place for washing sheep before shearing. Thus 142 sheep were shorn there in the summer of 1372, including some sent from the episcopal manor of Withington, further to the north-west in Gloucestershire.[83] For Michaelmas 1389 there were 190 sheep at Bibury.[84] As late as the middle of the fifteenth century Bibury still remained one of the few episcopal manors specializing in sheep farming, alongside Withington and Blockley.[85]

For the great manor of Henbury Saltmarsh, outside Bristol, partial accounts survive for 1363 and 1369, but no account for a complete year exists before 1375/6. For Stoke Bishop, adjoining it to the north-west, the first complete account survives from 1372/3. That year the reeve delivered £42 13s 9d in cash to the bishop's receiver,[86] surpassing by £6 the net revenue in 1302/3. There was no large demesne at Stoke, but the bulk of the income came from the rents and renders of its numerous tenants. The structure of the bishop's income from Henbury was similar; a small demesne, but income from rents was high. I shall provide more details later, using the first surviving account under Bishop Henry Wakefield (1375–95).[87]

The Worcester survey of 1299 shows Hampton Lucy and Hatton to have been two prosperous villages.[88] Hampton lies to the west of the Avon in a bend of that river. Hatton was sited about one mile further to the west. The two estates, belonging to Worcester since the eighth or ninth centuries, were saddled with both heavy rents and services, unusual in the surrounding area of Warwickshire. They had a joint reeve, and were treated as a single accounting unit. Hampton lay on easily drained, fertile, gravelly soils.[89] Hatton, fairly close to the Avon, may have been more suitable for pasture. At least, its later history suggests this. In the first half of the fourteenth century Hatton seems to have been slightly more prosperous than Hampton. But Hatton's population (unlike Hampton's) consisted almost entirely of villeins holding standard servile holdings, excessively burdened with rents and services. Each virgate in Hatton rendered aggregate dues 40 per cent higher than a virgate at Hampton. This would help to explain the almost complete desertion of Hatton in the last quarter of the fourteenth century. But this exodus had barely started when Bishop Wakefield succeeded to the see of Worcester in October 1375.

I have mentioned the high cost of hiring temporary labourers at Hampton in the autumn of 1372. In the account for 1371/2 the reeve charged himself with receipts (including some arrears) amounting to £58, nearly double the receipts of 1302/3. After deducting arrears at the end of the account £13, this left the balance of £45. But £35 15s was consumed by expenses, so that his cash deliveries to the bishop's receiver totalled only £13,[90] compared with £19 8s in 1302–3. Direct exploitation of demesnes was becoming less rewarding here in the changed circumstances after the Black Death. In section VI of this chapter I shall chronicle some dire disasters at Hampton after 1374 and the total collapse at Hatton.

VI

Using the manorial accounts and court rolls, supplemented by more general estate surveys compiled by the bishop's officials, Professor Dyer has produced a fascinating account of the economics of the bishop's estates in the last third of the fourteenth century.[91] This can now be further supplemented by Professor Farmer's study of price statistics.[92] During the first half of the 1380s prices of corn were fairly high, though not excessively so. This gave a fresh boost to the desire of landlords to continue direct exploitation of their demesnes. Difficulties with tenants intensified and costs of hired labour were rising, but the maintenance of good income from the sale of agricultural products made it possible for a time to face these higher expenses and to put up with resistance from the servile tenantries. Here the greatest danger was that servile tenants might abscond from episcopal properties, leaving vacant holdings which could not be filled on terms that were acceptable to the bishops and which would remain untenanted for long periods, while the buildings attached to them became neglected and unusable.[93]

These difficulties with the permanent servants, hired labourers and servile tenants formed the underlying structural weakness that was bound ultimately to call the whole enterprise of direct management into question. Professor Dyer's *Lords and Peasants in a Changing Society: The Estates of the Bishopric of Worcester, 680–1540*, provides much evidence about this complex of difficulties, but it is scattered through a number of chapters. It is necessary to draw it all together, as well as to survey other connected information not included in his book.

Speaking of the management of its estates in the second half of the fourteenth century by the Abbey of Westminster, Dr Barbara Harvey has remarked that, 'Never sensitive to economic trends, the monks of Westminster were never more heroically indifferent to them than they were in this period.'[94] She is reminding us that the preservation of the abbey's traditional lordship over its dependants was more important to its monks than the purely economic calculation of whether or not it continued to be financially profitable to do so. Increasing personal challenges to this lordship were more disturbing than was the decline of revenues from its estates.

We get the same impressions of a tenacious desire to maintain traditional conditions of lordship in a document from the Abbey of Evesham dating from 1368/9. This is of special relevance here as the abbey's estates lay in close proximity to several of the properties of the Bishops of Worcester. As the abbey was finding it difficult to find new customary tenants for some of its vacant holdings, it was granting them out instead on leases for life. One of the attractions was that no fines for entry were demanded from these lessees. But 'the life leases are often qualified with the statement that at the end of the tenant's life it must revert to old customary terms'. As Professor Hilton justifiably comments, one has 'the impression of a conservative institution attempting to preserve customary relations between itself and its tenants when the conditions which had permitted these customary relations to develop no longer held good'.[95]

The Bishops of Worcester included more businesslike administrators than the senior monks at Westminster. This was especially true of Bishop Henry Wakefield, a former keeper of Edward III's wardrobe and royal treasurer who governed the bishopric in the crucial years of deepening difficulties between 1375 and 1395. But the need to preserve effective personal lordship was just as important to them. The erosion of it through increasing friction with the peasantry discouraged the continuation of direct exploitation of the episcopal demesnes. Bishop Wakefield showed in his last will that he was aware of the oppressiveness of his rule, by leaving a bequest of £100 to be distributed 'among his poorer tenants and especially those that he had injured'.[96]

The estate reeves, normally recruited from among the servile tenants, were the men whose discontent might be particularly dangerous. One has the impression that under Bishop Wakefield his estate auditors were treating these officials harshly, surcharging them over a variety of transactions. It is impossible to tell how often such surcharges were justified.[97]

Reeves often stayed in office for several years and a rapid succession of these officials on any particular estate points to a history of troubles. This was certainly the case at Hampton Lucy with Hatton. There was here a fast turnover of reeves, nine different holders of that office appearing between 1371 and 1393 'in the eleven years for which accounts survive'. Walter Shayl, reeve from September 1375 to June 1377, was a substantial tenant at Hatton, cultivating about 50 acres. There had been a drought in 1375 and no demesne crops were harvested in the autumn of that year. Lack of seed presumably explains why only 17 acres of demesne were sown in that autumn (11 per cent of the acreage sown in the account for 1376/7). In that year there was 'a high mortality among the demesne sheep flock because of disease in the winter of 1376/7'. Shayl's account for 1375/6 reveals that the bulk of his receipts were consumed by expenses and he owed the balance of £5 10s 8½d. Nothing had been delivered to the bishop's receiver. Tenants were fleeing from Hatton and by September 1375 4 virgates were vacant there. Shayl's flight on 1 June 1377 increased this total to 6 virgates. He fled because by then he owed the bishop £20 5s 9½d, an amount he could never hope to repay. Following this disaster, a new office of rent collector was introduced at Hampton, to relieve future reeves of one cause of mounting debts.[98]

There is no evidence of any serious troubles on the episcopal estates in the summer of 1381, but peasant discontent must have been rife in the diocese of Worcester. 'The conflicts on the estates of the Worcester Cathedral Priory over the performance of labour services led in July 1379 to a general seizure of all the goods and chattels of the servile tenants' on all its manors. It was, presumably, a purely formal sequestration as an effective seizure would have been 'beyond the capabilities of the estate officials'. It would enable the priory to punish, by detention of goods, selected, particularly troublesome, tenants, followed by their release only on payments of fines. Walter de Legh, its prior, was terrified to leave it early in July 1381 in order to attend the Benedictine General Chapter. He alleged that there was violent agitation among both his free and his unfree tenants, who had withdrawn the services that were due. He claimed that they were preparing an armed insurrection and demanding the abolition of serfdom. There was a second sequestration of the goods of the priory's servile tenants in January 1385.[99]

I discussed earlier the increasing cost of casual agricultural labour on some Worcester estates. This persisted in the 1380s.[100] A still more serious threat to the profitability of direct farming by landlords was the mounting expense of maintaining the permanent staff of the *formuli*, 'the full-time employees who performed the basic tasks on the demesnes, manning the ploughs, carting and looking after animals'. Under the labour legislation after 1349, they were supposed to be hired on annual contracts, but 'the contemporary records of the enforcement of the labour laws show a persistent reluctance of wage-earners to enter into annual contracts', as the chances of higher earnings in casual employment were better than ever before.[101] Rises in money wages of the *famuli* and in the quality of partial payments to them in kind occurred on Worcester estates in the late 1370s and 1380s. They may have represented an indirect consequence of the growing peasant unrest and particularly a response to the unease of the bishops after the revolts of 1381.

As there was a spell of good prices for corn from 1379 to 1387 and again between 1389 and 1392,[102] the episcopal estates could afford for a while to treat these invaluable *famuli* better. A *fugator* (driver of the plough team) at Henbury and Stoke, who received 6s a year in the 1370s, was given 7s in 1380 and 8s from 1384.[103] The last rate was much higher than the Winchester manors were paying in 1383.[104] The two Hampton ploughmen received 9s and 13s 4d by 1377 and from 1384 they were both paid at the same rate of 13s.[105] It is important to stress that when a fresh royal statute in 1388 for the first time laid down precise maximum wages for *famuli*, it prescribed only 7s as the yearly wage for the ploughman.[106] 'The quality of the grain livery of the *famuli* was improved' at Bibury in 1385 and at Hampton in 1388 'with the introduction of a small quantity of wheat and the wheat content of the Stoke liveries increased in the 1380s.'[107] At Bibury a ploughman had his yearly cash wage increased in 1385 from 8s to 10s.[108] The same thing was happening elsewhere in England. In Sussex, where the services of skilled ploughmen were in particularly high demand, the one ploughman on Battle Abbey's estate of Marley attained by 1384/5 the huge yearly wage of £3, a large increase occurring after the revolts of 1381.[109] On the Surrey manor of Merstham, belonging to the Cathedral Priory of Christchurch, Canterbury, a ploughman's yearly wage more than doubled between 1379 and 1389 (from 7s to 16s) and there were increases, though not so huge, on the priory's Kentish estates.[110]

On the estates of the Bishops of Worcester, the revolts of 1381 may have led to the abatement of some servile renders. There was a notable decline in the entry fines demanded on some estates from new tenants. They were halved in the 1380s at Whitstones, the bishop's manor beyond the walls of the city of Worcester.[111] Such concessions were presumably caused by fears that vacant tenements would otherwise remain unoccupied. High merchet payments for granting servile women permission to marry are recorded before 1381 at Whitstones, amounting to as much as £1. In the 1380s and 1390s they were reduced to between 13s 4d and 3s 4d and the same thing was happening at Kempsey by the first half of the fifteenth century.[112]

In her studies of the estates of Westminster Abbey Barbara Harvey has provided a remarkable reconstruction of the abbey's strategies for dealing with the situation created by the Black Death of 1348/9 and the subsequent epidemics of plague: how to fill vacant holdings, while maintaining, as far as possible, the old system of direct manorial management. Down to the last decade of the fourteenth century the monks' ideal was to return ultimately to the pre-plague arrangements. Any dealings with the servile peasantry which departed from this were regarded as temporary and, as far as possible, the abbey tried to safeguard the possibility of reversing them in the future.[113]

Among the abbey's servile tenants, as elsewhere, there was a growing pressure to have liability to customary renders and to labour services commuted for fixed annual payments and for these new arrentations to be merged with the older money rents. We are watching hasty improvisations. 'Every kind of source betrays the lack of vocabulary to describe the changes that were so rapidly in train.' The resultant imprecision of our information makes 'the surviving evidence . . . treacherous to a degree . . . To our great confusion, one overworked word, *firma*, is used to describe' different types of new arrangements, 'a tenancy at will, a lease, the tenure of a villein whose services had been commuted into a money rent, and the rent that was owing in each of these cases.'[114] The same term was also used for rents from leases of demesne, of mills, quarries and fishery rights. To cite a parallel example from the account for 1383–4 for Blockley, one of the most valuable estates of the Bishops of Worcester, under the heading *firme* are jumbled together £5 from the leased demesne paid by the tenants of Paxford, a subordinate member of Blockley, 1s for the rent for the fishery rights in the same village and 5s for an annual payment from a leased quarry at Blockley.[115]

From the last quarter of the fourteenth century the evidence of the miscellaneous new arrentations on the estates of the see of Worcester is not as explicit as the detailed information marshalled by Dr Harvey for the properties of Westminster, but the developments on these two estates were roughly similar. On the huge manor of Henbury Saltmarsh just outside Bristol, the most valuable Worcester estate alongside Blockley, there were, in November 1375, sixty-seven tenants holding between them 22½ virgates, and twenty-nine lesser tenants, some of whom, at least, were serfs.[116] The account for 1375/6 records 1 arrented virgate free of charges other than a money rent. The account for 1377/8 reveals further new arrentations for 1 virgate and 3 half-virgates. In 1379/80 were added 3½ virgates more and in 1382/3 another 3 virgates, so that by that date nearly half the virgates had been arrented, though direct management of the manor's demesne by the bishop persisted until 1395. In the account for that year revenues included £5 1s 10¾d of supplementary rents from newly arrented servile holdings.[117]

A striking example of these changes is provided by the court roll for the court held at Bredon (south-eastern Worcestershire) on 12 October 1389. In 1299 servile tenants exploited here 33 virgates, of which 30½ were occupied again in 1389. The court roll records that holders of 17½ of these offered to pay that year a further £11 13s 4d as commutation for labour services and several customary renders, at the rate of 13s 4d per virgate. The group was made up of the holders of 14 virgates and 7 half-virgates at Bredon itself and its outlying settlements at Hardwick and Norton. This commutation was only granted for one year.[118] The bishop was unwilling, as yet, to make permanent concessions. But, in practice, this was a point of no return and the same concession was repeated henceforth annually.[119]

The increase in rents may have been one of the reasons why a separate receiver of arrears was appointed for the estates of the bishopric. By 1389 that office had been held by five successive officials and they owed between them an aggregate debt of £30 16s 7¾d.[120]

Much (or perhaps all) of the demesne at Fladbury in north-eastern Worcestershire had been leased by 1392. In that year the farm amounted to £2 17s. There was a corresponding increase in newly arrented servile holdings. These new arrentations yielded in 1392/3 the additional revenue of £5 17s 3½d, almost as much as the old assized rents (£5 18s 4½d).[121] From the same year of account there is evidence of new arrentations at Kempsey on the Severn, slightly to the south-east of Worcester. Here assized rents yielded £20 14s 5¼d. But new arrentation contributed an additional £17 2s 5½d. The bulk of this (£15 7s 1½d) came from 'terra nativorum arrentata diversis' ('servile land let out for rents to various'), and £1 15s 4d was received from vacant tenements which had lapsed into the bishop's hands and were conceded to temporary holders.[122]

The effectiveness of the bishop's lordship was being gradually undermined by these and other piecemeal concessions. It was this, as much as purely economic calculations of declining agrarian revenues, that was bringing near the moment when direct exploitation of demesnes would be abandoned on one manor after another and all the labour services would be commuted for rents.

VII

The episcopate of Henry Wakefield (October 1375–March 1395) witnessed the last stage of direct farming by the bishopric's officials on fourteen estates. The overall income was still holding up, but rising costs of labour and difficulties with the unfree tenantry were making the old system of management an increasingly hazardous enterprise. The best chances of enhancing income lay in securing more revenue from rents of servile tenants, but this could only be achieved by commuting the labour services of those tenants. Exploitation of demesnes became dependent on the exclusive use of permanent servants and hired labour, thus raising costs still further.

The prospects of profitable farming slumped after 1392, as prices of corn were beginning to follow a long-term downward trend.[123] Thus, in the last years of Wakefield's episcopate manorial profits were reaching a point 'where the differences between the returns from direct management' of demesnes and leasing them were becoming slight, 'and leasing offered advantages of stability and convenience'.[124]

It is impossible to estimate precisely Bishop Wakefield's annual income, but the value of the bishopric at the end of his episcopate may have been roughly the same as it had been at the start of the fourteenth century and, possibly, even slightly higher. From 1299 we have the valor (or valuation) of the bishopric estimated at £1,191 10s 6¾d.[125] It can be compared with the receipts of Humphrey de Walden, the custodian of the bishopric for thirteen months in 1302–3.[126] His receipts amounted to £903 5s 8d. Payments into the exchequer and other disbursements on the king's behalf totalled £536 13s 4d, but he was also allowed £341 11s 9d for the value of the corn remaining on the lands of the bishopric when he returned them to the next bishop. His receipts did not include, apparently, the revenues from the bishop's spiritual functions (? c. £100 a year). Presumably they also included less than the average income from wool and sales of sheep, as the executors of the deceased Bishop Godfrey Giffard were likely to have sold most of these animals.[127]

The survey of permanent revenues by the auditors of Bishop Wakefield based on the accounts for 1392/3[128] provides a starting-point for the estimate of his revenues and I have combined them with figures (usually higher as they include casual income) from a number of manors where accounts of approximately the same date survive. Alvechurch is missing from the record of 1392/3, but Professor Dyer has plausibly estimated its income at about £50 and he suggests that the total for the revenue from courts (one item of casual revenues) as c. £100.[129] The sales of wool and of corn from tithes, as at Blockley, yielded £170 10s in 1389.[130] Adding my figures for 1392/3 (£839 1s 5d) to the wool and tithe income and to Professor Dyer's estimates gives the total of £1,160 9s. It should be augmented further by the farm of Hillingdon in Middlesex, while Bishop Wakefield's spiritual revenues produced £85 13s 11d in 1380.[131] This gives the grand total for gross revenues of £1,272 12s. The figures in the survey for 1392/3 were regarded as basically net income, but the total average net income cannot be computed on this evidence.

The contents of the episcopal revenues had, however, appreciably changed between 1300 and Bishop Wakefield's episcopate. In 1303 as many as 3,413 acres of the demesnes were under crops and there were sixty-one demesne plough-teams. Only twenty plough-teams were maintained by the bishop in 1380,[132] and the cultivated demesnes were much smaller. A survey of figures for a few estates will bring this out. But the revenue from courts was well maintained. There was a loss on the old-established assized rents, because of some holdings remaining obstinately vacant. In 1392/3 on eight estates this deficiency amounted to £35 8s 9¼d[133] and by 1385 a further £5 17s had been lost at Hatton, which was becoming gradually deserted.[134] But, as has been explained in the preceding section, overall revenue from rents was rising because of much commutation of labour services, replaced by increased rent charges. The sales of the bishopric's wool, as revealed by the Blockley account for 1383/4, amounted to c. £133[135] and contributed perhaps one-seventh of the bishop's income. There were also additional receipts from sales of sheep and of skins of dead animals on individual estates. A look at a few estates for which accounts survive shows, in most cases, a recovery of incomes from the disaster of 1348/9, though there were some permanent casualties, most notably Hatton in Warwickshire, where only 4 out of the original 14 virgates were still occupied in 1393.[136]

The history under Bishop Wakefield of the three estates where the demesnes were leased between 1392–5 (Bibury, Hampton Lucy and Henbury Saltmarsh) would be more conveniently deferred until chapter 5, where I discuss the background to the leasing of these estates. Of the three, only Henbury Saltmarsh continued to prosper throughout Wakefield's episcopate, yielding almost as much in 1393/4[137] (cash deliveries and expenses of £93 7s 10½d) as it had done in 1379/80[138] (cash deliveries and expenses of £99 9s 9½d).

The great estate of Blockley (Gloucestershire), comprising several outlying members, was the most north-easterly property of the bishops.[139] Only one account, for 1383/4, survives for the period that concerns us here[140] and there are no further known accounts until 1458/9.[141] It was, alongside Henbury Saltmarsh, one of the two most valuable episcopal estates. The great bulk of the bishop's sheep who gathered here during early summer for shearing.[142] The tithes of Blockley and its component members were appropriated by the bishops. In 1383/4 the reeve and other officials and debtors delivered to the bishop's receiver £70 5s 9¼d, the largest component being £38 6s 8d paid for the previous year's tithes, surpassing the amount due from rents of free and servile tenants. These deliveries of cash and the expenses of the reeve and other officials amounted together to £147 5s 7½d. Slightly more than a third of this total was spent on sheep and on the two sheepfolds needed for them (£50 4s 9½d).[143] The use of Blockley as the main centre of the bishop's sheep-farming was possible because of the presence of abundant pastures. That year £1 7s 6d was received from leases of pasture while pastures worth slightly more (£1 8s 4d) were used for the bishop's own sheep. In the same year 146 acres were sown with various crops and thirty tenant ploughs were used. There was a permanent staff of nine manorial servants, including one shepherd employed for the whole year. Two other shepherds were employed seasonally. The bishop's auditors accepted a wage bill of £4 16s,[144] though a further expenditure of 4s had been claimed by the reeve. Casual labour hired for harvesting was paid at the rate of 8d per acre, which was regarded at that date by the bishop's auditors as the normal rate.[145]

At Blockley and its members there were at least fifty-four servile tenants still owing some labour services,[146] besides others whose *opera* (labour services) had been permanently commuted for additional rents. By 1383/4 10 half-virgates had been freed from labour services and their holders paid only rent. Some recent increases of rent had been secured from certain tenants. Thus eight holders of virgates at Ditchford, who used to render between them annually £3, were now paying another £1.[147]

If one moved south-west from Blockley across Gloucestershire and south-eastern Worcestershire, there were in the time of Bishop Wakefield two estates for which several accounts survive. Bishop's Cleeve (Gloucestershire) had in 1393/4[148] probably fifty-five servile tenants, compared with fifty-eight in 1299. In 1393/4 125 acres were still sown with crops, and 350 sheep were shorn, their wool being valued at £9 16s 4d. Twice as much was due from assized rents. The net cash deliveries amounted to £38 4s 2½d, nearly £10 more than in 1372/3.[149] If cash deliveries and expenses in 1393/4 are added together, they amounted to £60 18s 2½d.

Bredon (Worcestershire) had recovered by Bishop Wakefield's time from the disasters it had suffered in 1348–9 and 1364. In 1302 its unfree tenants had paid £3 0s 4d in seignorial tallage and 'spenyngfee' at the rate of 1s per virgate. This total slumped to 10s in 1364. In 1375/6 the rate per virgate was half the previous one (6d per virgate), but tallage yielded 17s 6d, reflecting a partial recovery in the numbers of servile tenantry and in the virgates occupied by them.[150]

In the mid–1380s Bredon was yielding roughly the same amount of revenue as in 1302/3, but expenses were lower, as the scale of demesne exploitation had declined and net cash revenue was correspondingly higher. The joint figure for expenses and cash deliveries in 1302/3 was £59 16s 4½d. The comparable figure in 1384/5[151] was £55 1s, but net cash deliveries were higher by £17 14s 7¼d in that year than they had been in 1302/3. Some hundreds of sheep were pastured at Bredon in Bishop Wakefield's time, but its sheep-farming was an appendage to Withington (Gloucestershire) further to the south-east, on the edge of the Cotswolds. In 1393/4 a flock of 224 sheep was driven from Bredon to Bishop's Cleeve, and then to Withington.[152] Seventy-eight acres of the demesne arable had been leased by 1375/6,[153] but the direct exploitation of the rest continued into the first decade of the next century. In 1392/3 rents received from the farming of a portion of demesne and of some vacant holdings yielded £6 2s 2d.[154] By 1408, when the entire demesne was already leased, the revenue from farms amounted to £24 17s.[155]

As I have mentioned in the preceding section, commutation of labour services for rents had increased apace at Bredon in the last quarter of the fourteenth century. The account for 1375/6 mentions commutation of services for 2 virgates and 4 half-virgates.[156] In October 1389 came the collective commutation, for additional annual rents of £11 13s 4d, of a further 17½ virgates (out of a total of 30½ virgates held by servile tenants).[157] Thereafter the remaining demesne was cultivated chiefly by permanent servants and hired labour. Payments of £1 10s to four permanent *famuli* are mentioned in the account for 1384/5.[158]

In the last years of Bishop Wakefield's episcopate there was a succession of inquiries into the

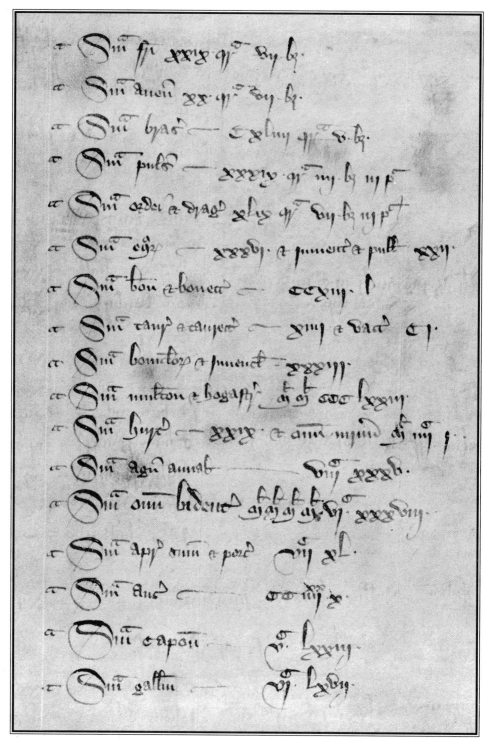

A list of animals on the estates of Bishop Henry Wakefield of Worcester, Michaelmas 1389 (Reproduced by permission of the Bishop of Worcester: Worcester Record Office: BA 2636/193, pcl 193, no. 926284/9v)

revenues from his estates and into their assets. Late in 1389 a survey was made into the accumulated arrears on all the properties. The total at Michaelmas 1389 was £464 16s 4¼d.[159] But two items from Blockley, amounting to £170 10s, should be subtracted for debts for wool and corn from tithes sold at Blockley, as these were always paid for after a delay of about a year. The remaining £294 6s 4¼d represented debts due from various estate officials. These do not look very grave. The two highest amounts were on the two most valuable estates, Blockley (£39 0s 8¼d) and Henbury Saltmarsh (£30 4s 7d). Wick and Whitstones, adjoining the city of Worcester, came next, with joint debts of £35 15s, while Stoke, adjoining Henbury, owed £26 12s 10¼d. All were estates where the money was likely to be collected sooner or later if the bishop's officials were efficient enough. The special receivers of arrears owed £20 16s 7¼d, due from five different officials. Previous farmers of demesnes at Throckmorton and Aston owed £5 6s 2d. If all these items are deducted, this leaves £136 10s 5d divided between thirteen different estates. Proportionately most indebted of these were the two properties of Bishop's Cleeve (£19 6s 8¾d) and Withington (£21 3s 6½d) in south-eastern Gloucestershire, though one may suspect that some of their debts arose out of sales of wool on credit and could be discounted just as much as the similar debts at Blockley.

The document containing this list of arrears has on the dorse a list of stores of crops and of animals on all the estates at Michaelmas 1389. The figures for animals are worth citing. There were 58 horses, 361 of various types of cattle (including 101 cows), 4,638 different types of sheep, 840 pigs and 1,530 poultry (chickens, ducks and geese).

In the spring of 1394 the bishop's auditors were compiling an inventory of permanent revenues ('rotulus . . . de annuis redditibus et firmis') on all the estates. They assembled figures for the last full accounting year (1392/3) and the resultant record was preserved by the bishop's central administration. One item, under Wick by Worcester, confirms that casual revenues were deliberately omitted.[160]

Since 1391 calculations of value began to be recorded for different items of demesne revenues. These notes are quite detailed and informative on several accounts for 1393/4. 'The Bibury account contains valors of 11s 4½d for grain, 4s 6d for stock, £11 13s 9d for wool and £18 1s 10d for the entire manor.[161] At Bishop's Cleeve the value of the wool of 314 sheep was estimated at £9 16s 4d.[162] At Bredon the total value of the manor was given as £63 12s 1d, though it is impossible to discover how the auditors arrived at this sum. The actual total of expenses and cash deliveries amounted, in fact, to £72 1s 9d. Some of the details show that much care was taken to arrive at estimates. Thus the total of the value of animals, given as £12 11s 10½d, mentioned the inclusion of one cow received as heriot. Marginal notes against the total amounts of corn produced mention the proportion of yield to the seed sown as four-and-a-half times for wheat and five-and-a-half for barley.[163]

The practice of recording valors was generalized from the start of the episcopate of Wakefield's successor Tideman of Winchcombe. These later figures are more easily accounted for. For Henbury Saltmarsh it was in 1395/6 the total of cash deliveries (£61 14s 4d) augmented by £3 of 'recognition'.[164] At Bibury, in the same year of account, the figure given is identical with cash deliveries followed by a note that an additional £4 16s 8d had been spent on houses.[165]

These various attempts to evaluate the bishop's income may have played a part in starting a wave of demesne leasing on the episcopal estates, which started in 1392 and widened on the accession of Wakefield's successor in 1395.[166] It extended to virtually all the episcopal properties during the early years of the fifteenth century.[167]

CHAPTER 5
Some Examples of the Early Leasing of Demesnes

I

As was amply explained in my introductory chapter, in the century after 1350 the most important change in the organization of estates was the gradual leasing of demesnes. This happened in every part of England and produced a profound transformation in the relations between owners of manorial estates and their peasants. However, if individual manors are studied in detail, there emerges a great variety of causes and consequences of this change. Each case is likely to be slightly different from all the others. The existing literature has provided enough varying examples to allow one to formulate a provisional questionnaire. But many more studies of individual cases are needed. This chapter attempts to give examples of different types of early leases (mainly before 1400) and to add some fresh evidence, derived mainly from the estates of the Bishops of Worcester.

The leases in the second half of the fourteenth century were often not intended to be permanent. Many landlords still regarded them in that period as temporary expedients, which they were hoping to reverse when better times returned. '*quousque mundus melius relevatur*', as the council of the Countess of Warwick put it in 1401.[1] The consequent concessions to their tenants, and especially the servile ones, were viewed with nervousness by the peasantry, who dreaded their reversal.[2] At that early stage leases tended to be for fairly limited periods and on terms that did not produce irrevocable changes. Thus, on the estates of the Abbey of Westminster, the early leases included some livestock and equipment, so that, should the demesne be resumed by the abbey in direct management, it would be available stocked with 'the basic equipment'. This practice was abandoned on the Westminster properties early in the fifteenth century and, indeed, 'none of the demesnes then on lease was taken in hand again within the medieval period'.[3] In the course of the fifteenth century, too, the length of leases awarded to the particular farmers tended to become much longer.[4]

The leasing of demesnes was mainly an economic operation, designed, above all, to arrest the decline in the income from estates.[5] But some of the leases went to influential people whose support was desired. This was particularly true of ecclesiastical properties. I shall be illustrating this development in Worcestershire, where a group of royal officials and local squires established a profitable hold over some of the monastic and episcopal estates and retained it for much of the fifteenth century.

II

On Sunday 11 June 1368 the chief steward of the demesne of John of Gaunt, Duke of Lancaster, and others of the lord's council assembled in the parish church of the ducal manor of Long Sutton in Lincolnshire.[6] They were making permanent an earlier, temporary arrangement, dating from the time of John's father-in-law, Duke Henry of Lancaster (1345–61), under which the 1,000 acres and half a rood of [arable] land, meadow and pasture making up the manorial

Long Sutton Church, Lincs., where the chief steward and the council of Duke John of Gaunt met in June 1368 (By permission of the Local Studies Library, Lincoln Central Library)

demesnes, together with all the fisheries, had been leased collectively to the unfree tenants of the manor. The grant was now made to the whole homage [of servile tenants], 'to have and to hold by the aforesaid homage and their heirs in bondage, to be divided among themselves according to the condition and ability of each of them, as appeareth in the roll of the court of Sutton . . . paying per annum £162 4s 6d'.

Several features of this transaction deserve comment. A lease by a lord to 'the homage and their heirs in bondage' was a contradictory and legally unacceptable form of words according to the strict principles of Common Law. Servile tenants were not supposed to have any legal heirs. But it was becoming not unusual in the later fourteenth century. Economic realities were obliterating the existing legal rules. As Barbara Harvey had noted in discussing the estates of the Abbey of Westminster, 'every kind of source betrays the lack of a vocabulary to describe the changes that were so rapidly in train'.[7]

Secondly, the demesne at Long Sutton had maintained a large flock of the lord's sheep. There had been about a thousand in 1314. Now they were being sold to the unfree tenants, presumably 'for cash down at the same time as they leased the pastures'.[8]

The partitioning of the demesne among the tenantry meant that the change was virtually irrevocable. It made it likely that the duke's servile peasants would be able in future to alter the conditions of the grant to them in their own favour. This is precisely what happened at Long Sutton, where, by 1439, the annual collective rent amounted to only £128 13s 6d. The difficulties experienced by the manorial lords in maintaining the level of rents secured by them in their initial leases will form one of the recurrent themes of this book.[9]

Several of John of Gaunt's other leases of demesnes were undertaken as more temporary expedients, that could still be reversed. This is the situation revealed by a general survey in 1388 of most of Duke John's estates in the Midlands and the south-east.[10] It makes melancholy reading. The risings of 1381 had had a disastrous effect on his income, as the great repository of his records at his London palace of the Savoy had been destroyed when that palace was blown up. There had also been widespread destruction of his records on particular manors, as the duke had been exceptionally unpopular.[11] The bailiffs of his franchises across much of southern England had not accounted for their judicial revenues since the rising, as all their previous accounts and other records ('*remembrances*') had been destroyed at the Savoy.

Perhaps the condition of the estates was unusually bad in 1388 because Duke John had been abroad since 1386 and there may have been a slackening of central controls over his properties. Direct exploitation of many estates had proved ruinous, as costs had exceeded income. That had happened at Higham Ferrers and Raunds in Northamptonshire and the ducal auditors had recommended that the 'demesne lands should and can be leased at farm as in other places'.[12] At Higham this advice was followed and the demesne pastures and meadows were leased to two men for ten years by the duke's chief steward, Thomas Hungerford. Be it noted that this was still a temporary lease, as leases to one or a small number of individuals were usually in the initial period of the farming of demesnes.[13]

When Methwold, near Lynn in Norfolk, had been at farm in 1387 it had yielded £80 that year. However, the lease was terminated, apparently because the farmers were neglecting the ducal properties. In 1388 it was administered again directly by ducal officials in order to restore it ('*en approwement*),[14] but yielded only £28 11s 2d, 'with the sheep dead of murrain, husbandry at great loss ['*a graunde meschief*'], houses and tenements of the tenants in ruinous condition'.[15] The auditors also recorded that the 'rentals, manorial extents, custumals and other evidences' had been destroyed during the rising of 1381.[16] At another Norfolk manor, Snettisham, the farm had yielded in the past £86 a year, but in 1388 it only produced £50. That manor, too, was in the hands of ducal officials in order to restore it.

These two examples, with their story of neglect by the temporary farmers, illustrate the dangers of short-term leases. The farmers tried to get out of them as much as they could during the restricted time promised to them. Longer leases combined with stringent safeguards to ensure proper maintenance of properties could obviate such perils and this was the solution adopted later by the more experienced landlords, like the Abbey of Westminster.[17]

By 1392 John of Gaunt's manor of Methwold was being farmed by John Bolt, one of the leading men of Lynn. He agreed to pay £50 a year for the demesne and this 'together with the un-leased rents and court profits brought the total value [again] to about £70'.[18] A prosperous merchant was one possible type of farmer whom landowners did find very attractive. Lynn was one of the most important English corn-exporting harbours[19] and a man described as one of the *potentiores* of Lynn could regard control of Methwold as particularly rewarding.

Westminster Abbey owned a few outlying properties in the west Midlands. In 1373 it leased its demesne at Hardwicke in western Gloucestershire to John Monmouth, merchant of Gloucester. There were 200 acres of arable under crops and ample pastures. Monmouth had the resources to undertake the rebuilding of a grange. The annual rent he offered, of £8, was very moderate and it was still the same in 1427.[20]

There was a very different story at Earl Thomas of Warwick's manor of Flamstead in Hertfordshire. Here, too, the lease of the demesne had been taken up at 40 marks *per annum* by a

Peasants gathering in the harvest under the supervision of the lord's official (By permission of The British Library: Royal MS. 2.B.vii, f. 78v)

townsman, Nicholas Pyk, a member of a prominent London family. However, he had withdrawn from the lease and on 1 December 1374 the earl's council had assembled to look for a substitute. A servile tenant of the earl, Thomas Payn, agreed to take over the farm for a term of years, but only on condition that he should be excused £6 for the first two years. After that he agreed to pay the full annual rent of 40 marks (£26 13s 4d).[21] Here, as at Long Sutton, a lord's serf was bargaining as an equal party with the earl's councillors.

The most common type of early lessees of demesnes were the lord's estate officials.[22] I shall illustrate this type of arrangement in a moment from the properties of the Bishops of Worcester, by citing the example of Bibury in 1395. These seignorial officials knew better than anyone else how to make leases profitable. As lords' manorial officials they had often embezzled their masters' funds and misused their prerogatives:[23] they knew how to protect themselves from becoming victims of similar malpractices. Chaucer's picture of a manorial reeve is of an astute rascal: 'there was non auditour coude on him winne'.[24] However, at least the competence of those who had been estate officials for some time was well-attested. If many of them were rascals, they were, at least, experienced rascals.

The estate officials were recruited from among the more prosperous peasants. Lords preferred to appoint as reeves men who were their serfs.[25] Thus the majority of the takers of the early leases of demesnes were either richer peasants or men who had emerged quite recently from that group of villagers. The one typical example I want to cite here is of special interest, as we can trace the origins of this particular family of demesne farmers for two centuries.

Weedon Bec in Northamptonshire was an estate of the Norman abbey of Bec-Hellouin. In the reign of Edward IV it finally became the property of Eton College and we owe to this the preservation of its manorial records. Around 1248 a man by the name of Brother was a tenant there of 1 virgate. In 1365 there were three members of that family holding, at least, 1 virgate each. 'By 1439 John Brother was farmer of the demesne land of the manor for £45 annually' and in 1447–8 William and Richard Brother were leasing it from Eton College for £40.[26]

III

The last two decades of the fourteenth century were a period of lower prices for all kinds of crops.[27] On the estates of the Bishops of Worcester this was probably the main reason for leasing all the manorial demesnes in the 1390s and the first years of the fifteenth century.[28] As was bound to happen on episcopal estates from time to time, changes were hastened by the vacancy of the bishopric after the death of Bishop Henry Wakefield on 11 March 1395. All the moveables on the episcopal estates became the property of Wakefield's executors, so that if direct farming were to be carried on by his successor, he would have to restock all his properties. The situation remained somewhat better in 1395 than it would be normally, as Tideman of Winchcombe, a native of the region and the king's physician, had been previously the Bishop of Llandaff and moved to his new Worcester possessions some of the stock from his former Llandaff properties.[29] But Tideman decided to curtail at once the direct exploitation of two estates in Gloucestershire, and perhaps some others as well.

Bibury at the southern edge of the Cotswolds was one of the bishop's less valuable estates, but it contained good pastures and several hundred sheep were always kept there.[30] It is a perfect example of a manor where a reeve of long standing, Robert Giffard, became the first farmer of the demesne. He was reeve already in 1388/9 and continued as reeve until the death of Bishop Henry Wakefield on 11 March 1395. At that point he owed no arrears.[31] In the first account under Bishop Tideman (21 July–29 September 1395) he reappears as the farmer of the demesne, and, indeed, at that initial stage, of the whole manor.[32] A Robert Giffard, either our former reeve or a relative of the same name, was the farmer in 1407/8 (with a partner). In the first account for a full year under Bishop Tideman (Michaelmas 1395 to Michaelmas 1396) Robert Giffard was still the only person in charge, both as reeve and as farmer of the demesne. In both 1388/9 and 1395/6 just over a hundred acres of arable had been under crops: wheat, barley, oats, drage (a mixture of several corns). For farming the demesne he was to pay £4 6s 8d a year. The leasing of the entire demesne to him appears to have been negotiated in a hurry, as the account for 1395/6 records that no agreement had been reached as yet about the duration of his lease and the bishop was to be consulted by the auditors.[33]

Bishop Wakefield's executors sold at Bibury the entire flock of 516 sheep.[34] It may be that in the summer of 1395 there was no immediate intention of resuming sheep-farming. However, the terms of Giffard's lease included permission for him to use the bishop's sheepfold in winter to shelter his own sheep.[35] The production of wool had always been one of Bibury's main assets and the manor was one of the three estates where sheep were under the control of the bishop's master shepherd as late as 1450.[36]

The account for 1395/6 gave the details of various perquisites awarded to Giffard as part of his farm. He was to have all the amercements for breaches of manorial regulations. He was also entitled to exact all the services of the customary tenants who occupied twenty-four tenements. There is also a list of expenses for which he remained responsible, including the maintenance of buildings and payments to the bishop's steward and other officials when they visited the manor.[37]

Under the next bishop, Richard Clifford, the terms of the lease were reorganized (in 1403/4). Giffard was to render £6 a year and hold the lease at the lord's will. Alongside him there was now a beadle and a collector of rents, Walter Thrift, who shared the farm with him.[38]

One of the principal advantages of leasing the demesne and of giving up direct exploitation was a notable saving on costs.[39] In a later chapter I shall illustrate this in a striking way from the

Archbishop of Canterbury's Kentish estate at Otford. The leasing of demesne in 1444 resulted there, in the second half of the fifteenth century, in an average net increase in annual revenue of some £60.[40]

The lease of demesne in 1395 on the Bishop of Worcester's estate of Bibury produced the same result, though not on such an impressive scale. Henceforth more ready cash was available for delivery to the bishop's receiver. While Giffard was still only a reeve, the revenues from Bibury were at a low ebb. Nearly a quarter of the customary holdings were vacant in 1390 (five out of twenty-four).[41] As reeve, in 1388/9, Giffard had delivered no more than £5 in cash, a third of what an earlier reeve had paid to the lord's receiver in 1380/1. In 1388/9 the auditors allowed Giffard the combined cash payments and expenses of £16 15s 3¾d. In his first year as both farmer and reeve the corresponding total was £14 13s 4d, but the delivery of cash amounted to £9 16s 8d. In 1407/8, despite the raising of his annual farm to £6, he managed to deliver £12 6s in cash.

The other episcopal demesne leased by Bishop Tideman in 1395 was at Henbury Saltmarsh at the north-western edge of the city of Bristol. It was one of the most densely populated and valuable episcopal manors.[42] But its demesne was always relatively modest for a manor of this size. Even at the height of direct farming by the bishops, in 1299, it amounted to no more than 141¼ acres.[43] Eighty-six acres were still cultivated in 1378/9.[44] The bulk of the bishop's high income came from rents of numerous free and unfree tenants. The 'recognition' of the new bishop (Henry Wakefield) in November 1375 listed sixty-seven servile tenants holding between them 22½ virgates, three men holding 2 free virgates, and twenty-nine lesser tenants, some of whom, at least, were serfs.[45] There was here considerable competition for land and every incentive for raising the bishop's income still further by commuting the abundant labour services, far in excess of what was required for the cultivation of the demesne. In the quarter of a century before direct exploitation of the demesne was abandoned in 1395, the chief increases of the bishop's income came from the gradual commutation of the labour services of many of the tenants for additional rent payments, which were recorded in the newly compiled 'rental' of the manor.[46]

The actual leasing in 1395 of the remnant of the demesne was part of this pattern. The account for Michaelmas 1395 to Michaelmas 1396 mentions a new revenue of £3 16s from the farms of the demesne. There were no single farmers here, but the bishop's arable land had been parcelled up among a number of lessees holding 'at lord's will as long it pleased him'.[47] Given the scale of the revenues from Henbury (cash delivery of £93 7s 10½d in 1393/4 and of £76 12s 11¼d in 1395/6),[48] the actual change in the bishop's income was quite small, though there was some saving on the expenses.

At Hampton Lucy in southern Warwickshire and its dependency of Hatton the leasing of the demesnes occurred in October–December 1392.[49] The two estates had had a chequered history in the preceding years and by 1392 all the servile tenants had gradually migrated from Hatton.[50] I lack evidence to calculate how far the leases in 1392 produced substantial savings in costs, though the first year when the manor was farmed produced a higher cash return to the bishop (£47 4s 3d)[51] than any annual revenues from Hampton and Hatton during the preceding two decades. The details of the leases in 1392 are, however, worth recording, as they provide an illuminating example of how such changes were effected.

The main lease of the demesne at Hampton was recorded in the court roll for 1 October 1392.[52] The bishop was not as yet completely giving up direct exploitation; that would only come in 1419.[53] In 1392 the lease was granted to Walter Smyth and William Baron, who was a

Binding corn: a misericord in Worcester Cathedral (Courtauld Institute of Art: Conway Library)

former reeve. The bishop's officials may have been specially anxious to arrange the lease, as by the bishop's special writ directed to his auditors Baron was excused 13*s* 4*d* of his former debts as reeve.[54]

If Walter Smyth was the father (or grandfather) of a Richard Smyth who was conceded land by the bishop's steward in 1410/11, this might mean that Walter was of servile origin. Richard was claiming in 1453 to be a freeman contrary to the beliefs of the episcopal officials.[55] By that date a different group of tenants was controlling the administration of Hampton and Hatton: Richard was permanently at odds with them.[56]

The lease of the main portion of the domain was granted to Smyth and Baron for seven years, with meadows and pastures adjoining, at the annual rent of £10 13*s* 4*d*. In 1389/90 the arable under crops had comprised 138 acres of 'Northfield', in what was clearly a two-field village.[57] But the bishop continued to retain another area to the north-west of Hampton. This was called 'Gravefield', the present 'Grove Fields' in the loop of the River Avon (arable, meadows, pastures and fisheries). As we learn from a later list of arrears (in 1412), the bishop had his park there. By that date the Grove Fields were also being farmed for £12 a year.[58] The other things retained in the bishop's hands after 1392 were rents due from free and servile tenants, the revenue from the manorial courts, the lord's park, and woodland with pasturage for 30 oxen.

On 16 December 1392 a separate lease was arranged at Hatton, where there were now no tenants left.[59] Three men of Hampton leased 7 of the vacant virgates for seven years at an annual rent of £1 15*s*. One of them was Thomas Rowes (or Rolves), whose descendant was farming the whole of Hatton in 1453 for £8 of yearly rent. In 1392 the bishop still reserved to himself meadow and pasture for 240 sheep and the farmers were to maintain the bishop's shepherd.[60]

IV

The estates of ecclesiastics were very vulnerable to the pressure of local notables. These men were able to supplement the income from their own properties by exploiting their ecclesiastical neighbours or overlords. They farmed some of these properties on terms favourable to themselves, while at times withholding the payments due from them. The same thing happened with the rents due to their ecclesiastical overlords for their freeholds. While Westminster Abbey was usually quite successful in controlling its farmers, it failed to do so in the case of John Cassy, a farmer of Deerhurst in Gloucestershire since 1488, who accumulated arrears of debt to the abbey amounting to £21 13s 4d. There was no remedy to be had against him in the ordinary course of law, 'by cause of his grete might, kynne and alyance'.[61] Men of this type also enjoyed fees for life from their ecclesiastical patrons, acted as the latter's estate stewards or auditors, and accumulated all manner of other perquisites. They were, of course, county officials and repeatedly represented their shires in parliament.

One such strongly entrenched group flourished in Worcestershire and Gloucestershire, profiteering at the expense of the Abbots of Westminster (who owned properties in the west Midlands) and the Bishops of Worcester.[62] The leading members of this group of notables caused a disaster for the bishopric when they acted as its custodians during a prolonged vacancy between 31 August 1433 and 15 April 1435. By reviving obsolete demands, that went back to conditions prevailing before the Black Death of 1348/9, they left a legacy of conflict with the servile tenants on the estates of the bishops that led to a permanent loss of episcopal revenues.[63]

This group of custodians of the vacant bishopric belonged to a number of families, some of whose members were doing very well out of their connection with the Bishops of Worcester over a number of generations. They were minor landowners in their own right, but were eager to acquire additional income and to enhance their standing as local notables. The custodians were: John Throckmorton, the under-treasurer of the king's exchequer between August 1433 and July 1443; John atte Wode, the younger, steward of the bishopric's temporalities; John Vampage, the elder, the royal attorney-general since 1429; William Woollashill, whose daughter and heiress married in 1436 Vampage's son and heir, another John; William Pullesdon, sometime bailiff of Worcester and three times Member of Parliament for that city.

The most important magnates in Worcestershire were the successive Earls of Warwick. Professor Dyer has plausibly conjectured that the close connection of the families of most of the vacancy custodians with the earls 'may well have influenced successive bishops in appointing them to offices'[64] and granting them various perquisites. The most significant members of this group were the Throckmortons, generations of whom had been in the service of the earls.[65] The earls were hereditary sheriffs of Worcestershire. Four out of five of the custodians served at one time or another as their deputies (under-sheriffs of the Earl of Warwick),[66] the one exception being Pullesdon.

Thomas Throckmorton (d. 1411), retained by the earls since at least 1396, had been in 1395 one of the executors of Bishop Henry Wakefield and was the chief steward of Bishop Thomas Peverel, at least in 1409/10.[67] His much more important son, John, served in the retinue of Earl Richard (1403–39) in Normandy in 1417/18 and became one of his councillors. In 1431 he was retained by the earl for life with an annual fee of 20 marks as a legal expert ('legis peritus').[68] During the earl's absence from England in that year he acted as his general proctor. He was evidently by then one of the earl's most trusted confidants.[69] In 1419 Earl Richard nominated Throckmorton as one of the two chamberlains of the royal exchequer (the hereditary property of the Beauchamp Earls of Warwick) and John Throckmorton retained this office until his death in

April 1445. His permanent position at the exchequer of receipt paved the way for his appointment as the under-treasurer to Ralph, Lord Cromwell, throughout the latter's tenure of the treasurership (1433–43).[70] When John Throckmorton accounted for the custody of the Bishopric of Worcester in 1433–5, he was having his accounts audited by close colleagues. I shall have much more to say about his relations with the later bishops and the ambivalent record in the service of Bishop John Carpenter of his son, Thomas (d. 1472).[71]

The elder John Vampage of Pershore had farmed the Abbot of Westminster's estate there since 1391. In the same period he acted as one of the Bishop of Worcester's auditors (1391–6). By the time of the Worcester vacancy of 1433–5 he was, of course, a far more important notable, having acted since 1429 as the king's attorney-general,[72] an office he kept until 1452. John atte Wode, the younger, held properties in eight localities in Worcestershire and Warwickshire. He became the steward of the bishop's temporalities in 1426 and held that office until 1448.[73] William Woollashill, a follower of the Earls of Warwick, held lands in seven Worcestershire villages.[74] His principal manor was at Woollashill. High rents were being exacted from his tenants, which may explain why they were gradually drifting away, so that the manor became completely deserted some time after the middle of the fifteenth century.[75] It may be significant that a lord of this kind of village should have been one of the keepers of the vacant bishopric, whose insensitivity to the condition of the tenantry produced a major crisis.

A list of allowances conceded to the five custodians in the exchequer account for the vacancy of 1433–5 provides an illuminating record of the income that they were deriving annually from the Bishops of Worcester,[76] though this has to be supplemented from other sources of evidence. To start with the Throckmortons: their main properties had been held of the Bishops of Worcester since at least the early thirteenth century.[77] The place from which they derived their name is an outlying village of the episcopal manor of Fladbury in eastern Worcestershire. Until the 1470s that village remained their chief residence.[78] In 1407/8 Throckmorton was reckoned to yield annually just over £14 a year.[79] In 1410 it was farmed to John Throckmorton (d. 1445) at an annual rent of £12. He did make some payments (£3 in 1419).[80] In the vacancy account of 1433–5 the manor of Throckmorton contributed £17 10s, that is almost the entire amount due from John Throckmorton for a year and a half.[81]

John atte Wode, the younger, was the son of another John, who had been a Member of Parliament for Worcestershire five times between 1372 and 1380. By a concession of Bishop Peverel (1407–19) the younger John held for life the farm of the manor of Whitstones, a valuable group of lands immediately to the east of the city of Worcester, adjoining the cathedral. Bishop Peverel also excused him £6 a year out of this farm and conceded to him rents from various tenements there, free of charge, worth £2 1s 8d according to the vacancy account.[82] On 1 November 1426 Bishop Thomas Polton appointed Wode to the office of the steward of temporalities with an annual fee of £13 6s 8d and, also for life, of a fee of £20 to be deducted from the farms of Whitstones and Knightswick (also farmed by Wode).[83] Though the Worcester vacancy lasted only a year and a half, Wode made sure that he received £40 from the custodians as two years' fee.[84] The vacancy account also mentions that there were due from Wode £23 6s 8d of arrears from his lease of Whitstones and £11 13s 4d of like arrears from Knightswick.[85]

William Pullesdon enjoyed an annual fee from the bishop for life of £5 and the vacancy account included £8 15s paid to him.[86] Lastly, the vacancy account mentions that George Polton, a nephew of Bishop Thomas Polton, had been conceded for life the farm (worth £4 a year) of the manor of Aston, another property (like Throckmorton) connected with Fladbury, for which George was obliged to render annually only 13s 4d. Polton owed £5 of arrears of this rent.[87]

The custodians collectively received £84 11s 5d as remuneration for keeping the bishopric (at £1 per week) and were allotted a further 100 marks for their expenses.[88]

If all these exemptions from payments, arrears of unpaid farms (including George Polton's) and the award of remuneration and expenses to the custodians are added together, we get a total of £252 1s 4d. Compared with the total of cash delivered by the custodians to the king (£1,304),[89] this amounted to a further 19 per cent over and above that sum.

V

Some of the custodians of the bishopric in 1433–5 and their descendants continued to be connected with the bishops after 1435. John atte Wode acted as the steward of the temporalities until 1448. His son, William, was appointed for life to the keepership of the bailiwick of Hanbury by Droitwich in Worcestershire as the administrator of the bishop's judicial franchise there. At the same time he was appointed to the wardenship of two forests, at Feckenham inside the manor of Alvechurch (to the north-east of Hanbury) and at Fladbury in eastern Worcestershire.[90]

William Pullesdon, in the first year of the episcopate of Thomas Bourchier, on 3 October 1435, was granted the lease of the manor of Wick, west of Worcester, at the annual rent of £12, including all the houses, arable, meadow and pasture pertaining to the demesne, with all the rents as well as customary renders. This grant was renewed by Bishop John Carpenter on 6 October 1449. Pullesdon surrendered his right to the rents and customary payments of the tenants and retained the demesne at £1 5s per year. His surrender of the rents and customary payments was described as for the convenience of the tenants,[91] suggesting that there might have been friction between them and Pullesdon. This helps to explain something that happened in 1452. In an inquiry in that year into arrears and malpractices on the episcopal estates there was an investigation of complaints that Pullesdon was occupying more than had been granted to him and whether, through the enclosures and ditches he had constructed and dug, he might have done damage to the bishop and to the other tenants.[92] Whatever the truth of these charges, we find him acting as one of the bishop's auditors between 1453 and 1459.[93]

Even more complex and ambivalent were the relations of the bishops with the Throckmortons. In 1435 John Throckmorton was one of Bishop Bourchier's numerous creditors. At his accession to the bishopric Bourchier owed total debts of, at least, £754 2s 4d. The debt to Throckmorton, of £40, was one of the largest.[94] This may, perhaps, help to explain why on 13 April 1439 Throckmorton entered into an exchange of revenues with Bishop Bourchier which suited his interests, though it proved very unsatisfactory for the bishop. Instead of paying £12 a year for the farm of the village of Throckmorton, he was to pay in future rents totalling only £10 a year (with a saving of £2). Two-thirds (10 marks) were to be discharged by various tenants of the Throckmortons, who owed them rents in various villages in Gloucestershire, while Throckmorton was to pay each year the remaining one-third (5 marks).[95] The sequel was quite disastrous for the bishops. It is an example of what K.B. McFarlane has described as the 'obstinate determination not to pay on the part of those who' were powerful enough not to do so.[96]

After John Throckmorton died in 1445, his son, Thomas, ceased to feel any obligation to continue paying rent to the bishop. Henceforth the 5 marks due from him personally remained unpaid and his tenants, who owed rents in Gloucestershire, likewise defaulted on their share (10 marks a year).[97] Nothing was rendered under Bishop Carpenter by, or on behalf, of Thomas until 1469. But, as a follower of the all-powerful Earls of Warwick, he continued to be an important man[98] and acted as the steward of the bishop's temporalities from 1459 to 1470, with an annual fee of £20.[99] After Thomas's death in 1472 the accumulated arrears of debt on the exchange of 1439 were estimated by Bishop Carpenter's officials at £160 11s 5d. His total debts to the bishop amounted after his death to £230.[100] A partial settlement had, however, been reached between Bishop Carpenter and Thomas Throckmorton on 13 January 1469. The date may be significant, as this was a time of temporary eclipse in the political importance of Throckmorton's patron, Richard, Earl of Warwick. Thomas had to settle on the bishops a perpetual rent of £12, secured on his property at Severnstoke in Worcestershire.[101] He ceased to be Bishop Carpenter's steward in 1470. His successor was Humphrey Stafford of Grafton,[102] a prominent supporter of the Yorkist kings and the under-sheriff of Worcestershire for ten years. Remaining loyal to the Yorkist cause, he rebelled in 1486 and was executed by Henry VII.[103]

CHAPTER 6

Sheep and Wool of the Cotswolds

I

The Cotswolds, stretching from southern Warwickshire, through eastern and central Gloucestershire and the western parts of Oxfordshire, were throughout the later Middle Ages one of the main areas of England producing fine wool.[1] Its sheep appear to have been quite different from the animals pastured in the same area in modern times. They were certainly smaller and produced shorter fleeces.

Along the Welsh border, especially in Shropshire and Herefordshire, there was wool of even higher quality, the best in medieval England, but flocks of sheep kept there were never large. This 'March wool' was short and curly, well suited to the manufacturing of heavily fulled broadcloths specially prized by the medieval manufacturers of the best woollen textiles. The better Cotswold fleeces may have been somewhat longer, but as late as the fifteenth century they still belonged to the 'short' variety. They were the product of local breeds of sheep. We are told in one of the letters of the Cambini of Florence, who bought Cotswold wools for the Tuscan manufacturers, especially the Datini of Prato, that after a murrain of sheep had decimated the local flocks in 1402, the value of some of the wools available thereafter in the Cotswolds temporarily declined, because many sheep had been introduced from outside the area to replace the lost local animals.[2]

In the first quarter of the fifteenth century the best Cotswold wools were nearly as valuable as the best March wools. This is clear, for example, from the records in 1420–3 of a firm owned by one of the wealthiest Florentine families, the partnership of Lorenzo, son of Palla Strozzi, and associates. The price of March wool marketed by it oscillated between 38 Florentine pounds and 42½ Florentine pounds per 100 lb of wool. But the highest valuations for Cotswold wool ranged between 35 and 40 Florentine pounds per 100 lb. The most highly priced wools came from reputable wool-producers, especially religious houses. Fleeces bought up from a multitude of lesser men (the '*collecta*', or '*coglietta*' in Italian) were valued in the Strozzi records towards the bottom of their price range, at 36 Florentine pounds per 100 lb.[3]

Before the last years of the fourteenth century the wools of the Welsh March and the Cotswolds, though highly prized, did not dominate the English wool trade. Indeed, through combining the evidence of the Datini archive at Prato with the English customs accounts, I shall be able to pinpoint the time when the Italian wool experts decisively transferred their demand to the wools of the Cotswolds, destined henceforth for Italy (*c.* 1398).

Earlier in the fourteenth century, and long before, the bulk of the English wool exports were destined for the textile industries of the Netherlands, where there was a demand for a wide variety of wools of diverse qualities best suited for manufacturing Flemish and Brabantine woollens of many different types. Wools of Yorkshire, Lindsey and the north-eastern Midlands loomed large in the exports of the late thirteenth and most of the fourteenth centuries.[4] Hull, Boston and the East Anglian ports exported between them in many years nearly as much wool as London.[5]

Sheep at Cleeve, Glos., a leading sheep-farming estate of the Bishops of Worcester (The Bodleian Library, Oxford: MS Gough Liturg. 2)

A series of considerable changes took place in the late 1370s. One can trace the interaction of several different factors and I shall try in a moment to unravel this complex story. One new long-term trend was for shipments of wool directly to Italy, chiefly from Southampton, and predominantly only of fleeces of high quality. Only these were needed by Tuscan woollen industries, and the wools of the Cotswolds, so conveniently near to Southampton, made up the bulk of the shipments from the Hampshire harbour. Some wools from the area to the south of the Cotswolds (Wiltshire and Hampshire) were exported in certain years, but by denizens rather than Italians. Thus, Bishop Henry Beaufort of Winchester shipped from Southampton the wools from his own estates in May 1431 (261 sacks) and 1446/7 (83 sacks).[6]

In the course of the fifteenth century the Cotswolds became also the most valuable source of the fleeces exported by English merchants to the Wool Staple at Calais.[7] Lesser varieties of English wool from other regions came to be used predominantly by the expanding native woollen industries, though these competed also with the exporting merchants for supplies of the better Welsh March and Cotswold wools.[8]

My account of the emergence of the Cotswolds as the most important source of fine wools differs from previous treatments by scholars through a much fuller use of the business correspondence of the firm of the Datini in the Archivio di Stato at Prato. The series virtually begins in 1383 and becomes immensely rich from 1395 to Francesco Datini's death in 1410. The late Federigo Melis, who made the archive much more fully available to scholarly use, published numerous studies based on it,[9] some of which I shall use here.[10] He arranged for one of his expert assistants, my friend Elena Cecchi, to send me the transcript of a part of the correspondence sent to the Datini by the firms who consigned goods to them from England. These letters of Giovanni Orlandini and Co. of Florence[11] and of the Cambini of Florence supply a wealth of fresh information about the trade in Cotswold wools between 1395 and 1405 and make it possible to reconstruct it in considerable detail.[12]

My other main source of partly unpublished material comes from the records of the Bishops of Worcester between 1381 and 1458. Professor Christopher Dyer made a splendid use of much of this material in his *Lords and Peasants in a Changing Society: The Estates of the Bishopric of Worcester, 680–1540* (Cambridge, 1980) and it would be superfluous to repeat most of the details recorded in his account. I draw a great deal on the materials assembled by him in my outline of the episcopal sheep husbandry, supplementing them from some records that have escaped Professor Dyer's attention and asking some questions different from those which he has tried to discuss.

II

In the twenty years after 1378 there was a dramatic change in the fortunes of the wool trade of the Cotswolds and of the maritime trade of Southampton. In that year alien merchants, which meant in practice chiefly Italians, were allowed to export directly to the Mediterranean, ignoring the English Wool Staple at Calais, on payment of a small supplementary duty, 'the Calais money' (19*d* per sack). The foreign exporter had to seal an indenture at the harbour of shipment pledging him to take the wool 'to the parts of the West', and not elsewhere, on pain of double the value of his cargo of wool.[13] During the first twenty-one years of this 'new deal' (1379–1400) alien exports from Southampton amounted to 33,330 sacks of wool.[14]

Several developments account for this expansion. Dr A. Ruddock has suggested that England benefited from the revolutionary disorders in Flanders from 1379 to 1385 which compelled Italians to seek woollen cloths elsewhere.[15] This would explain why there was a sudden jump in the exports of English woollens through Southampton from 1380 onwards.[16] As a by-product of this expanded traffic Italians also started bringing to Southampton increased quantities of dyes and alum needed by the English textile industry and to fetch in return not only English cloths but wool from the Cotswolds. But the temporary change brought about by the Flemish troubles began a permanent new trend. This needs explaining and we must turn to long-term changes in the business methods of the Genoese and the Venetians, who provided the shipping, and of the other Italian merchants who used their fleets.[17]

After 1381 the Genoese fully regained control over the alum mines of Phocea from which came the best and the most plentiful supplies of this chemical needed by all the European woollen and leather industries. During the next few years a group of leading Genoese businessmen were able to organize the transport of alum and various dyes needed by the textile industries in an exceptionally efficient and cheap manner. Federigo Melis found mention in the Datini archive between 1383 and 1411 of 437 ships that travelled in those years between the Mediterranean and the harbours of England and the Netherlands, out of which 120 were Genoese. Half of the latter were large ships[18] and some of them were so huge as to merit being described as 'castles'.[19] In their letters from London to Francesco Datini, the Orlandini of Florence repeatedly stress the solidity of these ships and the security offered by their large

A sailing ship carved on a bench end in Bishop's Lydeard Church, Somerset (Courtauld Institute of Art: Conway Library)

crews.[20] These large *'naves'* ('sailing-ships') were purpose-built for moving bulky commodities. A ship of Francesco Doria travelling from Bruges and Southampton to Pisa in the spring of 1407 carried goods, including wools from England, estimated to be worth 180,000 Florentine florins (c. £29,700)[21] at a time when the annual revenue of the Bishops of Worcester oscillated around £1,000. Already in the earliest years of the fifteenth century some of these Genoese carracks would come from Bruges to Southampton expressly to pick up the new Cotswold wools available after the shearing of sheep in June. Thus in a letter of 16 April 1402 the Orlandini reported that two of these giant Genoese vessels had come to Southampton and were prepared to wait there until the 'new wools' were available for shipment.[22]

This group of Genoese capitalists was able to impose their terms on shipowners and ship operators so that freight charges for long-distance voyages could be reduced and permanently maintained at a comparatively low level. Thus charges on wool varied between 3.7 and 4.3 per cent of their purchase price.[23]

Venetian state galleys started visiting England in 1392 and came to London fairly regularly from 1395 onwards. They were the safest vessels afloat, but they carried much less cargo than the large Genoese carracks and their freight charges were higher.[24] Valuable Cotswold wools might, however, be shipped on them if no Genoese or Catalan vessels were readily available. In June 1401 the Orlandini loaded 11 pockets of wool destined for the Datini on three Genoese carracks, the costs of shipment averaging £6 per pocket. But in August 1401 the Venetian galleys took a further 8 pockets at a cost averaging £6 13s 4d per pocket (pockets are canvas packages of wool of variable weight).[25]

A letter of 13 June 1402 from the Cambini to Francesco Datini contained an illuminating comment on the recent expansion of the demand for the wools of the Cotswolds. As one of the reasons for the recent rise in the price of wool there, they described the change in the habits of the Italians exporting wool from England. The Milanese and others (chiefly, it seems, Florentines) who used to export Lindsey wool, shipping it from the eastern English harbours, 'have now all shifted to the Cotswolds'.[26] A glance at the customs accounts can pinpoint the time of this change. There were virtually no exports of wool by aliens from Hull, Boston and Lynn after 1398.[27]

III

The core of the Cotswolds was an area over 400 ft above sea-level,[28] today a plateau largely denuded of trees, though more densely wooded in the late Middle Ages. It was a region of mixed arable farming and sheep husbandry. Much of it was too dry and lacking in meadows to sustain large herds of cattle. Flocks of sheep were here the essential factor in the successful growing of crops. The soils were fairly thin and exposed to erosion, especially as there were steep slopes on the boundary between the elevated ground and the lower areas to the west and the east, as well as above river valleys. The folding of sheep on these vulnerable soils was indispensable to maintain their greater firmness, as well as preserve their fertility for the growing of arable crops. The Cotswolds were thus peculiarly suited to a mixed economy of corn-growing and sheep-grazing. Sheep require less water than cattle and the relative dryness of much of this area protected them from foot-rot, one of the greatest menaces to the health of sheep.[29]

I shall be especially concerned here with three ecclesiastical landlords whose sheep husbandry was highly developed on their estates in the Cotswolds: the Bishopric of Worcester, the Abbey of Cirencester and the Abbey of Winchcombe.

The greatest threat to the continuous success of direct farming by the bishops was the loss of the crops and animals after the death of each prelate, as all the moveables on the episcopal estates went to the executors of the will of the deceased bishop. In the late fourteenth or the early fifteenth centuries that might become the occasion for the final leasing away of the episcopal demesnes. As I have shown in my last chapter, this is what happened after the death of Bishop Henry Wakefield of Worcester on 11 March 1395 on the Cotswold manor of Bibury.[30] To quote the example of the loss of animals on this occasion, at Bibury 516 sheep were given to the bishop's executors, including 260 brought for this purpose from the lowland estate of Bredon, and the whole flock was sold by them to John Cassy of Deerhurst, probably originating from the bishop's manor of Droitwich, and owner of several Gloucestershire estates as well as being a high exchequer official.[31]

Wool was, however, so highly valued by the Bishops of Worcester that down to the middle of the fifteenth century flocks were rebuilt from scratch by each successive bishop, at a time when all the arable demesnes were gradually leased to farmers. Unlike arable farming, which entailed large expenditures on labour, only a few shepherds were permanently needed to look after sheep. The annual shearing lasted only a few days and the resultant expenditure on hired labour would be modest. Thus, in 1485 at Sherborne, the headquarters of the sheep husbandry on the properties of the Cotswold Abbey of Winchcombe, 2,900 sheep were washed and shorn in four days.[32] There were, of course, all through the year, other incidental costs and in a moment I shall try to compare the Bishop of Worcester's receipts from the sales of wool with a partial estimate of their annual expenditure on sheep. As long as prices for Cotswold wool remained high, their sheep-farming seems to have remained profitable. At least, they thought that it was. Why all this changed in the 1450s will be a matter for a later inquiry. I shall argue that one important factor was damaging competition from peasant flocks, where costs were much lower.[33]

The flocks of the Bishops of Worcester were much smaller than those of the much richer Bishops of Winchester south of the Cotswolds, though the Worcester wools were more valuable. In the 1420s Bishop Henry Beaufort had between ten and twelve thousand sheep.[34] At Michaelmas 1381 Bishop Henry Wakefield of Worcester owned 4,077.[35] This total rose by Michaelmas 1389 to 4,638 animals, divided between eleven estates.[36] Four of these were within

Sheep shearing, a misericord in Beverley Minster, Yorks. (Courtauld Institute of Art: Conway Library)

the Cotswolds proper: Blockley, the headquarters of the bishop's sheep husbandry, Bishop's Cleeve, Withington (second only to Blockley in importance) and Bibury. Three more of these manors, to the north and west of the Cotswolds, still lay near land at least 200 ft above sea-level: Hampton Lucy, Fladbury and Bredon. Still further to the west there were sheep at Whiston and Kempsey near Worcester and at Ripple, all in the valley of the Severn. Lastly, at the southern end of Gloucestershire, Stoke Bishop (by Bristol) was used for breeding lambs (3 ewes and 216 lambs at Michaelmas 1389).

The sheep on these eleven properties were treated as a single unit, with frequent movements of animals between different estates. In 1389 the lowland manors were mainly used for breeding, while in spring and summer substantial numbers of fully grown animals were moved to the upland pastures of the Cotswold estates.

For shearing, the great majority of animals were moved each year in the late spring to Blockley, the most north-easterly of the bishop's properties in the Cotswolds. As Professor Dyer has noted, 'If animals on the more distant manors were sheared locally, the wool was often carried to Blockley for sale.'[37] The village lies in a hollow largely surrounded by abundant hill pastures. The Blockley Brook which still flows through the village provided water to wash the animals before shearing.[38] In the late spring of 1384 3,126 sheep were shorn at Blockley. The resultant 14¼ sacks of wool were sold for £133 to William Grevel of Chipping Campden.[39] In 1389 Grevel owed £134 6s 8d to the Bishop of Worcester for wool, which suggests that this second sale was of roughly identical amount. On this occasion he had a partner, Francis Ion', who may have been an Italian.[40]

The price in 1384 of £9 6s 8d (14 marks) per sack was substantially higher than the average price of good Cotswold wool, as quoted in the letters of the Orlandini of Florence to the Datini between

The house of William Grevel (d. 1401), a leading wool merchant of Chipping Camden, who bought wool from the Bishops of Worcester (Margaret Lister)

1395 and 1400 (£7 to £8 per sack).[41] This points to the exceptionally high quality of the bishop's fleeces. They were presumably carefully packed and free from fraudulent mixing of wools of different sort in the same pockets.[42] This is attested also by the high reputation of the purchaser, William Grevel. The inscription on his tomb at Chipping Campden, a few miles to the north-east of Blockley, calls him the 'flower of the wool merchants of all England'.[43] That this was not just vainglorious rhetoric is confirmed by a comment of the Cambini of Florence in a letter to Francesco Datini of 29 July 1402, a year after Grevel's death.[44] In stressing the temporary decline of wool production in the Cotswolds, because of a recent murrain of sheep, the Cambini remarked that in times past Grevel alone had been acquiring annually some 300 sacks. Besides buying the wools of the Bishops of Worcester, he also made block purchases from the Earls of Warwick, acquiring, for example, in 1397 some four thousand of their fleeces for £143,[45] which would suggest the sale to him of slightly more than 15 sacks. The Cambini obviously regarded Grevel as the most important English 'woolman' (middleman dealer) in the Cotswolds. His purchases of estates led to the founding of two knightly families, one of which was raised to the peerage in the seventeenth century.[46]

Looking at the eastern episcopal estates in the 1380s one has the impression that the whole organization existed above all for the production of high-grade wool, with different types of animals kept on different estates, the annual transhumance between the winter and the summer pastures, the concentration of sheep at Blockley for the shearing and the sale of wool. The costs of this elaborate organization were considerable, though the high prices, while they lasted, seem to have kept it profitable. One doubts, however, whether the bishops tried to compare the receipts from wool with the cost of its production throughout their properties. We cannot do so adequately any more, as the accounts are missing for some of the crucial estates, like Withington. Professor Dyer has, however, concluded that at Hampton Lucy (Warwickshire) there was in 1377–8 a net profit on sheep and wool of £5 on an outlay of £6. There is, of course, no way of estimating the value of sheep manure, crucial for the cultivation of this important arable estate. At Bibury in 1383–4 there was a net profit of almost £8 on an expenditure of nearly £6.[47]

The starting-point for any overall calculation must be sought in the accounts for Blockley. In 1383–4 the £133 raised from the sale of the entire wool clip to William Grevel must be set against costs on sheep and wool amounting to, at least, around £50.[48] Admittedly these expenses were singularly high in that financial year (starting at Michaelmas 1383), as the existing sheepfold at Blockley had to be repaired and a second large sheepfold was constructed. That new structure was some 120 ft long, with an expensive roof of stone tiles. The expenditure on the two sheepfolds amounted to at least £14 3s 4d, constituting about 10 per cent of the expenses and cash deliveries at Blockley in that year (£147 5s 7½d).[49]

I shall be arguing later that when prices for wool seriously slumped the whole elaborate enterprise ceased to be competitive in comparison with simpler and cheaper units of wool production run by lesser men. These sheep of peasants might be less pampered than the episcopal flocks. Wool from lesser producers was regarded by the Italian buyers in the Cotswolds as less reliable. But by the middle of the fifteenth century their production was apparently squeezing out the wools of a great landowner like the Bishop of Worcester. In the unforgettable phrase of Eileen Power, 'Hodge rules the field; it was the day of the small man.'[50]

The largest producer of wool in Gloucestershire was the Abbey of Gloucester. Its chronicler recorded in the early fourteenth century that it owned then some ten thousand sheep, producing for sale 46 sacks of wool a year.[51] Leading Venetian merchants were certainly buying its wool in the 1440s.[52]

The market place, Cirencester (From the Local Studies Collection, Cirencester Bingham Library)

More is known about the details of the wool trade at Cirencester. It was the most important town of the Cotswolds. In the first years of the fifteenth century the Cambini of Florence regarded its abbey as the second most important producer, after Gloucester, of fine Cotswold wool. In a letter of 29 August 1402 to Francesco Datini they wrote that they had purchased for him 13 sacks of Cirencester wool priced at £9 6s 8d per sack, which was well above other Cotswold prices that year. They added that the town of Cirencester was the best market for wools because there was an exchange for the Florentine gold coinage and because, above all, there were no medium wools offered for sale but only those of the best quality.[53] Forty years later Federigo Corner, one of the richest Venetian merchants trading to England, purchased from the Abbot of Cirencester 19 sacks of wool valued at the exceptionally high price of £10 per sack. His other purchases on this occasion consisted of 33 sacks, 32 cloves of diverse other Cotswold wools, bought at prices ranging from £9 to £9 10s per sack.[54] (A sack was a statutory measure of wool, consisting of 364 lb. It contained 26 stones, of 14 lb each, and each stone contained 2 cloves, of 7 lb each.)

The Augustinian Abbey of Cirencester, founded by King Henry I in the last years of his reign, had been endowed by him with a chain of churches and lands chiefly on the edge of the Cotswolds. Six lay fairly near the abbey, to the east and south-east, in Gloucestershire and northern Wiltshire. There were also four other properties in western Gloucestershire, two more in central Wiltshire and four in Berkshire besides some outlying possessions in more distant counties (Somerset, Dorset, Northamptonshire).[55] The abbey had thus plenty of land in areas well suited to producing good wool.

The Abbey of Winchcombe, on the western edge of the Cotswolds, was one of the richest religious houses of that region. The organization of its wool production and marketing resembled the pattern on the estates of the Bishops of Worcester.[56] It owned ten upland manors in the Cotswolds, as well as some lowland properties. The shearing of its sheep was each year concentrated at Sherborne in the valley of the River Windrush flowing out of the eastern edge of the Cotswolds. Sherborne lay half-way between the sites of the two great annual fairs for Cotswold wool, at Burford further to the east, always held in the last fortnight in June, and at Northleach to the west, where the annual fair was held somewhat later. Sherborne was a large manor, 'fully capable . . . of providing the extra victuals, fodder and labour necessary at the shearing'. It was the only manor of Winchcombe where we find the exaction of the labour services of washing and shearing the sheep. The Sherborne Brook, a tributary of the Windrush, 'wide and shallow, would provide the water for washing 2,000 or 3,000 sheep'. These are the numbers mentioned in accounts in the second half of the fifteenth century.

Sherborne was leased to a farmer in 1464, but unlike the Bishops of Worcester and the Abbots of Westminster at Bourton-on-the-Hill[57] (near Blockley), the monks of Winchcombe continued to run their sheep farms. Perhaps the position of Sherborne near to, and between the two main wool fairs at Burford and Northleach, encouraged this decision.[58] The farmer of the manor of Sherborne simply acted as Winchcombe's agent in handling the expenses connected with the sheep. Under his supervision 1,900 were shorn at Sherborne in 1468. But by 1485 one of the monks was again directly in charge of the sheep at Sherborne and using it as the centre for shearing all its flocks. In that year 2,900 were shorn under his supervision and the wool was packed into 14 sacks.

IV

The information contained in the letters of the Orlandini and the Cambini to Francesco Datini is of first-rate value, as they were among the four leading Florentine firms exporting Cotswold wool.[59] In the case of the Orlandini one can test this also by the evidence of the customs accounts at Southampton. The Datini were only one of several firms which the Orlandini supplied with wool. In a letter of 25 April 1401, addressed to the Datini, Giovanni Orlandini expressly referred to many others ('*piu altri*') to whom his firm was sending English wool.[60] While the average Orlandini consignment for the Datini amounted to about 15 sacks, we find them shipping from Southampton, between Michaelmas 1403 and 25 March 1404, 174½ sacks, or almost one-fifth of all the wool exports recorded in that account. On 10 March 1405 they exported 316¾ sacks in a single Genoese carrack.[61]

The letters sent to Francesco Datini from London by the Orlandini and the Cambini of Florence reveal a wealth of information about the marketing of Cotswold wool between 1399 and 1405.[62] Some of it is quite new. The greatest surprise is the existence of the two annual wool fairs. The Italian purchasers of wool journeyed to both of them. The first was held at Burford in late June and it determined the price of wool that summer, though this might be altered later in the year by new developments. The Cambini, in a letter of 21 June 1403, said quite plainly that the valuation of wools at Burford determined the prices in the entire Cotswolds.[63] The second fair was held somewhat later at Northleach.

The supply of wool fluctuated from year to year because sheep were subject to a multitude of dangerous diseases. So did the quality of their fleeces, affected by changes in their health and vagaries of the weather in the months before they were shorn. The Italians tried to exploit these changes and to dominate the market for wool. One has the impression that in these early years they were fairly successful in this and that the local middlemen (woolmen) had less complete control over the wools of the Cotswolds than they acquired later in the fifteenth century. Perhaps no English woolman could step into the influential position of William Grevel after his death in 1401.

When wools seemed poorer in quality than usual, and their prices seemed, therefore, excessive, the Italians were in a strong enough position to delay purchases in order to force prices down. This happened in the later months of 1400. The Orlandini refused to buy Cotswold wools at the average price of £7 16s 8d a sack, hoping to depress it to at least £7 6s 8d, or even less (letter of 18 October 1400), and in a later missive of 29 December 1400 they reported with glee that some 450 sacks still remained unsold in the Cotswolds.

At that early stage in the history of the Italian wool exports from Southampton not everything was of high quality. The Cambini reported on 9 May 1402 that three Genoese carracks were about to sail for Italy carrying some 1,700 pockets of wool (perhaps some 800 sacks). Two-thirds of these were fine wools, including 27 pockets of fleeces from Hailes Abbey, near Winchcombe, purchased by the Cambini for Francesco Datini.[64] But the remaining third were described in the letter as 'lane grosse per Lombardia' ('gross wools for Lombardy') and, slightly later, they were called 'Lane chomuni' ('common wools'). The Milanese appear to have been chiefly responsible for the shipment of these lesser wools for the industries of the Lombard cities and it is possible that they did not even come from the Cotswolds.

The new wool clip of 1402, available from June onwards, represented a radically different situation. Disease had killed in the winter of 1401–2 very many sheep in the Cotswolds. In a letter of 4 July 1402 the Cambini reported a decline of one-third in the supply of wool. Next month (on 29 August) they estimated that not more than 700 sacks derived from the new wool clip were available in the Cotswolds. That would suggest that the normal supply of wools here of good, or, at least, of medium quality should have averaged some 1,050 sacks. The Italians exploited the shortage by partly monopolizing the purchases. They formed a group of five firms, one Milanese and four Florentine, including the Orlandini, the Cambini and the Alberti (letter of the Cambini of 13 June 1402). A month later the Cambini reported that between them they had acquired some 400 sacks. As we have seen, the Cambini's share included the superb wools of the Abbey of Cirencester. That Cirencester consignment was in January 1403 being loaded on to a Genoese carrack at Southampton as part of a cargo of 300 sacks of wool belonging to the Florentines.[65]

After the Burford fair of 1403 the Cambini reported on 21 June that genuine Cotswold wool still remained expensive and that there was a large quantity of medium wools from sheep which had been bought from other regions to fill the gaps caused by high mortality among the local sheep. These imported animals could not be regarded as producing wool comparable to true Cotswold fleeces. The Florentines had bought between 120 and 130 sacks of the best Cotswold wools and much had been acquired by the clothiers of London and Bristol. This mention of purchases for the fast-developing English cloth industry is an interesting testimonial to the changing pattern of the demand for the wools of the Cotswolds.

The leading Italian buyers tried to secure supplies above all at the fair of Burford or the subsequent fair of Northleach. As a letter of the Orlandini of 12 April 1402 put it, there was a great advantage in buying directly at the fairs as wools there were of better quality and of better weight. This may mean that the fleeces were of the right length, a feature which enhanced their value.[66] Purchases at the 'common markets' were less satisfactory and it was better to follow up attendance at the fairs by bargains with individual religious houses. As we have seen, in 1401/2 the Cambini purchased the fine wools from the Cistercian abbey at Hailes inside the Cotswolds, slightly to the north-east of Winchcombe, and, later in 1402, they bought the excellent wools of the Abbey of Cirencester. In 1403 the Orlandini acquired very fine wools from the Abbey of Osney (outside Oxford) and from Llanthony Priory, near Gloucester.[67]

It is not true that purchases by Italians were entirely on credit. In the middle of June they were reporting a need for supplies of cash before they proceeded to the fair at Burford.[68] Presumably they had to pay at least one-third in ready money at the time of the delivery of wool to them. This was expected of the English Wool Staplers in the last third of the fifteenth century.[69] The mention by the Cambini of the existence at Cirencester of the exchange for Florentine gold florins[70] confirms that supplies of cash had to be secured before bargains could be concluded.

V

The collapse of the Anglo-Burgundian alliance in 1435, followed by the war between England and the Burgundian state from 1436 to 1439, led to a severe dislocation of English trade with the Netherlands. There was another prolonged economic crisis after 1449, starting in May of that year, with a commercial war with the German Hanse. The recurrence of hostilities with France and the Burgundian state between 1449 and 1453 led to the loss by England of all the French territories save Calais.[71] Italians were the chief beneficiaries from the severe disruption of most of England's traditional trades.[72] They continued to export some of the best English wools and increased their share of the trade in English woollen cloths. The maritime trade between England and the Mediterranean continued to flourish until 1458, when Henry VI's government seized the goods of all the Genoese merchants in this country.[73] Also in 1458/9 the Bishop of Worcester gave up production of wool on his estates. There may have been some connection between these two events.

Italian merchants enjoyed important, long-lasting advantages in their commerce with north-western Europe and, in particular, with England. Italian trade was favoured by a profound contrast between the economies of England and of parts of northern and central Italy, as there was a marked difference in price levels between England and the more developed parts of Italy.[74] This situation was not new,[75] but the contrast was sharpened by the smallness of the English population in the middle of the fifteenth century and the consequent low demand for the basic commodities. Italians could buy goods cheaply in this country and sell them very profitably in Italy and also some other parts of the Mediterranean area. One corollary was that sales of imported goods in England often did not suffice to finance purchases for export and Italians had to bring into England considerable amounts of capital. The sophisticated development of Italian banking and other financial services, however, made this possible.[76] Because in the fifteenth century the more developed parts of Italy formed the most advanced consumer society in Europe, there existed in those regions a demand for goods of superior quality.[77] Fine wools such as those from the Cotswolds enjoyed here a special advantage. By the second half of the fifteenth century Italy had to import much vaster quantities of Spanish wool, but fine English wool continued to be much more highly prized. In the Pisan customs accounts of the second half of the fifteenth century English wool was rated at about double the value of Spanish fleeces.[78]

For the two decades after 1435 there is a rich variety of documentation about the wool of the Cotswolds. From the estates of the Bishops of Worcester there survive two accounts of the bishop's master shepherd (1448–50). A bout of zealous enforcement of the Hosting regulations imposed on the foreign merchants had provided us with valuable Hosting accounts at London between 1440 and 1443.[79] The high profitability of the exports of English wool and cloth influenced the decision of two leading Florentine banks, the Medici and the Salviati, to establish branches in London in 1445/6.[80] The resultant records of the Salviati are today very fully preserved at Pisa. There is a good series of particulars of customs accounts at Southampton and, lastly, the Brokage Books of Southampton provide valuable information about the overland movements of goods transported out of the Hampshire harbour or brought into it by road. These records survive particularly well from the 1440s.

The Brokage Books show that several of the principal wool markets of the Cotswolds lay on an important road from Southampton to Coventry, one of the leading centres of the English woollen industry. The waggons engaged in the trade passed through Burford, Stow-on-the-Wold and Chipping Campden. They brought each year from Southampton large quantities of canvas for making the pockets or sarplars into which wools were packed. The chief suppliers were the Genoese. On their return journeys from Coventry the waggons picked up wool for carriage to Southampton.[81]

In the four years after Michaelmas 1441 alien exports of wool from Southampton averaged annually slightly over 1,000 sacks[82] and one can safely assume that most of it came from the Cotswolds. There was plentiful shipping awaiting wool in the Hampshire harbour. Thus, in the year after Michaelmas 1443, as many as twenty-one Italian and Spanish ships called at Southampton. At least nine were Genoese or from Liguria, including some huge Genoese carracks. The largest amount of wool, valued at £6,885, was exported in April 1444 on two Florentine state merchant galleys.[83] To get some idea of what this figure meant it should be recalled that in around 1433 the yearly royal income from all the duties on foreign trade was estimated by the royal exchequer at about £30,700.[84]

Florence began in 1425 to send to England one of its state galley fleets. Its chief objective was to fetch wool of high quality for the Florentine woollen workshops. Down to the 1470s they visited England in most years.[85] In 1443/4 the two Florentine galleys chiefly fetched wool belonging to Florentines, but they also carried wools of other Italians and of some Englishmen,[86] who on this direct sea route to the Mediterranean had to pay the higher alien rate of duty.

In May 1451 John Balmayn, an agent of William Cantelowe, a leading London mercer, set out for Florence with a consignment of 264½ sacks, 5 cloves of fine wool.[87] Cantelowe had licence to ship this wool directly to Italy, free of a part of custom and subsidy, in repayment of a consolidated debt of £10,700 due from the royal government to the Company of the Staple. Cantelowe had been the chief negotiator of this arrangement and the shipment of 1451 completed the recovery of his share of the loan.[88] The shipment on three Genoese galleys was arranged and financed by the Salviati of Florence, who had had a branch in London since 1445 and acted as Cantelowe's habitual bankers. The wools had been purchased by Tommaso Alberti, a veteran Italian business agent resident for many years at Southampton.[89] The composition of this consignment of wool is particularly interesting. Pockets of March wool (from Abbey Dore), more valuable than the Cotswold fleeces, amounted to 7 per cent. The bulk of the rest were fine Cotswold wools (399 out of 466 pockets). Purchases had been made chiefly at Cirencester. Sellers included Henry Garstang, woolman of Cirencester, and two gentlemen from that town and its neighbourhood. In Florence 448 pockets were sold speedily and very profitably to various

Loading ships at the quayside (The Bodleian Library, Oxford: MS. Douce 208, f. 120v)

local cloth manufacturers. In a letter of 27 August 1451, written by Balmayn at Florence,[90] he cited the advice of Jacopo Salviati that Cantelowe should send a further 100 or 200 sacks. They would have a ready sale provided that they were of very high quality ('ye moste bye of ye beste'). He added that the Strozzi and the Medici had failed to sell 60 pockets that were 'right good', but not quite of the highest grade.

VI

At the very time when the best Cotswold wool could still be sold very profitably at Florence, the Bishop of Worcester's sheep-farming was coming to an abrupt end. Why this happened can only be a matter of speculation. Though his fleeces did not rank among the best wools, their quality, to judge by earlier prices, was still very good. The explanation lies, probably, in the combination of a general economic crisis after 1449 and local difficulties on the episcopal estates.

Some of the best wools were often shipped to Italy on Venetian galley fleets, because of their assured safety. This was expensive. A decline in wool prices might discourage such shipments.

Merchant ships setting out from Venice (The Bodleian Library, Oxford: MS 264, f. 218r)

According to Professor D.L. Farmer's index of English wool prices, they started declining in 1449–50 and reached their lowest point in the fifteenth century in 1452/3.[91] It is interesting to note that no Venetian galley fleet came to England in 1452.[92] The lowness of wool prices is corroborated by the evidence of Italian purchases in the Cotswolds. The manager of the London branch of the Medici, Simone Nori, 'late in the summer of 1453 rode into the Cotswolds to buy wool. He intended to buy only 60 sacks, but as the clip was unusually fine and prices low', £7 6s 8d a sack, he ended by buying 100.[93] According to Farmer's index, 1455/6 was also a time of low prices for wool.[94]

In 1456 the Venetians again did not send a galley fleet to England. The low prices for even the best wools persisted until the end of the civil war in 1461. They were particularly low in 1459/60 and 1459 was another year when no Venetian fleet came to this country. Prosecutions of numerous Gloucestershire wool dealers for selling wool on credit to various Italians in 1457 reveal average prices at the lower end of normal costs of Cotswold wool: £7 per sack for 16 sacks sold by a dealer of Chipping Campden, £7 2s per sack for 147 sacks sold by a man from Lechlade and the same price for 52 sacks sold by a dealer from Chipping Norton. Two sales by John Briddock, a woolman from Northleach, reveal a wider range of prices. In each case Bartolomeo degli Sciatti of Lucca was one of the buyers. Eleven sacks were sold at £7 6s 8d each

and 17 sacks were sold at the very high price of just over £12 per sack.[95] The average price in the cases brought to trial in 1459/60 worked out at £7 per sack (1,234 sacks worth £8,643),[96] though one cannot be sure that they all concerned Cotswold wool.

To return to sheep-farming on the estates of Bishop John Carpenter of Worcester (1444–76). Between 1447 and November 1450 he was still maintaining a separate administration for his sheep with a master shepherd in charge (Richard Harris).[97] He kept about 60 per cent of the flocks of the 1380s, concentrated at Blockley, Withington and Bibury. Though on a smaller scale, the involvement in sheep-farming was seemingly still quite well-established, but some of the details suggest structural weaknesses. The sheep kept were mostly wethers, producing especially good wool, but forming no basis for a permanent flock. There were almost no ewes or lambs and these are mainly mentioned only as being sold to others. In order to maintain the supply of sheep large annual purchases were needed. In the account for 1448/9 the purchase of 702 sheep is mentioned, costing £74 19s 7d. The account for the next year (November 1449 to November 1450) mentions the purchase of a further 400 sheep, costing £35, using money provided for this purpose by the bishop's receiver general. The other element of weakness was the inadequate supply of pasture. Even at Blockley, the traditional centre of the episcopal sheep-farming, additional pastures had to be leased for 80 sheep, at the cost of 26s 8d.

The brass of John Fortey, wool merchant (d. 1458) in Northleach Church, Glos. His belt carries a pendant with his woolmark and the six medallions around him also bear this mark (By permission of Northleach PCC)

In the account for 1448/9 there is a mention of the shearing of 2,927 sheep, only slightly fewer than the 3,126 shorn at Blockley in 1384. In that earlier year 14½ sacks had been sold, as compared with 12 sacks, 10 stones collected in 1448/9. In November 1448 the master shepherd owed to the bishop £125 15s for wool sold to an Italian, John de Leona.[98] If this debt arose entirely out of this one sale, this would give a price of around £10 per sack, slightly higher than the average price of £9 6s 8d per sack for wool sold in 1384 to William Grevel of Chipping Campden (total receipt of £133).[99]

Decline may have started in 1449/50. Only 2,780 sheep were shorn, yielding 10 sacks, 18 stones, and the wool was sold directly by the bishop – a sign, perhaps, that all was not well with

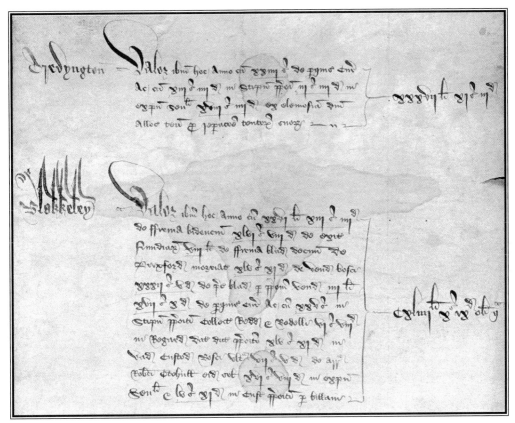

A membrane from the Valor of the estates of John Carpenter, Bishop of Worcester (Reproduced by permission of the Bishop of Worcester: Worcester Record Office: BA 2636, pcl 175, no. 92477)

the whole organization of sheep-farming. It may have collapsed by 1452. An inquiry of that year into the income from the bishopric speaks under Blockley of Richard Harris as the *former* master shepherd. He had been arrested for debts to the bishop, but there is a marginal note that he had nothing.[100] The same record, under Withington, recommends that the demesne should be leased, as this would be more profitable for the bishop. By 1457 Thomas Bleke, who was renting the bishop's sheep, had become farmer of the demesnes at Withington and Bibury.[101] The Valor of the bishopric at Michaelmas 1457 speaks of a payment by him directly to the bishop in the preceding year of account of £37 5s 4d for the farm of sheep, as well as the leases of pasture at Blockley and Withington, and of £6 for the farm of the demesne at Bibury.[102] He was farming the lord's flock of sheep for an annual rent of £26 13s 4d. The account for Blockley for 1458/9 mentions the payment directly to the bishop of a further £35 15s 4d of his arrears. It also supplies the details of his leases of pasturage at Blockley. Bleke had leased four different areas of pasture, some of which were explicitly described as previously used for the bishop's sheep. He was also required to maintain the bishop's shepherd, which suggests that there were still some expectations of reviving direct exploitation of sheep by the bishop. However, the account for 1458–9 records that in the course of that fiscal year the whole flock was sold to Bleke.[103] This was the end of

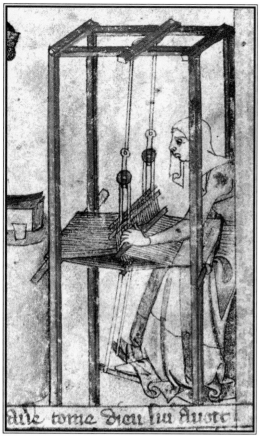

Weaving, c. 1350 (By permission of The British Library: Egerton MS. 1894, f. 2v)

many centuries of sheep-farming by the Bishops of Worcester.

Perhaps the exceptional threats in 1458/9 to the Italian trade in England may have hastened this decision. The government of Henry VI, preparing for the expected Yorkist attack, was trying to raise money by despoiling foreign merchants. The prosecutions of foreigners buying goods on credit has already been mentioned. In 1458 there was a seizure of the goods of all the Genoese in England.

While conflicts with Hanseatic and Italian merchants were affecting adversely the export trade in wool, the decade after 1448 was also a time of considerable contraction in the manufacture of cloth. In many parts of England these were years of distressing economic depression leading to a decline in the demand for cloth and other manufactured commodities.[104] There are indications that some of the wools from the episcopal estates may have been destined for local cloth-making[105] and their sales were likely to be curtailed or to become less profitable. It should be stressed that medieval wools did not keep well and prices for old wools were lower.[106] Prolonged storage of wools that could not be sold quickly was likely to be unprofitable.

The wools of the bishops were probably also facing the competition of more cheaply produced peasant wools, 'Our knowlege of peasant stock-keeping depends largely on chance references.' Professor Dyer has collected some information about flocks of hundreds of sheep kept in Worcestershire and Gloucestershire by individual peasant owners (such as two tenants at Bredon having jointly a flock of three hundred in 1406).[107] Records of tithes suggest very large cumulative totals of peasant sheep flocks. Tithes paid on lambs at Bishop's Cleeve between 1389 and 1397 show that between 1,020 and 1,340 new lambs were born each year. Tithes of wool point to a production of over 14 sacks in a year. Thus the peasant flocks of one of the bishop's villages produced as much wool as the entire episcopal estates of the bishops in the 1380s.[108]

There is every reason to believe that the same situation persisted into the middle of the fifteenth century and it is probable that peasant flocks were becoming even larger than they had been in the past. Dr Britnell has noted that 'the numbers of sheep reported by manor-court juries for trespassing increased'.[109] On some of the Bishop of Worcester's estates there is evidence from the 1450s of acute friction over the exploitation of pastures.[110] Competition from cheaper peasant wools could become disastrous for episcopal sheep-farming if prices of wool declined unduly and continued to be low over a number of years, as happened in the 1450s.

CHAPTER 7

Sheep and Wool of Central and Western Counties of Southern England

I

If one travelled in the fifteenth century from the Gloucestershire Cotswolds into Wiltshire and the adjoining southern counties one was in a world of different species of sheep and varieties of wool. Instead of wools attaining up to £10 per sack, as in Cirencester, one was dealing with average prices of roughly half that amount. A selection of wool prices from the early 1440s on the estates of the Duchy of Lancaster supplies a good example. At Chipping Lambourne in West Berkshire 1 sack, 5 tods (1 sack and 140 lb) sold in 1441/2 fetched £5 13s 4d per sack. The same price was secured for 3 sacks and 163 lb from the nearby manor of Aldbourne in East Wiltshire. One sack and 294 lb from Everley, further to the west in Wiltshire, was sold at £5 4s per sack, and wool from Everley fetched the same price in 1442/3. Wool from the two Dorset estates of Shapwick and Kingston Lacy fetched in 1441/2 a slightly higher price of £5 6s 8d per sack.[1]

Higher prices were achieved on a few estates especially renowned for good sheep-farming. Thus the Cistercian abbey at Quarr on the Isle of Wight may have marketed in 1420/1 the wool of some seven hundred sheep. Its best fleeces, amounting to 2¾ sacks, 3 stones, were sold to one Garado, an Italian or Spaniard, at £7 10s per sack. The bursar's receipts from wool (including

A sheepfold; sheep were valuable for their meat, their wool and their milk (By permission of The British Library: Add. MS. 42130, f. 163v)

also some coarser fleeces) amounted that year to 14 per cent of his total income.[2] A sale to a man from southern Europe suggests that the wool was intended for export. This was different from the presumed destination of most of the wools of that region, which were generally used by the English or Norman cloth industries.

While this assumption is doubtless correct, it is only rarely that we have assured evidence to prove this, or, at least, information pointing that way. This is important, because it was the essential condition of the growth of the English woollen industry that the bulk of its products should be fairly cheap. Wool constituted the most costly element in the production of medieval cloth[3] and only by using moderately priced wools of southern and eastern England could English woollens find ready sale in England and attract foreign exporters. It is, indeed, probable that the wools of these regions had consistently to remain fairly cheap in order to be acceptable to the native textile industry, but not excessively cheap, lest sheep-farming might cease to be sufficiently profitable. The compromise between these two extremes was hard to maintain.

Ultimately the contraction of demand for cloth among the shrunken English population pushed wool prices still further down, to the point where the dismayed wool producers avoided selling some of their stock, hoping for the advent of better time.[4] That point was reached in the middle decades of the century and was a major feature of a slump that lasted in much of England until, at least, the 1470s.

If one looks at exports of English cloths in the 1440s by the Venetians and the Florentines[5] the great bulk of them were medium-priced cloths valued at between £1 4s and £2 each. Bertuccio Contarini, subsequently (1456–60) the Venetian consul in London, bought in 1439–41 cloths worth £2,384, nearly three-quarters of which consisted of woollens in that price range. They were either 'Westerns', clearly products of the area stretching westwards from Wiltshire, or else 'bastards'. The latter were light draperies, probably not fulled, and not requiring wools of high quality. We hear of 1,432 'bastarde de la West' priced at £2,866 (i.e. almost £2 per piece) shipped by two Venetians from Southampton. There was clearly a large output of these 'bastards' in the same area.

The average value of 782 cloths exported in 1439 by a Florentine galley fleet from Southampton was £1 16s per piece. In 1448 the Florentine galleys shipped from the same harbour 538 cloths estimated on average at £1 15s. If we compare these figures with the prices of wool, a Wiltshire woolsack worth £5 would yield 4⅓ cloths, with the cost of wool in each amounting to about £1 2s.

In the case of Wiltshire cloths made for the home market in the Salisbury region, the chief Wiltshire centre for the marketing of textiles, 'production was confined mainly to cloths of the middle price range, such as would be bought by the middle classes, by the more prosperous peasants and artisans, or by the upper classes for their household servants and retainers'.[6]

The evidence about the provenance of the wools used by the English textile industries is widely scattered, but a good deal can be pieced together. There was a small quantity of very highly priced English cloths, produced in a few very specialized centres. These used the most highly priced varieties of wool, like the ones exported by the foreign merchants to the Mediterranean or sent to the Wool Staple at Calais. Such were the cloths of Ludlow, woven, from March wool, the most expensive fleeces in England. In 1439–41 Bertuccio Contarini, whose large purchase of medium-priced woollens have been mentioned earlier, also acquired a few Ludlow cloths valued at £3 each. But Ludlow' production always remained fairly small. In 1442 Lorenzo Marcanuovo, the Venetian consul in London,

A clothworker, carved on a pew at Spaxton, Somerset (Courtauld Institute of Art: Conway Library)

bought 140 pieces of cloth of Ludlow (at £4 each) and also cloths called 'Cotswolds'.[7] These were manufactured from Cotswold wool, probably in Gloucestershire. The famous red 'Stroudwaters', manufactured in the Stroud valley in the south of that county, belonged to this type of luxury cloth.[8]

Wools used in the cloths of non-luxury textiles often did not come from the manufacturing regions, though they might have been brought from adjoining areas.[9] Wool transport was well-organized in medieval England and costs were not high.[10] One of the main areas of Wiltshire textile industry lay in the west of that county, partly in a stretch of heavy clays not suited for the keeping of sheep, menaced by footrot on wet lands. The main area of large flocks lay on the permeable chalklands in the eastern part of the county and in the adjoining areas of Oxfordshire and Berkshire.[11]

In her article on the medieval agriculture of Wiltshire, Richenda Scott recognized that 'for the most part the destination of the Wiltshire wool in the Middle Ages is unknown to us'.[12] All the more valuable are a few crumbs of information pointing to its use by the local textile industries. W.G. Hoskins was certainly right in assuming that the growth in the later fourteenth and fifteenth centuries of the woollen industries of western Wiltshire 'stimulated the production of wool locally'.[13]

Among the most substantial pieces of evidence for the use of wools of this region by the industries of southern England and Normandy (under English rule between 1420 and 1450)[14] are the licences to Henry Beaufort, Bishop of Winchester, to export wool to Normandy, where it was, presumably, destined for the local cloth industry. In March 1427 he had a licence to ship 800 sacks to Cherbourg and sell them there, and in November 1446 he had a licence to ship 100 sacks to Normandy. On that second occasion we are told that he shipped 83 sacks in 1446/7 and that they came from the episcopal estates,[15] which lay partly in Hampshire and Wiltshire but mainly in other counties of southern England.[16]

In 1466 at the central manor of the Lords Hungerford at Heytesbury were shorn 1,526 sheep. They came from a number of estates in western Wiltshire and just over the border in Somerset.[17]

Two years later, 40 sacks of 'pure white wool' of the Hungerfords were bought by James Tucker (alias Terumber of Trowbridge), one of the leading manufacturers of cloth in western Wiltshire.[18]

Longbridge Deverill and Monkton Deverill were two manors of Glastonbury Abbey in south-west Wiltshire. We know the names of two local purchasers of wools from these manors in 1452–4, a man from Glastonbury and another from Wells. In other years the purchasers dealt directly with the abbey's chamberlain, making their payments to him and merely collecting from Longbridge the wool for which they had contracted. Most of the buyers one can identify came from within a radius of 15 leagues.[19] Presumably, these were purchases for local textile industries.

The same was, no doubt, true of the sale of wools of the Bishop of Bath and Wells in 1459/60. There were flocks on four of his manors in Somerset, all on the western edge of the Mendip Hills, at Barnwell, Cheddar, Westbury and Evercreech. Nearly a year's clip (6 sacks, 3 tods, each tod of 32 lb) were sold to John Payn of Axbridge, one of the episcopal manors in the same area. That this wool was destined for the local cloth industry is confirmed by its low price of about £3 16s per sack.[20]

II

On the chalklands of eastern and central Wiltshire sheep-farming flourished in the late fourteenth century and the early decades of the fifteenth. The Cathedral Priory of St Swithun's, Winchester, owning some thirty estates, mostly in Hampshire and Wiltshire, was an outstandingly efficient landlord. In 1390 it possessed some twenty different flocks, comprising 20,357 sheep. Most of its arable demesnes were leased between 1420 and 1450, but 'on many of the chalkland manors the monks continued to operate large-scale sheep flocks long after they had leased their arable lands', as did several other monastic landowners of this region.[21]

There was such specialization on the estates of St Swithun's. Some manors were used for breeding, while others had only flocks of wethers, which produced better wool. As was normal on complexes of manors belonging to the same owner, there were routine movements of sheep between different properties. All the wool was sent to the priory. Unfortunately, in the absence of its central accounts, we do not know who was buying it, or for how much.[22]

The Bishops of Winchester were the other owners of huge flocks of sheep in the same region. From 1388 to 1397 there was an average of 33,000 on the Winchester demesnes. There followed a rapid decline of about 8,000 at the turn of the century, which was never reversed.[23] Crawley in Hampshire, one of their best known properties, was yielding annually between 5 and 6 sacks of wool from 1350 to 1357, but its wool production was always below 3 sacks after 1430/1. This was due not only to the decline in the number of sheep, but also, to some extent, to the fall in the weight of marketable fleeces produced by each animal, which declined notably on the Winchester properties in the 1430s. A colder climate and the spread of debilitating diseases among sheep have been suggested as possible explanations.[24]

Crawley's arable demesne had been leased to its reeve in 1407, but the sheep were retained by the bishops until 1448. It is possible that after 1407 wool production at Crawley may have also been affected by troubles with servile tenants. In 1410 they were collectively fined £1 for refusing to shear lambs as they were customarily obliged to do.[25]

In the 1420s Bishop Henry Beaufort of Winchester had still between ten and twelve thousand sheep, mainly in Hampshire, Wiltshire and Oxfordshire. As in the case of St Swithun's, the bishops' wool was centralized at the episcopal palace of Wolvesey and we know little about the sales of it.[26] These flocks of the bishops and of the cathedral priory were larger than the number kept by even the most important Cotswold landowners. Their huge size compensated for the greater cheapness of the wools. Smaller but profitable flocks were kept in the same areas by other ecclesiastical landlords, like the Abbey of Glastonbury and the Priory of Edington, as well as by major lay landowners, like the Lords Hungerford.[27]

The costs and profit of wool production can best be calculated from the estates of the Duchy of Lancaster in the region. No complete estimates are possible, as the indirect value of the manure of the flocks must be excluded. Up to 1440 I am using the evidence collected by Dr J.N. Hare,[28] while for the last years of the duchy's wool-farming I am relying on the manorial accounts for 1441–4.[29]

Sheep were kept on nine southern estates of the Duchy: Chipping Lambourne in Berkshire; Aldbourne, Collingbourne, Everley and Berwick, all in east Wiltshire; Somborne and Longstock in Hampshire; and Shapwick and Kingston Lacy in Dorset. The relatively sheltered valley manor of Collingbourne in east Wiltshire maintained at Michaelmas 1441 the breeding flocks of 30 rams and 596 ewes and supplied 'hogasters' (second-year animals) and wethers to the more open downland manor of Everley, slightly further to the north-west.[30] Sixty-two wethers were moved from Collingbourne to Everley in 1441/2. The other breeding manor was at Somborne in Hampshire, where at Michaelmas 1441 there were 15 rams and 393 ewes. Altogether at that date there were on the nine duchy manors 6,140 sheep. During the course of the accounting year 1441/2 505 were bought, and 4,573 animals remained at Michaelmas 1442.

Seventeen sacks, 123½ lb[31] were sold on all the nine southern estates of the Duchy in the accounting year 1441/2. They yielded £58 3s 3½d. A comparision with the sales of the Bishop of Worcester a few years later is instructive. On Worcester estates the clip of 1448/9 produced 12 sacks, 19 stones.[32] To provide this amount of wool 2,927 sheep had been shorn. The clip of the previous year was, presumably, roughly the same and had been sold for £125 15s.[33] A smaller quantity of Cotswold wool, but much more valuable, was producing a larger income.

III

Average profits from sheep-farming were higher on the Duchy of Lancaster's southern estates in the first decade of the fifteenth century than they became by 1441/2. The only detailed comparison is possible for Aldbourne in eastern Wiltshire. This was a very valuable manor, with gross revenue amounting in 1441/2 to £159 14s, out of which £132 16s were actually delivered in cash to the duchy's receiver.[34]

The figures for 1400–7 are averages based on estate valors.[35] They may not always correspond accurately to the real values, though the figures connected with wool are probably correct. My evidence from the estate accounts is certainly dependable. Both sets of figures take into account the sales of wool and animals and the general expenses incurred over these flocks. Dr Hare's averages for 1400–7 also include the cost of purchasing sheep. My evidence does not cover that, but for Aldbourne I have assumed an average price of 1s 2d for each wether, as 120 wethers were sold there at that price in 1441/2.[36]

The average annual profit on wool and sheep at Aldbourne in 1400–7 amounted in £15 14s. The comaprable figure there in 1441/2 was £11 12s. For Collingbourne and Everley, very near each other, the joint average profits amounted in 1400–7 to £40. As there were no wool sales in Collingbourne in 1440–43, no comparisons are possible, but the amount of wool produced in these years on that estate and at Everley could not have produced the high profits of 1400–7.

The profitability of the Duchy's sheep-farming had been declining from at least 1434. Both T.H. Lloyd's and J.N. Hare's figures point to this.[37] However, their averages include the wholly exceptional, disastrous years of 1438 and 1439, a time of famine and epidemics, a time also of unusually wet summers, leading to the spread of footrot among sheep.[38] The disasters of these years caused a decline in what the shrunken and impoverished population could afford to buy. Cloth production slumped and with it a demand for wool. It is interesting to note that on the nine wool-producing estates of the Duchy of Lancaster in southern England the worst crisis came not in 1440–2, but in the following accounting year (1442/3), as, presumably, the people making cloth were being threatened with ruin unless they cut their costs. For their part the officials on the Duchy's manors seem to have resisted selling wool at £5 per sack or less. The result was a collapse of sales. Nearly a year's clip was retained by them from the sheep shorn in the summer of 1440/1. As medieval wools soon deteriorated in value, in the accounting year 1441/2 they sold a part of these accumulated stocks, while witholding the fresh wools shorn in that year. In the following year (1442/3) almost no wools were sold.

In 1441/2 net profits on wool and sheep still amounted on the nine estates to £37 18s 2d, with prices ranging from £5 13s 4d per sack (at Berwick and Aldbourne in Wiltshire) to £5 4s (at Everley in Wiltshire).[39] In 1442/3 this changed to an overall loss of £12 19s 10d. Clearly, a drastic change of policy was needed. Restocking still continued on the two Dorset manors of Kingston Lacy and Shapwick, but elsewhere the flocks were run down. The end of direct sheep-farming on the Wiltshire and Berkshire properties came at Michaelmas 1443. Some months earlier, in the summer of that year, the trustees in charge of the Duchy's manors, acting as executors of the will of Henry V, had surrendered their control in favour of a new batch of trustees, acting on behalf of Henry VI, as executors of his will. This was a natural opportunity to introduce new arrangements.

Some of the accumulated stocks of wool were sold off during 1443/4, this time at lower prices. Thus at Chipping Lambourne in Berkshire wool was sold at £5 per sack.[40] But the flocks were now farmed there for five years, at the annual rent of £2 3s 4d, to John Stamford, previously stockman of the southern estates of the Duchy. He also bought outright the breeding stock of 691 animals at Collingbourne and 484 wethers at Everley, paying £76 17s 3d (payable over two years) for these 1,175 sheep. Furthermore, he rented the demesnes at Collingbourne and Everley for the annual rents of £25. This included an increase of £12 6s 8d over the previous annual farms, to cover the demesne pastures not leased previously. At Aldbourne Thomas Goddard, the reeve in 1441–3, similarly bought 825 wethers for £61 17s 6d and leased the demesne for £26 3s 4d yearly, including an increase in rent of £15 7s 8d, to cover the demesne pastures.

The readiness of these men to take over the flocks and the demesnes, including heavy increases of rent to cover pastures, suggests that sheep-farming still promised to be profitable. These experienced men were clearly ready to invest heavily in such a venture. One wonders whether they had served as efficiently the interests of the Duchy's trustees as they were prepared to manage these flocks for their own benefit.[41]

IV

The two men who took over at Michaelmas 1443 the sheep, the demesne pastures and the farms of the Duchy of Lancaster manors in Berkshire and Wiltshire were very prosperous agricultural entrepreneurs. John Stamford seems to have come from a family of substantial freemen of Rushall, a small village to the west of the Duchy's principal Wiltshire manors. He was the stockman of the Duchy's southern manors at least from the early 1420s. Already in 1423 a man of that name was leasing the pastures in Upavon near Rushall. Between 1439 and 1452 Stamford was leasing Rushall itself and between 1439 and 1446 he held an estate of an alien priory at Charlton. As stockman of the Duchy's manors he had to tour these properties, 'seeing to the upkeep of the stock, selling wool and sheep, and buying new stock'. Between 1432 and 1443 all the accounts for animals and wool on the Duchy's southern estates are in his name. All the manors that he was farming personally (as opposed to his activities as the Duchy's stockman) are to be found in a very restricted area of Wiltshire and Berkshire, 'with each manor lying adjacent, or almost adjacent, to another of the manors on which he had secured a lease'. His family remained prominent in this area in the later part of the century.[42]

The Goddards seem to have been an Aldbourne family of villein origin, but quite prosperous already in the later fourteenth century. Dr Hare is hesitant to treat them as descending from villeins, but much evidence points in that direction.[43] One branch of the family had in the

A flock of sheep from a bestiary of the first half of the thirteenth century (The Bodleian Library, Oxford: MS. 764, f. 35v)

middle of the fifteenth century trading interests connected with Marlborough. Thomas, the lessee of Aldbourne in 1443, may have been identical with the man who in 1445 leased for a yearly rent of £50 the twin manors of Ogbourne St Andrew and St George, the most valuable of the former properties of the Norman Abbey of Bec. Ogbourne came to belong to King's College, Cambridge. Members of the Goddard family recur as lessees of Aldbourne and Ogbourne far into the first quarter of the sixteenth century and by then some of them were styled gentlemen.[44]

The activities of John Stamford and Thomas Goddard point to their belief in the potential value of sheep-farming. At Michaelmas 1443 John Stamford leased the demesne arable and pastures of Collingbourne and Everley for ten years and Thomas Goddard leased the same at Aldbourne for seven years.[45] Edington Priory in Wiltshire, while leasing in 1421 the demesnes at Coleshill, just over the Wiltshire border in Berkshire, retained the demesne pastures and kept flocks of between one and two thousand sheep down to 1459.[46] The Cathedral Priory of St Swithun's, Winchester kept the various flocks on its Wiltshire estates far into the third quarter of the century, or even beyond. Only by 1484 had it 'ceased to run its own flocks except at the home manor of Barton'.[47] When Henry Beaufort's successor, William Waynflete, decided in 1447/8 not to restock some of its demesnes but to lease them, he still continued to be interested in their wool. Thus, at Crawley in Hampshire the annual rent was fixed at 10 marks together with each year's wool clip.[48] Most of Wiltshire's monastic landowners retained their flocks far into the fifteenth century. St Mary's Nunnery at Winchester kept its sheep at Urchfont until the late 1470s and at All Cannings until the early 1480s, 'long after it had leased the demesne arable'. Netley Abbey 'kept flocks on its chalkland manors of Kingston Deverill in Wiltshire and Waddon in Dorset' until the 1490s, even though the former's arable had been leased a century before. But it did not retain sheep on properties outside the chalklands. Wilton Abbey, 'most of whose estates lay in the chalklands', was involved in the wool trade as late as 1521.[49]

CHAPTER 8

After the Peasants' Revolt:
General Trends, *c.* 1381–*c.* 1430

I

In the half century after the Great Revolt of 1381 direct exploitation of manorial demesnes was largely given up on lay and ecclesiastical estates in every part of England. The early stages of this change have been illustrated in two previous chapters (chapters 4 and 5). In the second half of the fourteenth century landlords often do not seem to have regarded the resultant changes as irrevocable, but this was ceasing to be true in the period studied in this chapter.

The move away from direct exploitation of demesnes was more typical of major landlords owning numerous properties than of resident squires living on their few ancestral estates and managing them through their household officials or estates managers. Two examples are properties that came later into the hands of John Hopton, a Suffolk gentleman (d. 1478). At Swillington in the West Riding of Yorkshire (near Leeds), the receiver of Sir Roger Swillington received in 1408/9 from sales of grain and stock over £70 while the costs of production were £11 and other payments amounted to £12. There was, of course, also revenue from rents of tenants. He delivered over £60 in cash to Sir Roger. In 1429/30 Ela Shardlow, mother of Sir John Shardlow, knight of the shire for Suffolk in the parliament of 1432, managed directly the manor of East Bavent in that county. The estate was run almost entirely to provide supplies for Ela's household. Out of the bailiff's charge in 1429/30 of £55 8s 2d he discharged almost all of it (owing a debt of only 6s 8d). Half his charge was paid up in the value of provisions supplied to Ela's household (£27 7s 4d).[1]

Professor Bean has listed a number of well-documented examples drawn from East Anglia and the northern Midlands, where landowners of this sort 'retained methods of direct management, both of arable and of pastoral, through the fifteenth century'.[2] In some regions, as for example in the south-western Midlands, such estates remained quite numerous and some of the squires exploiting them also took leases of properties of their more mighty neighbours, like the Bishops of Worcester and the Abbots of Westminster.[3]

As has been amply illustrated from the estates of the Bishops of Worcester,[4] the leasing of demesnes usually meant the final abandonment of most, or all, of the remaining labour services. Indeed, because of the increasing disaffection of the tenantry, at least partial abandonment of the labour services frequently preceded the leasing of demesnes. Such agricultural operations as were still carried on by landowners had to be maintained largely, or even entirely, through the use of permanent servants supplemented by temporarily employed labourers. The procuring and maintaining of a satisfactory, paid labour force was becoming increasingly difficult and costly.[5]

A moment ago I drew attention to the contrast between the almost wholesale leasing of the properties of major landowners and the maintenance of direct exploitation by many owners of single estates or of a small number of closely adjoining properties. But even on properties of major landlords the chronology and manner of changes from direct management to leasing was far from uniform. On the exceptionally well-organized estates of the Bishops of Winchester their officials were still cultivating nearly three-quarters of their pre-1348 area of arable in the second decade of the fifteenth century.[6] But expenses were rising. At Burghclere in Hampshire expenses amounted to 20 per cent of the receipts in 1376 but rose to 30 per cent of the receipts by 1421. At Fareham in the same county they doubled between the same dates.[7]

Some religious establishments, both households of bishops and religious houses, retained a few home-farms through much, or even most, of the fifteenth century. One motive might be that they were favourite country residences of their bishops or abbots who wanted to retain well-supplied manors when they visited them. Denham in Buckinghamshire, belonging to the Abbots of Westminster, was such an estate. It was the last of their properties to be leased, only in the 1430s.[8]

When King's College, Cambridge, the favourite foundation of King Henry VI, and lavishly endowed by him, made its first purchase of property in 1452, it acquired the manor of Grantchester, only some two miles from Cambridge. For fourteen years it retained it as a home-farm to assure good supplies of wheat and of barley for malt, not for financial profit, though the lack of sufficient returns led to its being leased away in 1466 to its bailiff in partnership with a man who had been buying some of its corn.[9] The manor of Alciston in east Sussex, belonging to the Abbey of Battle, an exceptionally large and prosperous estate, was retained by the abbey as a home-farm until 1496.[10] Most of the demesnes of the Bishops of Winchester were leased by 1472, but they retained the manor of Fareham in Hampshire as a home-farm throughout the fifteenth century. Only 95 acres of demesne arable were cultivated there in 1498, however, as compared with 195 acres under crops in 1320.[11]

Even on the properties of major lay landlords and leading ecclesiastical landowners direct exploitation of flocks of sheep and herds of cattle was often maintained much longer than arable cultivation, lasting in several instances until the disastrous economic slump in the middle decades of the fifteenth cenuty. On properties of lay magnates the final abandonment of direct pastoral exploitation was just as likely to be precipitated by political and administrative changes as by economic considerations. Thus, as we have seen, the giving up of extensive sheep-farming on the estates of the Duchy of Lancaster in southern England coincided with the surrender in the middle of 1443 by the trustees of the will of King Henry V of their immense land-holdings, in order to pave the way for a new trust set up to execute the will of King Henry VI.[12]

Except for one year of exceptionally high prices for corn (1390/1), harvests were good and prices for foodstuffs correspondingly low in the decade 1386–96, with a marked decline of prices in 1392–5.[13] Prices may have been pushed down further through landowners trying during these years to compensate for rising costs of labour by increasing their production and sales of corn. At Alciston in Sussex some of the largest recorded arable acreages were sown in 1387/8, 1390/1 and 1396/7.[14] Professor Farmer has suggested that good harvests and low prices may have likewise driven peasants to grow more grain for sale.[15] Professor Dyer's remarks about what happened on the estates of the Bishops of Worcester in the last quarter of the fourteenth century might be applied much more generally. For a time 'falling grain prices were probably seen as a temporary aberration and it was not until the 1390s that the estate officials would have been convinced that prices were following a long-term trend downward'. Besides, 'the conservatism of the management may have also influenced them' in failing to recognize for quite a time that direct exploitation of the demesnes needed abandoning: 'the directly managed demesne represented an element of the old order'.[16] I have described in chapter 4 the enquiries

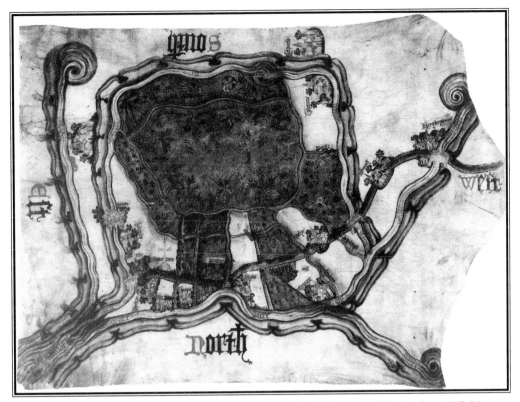

Inclesmoor, Yorks.: a slightly later copy of a map drawn in about 1407 (Public Record Office, London: MPC 56: Crown copyright)

carried out on Worcester estates which may have influenced the final changes.[17] The same conservatism was tending to delay changes on the estates of the Abbots of Westminster and, no doubt, on most other estates.

Until about 1430 the move away from direct management of demesnes to the farming of them for fixed rents was not cutting down revenues too seriously. It is true that the leasehold rents, initially secured, often could not be maintained. The persistence of a low level of prices for agricultural products made this inevitable. Also farmers of demesnes were taking advantage of the fact that the change over to leasing had become practically irreversible. They could, therefore, safely lower their offers at the renewals of leases.[18] But the rate of decline was not, as yet, very drastic and it was counterbalanced by the gains of the leasing landlords from notable falls in costs.[19]

Compared with the agrarian, and later commercial and industrial, slumps, from the 1430s to the 1470s,[20] the first decades of the fifteenth century were a period of relative stability. There were widening differences between different regions and the more prosperous areas may even have witnessed for a time 'a decisive check in the downward trend in agrarian economy'. The keeping of sheep and cattle was yielding better returns than the growing of crops. This was very evident, for example, on some estates of north-eastern England.[21]

A temporary cessation of serious epidemics may have been an important factor. There were four generalized outbreaks of grave mortalities, probably from plague, between 1390 and 1413 (1400 and 1407 being the other two years), but, outside London, twenty-one years 'separated that of 1413 from that of 1434'.[22] More disasters followed, however. There was a grave failure of crops in 1437–9, leading to a famine in 1438/9, the most serious of the fifteenth century. Another widespread epidemic occurred in 1439.[23] If in the reign of Henry V and during the minority of Henry VI it may have briefly seemed to contemporaries in some parts of England that decline and depression were easing off, there was a rude awakening from this illusion in the second third of the century.

The gradual abandonment almost everywhere of the labour services of villein tenants meant the disappearance of economic reasons for the maintainance of servile tenure. There were two alternatives. One was the continuation of customary tenure on changed terms. The other was the creation of contractual leases. On many estates both methods were tried side by side.

If customary villein tenure was maintained additional rents in money (sometimes in kind) were imposed, while other renders and taxes of servile tenure continued to be exacted without any change, or with slight alterations. In the circumstances of the period after 1349, when landlords tried to retain by all means such tenants as still remained, this meant hereditary tenure in practice, or life tenure at least, according to the custom of each manor. At the behest of lawyerly advice many landlords renewing customary tenures of fresh tenants added at the end of the record on the manorial court roll: 'to be held at the will of the lord according to the custom of each manor'.[24] It was one of the central doctrines of the Common Law that 'tenure at will' could not confer a *free* tenement and, therefore, could never come under the protection of the king's courts. The insertion of this phrase thus served as a reminder that customary tenure continued to be a servile tenure, unprotected by the royal Common Law, though in the circumstances of that time it did not mean that the tenure was insecure in practice. The alternative of contractual leases did permit very great flexibility. Each lease would be the outcome of individual bargains. It might be for a stipulated term of years or for life and for rents and fines for entry agreed upon at its start. In section VI of this chapter I shall illustrate the changing practices of different landlords over the admissions of new tenants. In chapters 15 and 17 I shall discuss the legal consequences of each of the two alternatives mentioned here.

II

Though in the half-century after the revolts of 1381 most important landlords were managing, on the whole, to avoid disastrously large losses of income, their grip on their dependent peasantries was weakening. This was undermining their capacity to cope with the more far-reaching economic depression in the second third of the fifteenth century.

That century witnessed a spectacular increase in the mobility of the peasantry.[25] Not all the migrations of servile tenants were in defiance of their landlords. Some villeins had permission to stay away from their native manors on annual payment of 'chevage', though, if their absence became prolonged, they might begin to default on these payments. Some of the allegations of peasant flights in the manorial court rolls really concerned such long-term absentees, who had ceased to pay chevage.[26] But there were also numerous real flights.

The reluctance of some landlords to make necessary concessions to their shrinking peasantry contributed to the increase in this exodus of tenants. It was particulary extensive on some estates which are known to have been badly run. But the general causes encouraging migrations operated throughout England. Labour was becoming increasingly scarce, able-bodied migrants could be sure of finding employment and they could reckon on driving satisfactory bargains about securing good wages. Ths Statutes of Labourers became increasingly unenforceable. A statute of 1427 expressly exempted the employers of labour from prosecution for all breaches of the labour legislation 'because the punishment . . . is too hard upon the masters of such servants, forasmuch as they shall be destitute of servants if they do not want to bypass the ordinance of the statute'.[27]

If the migrating peasants were in a position to take up fresh holdings on estates of new landlords, away from their native villages, there were abundant opportunites for doing so, as most landowners had some vacant peasant holdings on their land. One major incentive for migration was the escape from serfdom, as new landlords were only too glad to secure fresh tenants and their rents. They would avoid asking any questions about the status of these new arrivals. Many fugitives at first found employment as permanent agricultural servants, as is revealed by the attempts of their former landlords to find out what had happened to their absconding serfs.[28] Their new employers were unlikely to worry that they were violating the labour laws.

When good series of court rolls survive, as they do on the estates of the Bishops of Worcester, they reveal repeatedly that when holdings became vacant through the death of servile tenants, their adult sons, who were known to live outside the bishop's lordship, did not come forward to claim succession.[29] To have done so would have made them serfs also. Some villeins were expressly freed by their lords in order to retain them. Thus, in 1452, William Wattes was freed from serfdom by the Abbot of Ramsey at Abbots Ripton (Huntingdonshire) on condition that he should maintain for the rest of his life the tenement that he held from the abbey.[30]

However, in migrating from their communities, peasants did run new potential risks. If through accident, illness or other misfortune they fell on evil days, they were less likely to receive charitable support in places where they were strangers and might be viewed with distrust. This was happening in a society where peasant communities were becoming more polarized between prospering minorities and the rest, and where local charity was likely to be administered more stringently.[31]

Many of the problems facing landlords in dealing with their peasants arose directly out of the leasing of demesnes. The disappearance of the daily routine of the enforcing of labour services undermined the regular contacts between seignorial officials and the servile tenantry. It became harder to ensure that the servile dependants would stay on the estates. Dr Britnell has rightly remarked that while peasant migrations and flights were not a new phenomenon, the influence of this mobility 'to bring about social change was increased. The movement of villagers away from their family lands to bargain for higher incomes or freer status was especially noticeable at the end of the fourteenth century and the beginning of the fifteenth, when manorial custom was crumbling rapidly'.[32]

In this routine matter of stopping the peasants' illicit migration from thier manors, lords were becoming less able to control the movements of their servile dependants because their manorial officials were becoming increasingly unwilling or unable to enforce the customary restrictions. Estate officials were intimidated by the passive resistance of the tenantry backed up by threats of violence and even occasional physical attacks. Even more demoralizing to the lords' agents was the threat of financial ruin hanging over them, as they were usually held liable for the mounting arrears of debts from rents and seignorial dues witheld by the fractious peasantry. I shall be illustrating this especially from the estates of the Abbot of Ramsey in the early decades of the fifteenth century.[33]

Even the private seignorial courts were on some estates ceasing to be wholly dependable instruments for enforcing the will of their lords. Landlords were becoming less sure of having all their orders carried out by frightened and demoralized officials. One strange case should be mentioned, where a lord may have been openly defied in his own court. A receiver of Lord John Talbot at Whitchurch in Shropshire, put on trial in 1433 before the court leet[34] of his master, was acquitted of corruptly enjoying certain 'profettes' at his master's expense, which were set at just under £15. It may have been a piece of blackmail to force him into some private settlement with his master, but lords did not normally put their agents on trial by a jury of their own tenants unless they were counting on a conviction. It is probable that Lord Talbot's normal expectations were frustrated on this occasion.[35] This was, presumably, an extreme case, but it is significant that such things could now happen.

III

The attempts at enforcement of the Statutes of Labourers, and partial failures to do so, provide a kind of indirect index to the movement of wages. However, any study of the application of those laws has to be conducted with caution. The prosecutions before the King's Bench in Essex in 1389/90, during which 791 persons were indicted for offences against the labour laws, reveal a very ambiguous pattern of charges. It is noticeable that the men who are known to have been taking up leases of manorial demesnes do not appear as prosecutors of their employees. Presumably their profits depended not on economies over wages but on other factors. A few of these enterprising farmers, however, saw their labourers prosecuted at the behest of their manorial lords. It was done, for example, by the bailiff of the Earl of March, still a minor, at Thaxted in Essex. This was designed as a form of pressure on the farmers shortly before their leases were up for renewal. Some of the proceedings were, obviously, part of an obscure pattern of economic rivalries, feuds and jealousies, where it suited someone's interest to prosecute.[36]

In the 1380s there were still some harsh additions to the existing legislation. A statute of 1388 for the first time tried to regulate the wages of the permanent *famuli*.[37] The rates it laid down were lower than the payments made by the Bishops of Worcester and the Abbots of Battle,[38] though higher than the wages paid by the Bishops of Winchester, usually very successful in regimenting their peasantry.[39] The statute contained an extremely oppressive provision that children who had worked in agriculture before the age of twelve were to remain for ever 'at the same labour without being put to any Mystery or Handicraft'.[40]

In 1390 a more realistic enactment tried for the first time to impose regulations that were more capable of enforcement. Each group of justices of the peace was empowered to fix local wages at their discretion from year to year, having attention to the changing prices of victuals.[41] Unfortunately, our fullest documentation of proceedings under these new rules comes from the city of Oxford in 1390/4 and not from the countryside.[42] The justices here do not appear to have promulgated temporary new schedules of wages, as they had been empowered to do. Many of the alleged offenders were now genuinely unsure whether the wages that they had received had broken any regulations and the justices were behaving very hestitantly. They were avoiding the application of the notoriously unenforceable rules compelling servants to enter into annual contracts.

In the first half of the fifteenth century the labour legislation, while constituting a constant irritant in the eyes of the peasantry, was not solving the problems of landowners. 'By the end of the fourteenth century the profitability of medieval agriculture had been undermined by the continued low prices for grain . . . and by labour costs which the combined powers of legislation, stringent auditing [by seignorial auditors] and market forces could not push back to the pre-Black Death levels.'[43] As has been noted earlier, the exemption in 1427 of employers from punishments for breaches of the labour legislation was a practical confirmation of its ineffectiveness.

A chronic shortage of dependable labour would by itself explain why wages continued to rise throughout the later fourteenth century and most of the fifteenth. Besides, the wanderings of a large group of uprooted, restless, migratory labourers tended to raise wages still further, but the variable effects of this cannot be traced in the existing documentation. A glance at the movement of wages of a particular type of labourer or at the oscillations in differentials between workmen of unequal skill, as they can be studied for example on the estates of Crowland Abbey between 1381 and 1417,[44] reveals puzzling variations that cannot be fitted into any intelligible pattern. In order to explain them we would have to know a good deal about each of these labourers and about the fluctuating impact of migrant labour.

Individual employers tried to retain good servants by exceptional favours. In 1393, at the Abbot of Ramsey's manor of Warboys (Huntingdonshire), 'a carter and a ploughman received 8*s* each extra because they were freemen'[45] in order to retain them, as their free status entitled them to depart at will. In 1401 on the Kentish manor of Wrotham, belonging to Archbishop Arundel of Canterbury, wages of all the agricultural servants were raised, 'so that they should conduct themselves better in the lord's service'.[46]

Those landowners who still continued to exploit personally some demesnes tried to counter the rise in wages by employing fewer permanent agricultural *famuli* and expecting them to work longer hours. Two exceptionally well-managed estates (Otford in Kent and Alciston in Sussex)

Ploughing (By permission of The British Library: Add. MS. 42130, f. 170)

provide instructive examples of this, though in both cases an excessive rise in wages could not be avoided in the long run.

Alciston in east Sussex, one of the largest and most valuable properties of the Abbey of Battle, was retained by it as a home-farm until 1496.[47] It was exploited with exemplary efficiency. The chief crop was wheat and, in the fourteenth century, about half was sent normally to the abbey. The number of its sheep at times surpassed two thousand, and it formed the centre at which wool from the surrounding abbey estates was collected. The use of tenant labour had caused problems in the fourteenth century and, at the time of the Peasants' Revolt, a large amount of hired labour had to be used because of a temporary strike of the abbey's villeins. Some twenty-three permanent agricultural servants were employed in the decade after the revolt and by 1408/9 the use of tenant labour had been virtually given up. Thereafter the abbey continued to exploit Alciston with the labour of its *famuli*, though cutting down gradually on their number and increasing the amount of work demanded of them. In 1418/19 all the *famuli* received substantial increases of their annual salaries, in many cases an increase of one-third. The next crisis came in the 1430s. Rises in grain prices may have necessitated further increases of wages.[48] Sheep-farming on the estate was badly hit, with murrains between 1432 and 1438 reducing the flocks at Alciston to only around a hundred animals. There had to be further increases in wages for some *famuli* between 1438 and 1445, including one for the shepherds, who had rises in 1441 and 1445.[49]

Otford in west Kent was the last of the properties of the Archbishops of Canterbury to be retained as a home-farm, its direct exploitation lasting until 1444.[50] As at Alciston, wheat was its chief crop and it was retained in hand so long chiefly to assure direct supplies for the archbishop's household. Its 'demesne arable was increasingly underexploited from the mid-fourteenth century onwards'.[51] Bits of it were leased piecemeal, while the demesne still cultivated by the archbishop's servants in the last year of the fourteenth century amounted to only 168½ acres, compared with 315½ acres in 1315/16.[52] As at Alciston, there were serious troubles here in 1381. After the murder in London of Archbishop Sudbury by the rebels in June 1381, the men of Otford defied the royal custodians of the vacant archbishopric and refused to perform customary services.[53] In any case, the amount of labour due from them was never large. Until about 1393 six ploughmen were permanently employed by the archbishops, but thereafter their number was reduced to four. Until *c.* 1428 the annual labour bill rarely reached £10 and was maintained at that level, but in the renewed agrarian crisis of the 1430s that annual limit began to be breached regularly. There were also difficulties with piecemeal leasing of portions of demesnes and with finding labour for the cultivation of the rest. At the adjoining property at Shoreham only 23 acres of demesne could be leased in 1437/8, a bad year, and the rest could not be cultivated because no *famulus* could be found to act as a ploughman ('*conductor*').[54] In 1443/4, the year of the death of Archbishop Chichele, the wage bill rose to nearly £23. There were then six *famuli* at Otford – four ploughmen, a carter and a shepherd – supplemented by temporary hired labour. In 1443/4 the archbishop's surveyor 'had not only to convert the corn liveries of the *famuli* to money at a rate favourable to them', but the estate had to be subsidized by the archbishop to maintain its farming.[55] It is not surprising that Archbishop Stafford, Chichele's successor, decided in 1444 to lease the entire demesne. There was a huge immediate saving on expenses. In the years preceding 1443 'Otford had yielded an average of £76 a year and had cost an average of £67 to maintain'. In 1444 Otford was leased for eight years at an annual rent of £15 6s 8d to a single farmer who also bought the sheep and other animals for £20. Under this new arrangement the archbishop's gross revenue from Otford rose to £84 (chiefly rents of tenants and the farm of the lessee) while costs amounted to an average of only £14,[56] a rise in net annual income from £9 to £70.

IV

One of the worries of the landlords who had leased their demesnes was whether they could maintain the level of farm rents initially secured by them. In the first third of the fifteenth century this was ceasing to be possible in the majority of cases.

Dr Barbara Harvey's studies of the estates of the Abbey of Westminster provide exceptionally well-documented examples of what was happening.[57] They also illustrate that circumstances varied from one property to another. In this particular case the policies of the abbots differed markedly from those of their convent and I shall be chiefly concerned with the former.

On the estates retained by the Abbot of Westminster, there had been temporary experiments with the lesing of demesnes early in the fourteenth century,[58] but a more generalized wave of leases started around 1370. The prior and convent did not follow the same policy on several estates until the early fifteenth century. Most of these early leases included seed-corn and animals. There was initially a clear hope that the demesnes might be resumed into direct exploitation at some not too distant date and it was essential that they should be easily recoverable and well-equipped. Thus at Launton (Oxfordshire), forming the portion of the prior and convent, the demesne of some one hundred cultivated acres was leased in 1386 to the rector of the parish for £12 a year, but he also bought seed and corn worth almost as much (£11 7s 8d). The custumal of Islip (Oxfordshire), exploited by the abbot, was drawn up in 1391 and testifies to the same hope of continued direct exploitation. Though all regular labour services (week-work) had been commuted for rents in 1386, the custumal still 'records the proper customary rents and services for each tenement then at farm', though in reality only a half-virgate was ever held again on former customary terms.[59]

Another early experiment, later discontinued, was tried at Islip in 1395. This was an estate with one of the largest abbatial demesnes (400 acres) and it had previously supplied to the abbots large liveries of corn. In 1395 the lease of the demesne stipulated that almost the entire rent of the farm was to be sent in corn. However, as corn prices were temporarily higher between 1395 and 1403,[60] the lessee must have found it unduly onerous and by 1400, under a fresh contract, the demesne at Islip was again on lease for a money rent. 'In the course of the fifteenth century corn renders became unusual anywhere on the abbot's portion of lands',[61] though they persisted on several properties of the prior and convent.

The gradual fall in the yearly return from the farm of the demesne is well documented at Launton, an estate of the prior and convent. In 1408/9, the eleventh year of a thirteen-year lease, £2 were remitted to the lessee out of a farm of £12. In the next contract it declined to £6 and in 1423 the farm fell to £4.

Except for two estates in the foothills of the northern Cotswolds (see below) the rents from the domanial leases of the Abbots of Westminster mostly showed 'a tendency to sag in the first half of the fifteenth century'.[62] For example, at Islip annual rents fell between c. 1400 and c. 1423 from £15 to £12. A new stage in the 'domanial' policies of the abbots began in the 1420s, perhaps connected with the election in 1420 of a new abbot, Richard Harwden. Leases including seed and stock began to be discontinued: Harwden, presumably, no longer believed that direct exploitation of demesnes could ever be resumed. That meant a downward revision of rents from farms of the demesnes. Thus, Pyrford (Surrey) was leased for the first time without livestock in 1421 and Islip in 1430,[63] with the farm abated to £7 3s 4d. The declining rents in the 1420s and 1430s on these and other estates caught up belatedly with the decline of corn prices. In the first two decades of the fifteenth century the abbots were enjoying higher real rents at the expense of the demesne farmers, whose incomes had been declining. The new reductions of farms under Abbot Harwden (1420–40) 'tardily adjusted the balance in favour' of the farmers and 'for several decades to come . . . the mainly sagging rents on the Abbey's demesnes matched generally sagging prices in the wider market'.[64]

The two exceptions to the downward movement of farms were Todenham in Gloucestershire and Sutton-under-Brailes on the southern border of Warwickshire. Todenham was one of the five abbatial estates where the demesne exceeded 300 acres. It was smaller at Sutton, but still sizeable (200 acres).[65] In the 1420s the annual farm rent at Todenham rose from £8 to £9. Under a contract of lease concluded in 1423 the lessee of Sutton-under-Brailes undertook to pay at first £2 13s 4d per annum, but promised to start paying after fifteen years £3 6s 8d annually for the remainder of his lease, concluded for thirty-five years.[66] It is significant that in 1423 prospective lessees in this part of England were expecting continued and rising prosperity. On a few of the neighbouring estates of the Bishops of Worcester some domanial farms were also showing a tendency to rise in the first third of the fifteenth century, though in more cases they were declining or were, at best, stationary.[67]

There is very little evidence of special premiums (fines) being paid to the Abbots of Westminster at the start of domanial leases. But the lessees were always obliged to maintain buildings in good repair and were closely supervised to ensure that they did so. New lessees had to give security bonds to guard against accumulations of arrears and it was very seldom that these were allowed to occur.

As has been mentioned before (chapter 5), the most frequent lessees of the Westminster abbatial properties were the local manorial officials. One gets the impression that the abbots were more concerned with the continued goodwill of these essential people than with securing the highest possible returns. In the words of Dr Harvey, 'the prevalence of the ministerial-type lessee . . . suggests, that the need to favour the families on whom [the abbot's] local administration had come so largely to depend was a foremost consideration when it came to arranging terms'.[68] This would explain why many of these leases were made for surprisingly moderate rents and why the duration of leases tended to be extended as the fifteenth century went on. 'Down to the end of the fifteenth century the monks [of Westminster] probably did as well on their demesnes as any landlord of the period could.'[69]

The very profitable opportunities available to some manorial officials can be illustrated from the Duchy of Lancaster's estate of Donington Castle in Leicestershire. William Baron was its bailiff in 1421. He was one of the four customary tenants who held 2 virgates each. The rest held less. In 1421 he also leased 6 virgates and 1 bovate of arable, in the lord's possession because of a lack of tenants. 'Thus he had in his hands a farm of about 215 acres of arable.' He was rendering much less for the vacant tenements than their former tenants used to pay, his liability being smaller by £3 6s 8d. In 1429 he was also leasing 24 acres of demesne arable and 10½ acres of demesne meadow, paying 3s 9d less than they used to yield in 1421.[70]

V

The servile tenantry caused most landlords increasingly intractable difficulties. I shall illustrate later the different strategies adopted by some landlords to deal with this problem. Before considering the changes in the types of tenure it is desirable to look at the challenges presented by flights of tenants and the ruin of buildings belonging to abandoned tenements.

Buildings became 'one point of friction'.[71] Tenants who were planning to leave their villages recurrently ceased to maintain their houses and farm buildings, ultimately abandoning them in a ruinous state. When a landlord created large tenements out of what had been previously several holdings, only one set of buildings, those actually occupied by the new tenant, was sure to be properly maintained. The other dwellings and agricultural buildings connected with them (including granges, barns, byres and sheepfolds) were likely to collapse through neglect or even to be dismantled so that their components might be sold. In the west Midlands such unoccupied assemblages of former farmhouses were called 'tofts'. Landlords rightly feared that such decay of buildings amounted to what they regarded as the waste of their assets. 'They seem to have lived in expectation that in the near future' the supply of tenants might recover and that the merged holdings could again be rented separately. The loss of buildings threatened this hope. Manorial court rolls of the late fourteenth and the fifteenth centuries are full of injunctions to servile tenants to maintain buildings or rebuild abandoned and ruined ones. This was especially a feature of bargains with new tenants. Thus landlords were 'seeking to preserve wasting assets in a bleak economic climate',[72] though they were often fighting a losing battle.

The increasing inability of manorial officials to collect some of the revenues due to their lords, especially rents from abandoned holdings, or disaffected tenants, plunged them into growing indebtedness. Some of the previously most prosperous villein families were in dire trouble because of this. The disruption of traditional village society caused by the impoverishment or disappearance of long-established servile families reduced the opportunities for many of the remaining villagers. This in turn led to still larger migrations. A chain of events was set in motion which led to the virtual depopulation of some localities.

The vastly increased mobility of the peasantry is abundantly attested in manorial court rolls. Attempts to present this evidence statistically are, however, full of pitfalls.[73] Heredity of surnames was not yet securely established in the fourteenth century, or even later. Often we cannot be sure that we are not treating as single individuals several people with identical names. Above all, when historians are using the evidence of surnames to describe the survival or disappearance of long-established peasant families, they are ignoring the inheritance of holdings by descendants of female relatives. This is also a problem facing the student of the upper classes, but in their case there is often sufficient genealogical evidence, whereas this is usually lacking for peasant families.

The wide prevalence or relative paucity of flights of servile tenants was partly a regional phenomenon. Widespread vacancies of holdings seem, for example, to have been less of a problem near London. Thus, on the properties of Westminster Abbey, the prior and convent, whose portion consisted mainly of manors in the Home Counties, were troubled less by this problem than were the abbots, with their much more widely dispersed properties.[74] Much depended also on the individual landlord's perception of change and on his capacity to adopt sensible policies towards tenants or, instead, obstinate failures to do so.

Some of the best-documented evidence of extensive migrations of the peasantry, including numerous flights of servile tenants, comes from Cambridgeshire and Huntingdonshire. There had been large mortalities from plagues in Cambridgeshire and the adjoining counties. By 1381 Chippenham in Cambridgeshire appears to have lost over half its population of 1279.[75] At Coltishall, 7 miles north of Norwich, the population of tenants appears to have been reduced by 80 per cent in the two decades after 1349. 'Thereafter the downward trend in numbers seems to have slackened but not to have halted.'[76] There is every reason to think that these shocking figures were not untypical. The voids thus created opened up good opportunities for migrant new settlers.

Village of Wilburton, Cambs. (Cambridgeshire Collection, Cambridgeshire Libraries: Y. Wilb. K3, 14101)

At Wilburton, a manor of the Bishops of Ely, lying in the Isle of Ely, on the edge of the Fenland, flights of villeins multiplied from the last years of the reign of Edward III. 'For many years orders were given at every successive court for their recapture . . . though nothing seems to come of it.' The whereabouts of migrant villeins were often known and, in some cases, it must have been obvious from the outset that they could never be recovered. Thus, in 1380, one holder of a virgate (24 acres at Wilburton) had left with his chattels for Chesterton, a manor on the Ancient Demesne. In this case there was no talk of seizing him.[77]

The numerous court rolls from Crowland's manors of Cottenham and Oakington (both in Cambridgeshire) reveal badly run estates.[78] 'It was evident that the Abbot could not hold his tenants to the old conditions, yet no attempt was made to alter them' by concessions from above. At Oakington, between 1368 and 1378, the huge number of 161 offenders were presented for waste and destruction. In one court in 1395 'there were no fewer than 48 instances of trespass upon the lord's hay and grain by cattle of tenants straying into his crops'. The pasture regulations and by-laws were ignored and the common pastures were overloaded with the beasts of men having no common rights. It is evident that this was a demoralized community where 'the safeguards of the open-field system were being over-ridden with comparative impunity'.[79] There was a continued history of varied troubles during the first third of the fifteenth century, but only in 1430 did the abbot finally decide to give up the exploitation of the demesnes at Cottenham and Oakington and lease those much disturbed estates.[80]

The large-scale exodus of Crowland's tenants was one consequence of this unsatisfactory state of affairs. Flights of villeins, numerous since 1350, became a stampede from around 1395 onwards. In 1396 slips of parchment began to be attached to the manorial account rolls recording the debts owed by the fugitives. The peak of flights was reached in the first quarter of the fifteenth century. Thirty-eight were recorded as fleeing from the Cambridgeshire estates between 1400 and 1415, including two rent collectors from Dry Drayton, who absconded with 49s 5¾d of arrears of cash. In 1425, at Cottenham, twenty-two villeins were reported as missing.[81] Almost every outgoing or fleeing tenant left the buildings of their holdings in disrepair, and some of the fugitives, having anticipated the opportunity to leave for some time, abandoned their tenements in a state of utter neglect.

A story of one fugitive family, the Thankrets of Cottenham, can be reconstructed in considerable detail.[82] They belonged to one of the principal families of the village. When in 1394 John Warlock, tenant of a large accumulation of 10 customary virgates, died, and nobody was willing to take them over, William Thankret and two other men were declared to be sufficient for taking over this holding and were forced to do so, though no entry fine was demanded from them as the tenement 'impositum est super eos' ('[was] forced upon them'). They were to keep it as a hereditary holding, as was normal with customary land on this estate. We next hear of members of the Thankret family nine years later, when they were in conflict with the abbey. A Thomas Thankret, possibly a son of William, was being prosecuted on 19 February 1403 for having failed to repair his tenement, then in a ruinous state. Another charge, which may have concerned a different building, required him to rebuild a cottage destroyed by fire. At a court held on 7 March 1409 William Thankret, described as 'the lord's serf by blood' ('nativus domini de sanguine'), was presented as having fled suddenly with his sons John, Thomas and Henry. That he was probably identical with the man forced in 1394 to take up a share of the holding of John Warlock is shown by the fact that he still held some of Warlock's land. The fugitives left behind one horse, two cows and a variety of equipment. The sequel to this story appears in the next court roll of 16 April 1409. John Thankret returned by night, broke into an enclosure belonging to the abbot, seized a cart worth 5s, loaded it with goods (presumably his former possessions) and with the help of a relative, and other men unknown, drove it to Cambridge.

The court of 7 March which recorded the flight of the Thankrets also presented that Simon Bonde, likewise the abbot's serf, had fled with one son and two daughters, abandoning 1½ virgates. Another serf, Thomas Bonde, a holder of 1 virgate, had also fled with a daughter, taking with him various household goods.[83] These were clearly all men of some substance. It is not surprising that in October 1409 there were at Cottenham nineteen vacant holdings in the lord's hands.[84]

One more case of flight must be mentioned, because it illustrates the accompanying waste of a tenement. On 18 May 1430, in the court of Oakington, it was presented that Simon Sperner, a holder of 2 virgates, had fled to Ely with his wife, two daughters and two sons, leaving his two houses and the land held with them in condition of grave devastation. Some of the land abandoned by him had been sown with wheat. This fact, as well as the details of some of the other cases of flight, shows that men decided to flee in spite of this involving some immediate losses.[85]

The abbot's officials were able to trace the whereabouts of some of the fugitives. One woman had become the servant of the 'Prioress of Ikelyngton'. Some of the serfs had ended up in London, Leicester, Bedford, Wisbech (in the Liberty of Ely), and various surrounding villages.[86] The predominance of migrations to nearby villages is revealed by an inquiry held by the officials

The gatehouse of Ramsay Abbey, Hunts. (A.F. Kersting)

of the Abbey of Peterborough (Northamptonshire) in 1391.[87] This was also true of migrations from Kibworth Harcourt in southern Leicestershire, belonging to Merton College, Oxford, and from Warboys (Huntingdonshire), belonging to the Abbey of Ramsey in that county.[88]

Ramsey Abbey was among the landowners in deep trouble between the 1390s aand 1420. After that date there is a gap of twenty years in the surviving manorial accounts, but when they restart in 1440 they reveal an even more disastrous decline.[89] The abbey maintained direct exploitation of some of its demesnes far into the fifteenth century, though on other estates they were leased between 1400 and 1410. On the estates managed directly by the abbey labour services continued to be exacted until the final leasing of demesnes. This continued exaction of customary services was one of the causes of the resentment of its tenantry against its lordship. The clearest revelation of mounting troubles comes from the rapid increase of debts by officials on some of the estates.[90] At Slepe (Huntingdonshire) debts of former and current officials amounted in 1418/9 to £49 19s 7d. Rent collectors (beadles) owed four-fifths of this total. A previous farmer of the manor owed £59 8s 6d and was described as '*mendicus*' which seems to mean that he had no assets out of which his debt could be levied. This was also the description of two former beadles. A former reeve, who owed £7, had fled.[91] At Houghton (Huntingdonshire) £53 9s 9d were owed by officials in 1418.[92] At Upwood in the same county numerous officials were in debt to the abbey in the first decade of the fifteenth century, with rent-collecting beadles again contributing a notable group of debtors (£7 14s 3d out of the total of £17 9s 7d). 'The aura of indebtedness must have come down hard at least on the morale of even the most prosperous villeins. It may be for this reason that a good many scions of leading Upwood families left the village about this time.' Some of the liabilities of the beadles arose from the flight of some of the tenants who had left nothing from which money could be collected.[93]

Villein migrations, often by flight, became numerous on some of Ramsey's manors around 1400. In the first decade of the fifteenth century it coincided on those manors with the leasing of the remaining portions of the abbot's demesnes. Hitherto the gradual leasing by the abbots of some bits of demesnes may have helped to retain some of the peasantry in the village. Once their chances of getting more of the lord's land had gone, a larger exodus began. Throughout the first half of the fifteenth century the abbots did everything in their power to stop the flight of their villeins, but they were largely helpless. For over a century after 1349 'Ramsey Abbey spent substantial sums on repairing buildings not taken up by the peasantry. The monks looked for a restoration of the old order, but that was not to come.'[94]

At Warboys the abbey's tenant families numbered eighty in 1400. Only sixty-one families were left by 1430. On another of Ramsey's estates, Holywell-cum-Needingworth (Huntingdonshire), the period of most rapid decline of tenant population was from 1390 to 1410, when the number of tenant families declined from sixty-one to forty-one.[95]

At least fifteen families lived in 1363 at Brookend, an Oxfordshire manor of the Abbots of Osney. Flights of villeins first became a serious problem in 1381. During the subsequent years the abbots tried to check it by imposing collective fines on the whole population in order to compel the return of the fugitives. This had, however, the opposite effect, of provoking further flights. The vacated holdings were engrossed by a few richer tenants. 'When a tenant engrossed several holdings the lord tried to insist that he keep all the buildings in good repair. This was very unpopular with the tenants. Many of those who left Brookend did so because they were harassed by the lord to carry out repairs.' The abbot was fighting a losing battle, and once the vacated homesteads fell into ruin, it became certain that they would never attract new settlers. By 1441 there were only three permanent landholders.[96]

Brookend was depopulated against the wishes of its lord. The same thing appears to have happened in many of the localities of the south-western Midlands, partly or wholly deserted in the late fourteenth and the first half of the fifteenth centuries.[97] The village of Woollashill in Worcestershire belonged until 1436 to the family of that name, who owned no other entire village and had concentrated all their serfs on this one manor. Before 1348 there were twenty-two tenants, of whom as many as twenty were servile villeins. Rents of servile holdings were as high as on the heavily burdened episcopal manor of Bredon, slightly further to the south (10s per half-virgate). This may explain the gradual drifting away of Woollashill's inhabitants, especially as its soil was not very fertile. There were thirteen tenants in 1424, amd this figure had dwindled to nine by 1442, with several vacant holdings in the hands of its new lord, John Vampage, the royal attorney general (1429–52).[98]

VI

As the evidence used in this chapter comes mostly from records of ecclesiastical estates, one legal problem that is peculiar to them needs explaining.[99] Under the royal mortmain legislation of 1279 any acquisition of fresh property by ecclesiastics required a royal licence, which had to be paid for. After some initial confusion, however, it became the established rule that escheats reverting to ecclesiastical lords did not come under the statute. Nor did resumptions of leased lands after the lease had expired. Hence leases at will or for terms of years, or even some types of leases for life, were all licit. The variant adopted on some estates, of leases for lives of a tenant and of two other members of his family, were permissible, so long as the death of the tenant was followed by a formal renewal of the leases to the two survivors (with a new third lessee often added), a new fine for entry being normally demanded at each renewal.

Of course, landlords could always freely re-enter land which was indisputably servile, but in the late Middle Ages the exact legal status of much land became uncertain and the rules about exemptions of leases from mortmain were of increasing importance to ecclesiastical landlords. This was also the case with the recognition that they could freely re-enter vacant and abandoned lands held of them.

In the last decades of the fourteenth and the first quarter of the fifteenth centuries the balance of advantage in the dealings of landlords with their servile tenants was swinging 'perceptibly if not decisively in favour of tenants'.[100] Much depended 'on the landlords' perception of change' and how soon they realized where their true interests lay in the changing situation. Most were slow to grasp what concessions were needed, though the Great Revolt of 1381 seems to have sometimes quickened the realization that they must accommodate their peasantry to some extent. For example, there is no evidence that there were in that year any disturbances at Kibworth Harcourt in Leicestershire, which belonged, as previously stated, to Merton College, Oxford. But the manorial account for that year records some important concessions over the college's demands on its reeves, lessening, in turn, the pressures on the tenants.[101] On Westminster estates there were in 1381 disturbances on some manors within the counties where there occurred widespread troubles: at Pyrford in Surrey, Moulsham in Essex, and Wheathampstead, Harpenden and Great Amwell in Hertfordshire. On that last estate manorial court rolls were burnt. There may be some connection between this and the appearance a few years later (from *c.* 1386) at Great Amwell of grants of holdings to tenants, their descendants *and assigns*, recognizing permission to alienate to other persons.[102]

Another example of concessions imposed upon an ecclesiastical landlord by events outside his control comes from Binham Priory in Norfolk. It was a dependency of the Abbey of St Albans. There was a history of bad relations between the priory and its servile tenants. In 1381 John Lister of Binham, one of the rebels in this part of Norfolk, was responsible, with Geoffrey Lister, the leader of the Norfolk rebellion, for burning the records of Binham Priory.[103] Half a century later its bond population was again at odds with its monastic lord. Bishop William Alnwick of Norwich, during a visitation of the priory in 1431, had listened sympathetically to the complaints of the tenants. The priory decided that it would be wise to make some concessions. By an agreement concluded on 14 September 1432 the priory halved the fines for entry of new tenants of servile holdings. Previously arbitrary fines for taking up dwellings without tenements attached to them were to be fixed henceforth and concessions were made to the priory's tenants over their usage of common pastures.[104]

As was to be expected, F.W. Maitland was a pioneer (in 1894) in tracing changes on an estate of a major landowner, with his customary attention to every significant detail and masterful precision in summarizing social and legal changes.[105] Wilburton was one of the lesser manors of the Bishops of Ely. It formed part of its original tenth-century endowment and labour services were heavy, though customary rents were light.[106]

The courts rolls for the reign of Richard II start in 1379. They reveal recurrent abandonments of substantial holdings by tenants (including several virgates of 24 acres) as well as escapes of villeins. Several holdings continued to remain in the lord's hands for lack of new takers. 'On the whole . . . our conclusion will probably be that, in the then state of the markets for land, labour and food, the value [of a virgate] . . . of the manor of Wilburton, to be held by the ancient services, was extremely small, and was often accounted a negative quantity by the tenant – that is to say he would rather not have the land than have it'.[107] When tenements that had lapsed into the lord's hands were leased, heavy annual rents were demanded. A virgate was leased in 1382 at 13*d* per acre and another in 1385 at even 14⅔*d* per acre.[108] For comparison, it might be noted that the reeve of John of Gaunt's very valuable estate of Colham Green (Middlesex) in 1388/9 was taking on lease 16 acres at the annual rent of 15*d* per acre and another 8½ acres at as much as 16*d* per acre, but this was within easy access to London and likely to be very rewarding. The reeve must have thought so, because his main lease was to run for thirty years.[109]

There is a gap in the surviving records of Wilburton in the second decade of the fifteenth century. By 1423 the labour services had been almost entirely commuted and most virgates were now paying instead annually 24*s*, at the rate of 12*d* per acre. Leases of the former villein holdings which had lapsed into the lord's hands had come to yield annually nearly £10 in the course of the reign of Richard II. In 1423 the account speaks of £22 as 'rent of bond land'. Then, in or about 1426, the manorial demesne of 246 acres of arable and 42 acres of meadow was leased to Wilburton's reeve for £8 a year. Later in the century the farm of the demesne declined to £7 a year, while the rents for the former customary holdings abated to 20*s* per virgate and in the reign of Edward IV were yielding annually only *c.* £17,[110] a decline of £5 since 1423.

The strategies adopted by different landlords for replacing customary tenure of servile holdings resulted in a bewildering variety of practices. They might vary considerably on the estates of the same owner, as was the case on the properties of the Bishops of Worcester.[111] Local circumstances would determine in each case what was practicable.

The chief feature of these new arrangements was the increasing number of individual bargains struck between landlords and new takers of holdings, necessitating more detailed and precise statements in the manorial court rolls of the terms agreed upon in each case.[112] Often the landlord's rights are expressly safeguarded by the description of the tenure as being 'at the will of the lord', though one need not regard the presence, or absence, of this stipulation as being, necessarily, of great practical importance,[113] in an England where lords were, above all, anxious to retain tenants and assure continued payments of rents by them.

The insecurity of the northern counties, exposed to bouts of vicious Anglo-Scottish warfare, was one major reason for the prevalence there of short-term leases, both of demesne farms and of tenant holdings. As far as demesne leases were concerned, 'the danger of Scottish raids made profitable demesne farming more hazardous than it was elsewhere and militated against the willingness of one man to risk his money in taking long-term lease'. In 1427, for example, the receiver of the Duchy of Lancaster's lordship of Dunstanburgh in Northumberland was unable to lease the demesnes at Embleton. One reason was undoubtedly its vulnerability to attack from north of the border. The receiver was instructed to find a farmer for at least three years or, 'if he could not do this, he was to lease them for a year at the highest obtainable rent'.[114]

This may also have been a factor further south on the estates of the Cathedral Priory of Durham, though it is unlikely to be the only explanation. The priory after 1380 increasingly had recourse to short-term leases of peasant holdings to its servile tenants. In south-east Durham 'already by 1400–4 more than half of all land transfers were taken up on leases of nine years or less and by 1430 leases for the life of the tenant had been completely replaced by leases mostly for three or six years.[115] The lessees had at least the advantage of seldom having to pay fines for entry.[116] But these developments remain puzzling, especially as the priory had a bad reputation for inefficient estate-management, which produced some disastrous breakdowns of revenue.[117]

Merton College's manor of Kibworth Harcourt in Leicestershire provides an example of recurrent troubles with tenants because of a landlord's reluctance to make the concessions demanded by villeins. The college capitulated only after the loss of nearly £100 in withheld rents.[118] The college had already abandoned direct exploitation of its demesne here in the late thirteenth century, but rent charges were heavy, with commutation of the labour services (6s 8d per servile virgate) accounting for nearly a third.[119] Exaction of fines for entry of new tenants appears to have been abandoned after the Black Death of 1348/9, but the college insisted on maintaining other disabilities of servile tenure and the heavy rents. Arrears of unpaid rents began to accumulate. Matters were made worse by continued migrations of several villeins, though most of them moved only to near-by villages, where presumably land could be secured on less onerous terms. Arrears of unpaid rents formed a fifth of the reeve's total charge in 1361 and in two years of accounts, in 1362–4, the reeve was unable to collect rents from thirty-seven tenants. As R.H. Hilton has remarked, 'these documents may be telling us of something like a rent strike'.[120]

The risings of 1381, though they did not spread to Kibworth Harcourt, seem to have had a chastening effect on Merton College, for in the account for that year there was a remission of arrears due from several former reeves (at least £28 9s 10½d).[121] Also the college now 'abandoned the idea that for every vacant holding there was an heir to be found. Previously the reeve had been charged for any vacancy' and this was partly responsible for the accumulated debts remitted in 1381. Thereafter, the reeves ceased to be held responsible for lost revenues from vacated holdings.[122] Nevertheless, the arrears continued to pile up in spite of the decision in 1387 to abandon the exaction of small debts. In that year arrears amounted to £36 13s 2d and the college refused to write off this item until 1421.[123] By that time there had been recurrent outbreaks of resistance by the servile tenantry. The accumulation of several holdings by many tenants was leading to the presence of numerous unoccupied houses. An attempt to check this in 1401 by the imposition of heavy fines on twelve tenants led to a protest surrender of their holdings by these and by thirteen others: the college then abandoned the exaction of these obnoxious fines.[124] In 1407 the four chief pledges refused in the manorial court to present the names of villeins who had illegally left the manor and after 1409 the list of those absentees was abandoned.[125] It may be evidence of the state of unrest prevailing in this southern corner of Leicestershire that a dozen men from Kibworth Harcourt and adjoining villages were involved in the abortive Lollard rising of January 1414.[126]

The chronic conflict between the villeins of Kibworth Harcourt and its collegiate lord increased the dependence of the college on its local officials. After 1375 two successive reeves 'had held office for seventeen and nineteen years respectively'. Robert Polle, from one of the manor's long established families, had his yearly reeve's salary increased in 1417 from 6s 8d to 40s.[127] The conflicts between Merton College and its villeins came to a head between 1421 and 1423. The tenants were demanding the abrogation of their servile status and the abatement of rents exacted from servile holdings. A considerable number, in order to put pressure on the college, abandoned their holdings, and after 1423 one-third of the manor was without tenants, with 11 bond virgates and all the demesne virgates (previously held on leases) being in the reeve's hands. The reeve now had an accumulation of 469 acres in his custody and there was an annual

Harvesting: two men with toothed sickles cut wheat while a woman binds corn into sheaves; another woman arrives carrying a basket with provisions (The Bodleian Library, Oxford: MS. Gough Liturg. 7, f. 6)

loss of about £10 in rents, only partly offset by temporary leasing of some of this land for pasture. By 1433 the college had lost some £95 in unpaid rents.[128]

In 1427 there was a partial capitulation by the college. The remaining 18 servile virgates were henceforth not to be treated as 'in bondagio'. Thereafter they were described as held 'at the will of the lord' but also 'according to the custom of the manor'. This complex formula was probably introduced on the advice of the college's lawyers. Its purpose was to ensure that the tenants had no rights under Common Law.[129] In the circumstances of the early fifteenth century these tenants enjoyed, of course, effective security, as the concession of the holdings to them on these new terms had been made for the express purpose of retaining them. The new conditions of tenure included an abatement of servile rents by 3s 4d per virgate.[130] To begin with, only some of the tenants accepted customary holdings on the new terms and lengthy negotiations to attract others continued for over a decade. Some previously servile tenements 'remained on the vacant list until 1439', as did 7 out of the 8 demesne virgates, until the college agreed to abate the rent for the latter by 6s per virgate. After that settlement a part of the demesne land was let to tenants without further delay.[131] As for the reduced rents for the former servile virgates, they were treated henceforth as if they were fixed free hold rents and remained at that same level as late as 1700.[132]

One of the best documented studies of the changing relationships of major landlords and their tenants is provided by Dr Barbara Harvey's writings on the estates of the Abbey of Westminster. The abbey's lordship was strong.[133] It was for a long time able to deny many of its tenants the concessions they desired. It was also more successful than most other landlords in preventing too many vacant holdings from persisting on its estates for long.

Until about 1390 the abbey's ideal was to return as soon and as widely as possible to its traditional methods of exploitation, based on the heavy use of labour services and on the framework of customary holdings that provided them. To mention again Dr Harvey's fascinating generalization: 'never sensitive to economic trends, the monks of Westminster were never more heroically indifferent to them' than in the forty years after the Black Death of 1348/9.[134] The charges of customary holdings, their labour services supplemented by money rents and customary taxes, were more valuable to the abbey in the existing economic conditions than any rents that could be secured from alternative arrangements. At Islip (Oxfordshire) a half-virgate held on customary terms yielded in 1391 yearly services and rents worth 11s 3½d, over a shilling more than half-virgates held on lease for money rent only (10s 2¾d per year)/[135] The cost of hiring labour was substantially greater than the labour that could be exacted from traditional servile holdings. The abbey became at times very oppressive trying to maintain the old system. At Hardwicke in Gloucestershire the almost entire labour-service obligation of the customary tenants was commuted in 1349 for rents, with the exception of three days' mowing per half-virgate. The yearly rent of a half-virgater was correspondingly raised from 3s 4d to 5s. Yet by 1366 the customary half-virgaters were again deemed to owe six days' work a week during the three weeks of the harvest season, though they nevertheless continued to pay the additional rent demanded of them as the price of commutation in 1349.[136]

The servile tenantry wanted to profit from the shortage of labour and of tenants after 1349 to get rid altogether of the labour services and to hold land only for rents. On some Westminster estates they were able to force the abbey to some extent to replace customary tenures by purely rent-paying alternatives, but on nothing like the scale that its peasantry would have desired. Conceding such alternative arrangements was the condition of avoiding numerous vacant holdings. But these alternatives were mostly of such a nature as to leave the future open and allowed the monks to hope that they would be able to return to a regime based predominantly on traditional villein tenures burdened with regular labour. 'The institution of villeinage, articulated . . . in the classic system of rents and services, stood . . . for the right of the aristocracy to the support of a dependent class of labourers.'[137]

There had been serious riots in 1381 on several of the abbey's estates in Essex, Hertfordshire, Middlesex and Surrey, involving the wholesale destruction of manorial court rolls.[138] This may have hastened concessions to tenants on some of these estates. There may also have existed some connection between this quickening of changes and the replacement in 1386 of the very aristocratic Abbot Nicholas de Litlington by the humane and compassionate William Colchester. But it can be at best a partial explanation and Dr Harvey prefers to stress the influence of the general changes in the country at large.[139]

The concessions gradually made to tenants by the Abbey of Westminster between c. 1390 and c. 1430 do not add up to any tidy pattern and they differed considerably from one manor to another. The abbots appear to have been more ready to face changes than did the more conservative Westminster Convent. Fear of a large number of deserted holdings remaining unoccupied for long periods was the main incentive for paying more attention to the demands of the servile peasantry. But 'the changes took much longer to work themselves out than might have been expected in the circumstances; not even by the middle years of the fifteenth century were the monks' demands on their tenants always such as the land would readily bear'.[140] As leases of demesnes spread to an increasing number of manors there was tenant pressure for permanent commutations of labour services. At Todenham in Gloucestershire this happened in the accounting year 1390/1, but the money rents substituted for labour proved unduly high and within a few years they had to be abated somewhat. The yearly rent for a virgate, fixed in 1390 at 10s, had to be lowered by 1406 on 6 virgates to 9s or even 8s.[141] Cumulatively more important were piecemeal concessions made to new tenants as a condition of their acceptance of holdings. This is how the alternatives to traditional hereditary tenure for accustomed services began to spread.

As on other properties, these alternatives were diverse contractual tenures. Tenements were to be held predominantly for rents, though some labour services might be stipulated (usually only boon works). Three types of arrangements should be distinguished. There were very temporary leases, at the lord's will. These were often merely stop-gap devices to assure continued exploitation of land that had become suddenly vacant. No fines for entry were expected, nor heriots. Much more important were leases for a term of years or, at most, for the life of the lessee. There might be initial fines for entry, but they were normally quite light. The fine was the recognition of the security of tenure within the terms of the lease, as opposed to the entirely precarious concessions of tenancies at will. At the surrender of the leased holding no heriot would be expected. To take one example of a clear statement of this rule, in 1394, at Launton (Oxfordshire), William Jones owed a heriot for the messuage and virgate of land which he held in villeinage, but not for another holding which he had on lease for his life, 'because he held it at farm and not for services and customs'.[142]

Another variant was a grant for a term of years or life of a tenement 'according to custom', owing only money rent but subject to all the customary taxes and suit of court of a servile tenement. The rent was likely to be lighter than the full burdens of a customary tenement. Dr Harvey assumes that some people preferred this arrangement to a pure lease, because 'such a tenant, though nominally holding for a term, had an expectation of passing on his holding to his heir that other lessees for life did not enjoy. His heir could not claim the *right* to succeed, but custom may soon have allowed something akin to the first refusal of the lands on terms little changed, if indeed they were changed at all.' This type of arrangement was, very likely, the origin on Westminster properties of copyhold tenure *without the right of renewal*.[143] But such temporary concessions in villeinage seem to have been 'used sparingly' before *c.* 1390 and 'the real importance of the institution was' then 'still in the future'.[144]

Two Oxfordshire manors, a short distance from each other, can illustrate the divergent policies pursued by the abbots and by the Convent of Westminster. Launton was a conventual manor. Its demesne had been leased continuously since 1372 and the rent from the farm had declined by 1423 to £4 per year. The bulk of the revenue was derived from the rents of tenants. In the fifteenth century there was here only one freeholder; all the other tenants were servile villeins. As vacant holdings multiplied after the Black Death, reaching the total of nearly 10 virgates by 1361, the convent resorted to contractual leases more acceptable to new tenants. Vacancies were thus reduced to about 4 virgates for the rest of the century and during the opening decades of the fifteenth century. The custumal of *c.* 1416/17 lists 11 customary virgaters, 3 customary half-virgaters, 16 leaseholders and 6 tenants of composite holdings combining customary tenements with leases. The latter formed the wealthiest group, each of its members possessing more than 1 virgate. Between 1421 and 1423 the convent made a determined and successful effort to eliminate altogether vacant holdings, so that 'vacancies were negligible for the remainder of the century'.[145]

On the abbatial manor of Islip 13 half-virgates were farmed by 1391 for money rents and only one of these ever returned to tenure by customary services. Fifteen composite holdings, some of them held by the wealthiest tenants, included both lands held at farm and customary half-virgates. 'It was by the grant of farms and leaseholds that the Abbot of Westminster kept all land in Islip under cultivation.' The commutation of week-work was completed about 1386, though some other services were retained until 1433. They were available to the farmers of the demesne leased continuously since 1395. Here, likewise, the gradual decline of the farm for the demesne made the rents from tenants into the main source of revenue. Recurrence of flights by tenants led to further concessions after Richard Harwden became abbot in 1420. 'The new policy shows itself in the occasional remission of heriot, entry fine, and the first year's rent if the tenement taken by the incoming tenant was waste, and by a general reduction' in such fines as still continued to be exacted. When in 1433 Abbot Harwden commuted the remaining labour services, each half-virgate became charged with the annual rents of 10s 6d. 'This, if not too heavy a burden at the time, may quite soon have become so.' By the middle of the century there was a recurrence of the flights of tenants and of vacant holdings.[146]

Widespread commutation of labour services was making personal serfdom an economic anachronism. But scholars have tended to exaggerate the speed with which it was disappearing. There were some areas where the personal disabilities and financial charges arising out of it continued to be tenaciously enforced. The south-western region, stretching from Wiltshire and Hampshire into Dorset, Somerset and Cornwall was one such particularly backward region, as will be shown in chapter 13.

Serfdom lingered on many estates because of the money that could be exacted for chevage paid by serfs residing outside their native manors, for payments of merchet on the marriages of servile womenfolk and other customary exactions that could be collected from 'serfs by blood'. Manorial lords were especially interested in preserving evidence about the personal serfdom of the better-off servile families, who alone could be profitably exploited.[147]

One finds on many large estates a trickle of gradual emancipations in return for payments. As it was an irreversible operation, there was every incentive to exact considerable sums. A particulary odious abuse was the seeking out of alleged former serfs who had settled in distant places. Thus, in 1415 Earl John Mowbray of Norfolk, in order to raise money to equip his retinue for the French campaign of that year, tried to claim prosperous townsmen as runaway villeins and to extract money from them for their blackmail manumissions. A citizen of Norwich 'belonging to the manor of Forncett' in Norfolk paid £20 and 'so did an alleged *nativus* of Chacombe' in Northamptonshire. This practice became increasingly common later in the century.[148]

On some large estates emancipations of serfs appear to have been particularly numerous during the years of economic crisis in the middle decades of the fifteenth century. However, on some estates the main wave of manumissions occurred earlier. This was so on the properties of the Cathedral Priory of St Swithun's, Winchester, in Wiltshire and Hampshire. Thirty-seven manumissions are recorded between 1390 and 1450, 'with by far . . . the highest concentration in the decade 1410–19, when fifteen grants were made'.[149]

The longing of serfs to gain freedom for themselves and their descendants was memorably conveyed by an elderly bondman of the Abbot of Malmesbury in the 1430s. He wished to be free before he died, and his heirs and blood after him, 'and if he might bring that aboute it wold be more joifull to him than any worlelie goode'. He borrowed £10 from another peasant to make this dream come true.[150]

CHAPTER 9

The Estates of the Bishops of Worcester, *c.* 1395–1436

I

The main fact that stands out from a survey of the estates of the Bishops of Worcester from *c.* 1395 to 1436 is that, at least down to *c.* 1420, they managed to maintain fairly well the previous level of their revenues.[1] This was not an isolated success in this region. If one compares eleven estates of the Earls of Warwick in Worcestershire[2] between their forfeiture to Richard II in 1397[3] and a valor of 1434/5, commissioned by Richard, Earl of Warwick,[4] their estimated total value was almost the same at both these dates. The figure for 1397 was £351 and for 1434/5 it was £345.

The surviving survey of the arrears due to the Bishop of Worcester in 1412[5] shows that the bulk of them arose out of the usual medieval delays in cash payments, which would be ultimately forthcoming. There was as yet no serious problem, certainly nothing comparable to the disturbing mountain of arrears that was to build up by the middle of the century. Most, perhaps all, of the episcopal demesnes were leased by 1410 and, like other landlords, the bishops were often unable to maintain the initial level of the leasehold farms.[6] But because of the ancient origin and great power of the bishop's lordship, the revenues arising out of their authority over their servile tenants remained high. The episcopal valor, based on yearly accounts for the year ending on 30 September 1406, reveals £15 3s 9½d of the value of heriots collected on eight estates and this is clearly only a part of what had been levied.[7] On the estates for which adequate information is available, the revenue from labour services commuted into rents and from servile taxes amounted in 1419 to almost a quarter (23 per cent) of the total income from these properties (£114 from commuted services and £36 from servile taxes out of the total revenue of £629). It is interesting to note that the income from commuted services was slightly higher than the value of the rents received from the farming of demesnes (*c* £105).[8] After 1433 the burdens arising from the legacies of serfdom became the special target for the resentment of their peasantries.[9] In 1419 the bishop's 'spiritual' revenues reached their highest recorded medieval total of £217 12s 11d,[10] though the reasons for this are mysterious.

Where we have new rentals, as at Hanbury by Wich (1410/11),[11] Kempsey (?1410/11)[12] and Stoke,[13] they reveal the disappearance of the old uniformities of tenure. Instead there is a mosaic of variable bargains between the bishops and their servile tenants, with rents differing widely for the same amounts of land. If we had the information about the fertility and varying agricultural prospects of each holding, known to every villager but never available to us, that pattern of differing rents would probably begin to make more sense. We also know nothing of the economic potential of each tenant's household and the number of relatives available to help with labour.

While agricultural prospects seem to have been relatively stable during the first three decades of the fifteenth century and prices of the main grain crops were not unduly low, one suspects that the bishops' servile tenants may have found it difficult to market their produce with sufficient margin of profit to pay easily for the heavy, enhanced rents demanded of them. When,

Mowers with scythes, a misericord in Worcester Cathedral (Courtauld Institute of Art: Conway Library)

during the long vacancy of 1433–5, the tenantry complained of being impoverished,[14] that may have been partly due to recent disasters, but it seems probable that many of them had been suffering from a more prolonged period of mounting difficulties and indebtedness.

Worcester's successive bishops may not have been an ideal group from the point of view of safeguarding adequately the properties of the bishopric. Richard Clifford (1401–7), a royal councillor, was in his diocese only seventeen months out of six years. Bishop Thomas Peverel (1407–19) did try to survey anew the episcopal revenues and arranged for the compiling of some fresh rentals. But a visit to his residence in 1417 by Margery Kempe revealed a disordered household. She was so indignant at what she saw that she told his entourage that they were 'more like the devil's men'.[15] Bishop Philip Morgan (1419–26) was an important member of the royal council.[16] His successor, Thomas Polton (1426–33), had been formerly a high papal official and was used repeatedly by the royal government for dealings with the papacy. Both Morgan and Polton had to be absent frequently from their diocese. Indeed, in 1421 Pope Martin V had stopped the appointment of Polton to the Bishopric of London on the ground that such an important see needed a resident bishop.[17] When Bishop Thomas Bourchier finally acquired the Bishopric of Worcester, in April 1435, after a long delay, he claimed compensation from Polton's executors for neglect of castles, manors and houses and for other losses. He secured the huge sum of £800 in damages. This was a most unusual happening and Bourchier owed it to the pressure of his relative, the all-powerful Cardinal Henry Beaufort of Winchester, whose intervention is expressly mentioned in his first account for the bishopric.[18] Polton certainly conferred advantages on an 'irresponsible scale' on the chief steward, John Wode, and on his own relatives. Bourchier himself maintained a luxurious household,[19] as befitted his high aristocratic rank. One has to wait for the long episcopate of his successor, John Carpenter (1444–76) to find a resident, zealous and cultivated bishop, who fully lived up to what could be expected of his office.[20]

II

The principal sources used in this chapter require discussion, as their usefulness, and limitations, vary. The accounts and court rolls surviving from a minority of estates are used where they yield significant information. They include Bredon and Hanbury by Droitwich in Worcestershire, Hampton Lucy in Warwickshire, and Bibury, Cleeve and Henbury Saltmarsh in Gloucestershire. Above all, all the more general records covering some or most of the estates are used.

We have a valor for the majority of properties compiled from accounts for the accounting year 1405/6, ending on 30 September 1406. The details mentioned in it inspire confidence that we have here a record of real cash revenue and real expenses incurred by the estate officials.[21] A copy of a royal inquiry held on 1 November 1407, during the vacancy of the bishopric between 22 June and 20 November of that year, gives a list of assized rents on all the Worcestershire estates. It appears to lump together the old assized rents and new arrentations and to deal only with rents from holdings that were actually occupied. It also specifies the size of the demesne arable and meadows on each manor, ignoring any demesne leases and treating all domanial lands as integral parts of the bishop's properties.[22] In the year after this vacancy the new bishop, Thomas Peverel, ordered the drawing up of an 'extent' of all his estates, based on accounts for the year ending at Michaelmas 1408.[23] It excluded all recognized allowances of rents and other dues which had lapsed because the relevant holdings lacked tenants. It also did not include certain casual revenues, specifying among these the value of herbage on the bishop's meadows and the perquisites of the manorial courts. Therefore, its figures are less complete than the information provided by the 'valor' for 1405/6, but it does appear to give a fairly reliable record of the *permanent* revenues expected at that time. From Peverel's episcopate there survives also a very instructive list of arrears at Michaelmas 1412.[24]

There was again an episcopal vacancy from 1 March to 18 October 1419. The next bishop, Philip Morgan, began his tenure of office by ordering another detailed survey of the episcopal revenues in the accounting year 1418/19. The resultant record does not include some servile taxes collected by the royal escheators during that year, but seems, otherwise, to be fairly complete and is very instructive.[25]

The long vacancy of one-and-a-half years in 1433–5 can be studied in a number of records.[26] There exists an account of the receiver appointed by the royal custodians.[27] A copy of the account presented at the exchequer by the custodians is preserved,[28] as also is its enrolment at the exchequer and the record of various proceedings there.[29] The custodians presented two petitions for allowances on their account.[30] The sequel to the vacancy, which produced a serious clash between the custodians and the tenantry, can be pursued in the first account (for 1435/6) of the new bishop, Thomas Bourchier.[31]

III

Three episcopal vacancies in fairly quick succession (1395, 1401, 1407) may have hastened the leasing of the remaining Worcester manorial demesnes, as each new bishop had to decide whether it was worth restocking the estates still directly exploited by his officials. Bishop Tideman started his episcopate by leasing the demesnes at Henbury Saltmarsh and Bibury,[32] and, possibly, also, on some other properties. Most, perhaps all, remaining demesnes may have been leased by 1408, though the precise dates are not certain. Cleeve (Gloucestershire) was still exploited directly at Tideman's accession in 1395, but its demesne was leased by Michaelmas 1408.[33] Also leased were the demesnes at Wick and Wichenford, Kempsey and Fladbury in Worcestershire and at Stoke and, possibly, Withington in Gloucestershire.[34] At Bredon, in Worcestershire, the enclosures for cattle, pigs and sheep were being repaired at the bishop's expense in March 1408, perhaps as a preliminary for farming away the manor (activities of farmers are mentioned in May of that year and again in 1409).[35]

The retreat from direct exploitation was never quite completed. The maintenance of flocks of sheep by the Bishops of Worcester down to the early 1450s is discussed in chapter 6. Demesne meadows on a number of manors were kept in the bishop's hands throughout the fifteenth century, and beyond it, to provide hay, and demesne woodlands were likewise retained.[36] For centuries direct exploitation of their demesnes by the bishops dominated the lives of thousands of peasants on their properties. Yet, leased away in the fifteenth century, they were contributing between 1406 and 1419 only just over a fifth (c. 22 per cent) of their economic income. The figures on which this conclusion is based derive from a combination of evidence from Michaelmas 1406 and Michaelmas 1408, the new rentals of 1411/12 and the accounts for 1418/19.[37] The figure for the total revenue from properties is based mainly on the valor for Michaelmas 1406 (£1,137 15s 11d by my addition). The figures for income from the farming of entire manors, or merely of manorial demesnes, chiefly derive from the valor for Michaelmas 1419, but if they are missing in that record they have been supplied from other evidence in 1408 and 1411/12 (c. £267). As I am only aiming at establishing an approximately correct order of magnitude, these combined figures are adequate for this purpose.

Like other landlords, the Bishops of Worcester were often unable to preserve the level of the rents secured originally from their farms of manors, or of the demesne lands within manors. Something catastrophic happened at Bredon. In 1419 a group farming that manor for the annual rent of £23 gave up their farm. A total of £10 0s 6d was secured that year from temporary leases. In Bishop Bourchier's first account (1435/6) the annual farm stood at £14. Bredon will cause grave difficulties for Bishop Carpenter during a period of exceptional crisis in the 1450s.[38]

At least eight other items of revenues from farms declined by 1419, amounting to £16 15s 11½d. The fall is calculated either from the time of original leasing or from 1408.[39] The evidence about Hanbury by Droitwich is particularly odd. The revenue from the farm in 1419 was lower by £2 6s 4d than it had been in the past. William Webbe, esquire, who in 1418 had secured a lease of a part of its demesne for life at the annual rent of £3, owed £18 2s 5½d of arrears in 1430/1. By that time a large part of the former demesne arable had been converted to pasture. Yet Webbe at the time of his death in 1446 held in addition to the demesne an accumulation of eight free holdings, and seven heads of cattle were taken as heriots.[40] Several of the lessees of the episcopal manors and demesnes secured their farms not for purely financial considerations but because they mattered for other reasons. Such leases were being granted on privileged terms and some of this group of lessees were apt to be often, or permanently, in arrears with impunity. William Webbe at Hanbury may have been one of those people.

To come to some better known notables.[41] John atte Wode had been granted by Bishop Peverel the lease of the manor of Whitstones for life, with £6 of annual rent remitted. He was also conceded rent there of £2 1s 8d, free of charge, Furthermore, he farmed Knightswick at an annual rent of 10 marks. In 1426 Bishop Polton appointed him steward of the bishopric's temporalities. In 1433–35 he owed on his various farms arrears of £34 14s and he was also receiving yearly fees of £33 6s 8d secured on episcopal demesne farms.

John Throckmorton farmed since 1410 the manor of that name. Though valued at slightly over £14, it was leased to him for an annual rent of £12 12s. George Polton had received the lease of Aston for life from his uncle, Bishop Thomas Polton. Though it was worth annually £4, his yearly rent was reduced to 13s 4d. He never paid a penny in his uncle's lifetime. Lastly one should mention that Humphrey I Stafford of Grafton (d. 1450),[42] a member of an important landed family in the west Midlands, was retained in 1430 by Bishop Polton as a member of the episcopal council with an annual fee of 66s 8d, payable out of the revenues of Hanbury by Droitwich.[43] His heir, Humphrey II, under-sheriff of Worcestershire for ten years, became the chief steward of the bishopric in 1470.[44]

IV

As has been explained in the preceding chapter, in the late fourteenth century and the early decades of the fifteenth, the earlier uniformity of servile tenures was rapidly disintegrating on many manors. Landlords were striving to strike bargains with individual tenants in order to retain them on their estates. The continued abundance of land, and shortage of men ready to exploit it, was leading to the accumulation of previously separate holdings in the hands of a richer group of peasants. Each of these richer tenants would occupy only one house and a connected group of farm buildings (his 'croft'). The other complexes of buildings would not be needed and would remain deserted. They were sure to collapse through neglect. In concluding bargains with new tenants, landlords tried to compel them to maintain most or all of the buildings or to re-erect the ones that had decayed, but they were often fighting a losing battle.[45]

The same processes can be observed in the west Midlands. There is a particularly instructive documentation in the court rolls from the estates of the Cathedral Priory of Worcester, scattered through the same countryside as the properties of the bishops.[46] Some of the episcopal estates yield similar evidence, though one has the impression that the bishops maintained a more effective grip on their dependent peasantry in the period covered by this chapter.

The word used in the western Midlands to describe buildings which had ceased to be occupied was a 'toft'[47], as opposed to a 'croft' of a tenant who combined his agricultural holding with a farmhouse. Episcopal court rolls of Whitstones in 1386 and 1399 mention in two new grants of servile holdings an obligation to rebuild buildings on the tofts thus conceded to villeins.[48] Another court roll, at Kempsey, probably dating from 1 July 1433, records that a tenant had failed to carry out a pledge, given six years earlier, to build a new house on a holding of 6 acres given to his son.[49] When tenants combined free and servile holdings, as richer tenants were increasingly doing, they naturally chose to reside on their free crofts, where the lord could have no say about their maintenance of buildings, felling of trees or any other operations. Thus, in 1377, at Hanbury by Droitwich, Thomas Elvyns, who combined both an inherited servile tenement and freehold land, opted to live on the freeholding.[50]

Bishop Peverel ordered the drawing up of new rentals on episcopal estates in order to record the changing tenurial arrangements. The most instructive of all is the rental drawn up in 12 Henry IV (1410/11) at Hanbury by Droitwich.[51] This was a large estate, with much woodland and pasture as well as stretches of good arable.[52] It had been severely stricken by plague and was one of the first to be leased to a farmer, though some of the bishop's buildings were not abandoned until 1407.[53]

At the start of Bishop Wakefield's episcopate his officials were finding great difficulties in

Felling trees, c. 1500; from a manuscript of George, Earl of Shrewsbury (The Bodleian Library, Oxford: MS Gough Liturg. 7, f. 2)

inducing new tenants to take up the customary half-virgates at Hanbury. While in 1302/3 there had been thirty-nine holders of these standard tenements,[54] in 1376 twenty-five of them were said to be lying 'in the lord's hands', which meant that, at best, they might be let on short-term leases, normally for a year at a time.[55] The rental of 1410/11 reveals that a solution had been evolved by then, based on a series of bargains with individual tenants.[56] This rental also reveals a pattern of holdings that parallels the new pattern on the estates of Westminster. There were now two categories of tenements. There was one group held according to the custom of the manor, probably mainly the holdings to which tenants had succeeded by inheritance. The second category consisted of temporary concessions. These were tenements that must have lapsed at some stage into the bishop's hands and had been regranted on variable terms arising out of fresh bargains.

The Hanbury rental mentions forty-one free tenants and seventeen or eighteen holders of servile virgates, holding between them 25 half-virgates, with only 2 half-virgates left in the lord's hands. The servile holdings were divided into ten held according to the custom of the manor and fourteen held at the bishop's will ('*ad voluntatem*'), as the result of individual bargains. As had been explained in the previous chapter, the insistence on treating the new tenures as 'at the will of the lord' was the lawyers' way of safeguarding that these contractual tenures were not protected by Common Law, but these tenants were secure enough in the circumstances of the time.[57] Their holdings 'at will' appear to have been conceded without exacting a fine for entry. If such a tenement continued to be regranted over a period of years, as often happened in practice, a heriot might ultimately be exacted when the tenant died or relinquished his holding. Thus a tenement of 1 virgate at Henbury Saltmarsh was charged in 1435 on the death of its tenant at will, John Joyce, with a heriot of an ox worth 12s. His widow, who was allowed to retain the holding for her life, did not have to pay a fine for entry.[58]

The *customary* holding at Hanbury were normally liable to fines for entry from new tenants and delivery of heriot of the best beast when a tenant died or vacated his holding. They paid annual rents varying from 3s 4d to 4s and rendered yearly 7s for servile taxes. The rents and taxes for tenements at will ranged between 8s and 10s and were, therefore, somewhat lighter. Three tenants combined both types of holdings. Where a man had two holdings, as, for example, J. Meuske, one of them was described as including a toft, that is an unoccupied house. His rent for the customary messuage and half-virgate was 10s. The rent for the other half-virgate with a toft, held at will, was 9s. There were also some lesser servile tenants and the rental included holders of small assarts (pieces of land newly reclaimed for cultivation, of which there were twenty-five, held for 35 pence) and further miscellaneous bits of land, some of which were small parcels of leased demesne. The overall picture is of much diversity.

The two other rentals of roughly the same date, from Kempsey in Worcestershire and Stoke in Gloucestershire, do not list these two categories of holdings but, again, display a comparable diversity of rents for tenements of the same size. At Kempsey[59] tenants occupying more than one tenement held tofts; one John Hurst possessed a messuage with a garden (rent of 1s 6d) and two tofts with a garden and 1 acre (presumably of arable) at the joint rent of 2s 10d. At Stoke, near Bristol, the rental of 1410[60] reveals heavier charges than the rentals of Hanbury and Kempsey. Land was more valuable here. Some virgates bore rents of 23s or 25s, apparently including annual servile taxes. Half-virgates were charged at a rate of 10s 6d or 11s 6d. The manorial cowherd paid only 9s for his virgate and held also a field described as 'Herdersfeld' for a further 2s 8d. In the thirty years since 1381/2 the number of servile holdings still occupied by tenants had decreased considerably. In 1381/2 labour services had been due from 28 virgates. In 1410 there were only 9 or 10 servile virgates and 6 half-virgates. Fourteen tenements of 5 acres each had been replaced by only seven, but there were in 1410 eighteen still smaller holdings.[61]

V

The list of arrears at Michaelmas 1412 shows that there was nothing radically wrong, as yet, with the finances of the Bishopric of Worcester.[62] The bulk of the arrears represented merely typical medieval delays of payments. The entire sum of £252 9s 2½d was recovered fairly rapidly. Debts arising out of sales of wool amounted to £34 14s 1d, out of which £21 9s were due at Blockley. It was, of course, normal to sell wool on credit, usually for at least a year. The same was true of £99 6s 4d due for tithes belonging to the Church of Blockley, collected at that township and its various adjoining villages and hamlets. The bishop's chief receiver owed £16 6s 6d and Thomas Boldying, formerly a senior official of the bishops and Provost of St Wulfstan at Worcester, accounted for £15 18s 7½d, including £4 9s 21½d for wools. Arrears of domanial and other farms amounted to £22 7s 10d, but these too were promptly recovered. They were due at six different manors and only the debt due for Grovefield, north of Hampton Lucy, and for the bishop's park there, was of any size (£12).

A more disturbing picture is revealed by the account of the custodians of the bishopric between 31 August 1433 and 15 April 1435. The apparently irrecoverable arrears amounted to only £46 9s 4¾d,[63] but the custodians met with tenacious opposition from the tenantry over some of their demands. The two custodians who accounted at the exchequer were John Wode, the steward of the temporalities, and John Throckmorton, a former steward and member of the bishop's council. The other three had all at some time served as auditors or receivers on the bishopric's estates.[64] One may conjecture that those five custodians, very representative of the Worcestershire and Gloucestershire notables, were viewed with distrust by the peasantry of the bishopric. At the start of that long vacancy the episcopal estates appear to have been in a neglected condition. I have reviewed elsewhere some of the information pointing to this. The unusual payment in 1435/6 to Bishop Bourchier of £800 as compensation by Bishopric Polton's executors is one crucial piece of evidence.[65]

In a petition for various allowances the custodians claimed in January 1439 that 'the customary tenants of the aforesaid lordships and manors were at the time of the vacancy . . . in great poverty. . .'. Earlier in the same petition it was claimed that 'there had been many plagues ['pestilentia'] in the aforesaid lordships so that the major part of the aforesaid tenants had died'.[66] Chroniclers do indeed report a plague in 1434, 'but the absence of court rolls during the vacancy prevents us from checking the evidence for a high death rate during that year'.[67] I am inclined to treat seriously these claims of high mortality among tenants and of the impoverishment of many of them. Among the sums that the custodians had failed to collect, and were asking the exchequer to remit (successfully), were £46 9s 4¾d of arrears due from manorial officials on twelve different estates. At Alvechurch £3 4s 8d was due from the reeve, which could not be collected as it was due from tenants who had departed from the manor, leaving behind nothing from which payments could be distrained. The same claim was made concerning £9 11s 6¼d at Blockley, Wick and Wichenford. As defaulting officials were listed the rent collector (beadle) of Blockley, the former reeve and beadle of Wick and Wichenford and the former farmer of these last two closely connected estates.

No migration of tenants was mentioned on eight other manors, but it was claimed that £33 5s of arrears due there could not be collected because of the poverty of the tenants. The list of the defaulting officials consisted of the reeve at Withington, the reeve and the beadle at Bibury and several reeves of Cleeve, all in Gloucestershire, the reeve of Whitstones, the reeve of Ripple (£10 5s 7½d), the beadle of Kempsey and the rent collector at Bredon, all in Worcestershire, and the bailiffs of the borough of Stratford-upon-Avon in Warwickshire.[68]

The resistance of tenants was apparently aggravated by the demands of the custodians at the start of their control of the vacant bishopric. Their initial action had been to demand the 'recognition' due from the customary tenants to the new lord of the estates.[69] The last evidence of this payment that I have been able to find on Worcester properties was in 1395, when Bishop Tideman of Winchcombe collected it on some manors, though this negative argument is far from conclusive. Be that as it may, the worst decision of the custodians was not a demand for the recognition, but the requirement of payments at a rate prevalent before the Black Death of 1348/9, when the population of customary tenants had been much larger. The amounts demanded, with a few differences, were those received by Humphrey Walden, keeper of the bishopric for thirteen months in 1302/3.[70] He had collected £40 7s 4d, while the custodians demanded in 1433 a slightly smaller amount of £38 4s, mainly because Tredington and Aston were missing from the list of 1433.[71] This ill-considered and anachronistic demand led on this occasion to the refusal of the tenants to pay anything at all.

The tenants on the episcopal estates presumably knew in 1433 that the recognition had become much lighter from 1349 onwards. In that year the royal custodians of the vacant bishopric collected a mere £1 18s. 8d in Worcestershire and Warwickshire. The next bishop, John Thoresby, may have carried out a revision of the quotas due from each village. At any rate, after his translation to York in 1353, the royal custodians put into operation a reduced scale of payments and collected no more than £3. In 1361, after another heavy mortality from plague, the recognition yielded only £2 6s 6d. There was an increase to £5 0s 8d in 1364, partly because there had been a rise of £1 6s 8d in the quota of the wealthy and populous manors of Henbury Saltmarsh and Stoke, adjoining each other on the edge of Bristol.[72] In 1375 we have figures for a few estates. Henbury paid £2 to Bishop Henry Wakefield, the same as in 1364 (compared with £10 in 1302/3) and Hanbury by Droitwich 10s (a rise of 6s 8d compared with 1364).[73] In 1395 Bibury paid 6s 8d (compared with 2s in 1364) and recognition was also collected at Henbury Saltmarsh and Bredon. But by demanding £38 4s in 1433, the custodians killed the recognition for ever. In their subsequent petition, asking to be excused from collecting this impost, the custodians alleged that the customary tenants had threatened to abandon the bishop's estates and move elsewhere, so that they did not 'dare' to enforce their demand.[74]

That this was not altogether an idle threat is suggested by one of the manors of Earl Richard of Warwick in 1437. This was Lighthorne, a large estate about 7 miles south-east of Warwick. It had been farmed to the rector of the parish in 1398 and there had been a gradual loss of tenants. In 1437 the earl instructed his officials to moderate further the rents. 'The reason given was that the tenants had complained that the rents were so heavy that they could not keep alive. This was why so many holdings were in the lord's hands for lack of tenants. . . . They had protested to the Earl that unless rents were reduced they would have to quit the manor so as to be able to gain a living.' Their rents were reduced by nearly a third, from 15s 6d to 10s 6d for each customary virgate, and the cut was maintained henceforth. Thus 'the tenants of Lighthorne', by threatening to leave, 'won their case and maintained their gains in the face of one of the most powerful lords of fifteenth-century England'.[75]

With regard to the bishopric of Worcester, Professor Christopher Dyer, surveying these events, has argued[76] that the tenants of the episcopal estates could have paid some of the money demanded of them for the recognition and (perhaps)[77] could have discharged some of the arrears. But this could have only happened if there had been goodwill on all sides, and that was clearly lacking: hence 'the concerted non-payment of the recognition and . . . the refusal of other rents which appear as arrears charged to manorial officials'.[78]

There is no evidence that the next bishop after the vacancy of 1433–5, Thomas Bourchier, did receive any recognition.[79] His successor, John Carpenter (1444–76), did try to return to the high quotas demanded by the custodians in 1433, but met with complete defiance, which extended to other servile burdens. His losing battle with his tenantry will be traced in chapter 11.

The period for which the custodians accounted (31 August 1433 to 15 April 1435) was longer by two months than the time covered by the first account of Bourchier's receiver (15 April 1435 to Michaelmas 1436). Two harvests were covered in each case, which justifies a comparison between the receipts from the estates in both accounts.[80] Bourchier's receiver collected £243 15s 6½d less and on only two estates were his receipts larger (Blockley and Henbury Saltmarsh, the two wealthiest properties). The falls were largest at Fladbury (£34), Hampton Lucy (£33), Wick and Wichenford (£32), Ripple (£28) and Alvechurch (£22). Except for Wick and Wichenford, they form a geographic block in the north-eastern and eastern portions of the episcopal estates. One wonders whether this was an area particularly affected by mortality from the epidemic of 1434.

Bishop Bourchier took over a very encumbered complex of properties. In addition to the figures of decline just cited, one must note that in his receiver's first account arrears of the farms of nine manors by themselves amounted to £77 17s 4d. The receiver's debt at the end of this account came to £174 8s 3d. The bishop personally owed then £754 2s 4d due to various creditors. These debts had been incurred in order to discharge the extraordinary expenses of acquiring his episcopal dignity. The bishopric was entering upon an age of increasing financial difficulties.

CHAPTER 10

Crisis: Economic Depression, *c.* 1430–*c.* 1470

I

The years *c.* 1430 to *c.* 1470 witnessed 'one of the most sustained and severe agricultural depressions in documented English history'.[1] Speaking of a decline of agricultural values over much of England from the late fourteenth century onwards, Dr J. Hatcher has remarked that 'the bottom of the trough was reached in the middle of the fifteenth century or a little later'. There were some fortunate exceptions that escaped serious decline, but 'even the exceptional regions experienced a . . . mid-century recession'.[2] This chapter illustrates from concrete examples the accelerating decline towards this 'mid-century trough', followed by some instances of what was happening in the third quarter of that century.

Professor R.B. Dobson, in a survey of urban impoverishment, has commented that 'only the existence of prolonged and remorseless demographic attrition in England as a whole'[3] can explain the widespread economic decline or, at best, stagnation. One set of statistics is worth citing. In 1433 the yield of the fixed fifteenths and tenths was cut by £4,000. A second reduction of £2,000 came in 1446. As a result of these two remissions, between 1433 and 1472 successive royal governments lost over £60,000 in direct taxes. Medieval individual remissions always demand suspicious scrutiny, as political pressures might have been responsible, but, cumulatively, remissions on this scale by a financially hard-pressed government reflect realities, 'an acknowledgement that any attempt to enforce payments would produce no profit'.[4]

From the later 1420s onwards there was a succession of disasters. Recurrence of plagues, the worst famine of the fifteenth century (in 1438/9), as well as devastating epidemics among sheep and cattle, made the years up to 1440 a grim period.[5] The early 1440s, though not marked by comparable disasters, continued in many parts to be a time of low economic vitality, due, it seems, principally to a depleted population. The decline in the demand for food was reflected in the low prices of wheat. The average price in the 1440s was the lowest in the century and one would have to go back to the last decade of the fourteenth century for even lower figures.[6] And that earlier decade was the time when many landlords had decided to give up, or seriously curtail the direct exploitation of their arable demesnes.

There were, of course, some more positive developments as well. One sees a shift, in suitable areas, from the growing of crops to the rearing of sheep for the expanding cloth industry and of cattle for meat. These were the precursors of a more widespread transition from arable to pasture in the second half of the century.

Returning to the 1440s, the last years of that decade were a time of renewed crisis, which lasted until at least the 1470s. Its long duration was fundamentally a reflection of the situation that by the mid-fifteenth century 'the supply of pastoral as well as arable products was considerably in excess of demand'.[7] The customs' accounts reveal a catastrophic fall in the export of wool in the year from Michaelmas 1448 to Michaelmas 1449, while the slump in the shipments of cloth lasted until 1450. This was the combined effect of the start of a commercial war with the German Hanse (a Hanseatic fleet was seized off the English coast on 23 May 1449) and the revival of the war with France and the Burgundian state in the summer of 1449.[8] Normandy was effectively lost after the disastrous defeat there of an English army on 15 April 1450 and widespread popular uprisings in England occurred in the summer of that year. Gascony was finally lost in July 1453 and England retained henceforth no possessions in France save Calais. Loss of Normandy and Gascony destroyed the trade with these regions and had a disastrous effect on the exports of English cloth.

The eruption of private warfare between noble factions seriously dislocated economic activity in some parts of England (as in Devon in 1451 and 1455, and in Yorkshire in 1453/4).[9] Recurrent bouts of civil war between 1455 and 1461, combined with vicious magnate feuds, prolonged the period of insecurity and economic disruption into the early 1460s. The disordered conditions returned during another bout of civil war in 1469–71. These troubles certainly impoverished landlords and peasants in some parts of the country. Insecurity and the fall of incomes hurt producers of cloth and their workers, merchants and craftsmen. When conditions were particularly disturbed, this discouraged foreign merchants and shipping from coming to this country.

Not all parts of England were equally impoverished between *c.* 1430 and *c.* 1470. Districts connected with leading centres of the cloth industry, like the villages around Colchester in Essex, or areas adjoining important tin mines, in parts of west Devon and east Cornwall, sustained by the demand of tin-miners for food and other essentials, escaped prolonged decline.[10] But over much of England there is abundant evidence of diminished economic activity, fall in demand for goods and prolonged periods of low prices.

While studies of conditions in the middle of the century usually confirm this dismal picture, it is often difficult to prove whether this was mainly the outcome of continued decline over the previous century or of the more recent series of crises that became aggravated after *c.* 1430. Thus, 'in the mid-fifteenth century land in north-central Essex could be leased for only half the rent per acre it had fetched before the Black Death'.[11] The Fenland of south Holland in Lincolnshire had been in the later thirteenth century one of the most densely populated and prosperous regions of England. But there 'seems little doubt' that its economy 'in the second half of the fifteenth century was depressed', above all 'through lack of people'. 'Decayed rents, rents much lower than some years before, lands in the lord's hand, sometimes escheated for failure to pay the rent, debts outstanding for a generation, flooded lands . . . all these are signs of decay. To these we could add a wholesale conversion from arable to pasture and meadow and from meadow to pasture.'[12] Neither in Essex nor in south Holland can one at present document the precise chronology of changes that produced such decline.

Most of our evidence comes from the records of important lay the ecclesiastical landowners. Many monasteries were particularly depressed in their incomes, as they had very little chance of acquiring new sources of revenue, unlike leading laymen, who through warfare, successful politics, or by contracting lucrative marriages could compensate for losses from their properties.

As far as one can tell, none of the lay and ecclesiastical notables were permanently crippled by the decline of incomes from their properties. Ruin did overtake some landed families because of their improvident political or military ventures. If economic difficulties contributed to their reckless feuding, as is probable in some cases,[13] the succession of financial crises may have been one indirect cause of the ruin of some nobles and gentry, but it is difficult to prove this conclusively in any particular case. However, many lay and ecclesiastical notables seem to have been forced into curtailing somewhat their ordinary expenditures and had to devote more attention to their finances and properties.

It is possible to show that on some estates, at any rate (for example, on those of the Archbishops of Canterbury and the Bishops of Worcester), a part of the fall in the lords' income was due to the refusal of their tenants to pay some of the customary servile dues. This happened on the estates of Bishop John Carpenter of Worcester throughout his episcopate of 31½ years (1444–76). At Bredon in eastern Worcestershire, up to the end of 1475, at least £48 15s 4d was lost through the refusal of the servile peasantry to give him the recognition which he demanded on his accession in 1444 (£2 10s) or to pay the annual 'common fine' and customary silver, amounting together to £1 8s 11d. The single payment of recognition and these annual taxes for thirty-two years, accumulating together, constituted by the end of his episcopate three-quarters of the arrears due at Bredon.[14]

Increasing financial difficulties affecting some of the peasantry may have been partially responsible for this hardening of resistance to servile dues. Probably of greater importance was the realization by peasants that they could defy their lords with impunity, because they did not need to fear the ultimate sanction of mass evictions. In the middle of the fifteenth century what most landlords feared was the loss of their tenants, many of whom could not be replaced.

During the series of economic crises between *c.* 1430 and *c.* 1470 countless peasants, craftsmen and lesser merchants were seriously impoverished and some were even ruined. Ordinary peasants had to sell some of their produce each year to procure cash for rents and various customary dues to their landlords, as well as royal taxes. When prices of corn and wool, their main source of cash, remained depressed and stagnant, they were in serious trouble. Nor, unlike their social superiors, did they have facilities for storing surpluses at times of exceptionally low prices in order to keep them until market conditions improved. It is they, rather than their social superiors, who suffered most during these difficult years, like, for example, some ruined farmers of the demesnes of Durham Cathedral Priory after the disastrous years 1438–40.[15] It is only in the second half of the fifteenth century that wholesale evictions of all the unfree tenants took place on any scale, where the owners of their villages decided to save or improve their finances by total conversions of arable to pasture.

II

The epidemic of plague in London in 1434[16] extended also to other parts of the country. I have mentioned in the preceding chapter that it may have contributed to the decline of the revenues of the Bishops of Worcester.[17] Parts of north-eastern England were badly hit. In 1434/5 there were sixty-eight more deaths than births in Scarborough, quite different from normal years. This was the beginning of the partial collapse of Scarborough as an important fishing harbour, which was made worse by the still greater disaster of famine and epidemics in 1438/9.[18]

The three summers of 1438–40 were exceptionally wet, that of 1438 being the most disastrous of all.[19] The yield of wheat on the four Winchester estates for which we have figures in 1438 was the lowest in the century after 1349.[20] The years 1438 and 1439 witnessed the worst famine of the fifteenth century. While in the years 1380–1430 average prices of a quarter of wheat oscillated normally between 5s and 6½s, in 1438/9 the treasurer of Westminster Abbey had to pay as much as 24s a quarter to buy wheat for the Westminster monks. The prices of other corns rose

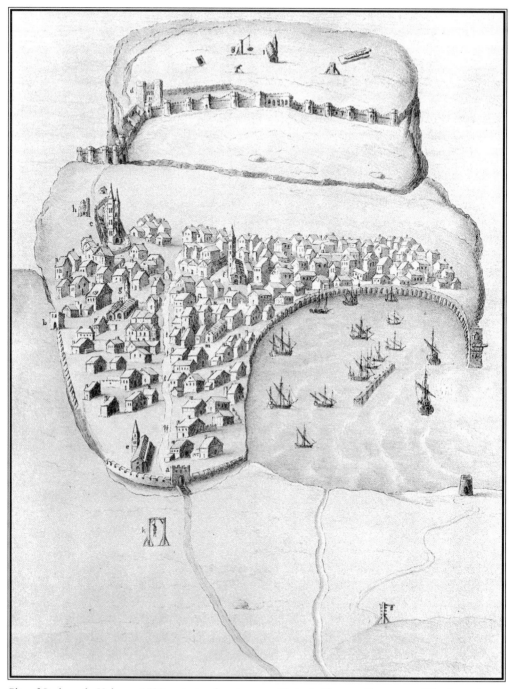

Plan of Scarborough, Yorks., c. 1590; a nineteenth-century copy (Rotunda Museum, Department of Tourism and Amenities, Scarborough Borough Council)

less than wheat and there was a marked increase only in the second year of shortage (1439/40). It was then that, according to a later London chronicler, Londoners had 'to eat beans, peas and barley more than in a hundred years before'.[21] In London the permanent legacy of that crisis was the building in 1439 of the public granary at Leadenhall.[22]

The famine furthered the spread of various infectious diseases, which caused considerable mortalities. There may have been some plague, as well as much dysentary and, perhaps, typhus.[23] Several chroniclers expressly mention that deaths were particularly numerous in northern England.[24] At Scarborough even more people died in 1438/9 than in 1434/5, 126 more deaths than births. Its fisheries were lastingly crippled.[25] To judge by wills at York, around 150 people of some means died there in the summer and autumn of 1438.[26] The epidemics of those years abruptly terminated such modest revivals of prosperity as had occurred in the preceding years on a number of estates in north Yorkshire and the Palatinate of Durham.[27]

Epidemics among cattle and sheep were very common in medieval England, though, mercifully, they were often fairly localized. At their worst they could wipe out the entire stock of animals on a manor. Thus Eynsham Abbey (Oxfordshire) had in 1453 a flock of 1,238 sheep. But shortly after 1460 all but one of its 954 beasts died.[28] The abbey then abandoned sheep-farming for good. Where some animals survived in a village and seem to have acquired immunity, the lurking infection was likely to continue killing most of those newly born.[29]

There is an ample record of epidemics among sheep and cattle in the second quarter of the fifteenth century in south-eastern England. The years 1426–37 were particularly disastrous in Kent and Sussex.[30] The exceptionally wet summers of 1438–40, which led to a famine in those years, also witnessed the spread of foot-rot among sheep.[31] The high mortality among sheep between 1426 and 1440 was followed by a slump in the demand for wool in the next decade, because the shrinking population was purchasing less native cloth. To judge by the nine wool-producing estates of the Duchy of Lancaster in Berkshire, Wiltshire, Hampshire and Dorset, sales of wool at prices satisfactory to its officials were difficult since 1440/1 and became virtually impossible by 1442/3. This led to the withdrawal from sheep-farming of the duchy's officials and its curtailment on the properties of some of the other landlords in this region.[32]

III

The south-eastern counties probably 'did not experience as deep an agricultural recession as the rest of England'. Kentish agriculture profited from its proximity to London. While here, too, there was some decline, probably it 'was not as severe as that experienced by most other counties'.[33]

One of the most important Kentish landowners was Canterbury Cathedral Priory. By 1437 its revenues had declined considerably from a high peak reached in 1410,[34] but the account in 1437 of Prior William Molash still showed a small credit balance. Disastrous lapses into indebtedness only occurred in the 1450s and the 1460s. The earlier decline in the second quarter of the fifteenth century was caused partly by losses of sheep through murrain on several of its manors, as happened in 1425/6 and in 1430–2.[35]

Battle Abbey, with its valuation in 1535 of £909, was the second wealthiest monastic house in Sussex.[36] The properties which supplied it with cash were mostly leased by 1400. But there was a group of particularly fertile, large manors near the Sussex coast, which had always supplied the monastery with food and which remained under direct management much longer. Two,

Lullington and Alciston, were only leased in the 1490s. Here, too, there was a decline in the extent of the demesne under crops but, at Alciston at least, the decline in acreage was chiefly on marginal lands used for fodder crops. The more fertile lands, well-marled, were kept in cultivation much more fully. In the century after 1380 acreage under wheat grown on these better soils declined by only a quarter. These manors were model farms, yielding 'heavier harvests' than was usual in medieval England.[37]

However, these manors, too, had their share of tribulations in the second quarter of the fifteenth century. At Alciston, in 1433, some 50 acres of land previously held by customary tenants were unoccupied.[38] A series of epidemics between 1428 and 1438 reduced its normal flock of over 2,000 sheep to 998 (at Michaelmas 1438) and it was not until 1444/5 that its flock again surpassed 2,000. At the neighbouring manor of Appledram the flock was nearly wiped out.[39]

The small monastic town of Battle, adjoining the abbey, was surrounded by a large block of agricultural lands likewise belonging to the monks (its *leuga*). William the Conqueror, the founder of Battle, while endowing it with exceptional privileges and immunities, had insisted that the monastery must be placed on the exact site of his victory over King Harold. The *leuga* consisted of land not suitable for successful arable cultivation, with soils 'indifferent or worse' and no satisfactory water supply.[40] In the first half of the fifteenth century much of the district surrounding the abbey was going out of cultivation and was 'becoming derelict'. From approximately the 1410s to the 1450s men did not, on the whole, want *leuga* lands, and certainly they did not want them on the abbey's traditional terms. Heirs refused to accept their fathers' holdings. Some men accepted, but they soon defaulted upon leases. In the 1420s no farmer could be found for Marley Farm, to the north-east of Battle.[41]

The cellarers of the abbey had increasing difficulties in enforcing labour services allotted to them. The most vital of all were the carting services for bringing foodstuffs from Alciston and other coastal manors and timber from the abbey's properties in the woodlands of the Sussex Weald. The court rolls surviving from 1432 to 1459 'show that all tenants of customary land resisted the services and some few refused outright'. In 1439 the cellarer reported that the performance of wine-carting was two years in arrears. Seizure of holdings was threatened 'and one tenement was indeed seized into the lord's hand, because its holder had refused to pay his rent, repair his house or perform his services'. But this was no remedy against the bulk of the tenantry, where so much land already 'has been in the lord's hands for the lack of a tenant' and entry fines had been abandoned. It all merely ended with amercements on the rest of the defaulting tenants. Then, in 1457, all services were commuted for a money payment, except for an obligation to carry firewood to the abbey.[42]

I have discussed elsewhere the increasing difficulties faced by Ramsey Abbey (Huntingdonshire) in the first two decades of the fifteenth century.[43] When, after a gap of two decades, its accounts begin to survive again from 1440 onwards, they clearly reveal 'that conditions worsened with increasing intensity'.[44] In the 1450s there was a huge increase in arrears in the abbey's key home manors and there was a still further deterioration in the next decade.[45]

The 'economic confusion' and chronic mismanagement on the estates of Crowland Abbey in Holland (Lincolnshire) have been amply illustrated in an earlier chapter.[46] An entry on one of its court rolls in 1435 highlights the persistent inefficiency of its administration. Its manors of Oakington and Cottenham, both in Cambridgeshire, had been leased in 1430 to two of its

Aerial photograph of the abbey and town of Battle, Sussex (By permission of the University of Cambridge Committee for Aerial Photography)

villeins. Yet only five years later a vague inquiry is recorded on the court roll of Cottenham asking 'how many years the manors had been let'.[47]

One of the worst tales of decline in the 1430s comes from north-eastern England.[48] While parts of south-eastern Durham and northern Yorkshire had been experiencing a degree of economic stability and even improvement before *c.* 1430, the mortalities and agricultural decline of 1434/5 and 1438–40 reversed this disastrously for a considerable number of years. 'The crisis of 1438–40 was thus a major shock of the utmost importance for the later economic history of the North-east.'[49] In the countryside of northern Yorkshire and the Palatinate of Durham predominantly arable areas in the lowlands were more heavily hit than the upland, pastoral districts. Thus on the estates of the Bishop of Durham in the predominantly arable Darlington ward, the revenue which stood at £667 in 1434/5 fell to £495 in 1438/9. 'The main impact of the crisis of 1438–40, thus fell on arable husbandry.'[50]

Durham Cathedral Priory was one of the richest English religious houses. It had lost much income since the start of the Scottish wars in the reign of Edward I, but in the priorate of John Wessington (1416–46) it could still count in normal years on a revenue of about £2,000.[51] The greatest loss of income came from the decline in the value of tithes from churches appropriated to the priory. Part of this revenue came from districts lost to the Kingdom of Scotland or devastated by warfare. In 1436 the priory's income from this source, amounting then to £353, was estimated to have declined by at least £1,070 from its peak in 1293 (actually £1,467 in that year).[52] Depopulation and agrarian decline since 1349 had also caused major losses. These long-term causes of deterioration in income also cut down the priory's revenue from agriculture, though Wessington still estimated it, somewhat optimistically, at about £1,000 a year.[53]

Durham Priory's management of its estates created some special threats to its solvency. By Wessington's time most of its formerly unfree tenants held their tenements only on short-term leases, though they were normally renewed. One advantage enjoyed by the tenants was that they were usually not charged fines for entry.[54] Near the Scottish border the ever-present fear of the revival of warfare, or of raids by marauding gangs, had created a climate of fear which made men reluctant to take on long-term commitments or to offer rents that corresponded to the real value of their holdings. There are several instances from vills in Northumberland of men refusing to pay the traditional farms for lands or mills 'because of fear of the Scots'.[55] But the shortness of leases, both of isolated tenements and of manorial demesnes, meant that in times of sudden crisis it was very difficult to renew them on terms acceptable to the priory or, indeed, to renew them at all. This happened during the grave crisis caused by famine and epidemics in 1438–40. The inventory drawn up in the priory in 1446 'leaves no doubt whatsoever of the then reluctance on the part of villagers all over' the Palatinate of Durham 'to take up the available leases . . .'. In South Shields the situation was so severe that for several years up to 1446 'most of the vill lay waste and completely depopulated'.[56] The revenue from the farming of corn mills on the priory's estates fell to the lowest recorded level in the fifteenth century. It had declined from £76 in 1388 to £22 in 1446.[57]

The crisis of 1438 produced a spectacular upheaval in the priory's financial administration. The central figure in its finances was the monk-bursar. Between 1419 and 1432 three men had held that office in succession, 'none of whom had been particularly successful in keeping arrears, wastes and decays to a tolerable minimum'. Disaster followed under their successor, Thomas Lawson (1432–8), a former cellarer, admittedly not a competent man but appointed 'in the absence of a more suitable candidate'.[58] The level of current yearly arrears rose between 1433 and

Durham Cathedral, with the fulling mill below (Philip Nixon)

1436 from £115 to £265. 'Much more seriously, Lawson systematically suppressed mention of very heavy debts that he was incurring, as the report after his fall put it, concealed from the prior and convent.' Lawson was touring the convent's estates in the midst of the economic crisis of 1438 when news reached him that the full extent of his mismanagement had been uncovered by an inquiry by other officials. He fled in the middle of the night and disappeared into hiding. The debts piled up by him allegedly amounted to £1,210. A special tax had to be imposed on all the dependencies of the priory to cover the losses thus incurred. As no other monk was willing to take up the office of bursar, for seven years, from August 1438 to November 1445, the central management of the priory's finances was split between three officials.[59] During this new regime rents continued to decline and there was a failure to maintain the monastic buildings in a fit state of repair.[60] The agrarian depression was not only impoverishing the priory; it was also undermining several farmers of the priory's manors, some of whom became ruined ('*impotentes*') in the mid-fifteenth century.[61]

Prior Wessington resigned in 1446. His successor, Ebbchester, writing in that year to a fellow monk, described the state of the monastery as nearing collapse ('*non mediocriter est collapsus*').[62] The monks found it hard to live amid financial constraints and the decline in its income endured henceforth, though it still remained one of the wealthiest monastic houses. At their lowest point, in the 1450s, its revenues averaged less than £1,300 a year.[63]

In 1436 Bishop Thomas Langley of Durham, enjoying an average annual revenue of about £4,000, was probably one of the five richest English landowners. However, his revenues, too, were declining. While the income from the estates oscillated around £2,900 in the 1420s, it was only £2,568 in Langley's last surviving account for 1435/6.[64] There was a further drop to £1,914 in that disastrous period of 1438/9. Concessions had to be made to the bishop's tenants. Normally, on the episcopal estates in the south-east of the Palatinate of Durham approximately 75 per cent of the new tenants paid entry fines. In the decade following 1438 the proportion fell to as low as 20 per cent.[65] Only in the first decade of the sixteenth century did the Bishops of Durham regain the level of revenues enjoyed by Bishop Langley before the crisis of 1438–40.[66]

There is parallel evidence of serious economic damage inflicted by the crisis of 1438–40 on two northern secular estates, those of the Percys, Earls of Northumberland, and of the Lords Fitz Hugh. On the Percy properties the most marked decline was on their lands in Northumberland. Thus, their lordship of Alnwick lost about a third of its revenue between 1434/5 and 1449/50.[67] The centre of the Fitz Hugh properties was in north-western Yorkshire; their pastoral economy, based on the rearing of cattle, was prospering before the 1430s. The disaster of 1438–40 cut the rents received by them by about a third. They had to go out of their way to conciliate their tenants and to attract new ones, granting rebates of rents and bearing the cost of repairs to houses and farm buildings. They suffered some permanent losses of revenue over the next decade and a number of vacated holdings remained in the lord's hands.[68]

IV

I have discussed in an earlier chapter a number of villages where much of the population gradually drifted away, either out of poverty or because of excessive demands of local landlords. Encumbered with a growing accumulation of arable land that nobody wanted to take up, landlords might finally convert it to pasture.[69] Professor R. Hilton termed this development the 'Pre-History of English Enclosure',[70] occurring in the late fourteenth and the first half of the fifteenth centuries. Much more extensive conversions of arable to pasture occurred in the second half of the fifteenth century.[71]

In the second quarter of that century more profit could often be expected from the keeping of cattle rather than of sheep. As prices for wool of medium or lesser qualities tended to fall, production of meat instead of wool seemed to promise greater gains. The keeping of larger herds of cattle has been noted on a number of estates in the central Midlands. Forested parts of this area in northern Worcestershire, north-western Warwickshire (the Arden region) and Staffordshire had for a long time been famed for their pastoral enterprises and these were now being extended.

New conversions of arable to pasture expanded these activities. Thus at Hanbury, a manor of the Bishops of Worcester in a partly wooded area of northern Worcestershire, the account for 1430/1 reveals at least 400 acres of former arable put down to grazing. Parts of this consisted of former demesne arable and the rest were vacant tenant holdings in the bishop's hands.[72] In the adjoining area of north-western Warwickshire the evidence of the feet of fines suggests that the really decisive expansion of pastures came in the 1440s.[73] Between 1438 and 1457 John Brome, a minor landowner, but well connected at the royal court, created a profitable estate in the Arden area to the west of the River Avon. His principal manor was Baddesley Clinton, to the north-west of Warwick, where there was much enclosed grassland and wood. His other properties included the site of a deserted settlement, Woodloes, where he had a compact, enclosed estate consisting of pastures. He specialized in producing meat and supplied it to the royal household. His Lancastrian connections led him into serious trouble in 1450 when Henry VI's notable supporters were under attack. His house at Warwick was sacked and the labourers on his estates were so intimidated that they refused to work for him. It was much worse after he lost the protection of his Lancastrian masters in 1461. He was deprived of one of his properties by the Catesby family. In 1468 he was murdered by John Herthill, steward of the Yorkist leader, Richard, Earl of Warwick, who had been Brome's rival for Woodloes.[74]

Kingston, to the east of Stratford-upon-Avon, had been largely converted from arable to pasture at some unknown date before 1437. A few peasant landholders still remained in this shrunken village as late as 1461, when some rents were still being received from them. As with Brome's properties, political affiliations were important, as its owners in 1437 were the Verneys, who had acquired it recently and had prospered through service to the Earls of Warwick. Brothers Richard and John (Dean of Lichfield), who controlled this property, and had also acquired the neighbouring manor of Compton Murdak (later Compton Verney), were sons of Richard, who had been receiver-general to the Beauchamp Earls of Warwick. At Kingston, in February 1437, the younger Richard leased the manor to John Lichfelde, a prominent butcher of Coventry, for procuring supplies of meat. The annual rent from Lichfelde (leased for ten years at £26 13s 4d a year) was more than the gross receipts, less arrears, of the whole manor in 1395 (£17), and very much more than the cash handed over by the bailiff that year to its then Leigh lord (£11 11s).[75] Maxstoke Priory, in the north of the Arden area, had in 1442/3 a herd of 72 mixed dairy cows and beef cattle.[76]

Throughout the Middle Ages pastoral economy was very important in the forested parts of Staffordshire.[77] On the Duchy of Lancaster's properties of Needwood Forest in Staffordshire and the woodlands of Duffield Frith in Derbyshire the biggest portion of revenues came from the renting of pasture rights for cattle and pigs. In Needwood the total income from leases of pasture rose between 1400/1 and 1427/8 from £42 12s to £48 18s. In Duffield Frith a peak was reached in 1426/7 (£57 8s). The depression of the mid-century stopped further progress, however. 'The values of forest pastures stopped rising in the middle years of the fifteenth century and in many cases there were reductions in the leases.'[78]

The disastrous economic decline in the north of England during the 1330s had arrested for a period the widespread growth of pastoral economy in north Yorkshire and the Palatinate of Durham. The example of the estates of the Lords Fitz Hugh is particularly instructive. Between 1410 and 1425, 'when demand for dairy products and meat would appear to have been particularly buoyant', Lord Henry Fitz Hugh established three herds of cattle on his estates in Lunedale. In 1424 he was establishing yet another herd on lower lands, at Berwick-on-Tees (now Berwick Hill). This development was abandoned for twenty years after his death in 1425. His heir, Lord William Fitz Hugh, reverted to running a stock farm at Berwick-on-Tees and by Michaelmas 1450 he had there a flock of nearly 1,600 sheep and a herd of 108 cattle. But the net profits were very low, less than £2 in 1451. At his death in October 1452 his animals (746 sheep and 189 head of cattle) were sold for £108 10s by his executors and direct management of Berwick-on-Tees was again exchanged for a lease to farmers. Later Lords Fitz Hugh do not seem to have changed this policy.[79]

Opportunities of much more profitable sales of meat existed in the vastly more prosperous East Anglia. The farming operations of John Hopton in Suffolk provide an illustration of this. In 1448 he bought 60 bullocks fairly cheaply, probably for fattening. Such 'fat bullocks may have provided a large part' of Hopton's not inconsiderable income.[80]

V

We would wish to know what economic difficulties and social discontents underlay the widespread popular revolts in south-eastern and southern England in the summer of 1450, followed by much unrest in these regions during the following years. The risings of Kentishmen and men of Sussex from May to July of that year were above all demonstrations of political discontent and of hatred for the overmighty and corrupt group around King Henry VI and their henchmen in local government. The same was true of the disturbances in East Anglia and of the somewhat later risings in Wiltshire, Hampshire and adjoining areas, as well as of scattered troubles elsewhere in England.[81] The demands put forward by the Kentish leader, Jack Cade, and his chief supporters confined themselves chiefly to political grievances. The fullest and most generalized statements are to be found in the documents submitted to Henry VI during the abortive parleys between the king and the rebels in the middle of June.[82] These documents constitute chiefly a skilfully worded programme of political demands interspersed with protests at fiscal exactions, including the purveyances for the king's armies 'of wheat and other graines, beef, mutton and all other victuall', and denunciations of legal injustices. The one purely 'proletarian' complaint was the description of the Statute of Labourers as insupportable.[83] However, it is justifiable to assume that the prolonged economic stagnation of the 1440s, followed by a serious economic crisis from 1449 onwards, swelled the mass discontent among the population of the rebellious counties. For example, the prominence of textile workers in the risings in Wiltshire and Hampshire can be attributed to the slump in the demand for woollen textiles during those years.

A serious decline in the shipments of both wool and cloth occurred in 1449 as the result of conflict with the German Hanse (after May 1449) and the revival of war with France and the Burgundian state in the summer of that year. Wool exports slumped dramatically in 1448/9 to 1,858 sacks. After 1450/1 the level of wool exports remained persistently lower than it had been in the past. In 1448/9 the exports of cloth were lower by 36 per cent than they had been in the two preceding years and the depressed figure of that year (35,599 cloths of assize, each approximately 24 yards in length and 1½ to 2 yards in width) declined further to 34,465 cloths in 1449/50.[84]

Decline in cloth exports occurred even in areas like Devon where there had been a remarkable expansion of the industry between 1431 and 1448. There was a slump in exports of western cloths in 1449–51, which at Plymouth lasted until 1453. There was also a slump in the output of tin. In 1448/9 production in Devon 'was the lowest for any year on record'. So was Cornish tin production in 1450 and it remained much lower than in the 1430s throughout the third quarter of the fifteenth century.[85]

'Today . . . Cherbourg is gone and we have now not a foot of land left in Normandy', so James Gresham wrote to John Paston on 19 August 1450.[86] By 1453, as we have seen, England had lost all its French possessions except Calais. The loss of English territories in south-western France not only ended the importing into England of Gascon wines, but also destroyed a flourishing export trade in English cloth destined for the French Languedoc and the adjoining lands of southern France as well as Gascony.[87]

In chapter 7 I have surveyed the increasing difficulties experienced in the decade after 1435 by leading wool producers in Wiltshire and the adjoining counties of southern England. I have assumed that they were producing wool for English (or Norman) cloth industries rather than for export to the Mediterranean. Their increasingly frequent inability to dispose of their wool at prices acceptable to them must have presumably sprung from the slackening of demand for cloth in England. On the properties of the Duchy of Lancaster in this region, around 1440, the manorial officials were unwilling to sell wool at below £5 per sack. Sales were beginning to be delayed, apparently for that reason, from 1440/1 onwards and there were virtually no sales in the year between Michaelmas 1442 and Michaelmas 1443.[88] Lesser landlords could not afford to postpone sales so easily. On the estates of the Abbey of Syon in Sussex, early in the 1440s, its wool was regularly being sold to London merchants. In 1447/8 nothing was sold, and when a buyer was eventually found the next year, the fleeces were sold to him at the very depressed price of £2 12*s* per sack. Things got worse in the slump after 1449. By 1453 the abbey had accumulated the unsold clip of three years. Then, it handed over more than 10 sacks to Thomas Laughton, a London draper. There was a considerable delay before he could find a buyer and he finally disposed of this wool at the low price of £3 6*s* 8*d* a sack. 'At that point abbey officials seem to have decided that the market offered little opportunity for profit and for two years all their wool was made into cloth to be given to household members.'[89] Similarly, the prices fetched by the wools of the Bishop of Winchester reached their lowest level in 1453.[90]

Bishop Aiscough of Salisbury, one of Henry VI's leading advisers, was murdered in the risings of 1450 (on 29 June).[91] His various palaces and manors were ransacked and many of his muniments were destroyed. Except at Sherborne in Dorset,[92] his own peasant tenants are not known to have been involved in these attacks. 'In Wiltshire it was the cloth-producing areas in general and the men associated' with that industry 'who were heavily involved in the risings: of those indicted and whose occupations are described, at least 30 per cent' were connected with textiles. Of the four men specifically named in subsequent indictments as the murderers of Bishop Aiscough of Salisbury, or as participants in the attack on him, three came from Trowbridge and one from Heytesbury, both leading centres of the new textile industries of western Wiltshire. Three were described as a weaver, a tailor and a fuller while the fourth was a tanner.[93] Dr J.N. Hare is clearly justified in thinking that the prominent part played by textile workers in this western rising 'reflected the economic recession that had struck those areas, increasingly dependent on the manufacture and export of cloth'.

The fall in incomes from agriculture, because of the marked decline of corn prices in the 1440s,[94] was exacerbating opposition to customary payments exacted by landlords or, at least, was leading to demands that they should be scaled down.[95] The risings of 1450 brought these resistances to a head on several major estates in Kent and Sussex. The annual tax of the common fine was withheld in 1450 on a number of manors of the Pelhams in Sussex. The same thing happened that year on the properties of Battle Abbey, where nothing was received from this tax 'on account of the insurrections and disobedience of the people rebelling against such customs'. However, the Battle officials were again able to collect the common fine in 1451.[96]

Resistances were more persistent on the estates of the Archbishops of Canterbury. There was lasting resentment in Kent against Archbishop John Kemp (1450–4), himself a Kentishman, for his alleged duplicity in negotiations with the rebels in 1450. During the later, abortive risings in 1452 and 1453 he was one of the notables whose death was desired.[97] When Thomas Bourchier succeeded him in the summer of 1454, there was a general refusal on all the estates of the archbishopric to pay the recognition due on the accession of a new lord. A total of £186 10s was lost, and though recognition continued to be demanded for many years, it could never be collected. In the 1460s the tenants on the archiepiscopal lands also began to withhold the common fine, though a partial settlement was reached in 1468.[98]

VI

Kent and Sussex were not affected as severely by agricultural decline as some other English regions, but here, too, the third quarter of the century was a difficult time. For example, the Cathedral Priory of Canterbury experienced a prolonged decline of income. Its revenue of £2,382 in 1437 fell to £2,116 in 1454 and the monks owed that year £663 13s 5¼d to their creditors. Two years later its revenue fell further to £2,060 and its debts rose to £1,158 11s 6d. In 1468 the debts were still almost the same as in 1454 (£661 5s 2½d). It probably continued to be in a state of persistent indebtedness, but without ever incurring financial disaster. After all, an income of £2,000 a year still equalled the annual revenues of several earls.[99]

On the estates of the Archbishops of Canterbury difficulties increased in the middle of the century. I have already mentioned the revival of resistance by its tenants after 1450. On some manors it became harder to arrange satisfactory leases of the demesnes. On those estates in some years no farmers could be found. Only piecemeal leases were possible and for short periods. This happened at Northfleet (north-central Kent) in 1450/1. The farmer of Northfleet Rectory was pardoned £26 13s 4d of arrears in 1463 'by reason of a great detriment touching him with his farm in previous years'. The demesne of Northfleet had to be leased again piecemeal in 1467. At Petham in east Kent, in 1467, the farmer of demesne was unable to raise the money needed to pay off arrears.[100] In the bailiwick of Otford in west Kent the period of the greatest difficulties in finding single farmers was in the 1450s. The revenue from the bailiwick amounted to a yearly average of £303 in the 1450s and to only £262 in the 1460s.[101]

Not only the profits from arable farming, but also those from pastures, were in the doldrums. Thus the pasture of Bishopfield on the manor of Otford, which could be leased for 16s 6d a year in 1402, was repeatedly in the archbishop's hands between 1440 and 1455/6 for lack of a taker. A lessee was found in the latter year, but only for a yearly rent of 6*s*. Similarly, on Battle Abbey's manor of Wye in east Kent demesne meadow which had been selling for 6*s* or 7*s* an acre early in the century was renting for only between 3*s* and 4*s* an acre in the 1460s.[102]

Arrears carried forward from one annual account to another went on increasing in the middle of the century. Wye was one of the two most valuable of Battle Abbey's manors, but the arrears due from its officials and tenants in 1463/4 amounted to £401 9*s* 5¼*d*. This incredible amount had gradually accumulated over twenty years.[103] Here, as elsewhere, arrears were inflated by the reluctance of landlords to face up to falling land values and charge lower and more realistic rents. There were also prolonged refusals to accept that many of the accumulated debts could never be collected; there were frequently long delays before these hopeless debts were written off. The reeve of the archbishop's manor of Otford was by 1450 receiving a regular yearly allowance of 50*s* for lost rents, but for nine years up to 1460/1 he was requesting a further allowance of 42*s* 'for the loss of different lands and rents lying in the hands of the lord and no way could they be levied'. This claim was only conceded in 1460/1.[104]

Average rents for arable in Sussex in the 1440s were high, often amounting to as much as a shilling per acre. Some tenants were coming to find this burden excessive as their income from corn and wool was falling. Alciston, near the Sussex coast, was, alongside Wye, one of the two richest Battle manors, but its court rolls 'for the period 1440–70 frequently refer to the poverty of tenants and the difficulty of finding takers for customary lands'. During that period twelve holdings escheated to the lord 'either for lack of heirs or because of the poverty of tenants'.[105]

The Archbishops of Canterbury, the Cathedral Priory of Canterbury in Kent, and the Abbey of Battle in Sussex, despite temporary difficulties, continued to be among the richest and most efficient ecclesiastical landowners.[106] For a story of a temporary near-disaster we should turn to the properties of Ramsey Abbey, chiefly in Huntingdonshire and western Cambridgeshire. It was a house notoriously slow to make necessary concessions to its tenants. Its troubles with them earlier in the century have been chronicled in section V of chapter 8, but things got still worse thereafter. In the words of its recent historian, Professor Ambrose Raftis, Ramsey was experiencing 'the deepest and most prolonged depression in manorial revenues . . . revealed for any period in the abbey's history'.[107] By the third quarter of the century the accumulation of debt 'was often phenomenal'.[108]

The abbey's manorial accounts are inexplicably missing for the years 1420–40, so that comparisons must be made between revenues and debts at the start of the century and after 1440. Raftis has tabulated the revenues by the cellarar in 1405 and 1453. This official handled the bulk of the income centrally received and these figures reflect therefore the deterioration in the abbey's finances. Between 1405 and 1453 there was a drop in the cellerer's receipts of about a quarter (from £628 7*s* 2*d* to £475 8*s* 4*d*).[109] Comparison can be made with figures of cash liveries and arrears on six of the abbey's manors, all in Huntingdonshire. I have used the figures from either the same years, or where Raftis does not cite them, from dates as near as possible. The six manors are Ellington, Hemmingford Abbots, Houghton and Holywell in the south of the county and Warboys and Upwood, further to the north, nearer the abbey. Their collective cash deliveries around 1405 amounted to £213 19*s* 4*d*, nearly twice as much as the accumulated arrears at that time (£122 1*s* 3*d*). By around 1453 the cash deliveries declined by about one-fifth to £168 2*s* 1*d*, while the accumulated arrears more than quadrupled to £499 7*s* 11*d*. The highest arrears were at Hemmingford Abbots (£102 4*s* 4*d* in 1454) and at Houghton (£170 0*s* 9*d* in 1452). On that last estate they rose further to £261 by 1456.[110]

It is difficult to explain what was happening on Ramsey's properties, but the various publications of Professor Raftis provide elements for a partial judgement.[111] The abbey's notorious reluctance to face up to changing realities 'may perhaps best be seen in the fact that services were commuted on some manors after 1400 upon the express condition that they be revocable after a decade or two'.[112] Of course, such a return to the past never became possible.

In the fourteenth century the abbey depended increasingly for some of its income on piecemeal leases of parts of the demesnes to local tenants. 'Solvency in the demesne economy turned more and more upon the prosperity of the village community'[113] and on Ramsey properties this was fast declining in the first three-quarters of the fifteenth century. The continuous migrations of tenants attracted by better economic opportunities elsewhere were a major factor of decline. Of the hundreds of Ramsey men and women who left their home manors in the later fourteenth and the fifteenth centuries, the court rolls indicate specifically that only twenty-one returned.[114] Impoverishment was the lot of many of those who tried to stay in their ancestral villages, while only a small minority of peasants prospered at their expense, accumulating more land. Many of the Ramsey villeins fell into a chronic state of indebtedness for their home tenements from the end of the fourteenth century, that neither discounts on rents nor relaxations of services could counteract.[115]

All sorts of indications point to the abbey's increasing inability to impose its will on its tenants and to the weakening of its bargaining power in dealing with them. Fines for entry of new tenants repeatedly remained unpaid. Raftis lists the occurrence of this between 1433 and 1460 on sixteen manors. Possibly, as many as fifty-seven cases of non-payment occurred at Ellington between 1440 and 1454. Court rolls of Weston record thirteen between 1450 and 1455. The offending tenants did not seem to be worried by the refusal of the abbey to give them copies of the entries on the court rolls recording their admissions. Obviously they did not fear eviction for non-payment.[116]

By the fifteenth century the officials of the abbey were not in a position to enforce traditional penalties for dilapidation of buildings attached to servile holdings. Heavy fines were in theory due for this offence since the late fourteenth century, but no attempt was made to levy them. Instead, only tiny amercements were imposed. Twenty-one cases of dilapidation were recorded on the court rolls of Wistow between 1446 and 1457. There were nineteen at Warboys between 1448 and 1462.[117]

The abbey's weak bargaining position and the distrust of its tenantry is suggested by a variety of transactions. In the Ramsey *liber gersumarum*, recording payments of fines by new servile tenants on many of its estates between 1399 and 1458, the earliest mentions of tenure by copy (between 1449 and 1453) are normally accompanied by a peculiar security clause specifying that, if the tenant should default on the payment of rent, the lord has the right to reoccupy the holding 'notwithstanding the payment of the entry fine'.[118] The abbot was clearly nervous that the possession by the tenants of 'copies' might somehow curtail his power to re-enter their holdings. This evidence of distrust is reinforced by an entry of 20 September 1457. The abbot had re-entered a tenement held by copy after its tenant had fallen in arrears with rent for two years. The holding had been regranted to another tenant, not in customary hereditary tenure but for life only, and no copy had been delivered to the new holder.[119]

Professor Raftis tabulates the manumission of former serfs granted by the Abbots of Ramsey between 1431 and 1492. There is no assurance that we have a complete record of the abbey's manumissions, but in this list the most numerous grants (eighteen) belong to the 1460s. The abbey was trying to compensate for the drop in its ordinary revenues by selling freedom to its richer tenants. Some of those bargains 'well represent the lord's disadvantage in the land market of the period'. In 1452 William Wattes was freed at Abbots Ripton on condition that he would remain on his former servile tenement. Should he leave it, he was to find a successor and he also pledged himself to maintain the buildings in good repair. Retention of a tenant and a promise of good maintenance of a holding were clearly worth a villein's freedom. In 1437/8, at Walsoken, Richard Hunter appears to have agreed to farm Ramsey's hamlet of Poppenhoe in that village only on condition that he would be allowed to buy his freedom. A few manumissions include a remarkable security clause again testifying to the abbey's disbelief in the goodwill of its peasantry. Thus, John Milis of King's Ripton in 1439 bound himself to the abbot in £40 as a guarantee that he 'shall never henceforth himself perform or have brought about ingratitude or trouble against the Abbot of Ramsey and his successors or tenants, or shall never stand against them in any case of plea, unless only in a case of title to a right'. In 1459, at Therfield, Thomas Colle and his son William refused to give such a guarantee, but nevertheless secured their manumissions.[120] The election in 1468 of a new abbot, William Witlesey, coincided with a wholesale pardon of the accumulated arrears. At Hemmingford Abbots the arrears of £100 13s 2d of 1455 dwindled to £10 3s 5d. At Ellington arrears of £43 10s 2d in 1455 were replaced by £6 8s 9d. Remissions continued under the next abbot, John Warboys, elected in 1473. Thus the arrears of £255 18s 2d at Houghton in 1462 were cut down to £11 0s 3d by 1475.[121]

The rest of the fifteenth century after 1438 was a bleak era in the economic history of the north-east of England.[122] The losses in men, incomes of landlords and lands under cultivation caused by the disaster of 1438–40 were often not repaired until the end of the century. 'In the agrarian sector the trough of recession seems to have been reached in the 1440s and 1450s.'[123] The figures of the declining revenues of the Bishops of Durham and the Cathedral Priory of Durham are the best witnesses to this period of troubles. While before the late 1430s the priory could still count in normal years on an income of about £2,000, 'the net receipts of the bursar of the priory rose slightly from an average of less than £1,350 in the 1450s and 1460s to just over £1,400 in the 1470s'.[124] In the last surviving account of Bishop Thomas Langley of Durham (1435/6) the income from the estates alone amounted to £2,568. But the receipts of the receiver general of the bishopric fell to an average of just under £1,900 during 1459/60. The year 1459/60 appears to have been the worst in the century. Receipts only totalled £1,761, lower even than the income of £1,914 in the disastrous year 1438/9. A modest improvement came only in the 1470s.[125]

A permanent contraction of land under the plough had occurred which had a lasting effect on rents and income,[126] enduring largely beyond 1500. Expansion of pastoral farming occurred over much of the north-east, but it was a very gradual development.[127] Such lesser landholders as managed to survive reaped the benefits of lower rents, opportunities to secure more land and various concessions by their landlords. But there were also temporary wholesale collapses of farming and some permenant disappearances of settlements.[128] Ketton manor (Durham), belonging to the Cathedral Priory, was not sown between 1456/7 and 1465/6 and no tithes were received. It did, however, produce tithes again from 1466 onwards.[129] On the manors of Cleasby and Clowbeck, on the northern boundary of Yorkshire, the Lords Fitz Hugh started granting regular rebates of rents in order to attract and retain tenants. 'In 1441, for instance, Henry Richardson took a tenement normally farmed at £2 19s 4d after securing an annual rebate of 6s 8d.' He renewed the lease for a further three years in 1444, after the annual rebate had been raised to 13s. Other landholdings, which remained vacant for a number of years, could only be leased when the Lords Fitz Hugh were prepared to accept lower rents. 'Some properties could only be let after repairs had been completed at the landlord's expense.'[130]

VII

Even the usually very prosperous areas of coastal East Anglia were experiencing unprecedented difficulties in the third quarter of the century. Normally they were one of the most developed agrarian regions of the kingdom. Thus, in north-eastern Norfolk, where lay some of the estates from which my examples derive, there were exceptionally rich soils capable of supporting heavy crops with less frequent fallowing than elsewhere.[131]

The evidence discussed here is unusual in yet another respect. It comes mainly from the estates of two prosperous families of the gentry, John Hopton, in north-east Suffolk, and the Pastons, in Norfolk. Hopton (d. 1478), who also had valuable properties in Yorkshire (especially Swillington), was until 1476 the wealthier of the two, with clear annual revenues of at least some £300, and probably more.[132] The Suffolk estates yielded a net income of around £200 a year. But, unlike the Pastons, Hopton appears to have kept clear of politics and of feuds with overmighty neighbours. He resided amid his fairly compact group of estates and he supervised personally their management. This seems to have been his main concern. Some of his properties were on the sandy soils of coastal Suffolk, possessing also extensive marshland pastures and with access to useful harbours. He could send some of his produce by sea to London, like the 2,200 rabbits sold to John Harpenden, a London poulterer, in 1466–8, fetching £12 10s.[133] Other adjoining properties lay inland on rich clay soils, including his most valuable Suffolk estate of Yoxford, likely to yield a net annual revenue of over £50.

One striking feature of Hopton's farming was that on several of his properties he 'slipped in and out of direct management as need required'.[134] This flexibility helped to ensure that the value of his properties remained intact. On most of the estates for which there is evidence there were no large accumulations of arrears. Only at Yoxford was there prolonged trouble in the 1440s with the farmer of the demesne, who chronically owed considerable arrears,[135] but that demesne was ultimately resumed into Hopton's hands. When tenant holdings became vacant they were added on several manors to the demesnes. Repeatedly these enlarged demesnes were used for the pasture of sheep and cattle. In 1448 60 bullocks were bought by the bailiff of Blythburgh (Suffolk), probably in order to fatten them on the marsh pastures of this seaside manor.[136] At no time is Hopton known to have kept much more than some 700 sheep (721 in December 1478, one month after his death).[137] Norfolk wool was of inferior quality and most of it was presumably destined to make the relatively low grade cloths of East Anglia. The wools of Sir Roger Townshend, Hopton's chief steward and husband of his step-daughter, were selling in 1479 at an average price of slightly below £3 per sack.[138]

One other point about Hopton's estates should be stressed. On most of them rents due from tenants remained very stable. At Blythburgh, from which there survive several accounts, 'the collection of rents seems to have proved no problem at all'. Hopton appears to have been a good lord to his men. On several estates there are repeated mentions of pardons of amercements and of remissions of rents due to him, because of the poverty of these men or 'out of charity'.[139]

The estates of the Pastons had a much more chequered history and they were, apparently, harsher landlords. Because of the unique survival of a great mass of their correspondence and other papers (over a thousand documents between *c.* 1420 and 1503), we can study the vicissitudes of their estates and survey their dealings with their farmers and tenants in a detailed way impossible for any other complex of fifteenth-century properties.[140]

The original estates of the Pastons were mostly near the coast of northern and central Norfolk. They lay mainly in areas of exceptionally rich soils. This was particularly true of the inheritance of Margaret Mautby, who had married John I in 1440, with its central manor of Mautby, only 3 miles from the coast, one of the most fertile estates in the country. The easy communications by sea to London and other east-coast towns made it possible to ship Paston grain and malt exceptionally cheaply.[141]

A brief sketch of the history of the Paston family and their estates is necessary in order to explain the special problems facing them as landowners. The founder of their fortunes was William, Justice of the Common Pleas from 1429 to his death in 1444. He was a son of Clement, a prosperous farmer at Paston. There is no *conclusive* evidence that their Paston ancestors were bondmen, though this was later an excuse for dangerous attacks on William's heir, John I (head of the family 1444–66). In the eyes of the landed élite of East Anglia the Pastons were upstarts, 'struggling newcomers among the gentry',[142] regarded with jealousy and inviting attacks before they consolidated their position. There were several attempts by leading notables to attack their estates and deprive them of some of their properties. The hostility to them may have been enhanced by their fraudulent attempts to claim descent from landed gentlemen of long standing. In 1442/3 Judge William acquired at Paston two holdings of servile peasants together with the persons of their tenants, in order to maintain that he had a proper manor there. Apparently, in 1466 his son John tried to procure from King Edward IV a recognition that since time out of mind they had possessed a manorial court at Paston and had been lords of 'many and sundry bondmen' and that they were 'gentlemen discended lineally of worshipfull blood sithen the Conquest'. If this document was ever issued (our text is only a draft), its contents were certainly pure invention.[143]

In November 1459 John Paston I inherited the very considerable fortune of Sir John Fastolf, a relative of his wife and a veteran commander in the French wars. He was one of the chief executors of Fastolf's will. His enemies alleged, probably unjustifiably, that the will had been tampered with by Paston.[144] The Duke of Suffolk in 1465 and the Duke of Norfolk in 1469 and 1471 violently attacked some of the Paston properties. Over a thousand of their sheep were carried off by Suffolk's men and some six hundred by Norfolk's followers.[145] John I's two sons (John II and John III) fought against Edward IV at Barnet in 1471 and were lucky to escape permanent ruin.[146] The Pastons were unable to retain most of Fastolf's lands, except for Caister Castle, recovered after Norfolk's death in 1476.[147] But after that year they survived with less challenge as one of the more important families of East Anglia. As a follower of John, Earl of Oxford, Henry VII's leading commander in 1485, John Paston III became the first Tudor sheriff of East Anglia. Ultimately, in 1679, the Pastons became Earls of Yarmouth.

The repeated challenges to the peaceful tenure of their estates greatly complicated their relations with farmers of their properties and their peasant tenants. Men delayed, or withheld, payments of rents on the disputed manors and the problem of finding good farmers was bedevilled by the inevitable precariousness of leases on these properties.[148] In contested properties rents might be partly collected by the Pastons, but partly by their opponents: 'each contesting lord got some rents until the conflict simmered down'. There is no evidence that the Pastons tried to collect for the second time the rents that their farmers and tenants had already been forced to pay to others. This meant that the income of the Pastons diminished. There are suggestions in the Paston correspondence that farmers of Paston property who had paid their opponents should be replaced by 'other folkes', but we know of no evidence that these threats were ever carried out. In practice, 'farmers and tenants being so hard to come by . . . had to be decently treated'. There was violence against Paston farmers, less often against their peasant tenants. There were also distraints on the beasts of their dependents. 'The husbandry of the tenants was undoubtedly interrupted' by these feuds, 'beasts driven away, barn doors sealed, ploughing delayed, fields unsown'. The Pastons willy-nilly had to take action when these things happened, incurring further costs and troubles. When the farmer of Titchwell, in January 1469, had three horses led away by armed followers of the Duke of Norfolk, the Pastons were plainly told by the local rector that they must intervene, because otherwise no man would be willing to hold land of them or act for them.[149]

While the Pastons were exceptionally plagued by the enmities that they had incurred, all Norfolk landowners had to face up to chronic economic difficulties in this period, particularly in the 1460s. Prices of their main products – barley, malt and wool – were low. All landlords shared the same problem 'of maintaining their livelihood in a period of stagnant or contracting demand'.[150]

In 1461 John I held eleven estates, yielding annually about £200, a smaller income than John Hopton's and less secure. Rents were chronically in arrears. The Pastons chose to believe that some of the delays in payments were deliberate rather than unavoidable. There were marked delays particularly in times of political uncertainty, as in 1461–3. But, in fact, the bulk of the arrears was due to their dependants being genuinely unable to sell their produce profitably. While Pastons could ship their goods to London or other harbours, which meant higher costs but ultimately better returns, their farmers and tenants had to sell locally at such meagre prices as were current there. Some years were particularly bad. The year 1469 was one such, partly it seems because of uncertainties caused by political upheavals. There were problems on all the Paston estates. By October John I's widow, Margaret, reckoned that she was owed over £80 by the farmer of Mautby and was never likely to recover this debt. Mautby was an exceptionally fertile manor, with a net annual income of about £20, but the rent demanded hitherto had been too high and nobody else was willing to farm it. Direct exploitation of the demesnes was, for the Pastons, a desperate remedy, but in 1470 Margaret had no choice. She resumed Mautby into her hands and administered it that year through her servants.[151]

On the whole, 'it was farmers and tenants who had the upper hand'. Their arrears had to be tolerated, some of the old debts had to be pardoned, rents were repeatedly lowered at each successive bargain. There were intricate negotiations at each renewal of a farm of demesne or a tenancy, with the level of rent, the duration of leases and the responsibility for maintenance of properties all being balanced against each other. Farmers who had the reputation of being satisfactory were at a premium and concessions had to be made to get them and keep them. Tenants were dealt with harshly at times, in order to force them to pay arrears of rents. Their corn might be distrained after the harvest. Agnes Paston, the widow of Judge William, was planning in 1477 to let eight defaulting tenants take their harvest into barns and then to order her servants to seal these and distrain the tenants into making payments. Altogether we get an impression of a harsh and aggressive Paston lordship, tempered only by fear of pushing their dependants too far.[152]

VIII

A small number of peasants profited from the migrations of their neighbours and the increase in the number of vacant holdings by accumulating substantial amounts of land. Dr R. Faith speaks of them as a peasant aristocracy.[153] But in the middle decades of the century their chances of establishing permanently the prosperity of their families were fairly precarious, though their prospects became better in the last decades of the fifteenth and the early years of the sixteenth centuries. Well-documented examples are hard to come by and each case may have had exceptional features. The few examples cited here are merely adduced as illustrations of what was happening on some manors.[154]

Coleshill in western Berkshire and the adjoining manor of Eastrop, just over the border into Wiltshire, were both estates of the Priory of Edington in Wiltshire. There is unusually full documentation of the developments discussed here. The outstanding feature in the fifteenth century 'was the rise of a peasant aristocracy which came to nothing'. In the sixteenth century, a different group of families came to dominate these villages.[155] The agrarian conditions that facilitated their temporary rise can be easily identified. There was much vacant land here in the fifteenth century. 'The record of land in the lord's hand shows that Coleshill was severely depopulated between 1379 and the mid-fifteenth century' and the fall was particularly steep in the first quarter of that century. Fines for entry into customary holdings, high in the early fourteenth century, were now exceptionally low, varying usually between 2 capons (or 6*d*) and, at most, 10*s*. A number of new tenants were admitted without paying fines. One of the reasons seems to have been the preference of the local men (particularly between 1433 and 1459) for leasing portions of demesne, 'especially grazing land and the piecemeal and short-term leasing of vacant holdings', as opposed to the more permanent acquisition of vacant customary holdings. The latter were burdened with customary rents and renders, unlike short-contract leases, for which favourable terms could be negotiated.[156]

The Cubbells of Eastrop and Coleshill were one of the families that prospered for a time in the fifteenth century. They had accumulated between 60 and 80 acres of arable together with much pasture and a mill. They were able to graze a hundred sheep and employ three or four labourers. They paid modest rents of 6*d* per acre and rendered very low entry fines for new holdings. But by the early sixteenth century they had left the two villages, though they were still prosperous men. When in 1505 an attempt was made to compel John Cubbell to return from Newbury as the lord's villein, he was described as 'worth 100' marks.[157]

Other leading families fared less well. Some rose originally as seignorial officials and farmers of the demesne. But on these two Edington manors the priory only leased such portions of the demesne as were less valuable, while retaining in direct management the land best suited for pasture.[158] The Kypping family were victims of this situation. A Kypping had been the lord's rent collector before he farmed a part of the demesne in 1421. His lease was for twelve years, but it was extended later. He took on the demesne arable, the dairy herd and a considerable amount of grazing land. 'He had to make a profit from 84 acres in bad years as well as good and was responsible for what might be very expensive repairs.' He owed £10 by 1443 and one of his successors owed £15 in 1464. At Wolestone, not far from Coleshill, belonging to St Swithun's, the Cathedral Priory of Winchester, the farmer abandoned the manor in 1440, without paying any of the farm, and carried off 87 sheep, 13 heads of cattle, 24 quarters of corn and other things.[159]

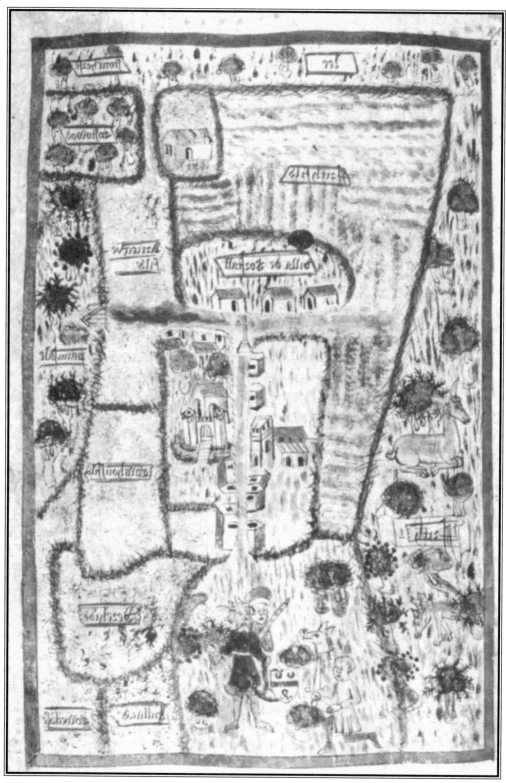

Plan of the village of Boarstall, Bucks., 1444. This is one of the earliest surviving village plans and shows the church and moated site surrounded by houses; beyond are the village fields (By permission of Buckinghamshire Record Office)

Durrington was a very prosperous village, ten miles to the north of Salisbury, with a large amount of fertile arable. The expanding textile industries of this part of Wiltshire led to a growing demand for foodstuffs and Durrington was one of the villages supplying them. We know most about the western part of the village, forming a manor that since 1399 had belonged to Winchester College. The annual cash liveries to the college reached their peak in the 1440s, averaging then annually nearly £42. The next two decades were here, like elsewhere, a time of decline, with cash liveries averaging annually in the 1460s only £27 13*s*. A succession of farmers, drawn mostly from the more prosperous local men, had farmed profitably the college's demesne in the first half of the century. But John Langford, who held the farm from 1458 to 1478, fell on evil times. When he gave up the farm he owed £58 1*s* 3*d* to the college, which had to pardon it to him two years later, as he had become insolvent. His successors, the Harvests, who held the farm from 1478 to 1512, were able to prosper again, as the times became more propitious once more.[160]

However, service to a manorial lord over several generations, and the farming of his demesnes, could produce an enduring success for a peasant family. Elmley Castle was one of the most important Worcestershire estates of the Beauchamps, Earls of Warwick,[161] succeeded in 1449 by Richard Neville (killed at Barnet in 1471). For a long time members of the Hamond family administered this manor for them in one capacity or another. A John Hamond paid in 1373 a fine to enter a holding of a messuage and half a virgate.[162] Edward Hamond was reeve and beadle (rent collector) in 1395–7. His arrears were quite small.[163] John Hamond, reeve in 1425–8, appears to have been equally solvent, as was Richard Hamond, reeve in 1434/5. For this office he had an annual allowence of 11*s* 1*d* to cover the rent of his holdings and customary taxes due from him.[164] Since 1433 Richard had also been farming, together with some unnamed associates, the lord's demesne for an annual rent of £10. The farm included both arable and pasture. A Richard Hamond was still farming with associates the earl's demesne in 1459/60. Their annual rent of £10 was still the same and he was reeve with the same yearly allowance of 11*s* 1*d*.[165]

A similar example of successful service comes from the bishop of Worcester's estate of Hampton in Warwickshire.[166] The successful family were the Kynnes, originally from Blockley, another episcopal manor further south. A Walter Kynne is mentioned in the account for Blockley of 1383/4. He must have been a substantial tenant, as he owed that year to the bishop £12 4½*d*.[167] When William Kynne first appears in the records of Hampton in 1430 he is described as 'of Blockley'. That year he took the farm of the episcopal demesne at Hampton for twelve years at the annual rent of £12 13*s* 4*d*.[168] There had been difficulties earlier on over finding a farmer. John Sheppard had farmed it in 1419, paying for it and for the pasture of Grovefield, to the north of Hampton, £14 13*s* 4*d*.[169] But he had abandoned it by 1427/8 and that year these lands were farmed to various tenants on short term for £11 14*s* 10*d*.[170] William Kynne's willingness to take it for £12 13*s* 4*d* provided a permanent solution. The farm included the bishop's manor-house and buildings attached to it.

By 1447 William had been succeeded by his son, Richard, who continued to farm the demesne for nearly thirty years. He was also reeve in 1450/1[171] and that office was filled fairly continuously by either himself or relatives (a John and a Robert) until, at least, 1482.[172] Richard became the bishop's trusted agent at Hampton. The record of inquiries in 1452 into the bishop's income on all his estates mentions in two cases the need to consult Kynne over defaults of Hampton's tenants, as he was the best person to advise the bishop's council ('*optime scit consilium domini inde informare*').[173] As reeve, Richard received a yearly allowance of 13*s* for the rent of his holdings. While there were yearly fluctuations in his accounts as reeve, one has the overall impression of competence and solvency. Thus his account for 1467/8, after nearly twenty years during which he and his relatives had functioned as reeves, ends with a debt of only £1 10s.[174] Richard also continued permanently as farmer of the demesne. There were some increases in rent, as he also took over some additional lands in the bishop's hands. The most substantial was the addition of 13s 4d for an enclosure made at the bishop's expense. In 1467/8, as farmer, he was paying £13 7s 8d.[175] In July 1470 his farm was renewed for thirty more years at an annual rent of 20 marks (£13 6s 8d).[176]

A Case Study of the Depression of the Mid–Fifteenth Century: the Estates of the Bishops of Worcester, 1436–76

I

One of the fullest documentations for the troubled years of economic depression between the 1430s and the 1470s comes from the estate archives of the Bishops of Worcester. Most of this period was covered by the episcopate of John Carpenter (active as bishop from February 1444 to the summer of 1476). Because of the economic depression as well as widespread tenant resistance the revenues of the bishopric reached their lowest point in the mid–fifteenth century. It is impossible to establish the exact figures as we have only fragmentary evidence about the income from the bishop's spiritual functions: a fragment covering the period from August to December 1452 reveals net receipts of £70.[1] No episcopal household accounts survive, which would have informed us about the various fines paid to the bishops and the other extraordinary payments received by them. The amounts of cash received directly from the estates do not appear to have fallen in any year below £900. The cash payments received from his properties by Bishop Carpenter in the year from Michaelmas 1447 to Michaelmas 1448 amounted to at least £1,064 and this is an incomplete figure.[2] A fuller record, for 1453/4, amounted to £901[3] and the comparable figure for 1456/7 was £964.[4] Carpenter's total revenue, even in those lowest years, must have surpassed £1,000.

If one asks what one could have expected of a reasonably satisfactory late medieval bishop, John Carpenter was clearly the best prelate that the diocese of Worcester had in the fifteenth century.[5] He appears to have come from Westbury near Bristol and to have descended from a family of episcopal tenants there, the only medieval Bishop of Worcester of such an origin. As he was ordained priest in 1421, he was presumably born in 1397, or earlier, and became a bishop in his forties. Previously he had been a provost of Oriel College at Oxford and chancellor of the University (in 1438). He had also been a king's clerk since at least 1430 and his promotion was clearly very acceptable to King Henry VI. He resided much of the time in his diocese and, unlike many contemporary bishops, seems to have devoted considerable time to his pastoral duties. Most of his income, which appears to have been fully sufficient for his needs, was spent on his diocese. Even in the difficult 1450s he was spending large sums on refounding the collegiate church at his native Westbury. In 1453/4 its buildings absorbed almost a third (32 per cent) of the cash receipts from the estates and the comparable percentage for 1456/7 amounted to one-quarter. Between 1456 and 1470 he paid out a sum equal to half an average year's income on the purchase of properties for the endowment of that collegiate foundation (£555).[6]

The resistance of the tenantry to some of the bishop's financial demands reached its peak during Carpenter's episcopate, but there was no armed rising against him in the dangerous years, 1449/50, in contrast to the attacks on the properties of the much more unpopular Abbot of Gloucester.[7] Carpenter's senior administrative staff (especially between 1448 and 1460) were efficient, but over-aggressive. More moderation followed after 1460 and by Carpenter's last years the worst of the confrontation with the customary tenantry was over, though at the cost of permanent losses of income. The details of this story will fill much of this chapter.

II

The principal source for this chapter is Professor Dyer's remarkable book published in 1980 on *The Estates of the Bishopric of Worcester, 680–1540*.[8] But on some details my conclusions differ from his account and I also sometimes ask different questions or study more fully some of the sources used by him. Professor Dyer used more completely than I have been able to do the manorial accounts and court rolls for particular estates.[9] We have both used the same general records, consisting chiefly of the accounts of receivers general, annual valors and lists of annual arrears. It is important to explain what kinds of information can be derived from each of these types of records.

Only the accounts of receivers general cover, for the most part, transactions that have really taken place. They list the sums received by this official from each estate in turn, specifying the people who have made payments to him. For the period that concerns us here there survive such accounts for 1435/6, 1447/8, 1453/4, 1456/7, 1460/1, 1463/4, 1464/5, 1465/6, 1467/8 and 1470/1.[10] These accounts also list payments to the bishop. To the account for 1447/8 there is still attached a copy of indentures recording all disbursements, enabling me to reconstruct their chronology. These accounts mean what they say only if the receivers general were honest and there is no assured way of checking on that. The account for 1447/8 ends with a series of claims by various people that they should have been credited with payments to the receiver, Richard Ewen, which he had failed to acknowledge. It is a suspicious circumstance that claims against him reappear in lists of arrears of later years,[11] after he had left Carpenter's service and had become the surveyor of the much vaster properties of the bishop of Winchester. The one limitation of the accounts of receivers general is that they only record cash that passed through that official's hands. As the household accounts of the bishops have disappeared, we lack evidence about many of the payments made directly to them. One of the most serious gaps are the fines paid by farmers of the episcopal demesnes for the granting or renewals of their leases. However, the payments made directly to the bishops by individual manorial officials can be found in the valors of the entire episcopal estates.

Valors survive for 1454, 1457, 1459, 1465 and 1466.[12] They are made up from valors for particular estates, recorded at the end of each annual manorial account, giving an estimate of the amounts that the estate should have yielded, though these sums are invariably larger than the actual receipts. Only the records of casual income at the end of each valor list the sums effectively received. The other real pieces of information are the lists of fees and wages paid to manorial officials and other items of local expenditure. After giving the annual total of all the particular valors, this type of record proceeds to break them down into particular types of income, starting with the rents of assize. This section is a mixture of what was expected and what had been received from casual and extraordinary sources. The bishop's advisers presumably thought that this was useful for devising administrative policies. For the same reason the valors also provided totals for different types of expenditures and of allowances given to manorial officials. These were real sums. Valors also listed the alleged accumulated arrears. This was another partly unreal item, as it included many sums that could never be collected. A real figure would then follow, of arrears which had been actually received in that year. Thus, the valor compiled for 1453/4[13] records alleged arrears of that year, totalling £401 11s 5¼d, followed by arrears pending in the valor of previous years, amounting to £1,111 18s 7¼d. Some of these items could be cancelled and £304 6s 9d was paid fairly soon. Intractable arrears of £792 5s 6¼d still remained outstanding, including many items that would never be received. Lastly, the valors also listed towards the end the sums for which special allowance was granted. These were chiefly items of authorized extraordinary expenditure, but also included some pardons of debt out of special favour.

For individual debts making up arrears, we have to turn to the individual accounts, where these survive.[14] In their absence much can be learned from general lists of arrears. We have such records for all the episcopal estates for 1460, 1462 and 1473,[15] and by analysing them it is possible to separate three categories of debts. Some were merely delayed payments. Professor Dyer has estimated that in the third quarter of the century up to a third of Bishop Carpenter's annual receipts consisted of outstanding arrears of the previous two years.[16] They were symptoms of economic depression, but not of serious trouble. Secondly, there were arrears due to deliberate resistance of tenants; these require a separate study. Lastly, there were charges arising out of the obstinate refusal of the episcopal administration to accept that economic decline had made some fiscal demands obsolete. Ultimately, though very grudgingly, many of these items were pardoned, chiefly after 1460.

III

In section V of chapter 9 I have described how the anachronistic demands of the custodians of the vacant bishopric in 1433–5 for payments of the recognition at the obsolete rates collected in 1302/3 led to a complete refusal to pay it. Behind this refusal there lay a concerted action between the tenants of *all* the episcopal estates. There is no mention of any recognition being received by Bishop Bourchier in 1435. There is abundant evidence that his successor, Bishop Carpenter, never received recognition on any of his estates, though his claims to it were never abandoned and it appears among arrears demanded by him to the end of his life.

Resistance began to spread to the payments of other servile dues. Some tenants at Bishop's Cleeve (Gloucestershire) refused to pay the annual common fine in 1441.[17] On the wealthy manor of Henbury by Bristol the tenants refused to pay the annual render for pasturing pigs on the lord's woods. It had yielded 18s 6¼d in 1379, but sank to 2s 9d by 1437/8 and a derisory 5d in 1448/9. The inquiry into the losses of revenues on all the estates in 1452 revealed that the tenants of Henbury were refusing completely to tolerate this impost. As a compromise solution, at Whitstones and Wick (near Worcester) in 1441 each of the customary tenants was paying annually ½d irrespective of the number of pigs he kept and the same arrangement was adopted in 1448 at Kempsey, to the south-east of Worcester.[18] From the start of Carpenter's episcopate the customary tenants of Bredon were refusing to pay their servile renders. This was the culmination of a long history of conflict and I shall return to its details later in this chapter. A similar refusal started on the Gloucestershire estates of Withington and Bibury, by 1451 at the latest. Like Bredon, all these properties lay within easy reach of the Cotswolds.

In 1448 Thomas Arnold of Cirencester was appointed as Bishop Carpenter's receiver general, the first layman to hold such an office on the Worcester estates. He acted until 1460 and then, for another twenty-three years, he was the auditor of the bishopric's estate accounts.[19] A royal pardon of 1459 granted to him for various commercial offences described Arnold as a gentleman, *alias* clothman *alias* woolman.[20] He may have been largely responsible for the vigorous attempts to recover lost revenues and to reorganize the administration of the episcopal estates. One of the first 'victims' was Nicholas Poyntz, a Gloucestershire gentleman who had farmed the demesne at Bibury since 1435. His original annual rent of £6 16s had been reduced in 1437/8 by £2, but his payments continued to fall into arrears, especially after 1445. He paid nothing in 1447–9 and was deprived of the farm in the following year.[21]

In 1450 Arnold was joined by another enterprising colleague, William Nottingham, appointed as chief steward. He had been justice of the peace and escheator. Like Arnold, he remained steward of all the estates until 1460; subsequently he continued to be steward for only Gloucestershire properties until 1470. He served as one of the royal Barons of the Exchequer throughout the reign of Edward IV.[22]

'The court rolls throughout the estate for 1450/1 were unusually lengthy and detailed and contain references to attempts to discipline tenants in a manner which had not been known on the estate' in the first half of the century. The most dramatic confrontation between Nottingham and the tenants occurred in the spring of 1450, a few months before the revolts in south-eastern England. At the court for Wick and Whitstones (two suburbs of Worcester), held on 12 April various offences were prosecuted. A jury was empanelled to reveal whether there had been concealments of them by the manorial juries in previous years. It included some substantial freeholders as well as customary tenants. That jury 'armed in a warlike manner . . . as insurrectionists and rebels against the peace' refused to make any presentments required of them. Each of its members was threatened with a penalty of £20. 'To avoid a breach of the peace' they were dismissed, but on being recalled the following day they still refused to make any presentments. Nottingham had seized several holdings which had been exchanged illegally, or were illicitly occupied. A 'smallholding had been declared forfeit because the tenant had neglected to pay the fine'. The jurors must have been particularly alarmed by the seizures of lands and the threats of forfeiture, 'seen as a danger to all tenants'. Their resistance seems to have been effective as there is no mention in subsequent court rolls of the collection of the penalties threatened against the jurors by Nottingham.[23]

The fullest evidence of tenant discontent and of the past failures of the episcopal administration is provided by a record of inquiries into all the properties owned by the bishop in 1452/3.[24] Professor Dyer could only date it to around 1450, but this can be narrowed through a comparison of this inquiry with other records. Two stages can be distinguished. The inquiries were apparently completed by the end of 1452. The final record was then scrutinized, probably soon afterwards, by the bishop's council and his senior officials. Hence we have various marginal comments recommending further action or ordering that Bishop Carpenter should be consulted. The evidence for precise dating comes from this annotation. Under the manor of Hampton (since the sixteenth century Hampton Lucy) there is a presentment about the unsatisfactory yield from Hatton, a deserted village adjoining Hampton. Against this entry a note was entered that Hatton was (subsequently) leased to Thomas Rowes, the bishop's *nativus*, for an annual rent of £8. The record of this leasing can be found on the court roll of Hampton under 20 January 1453.[25]

The returns to this inquiry reveal much mismanagement, neglect and discontent.[26] The margins are littered with recommendations, but much was clearly beyond remedy. Many of the practical recommendations about enclosures of pastures, repairs of farm buildings and mills, and other measures involving expenditures, were long delayed. Carpenter appears to have been much more interested in his new foundation at Westbury or repairs to his splendid residences at Worcester and Hartlebury than in spending much money on improvements to estates.[27]

The inquiry of 1452 noted the ruinous state of some mills and buildings on the episcopal estates and the urgent need for enclosing some of the bishop's pastures. At Hampton its virtually hereditary reeve, Richard Kynne, threatened to relinquish the farm of the demesne unless the bishop's pasture was enclosed, as it was being ravaged by animals from adjoining vills. He estimated the cost at £2. A marginal note recommended consultation with the bishop and his council. As Kynne was highly valued, his wishes were granted and part of the demesne, Polefurlong, was enclosed at the cost of £3 in 1454/5. Kynne agreed to pay an annual addition to his farm of 13s 4d. A new water-mill was demanded at Hampton, as the existing one was wholly ruined. It was built only in 1460/1 and there were improvements to the sluice gates in 1467/8, at the combined cost of £12 16s 10d. The mills at Stratford-upon-Avon had always been profitable and, in order to maintain this income, in 1460/1 the floodgates were repaired at a cost of £16 15s 3d. More than half of the cost was provided by Richard Kynne, reeve and farmer of the neighbouring manor of Hampton. Various recommendations of the 1452 inquiry about repairs of farm buildings were carried out belatedly, with a new barn constructed at Fladbury between 1458 and 1461 at the cost of £14 4s 4d, while £6 4s was spent on barns at Henbury Saltmarsh in 1462/3 and £11 14s 9d at Northwick (outside Worcester) in 1465/6. But as Dyer rightly warns, the level of all this capital spending was never very high. In the middle years of the century the total was only about 3 per cent of net income. Clearly Bishop Carpenter could have spent much more on improvements in his estates 'if there had been a will to invest'. But his priorities lay elsewhere. Like many late medieval landlords, he was content to raise as much revenue as possible from existing assets, rather than invest in improvements for the future.[28]

Dyer noted some vigorous measures during the inquiry of 1452. 'If a jury failed to give a satisfactory answer', as in a case of eight 'missing' virgates at Stratford, they were sent away 'to enquire better'. When one of the tenants of these 'lost' virgates was rediscovered, he was distrained to pay the old rent. 'If tenants claimed to have had their rent reduced in the past, they were ordered to produce their charter or copy of court roll. Unsatisfactory responses produced the drastic order that the holding should be seized.'[29] This display of vigour, though effective against some individual peasants, ran into insuperable obstacles where important free tenants were concerned, or if there was well organized resistance of entire peasant communities.

The inquiry of 1452 and other records show that the bishops had largely lost control over their more important free tenants and could not collect the large arrears due from them. I have traced earlier the story of defaults by the Throckmortons, the greatest 'culprits'.[30] In that disturbed mid-century churchmen were at a disadvantage in dealing with powerful lay neighbours. The inquiry of 1452 attempted to investigate tenants by knight service. For example at Bibury (Gloucestershire) eleven free tenants were mentioned, of whom five were 'magnates', withholding the suit of bishop's courts. By 1460 attempts to obtain revenues from wardships of the heirs of knightly freeholders seem to have been abandoned.[31]

In section V of chapter 9 I have mentioned that during the Worcester vacancy of 1433–5 some of the customary tenants secured an abatement of financial demands on them by threatening to leave, as poverty compelled them to do so. The same thing happened in 1437 on one of the Earl of Warwick's estates. In the middle of the fifteenth century many peasants of the western Midlands were becoming impoverished or, at least, feared that this might happen to them. They were possibly hit even harder by the general economic depression than were their lords. This would explain the widespread 'rent strike' in the time of Bishop Carpenter on Worcester properties, as well as on some other estates of that region. On the other hand some of the episcopal tenants were certainly well above the poverty line and were exploiting the eagerness of their poorer neighbours to support them in the resistance to their common master.

We must distinguish between the refusal to pay certain obnoxious renders, chiefly confined to the servile dues, and a more generalized pressure for a scaling down of rents and other burdens of customary tenure. The servile taxes which were particularly resented were not very onerous but were hated because of the stigma of servility attached to them. Much of the most determined resistance to these renders, on episcopal properties, was confined to a group of estates in eastern Gloucestershire and properties closely adjoining them. Bredon, in the south-eastern tip of Worcestershire, and Bibury, Withington and Bishop's Cleeve in Gloucestershire, all close to the Cotswolds, formed the most obdurate core of resistance. The last two lay near to the Nunnery of Syon's estate of Cheltenham, where there had been similar prolonged troubles between 1445 and 1452. That story should be told first, as it was feared in 1452 that the tenantry at Cheltenham might resort to violence. From 1445 onwards they had refused to pay a yearly render of £10 0s 7¼d for commutation of their labour services. It required two visits of a magnate arbitrator, Lord Sudeley, before a settlement could be reached. On the first occasion he deemed it necessary to bring with him twenty-four mounted attendants and for the final arbitration, in September 1452, he was followed by as many as forty-six horsemen. The hated annual payment was reduced to £6 13s 4d.[32]

The greatest loss of tenant taxes suffered by Bishop Carpenter was at Bredon.[33] From the start of his episcopate, and perhaps earlier, its tenantry refused to pay annual renders of £1 8s 11d. This amount was made up of two different payments. One was the 'common fine', in recognition of the bishop's franchisal jurisdiction, his right to hold annually the 'view of frank pledge'. Both free tenants and customary serfs were theoretically liable to it (9s 4d). The other render was 'worksilver', in commutation of labour services (19s 7d). This had a long history behind it. Already in 1384/5 the reeve of Bredon had been unable to collect £2 4s 4d of servile taxes.[34] This resistance probably explains a temporary settlement reached at the manorial court held on 2 October 1389. Tenants of 17½ virgates were henceforth to pay the rent of 19s 7d per virgate. This included 2s 6d for partial commutation of labour services and the absorption into rent of all servile renders except for the common fine and the annual payment, by the entire tenantry, of another 19s 7d. This concession was made for only one year and its longer continuation was to depend on the will of the lord. Certain carriage and other labour services still remained reserved to the bishop.[35] In practice, the new arrangement was continued henceforth, but from the start of Carpenter's episcopate the tenants of Bredon refused to render each year this residue composition for labour as well as the common fine (jointly £1 8s 11d per annum). The inquiry of 1452 showed that the tenants were willing to make another compromise settlement, offering to pay each year 3s for the common fine.[36] The offer was presumably refused, as nothing was rendered for the rest of Carpenter's episcopate. From 1458 onwards the tenants of Bredon refused also to pay the annual render of £1 for the right to fish in the Avon. By Carpenter's death in 1476, he had lost at least £63 5s 4d from the taxes withheld by the men of Bredon, nearly half the total losses from revenues withheld on his estates. A fortunate survival of some schedules[37] attached to the court roll of Bredon for 1455/6 shows that there was trouble at the manorial court. One John Scotarde, for example, was fined 6d for insulting the bishop's

A membrane of the arrears roll of the estates of Bishop John Carpenter of Worcester, Michaelmas 1462. Bredon was one of the centres of resistance to the payment of servile dues (Reproduced by permission of the Bishop of Worcester: Worcester Record Office: BA 2636, pcl 176, no. 92488) steward 'in open court'. Of the charges imposed as the result of court proceedings in that year (£1 6s 10d), little more than one-eighth was actually collected (3s 11d).[38]

At Withington, from at least 1451, the servile tenants refused to pay annually £1 6s 8d for servile tallage. They alleged at the inquiry of 1452 that this payment had been excused by one of Carpenter's predecessors, though they did not specify his name.[39] By the end of his life Carpenter had lost at least £32 at Withington. At Tredington in Warwickshire £8 12s was lost between 1444 and 1476 through the refusal of tenants to pay the yearly tax of 5s 4½d for permission to use the bishop's woods ('woodsilver'). Partial losses of the common fine at Bishop's Cleeve and Fladbury appear to have been incurred since 1444 (£10 4s during the thirty-two years of Carpenter's episcopate). At Bibury the common fine (6s annually) was unpaid from at least 1450. 'Churschscot' was an ancient Anglo-Saxon render, initially paid by free peasants, though by the fifteenth century it had become a servile tax. It was withheld at Bibury (1s 8d annually) and at Tredington (2s 6d annually). Altogether Bishop Carpenter lost during his episcopate in unpaid taxes at least £134 16s 10d,[40] without counting the anachronistically high recognition demanded by him at his accession (assessed at £38 4s).

Behind all this resistance lay the conviction of tenants that the bishop could not resort to serious collective sanctions against them at a time when demand for tenements was slack and rents were declining. This explains also the erosion of various individual servile payments. The burden of heriots was alleviated by changes in arrangements for their collection. 'A customary tenant who had a multiple holding made an agreement that constituent parts should be regarded as one tenement for the purpose of heriot payment.' This was particularly frequent at Kempsey and Whitstones (near Worcester), where there were numerous small-holdings. 'A parallel development, especially after 1460, was an agreement that one of the holdings in a multiple tenement should pay only a cash heriot.' Fines paid by new customary tenants were generally low between 1430 and 1470. Quite often they do not seem to have been exacted or were reduced to slight, token renders.[41] The size of merchets (payments for the marriages of servile women), declined in the third quarter of the century. After 1450 payments of 2s or 1s became normal everywhere. However, at some manors, notably Whitstones and Kempsey, they seem to have been largely avoided altogether after that date.[42] Tolls on the sale of animals, usually of 1d or 2d, disappeared from manorial accounts in the fifteenth century, except at Henbury by Bristol, where they were last recorded in 1464. The officials in charge of the episcopal woods exacted payments to compensate for likely damage. Early in the fifteenth century they still amounted annually to 10s at Bredon. They disappeared everywhere in the second half of the century.[43]

From 1450 onwards the episcopal officials started to compile periodically lists of serfs 'by blood' on particular manors. The main motive seems to have been the encouragement of their emancipation for payments. At least fifty were negotiated between 1450 and 1479, often collectively for a whole family.[44] But, like other landlords, the bishops were finding insuperable obstacles in recovering or punishing serfs who had successfully absconded, though their whereabouts might be perfectly well known. The lack of 'good governance', of which the subjects of Henry VI complained with good reason, affected adversely the capacity of the landlords to cope with the rebelliousness of their tenants and to ensure the obedience of their manorial officials. The records of the manors of Wick and Wichenford near Worcester provide a clear illustration of this. In the 1430s William Boys had succeeded his father as farmer of the bishop's demesne at Wick and at various times he had served as a reeve and a rent collector. A Wick jury testified many years later (in 1457) that he 'is the lord's serf by blood . . . and all his ancestors are and were serfs time out of mind'. In 1452 his brother John, who was still living at Wichenford, admitted his serfdom. But William had migrated from Wick some time earlier and was living at nearby Kenswick, outside the bishop's property, though within his episcopal hundred of Oswaldslaw. The inquiry of 1452 denounced him for denying his serfdom, but he managed to do so with impunity and in 1457 he was farming the demesne of another landlord at Kenswick.[45]

IV

A look at the farming by Bishop Carpenter of the tithes at Blockley and of the manorial demesnes points to an economic depression in his diocese. Delays increased in the paying of the farms. Arrears of between one and two years had always occurred in the payments of the farms of tithes. But the account for Blockley in 1458/9 included the unpaid arrears of £13 5s 8d (over one-third of the average annual income from tithes), going back to the troubled years of 1449–51.[46] Still more disturbing was the gradual decline in the sums offered by prospective farmers of tithes. In the Blockley account for 1383/4 these totalled £42 10s.[47] The figure for 1458/9 was £36 6s 8d.[48] It declined to £31 3s 4d by 1464/5 and £29 3s 4d by 1465/6.[49]

The decline in prices of agricultural products made it harder for some farmers of episcopal demesnes to find cash for their annual rents. The appearance of partial renders in kind is one indication of this. Grain and hay worth between £8 and £15 a year were delivered to the bishop's household instead of cash payments between 1454 and 1466.[50] The economic depression did, however, encourage some farmers to feel that they could delay or altogether withhold payments with impunity on the basis that the lord would find it hard to replace them. The example of Richard Bayly is instructive. He was a Bristol merchant, who in 1447 leased the demesne at Stoke very near that city. Like the neighbouring manor of Henbury, it was one of the more prosperous episcopal estates. In 1470/1 the two together provided Carpenter's receiver with nearly one-ninth of his cash income (£112). Yet Bayly, as a demesne farmer, paid nothing between 1451 and 1457. In 1458 he agreed to pay £10, but only on condition that his accumulated arrears of £34 were pardoned. He soon, however, started to default again on his farm. The list of arrears at Michaelmas 1462 revealed new debts of £22, of which £17 was from arrears of previous years. The same list reveals a debt of £10 3s 6½d, going back seventeen years, due from the farmer of the demesne at Withington and obviously irrecoverable.[51]

Unlike Stoke, the manor of Bibury at the south-eastern edge of Gloucestershire was one of the poorest episcopal estates, being severely depressed in its economy. The farmer of Bibury demesne, who after 1451 was supposed to render £7 6s 8d each year, owed £22 by 1459. After some pardons he paid up £13 6s 8d in 1461/2.[52] However, the majority of the farmers of demesnes, though often delaying payments, discharged their obligations reasonably well.

Professor Dyer has investigated in great detail the story of the farm of the salt-works at Droitwich. The annual rent of £2 6s 8d was raised by Bishop Bourchier in 1439/40 to £2 13s 4d. From 1443 at the latest it was farmed by George Clent, who held it until at least 1463, but he refused to pay the increase and in Carpenter's early years he paid only the old rent. Then, in the early 1460s, when the salt prices reached a low point, there was a total cessation of payments for four years (1462–6). After the building in which the salt brine was boiled had been repaired in 1465/6, at the cost of £3 5s 4d, partial payments were resumed, perhaps by Clent's successor. Richard Wyche was farmer in 1468, when he already owed arrears of £6.[53]

V

Economic depression and tenant resistance to the bishop's fiscal demands were only two of the major features of life on episcopal estates in Carpenter's time. There were also feuds between rival groups of village notables, including conflicts between those local officials who were virtually in hereditary employment by the bishops, and others, perhaps equally prosperous, who were kept out of office, and competition for pastures for flocks of sheep and herds of cattle, perhaps increasing in size, between members of the minority of more successful peasants. All these things can be documented in the third quarter of the century at Hampton Lucy in Warwickshire and the depopulated former village of Hatton adjoining it.[54]

My story centres on three local families, the Smyths, the Kynnes and the Rowes (also spelt at times as 'Rolles' or 'Rolves'). When the episcopal demesne was first leased at Hampton on 1 October 1392, Walter Smyth was its first farmer, together with a former reeve, William Baron.[55] It is probable that both were of servile origin. Smyth had already been leasing three years earlier a parcel of land in the bishop's garden.[56] The lease of demesne to him and Baron was for seven years and included the meadows and pastures in the bend of Avon at Grovefield, to the north of Hampton. The annual farm-rent amounted to £10 13s 4d. On 16 December 1392 Thomas Rolves, whose descendants were later described as serfs ('nativi'), was granted, with two partners, the lease of 7 virgates at Hatton,[57] already depopulated and used as a large pasture. Thereafter the careers of these men and their descendants diverged. At a manorial court held at Hampton in 1410/11 (12 Henry VI) a Richard Smyth, who may have been a son or grandson of Walter, was allegedly confirmed by Thomas Throckmorton, the bishop's steward, in the tenure of an enclosed holding at Grovefield; or so he claimed in 1453. An investigation was ordered and, in the court held on 1 October 1457, his detention of this land was declared to be unjust and without the lord's licence. He was to be fined 6s 8d.[58] These proceedings came after a long series of other conflicts between Smyth and the episcopal officials and there may have been prejudice against him, though what I shall be saying about his other activities suggests that he was probably guilty here of wrongdoing.

In 1419 a Thomas Rowes, either the Hatton farmer of 1392 or a descendant, was leasing 5 virgates at Hatton for £2 a year. One of his partners was John Shepurd, who was then farming the demesne at Hampton.[59] These men, with other partners, were still leasing the pastures at Hatton in 1427/8, at a slightly lower annual rent of £1 18s. That lease still continued in 1438/9, but a John Rowes appeared as one of the lessees instead of Thomas. Thomas Rolles served as reeve of Hampton in 1437/8.[60]

The first appearance of William Kynne of Blockley at Hampton was in 1430, when he took over the farm of the demesne there at the annual rent of £12 13s 4d, replacing the temporary leases at lower rents held since 1427 by a group of tenants.[61] His son Richard had succeeded him by 1447, still paying the same rent.[62] The farm included the bishop's manor-house and the buildings attached to it. Richard proved a satisfactory farmer, and his tenure continued to be extended, the last time for twenty years at a somewhat higher rent of £13 6s 8d. In 1450/1 he served also as reeve. He held this office henceforth in most years during the next two decades.[63] As commented on in the previous chapter, he became the bishop's trusted agent at Hampton, as indicated by the record of inquiries into the bishop's estates in 1452, which mentions in two cases the need to consult him over defaults of Hampton's tenants, as he was the best person to advise the bishop's council.[64] In 1458 confiscated goods of Simon Workman, who had to abjure

The village of Hampton Lucy, Warks., an estate of the Bishops of Worcester in the Middle Ages (Warwickshire Museum: B2567/B8595)

the realm for a felony, were entrusted to Richard, called here the bishop's farmer.[65] It was possibly this position of trust that brought him into collision with Richard Smyth. At the Hampton court of 20 January 1453 Smyth was fined 6s 8d for bringing a writ against Kynne in the king's court, in defiance of the local ordinance prohibiting this, thus vexing Kynne.[66]

Professor Dyer has noted that at Hampton, after 1450, very few tenants were succeeded by men bearing the same surnames.[67] This does not take account of succession by widows or by families of tenants' sisters, but it nevertheless suggests a disturbed community. Certainly in the 1450s it seems to have been riven by feuds and Richard Smyth was one of the leading troublemakers.

On 17 January 1450 the court at Hampton prohibited the men of that village from unjustly using the common pasture at Hatton belonging to the bishop and his tenants there (that is, the farmers of the Hatton pastures). They were to desist from doing so in future or pay a fine of 20s for each recurrence of this offence. The next court, on 23 April, actually imposed this fine and Richard Smyth was named as one of the offenders. The same injunction, on pain of a fine of 20s, was repeated at the court of 2 October 1451. On 20 January 1453 Thomas Rowes, either the

Hatton farmer of 1419 or a relative, was granted a farm of all the pastures at Hatton (formerly 14 virgates), with the manorial hall there, at £8 a year. He acted as the lord's agent in maintaining at his cost 40 of the bishop's sheep over winter, and 100 after Easter, and he was described as the lord's serf ('*nativus*').[68]

In October 1453 Rowes renewed his lease, adjoining to himself a relative called Thomas Rowes junior. The farm was increased to £9 6s 8d. In return, Rowes procured the threat of larger amercements on the people of Hampton invading the pastures at Hatton. The imposition of collective fines of 20s clearly did not stop this malpractice, as at the court of 4 October 1453 he bitterly complained of the losses suffered by him from this continuing pasturing of cattle and sheep belonging to men of Hampton on his grange at Hatton. This time each of the offenders was individually threatened with a penalty of 6s 8d. There is a long list of them, headed by the rector of Hampton. Richard Smyth comes second, presumably as one of the ringleaders. The other offenders included two former reeves, William Bernard, Kynne's predecessor in 1449/50, and Thomas Pathelow, who can be identified as the holder of 1 virgate (in 1460). It was clearly a group of leading villagers.[69] It may be pertinent to this glimpse of local feuds at Hampton to note that on 23 April 1450 William Sclatter had been accused of having, with 40 animals and more, destroyed the corn and herbage of four other tenants, including the afore-mentioned William Bernard.[70]

The farming by the two Rowes at Hatton did not prosper, perhaps because of the continuing invasions of Hatton by stranger flocks of sheep and herds of cattle. By 1458 they owed £9 6s, part of which was pardoned. In 1459/60 Thomas Rowes was farming with a new partner, Robert Walton. Of arrears of their farm due that year £2 13s 4d, £2 10s was charged to Rowes. The following year Rowes had ceased to be a farmer, though Walton was carrying on with another partner.[71]

To return to Richard Smyth: between 1450 and his death by the summer of 1463, there are diverse records charging him with various offences or, at least, suggesting devious dealings by him. He may have been at odds with the bishop's trusted men, like Richard Kynne, but he was not completely an outsider. Thus, in October 1451 he was elected to the office of local constable in the county court.[72] It is improbable that he was merely victimized. The recurrent proceedings in which Smyth was involved suggest an unscrupulous, deceitful and violent man. On 2 October 1451 he was presented as guilty of appropriating a parcel of the bishop's demesne and ploughing it up. He was fined 3s 4d. He restored this land to the demesne, but the fine continued to be charged to him and, of course, remained unpaid. As Richard Kynne was reeve and farmer of the demesne in 1450/1, the complaint must have originated with him. But Smyth was incorrigible, for he again appropriated the same parcel of the demesne in 1457 and was fined 6s 8d for this in Hampton court held on 16 June.[73] Kynne, as farmer of the demesne, was, presumably, again responsible for this charge.

The inquiry into the episcopal estates in 1452 mentions Smyth several times. We learn that he had bought for £3 3s 4d a tenement in Grovefield, north of Hampton, paying 6s a year to the bishop. This shows that he disposed of surplus capital. There was no suggestion here of any wrongdoing. It was different with two other charges. Smyth held 2 customary virgates, for which he should have paid £1 0s 6d, as well as rendered customary services and contributed to servile renders. He was only rendering 10s 10½d and denied that he owed anything else. He claimed that he was holding in free tenure and had received these tenements in free grant by charter from someone called Power. The charter was said to be undated, which increases one's suspicions about the truth of Smyth's statement. The matter was adjourned for discussion with Richard Kynne as farmer of the demesne.[74] It looks as if no one dared to question Smyth's free status.

Enough has already been said about the prominent part played by Smyth in invading wrongfully, with others, the farm of episcopal pastures at Hatton. At the court of 16 June 1457, where he was charged with cultivating illegally some demesne land, a more damaging accusation was also laid against him: that he was occupying unjustly and without licence an enclosure at Grovefield, presumably used as pasture. He was fined 6s 8d on the first charge and ordered to compensate the bishop for loss suffered by the farmer of the demesne. On the second charge he was threatened with another fine of 6s 8d, unless he vacated the holding in Grovefield. There was in addition a mysterious charge that he was 'a common harbourer of suspect people' ('communis receptor suspectorum'). He was to expel them on pain of a fine of 20s.[75] This could mean that Smyth was maintaining a group of malefactors, perhaps for his protection. But it could also mean that, at a time when the royal government was suspecting Yorkist conspiracies and facing open defiance in parts of Wales,[76] he had been welcoming some Yorkist supporters. By 25 July 1463 Smyth was dead. We learn of this from an order to seize an acre of customary land which Smyth had been occupying in his lifetime, claiming that it was free land. It was to remain sequestrated pending an inquiry.[77] It is fitting that the last mention of him should be of this ambiguous sort.

There is one other incident that could conceivably refer to Richard Smyth of Hampton. At a manorial court at another episcopal estate, Bishop's Cleeve, a Richard Smyth and his two sons addressed 'opprobrious words' to the steward and assaulted him. The steward would have been Sir William Nottingham, acting for the Gloucestershire estates since 1460. He was the man who had presided over inquiries into Smyth's doings at Hampton in 1452. The offenders at Bishop's Cleeve were fined the enormous sum of £100.[78] A man like Richard Smyth of Hampton, who had been for a long time affronting the episcopal officials, might have provoked the imposition of such an exorbitant fine.

VI

A poem written in 1401 in the dialect of the south-western Midlands complained that lords would never take any notice of what grieved the 'comouns' unless payments of rents ceased.[79] The total or, much more often, partial withholding of rents was something quite familiar to landholders of this region. It was more widespread than other forms of tenant resistance on the episcopal estates of Worcester. As Professor R.H. Hilton has observed, 'at what stage the normal medieval dilatoriness in making any cash payment on time merges into what could be called a *rent strike* it is impossible to say', but, in his view, 'that stage seems to have been passed' on Worcester estates by the middle of the fifteenth century.[80]

Peasant tenants did not, as a rule, default completely on their rents. That was the privilege of people much higher up on the social scale, like the Throckmortons or the Vampages, another family of influential gentleman among the free tenants of the Bishop of Worcester.[81] Lesser men could not risk going that far; they merely claimed that they ought to be paying less. Some of the peasants alleged concessions by the previous bishops or else, like Richard Smyth of Hampton Lucy, asserted that they were personally free and therefore liable to smaller, fixed payments. Of course, some of these claims were untrue, but they were often hard to disprove, especially if tenants had the backing of influential people.[82] Prolonged refusals to pay more than a part of their rents were likely, in the conditions prevailing in the middle of the century, to force the bishops to accept the tenants' offers sooner or later, as the best that could be got out of them. One of the most striking features of the whole situation was the reluctance of the bishop's officials to take any measures more drastic than imposing fines on the recalcitrant tenants, knowing full well that even these might not be paid.

In their zeal to enforce Bishop Carpenter's rights, his officials compiled a multitude of new rentals. They were drawn up for twelve estates, in many cases between 1450 and 1456. Eight more rentals followed during the rest of Carpenter's episcopate.[83] In the long run they helped to stabilize the bishop's claims, but in some cases the immediate effect may have been counter-productive, only stiffening tenant resistance. Thus, the list of arrears compiled in 1460 includes a debt of £11 15s 2d accumulated during the preceding seventeen years (that is, since Carpenter's election), arising out of charges of 'rentale tenentium' (the list of rents due from tenants) at Whitstones, which the tenants were refusing to recognize. This debt increased to £20 15s in the list of arrears drawn up in 1473.[84]

One cause of the decline in the revenue from rents was the slackening of the demand for land among peasants, unless they could secure it on terms that suited them. The account of 1458/9 for Blockley reveals a net annual loss of £6 17s 6½d, because 12 full virgates which had lapsed into the bishop's hands were not yielding their accustomed rents. The decline had occurred over a long period, going back in a few cases to the early years of the reign of Henry V (1413–22). All these holdings had been taken for varying terms by tenants who paid lower rents and were not being treated as customary tenants, because they were not liable to servile taxes or the residual labour services.[85]

It is very difficult to calculate the proportion of a year's income from rents withheld by the tenantry, because of the scattered nature of the evidence. Rent strikes largely took the form of individual refusals of small amounts of money, which were rarely recorded separately in the lists of arrears, being concealed in the arrears of the manorial officials. The inquiry of 1452 into the episcopal revenues provides some welcome details. Each sum was small but their formidable numbers produced large totals from some manors, £2 12s 4½d at Northwick, outside the then walls of Worcester, and £1 18s 6d at Stratford-upon-Avon. Urban tenants figure prominently. A list dating from the middle of the century shows that forty-six holdings in the city of Worcester withheld rents worth annually £4. Such urban evasion was facilitated by the difficulty of collecting rents in an exceptionally active economic centre, where sales and leases could be very complex and very frequent.[86]

Professor Dyer has tried to compare the level of rents expected in the bishopric's *Red Book*, compiled in 1299, with the average rents on seven estates in the fifteenth century. That second set of figures can be used only with great caution, as it extends over too long a period of fluctuating economic fortunes. It does, however, seem to reflect real contrasts between different manors. The greatest decline (58 per cent) is at Bibury, which we know to have been economically decaying by the middle of the fifteenth century. Nor is it surprising to find almost no decline at Bishop's Cleeve, an important centre for the movement of goods from the middle Cotswolds towards the Severn near the point where large shipments of corn and other goods could begin at Tewkesbury, with Bristol as the main destination. The flourishing manor of Henbury, just outside Bristol, reveals a decline of only 11 per cent. Declines of between a fifth and around a third are listed by Dyer (in increasing order) at Bredon, Whitstones (outside Worcester), Hanbury, Hampton and Kempsey.[87]

If the rents withheld by the Throckmortons and the Vampages, and other debts not connected

The last page of the account of John Salwey, Receiver-General of Bishop John Carpenter of Worcester, 1470–71 (Reproduced by permission of the Bishop of Worcester: Worcester Record Office: BA 2636, pcl 174, no. 92473)

directly with the peasantry, are put aside, the remaining arrears due to Bishop Carpenter in 1462 amounted to some £930, corresponding to slightly less than a year's revenue. This includes taxes that tenants of several manors refused to pay, as well as rents withheld by the tenantry. If particular estates are examined, one discovers arrears amounting to more than a year's income on eleven properties, that is on slightly more than half of Carpenter's manors. This was very embarrassing, but he was far from being ruined.[88] In the long run good relations with the episcopal officials on individual manors could only be safeguarded by pardons of obviously irrecoverable debts. That began to happen around 1460.

Three sets of developments may help to account for the relaxation of pressures on the tenantry of the Worcester estates from about 1460 onwards. The economy of the whole country was much disturbed between 1457 and 1462.[89] Political uncertainty was clearly an important factor, as was the recurrent serious fighting between Henry VI's supporters and the rebel Yorkists. Probably even more disturbing, because more widespread in its effects, was a huge increase in disorder and crime unleashed by the partial breakdown of government. 'The first few months of Edward IV's reign probably saw a higher level of disorder than any other period in the fifteenth century.' Gangs of seditious vagabonds roamed through many Midland and southern counties, killing and plundering. Margaret Paston wrote in 1461 from Norfolk that, 'I heard never say of so much robbery and manslaughter in this country as is now within a little time.'[90] The resultant high degree of apprehension and alarm felt over much of the country must have had a sobering effect on landlords, fearing an outbreak of violent discontent among their tenants. That the west Midlands were much disturbed is shown by an outbreak in 1460 of a private war between the men of Gloucester, supported by some of the gentry of the surrounding countryside, and the inhabitants of the Forest of Dean. In January and early February 1464 there was a rising against Edward IV's government over a considerable area of the west Cotswolds and the Vale of Gloucester.[91]

While there is no evidence of risings against the Bishop of Worcester, greater leniency towards his peasantry was presumably to be recommended. The replacement in 1460, as receiver general, of the enterprising but rigorous Thomas Arnold, by a more flexible John Salwey, deputy to Arnold for some years previously, was probably an important cause of changes in estate policies.[92] In Professor Dyer's words, 'The high total of debts that accumulated in the 1450s was the result of the irresistible force of tenant truculence, meeting the immovable object of a determined administration.' From 1460 onwards there was an appreciable change. Allowances of charges and pardons of debts reduced the arrears total of the whole estate by about £400 between 1460 and 1465. A new build up of arrears was prevented henceforth by a continued series of concessions. Small sums were regularly pardoned and allowed. For the remainder of Carpenter's episcopate his chief administrators continued to make concessions on arrears while still clinging to the old rent demands.[93] The pardons and allowances encouraged officials and farmers of various episcopal assets to make more payments. On some estates one can note a dramatic scaling down of the arrears that were still exacted. At Blockley they amounted in 1458/9 to £52 5s 6d, but only to £6 18s 6¾d at Michaelmas 1462. But at Bredon, where the episcopal officials continued to insist on the payment of taxes, which the tenants had been systematically withholding, arrears still amounted to £95 at Michaelmas 1462.[94] A comparison of the three surviving arrears rolls for all the episcopal properties is instructive, as long as it is remembered that they consisted of very diverse elements and included much that was irrecoverable. The total at Michaelmas 1460 was £1,497 17s 9¼d. The net amount due at Michaelmas 1462 (after deductions of some allowances) was £1,114 16s 8d. At Michaelmas 1473 the arrears that were still being charged amounted to only £896 3 4¼d.[95]

CHAPTER 12

Depopulation and Evictions:
the Midlands, *c*. 1440–*c*. 1520[1]

I

In 1971 Professor M. Beresford and Dr J.G. Hurst knew of 2,263 localities which certainly, or probably, were sites of medieval villages and hamlets deserted at various times.[2] Some were already lost before 1348/9. The successive epidemics of the Black Death depopulated some places and depleted many more so seriously that they were gradually abandoned during the long economic *malaise* of the later fourteenth and much of the fifteenth centuries. But deliberate moves away from arable cultivation to its replacement by pastures for cattle and sheep became an increasingly notable feature of changes in some parts of England from *c*. 1440 onwards. This was especially true of the central and eastern Midlands. The changes in this area between *c*. 1440 and *c*. 1520 are the main subject of the present chapter, though I shall need to cite some texts dating from the whole of the Tudor period, and even beyond it. A considerable proportion of the disappearances of other localities was due to further changes in the late sixteenth and the seventeenth centuries. My story, chiefly of the 1440–1520 period, divides in 1485. This is partly for evidential reasons, though the accession of Henry VII really did begin a new age of some active governmental concern about depopulation.

From Warwickshire we have a list of wholly or partly depopulated villages drawn up at the start of Henry VII's reign by a well-informed and scholarly local man, John Rous, a chantry priest in the service of the Earls of Warwick. He can be corroborated and supplemented by Sir William Dugdale's *Antiquities of Warwickshire* (1656).[3] No other English county had in the seventeenth century such a splendid study of its history. John Hales of Coventry, a member of Cardinal Wolsey's commissions enquiring into depopulation in 1518 and one of the chief inspirers of Protector Somerset's commissions in 1548,[4] was possibly influenced, above all, by what happened in Warwickshire when he stated in 1548/9 that, 'The chief destruction of towns and decays of houses was before the beginning of the reign of Henry VII.'[5]

The next, much larger body of evidence, comes from the presentments made to special commissions sent out by Cardinal Wolsey to inquire into depopulations caused by landlords since Michaelmas 1488, though some of the alleged changes went back to at least 1486. For the first time royal government was trying to enforce a statute enacted in 1489. The presentments of enclosers were followed by prosecutions by the crown. Altogether at least 482 localities are known to have been named to the commissioners of 1517/18,[6] with the greatest number in the Midlands. While Professor Beresford writes of at least seventy-five Warwickshire localities depopulated between *c*. 1450 and 1520,[7] fewer places in that county were investigated by the commissioners than in Leicestershire or Northamptonshire. It does look as if a large proportion of Warwickshire places particularly vulnerable to depopulation, followed by enclosures for pastures, had suffered that fate already by 1485. This agrees with Rous's list of nearly sixty localities and confirms the view of John Hales. To a lesser extent his conviction that particularly numerous villages wholly or partly disappeared by 1485 most probably applies also to other Midland counties, but it is very difficult to prove this. Outside Warwickshire we must, in most cases, mainly use the evidence produced to Wolsey's commissions.

How landlords managed to evict tenants still remains largely a mystery. Historians have discussed the legal weaknesses of manorial custom in many villages giving imperfect security of tenure to the populations of these localities. But this assumes that evictions occurred only when the tenurial framework made this legally possible. In Lawrence Stone's words, 'The fortunes of different classes of tenants varied arbitrarily according to the hazard of their legal circumstances.'[8] That is true. But it remains mysterious how some landlords were able to evict *at the same time* quite large numbers of people (the eviction of 120 is the largest number in a single village reported to Wolsey's commissions). Prolonged harassment of tenants combined with threats of evictions at the slightest legal opportunity may have achieved some of the mass evictions. I am assuming that violent use of force, or threats of the same, may have accounted for many of these tragic expulsions, particularly during the disordered years 1450–85. There is some concrete evidence of lawless procedures. I shall be considering all these possibilities in some detail in section IV of chapter 15.

In Warwickshire the area chiefly affected consisted of the Knightlow and Kineton hundreds in the south-east of the county, known as the Feldon region, with its northerly boundary running above the valley of the Avon. Its prolongation further east covered much of Leicestershire and parts of Northamptonshire. These were areas of heavy clay soils, capable of yielding good harvests, but requiring much effort in cultivation and liable to produce disaster if there was too much rain.

> Even today the farmers of southern Warwickshire require a good dry spell before they can tractor-plough their heavy clays. If they are able to do so in a dry autumn then the action of winter frost breaks down the heavy clods and sowing in a dry spring is easy. But if a wet autumn is succeeded by a wet spring, the land may never be ploughed in time to crop that year. . . . A succession of only two wet autumns and springs would . . . bring famine to peasants farming the heavy clays.[9]

The localities with these heavy soils were better suited to pasture than to arable. From the point of view of agrarian efficiency the replacement of arable by pasture in this belt of land could represent agrarian improvement and so it has been treated by some modern historians.[10] Thus, those parts of Leicestershire (chiefly in the south and the east) which underwent much conversion to pasture in the Tudor period 'have remained for the most part in permanent grass to this day'.[11]

Unfortunately, in the later Middle Ages this Midland region was one of the most densely populated areas of the open-field countryside.[12] Its peasantry had to remain arable farmers and practise their agriculture within a traditional and tightly organized system of communal arrangements. It was a system of farming that offered a maximum of obstruction to piecemeal and painless enclosure.[13] In the conditions of the fifteenth and sixteenth centuries wholesale enclosures in the open-field parts of this Midland area were often only possible through complete destruction of the previous village communities. And this was a region where these displaced people found it difficult to exist anywhere else, because it was so overpopulated.

Parts of East Anglia, especially eastern Norfolk, were also areas of dense population. But, as is stressed by K.J. Allison, few depopulating enclosures were presented here to the commissions of 1517/18. Some of this region had sufficient pastures. Where this was not the case, the special features of East Anglian field systems, combined with elaborate arrangements for adequate manuring of arable, made changes from arable to pasture unnecessary, and often even undesirable. There were conflicts between peasants and landlords arising out of overgrazing by some of the latter, but this problem became acute usually only in the sixteenth and seventeenth centuries.[14]

The period covered by this chapter consists of two distinct economic phases. From *c.* 1440 to *c.* 1485 transformations of arable into pasture were a way for landlords of minimizing their difficulties during a time of generalized economic crisis in the middle decades of the century. The years from the accession of Henry VII to Wolsey's inquiries into depopulation were a time of accelerating expansion for the English cloth industry and for the export abroad of its products. There was a growing demand for wool. Unlike in the previous period, where cattle-farming was as profitable as raising sheep, or even more so, conversion of arable into sheep pastures was the more prominent feature of the changes revealed by Wolsey's commissions over the years 1488–1518, though soils most likely to be very wet remained more suitable for cattle than sheep. An inhuman feature of many recorded evictions was their concentration in winter or autumn, often late autumn. A notable expansion of population and a more general agrarian boom occurred mainly in the second half of Henry VIII's reign, but that is outside the scope of this book.

II

The word 'enclosures' has often been used to sum up the changes leading to rural depopulation, but that word covers only some of these happenings. The preamble to the statute of 1489 speaks not of enclosures but of 'great inconvenyances which daily doth encrease by desolation and pulling down and wilfull waste of houses . . . so that the husbandrie which is one of the grettest commodities of this realme is gretly decaied'.[15] Besides, the term 'enclosures' involves ambiguities. As will be explained more fully later, some enclosures were *good*, desirable; only those leading to decline in the growing of food-crops and to depopulation were *bad*. Secondly, 'the enclosures which caused indignation and the breaking down of hedges were those in which a lord or his tenant rode roughshod over the rights of others'.[16]

Besides, depopulation was not necessarily caused merely by conversion of arable to pasture followed by the fencing of these closes. The same evil consequences could result from combining smaller farms into one larger unit. This was known as the 'engrossing of farms' and might result in evictions of previous, lesser landholders. Such engrossing of farms was occurring in every part of the country, and, unlike conversions of arable to pasture, followed by enclosures, was not mainly peculiar to the Midlands. In 1489 the earliest Tudor statute against depopulation referred to nothing else. It was concerned only with the Isle of Wight, where the engrossing of farms was leading to an alarming shortage of inhabitants and was endangering its defences.[17]

The communal customs of the open-field villages of the English Midlands, with which I shall be chiefly concerned here, were, apparently, a cultural inheritance of the people settled there. If we want to single out an important *economic* feature of open-field arrangements, this consisted in the need to organize tightly its entire farming in order to make the most effective use of such pasturage, often inadequate, as was available to them. Hence the number of animals each landholder was allowed to put out to pasture on the common waste was often 'stinted', that

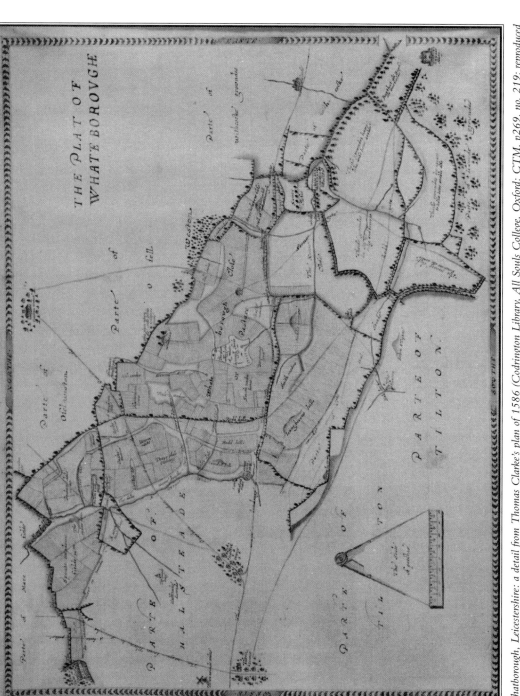

THE PLAT OF WHATEBOROVGHE

Whatborough, Leicestershire: a detail from Thomas Clarke's plan of 1586 (Codrington Library, All Souls College, Oxford: CTM, p269, no. 219; reproduced by permission of the Warden and Fellows of All Souls College, Oxford)

number being related to the size of each person's holding. Pasturing on the commons of an excessive number of animals by manorial lords, or by the men who leased from them manorial demesnes, was a potent cause of conflict. It caused more local riots in the sixteenth century than any other happening,[18] and was one of the experiences that impelled landlords, or their lessees, to take over the entire manors and enclose them.

In an open-field village the arable had to be used for pasturage when not under crops. This meant that each unit of cultivation (each of the two or three main fields) had to be sown with the same crops, so that harvesting could take place at the same time. If more varied and individualistic crop rotation was desired, it could only be done by enclosing one's arable, but in a typical open-field village this was often very difficult, as each landholder's arable was likely to consist of strips scattered through all the main fields. However, in some places the manorial demesne was owned in compact blocks, which did permit its enclosure without destroying the tight open-field discipline of the rest of the village. This happened in 1501 at Cotesbach in Leicestershire, where Thomas Grey, Marquis of Dorset, took over 100 acres of demesne, held hitherto by five lessees, and enclosed it,[19] while the enclosing of the rest of the village was delayed until the next century. But if a manorial lord, or the principal farmer of his demesne, wanted to proceed to a really extensive expansion of animal husbandry, usually this could only be done by destroying completely the communal disciplines of an open-field village. The tenantry had to be deprived of their usage of the common waste and of the right of access to seignorial meadows after hay had been harvested. An end had to be put to the regime of cultivated strips scattered through the arable fields. Usually only the eviction of all, or most, of the tenants could ensure all this. Enclosure was, however, expensive and, once carried out, could not be lightly reversed. When in 1469 Leicester Abbey enclosed its estate at Ingarsby in Leicestershire, in order to maintain the manor's seignorial flock of 400 sheep, the enclosed land was surrounded by a fence and a ditch at a cost of £74 11s 9d.[20]

Of course, it was widely recognized that enclosures were likely to increase the productivity of land by promoting more efficient exploitation. Arable closes could be better manured, permitted more varied crop rotation and, on good soils, could even be cropped continuously, dispensing altogether with a period of fallow. Pasture closes could be grazed more carefully than the open stretches of commons. Even John Hales, the most determined enemy of depopulating enclosures of the early Tudor age, acknowledged that 'experience sheweth that tenauntes in common be not as good husbandes [husbandmen] as when every man hath his part in several'.[21]

In the Arden region of north-western Warwickshire, where there was much forest and abundant pastures, enclosures did not cause depopulation, as piecemeal enclosures for improved arable cultivation were easy and enclosures by agreement among most of the landholders in a village could be arranged. Thus, 'at some time between 1445 and 1472 sixteen half-yardlanders of Sambourn agreed that all of their land would be kept several at all the times of the year; they consolidated their holdings by exchanging scattered strips of land, erected hedges and gates, and agreed to keep them in good repair'.[22] These were the *good enclosures* and contemporaries exempted them from condemnation. But enclosures which led to displacement of people caused distressing social and financial consequences that outweighed in the eyes of several leading Tudor statesmen any economic advantages. These were the *bad enclosures* and the target for parliamentary statutes and royal proclamations. One of the most eloquent was Protector Somerset's proclamation of 1548 reminding the king's subjects that 'his Realme . . . must be defended ageynst the enemye with force of men . . . not with flokes of sheepe and droves of

Aerial photograph of the fields of Water Eaton, Oxon., showing underneath their surface the medieval pattern of ridge and furrow (By permission of the University of Cambridge Committee for Aerial Photography)

beastes'.[23] As late as 1607, when the contribution of enclosures to agricultural improvements was becoming increasingly appreciated, John Norden, a professional surveyor and a very experienced advocate of such improvements, nevertheless denounced depopulating enclosures as the 'bane of common wealth, an apparent badge of Atheisme and an argument of waspish ambition or wolfish emulation'.[24]

A succession of Tudor statesmen tried to do something to check this evil: Wolsey, Thomas Cromwell, Protector Somerset, Secretary Robert Cecil.[25] But John Hales put his finger on the chief obstacle to any effective government action when, in his proposals for legislation in 1548, he insisted on bypassing the justices of the peace. They and their class were truly among the chief enclosers and evicters. In his third bill, introduced into parliament in 1548, he proposed that surveys of pastures were to be made annually by the parish priest and two parishioners associated with him and the offenders against the law were to be presented for trial. Parliament refused to enact this.[26]

The desirability of effective legislation, but also a recognition of how little it would really restrain landowners, comes from a speech of an anonymous Member of Parliament in 1597 preserved among the papers of Secretary Robert Cecil. He refers to the persistent lobbying of the great sheep-farmers against the proposed legislation: 'the ears of our great sheepmasters do hang at the doors of this house'. He contrasted the proposed 'trifling abbridgement to gentlemen' with 'balancing of the misery of the people and the decay of the realm's strength'.[27]

The main area of large-scale enclosures of former arable, followed by permanent conversions to pastures, was well defined in Thomas Cromwell's statute of 1536 against depopulation and conversion of ploughland to pasture. Except for the Isle of Wight, it was to apply only to a 'group of counties in central England extending from Lincolnshire and Nottinghamshire, south to Berkshire, Buckinghamshire and Hertfordshire, east to Cambridge and west to Worcestershire'. It included the counties that formed the core of the problem, 'Leicestershire, Rutland, Warwickshire, Northamptonshire, Bedfordshire and Oxfordshire'.[28]

Since the writings of Edwin Gay at the start of this century there has been a tendency among some historians to minimize the extent of forcible depopulation and to balance it against the benefits of increased agricultural efficiency. But, seen in the narrower context of the Midlands, it was a very disturbing experience for the peasantry of this most densely populated region of open-field England.[29]

Most of the statistics published so far are clearly incomplete and underestimate the amount of depopulation, of loss of arable cultivation and of social upheaval. Nor can this be merely a matter of statistics. Such evictions as occurred must have sent shudders of fear and insecurity through the entire countryside of the Midland counties. We find one echo of it in the pitiful statements to Wolsey's commissions: the jurors repeatedly expressed their belief that many of the victims may have perished.[30] Even if no immediate eviction threatened the peasants of a particular village, it was very disturbing for men to watch the progress of enclosure in and around it. The Midland peasant saw only 'more cattle and more sheep in the closes. He saw rich farmers taking up more and more land but giving less employment than ever before to the labourer.' It was difficult to keep a balanced outlook when one's livelihood or that of one's neighbours was at stake or might soon be destroyed.[31]

III

Various factors have to be considered in order to explain why numerous Midland villages and hamlets were partly or wholly enclosed in the fifteenth century and the first two decades of the sixteenth. That many of these changes occurred on soils more suited to pastures than arable cultivation provides one major explanation. On the higher ground of the Wolds of eastern and southern Leicestershire and the adjoining areas, further to the south-west of High Northamptonshire, lands covered by heavy, hard-to-drain boulder clays, the greater prevalence of enclosures for pasture between *c.* 1450 and *c.* 1520 represented a return to widespread pastoral usage in the earlier Middle Ages.[32] Besides, the Midland area, landlocked and debarred from transporting its crops cheaply by water, was not a region where there could be highly profitable corn production catering for distant markets. Most Leicestershire farmers produced corn chiefly for their own subsistence, and the market for any surpluses they might have was limited.[33] As an anonymous defender of the Midland graziers pointed out in 1607, cattle and sheep, unlike corn, did not need to be transported but could walk to the buyers.

However, all this does not suffice to explain why some villages disappeared while their neighbours, on similar soils, continued to survive. In earlier chapters I have mentioned a number of localities where loss of population occurred over periods of varying length in the late fourteenth and the first half of the fifteenth centuries, as one peasant after another withdrew from

Hillesden: this aerial photograph shows the surviving pattern of rectangular fields produced by Parliamentary Enclosure and beneath it a 'fossilized' medieval landscape of earthworks and ridge and furrow (By permission of the University of Cambridge Committee for Aerial Photography)

shrunken settlements to more promising places. This process was quickened by the economic depression of the mid-fifteenth century. Few of the Midland villages completely depopulated either then or in the early Tudor period had many inhabitants;[34] 'It would have been difficult, indeed impossible, for a landlord, however ruthless, to depopulate a large village.'[35] Thus many of the localities which disappeared in the Midlands had been decaying for a long time beforehand.[36] But destruction could come to not over-large but still quite viable village communities suddenly and brutally. The worst case of depopulation presented to the commission of 1517 was at Dodershall in Buckinghamshire, where, on 11 August 1495, Thomas Pigott, a leading lawyer ('*serviens ad legem*'), evicted twenty-four tenants, each holding a virgate of arable. The jury said that this involved 120 persons reduced to extreme poverty, who withdrew weeping and, according to the jury, perished.[37] The personality of the owner was an important fortuitous factor in the matter of depopulation. An example is the Feldon region of south-east Warwickshire, where the most numerous destructions of Warwickshire villages occurred. Coventry Cathedral Priory owned a number of Feldon estates and no serious depopulations occurred here until the dissolution of the priory in the late 1530s, because from the early fifteenth century it had been an easy-going landlord, leasing several demesnes to its tenants and showing no interest in expanding sheep-farming.[38] Of great importance also was the tenurial composition of the population in each village.

The increase in lawlessness through Henry VI's weak governance, exacerbated later by the disorders of the Wars of the Roses, may have facilitated the forcible evictions of 'inconvenient' tenantry. Some of the magnates were showing brutal indifference to what their followers were doing to hapless peasants. Bishop Edmund Lacy of Exeter recorded in his register that, during the private war between the Earl of Devon and Lord Bonville, in September 1451, some of his own tenants at Clyst, just east of Exeter, 'dared not occupy the land'. Worse was to happen at the end of 1455. After Lord Bonville had been defeated near Clyst Bridge on 15 December, this 'unleashed a systematic campaign of assault and looting' by Devon's men directed against Bonville's 'associates and tenants' in south-east Devonshire, which went on for nearly two months.[39] In January 1469 three armed men belonging to what Colin Richmond justifiably calls 'the Duke of Norfolk's mafia' despoiled one of the demesne farmers of the Pastons of three good horses. The vicar of the village of Tichwell (Norfolk), where this outrage occurred, appealed to the Pastons' chief bailiff to help the poor farmer who was 'likely to be undone'.[40] The civil wars also led to numerous confiscations of estates, which were subsequently granted afresh to new owners, who might be more likely to have recourse to radical innovations.

In the second half of the fifteenth century, the belief that the rearing of cattle and sheep was likely to be more rewarding than arable exploitation, or the dependence on declining rents from tenants, was shared by landlords in many parts of England. Some evidence about this has been discussed in earlier chapters. Such an enterprise was likely to be most profitable if carried on at a large, compact grange or a number of such units fairly near each other.[41]

The potential economic gain from changing an arable village into a large pastoral grange can be admirably illustrated from the estate of the Catesbys at Radbourne in south-eastern Warwickshire. This was a typical open-field village, where a vast pastoral estate could only be created once the landlord had appropriated all the common pasture, evicted all the tenants from their arable holdings and enclosed the entire locality. The Catesbys had gradually accumulated in the later fourteenth and early fifteenth centuries a considerable number of estates in the Midlands, chiefly in Warwickshire and Northamptonshire. The man whose agricultural enterprises chiefly concern us here was Sir William (d. 1478 or 1479), a devoted Lancastrian until 1461, a household squire of Henry VI (1453–61) and five times sheriff of Northamptonshire. The manor of Radbourne, belonging to the Catesbys since 1369, was initially a conventional manor, with the seignorial income derived from arable demesne, some pastures and tenant rents. In 1386 it was valued at £19. The rents still amounted then to £5 8s 10½d. By 1443 it had been entirely converted by the Catesbys 'to a single pasture without any arable or tenants', and in 1449 it was said to be worth £64. A breeding flock of sheep, kept there by the Catesbys, numbered 1,643 animals in 1448, but 2,742 in 1476. There were also a dozen cows in 1447/8, but as many as 54 in 1476, and the whole herd of cattle consisted in that year of 183 animals. A part of Catesby's enterprise consisted of purchases of young cattle from local peasant farmers or in a number of cattle markets of Warwickshire and Worcestershire. The purchases included animals brought by Welsh drovers. A century later, in 1560, there were 2,000 acres of pasture at Radbourne.[42]

In other parts of the country, where natural pastures were much more abundant, the turn to intensified animal husbandry could occur with little or no disturbance of arable farming.[43] This was, for example, happening on the estates of the Duchy of Lancaster in Staffordshire and

Derbyshire. A number of its manors adjoined large areas of forest, with abundant pastures. There had been a temporary fall of income from the sale of herbage in the 1450, and early 1460s, but by the early years of the next decade it was rising again. The pastures were used for horses, cattle and pigs much more than for sheep.[44]

In 1467 Richard, Earl of Warwick, thought it worth while to take back into direct management six closes and parks in his lordship of Middleham in northern Yorkshire. They were restocked in 1468/9 with 324 head of cattle and over 1,800 sheep, purchased at a total cost of £771 16s 7d. The dramatic ups and downs of his political career in 1468–71, ending with his death in April 1471 in the battle of Barnet, impaired this enterprise before it had time to prove itself.[45]

In all these three examples the importance of cattle, pigs and horses, alongside sheep, deserves to be stressed. Likewise, the Cistercian Fountains Abbey in Yorkshire was in the fifteenth century, when it still retained direct control over its numerous granges, as much a cattle-rearing (especially dairy-producing) as a sheep-rearing establishment.[46]

Sir Thomas More's *Utopia*, published in November 1516, castigated in unforgettable words the transformations of arable into pastures for sheep. He spoke of the houses of a depopulated village reduced to one 'shepehouse' placed in a former village church,[47] and of 'sheep [which] had become so great devourers and so wild that they eat up and swallow the very men themselves. They consume and destroy and devour whole fields, houses and cities.'[48] It was probably true of the time when he was writing that the keeping of increased flocks of sheep was one of the most obvious causes of these changes. This situation went back to at least the reign of Henry VII, when steadily rising exports of cloth stimulated an ever-growing demand for wool. By the later years of his reign cloth exports recorded in customs accounts were certainly higher than they had ever been in the past.[49] But enclosures before 1485 seem often to have been as much for cattle as for sheep.

Warwickshire and Leicestershire were the two counties with the highest number of depopulated localities. Exact statistics are not possible and some places were only partly depopulated. Writing in 1950, W.G. Hoskins knew of at least one-sixth of the villages of Leciestershire which disappeared between *c.* 1450 and *c.* 1600 (some 60 localities out of 370).[50] The number in Warwickshire was, apparently, higher.[51]

The main early settlements of corn-growing farmers in Warwickshire appear to have occurred on the easily ploughed and well-drained soils of the Avon valley and its tributaries. South-east of the Avon lay the Feldon region of heavy clay soils. Originally covered by forest, it was largely cleared for agriculture by the time of Domesday. It could provide rewarding harvests, but only at the cost of heavy labour with numerous plough-teams. In the early centuries of the Anglo-Saxon settlement Feldon villages had the use of the abundant pastures in the woodlands and heaths of the Arden region to the west of the Avon valley.[52] But connections with these were lost and by the thirteenth century the Feldon villages had to organize tightly their open-field economy in order to utilize to the full for pasture their common waste and their arable when not under crops. If their manorial lords wanted to expand their flocks of sheep and herds of cattle, they could only do so through wholesale enclosures of those villages and evictions of the tenants, as the Catesbys had done at Radbourne. This was the principal area of enclosures and of much depopulation. In the Arden region of western Warwickshire agrarian 'progress' could take place with hardly any depopulation and there, unlike in Feldon, deserted villages were rare.

John Leland's description of Leicestershire dates from 1535–43 and he visited several parts of

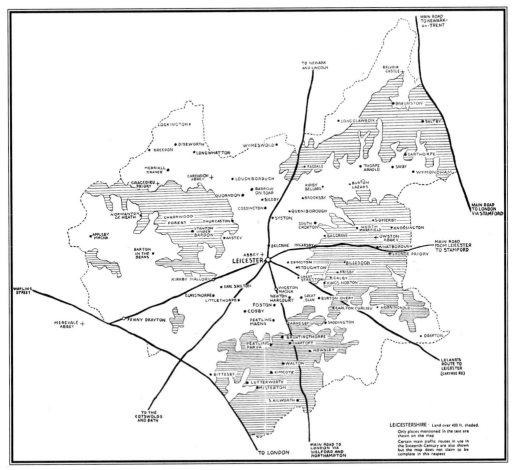

A map of Leicestershire indicating higher ground (where many of the depopulating enclosures took place) and naming many of the localities enclosed by 1550 (from W.G. Hoskins Essays in Leicestershire History, Liverpool, 1950, facing p. 128; reproduced by permission of Liverpool University Press)

it.[53] He described the south and the east as the open–field region.[54] It was 'a sea of clay dotted with small islands of . . . sands and gravel'.[55] Rye, which needs permeable soils, could only be cultivated on the latter and was rare. Only a small proportion of crops could be sown in the autumn. The heavy clay soils needed four or five ploughings each year for wheat and barley. Pasture had to be strictly stinted in this part of Leicestershire and there was very little woodland. Only in the west of the county did Charnwood Forest provide extensive pastures.

In the open–field region covering much of Leicestershire there were few spare pastures. Intensified animal husbandry by landlords was only possible after evictions of tenants and enclosures of parts of villages or of entire localities. It was, admittedly, a region wonderfully suited to conversion into vast enclosed pastures.[56] Only in the area inside and near Charnwood Forest are there no deserted villages, though much piecemeal enclosure did occur gradually for the better keeping of dairy herds.[57]

To return to my initial question: why were some Midland villages enclosed and depopulated

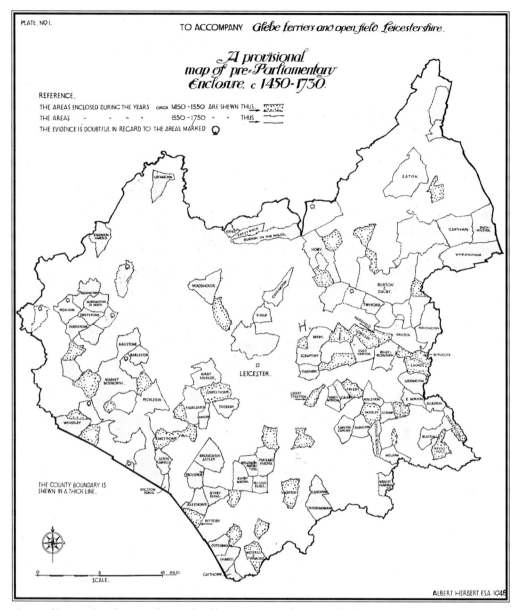

A map of Leicestershire showing villages enclosed between 1450 and 1730 and indicating separately localities enclosed between c. 1450 and c. 1550 (from W.G. Hoskins, Studies in Leicestershire Agrarian History, *Leicester, 1949, facing p. 76; reproduced by permission of the Leicestershire Archaeological and Historical Society)*

while their very similar neighbours escaped this fate? Differences in the tenurial position of the great majority of the inhabitants of otherwise similar villages often provide the essential explanation. The tenantries of some villages, for legal reasons, were much more vulnerable than the people of other localities.

Complete enclosure of an open-field village could only be carried out if all, or most, of its arable, was controlled by the lord of the manor, or the farmer leasing it from him. If all, or most of the cultivated strips scattered through the principal fields were held by peasants with no secure legal titles – the descendants of the former servile tenants – the lord could get rid of them. If there was a substantial element of freeholder tenants this would be well-nigh impossible, unless the lord was a great secular magnate, like the last Stafford Duke of Buckingham (executed in 1521), who thought that he could do as he liked.

The common waste of village, providing its main reserve of pasture, was open for use by all the landholders, but only freeholders could challenge in the royal courts its enclosure by the manorial lord, or by the farmer leasing from him. If only a few unimportant free tenants were present in a village, they might be persuaded to sell their arable and their claims to common waste, or might be intimidated into doing so. The presence in a locality of a substantial element of free tenants effectively protected their formerly servile neighbours from a threat of eviction.

I shall discuss in chapters 15 and 17 the legal situation of customary tenants at the end of the fifteenth century and try to explain why in the Tudor period, and later, their descendants often remained vulnerable to seignorial pressures. Here one need only quote R.H. Tawney's summing up. What was needed to protect them would have been the assimilation of customary tenures to the legal protection of freeholds. 'As it was', the descendants of the servile tenants 'were left fettered by the remnants of the legal rightlessness of the Middle Ages, without enjoying the practical security given by medieval custom, and felt the bitter breath of modern commercialism'.[58] One should add that the weaknesses of the tenurial position of many of them enabled landlords to transform gradually their customary tenures into short-term leaseholds. Once that happened, ultimate evictions became easy. Leicestershire furnishes several contrasting examples of adjoining villages experiencing different fortunes. Dr W.G. Hoskins has provided a fascinating study of Wigston Magna, four miles south of Leicester.[59] This was the biggest Leicestershire village recorded in Domesday Book, with some eighty-six landholders, fairly equally divided between free and servile tenants. In the fifteenth century, after sharing in the economic decline of its region, its population had diminished, but it still contained a vigorous community of free landholders in possession of perhaps 40 per cent of its arable. This was quite sufficient to protect the remaining 60 per cent of arable, divided between two different manors (desmesnes and servile tenants' land), from any threat of depopulating enclosures. Wigston was only enclosed in 1766 by a parliamentary Act.

At Knaptoft, 6 miles south of Wigston, however, Domesday Book mentions only two free sokemen and eighteen or twenty servile tenants. At that time 90 per cent of the arable belonged to its lord or his servile dependants. This pattern persisted for the rest of the Middle Ages. In 1269–79 there were some thirty-two households in Knaptoft. Later, new lords, the Turpins from Northumberland, who acquired the manor in the later fifteenth century, had it fully enclosed and turned into pasture by 1507. The principal enclosed fields were then leased to Thomas Bradgate of Peatling Parva, one of the richest men in Leicestershire.[60]

Bittesby, at the extreme southern tip of Leicestershire, was a flourishing village in the late thirteenth century. In 1279 it contained twenty-three villein families, each with a virgate of land, but only two free tenants, who shared a virgate between them. In October 1494 the Earl of Shrewsbury evicted the entire population of sixty people. The village, which maintained then nine plough-teams, was turned into sheep and cattle pastures.[61] This was one of the inhuman, autumnal mass evictions about which I shall have more to say later.

IV

A self-portrait of John Rous (d. 1491), from the Latin Warwick Roll of John Rous (By permission of the College of Arms: Ms. Cat. 39)

John Rous (d. 1491), a well-educated and idealistic priest in the service of the Earls of Warwick, was convinced that depopulating enclosures in his beloved Warwickshire were an economic disaster due to 'the plague of avarice' of greedy men.[62] He lumped together enclosing monasteries and leading lay notables. He was a scholarly student of the antiquities of Warwickshire and was shocked by its depopulation in the course of the fifteenth century. He presented a petition against it, no longer extant, during the Coventry Parliament of November 1459.[63] Presumably, Rous considered that some specific royal intervention could achieve results and could check depopulating enclosures by landlords or the farmers of their manors. The chief business of the Coventry Parliament was the proscription of Richard, Earl of Warwick, and other Yorkist lords defeated earlier that autumn. A petition about the fate of Midland peasants, especially as it was coming from one of Warwick's chaplains, was not likely to receive any attention. Rous presented similar petitions to subsequent parliaments, but always in vain, as he sadly recognized.[64] He returned to these deplorable changes in a work written a quarter of a century later,[65] in which he listed sixty villages 'of which the farthest is not much more than 13 miles from the town of Warwick', mostly in Warwickshire, though a few in Gloucestershire and Worcestershire.[66] Rous recognized that some of the places mentioned by him had been only partly depopulated. He made some mistakes about the people whom he regarded as responsible. Also, some of the villages had been depopulated earlier than Rous supposed. Thus, Hatton by Hampton Lucy had been deserted already in the late fourteenth century through the gradual migration of its inhabitants and not through any forcible eviction.[67] But the vast majority of the places listed by Rous had really dwindled or disappeared in his lifetime. He was apparently right in attributing the ruin of some to deliberate acts of landlords and demonstrably right in describing them as enclosed for parks or pastures.

Many of the places mentioned by Rous have been identified by modern scholars, though some have vanished utterly from any location on modern maps. Rous is our only detailed source for mass depopulation in the fifteenth century in one part of the Midlands before 1485. Indeed, using both his evidence and a variety of other sources, Professor Beresford, in 1951, knew of seventy-two localities in Warwickshire which had disappeared between *c.* 1450 and 1485; though not necessarily, in all cases, through forcible evictions of tenants. Be it noted that Wolsey's commissions in 1517/18 revealed only twenty-one more localities in that county where depopulation was alleged to have taken place after 1488.[68] It looks as if the great bulk of the villages and hamlets which their lords desired to depopulate and enclose had already suffered that fate in Warwickshire before the time of Henry VII, just as John Hales asserted.

Occasionally later reminiscences do reveal cases of deliberate depopulation in the middle of the fifteenth century. In 1440 Sir Robert Whittingham was given licence to empark 200 acres on his manor of Pendley in north-western Hertfordshire. This was probably the cause of its depopulation. In 1506 it was remembered that in the 1430s, it had still been 'a great town', where there were 'above 13 ploughs beside diverse handicraftsmen, as tailors, shoemakers and cardmakers . . . The town was afterwards cast down and laid to pasture' by Whittingham.[69]

Usually our evidence about depopulation becomes fairly full only for the years between 1488 and 1517/18 through the presentments to Wolesy's commissions and subsequent prosecutions of the alleged offenders. These sources provide the names of the numerous villages in the Midlands and, on a smaller scale, also for Lincolnshire and parts of Yorkshire.

Once, referring to Billesley Trussel (now Billesley, slightly to the west of Stratford-upon-Avon), Rous explicitly says that all the inhabitants had been expelled ('omnibus expulsis').[70] In some localities 'independent sources seem to confirm his [Rous's] version of events'.[71] Among the Warwickshire properties acquired by the Verneys before 1430 was Compton Murdak (now Compton Verney). The village had been declining earlier, with large arrears of rent revealed by a rental of 1406. Some of the landholders were tenants of the rectory appropriated to the Church of St Mary's at Warwick, which recorded in its accounts that these people had been 'expelled' by Richard Verney, probably in or about 1447. A rental of 1461 shows that there were extensive pastures there and it is mentioned by Rous among the 'destroyed' villages. He says that only a church and a manor-house remained, although formerly it had had twenty-seven holdings, either of villeins or free tenants.[72] Rous presumably got this figure from some record later than the Hundred Rolls of 1279, which attribute forty-one landholders to this manor.[73]

Another destroyed place listed by Rous was Caldecote (Calcutt in Grandborough), on the border of Warwickshire with Northamptonshire. It was held by Coventry Priory and a court roll of 1474 mentions the dismissal of three tenants from the tenements there, though some freeholders remained. Each of the three removed customary tenants is described as 'dimissus . . . de tenemento predicto'.[74]

In 1447 the Verneys acquired Chesterton Magna, to the east of Stratford-upon-Avon. By 1484 it belonged to John Peyto. According to Rous it had once had seventy-nine holdings, of which only three were left. In 1484 two tenants, who seem to have been freeholders, brought an action in the King's Bench for themselves and on behalf of other tenants complaining of the appropriation by Peyto of the common pasture, presumably by enclosure.[75]

Rous also mentioned three localities that can be identified as Hodnell, Chapel Ascote and Radbourne. This was a huge ranch for cattle and sheep owned by the Catesbys in the south-eastern corner of Warwickshire. There is little doubt that they were all enclosed by that family, who, presumably, also got rid of all the tenants.[76]

Acquisition of a manor by an enriched former native of it could spell disaster. Cestersover, north-east of Coventry, was not a large hamlet and it was declining by the middle of the century. It was not in an area of much enclosure. Henry Waver, who originated from it, but had prospered as a London draper and alderman in 1465–70, acquired it in 1460–6 and proceeded to turn it into a park in the latter year.[77]

For eleven places Rous gave the previous numbers of tenants, which he derived in part from the Hundred Rolls of 1279, as he himself mentions. These rolls recorded over three hundred landholders; by Rous's time in each village there were very few or none.[78]

In Rous's view the destruction of previously inhabited and corn-growing localities had contributed to shortages of corn, especially in years of bad harvests, so that poor people, who could not afford to pay the enhanced prices, were dying of hunger. He stressed the general decline in the demand for goods that had diminished trade and hit craftsmen.[79] In greater detail he described the growth of insecurity. Because of the destruction of Church Cherwelton, just inside Northamptonshire, where people travelling from Warwick to London had sought refuge in the past, travellers now had to deviate from the route which they had formerly followed. Cawston-over-Dunnismore, south-west from Coventry, once on the main route from that city to London, was now bereft of inhabitants and had become a hide-out for robbers and murderers, so that the former road had become dangerous. Rous blamed the Cistercian monks of Pipewell for this, as it was their grange.[80] He ended his list of lost villages by invoking God's vengeance on men who out of greed had caused these disasters.

Rous was justified in deploring the decline of food supplies in Warwickshire through the destruction of many corn-growing villages in the Feldon region. Coventry was still the largest city in the Midlands, particularly vulnerable to the scarcities of corn around it. There was one such crisis in the winter and spring of 1520, after an exceptionally bad harvest.[81]

Before 1488 we lack anything comparable to Rous's and Dugdale's evidence for the other Midland counties. Only very few cases can be adduced with certainty for Leicestershire. There is evidence of depopulating enclosures before 1485 in at least five localities.[82] Ingarsby, in the east-central part of the county, was enclosed, and apparently depopulated, by Leicester Abbey in 1469.[83] The hamlet of Hamilton, slightly to the west, belonging to the Willoughbys of Wollaton, was depopulated between 1423 and 1477,[84] and Keythorpe, to the south-east of Ingarsby, was depopulated by its new owner, Thomas Palmer of Holt, between 1450 and 1460.[85] At North Marefield in the same district, slightly to the north-east of Ingarsby, John Hartop, probably farming the village from Owston Abbey, sued four husbandmen in 1463 for hunting his sheep with dogs on his pastures and killing forty. This points to reprisals for at least partial enclosure and this village certainly became entirely depopulated by the mid-sixteenth century.[86] All these enclosures were in the eastern part of the county, where there were to be many more after 1485. The only exceptions were Woodcote, on the western border, changed entirely into pasture between 1446 and 1468,[87] and Castle Donington, likewise in the west, where some enclosure had started by 1482.[88]

Evidence of violent attacks by Leicestershire peasants on enclosed pastures raises a presumption that they were avenging wrongs suffered previously. In 1448 a husbandman of Hoton, north of Leicester, was charged with breaking down the enclosure of Richard Neel, a Justice of Common Pleas, and ploughing his pastures. Hoton never became a deserted village. Two other incidents concern villages fully enclosed only in the seventeenth century. In 1463 four husbandmen, allied with a merchant of Leicester, were accused of invading the enclosed pasture of the lord of Frisby, a little over 7 miles to the east of Leicester. They had pastured their own animals on it. A man who had leased 360 acres of pasture from the Abbey of Garendon at Eastwell complained in 1490 that his land had been forcibly ploughed up by a number of people.[89]

Farmers leasing the demesnes of ecclesiastical or lay landlords were responsible in several localities for high-handed enclosures with evictions[90] and they were dreaded for this reason by

Aerial photograph of the former arable fields of the village of Hamilton, Leics., showing the ridge and furrow pattern.
Hamilton was enclosed before 1500 (By permission of the University of Cambridge Committee for Aerial Photography)

peasants under their authority. Quinton, in the extreme south-western corner of Warwickshire (in Feldon), was one such village. It was bought by Bishop William Wainfleet of Winchester in 1475 and was subsequently given to Magdalen College, Oxford, which the bishop founded in 1480. An undated petition, probably in the mid-eighties (before Wainfleet's death in August 1486), addressed by the tenants to the President of the college, complained that John Salbrygge, the deputy farmer, had evicted several cottagers, each of whom had held customary tenements of between 1 and 3 acres out of the demesne arable, without compensating them for the crops that they had sown. Also 'for evyll wyll that he had' to the township he had ploughed up 30 leys of the common pasture. The tenants begged that he should cease to farm the demesne, as they were well nigh destroyed by him.[91]

Some time between Wainfleet's death, in August 1486, and August 1493, Thomas Elys, rector of Quinton, wrote to Richard Mayhew, President of Magdalen College, begging him not to renew the lease to Salbrygge's master, by name of Rose.[92] If his lease were to be renewed, he claimed that the village would decay further and nobody from outside would come to settle there. Elys reminded President Mayhew that Bishop Wainfleet, shortly before his death, had wondered whether it would not be better for the village if the community of the tenants were to take over the farming of it. Elys believed that President Mayhew inclined to this advice, but only if the tenants were to offer more in annual rent than any single farmer. Elys was begging him to desist from such auctioning of the manor to the highest bidder.

Elys was an Oxford MA. In his letter he combined practical considerations of continued revenues from the tenants with more idealistic considerations. He urged that it would be better

Lower Quinton, Warks.; this village was saved from enclosure in the late fifteenth century (Warwickshire County Record Office: PH 350/1699)

to support the community of the tenants than one man, 'yowr tenantes rathere then a strong man, the pore and the innocent a for [before] a gentylman or a gentylmans man'. He argued that, although there could be a short-term advantage in having a single farmer, in the long run the village would survive better if leased to the tenants, whose number, so he hoped, would increase again. He pleaded that the manor should be leased to the tenants for an annual rent of not more than £30, and that it should be shared among the eight tenants, or among a few of them on behalf of the others. He suggested that three might farm it together with him, acting for the rest, and he was prepared even to be the sole farmer on behalf of all the tenantry. The college appears to have accepted his arguments and Quinton survives to this day as a village.[93]

V

There has been a trend among some historians to question the credibility of much of the evidence presented to various royal commissions active between 1517 and 1607 inquiring into depopulation and enclosures. Scepticism has arisen out of the fact that presentments against particular landlords were followed up by a much smaller number of known prosecutions. Furthermore, Dr Eric Kerridge has demonstrated that not all the presentments about unlawful enclosures and depopulations were *legally justified*.[94] Some landlowners were able to show that the enclosures had taken place before Michaelmas 1488, or that they had been carried out not by themselves but by previous owners of these estates.

To disregard the evidence of depopulations because of absence of information about later prosecutions or because of the rebuttals of the charges on various legal grounds may be convincing to a lawyer and this tends to be Dr Kerridge's inclination. Other historians have been persuaded into caution by his publications.[95] I find such caution excessive. Most of the presentments made before the various commissions appear to have been true. Failure to follow up many of them by prosecutions can be explained on other, political or legal, grounds. Besides, as Dr John Martin has shown in the case of the accusations made to the commissions sitting after the 'Midland Revolt' of 1607, Dr Kerridge had considerably underestimated the number of prosecutions that did take place.[96] The same is probably true of the earlier prosecutions in the Tudor period. In any case, absence or presence of prosecutions does not diminish the credibility of the original presentments, nor do the acquittals of some of the landlords on grounds that do not disprove the truth of statements that depopulations had actually taken place. As Dr Martin has pointed out, 'Kerridge is unable to provide *one* instance in which an encloser was positively adjudged to have been innocent.'[97] He wrote this with special reference to the proceedings in and after 1607, but the same comment might be applied to the majority of the presentments made to the successive Tudor commissions. It is also true that a large number of presentments before the various commissions speak of only very few houses being demolished and very few tenants evicted. The cumulative effect on the countryside was nevertheless very considerable. It must also be stressed that the dismissed charges cited by Dr Kerridge do not include any of the brutal cases of mass eviction. Nothing written by him or other historians impressed by his arguments alludes to the inhumanity of mass expulsions, in autumn or winter.

In fairness to Dr Kerridge, one should also cite his initial recognition that the 'returns of inquisitions of enclosure and depopulation cannot be used as evidence of the extent of depopulating enclosure'.[98] This is very true of the commissions of 1517/18, which are the principal concern of the rest of this chapter. Kerridge stresses that most of the 1518 returns cannot be found, and that subsequent proceedings supply the deficiency only in part. His concluding remark is that 'it is not impossible that the area actually enclosed exceeded any that can now be deduced from the returns of the enclosure commissioners'.[99] This is patently true. I find Dr Kerridge's very cautious wording of this final conclusion to be unnecessary. Apart from the indisputable incompleteness of the evidence that we still have, there were other strong reasons why presentments should disclose only a part of depopulations. One must assume considerable hesitations of juries in presenting some notoriously violent and dangerous notables. The constable of Ascot in Oxfordshire and three husbandmen of the village complained to the Court of Requests that they had been threatened with the termination of their farms and ending of their tenancies because of the statements they had made to the commission of 1517. Cardinal Wolsey, in inquiring into the charges against the bailiff of Bungay in Suffolk of procuring evictions, was certified that the special commission sent there did not dare to proceed, as the bailiff had merely been carrying out the instructions of his master, Thomas Howard, Duke of Norfolk. The bailiff, backed by the duke's steward, had refused to give any answers.[100] It should be noted that Norfolk was the Lord Treasurer of England. John Hales mentioned varieties of malpractices over the behaviour of juries making presentments to the commission of 1548.[101]

As for the legal proceedings, Dr Kerridge assumes that the 'courts were entirely neutral in applying the law'. This is at variance with everything we know about that society. Sir Robert Brudenell, one of the favourite lawyers of Henry VII and of his mother and a royal justice from 1507 onwards (Chief Justice of the Common Pleas in 1521), earlier, in December 1496, had been responsible for a brutal mass eviction on his newly acquired manor of Holyoak in Leicestershire.[102]

In the cases of the evictions by Brudenell just cited, and of a number of others revealed in 1517/18, destruction came to some fairly viable villages suddenly and brutally. This may have been the result of political accidents. Steane in southern Northamptonshire was confiscated in 1485 with the other estates of Francis, Viscount Lovel, Richard III's Chamberlain. Sold by the king to Thomas Barker, it suffered the fate of other properties regranted to new owners, who were likely to introduce radical innovations.[103] The same thing happened at Wormleighton in the much depopulated area of Feldon in Warwickshire, near the Northamptonshire border. It was confiscated in 1495 when its hereditary lord, Sir Simon Montfort, fell victim to his close connection with Sir William Stanley, whom Henry VII wanted to destroy and who was executed for Stanley's alleged conspiracy. The estate was regranted in 1498 to William Cope, Cofferer of the Royal Household, who, in 1499, proceeded to depopulate it and enclose it for pasture, turning sixty people adrift.[104]

'Something like 70 per cent of the reported enclosures in the period 1485–1550 were carried out by the nobility and the squirarchy.'[105] In each county the men of this group were closely connected through intermarriages, common activities in running the local government and similar social outlook. They knew of each other's doings and influenced each other in introducing agricultural novelties. In counties like Warwickshire, Leicestershire and Northamptonshire, once the increasing profits from conversions of arable to pasture and from the consequent enclosures were demonstrated on some estates, others followed at a rapidly rising rate. The same inference of close contacts comes from noting the identical defences put forward by landowners of the same regions against prosecutions after Wolsey's commissions of 1517/18. There are striking examples of this in Warwickshire if one looks at the defences of John Spencer about Wormleighton and of Sir Edward Belknap about the closely adjoining Burton Dassett.[106]

Aerial photograph of the former arable fields of Lowesby, Leics., showing the pattern of ridge and furrow underneath the pastures (By permission of the University of Cambridge Committee for Aerial Photography)

Leicestershire was one of the counties most affected between 1485 and 1517/18 by depopulating enclosures, mostly through the replacement of arable cultivation by the keeping of cattle and sheep. The admittedly very incomplete presentments published by I.S. Leadam show that 88.9 per cent of the enclosed land was believed to have been used thereafter as pastures.[107]

One would wish that our evidence for Leicestershire were fuller. The surviving returns for the commission of 1517 start in the middle of a presentment on 27 August and we know that the commission had started acting at least a week earlier. We have no returns for the 1518 commission. We are worse off for Leicestershire than for a number of other counties.[108] Fortunately, as Leicestershire enclosures were numerous, we have records of several subsequent prosecutions. There is also the compensation of numerous modern studies.[109]

Leicestershire, in the landlocked central region of England, formed the core of an area where men perennially dreaded dearth. Complete breakdowns of crops were no more their experience, but they feared relative shortages raising prices beyond what poorer people could afford. A long and widely held tradition, which persisted in this part of England far into the seventeenth century, 'believed enclosures to be a major cause of dearth',[110] as John Rous had believed to be the case in Warwickshire.

My account of what happened in Leicestershire after 1485 is arranged in a roughly chronological order, corresponding to the sequence of changes in different parts of the county. We start with a 'tract of rolling country' a few miles to the east of Leicester. It is a district of over 400 ft in altitude on Liassic clays,[111] covered after enclosures with very succulent grasses. Ingarsby, on the western edge of this area, had been enclosed by Leicester Abbey as far back as 1469.[112] Between about 1485 and 1502 it was the turn of Baggrave, Quenby, Lowesby, North Marefield and Whatborough, and also of a few other places, the disappearance of which cannot be dated exactly. Lowesby and Quenby were enclosed by their lords, the Ashleys, between 1485 and 1489, arable being replaced by pastures for sheep and cattle. At Lowesby, not a large place (twelve or fourteen households were listed in the Poll Tax of 1377), depopulation took place, according to later proceedings in the Exchequer, on 6 February 1487. This is one of a number of inhuman evictions in the worst season of the year, to which I shall return. Whatborough had belonged to All Souls College at Oxford since 1437. Almost from the first, the college farmed it to the Priory of Launde, 'only a mile or two' from Whatborough. The priory depopulated and enclosed it in 1494/5. It was a mere hamlet by then, with only a few peasant families. North Marefield, belonging to Owston Abbey, had suffered the same fate by 1502. In Baggrave, Leicester Abbey owned about a quarter of the village and that was the part which the abbey enclosed in 1500/1, evicting thirty people. Later it acquired some 300 further acres and, presumably, likewise enclosed those. In this one corner of Leicestershire – the lordships of Ingarsby, Baggrave, Lowesby and Quenby (some 3,500 acres in all) – only eight families were left by the beginning of Elizabeth I's reign, where once fifty or more had tilled the land. Of the eight surviving families four were squires of the Cave and Ashby families. At Lowesby the Ashbys later built the finest Jacobean mansion in the county.[113]

Somewhat to the north of Baggrave and its depopulated neighbours lay Brooksby. It had belonged since the thirteenth century to the Villiers family. Sir John was cited before the 1517 commissioners for evicting twenty-four people on 6 December 1492 and converting 160 acres to cattle pastures. He was a violent man. Thomas, Marquis of Dorset, complained in 1519 to Cardinal Wolsey that Villiers had killed two of his brother's deer and stopped a jury from trying this offence by appearing with a retinue of armed men.[114] 'Doom fell upon the little hamlet of Willowes . . . in the wolds that look across the vale to Brooksby' on 10 November 1495, when its lord, Sir Ralph Shirley, evicted thirty persons and enclosed 200 acres. According to the presenting jury in 1517 the victims departed weeping and 'probably perished' ('ex verisimili perierunt').[115]

In the south-east of the shire, 'mainly upland country that made excellent . . . pastures', is a whole series of vanished villages. Holyoak, Noseley and Allexton were presented to the commission of 1517 and figured in subsequent legal proceedings. Holyoak was one of the earliest purchases in Leicestershire of Robert Brudenell. He evicted on 2 December 1496 thirty people from several arable farms to make way for cattle pastures. The jurors stated that they may have perished. As mentioned before, Brudenell was one of the favourite legal advisers of King Henry VII and his mother, Lady Margaret Beaufort. He was knighted in 1516/17 and in 1521 became Chief Justice of the Common Pleas.[116]

Noseley lay somewhat to the north-west of Holyoak. Its lord, Thomas Hazlerigg, was cited before the commission of 1517 for converting eleven farms to pastures for cattle in 1504 or 1505. This was done in winter and fifty-one people were forced to leave the village. Allexton, very near Holyoak, was partially enclosed (60 acres) by Walter, Lord Mountjoy. Eighteen people were expelled on 2 December 1509.[117]

The tomb of George Talbot, Earl of Shrewsbury (d. 1538), in Sheffield Cathedral (Geoffrey Wheeler)

If one adheres to a roughly chronological order, one should look next to the south-western part of the county. Brascote and Naneby, both enclosed in 1499, again lay on land above 400 ft. Bradgate, enclosed in the same year, lay on slightly less high ground. Lindley, further to the south-west, bordering on northern Warwickshire, was enclosed by the last of its Hardwick lords in 1500.[118] Some of the enclosure at Bradgate was the work of Thomas, Marquis of Dorset (d. 1501). He was also responsible, as custodian of Walter, Lord Ferrers of Chartley, a minor in his wardship, for the enclosure at Brascote and of the manorial demesne at Cotesbach.[119]

The southernmost tip of Leicestershire was the site of multiple depopulations. At Bittersby the Earl of Shrewsbury evicted on 2 October 1494 sixty people, who had held between them 24 virgates, creating an enclosure of 746 acres for sheep and cattle.[120] George, the fourth earl, who was responsible for this, was one of the few great nobles who had fought for Henry VII at Stoke in 1487. His heir's income from land was put in 1538/9 at £1,735. George lived beyond his means and incurred huge debts to Henry VIII and Cardinal Wolsey.[121]

In the middle of the fifteenth century Stormsworth was still a flourishing village. It belonged to the Abbey of Selby in Yorkshire, which had gradually swept away serious obstacles to complete control by buying out the various freeholders in the village. It was enclosed and depopulated by 1500, the enclosure comprising 1,620 acres.[122] Misterton and Poultney were depopulated and enclosed by 1500, or shortly afterwards, by their lord, Sir Thomas Pulteney, a descendant of one of the leading London financiers in the reign of Edward III. In 1524 Sir Thomas had the second highest assessment in Leicestershire to the subsidy on land. At the time of his death in 1540 he owned 1,000 acres of pasture at Poultney.[123] Knaptoft was probably wholly enclosed and depopulated by its lords, the Turpins, before 1507. A final concord of that year refers to 600 acres of pasture in what had previously been 'the Middle Field'.[124]

I have drawn attention several times to the inhumanity of some of the mass evictions carried out in the autumn or winter, after the harvest had been cleared and allowing good time to prepare the conversion to pasture, in utter disregard of the misery and possible danger of death from disease and exposure threatening the hapless victims during the most inhospitable part of the year. Leadam's tabulation of dates of evictions in Buckinghamshire allows one some statistical estimates. Of the acreage presented in 1517 as enclosed 81 per cent was converted to pasture.[125] If one confines oneself to localities where at least twelve persons were alleged to have been displaced, one gets a total of 444 persons evicted between October and March. This amounts to 39 per cent of the 1,131 people said to have been displaced in that county.[126]

At Burstone sixty people displaced in March 1489 were said to have departed weeping and to have subsequently been reduced to misery. At Castlethorp, a royal manor belonging to the Duchy of York, eighty-eight persons were evicted in November 1502, weeping and reduced to begging. This was done probably by John Clark, auditor of the estates of the Duchy. The only statement of the Buckinghamshire jurors recording that the evicted people had perished concerns 120 persons evicted somewhat earlier (11 August 1495) at Dodershall.[127] Several other presentments speak of the misery of the evicted victims.

Professor W.G. Hoskins, after listing the deserted villages of Leicestershire, turned to the Midland Revolt of 1607 against enclosures and cited an eloquent manifesto of some of the revolting peasants.[128] Lord Treasurer Dorset believed that it had been written by some Puritan clergyman.[129] He was certainly a literate man with some knowledge of the past:

> Wee, as members of the whole doe feele the smart of these incroaching Tirants, which would grinde our flesh upon the whetstone of poverty . . . so that they may dwell by themselves in the midst of theyr Hearde of fatt whethers. . . . They have depopulated and overthrown whole Townes and made thereof sheep pastures nothing profitable for our commonwealth. For the common Fields being layd open would yeeld as much commodity, besides the increase of corne, on which standes our life.

The manifesto goes on to warn that, should the harvest fail again for one year, 'there would a worse and more fearfull dearth happen than did in King Edward the seconds tyme, when people were forced to eat Catts and Doggs flesh'.[130] They were resolutely desperate:

> If you happen to show your force and might against us we for oure parts neither respect life nor living: for better it were in such case we manfully die, than hereafter to be pined to death for want of that which these devouring encroachers do serve their fat hogs and sheep withal.[131]

Some of the protesters were, soon after, killed in battle or executed.

CHAPTER 13

South-Western and South-Central Shires: A Region of Conservative and Oppressive Lordships

I

Medieval agriculture in the area stretching from Wiltshire and Hampshire to Cornwall was very diversified. There have been good recent studies of different regions within this area by Dr John Hatcher (the Duchy of Cornwall), Dr J.N. Hare (Wiltshire), Dr Edward Miller and Dr H.S.A. Fox,[1] and I will not repeat their accounts. However, despite the diversity, there was one common feature. It was an area of many long-established, very conservative estates, enforcing tenaciously and oppressively the rights of lords over their dependent peasants. For example, one can discover within it some very archaic and oppressive customs about the rights of manorial lords to take all the movable goods of deceased servile tenants. In Cornwall and Devon the backwardness of much agriculture until the fourteenth century, and the consequent poverty of large sections of the peasantry made these people particularly vulnerable to seignorial pressures. In 1377 Devon was one of the most thinly populated counties of England.[2]

Oppressive and 'backward' customs, affecting adversely the lives of servile peasants, existed in many parts of England. They were particularly widespread, for example, in the northern shires. They were also very noticeable in the south-western region discussed in this chapter. Rural life in this 'Thomas Hardy countryside' was, and long remained, a grim tale of endless hardship and misery for humble men and, especially, women.

II

The distribution of the slave population in Domesday Book is probably significant. 'The western and south-western counties have the highest proportion of Domesday slaves.' This was true of all the shires studied in this chapter: Wiltshire, Dorset, Devon, Somerset and Cornwall. Two of these counties are among the three recording the highest numbers (Gloucestershire being the third). Devon heads the list with over three thousand and Somerset had over two thousand.[3]

The south-west was in the later eleventh century a region of particularly large demesnes on major ecclesiastical estates. The bishoprics of Exeter, Salisbury, Wells and Winchester, and Glastonbury Abbey (the wealthiest of the abbeys in 1086), were among 'the very highest investors' in demesne plough-teams. Large demesnes directly exploited by their lords usually required in Domesday numerous slaves. The Bishop of Winchester's great manor of Taunton in Somerset, worth £154, with thirteen plough-teams, had seventy slaves. Most Winchester manors, especially in Hampshire, Wiltshire and Berkshire, had both substantial demesnes and notable numbers of slaves.[4]

There is, in all probability, a connection between the large presence of this lowest category of

Beaulieu Abbey's thirteenth-century stone tithe barn at Great Coxwell, Berks. (R.C.H.M.E.: Crown copyright)

men and women in these counties and the heavy burdens and oppressive customs to which many of their inhabitants were subjected in the later Middle Ages. About 70 per cent of the peasants whose status is specified in the Wiltshire inquisitions in the years 1349–75 were bondmen. A sample of twenty-four Devon rentals of the sixteenth century shows that 925 tenants (74 per cent) held by customary tenure and were the successors of medieval serfs.[5] When by the late fifteenth century customary tenure was evolving into copyhold tenure, copyholds for one life (usually at most three) were common in the south-west (and western Midlands), while copyholds of permanent inheritance were more usual in the rest of the Midlands.[6]

Ottery St Mary, in south-eastern Devon, was an Anglo-Saxon royal estate. This may explain why only eight of the 129 tenants were free in 1325. It was a rich village and it was taxed among Ancient Demesne manors, though it should not have been so treated, as Edward the Confessor had given it in 1061 to the canons of Nôtre Dame at Rouen and it did not figure therefore in Domesday as royal land in 1066. The Bishop of Exeter purchased it in 1335 and tried to exact more strictly what he regarded as the rents and services due to him. This provoked considerable resistance and in 1337 the bishop was forced to make concessions that made the terms of servile tenure much more certain. The bishop gave the estate to a collegiate church which he had founded at Ottery, but troubles recurred as the tenantry invoked their alleged Ancient Demesne status. In 1377 the warden and college were owed £36 of arrears of rent (out of an annual total of £76), as the tenants were refusing to pay part of the rents due from them.[7]

On many manors of this south-western region personal servile status lingered on far into the fifteenth century, and beyond it. As late as 1533 'Glastonbury Abbey had no fewer than 215 families of bondmen on its estates.' On the Cornish properties of the Duchy of Cornwall 'very few manumissions can be traced in the fifteenth century and . . . unfree status continued into the reign of James I'.[8]

By the 1440s there had been a blurring of the distinction between the types of land held by richer peasants on many English estates, with mixed parcels of land being held by many peasants for contractual rents based on individual bargains. Clearer distinctions persisted, however, on some estates of the south-west. In 1441/2, on the Duchy of Lancaster's very valuable estate of Kingston Lacy in Dorset, the manorial account still carefully distinguished between rents paid by different groups of servile peasants: 20½ holdings of customary tenants called carters, 12 of the tenants called 'davyns', 5 called 'forhors', 20 acremen, 20 'smalemen'. While rents of free tenants amounted to £6 10s, these seventy-seven servile dependants contributed £38 14s in rents, as well as servile tallage (£2 annually). Furthermore, there were labour services commuted for money. These servile payments constituted 22.5 per cent of the total gross revenue in that accounting year. On another of the Duchy's manors, Collingbourne in Wiltshire, the proportion of servile rents, renders and commuted payments rose in that year to 39 per cent.[9]

Chew Magna and Congresbury were two of the most valuable manors of the Bishops of Bath and Wells in northern Somerset.[10] In the two accounts available to me it is impossible to isolate all the payments exacted from servile tenants, but the incomplete totals which can be assembled show that they were heavy. In the accounting year 1458/9 there were still due at Chew Magna commutation payments for 5,292 manual labour services, besides ploughing and other works. After allowances had been granted for 5½ virgates in the reeve's hands, commutation payments were exacted from 17 virgates, 21 half-virgates and 64 fardells. 4,945 manual services alone rendered £10 6s ½d. Altogether payments for commuted services amounted to £28 5s 8¼d. Rents of the servile tenants called 'overlords' came to £28 6s 8½d. These two groups of payments alone amounted together to 43 per cent of the gross receipts that year.[11] At Congresbury rents of overlords and commuted labour services (£37 5s) amounted to one-third of the gross revenue in the accounting year 1474/5. The services were due from holders of 4 virgates, 12 half-virgates and 4 fardells. Furthermore, there was a commutation of services of eighteen 'mondaymen' (small-holders working for the lord one day a week) and thirty-eight tenants liable to the Old English rent of 'gafol'.[12]

Some of the details of seignorial regulations and exactions on various manors of Devon, Somerset and Dorset also reveal heavy-handed treatment of the peasantry. It is instructive to compare the fines for entry demanded by the Percys from their tenants in different parts of England. Fines equivalent to between one and one-and-a-half year's rent were usual in the first quarter of the sixteenth century on both their northern and Sussex properties. But they were much higher in 1520/1 on their chief manors in Somerset and Dorset, varying from about three to four years' rents.[13] Presumably, the Percys were taking advantage here of what was normal in this part of the country.

Devon was a region of 'tied cottages' rented to a lord's agricultural labourers only so long as they worked for him. Around 1360, at Stokenham, 59 per cent of the labourers' cottages were attached to larger farms, like that of John Shath, who owned 180 acres with two tied cottages. At Yarcombe the percentage in 1445 was 75 per cent of the cottages and it amounted to 80 per cent at Axmouth in 1483. The practice had spread considerably after 1348/9 and 'led to some degree of debasement of the condition of some labourers'.[14]

In 1378 a servile holder of 2 virgates at Great Burton in Dorset, besides familiar bond obligations of rents, labour services and liability to heriot, 'was also obliged to take a forced loan of wheat from the lord each year and pay for it at the highest summer price current in the neighbourhood'.[15]

A directive sent in 1391 by the council of Roger, Earl of March, who was still a minor, ordered his reeve at Odcombe in Somerset to cancel the demise of a free tenement to a free man. The reeve was forbidden to allow this to happen if servile tenants could be found instead, especially when they could be made to pay higher rents. In this particular case, a prospective bond tenant was available, who would pay annually 26s 8d more. This brings out the concern of the manorial lords that their servile population should be kept intact as one of their most valued assets. There followed a further general instruction that no serf of the lord 'by blood', male or female, was to be allowed to leave the manor so long as some sort of livelihood could be found for him or her'.[16]

The lordship of Dunster in north-western Somerset, forfeited in 1461 by the Luttrells, its Lancastrian lords, was held throughout the reign of Edward IV by the Yorkist Herberts. There survive three accounts of the receiver of Dunster, from 4 March 1461 to Michaelmas 1462 and for the accounting years 1465/6 and 1478/9. The manor of Carhampton Berton, slightly to the east of Dunster, was the most valuable member of the lordship, accounting for almost half its revenue in 1461/2. This included £19 7s received from leases of 155 acres of demesne arable to local tenants, on what seem to have been very onerous terms. The leases were for only one year, consisting of 84 acres under wheat and 71 acres under barley, at 2s 6d per acre. One might assume that the land was leased already sown with these crops, but, even so, these rents were exceedingly high. The same operation was repeated in the two other extant accounts, the leases being made in each case for one year. The tenants, who had no choice of what crops they might grow, were treated as a species of sharecroppers.[17]

The town and castle of Dunster, Somerset (Somerset Archaeological and Natural History Society)

One of the most oppressive features in the treatment of servile peasants found on a number of estates in Devon and Cornwall was the right of their lords to appropriate all or a part of the goods and chattels of the deceased tenants. This operated on sixteen out of the seventeen Cornish manors of the Duchy of Cornwall and on the estates of the Abbey of Tavistock on the western border of Devon. Apart from Tavistock itself, Werrington was one of that abbey's most valuable estates. In Domesday Book twenty-five serfs were listed there. In the later Middle Ages, if a relative took over a dead serf's tenement, he had to surrender a third of the movables on it or pay their value as assessed by a local jury. H.P.R. Finberg was, no doubt, justified in remarking that 'remembering the conservative outlook of the region . . . we may be sure that most . . . of the servile burdens we find the *nativus* bearing in the fourteenth century will have pressed with at least equal weight upon his forefathers in the twelfth and the thirteenth'.[18]

On the estates of the Duchy of Cornwall the prevailing tenurial customs were enforced more systematically and effectively after its administration was re-organized in 1333. While freeholders were only liable, on the death of a tenant, to a heriot (the best beast), the servile tenants suffered the forfeiture of all their movable goods. The exercise of this inhuman custom was not normally enforced to the full: 'On the death of an unfree tenant his movable estate was valued by six manorial jurymen, the expenses of the burial and wake were usually deducted, and third part of the final valuation was allowed to pass to his widow or next heir, without charge.' These mitigations still left a more onerous burden than the one-third exacted at Tavistock's Werrington. However, a further mitigation was allowed in practice. 'Goods ceded to the Duchy were frequently resold cheaply to heirs.' But the custom remained oppressive enough to provoke in 1382 a collective petition to the Duchy's council from the bondmen of two eastern manors of Climsland and Liskeard. They alleged that their children, in order to escape utter impoverishment on the deaths of their fathers, were migrating to other places. The date of this petition, one year after the risings of 1381, may be a testimony to the influence of the Great Revolt even in counties, like Cornwall, where no violent disturbances are recorded. The servile tenantry were asking that in future they should be only liable to heriots. The request was refused.[19]

One exceptionally terrible series of events, amounting to a revolt of serfs 'by blood' against their lord, occurred in 1425–6 at Faccombe in Hampshire, near the border with Berkshire, not far from Hungerford and Newbury. In 1425 three of the lord's bondmen by blood assaulted the lord. Two of them then removed sheep and corn seized on behalf of the lord. One of them, Richard Gosyn, had already refused to accept his villein status, having failed to perform his labour services and having married his daughter outside the lordship without permission. The manorial court had failed to present this offence. Obviously the other tenants, who included thirteen villeins by blood, were supporting these acts of defiance. In 1426 occurred an awful act of violence: 'Members of the Gosyn family and others dragged the lord outside the manor-house and killed him.' Twelve villeins were implicated, of whom four were hanged or forfeited their possessions, while eight others fled.[20]

III

Cornwall had very special tenurial customs.[21] They were not peculiar to the seventeen manors of the Duchy, but they are best documented on the Duchy's estates. They were enforced there very consistently after 1333, though their origins are much older. These customs had some very harsh features, which add to the general prevalence of hard seignorial pressures in this south-western corner of England.

Between 1333 and 1406 three categories of tenants are mentioned on the Duchy of Cornwall's Cornish estates. There were free tenants, paying fixed low rents and liable to reliefs in money on change of tenants, assessed at a fixed rate. At the other end of the tenurial arc were the serfs by birth. Their burdensome liability to the escheat of the bulk of their movables on the death of each servile tenant has already been described. But their rents were fixed. As there was hardly any demesne arable on the Duchy manors, their labour services were light. They were liable, however, to a variable and heavy annual direct tax (tallage). Its peculiar operation will be explained in a moment. They were also liable to the customary servile disabilities current throughout England. These included merchet (payable by their womenfolk on marriage), chevage (for permission to reside outside the Duchy's lordship) and the need for licences to send sons to school or to have them ordained as priests. This group never comprised more than a tenth of the Duchy's tenantry. They were found in greatest number on the eastern manors bordering on Devon.[22] There is, perhaps, some connection here with the large numbers of slaves recorded for Devon in the Domesday Book. There are no references made to hereditary servile tenure as a *separate category* after 1406, though servile status persisted, with all its customary disabilities. I shall explain later, more fully, the situation after 1406. The third and by far the largest group was that of the 'conventionary' tenants. There were approximately eight hundred on the seventeen Duchy manors in 1337. This type of special tenure was widespread throughout

A carving of sheep at Altarnun Church, Cornwall (Richard Muir)

Cornwall and there is some evidence that it was also practised in Devon.[23] But it is best studied on the estates of the Duchy in nearly a century of its most rigorous enforcement after 1333.

Conventionary tenure was a type of lease that lasted for seven years. Every seventh year, at Michaelmas, all the leases were terminated and a special group of assessors offered a fresh lease to the highest bidder for each holding. The existing tenants usually had the first option, as long as nobody else was prepared to offer more. There was no manorial common waste on these estates, as parcels of arable, meadow, pasture and waste were all offered for the highest bids. Thus, no tenant had any title, except to a seven-year lease. He could be removed within that period for unsatisfactory behaviour, or if he defaulted in his dues for more than a month. Rents for each holding usually remained fairly fixed, but the fines for admission constituted the variable element and bids were made for these. As the fines were spread over six years of tenure, they were, in fact, a kind of additional rent.

Both freemen and serfs were usually allowed to bid, though a servile conventionary tenant remained liable also to personal servile disabilities and the renders mentioned earlier. The serfs who did not take up conventionary holdings would have enjoyed an advantage through their payments of fixed rents, but the Duchy administration made sure that this was not allowed to happen, by adjusting the arbitrary, servile tallages. If fines had been raised at the beginning of a new seven-year conventionary period, servile tallages would be raised accordingly. By the beginning of the fifteenth century the increases in tallages were matching the periodic rises in fines. Obviously it made matters less cumbrous for the landlord if all servile holdings were assimilated to conventionary tenure, and this was done after 1406.[24]

The arrangement was very flexible and was the nearest thing to a systematic operation of a free market in leases anywhere in England. It bore hard on those who could not compete financially, though it was mitigated by assessing new conventionary fines on each manor at variable rates, according to what the assessing commission thought possible. We also find occasional charitable treatment of tenants who had suffered misfortunes or were sick, but all this was at the complete discretion of the Duchy's officials.

The system could only function profitably under an efficient administration and constant supervision.[25] There were periods of greater laxity, for example in the reign of Richard II. The agrarian depression in the middle of the fifteenth century resulted from the fourth decade onwards (1434–1485 period) in a virtual fixity of rents and to a shift towards fourteen- and even twenty-one-year leases. On the eastern estates, where the demand for corn-growing was sustained by tin-mining and the expansion of the woollen industry, the value of land was maintained up to a point. Here new fines were merely frozen, 'in sharp contrast to the previous hundred years which had seen an almost continuous increase in them'. On the Duchy's manors in central and western Cornwall reductions had to be allowed in new fines 'in response to a prolonged slump in demand for land'. From 1459 to 1484 the annual profits of the Duchy's manors averaged just under £500, or almost 20 per cent lower than they had been in the decade before the Black Death.[26] By the early sixteenth century there was a return to seven-year leases. New fines, as well as annual rents, remained fixed henceforth and sitting tenants were normally able in future to count on the renewal of their leases.

The normal expectation of most medieval English customary tenants was that they would be allowed to succeed their parents or other close relatives in the holding of their family tenements. Manorial courts of many villages normally upheld this as the binding local custom. Landlords were accepting this, partly because it was in their interests to do so. Otherwise, displaced relatives of tenants were forced to emigrate. King Edward III voiced these customary expectations, as well as the mixture of motives that encouraged landlords to uphold them, in a letter of privy seal addressed on 1 September 1337 to the officials in charge of his Chamber manor of Burstwick in Holderness, in the East Riding of Yorkshire. He had learnt that there was a custom there denying the right of inheritance to an infant child of a deceased servile tenant and allowing a stranger to receive the tenement if he offered a fine for it. This had driven descendants of former tenants to migrate elsewhere, to their great hurt and the king's loss. The king ordered that in future the rightful heirs, or their relatives, should have the first option of offering fines for securing such tenements. The king ordered that his directive should be applied retrospectively as well as to future cases.[27]

In the late fourteenth and the fifteenth centuries, as vacant lands became abundant in some parts of the country, the customary tenants tended to be less intent on enforcing these rules of inheritance, especially as migration from their native villages might free them from serfdom without any payment to their lord. But the customs presuming the right to inherit did persist and widows of servile tenants, in particular, were important beneficiaries.[28] The situation on Cornish and Devon manors was abnormal.

IV

According to the lawyers, villeins were supposed to derive their goods entirely from the lord or his ancestors, though there is little historical justification for this doctrine. Some contemporaries in the later fourteenth century were prepared to regard as extortion the seizure by a lord of any goods which his villeins had acquired by their own efforts. In the *Parson's Tale* Geoffrey Chaucer condemns this in a passage on avarice and 'covetise' that may, in its original form, date from before 1381. He identifies such conduct with 'harde lordshipes'. After citing the opinion of some stewards of certain lords that the 'cherl' had nothing that did not belong to his lord, he bursts out: 'But certes thise lordshipes done wrong that birewen hire bondefolk thynges that they nevere yave hem.'[29]

The south-western counties were an area where such extortions continued to flourish. I have quoted earlier the harsh customs about the lapses to lords of the goods of serfs on the estates of the Duchy of Cornwall, and partial such lapses on the properties of Tavistock Abbey in Devon. Dr John Hare, in a study published in 1992, has discussed some evidence about exploitations of serfs 'by blood' on a number of estates in Hampshire and Wiltshire.[30] He noted that in Wiltshire serfdom seems to have survived more fully on the chalklands in the eastern part of the county, with their combination of large expanses of arable cultivation and sizeable flocks of sheep, 'a reflection of the greater traditionalism of this area'.[31]

The information comes mainly from properties of ecclesiastical landlords. They were keeping a systematic record of families of the richer serfs by blood, as only those could be profitably mulcted. It was a dwindling group and, therefore, all the more a target for careful surveys. Sir John Fastolf at the Wiltshire manor of Castle Combe, Winchester College at Durrington in the same county, Glastonbury Abbey on its eight Wiltshire properties, and the Cathedral Priory of St Swithun's, Winchester, owning some thirty properties mainly in Hampshire and Wiltshire, were all taking care to record which of their customary tenants were unfree, or seeking to keep a note of the movements of their villeins. St Swithun's Priory was spending money on lawyers to assess the adequacy of evidence that a man was a villein.[32]

Sheep at Castle Combe, Wilts. (Wiltshire Record Office: Local Studies Library)

Over parts of the south-west many landlords profited from the expansion of the textile industries in the fifteenth century. One feature of this lay in attempts to exploit those textile merchants and manufacturers who were alleged to be of servile status. The Nunnery of Amesbury did this in the third quarter of the century by claiming as its serf John Halle. He was one of the principal merchants of Salisbury in the mid-fifteenth century, at a time when it was still the leading marketing centre for Wiltshire cloths. He served four times as its mayor. Yet he was accused by the Prioress of Amesbury of being her bondman. Her officials went so far as to seize some of his property. After arbitration in 1468 by George, Duke of Clarence, Amesbury Nunnery had to acknowledge publicly the freedom of Halle and of his family.[33]

One of the most outrageous cases occurred at Castle Combe in the north-western industrial textile region of Wiltshire. It shows how a particularly grasping lord, Sir John Fastolf, a veteran commander in the French wars, could squeeze a fortune out of his richest bondmen by merely enforcing his customary rights over them. Fastolf was taking advantage of the expansion of Castle Combe, with its production of fine red cloths as well as undyed white ones, by expecting his steward to let any vacant holdings to the highest bidder.[34] One of the most prosperous manufacturers was his villein, William Heyne, who, starting from very little, had built up a flourishing textile business. At his death in 1435 he owned not only a corn mill and a fulling mill, but also a gig mill, the earliest such device recorded in England. (It was used to raise the nap on finished cloth, preliminary to removing the sticking out portions and producing a smooth surface.) 'Hitherto the nap had been raised by the tedious process of drawing teasles over the whole surface of the cloth by hand.' By using a gig mill 'the cloth could be passed over a roller set with teasles and kept whirling by being attached to the spindle of a water wheel.'[35] At Heyne's death Fastolf's council chose to pretend that Heyne's goods alone were worth £2,000.

The local jury, which was clearly friendly to Heyne's widow, scaled this down to the net value of £200. They achieved this result partly by allowing for Heyne's outstanding commitments at the end of his life, such as £30 spent on the rebuilding of his house and £20 he had contributed to the rebuilding of the tower in the village church. Margery Heyne, his widow, had to pay £40 for permission to remain in her main dwelling and for the recovery of personal chattels. In 1437 she had to offer £100 for permission to remarry and to re-enter her late husband's remaining properties (including his industrial installations). Her new husband also had to pay a further fine of £40 for admission to his wife's property. On Margery's death in 1455 only £4 was exacted from her son, Thomas, to inherit his father's land, and in 1463 he was mulcted of a further £20 as the price of his manumission from serfdom. In the space of twenty-eight years Fastolf and his successors had extorted £204 from this one bond family. This figure excludes a fine that William Heyne had had to pay in the penultimate year of his life for the marriage of his two daughters and the annual rents that Fastolf was receiving from the Heyne tenements, which certainly surpassed £1 a year.[36] It is not surprising that in the less conservative parts of south-eastern England, which were also undergoing rapid industrialization, persistence of villeinage was regarded with abhorrence by the more prosperous villeins, as I have already illustrated from the example of Thaxted in Essex.[37]

CHAPTER 14

Some Evidence of the Effects of Warfare on Particular Regions or Estates

I

One of the aspects of the late medieval history of England and Wales that urgently requires much more research are the effects of warfare on agrarian economy. I have touched on this incidentally in other chapters, noting what was happening in Devon and in northern England in the middle of the fifteenth century.[1] In this chapter I will discuss some evidence about the effects of the invasions of the counties bordering on Wales by the followers of Owen Glyndŵr. The comparable ravaging of countryside and towns by the Lancastrian army descending from the north in January and February 1461 is also considered. The other incidents discussed here deal with two glimpses of how the Wars of the Roses affected particular estates or their peasantries. This is a subject on which very little has been published so far. I shall glance at the urgent attempts of Henry Holand, Duke of Exeter, to raise money from his estates for the warfare of 1471. A more detailed inquiry will be devoted to Elizabeth Luttrell and her activities in the lordship of Dunster in Somerset during the years 1461–85. Her husband, Sir James, who was reputed to have killed in December 1460 the father of King Edward IV,[2] had died of wounds suffered in a later battle in 1461. His lordship of Dunster was given to a prominent Yorkist, William Herbert, Earl of Pembroke, but his widow managed to appropriate and retain some of Dunster's revenues, partly, it seems, by violence and self-help. Her story has special features which probably make it untypical. One wonders, however, whether other similar occurrences, affecting estates and peasants on them, might not be discovered.

It is true that the properties of the leading participants in the civil wars continued to be administered in a routine manner. 'The accounts of the estates of Richard, Duke of York, in eastern counties for various years between 1447 and 1460 show no signs that their lord was engaged in a civil war.'[3] The account for 1459/60 of the reeve of Richard, Earl of Warwick, at his important estate of Elmley Castle (Worcestershire) invites a similar comment, though the failure to pay customary fees of £26 13s 4d (including 20 marks due to the Countess of Warwick) may point to some stringency or, perhaps, to the reeve's uncertainty about the future fortunes of his master.[4] However, there is an urgent need for a systematic scrutiny of all relevent accounts of the embattled magnates, most of which are still unpublished.

II

My account of the devastation and economic decline caused by the attacks by the Welsh followers of Owen Glyndŵr on the Marcher lordships will be confined to what happened in the Marches adjoining Cheshire and Shropshire.[5] It is not a simple story of devastation, as in some of the lordships, notably Denbigh, Chirk and the western areas of Oswestry, some of the local men joined the Welsh invaders, thus augmenting the number of subsequently deserted holdings. Plundering and destruction by English troops also added to devastation and general insecurity.

The town of Ruthin was partly burnt on 18 September 1400, in the initial Welsh attack and a few days later the town of Oswestry was largely destroyed by fire, but most of the countryside of its lordship was not seriously damaged at this stage.[6] With the exception of the Arundel lordship of Chirk, badly hit from the start by the rebellion of the earl's own officials and tenants, widespread devastation of the northern portion of the March was not caused by the Welsh raids until early in 1404. The mill at Sandford, in the eastern part of the lordship of Oswestry, which was farmed at £4 13s 4d a year was burnt by the Welsh raiders in the last week of January 1404 and all income from it ceased.[7] In April 1404 the inhabitants of Shropshire claimed that a third of the county had been ravaged by the rebels.[8] There followed another devastating raid into Shropshire in 1406 and, according to a tax roll, inhabitants of twenty-two localities around Shrewsbury were said to have fled.[9]

The long-term effects of the depopulation and destruction that I have been describing varied greatly. Further south, in the parts of the March and of Wales I shall not be discussing, recovery was speedy. This was true of the Bohun and Lancaster lordships.[10] In the region covered by me here, Ruthin seems to have suffered no enduring harm.[11] But in most of the lordships bordering on Shropshire there was prolonged decline. In the Mortimer lordship of Denbigh, for example, there was no income in most commotes (administrative districts) between 1405 and 1408. The revenue in 1406/7 (£114) amounted to only 15 per cent of that of 1396/7 (£749). The decline, though to a diminishing degree, continued henceforth for many years. 'It seems . . . that the lords' hold was permanently weakened. . . . They paid heavily for the exactions of their ancestors in the fourteenth century.'[12]

The years 1396–1404 were probably the most prosperous period in the late medieval history of the Talbot lordship of Whitchurch. At the start of the fifteenth century its annual value amounted to about £320, with the demesne farm alone yielding £47. The Welsh raid of 1404 changed all that. Much of the town was burnt, though the manor-house escaped destruction. In 1407/8 Whitchurch produced only 42 per cent of the annual revenue that it had yielded before 1404. The town mill was destroyed and was only reopened by 1411. The combined farm of the mill and tolls on trade, which had yielded £40 in 1403, produced only £7 16s in 1411.[13]

Moving south-west from Whitchurch one comes to the two Arundel lordships of Oswestry and Chirk. In the lordship of Oswestry only minor free tenants of the western parts joined the rebels in any numbers.[14] While for a few years after early 1404 the collapse of the lord's income was almost as complete as at Chirk, this was due mainly to the mass exodus of the bond tenantry whose houses had been burnt and whose livelihood had been completely ruined. The lists of these tenants in the previous years show that most of them bore Welsh names and held land by Welsh customary tenures.[15] Owen Glyndŵr's followers were here ruining Welsh peasants.

The account of the bailiff of the easterly townships of Sandford and Woolston for 1403–6 makes pitiful reading. While in the previous year the net revenue (cash deliveries and expenses) had amounted to £11 0s 3d, in the disastrous year of 1404 they dwindled to £4 10s 10½d. The bailiff asked for an allowance of £1 15s for renders of various tenements where houses had been burnt and tenants despoiled, so that the land lay wholly uncultivated and devoid of any labourers. Some of the tenants had fled into distant parts. An allowance was also requested for £2 3s 4d for lands controlled by the rebels. The financial situation was even worse in 1408/9. Cash deliveries and expenses declined to only £2 0s 11d. As late as 1410/11 the demesne could not be farmed as no one would take it.[16] In Ruyton, east of Sandford, £49 6s 3d of normal seignorial revenue had to be written off in 1406/7, after a fresh Welsh attack in 1406.[17]

In the more westerly Arundel lordship of Chirk there was for a while a complete collapse of the earl's revenue. The chief reason seems to have been the adherence to the rebels of some of his officials as well as of many bond tenants. The men of Chirk had been treated in the fourteenth century far more oppressively than the tenantry of Oswestry. Around 1400 the leading officials owed large debts, which may explain why some of them turned against their lord. The rebellious bond tenants deserted their holdings. As the lord's account puts it, no revenue was received in 1404/5 'because the tenants had become rebels'. The total collapse of income may have persisted for more than a year. The Welsh raiders were specially intent on destroying seignorial mills, both as symbols of seignorial authority and as valuable sources of the earl's income. Many of them were never rebuilt. The various farms at Chirk, including the leases of mills, had yielded £146 17s in 1397/8 but the revenues from them in 1407/8 dwindled to only £50 and they were still virtually as decayed in the following year (£52).[18]

The rebellion had undermined both the authority of the Arundel lords and the financial basis of their power. As late as 1416/17 the revenue from Chirk, of £173 17s, was smaller by some £200 than it had been in the late fourteenth century.[19]

III

Plunder by armies was inseparable from warfare. However, the ravages committed by the Lancastrian army moving from the north of England towards London in January and February 1461 were on a scale that vastly surpassed anything that happened elsewhere during the Wars of the Roses.[20] In the earlier warfare both the royal commanders for Henry VI and their Yorkist opponents had tried to prevent serious plundering in order to avoid popular hostility. In the motley Lancastrian host led south by Queen Margaret those restraints disappeared. The worst outrages were committed by her Scottish allies and by the English levies from the northern border innured to savage fighting and raiding against the Scots. These thoroughly undisciplined elements in her army were above all intent on plunder, though they were guilty also of outrages against women and other defenceless people. Villages were burnt. They treated the countryside that they were traversing as if it were foreign, enemy country.

According to the last portion of the so-called *Davies Chronicle*, covering the years 1450–61, and written probably shortly afterwards, the advancing army left a 30 mile wide swathe of destruction in its wake.[21] Admittedly some of the towns ravaged and partly destroyed could be treated as legitimate targets for a Lancastrian army. Stamford, the most important of them, formed part of the Duke of York's lordship. Some of the others, including Grantham in Lincolnshire, Huntingdon and Royston (Hertfordshire) also had Yorkist connections. Two towns clustering round major abbeys suffered the same fate. Peterborough was one. After the Lancastrian victory at St Albans on 17 February 1461 Margaret's troops ransacked both the town and its great abbey.[22] Rumour exaggerated still further the menace from this lawless host. Londoners were in terror of its approach. As a contemporary ballad by a Londoner, *The Rose of Rouen* (Rouen was Edward IV's place of birth) put it, 'we lived in mickle dread'.[23] A popular movement in London put an end to any attempt by its authorities to let Margaret's army into the city and compelled her return to the north, with her army continuing to ravage as much as before. The mass revulsion in London against this menace had saved the Yorkist cause.

Two later instances of plundering were specially notorious. The victorious Lancastrian right wing at the battle of Barnet, on 14 April 1471, followed the fleeing Yorkists into the village itself and started pillaging it. Their absence from the main battle contributed to the final victory of Edward IV. The English soldiers returning from the invasion of France in November 1475 plundered in Hampshire and Wiltshire and were ruthlessly punished for this by Edward IV.[24]

IV

Henry Holand, Duke of Exeter (1430–75, duke from 1450), was one of the most unscrupulous and brutal magnates of his time.[25] 'Cruel and fierce', a contemporary observer called him.[26] He was a consistent Lancastrian and, hated by Richard, Earl of Warwick, and a host of other enemies, he had no choice of being anything else. He returned from exile in February 1471 during the last months of Henry VI's 'Readeption'.[27] His estates were in the possession of his wife Anne, sister of King Edward IV. She had long been estranged from Duke Henry and was living with her lover, Thomas St Leger.[28] As a leading supporter of the newly restored Lancastrian regime, Duke Henry could not be denied access to his former properties.

Duke Henry's period of influence was brief, lasting only from February 1471 to the defeat of the Lancastrians at Barnet on 14 April. Henry did manage to get away and sought sanctuary at Westminster, but he was removed from there in May and lodged in the Tower of London.[29] His wife's officials had been forced to hand over some money to him while he was still influential. It is likely that he was desperately trying to raise money upon receiving news of Edward IV's return to England on 14 March and foreseeing a grim civil war in defence of Lancastrian rule. The payments that Duke Henry received from his wife's bailiffs appear as arrears requiring allowance from Anne in an account for the estates of the duchess for 1471/2.[30] We gather from it that Duke Henry had managed to collect money from the Holand estates of Stevington in Bedfordshire, Great Gaddesden in Hertfordshire and some Northamptonshire properties.[31] The various bailiffs who had to make those payments also claimed allowances for the expenses that they had incurred in doing this. The total came to £23 0s 5d, a tiny proportion of the income from Holand estates. One might conjecture that he might have obtained larger sums from the household and central financial officials of his wife.

My story of Elizabeth Luttrell extends over the whole period of the reigns of the Yorkist kings (1461–85) and beyond it. Her husband, Sir James, died before 4 March 1461 of wounds sustained in the second battle of St Albans.[32] Reputed to be the man who, on 30 December 1460, killed King Edward IV's father,[33] he had been attainted in the first parliament of Edward's reign and his lands were declared forfeit on 4 November 1461.[34] By Michaelmas 1461 all the Luttrell lands had come into the custody of Richard Willy, the receiver of William, Lord Herbert, Edward IV's chief representantive in south Wales. Apart from the Luttrell estates all his other properties were in Wales.[35] The core of the Luttrell inheritance was the lordship of Dunster along the northern coast of Somerset, but there were also two manors in Devon and two in Suffolk.[36] In the year from Michaelmas 1461 to Michaelmas 1462 Lord Herbert's receiver charged himself with £252 8s 8¼d due from the lordship of Dunster, out of which he delivered £216 to his master.[37]

Elizabeth was a member of the family of the Courtenays of Powderham, a junior branch of the Courtenay Earls of Devon. Her seven brothers were a warlike and formidable group.[38] This helps to explain her capacity to assert what she regarded as her rights against Lord Herbert's officials. In September 1462 Elizabeth was demanding the restoration of her jointure. The resultant official

The gatehouse of Dunster Castle, home of Sir James Luttrell (d. 1461) (Geoffrey Wheeler)

inquiry treated 29 December 1460 as the date of her husband's treason and forfeiture. That was the day before he killed Richard, Duke of York.[39] This was a legal fiction and she received after that date various sums from some of the estate bailiffs who do not seem to have regarded this as improper. I shall return later to the details of those payments.

The evidence about the sums which Elizabeth received 'normally' or collected forcibly comes from two account rolls for the revenues received by Lord Herbert in Somerset and Devon in 1461/2 and 1465/6 (in both cases from Michaelmas to Michaelmas). The first of these is partly damaged, but the missing items can be supplied from the second account, which contains a fuller record of what Elizabeth received or appropriated to herself.[40] In adding up all those items, I have tried to avoid counting anything twice and my total may be a slight underestimate. Certainly between 1461 (or late 1460) and Michaelmas 1465 her takings withheld from the Herbert officials amounted to at least £107 11s. Her actual income from the assets of the Luttrell estates was, of course, higher, as she exploited some of those lands.

During the earlier months of 1461 there was much confusion on the estates of the Luttrells. The royal escheator in Devon received some of the income from the two estates there in the course of that year. The officials in charge of the main block of properties in Somerset were clearly perplexed about their true allegiance. Sir James's heir was a child and Elizabeth was in charge of him. At least £17 1s 11½d was received by Elizabeth from manorial bailiffs previous to Michaelmas 1461 on three estates in Somerset and at Chilton Luttrell in Devon. Some payments to her may have been made before news of the definitive Yorkist victory at Towton (28 March) reached this remote corner of England. Of the rents for the Easter term (Easter fell on 5 April), £1 8s 5d received by Elizabeth at Chilton Luttrell might be accounted for in this way. The other payments preceded perhaps the take-over by the agents of the Herberts.

As indicated earlier, there is, however, also much evidence of Elizabeth appropriating money by forcible methods. At Carhampton Berton, slightly to the south-east of Dunster, where the bailiff charged himself in 1461/2 with £108 18s 1¾d, Elizabeth was alleged to owe 18s for diverse lands and tenements at 'Alred close'. This may be identical with the present-day Alter Farm to the west of Carhampton. Elizabeth had entered it after the death of her husband and was 'claiming hereditary right there'.[41] Her largest 'acquisitions' were at Quantoxhead, one of the eastern group of the Luttrell manors. In 1461/2 the reeve there charged himself with £43 14s 3¼d but he effectively handled only £14 4s 11d (the total of his cash deliveries and expenses), because Elizabeth had appropriated assets amounting to £28 17s 2½d. This manor formed part of

George, Duke of Clarence (d. 1478) and his wife Isabel, from the Latin Warwick Roll of John Rous (By permission of the College of Arms, MS. Cat. 39)

her jointure and she clearly thought that she should control its revenues.[42] The things she had appropriated constituted a miscellaneous collection. She had received £4 14s 6d of rents due at midsummer 1461. That may have been done peacably. A year later she could only repeat this by violent action. She collected £4 12s 6d of rents due at midsummer 1462, 'vi et armis' ('by armed force'). She had also occupied in 1461 the entire demesne sown with crops and had refused to pay anything. By Michaelmas 1465 she owed for it £58 16s 7d and had rendered nothing. She also occupied in 1461 the park attached to the manor and owed revenues from lands and pastures pertaining to it amounting to £3 15s 6d.[43]

There was also a series of other appropriations. At Carhampton Elizabeth pastured her sheep on the demesne meadow, thus diminishing in 1461/2 the bailiff's income by £1. At Ivyton (apparently near Carhampton) in 1461/2 she collected directly from tenants £4 0s 8d,[44] presumably in rents. At Kilton, east of Quantoxhead, and probably another estate of her jointure, she acquired revenues totalling £6 11s 4d, including rents due at midsummer 1461 amounting to £5 3s 4d (included in my total of £17 1s 11½d received before Michaelmas 1461, cited above). Some lesser amounts were taken at other places, which I have been unable to identify.

Lord Herbert (Earl of Pembroke since 1468) was put to death on 27 July 1469 by Richard, Earl of Warwick, at the start of Warwick's revolt against Edward IV. His chief ally at that time was George, Duke of Clarence, the treacherous younger brother of Edward IV. Elizabeth Luttrell's brothers and cousins (Courtenays of Powderham and of Boconnoc) were important supporters of Clarence. In 1470 Elizabeth's brothers and their relatives staged a revolt in the south-west in support of Warwick and Clarence.[45] It proved abortive but some of Elizabeth's brothers, the Courtenays of Powderham, managed to flee to France. They returned in the autumn of 1470 when Edward IV was in turn forced to flee into exile. Elizabeth's eldest brother, Sir William, became one of the leading men in the south-west. After Edward IV's final victory in 1471, Elizabeth's brothers, as followers of Clarence rather than of Warwick, managed to make their peace with the king. One of them, Peter, who had been secretary to Henry VI during the Readeption of 1470/1, retained the same position with Edward IV.[46] Clarence, now outwardly reconciled with Edward IV, was given on 7 April 1472 the custody of Elizabeth's dower and jointure. The other custodians were four of her brothers, including Peter.[47] This was, presumably, intended as preliminary to restoring them to Elizabeth Luttrell. The rest of Herbert's portion of Dunster was recovered by the Earl of Pembroke's widow,[48] probably through the pressure of Edward IV's queen, as her younger sister was married to Pembroke's heir. However, Elizabeth was able to enjoy her jointure and dower out of the Luttrell properties[49] and her portion is missing in the Herbert account of 1477–9 for the rest of Dunster.[50] In 1476 Elizabeth became godmother to one of Clarence's children. The arrest of Clarence in June 1477, followed by his execution on 19 February 1478, had, however, no adverse effect upon her fortunes and later in that year her brother Peter became Bishop of Exeter. The account of the receiver general of the Herberts for 1477–9 mentions some troubles among the tenants of Dunster, and Sir Giles Daubeny, the chief steward of the Herberts, received 25s 6d in expenses incurred in trying to restore order.[51] There is no evidence to indicate whether Elizabeth and her brothers were somehow implicated in this.

In 1477–9 the receiver of the Herberts charged himself with receipts from the lordship of Dunster totalling only £169 5s 4d,[52] some £80 less than its gross value in 1461/2. This would roughly indicate the value of Elizabeth's share, which she still owned at her death in September 1493. Its chief components were Quantoxhead and Kilton, Ivyton and Minehead, as well as some other properties, all in Somerset.[53] Her son, like other leading Lancastrians proscribed since 1461, was restored to his inheritance after the attainder on his father was reversed in the first parliament of Henry VII.

CHAPTER 15

Legal Aspects of Tenurial Changes

I

The disappearance of labour services on most late-medieval estates led to the emergence of two main categories of tenant holdings: firstly, contractual leases for varying periods of time and, secondly, customary tenures. The latter were likewise held for rents, but continued to be governed by the ancient customs of each manor regulating the renders and other liabilities of previously bond tenants as well as their customary claims to succession to the holdings of their relatives. In earlier chapters I have illustrated from a number of estates the emergence of this variety of tenures.[1] It is time to discuss the legal consequences of these developments. I shall also have more to say in this chapter about some features of the manumissions of former serfs 'by blood'. Lastly, I shall discuss legal and tenurial conditions that facilitated evictions of tenants in villages where their lords wanted to create parks or enclosed pastures.

By the late fifteenth century Common Law lawyers talked of customary tenures as constituting a definable legal category of 'copyhold tenures'. Sir Thomas Littleton in his *Tenures*, completed by 1481, and the only first-rate legal treatise composed in this country in the fifteenth century, included a brief account of what he regarded as a 'copyhold tenure'. He was providing a clear description for practical use by legal practitioners of what was, undoubtedly, happening by that time on many estates. He wisely qualified what he clearly regarded as a definable tenure by remarking that, 'it is to be understood that in divers lordships and in divers manors there be many and divers customs . . . and whatsoever is not against reason may well be admitted and allowed'.[2]

This was a fifteenth-century lawyer's way of looking at the England of his day. Though it had much foundation in observable facts, it was forcing into a single category a multitude of arrangements which had gradually sprung up because they were convenient, but nothing more than that. If one confines oneself to the court rolls and other estate records of numerous manors, one begins to realize that in the second half of the fourteenth century, and over much of the fifteenth, there was, as yet, no such thing as a 'copyhold tenure'. There was only a wide range of various customary tenures which, largely through the habitual inertia of manorial lords and of their officials, continued the practices of earlier times. Because of the greater complexity of the tenurial relationships on their estates, landlords often found it necessary to keep a more detailed record than in the past of the terms on which each of their tenants held their tenements. The court rolls of their manorial courts were the main repository of this information. The landlords might also make for their own use copies of entries on the court rolls concerning each particular tenant. Westminster Abbey was doing this by the middle of the fourteenth century and when many of its court rolls were destroyed in the Great Revolt of 1381, it could fall back on these alternative records.[3] Other landlords kept special registers of tenurial information, as did, fortunately, the Abbey of Ramsey. Its *Liber Gersumarum*, a register of fines received from new tenants as well as of some other payments made between 1399 and 1457/8 constitutes one of my most valuable sources.[4] Periodically new rentals were created by some landlords, like the series of such documents drawn up by the Bishops of Worcester. From their estates comes also a record of inquiries into arrears of revenues and of tenurial problems from 1452/3.[5]

Individual tenants were increasingly seeking copies of the entries on the manorial court rolls admitting them to their holdings. This gave them a feeling of increased security in case of any challenges to their position. Those 'copies' might, indeed, have set out more fully the terms of their tenure than the more summary entries on the court rolls. 'It is possible, for example,' that on the Westminster estates 'the permission to sublet was sometimes spelt out in the copy, but not in the roll'.[6] But the tenure of the customary tenants was not *validated* by the possession of such 'copies'. Not every manor had court rolls. The holding of courts involved trouble and some expense. Lesser landlords could be discouraged from holding them. Even if court rolls existed, no copies of entries on them were necessarily issued to tenants.

In the conditions of the late Middle Ages, where the main preoccupation of most landlords was to retain as many as their tenants as possible, it did not make much practical difference to tenants whether they possessed or did not possess copies of their admissions to tenements. Where dispute arose, the manorial court roll itself was the record that was inspected. If tenants had dated copies, that simply made it easier to find the relevant entries, thus sparing the lord's officials the tedious task of searching through numerous rolls. Dr Barbara Harvey concludes her eminently sensible account of the spread of copies by remarking that, on the estates of Westminster Abbey, 'useful though copies were to the monks and their tenants, even at the end of this period [i.e., around 1500], little or nothing in the records relating to the abbey's estates suggests that customary tenure would be called after them [i.e., "copyhold tenure"], much less that, as Littleton's *Tenures* show, this had already happened in some influential circles'. The abbey's tenants were said, as a rule, to hold 'by custom' or 'by the rolls'.[7]

II

The crisis in the relations between landlords and their villein tenants in the second half of the fourteenth century and the early decades of the fifteenth initially encouraged an increase in the practice of contractual leases. Tenants secured in this way the replacement of labour services by rents. Many landlords learnt that by striking individual bargains with many tenants they might avert, or at least mitigate, an exodus of their servile dependants. As these early leases were usually for a restricted number of years, landlords could speculate that, at the expiry of the leases, they could return to more onerous terms of tenure, though, as it usually turned out, this did not happen.

Short-term leases, though spelling immediate improvements for the tenants, were not free from potential dangers.[8] Tenants could not be sure of the renewal of their leases. If not leaseholders at lord's will, though they could seek protection of the royal courts if the landlord ejected them before the expiry of the lease (the action of *quare ejecit infra terminum*), in practice it was difficult, and might be dangerous, for a villein to sue his lord in a royal court. The protection against ejection by a third party was for long inadequate, and in any case a third party could act in collusion with the lord.[9] Against dispossession by others than the lord a leaseholder could use in royal courts the action of *de ejectione firmae*, but even if he were successful, this only gave him damages and not restoration to the leased holding. In such cases full restoration did not become available until changes in the Common Law occurred towards the end of the fifteenth century.

An even more precarious tenurial arrangement was adopted on many estates of the Bishops of Winchester. The bishops wanted to fill the numerous vacant holdings resulting from the plagues of 1348/9 and 1361 by finding new tenants willing to take them on the same customary terms as previously. This often proved impossible. Some peasants, however, were willing to take them on temporary tenure for fixed payments beyond customary rents, but without any fines. They were allowed to retain them until somebody came forward who was willing to pay a fine and to hold by customary tenure.[10] Thus at Witney (Oxfordshire), exceptionally devastated by the first plague, 21 virgates were entrusted to peasants on such precarious tenure for additional payments of 1s per virgate.[11] These arrangements persisted far into the late fourteenth century.

As the fear of the return of labour services gradually disappeared, this attenuated the pressure by tenants for short-term, contractual leases. Landlords, for their part, despaired of a return to earlier conditions, and feared a new set of tenurial relationships could emerge. On the estates of Westminster Abbey in the period immediately following the Black Death, 'when tenants were reluctant to take holdings in villeinage on customary terms, if these included labour services,' there was a spread of contractual leases. The abbey wanted to keep them short, thus reserving the future. By the early fifteenth century this phase was largely over. There was no going back on the exaction of nothing except rents, but the abbey wanted to revive and maintain all the other conditions of customary tenure. In return, it was increasingly ready to grant hereditary tenure, with stable rents and moderate fines for entry paid by new tenants. On those terms the abbey was able to avert any large-scale migrations of its tenantry.[12]

A similar evolution occurred on the estates of the Bishops of Worcester, though its exact chronology differed from one manor to another. At Bishop's Cleeve in Gloucestershire, in 1393/4, thirty-one customary holdings were let at 'farm' for terms of ten or twelve years, or at 'lords will'. But by 1426 almost all holdings were treated as customary tenements paying rents of assize (i.e. traditional rents) augmented by additions for commuted labour services. Only four holdings were then held on lease. At Hanbury by Droitwich in Worcestershire parallel developments took place more slowly. Sixteen of thirty-two customary holdings were 'at will' in c. 1410, though none such are recorded in the rental of 1466.[13]

Chippenham in Cambridgeshire, owned mainly by the Hospital of St John of Jerusalem, provides an example of a manor where the same thing happened. Here changes were dramatically hastened by a disastrous fire in 1446 which destroyed part of the village. This came on top of 'the already existing economic stagnation'. A period of confusion followed. The fire marked the end of leasehold tenancies in the village. Presumably customary tenure had lost the disadvantage of labour services, and there was therefore no inducement in the apathy and chaos which followed the fire for tenants to suffer the disadvantage of short, non-hereditable leases. The chief preoccupation of the Hospitallers was to retain as many tenants as possible and to encourage them to rebuild their houses. From 1457 onwards the holders of any sizeable tenements at Chippenham all held by customary tenure. As they all had by now 'copies' of the record of their admission on the manorial court rolls, they were all 'copyholders'.[14]

Of course, on many estates contractual leases persisted for local reasons (as, for example, on the estates of Durham Cathedral Priory). In the long run it could make the tenantry particularly vulnerable to eviction, but in the middle of the fifteenth century most tenants had no need, as yet, to fear that.

III

My previous introduction to the appearance of copyholds requires a more detailed expansion. I have noted that one reason for issuing 'copies' reciting the holdings of a particular tenant was the growing complexity of tenurial arrangements. The only court rolls surviving from the estates of the Earl of Warwick are the series fortuitously preserved for their manor of Elmley Castle in Warwickshire. Their tenants might have possessed 'copies', but they are almost never mentioned. The one notable exception occurs on the court roll for 19 May 1468. It deals with the holdings of Juliana Gosc, who had died in the previous April in possession of a large, miscellaneous assortment of tenements. There were two messuages with adjoining crofts, two tofts (unoccupied houses) with some arable and enclosures, 1 virgate of arable, a further, separate holding of 9 acres of arable, and, lastly, some meadowland. On 2 November 1465 Juliana had granted a reversion of all this to William Darrell by a 'copy' made before the lord's steward, which he now exhibited. He was admitted to this complex of properties on rendering, as heriots, one ox and one cow, worth together 19s 10d. Clearly this was a very special case.[15]

Changes in tenurial arrangements were reflected in the gradual evolution of customary terminologies. In the later fourteenth century, if customary tenements were being conferred on what amounted to hereditary tenure, the servile word 'sequela' ('brood') often still continued to be used contemptuously to describe the descendants of bond tenants, as if their children were a species of piglets. Its replacement by 'heirs', previously used only for relatives of free tenants, was only very gradual. Often landlords preferred a non-committal phrase; to 'a tenant and his' ('sibi et suis'). This was, for example, the usage adopted on some estates of the Bishops of Worcester, in temporary leases and concessions for life as well as for fully hereditary tenements, as a guarantee of the prior claims of one's rightful successors.[16] In the same gradual way that the use of the term 'heirs' became common, the word 'assigns' began to creep in after 'heirs', signifying the right to sublet, or otherwise to alienate to all other persons. Mention of customary holdings was often completed by the addition of the words 'at the will of the lord' to make clear that these were not free tenements and that they could not be protected by the royal Common Law.

As was to be expected, F.W. Maitland was a masterly pioneer in tracing the changes in tenurial nomenclature in a paper published in 1894.[17] He devoted to them a section of his study of the Cambridgeshire manor of Wilburton belonging to the Bishops of Ely, which I have already cited in an earlier chapter. Here, as in eastern England generally, significant changes in terminology were first noted by Maitland in the reign of Richard II. At Wilburton their first appearance antedated the permanent leasing of the manorial demesne and the final commutation of the labour services, which occurred only around 1410. Maitland noted that a hereditary grant combined with a servile wording first appeared in 1389, when two different concessions were made to two men and their *sequelae*. Such concessions multiplied henceforth. The alternative that also appeared frequently was an admission of a tenant to hold himself, followed by his family holding after him. The general phrase used was 'sibi et suis', implying, sometimes, a hereditary tenure. The same alternation of 'sibi et suis' and 'sibi et sequele sue' appears also from the late fourteenth century onwards in admissions to tenements of the customary tenants of Westminster Abbey.[18]

The novel formula of a grant to a man, his heirs and assigns first appeared at Wilburton in the last years of Richard II. This was ignoring the older nomenclature which had abhorred any recognition that villeins could have heirs, but the servile nature of the tenure was still safeguarded by statements that these customary tenements were 'held at the will of the lord according to the custom of the manor'. Westminster Abbey, too, was beginning to use this new formula of 'heirs and assigns', together with the same words safeguarding servile status.[19] At Wilburton, in the first half of the fifteenth century, concessions of holdings to a man and his *sequela*, or '*sibi et suis*', persisted side by side with concessions to a tenant together with his heirs and his assigns. Maitland also noted that while 'very few practical traces of personal servitude remain', we read of no formal emancipation of the bondmen by the Bishops of Ely, who were still careful to preserve the record of their bondage.

At Wilburton, 'in the middle of the fifteenth century it became common to describe the tenant as holding *per copiam*'. This was happening much more slowly on properties of some other major landholders, like those of the Abbots of Ramsey and the Bishops of Worcester. Up to the middle of the fifteenth century holding 'by copy' is mentioned rarely on the episcopal Worcester estates, for instance, though some of its occurrences make it clear that lots of tenants had 'copies'. But copies seem to have been treated as desirable out of evidential convenience and not as a legal requirement. In the fully developed Common Law about copyholds, as it was interpreted in the Tudor period, land that could be shown to have once been lord's demesne could never be held as copyhold.[20] But the inquiry of 1452 into the losses of episcopal revenues expressly mentioned that a number of tenants at Kempsey who held the leases of parts of the demesne had copies recording the terms of those leases. The rents paid by them were regarded as too low. For this reason their copies were to be annulled and a more profitable lease of the demesne was to be negotiated.[21] Obviously on the episcopal estates, despite the fact that lawyers were prominent members of the bishop's council, there was, as yet, no idea that the issuing of copies had to be restricted to holders of tenements in customary, unfree tenure. The word 'copy' was being used to describe any extract from the manorial court rolls, not as a technical, legal term.

In that record of 1452 copies were mentioned only in order to document losses of revenue through admissions of tenants at lower rents than in the past. Two such investigations at Hampton Lucy stipulated that the copies of two tenants should be inspected. In both cases rents had declined. One copy was for two cottages held for combined rents of 3s 9d. The other was for a messuage and a half-virgate. In the second case there was also ordered an inquiry to discover who had made this grant. A marginal note was added that this tenement had lapsed into the hands of the lord's reeve and had been subsequently conceded '*per copiam*' according to the testimony of Hampton's '*homagium*' (a jury of tenants). This implies that other tenements may not have been conceded 'by a copy'. This is also implied by a note to an entry about a half-virgate at Hanbury by Droitwich, that it was held '*per copiam*'. At Bredon a man who held 2 half-virgates for 2s less than they used to yield was expressly stated to be doing so 'without a copy' ('*sine copia*').[22]

The *Liber Gersumarum* of Ramsey contains 4,374 entries from the period 1399 to 1457/8. Nearly five hundred of these concern fines for permissions of marriage given to servile women as well as other miscellaneous matters. The rest are fines for admissions of new tenants, free as well as unfree, though the great majority concern bondmen. Most of these fines cover admissions not otherwise recorded on the court rolls of their respective manors, so that the latter complement the *Liber Gersumarum*.[23]

When the register begins, there is virtually no suggestion of any limitation on the abbot's absolute control over the servile tenements. A typical entry in May 1399 speaks of a concession, at Cranfield in Bedfordshire, of a messuage with a virgate held 'in bondage at the will of the lord according to the custom of the manor for the term of the tenant's life rendering annually all

Threshing (The Bodleian Library, Oxford: MS. Corpus Christi Coll. 285, f. 6v)

services and customary dues, entirely as the previous tenant had held them'[24] Thereafter the pace of change varied on different estates of Ramsey. Developments were very precocious at Lawshall in western Suffolk, perhaps because of the greater freedom of many peasants in that county. Its manorial court rolls mention no hereditary concessions of holdings between 1392 and 1401, but they came to constitute the great majority of concessions between 1402 and 1456 (119 out of 139 admissions of tenants). After 1456 all the holdings at Lawshall were conceded to tenants together with their heirs and assigns.[25] But, to judge by the *Liber Gersumarum*, around the middle of the century, concessions to a tenant and his heirs tended to be made only on some of Ramsey's outlying estates and not in the core region of its properties in Huntingdonshire and Cambridgeshire. There, concessions of holdings for one life or for terms of years still predominated. When hereditary concessions were made, the older servile wording was still recurrently used, granting a tenement to a villein and his *sequela* in bondage.[26] Some of the grants for life specifically prohibited subletting without the abbot's licence. Even when the grant was to heirs and assigns, the abbot's licence continued to be required, as for example in a concession of two tenements made in May 1460.[27]

References to copies given to tenants crept in very gradually in the Ramsey records. On the court rolls they do not, as a rule, appear in the main body of entries but as marginal notes added in a different hand, perhaps later.[28] The term '*copia*' first appears in the accounting records of the abbey's chamberlain in 1450/1, though after that it recurs frequently.[29] In the *Liber Gersumarum* the earliest mentions of admissions 'by copy' are normally accompanied by a peculiar security clause, specifying that, if the tenant should default on the payment of rent, the abbot has the right to reoccupy the holding 'notwithstanding this copy' or 'notwithstanding the payment of the entry fine'.[30] The monks of Ramsey were clearly uneasy that the possession by the tenants of copies might somehow curtail their power to re-enter holdings of delinquent villeins. The use of this security clause reflects Ramsey's ineffective management of its estates and the distrust of its tenants, on which I have commented before.[31] But it also suggests that we are watching early experiments with the issuing of copies to tenants. The impression of novelty is reinforced by an entry of 20 September 1457, cited by me once before. It specifically mentions that the abbot had re-entered a tenement held 'by copy' after its tenant had fallen in arrears with rent for two years and had regranted it to a new tenant not in customary hereditary tenure but for life only, without any mention this time of tenure 'by copy'.[32]

When new tenants failed to pay the entry fines demanded of them, as they did repeatedly in the first half of the fifteenth century, the Abbots of Ramsey did not punish them by eviction, at a time when their principal fear was the acccumulation of vacant holdings. They allowed the delinquent tenants to continue in occupation subject to payments of tiny amercements of 1*d* or 2*d* each year, a sort of recognition of lordship. On the margin of the court rolls there appear against these people notes like 'land without fine' or 'not fined for'. Once tenure 'by copy' began to be recorded in the middle of the century these defaulting tenants were denied their copies and came to be labelled in the court rolls as 'without copy' ('*sine copia*'), though, in practice, they continued to enjoy tranquil possession.[33]

By the late fifteenth century a stage was reached when possession of copies by tenants was becoming fairly commonplace on the estates of some of the major landlords. This was the case, for example, on some Westminster manors. Tenants who based their claims on copies were required by manorial officials to produce them. It was likewise increasingly common for customary tenants on the estates to the Bishops of Worcester to hold their tenements by copyhold tenure. 'There is no doubt that customary tenure became tenure *per copiam* on all Ramsey manors in the latter half of the fifteenth century.'[34]

IV

In section VI of this chapter I shall be surveying evidence about some protection offered by the central royal courts to villein tenants holding unfree tenements. Only the chancery did a little in this direction during the fifteenth century. It was prepared to enforce well-documented contractual obligations and to consider cases arising out of some breaches of the custom of the manor. But only very few cases have been discovered so far in the course of that century, interesting to a student of legal history, but seemingly not of any wider social significance.

I have said enough in earlier chapters about the effective security of tenure enjoyed by numerous servile peasants over much of England in the fifteenth century. Manorial customs often protected the claims of widows of tenants to adequate maintenance and favoured inheritance by the descendants of a deceased tenant, even if he only held his tenement for life. His legal heirs, at any rate, often enjoyed, in practice, the right to the first offer of succession.[35]

Landlords continued to enforce their right to evict particularly recalcitrant tenants, but it was in their interests to do so sparingly. On the court rolls of the estates of the Bishops of Worcester Professor Dyer has noted twenty cases of evicted tenants between 1440 and 1480. Most of them forfeited their holdings for neglect or destruction of buildings, but some were evicted for not living on their holdings or for illicit subletting. Some of the disgraced tenants were thrown out for being 'badly governed'. They may have been men of whom the rest of the village community likewise disapproved. Clearly, 'forfeiture was used sparingly in flagrant cases, or the number of tenants evicted for neglecting buildings or failing to pay their rents in full would have run into hundreds'.[36]

It was a different situation if a landlord wanted to get rid of all the tenants in order to change the whole village into pasture for cattle and sheep. In the introductory section of chapter 12 I stressed that the methods used to achieve this remain fairly obscure. What needs explaining, especially, is how lords could evict a considerable number of tenants all at the same time. Historians, in their search for legal explanations, have not fully faced up to this problem. It is true that in some cases mass evictions were possible through exploiting the weak tenurial position of the customary tenants and the loopholes in the customs of their manors, making tenants very vulnerable in the face of lords determined to get rid of them. I shall look later at these weaknesses of their legal position. But, as I stressed in chapter 12, I am sceptical whether this can provide an adequate explanation in all cases. Harassment of tenants, threats of violence or actual resort to violence may have occurred quite widely to procure evictions. The actual methods used by landlords are adequately documented in surprisingly few cases. I shall have to spread my chronological net very widely, going as far as the revolt of some of the Midland peasantry in 1607. Despite their late date these Elizabethan and early Stuart examples seem to be helpful in showing what may have happened earlier.

At Cotesbach, in the most southerly tip of Leicestershire, enclosure of the whole village was the work of John Quarles, a London draper and an influential contractor for the royal armed forces. He had bought the manor in 1596 from Sir Thomas Sherley, treasurer for the continental war. Sherley had been disgraced at the end of that year for alleged frauds, his assets had been seized by the crown and Quarles had gained control of Cotesbach only in 1602. He had suffered heavy losses through this delay and was determined to recoup them speedily. There were two major freeholders at Cotesbach. He bought out one and made an ally of the other. The third, who held only 2 acres, was too insignificant to need conciliation, though he was, ultimately, compensated with some land. All the other landholders held leases which, providentially for Quarles, had all expired by 1602. He offered to renew them, but at fresh rents so high that all the tenants declined. Through influence at Court he was able to secure a royal licence to enclose the whole manor. By 1607 Quarles had converted to grass 420 acres of arable. The majority of the former leaseholders were so impoverished that they chose to depart. Three (possibly five) were actually evicted and the population of Cotesbach declined by some eighty persons. This was one of the manors where the Midland rebels destroyed the enclosures at the end of May 1607.[37]

Another late example concerns the estates of the Treshams in Northamptonshire. Sir Thomas

Tresham's heir, Francis, died in the Tower of London while awaiting trial for his complicity in the Gunpowder Plot. Recurrent payments exacted by the crown from this leading recusant family were the chief cause of their heavy indebtedness. It is not clear how they were able to continue raising the rents of their tenants and to bully them into paying heavy entry fines ahead of the expiry of their leases. At Haselbach, in cooperation with some of the manor's more prominent freeholders, Sir Thomas Tresham was able to enclose the entire arable. For himself he created by 1599 a ranch of 960 acres of pasture. His action resulted in the virtual eviction of the leasehold tenants, 'who would not, and probably could not, pay the new rents'. Not one of them remained and 'some sixty people thus lost their livelihood'. This was another manor where enclosures were destroyed in 1607, as were other enclosures on properties of Tresham's relatives.[38]

These two examples show that, while the more substantial freeholders had to be conciliated, the rest of the tenantry could be very vulnerable. If they held short-term leases they could be denied renewal of these except on ruinous terms, through increases of rent and higher entry fines. While it is impossible to arrive at precise statistics, it appears that on the majority of manors entry fines for all types of holdings remained arbitrary.[39] Threats of higher fines could terrorize alike leaseholders and customary tenants for a term of years or for a lifetime. Leaseholders and tenants for a specified number of years could be intimidated by menaces of higher fines when they sought the regranting of their tenements. Tenants for life, who might normally expect that their lawful successors could follow them, could be told that much higher fines would be demanded of those successors. Such menaces to raise future fines could be an effective weapon for forcing sitting tenants to abandon tenements some time before their terms of tenure had actually expired. This is what Sir Thomas Tresham managed to do on some of his properties.

Manorial customs more frequently prescribed fixed rents. But tenants at will could have their rents raised annually unless they were also holding their tenements for specified terms. Even then manorial customs might not protect them from rises in rents. Besides, a lord could override manorial custom to get rid of tenants, as will be shown in some of the instances that follow.

One sure way to drive out the entire farming population was for a lord to enclose the common pasture of a village and much of the common waste surrounding it. Unless there were some independent freeholders on the manor, this could be done quite lawfully, though in defiance of the manorial customs. Such freeholders as there were could be compensated, while other tenants had no legal remedies. Such enclosure could deal a shattering blow to open-field arable cultivators.

Overcrowding of the common pastures by a lord's beasts or the animals of some other powerful notables could threaten the rest of the villagers very seriously and could equally compel them to leave the manor altogether. Large flocks of sheep would make it impossible to pasture cattle, because sheep crop grass closely, leaving little for other animals. There was a drift towards such a disaster at Rotherwick in Hampshire around 1484. Richard Rythe, gentleman, was overgrazing the common with his beasts. He was threatening to ruin men who were not his dependants but the tenants of Lord Strange (son of Lord Stanley). Some of the victims were substantial yeomen. Rythe was ready to back up his activities by violence. The local curate, who appears to have been supporting these peasants, was twice attacked in his church. After the second attempt to murder him, he fled from the village.[40]

The presentments to Wolsey's commission in Gloucestershire in 1517 accused Edward, Duke of Buckingham, of high-handed procedures on his great manor of Thornbury, where at the end

Thornbury Castle, Glos., residence of Edward, Duke of Buckingham (d. 1521) (Dr Malcolm Airs)

of Henry VII's reign he started creating an extensive park for hunting. Further additions to it were made in 1515. This included the enclosure of 159½ acres of common pasture previously used by the duke's copyhold tenants. A number of his tenants at will were evicted in 1515. Evidence presented at his trial in 1521, and further inquiries after his execution for high treason on 17 May, revealed violent and lawless proceedings. The duke, with characteristic ruthlessness, had terminated leases before their term had expired, evicting not only those tenants, but also a number of freeholders. Neither group was paid any compensation while he lived. The trespass upon the rights of freeholders was completely illegal.[41]

The Pilgrimage of Grace in the northern counties in 1536/7 encouraged a conspiracy for a similar rising in protest at the king's anti-Catholic policies in northern Norfolk, in the region around the Abbey of Walsingham. The conspiracy was betrayed in April 1537. Arrests and eleven executions followed. The plot had been partly fuelled by widespread economic grievances, especially against the monopolizing by the gentry of larger scale sheep-farming. They had abused their privileged position and overridden tenants' customary rights. The conspirators complained that the gentlemen 'have done them greett wrongs and taken away theyr lyvyngs'. The plan had been to capture the gentry and take their property, killing those who resisted. The plotters were predominantly yeomen and husbandmen. Sir Roger Townshend, who played the leading part in destroying this conspiracy, had been himself engrossing pastures on his estates and incorporating them into his personal sheep-walks. During Ket's Rebellion several of his tenants joined the rising and he himself fled from his Norfolk estates to the shelter of King's Lynn (1549).[42]

V

The traditional deed of manumission normally spoke of freeing a '*nativus*' (serf) and his '*sequela*' (brood). As was to be expected, leading magnates, advised by expert lawyers, continued to use this form of words in the fifteenth century. The officials of Humphrey, Earl of Stafford, did so on two occasions, in 1440 and (probably) 1442. Each deed stipulated the freeing of the entire *sequela* already born or yet to be born. The deeds of manumission do not mention the price of liberation, but they expressly recognize the freeing of all the land-holdings, both inherited and acquired, to be held at free rents, and the earl would warrant the freed tenants' titles to these, just as would be done in the case of a grant of freehold property.[43] Bishop John Carpenter of Worcester was using almost identical wording in his manumissions.[44] A manumission by John, Lord Dudley, dating from 8 January 1449, is, surprisingly, copied into Bishop Carpenter's register and is couched in very non-standardized terms. One might surmise that Lord Dudley was not issuing such documents habitually and may have lacked expert legal advice.[45]

Manumissions of men of servile status, so that they could be ordained priests, form a special group. A man freed for this reason and presented to a living would show a record of his manumission. Thomas Childe did so in September 1445 on being presented to the church of Withington (Gloucestershire), one of the manors of the Bishops of Worcester. The register of Bishop Carpenter contains a copy of the deed of his manumission by Henry, Duke of Warwick, subscribed in the duke's own hand: 'so that he be a preste and woll that this stande in effect'.[46] A deed of manumission for this reason by Humphrey, Earl of Stafford, of one of his serfs in Holderness (East Riding of Yorkshire) contained a restrictive proviso that it would become null and void if John Hogg, the freed serf, 'fails to be ordained'.[47] The Abbot of Ramsey, an abbey notoriously tenacious of its rights, in giving license in November 1400 to William, son of William atte Chirche, its serf, 'to receive all holy orders', expressly mentioned that William 'is not manumitted thereby' ('*quia per hoc non manumissus*'). William had to undertake that in future he would 'not denigrate the abbey, but . . . will stand in the service of the abbot and his successors, if required'.[48]

The Abbey of Ramsey freed, for payments, at least eighty-four serfs in the course of the fifteenth century. It was driven to do this in order to raise additional revenues and in order to stem the large-scale exodus of its tenants. I have mentioned earlier its distrust of former serfs and its demands for guarantees that they would abstain from all legal proceedings against the monks ('*sed ab omni actione iuris et clamei sunt exclusi per presentes*'). The abbey's need of money was, however, so great that it did emancipate even the serfs who refused to grant such guarantees. Except for these security clauses, Ramsey's deeds of emancipation were in the standard form, as used by the Earls of Stafford and the Bishops of Worcester.[49]

A man's manumission could be challenged if he did not possess the deed freeing him. Hence Richard Hogg of Tredington (Warwickshire), who had lost the deed of his manumission by Bishop Philip Morgan (1419–26), secured on 12 May 1447 a fresh letter from Bishop Carpenter, confirming his freedom.[50] Presumably he had to pay for this. Matthew Oxe of Staverton (Suffolk) escaped serfdom by flight in the mid-1430s. Some twenty years later 'he made a triumphant return to his native village' and 'proudly displayed a charter of manumission, dating from 1447, to the manorial court. He gleefully paid 6*d* to have a copy of the charter recorded' on the manorial court roll. It stated that he had been manumitted under the surname of Groom, perhaps a less servile name at Staverton than Oxe.[51] In 1537 the last Abbot of Malmesbury, having acquired by a subterfuge the deed of manumission of a formerly enfranchised serf, claimed him again as his bondman, despite the fact that the abbey had received previously at least £26 13s 4d (40 marks) for emancipating him.[52]

In the summer of 1536 the House of Lords considered a bill for a general manumission of serfs throughout the kingdom: *Billa concernens Manumissionem servorum vocat [orum] Bondmen*. The Lords rejected it on the third reading on 14 July. In the eyes of the peers manumission was tantamount to the wasting of their inheritance, as the Earl of Arundel put it in a letter to Thomas Cromwell.[53] This is the only known instance, since 1381, of a proposal to abolish serfdom through general legislation.

VI

Once many customary tenants were recognized to enjoy in practice an effective security of tenure, as had happened on a large number of manors by the middle of the fifteenth century, the entries in the manorial court rolls recording the terms on which they had been admitted to their tenements acquired a new and greater legal importance. The Courts of Common Law were debarred in the fifteenth century from paying any really effective attention to these changes, though we have a few opinions of some of their judges that they ought to have done so. But from at least the 1430s onwards we begin to find petitions to the Lord Chancellor asking him to enforce legal claims based on manorial court rolls. Eleven cases are known so far prior to 1485, none of them fully printed (though summarized by a few scholars).[54] I have studied the manuscripts recording all these cases. They exhibit such a wide variety of circumstances that it seemed desirable to rehearse the details of the ones that can further increase our understanding of that society.

A legal historian, Charles Montgomery Gray, has argued that these cases, and some other fragmentary evidence, do not suffice to prove that the Lord Chancellor, as yet, recognized the *right* of customary tenants to be protected by chancery against their lords or those lords' officials. He urges that the cases are too few. Furthermore, several of them may have been considered by chancery on more general legal grounds, in accordance with its evolving principles about the kinds of rules that it ought to enforce.[55] I am inclined to dissent from Gray's conclusions in this matter, but he has written an admirable book, clear, very well informed and closely argued.

Much of the uncertainty arises from the absence, before 1535, of chancery's decisions. We have only the petitions of the plaintiffs and the replies of the defendants, though we have sometimes more than one set of these plaints and rejoinders to them. Whatever may be one's opinion about the principles on which the Chancellors acted in these agrarian cases up to 1485, a few reasonable deductions can be made. Some customary tenants with claims against their lords were prepared to incur the expense of addressing the Chancellor. They, or their legal advisers, may have had some grounds for thinking that something could be gained thereby. They may have known of some earlier, successful cases. The paucity of surviving proceedings proves little where so much has been lost, though obviously there was no flood of such cases before 1485. Dr Gray has found six more between 1493 and 1502, with two further ones up to 1509. Some sixty such cases can be assigned to the reign of Henry VIII.[56]

The known proceedings show that already under Henry VI chancery treated the tenant plaintiffs and the lordly defendants on an equal footing. Chancery's powers to compel the attendance of parties were more effective than those of the Courts of Common Law[57] and it is clear that the lords had to appear in these 'manorial' cases, either in person or through their legal attorneys. They declared themselves ready to submit to the judgements of the chancery. They had also to submit in their rejoinders elaborate answers. This, above all, was an important new development. The pressure thus exerted upon landlords was bound to have some effect on their future conduct towards their customary tenants.

I shall not follow Dr Gray in speculating about the legal principles guiding chancery in hearing these 'manorial' cases. I shall omit those where the lords and their farmers, or officials, were not involved and shall merely summarize the relevant facts of the remaining disputes. After dealing with the cases prior to 1485, I shall look at some of the proceedings attributable to the reign of Henry VII, discussed by Gray.

In 1437/8 two daughters of a Southwark grocer, Thomas Stowell, petitioned chancery that they should be admitted to their parents' messuage and appurtenant holdings at Dulwich held of the Abbot of Bermondsey. They admitted that because these land-holdings were held 'by copie after custume of manoir' they were 'without remedie at the commone lawe'. Previously these holdings had been surrendered to the steward of Dulwich in order to be regranted to Stowell and his heirs (the two girls), but the steward refused to make an entry of this on the manorial court roll, because of a challenge by another man, who claimed to have a part-share in them. This was noted in an earlier record on the manorial roll registering a fine for entry. When Stowell died this other man, by the name of John Colcok, was admitted to the holdings by the lord, the Abbot of Bermondsey. Stowell's two daughters petitioned that chancery should summon both Colcok and the abbot's steward and that the latter should bring with him the manorial court rolls.[58]

The next example also turns on the alleged absence of a record on the manorial court roll. A man alleged, some time in the 1450s, that he had been excluded from the succession to his mother's copyhold tenement held of the Abbot of St Albans because the clerk of the abbot's court had previously omitted to enter on the manorial court roll the admission of the plaintiff's mother. A jury of tenants had confirmed that he was her heir, and the clerk's evasive replies suggested that he had suppressed vital evidence. The plaintiff asked that chancery should direct a writ to the abbot to certify the truth by examination of the court rolls.[59]

In November 1440 a copyholder and his wife petitioned chancery about an alleged wrong done to them by their lord, Arundel College in Sussex. They were admitted to a cottage and a virgate and an entry to this effect was made on the manorial court roll. However, subsequently, the college would not allow them to enter this holding for reasons that are not explained. The couple asked chancery to summon the authorities of Arundel College to appear in court. They were assuming that chancery could compel the appearance of their lord to explain why he 'against his own grant and court rolls hath put out the said beseechers'. Gray admits that this is one of the strongest pieces of evidence for the readiness of chancery to uphold manorial customs against lords of customary tenants holding copyholds.[60]

Another case recognized by Gray as offering 'acceptable evidence' for the protection by chancery of copyholders dates from the first decade of the reign of Edward IV (a petition to the chancellor, 1465–71, about some earlier events). Nicholas Kingston sued the lord of the manor of Toyfield Hall (Middlesex) for a messuage, garden and 5½ acres of meadow held previously by his now deceased father, John Kingston. The lord, John Giben, appears to have acted very shiftily. There was a series of successive proceedings which show, at any rate, that chancery deemed the lord's first rejoinder to be unsatisfactory and forced him to present further defences.

The lord's statements are contradictory, which confirms one's impression that he had a bad case against the plaintiff.

The plaintiff had been serving in Edward IV's army in Yorkshire against the Lancastrians. It was alleged that his father had ceased to be seized of his holdings in his lifetime, as they were conveyed to his daughter, Amy, and her husband, who were maintaining him in his old age. The plaintiff later denied that the woman was his sister and one suspects that she may have been illegitimate. He also denied that his father had not been seized of his holdings at the time of his death and the jury of tenants subsequently upheld this denial. When the plaintiff's father died it was, allegedly, believed by the lord that the son had been killed in the king's service and the lord, therefore, formally confirmed the alleged sister in the tenure of these holdings. The plaintiff then reappeared and a jury of tenants described him as his father's heir. The plaintiff paid to the lord the required fine for entry of £1 and also 10s 2d of arrears of rent owed by his deceased father. The lord accepted these, but subsequently refused to admit the plaintiff into the holdings and seized them into his own hands. The lord alleged that he was only holding them pending the settlement of the dispute between Nicholas and his alleged sister, Amy, about who was the rightful heir. Matters were complicated further by the death of Amy's husband and in the second statement of his case to chancery the lord claimed that, because of this, Nicholas should have started fresh proceedings and that his case should be dismissed for his failure to do so. The lord's collusion with Amy is brought out by his subsequent behaviour. According to the plaintiff, the lord declared himself to be his own steward for the purpose of holding his manorial court and then refused to convene any further sessions of it, so that Nicholas was deprived of all local remedies. The pleadings bear witness to the fact that chancery accorded fair play between the lord and his customary tenant. But the lord had many ways by which to evade allegations and the custom of the manor was by no means an easy thing to ascertain or enforce if the lord was not impartial.[61]

A case dating from 1450–4 raises contradictory issues. The plaintiff was a cousin of a deceased copyhold tenant of a messuage and a virgate at Melksham in Wiltshire and claimed to be his next heir. He also alleged that he had offered to pay what he claimed to be the customary fine there, of one year's rent (30s), but that the lord's steward had refused to accept it, as a stranger, without apparently any hereditary claim, had offered double that amount (£3). The plaintiff may not have had a strong case, as he did not claim that the custom of the manor had been broken and did not specify what his cousin's customary tenure was. Instead he based his claim on allegations that the steward had threatened 'to beat and mayhem him'. That was a good plea for invoking the chancellor's aid, but makes one doubtful whether the plaintiff had the manorial custom on his side.[62]

Two of the cases dating from the reign of Henry VII show that some copyholders thought it worth their while to apply to chancery against lords who had evicted them from their copyholds.[63] In a case dating from 1486–93 the plaintiff alleged that the lord of his manor had 'always been accustomed to grant the land by copy'. He had secured his tenement for life and had paid the required fine. Furthermore, subsequently, he had spent much money on improvements and had dutifully paid rent. Nevertheless, he had been evicted by the lord. In a second case, dating from 1500/1, the plaintiff and her husband had paid a fine of £10 to have their copyhold holdings for their lives. Nevertheless, after the death of the husband, the lord had evicted the widow 'contrary to his own grant'. A third case, that may date from 1486–93, or as late as 1504–15, is similar to the preceding one. The lord, who had received a fine of £5 for conceding a copyhold for life, later evicted that tenant, though he was himself the original grantor. The evicted tenant had petitioned the lord on several occasions for at least a refund of his fine and of his expenses on improvements, but had never been able to secure any compensation.[64]

As has already been noted, some of the copyholder complainants to chancery repeatedly stressed that they could seek no remedies at the Common Law. There was no effective change of this situation before a case in 1505/6. But in two cases, in 1467 and 1481, two Chief Justices of the Common Pleas, respectively Robert Danby and Thomas Brian, expressed *opinions*, though apparently they were no more than that, which diverged from the existing law. They came to believe that a tenant who had paid his fine for entry, and had not defaulted on rents or other services, ought not to be disturbed by the lord in his enjoyment of his customary tenement. Both justices recognized that no possessory action was available to such tenants, but on both occasions they expressed the view that the wronged tenant was entitled to an action of trespass against a lord who had wrongfully dispossessed him. If successful, the tenant would be entitled to a pecuniary compensation, though he would not be able to recover his tenement. The notice of these two opinions first appears in an addition made in 1534 to a new edition of Littleton's treatise, *On Tenures*. Danby's opinion could not have had any effect on the outcome of the case in 1467, as it was only loosely connected with it. There is no evidence regarding what effect, if any, resulted from Brian's opinion in 1481.

However, when in that later case the landlord's attorney demurred that no action could be allowed at Common Law because a copyholder could not claim that he was seized of a freehold, Chief Justice Brian made a very interesting comment. He drew a distinction that may have influenced later judges in the sixteenth century. While he recognized that such a tenant could not, indeed, claim freehold tenure, he could allege freehold *interest* created by his payment of a fine for entry and the due discharge of his services.[65]

The first case where the Court of Common Pleas was willing to recognize that a customary tenant could be vindicated against a charge that he had trespassed into his lord's land was tried in 1505/6. The tenant's copyhold had been appropriated by the lord and enclosed in breach of the custom of the manor. The tenant had broken the close and was sued by the lord for trespass. The case was twice adjourned and the outcome is unknown. However, in the course of it two justices expressed opinions upholding the tenant's defence of the legal justification for his action.[66]

'The evidence from the next half-century is inconclusive', but it seems that any precedent that the case of 1505/6 may have created was not followed. Probably only 'shortly after the middle of the sixteenth century did the courts come to the opinion already reached by the Common Pleas judges in 1506' that a customary tenant could bring an action of trespass against his lord for wrongful interference with the undisturbed tenure of his customary holdings.[67] This was the beginning of reasonings that by the late sixteenth century were to create an effective legal protection for those copyholders who could justifiably invoke the customs of their manors. The remedy came through the extension of the action of trespass to their special needs. The successful litigant in an action of trespass was, before the sixteenth century, entitled only to pecuniary damages. But the action of ejectment (*ejectio firmae*), which was a variety of action for trespass, came to be applied in ways that allowed a wronged tenant the *restoration of his tenement*, as well as damages. Indeed, freeholders began to use it instead of less convenient, older possessory assizes.[68]

CHAPTER 16

Oppression and Injustice on the Estates of Some Major Lay Landlords

I

The magnates of late medieval England were an arrogant group, proud of their superior descent, contemptuous of the lower classes of society, convinced that their power and influence would protect them from any serious penalties if they abused or disregarded the law of the land. There were some exceptions, as Chaucer's idealized picture of the knight suggests in the prologue to the *Canterbury Tales*. This character was derived in part from Sir Richard Waldegrave, whose conduct as the Speaker for the Commons in the first parliament after the Great Revolt of 1381 does reveal an unusually broad-minded man, very much aware of the oppressions and injustices habitually committed by many of the magnates.[1] In a speech that was remarkable for its truthful realism he castigated the abuses not only of royal but also of magnate officials. He spoke of 'grievous and outrageous oppressions done . . . by various servants of our lord the king and other lords of the realm'. He particularly blamed the lords for the perversions of justice and spoke of their keeping an outrageous multitude of embracers of quarrels and maintainers who acted like kings in the country, 'so that justice and law are scarcely administered to anybody.' He warned that still worse troubles were to be feared 'if good and proper remedy is not provided in time for the above-mentioned outrageous oppressions and mischiefs'.[2]

The late K.B. McFarlane confirmed this dismal picture of much of the magnate class. He spoke of their 'harsh efficiency': 'The commonest impulse detectable was to exploit every imagined right, to push every promising advantage to its limit. Hardly a collection of private papers fails to offer some piece of vivid evidence of lordly high-handedness or extortion in which neither tenants nor servants were spared.'[3] While most lords faced increased economic difficulties during the middle decades of the fifteenth century, the exercise of harsh and exacting lordship allowed some magnates to minimize this. This and the next chapter will offer a few well-documented examples. 'There is no sign whatever that even one of the comital houses . . . came to disaster by any other road than political miscalculation.'[4] In the course of the fifteenth century lords who had personal summons to parliament came to be regarded even more than before as a class apart. To offend them was highly dangerous. In 1481 a Nottinghamshire squire explained that he had remained inactive in the face of a forcible entry by Francis, Lord Lovel because, 'Considering he is a lorde, I may not so deale.'[5]

Magnates employed councillors and officials who, as a matter of course, implemented the harsh directives of their masters. They knew that they would be normally protected from retribution for any wrongdoing as long as they zealously pursued their lords' interests. Indeed, they were apt to go further in this than some of their masters deemed wise. While the magnates were a very conservative group in trying to enforce their traditional rights over their peasant dependants, 'the conservative attitude of estate administrators was as important as that of the lord'. John of Gaunt, Duke of Lancaster, son of Edward III, 'suspected that the attacks on his rural properties in the revolt of 1381 were partly the result of heavy-handed management by his local officials'. After the revolt he was anxious that these officials should not get out of control in inflicting punishments. No fines were to be imposed on individual villages without reference to his central council or without special mandate from John himself.[6]

II

An incident in 1390 at Wingham in Kent highlights the arrogant contempt of the English aristocracy for their inferiors and the readiness of some lords to humiliate their serfs as part of what they regarded as the maintenance of their rights and of the proper social hierarchy. It is a story of what was done by an Archbishop of Canterbury, William Courtenay: it is no surprise that he was a son of the Earl of Devon.[7]

Six of Courtenay's customary tenants at Wingham, instead of driving cartloads of hay and litter to his palace of Canterbury, as they were obliged to do by custom, brought it all secretly and on foot, so that they should be less conspicuous while performing this shameful obligation, which was otherwise not particularly arduous. The landed tenants on Canterbury estates were often prosperous men and these serfs were ashamed of their bond status. Courtenay's court treated their action as in contempt of the archbishop. For this they were sentenced to parade like penitents, semi-naked, round Wingham Church, each carrying on his shoulders a sack of hay and straw. Courtenay commemorated his triumph by recording the sentence in his archiepiscopal register, with a picture of a penitent villein in the margin.[8]

'One reason why lords insisted in the fifteenth century on maintaining the institutions of serfdom was, no doubt, because of deeply rooted ideas about social status.'[9] The contemptuous attitude towards serfs among some members of the landowning classes who dominated the House

Driving, with great difficulty, a cartload of corn; psalter of Sir Geoffrey Luttrell of Inham, Lincs., before 1340 (By permission of The British Library: Add. MS. 42130, f. 173v)

A page from the archiepiscopal Register of William Courtenay, Archbishop of Canterbury, showing a servile tenant of Wingham, Kent, on 10 April 1390, doing penance in Wingham churchyard as punishment for avoiding carrying service due to the archbishop (Reproduced by permission of the Archbishop of Canterbury and the Trustees of Lambeth Palace Library: Lambeth MS: Register of Courtenay, f. 337v)

of Commons is revealed by two petitions presented there in 1390 and 1391. The first, in the year of the Wingham incident, led to a statute prohibiting 'any kind of artificer or labourer' from taking or destroying 'beasts of the forest, hares, or rabbits, or other sport of gentlefolk'. Next year (1391) another petition demanded that sons of villeins should not be allowed to go to school lest they became clergymen. The request was justified by the need to maintain 'the honour of all the freemen of the kingdom'. The king refused to grant this unenforceable request.[10]

A horrible case of the abuse of legal rules about serfdom came to light after the death, on 23 February 1447, of Humphrey, Duke of Gloucester, the youngest son of King Henry IV. Humphrey had been arrested during a parliament at Bury St Edmunds by the king's order and had died, apparently of a stroke, five days later. Prisoners detained by him were released. Among them was John Whithorne, a Wiltshire gentleman of considerable wealth. Duke Humphrey, apparently quite falsely, had claimed that Whithorne was his serf from the manor of Bowscombe (on the Isle of Wight) which was owned by him. Whithorne had been seized by Humphrey's servants and taken to his castle at Pembroke. After a detention of more than seven years he was completely blind and deaf. Humphrey had seized Whithorne's properties, said to have amounted to 600 acres of arable, 30 acres of meadow and 6 acres of pasture, dispersed through eighteen localities in Wiltshire, as well as rents of 6s 8d at Salisbury, inspired, according to the royal letters patent by his 'great malice and insatiable avarice'. The royal letters patent of 16 July 1447, which record all this, restored to Whithorne all these properties. This dreadful case shows that when a landlord was a royal prince it was impossible for the supposed villein to prove his free status even when he was a gentleman who owned a considerable amount of land.[11]

I have referred several times to the reckless trampling upon peasantry of magnates engaged in private warfare. This happened in the early 1450s in the fighting in Devon between the Earl of Devon and Lord Bonville and the feud between the Nevilles and the Percys in Yorkshire. There was also the practice of forcible collection of rents from one's opponents' luckless tenants. In East Anglia the followers of the predatory Robert, Lord Moleyns, did this early in 1449 when wrestling the manor of Gresham from the Pastons. It happened again in the 1460s in the conflicts between John, the last Mowbray Duke of Norfolk, and the Pastons.[12] An earlier instance occurred in the early 1430s in the course of a bitter feud between the Talbots and the Berkeleys.[13]

In section V of chapter 12 I have referred to an inquiry by Cardinal Wolsey into the charges against the bailiff of Bungay in Suffolk of procuring evictions of tenants. It was certified that the special commission sent there did not dare to proceed as the bailiff had merely been carrying out the instructions of his master, Thomas Howard, Duke of Norfolk. The bailiff, backed by the duke's steward, had refused to give any answers.

Leading families of the gentry were apt to be as ready to defy the law and to behave as arrogantly and violently as many of the great lords. For example, in Derbyshire, in the period between c. 1480 and 1510, some of the worst maintainers of violent gangs and of perpetrators of various illegalities were some of its premier families, especially the Vernons. Sir Henry Vernon inherited the family estates in 1467 and in the later years of the reign of Henry VII was Treasurer of the Household of the Prince of Wales. The clear value of the Vernon properties, extending over seven counties, with their centre at Haddon in Derbyshire, must have been at least £500 in the later fifteenth century. A special commission of oyer and terminer was appointed in 1509 to investigate Sir Henry's numerous misdeeds over many years. As steward of the Duchy of Lancaster's lordship of High Peak, he had procured unjust prosecutions for debt and then

Lady Margaret Beaufort, mother of King Henry VII (Reproduced by permission of the Master and Fellows of St John's College, Cambridge)

appropriated the goods of the wrongfully condemned victims. He was accused also of wrongful enclosure (in 1484) and of unlawful disseizin (in 1508). Above all, there was a flagrant breach of the law at the Derby assizes in 1506. A lesser gentleman, Ralph Leech, had procured against him a writ of trespass. At the trial Sir Henry spoke threatening words to one of the jurors and the 'fearful jurors dared not try the issue'.[14]

While some of the lords' leading central and local officials were the 'skilled and willing instruments of extortion' from their peasant tenants, they themselves were 'also subjected to harsh measures for their failure to pay over what was expected of them'.[15] A list of uncollected debts compiled shortly before the death in 1459 of Sir John Fastolf (with a rent roll yielding an annual income of £1,450) shows that at different times half his estate officials had been gaoled for being in arrears with their dues. Even his receiver general was not exempt from his lord's severity.[16] That fierce old lady, Margaret Beaufort, the mother of King Henry VII, pursued her officials quite ruthlessly. John Knight was a long-standing auditor in her service. Yet in 1502 she was prosecuting his widow for debts owed by him. 'The most striking example concerns Roger Ormeston, Lady Margaret's chamberlain and one of her most loyal officers.' In 1506 she sued his widow and other executors for a debt of £22.[17]

An instruction commonly found in the late medieval testaments of magnates to their executors, that they should try to undo all the injustices committed by the testators, was no mere formula.[18] The example of Ralph, Lord Cromwell (d. 1456), is particularly instructive. He had been a notably enterprising and masterful King's Treasurer for ten years (1433–43).[19] During his tenure of that office he had defrauded a leading family of Nottinghamshire gentry, the Pierpoints, of a substantial landed inheritance.[20] Between 1429 and his death he had nearly doubled his income from land. Estimated at around £1,020 in 1429, it amounted to about £2,260 shortly before his death.[21] The executors of his testament found it necessary to restore to their lawful owners lands worth £5,500 which he had wrongly appropriated, 'as full greatly it moved the conscience of his executors'.[22]

III

We possess numerous estimates of the incomes of lay magnates in the later fourteenth and the fifteenth centuries. Much less is known so far about the details of the management of their estates and their treatment of peasant tenants. Materials for such studies are fairly abundant, but they are mostly unpublished and still await their historians. The three examples that follow (some Norfolk estates, the properties of the Lords Grey of Ruthin, and the lordship of Dunster in Somerset) have been selected because of their relatively full documentation. The Earls (later Dukes) of Norfolk were harsh landlords and provoked much resistance from their East Anglian tenants. Theirs was in the long run a losing battle. The Greys of Ruthin were hard men, but intelligent. They controlled their officials and their tenantry effectively, but were capable of devising compromise arrangements that assured for them steady income, while meeting also the wishes of their tenants, or, at least, the more prosperous among them. For over a century, from the 1390s onwards, the Greys were able to achieve a high and fairly stable income, which by the 1460s equalled roughly the revenues of the Bishops of Worcester. The Luttrells of Dunster were resident lords of a fairly compact group of estates, mainly in Somerset, and exploited them successfully. As was the case with other landlords in the very conservative south-west of England, they retained a high level of renders and services of a kind that was disappearing in the more developed parts of England. They lost their lands temporarily through adhering too vigorously to King Henry VI. The Herberts, who replaced them between 1461 and 1485, were absentee landlords and Welsh strangers and ran into much resistance from the surviving Luttrells and their relatives. They also appear to have been less successful in collecting the maximum amount of income. Lastly, in the next chapter (section VI), I shall tell the notorious story of the last Stafford Duke of Buckingham's rack-renting and otherwise brutal pressurizing of his servile tenantry.

Margaret, Countess (later Duchess) of Norfolk, who held the estates of her family from 1338 to 1399, was an unscrupulous, greedy and arrogant lady, proud of being a grand-daughter of King Edward I. She asserted tenaciously what she regarded, at times quite unjustifiably, as her rights.[23] In 1388, in pursuance of one of these unjust claims, her servants from the lordship of Chepstow killed three royal tenants.[24] By the last decade of her long life (she died aged about eighty) Margaret possessed an annual income little short of £3,000 (£2,839 in 1394/5). She tried to exploit her estates effectively, but her income had grown to this imposing total above all through lucrative marriages and windfall inheritances. At Bosham in Sussex, which she inherited in 1383, she did try successfully to increase the agrarian income. Like other owners of the fertile coastal lands of Sussex (notably the Abbey of Battle), she increased the annual income from sales of corn from an average, before 1383, of £13 to £40 and she nearly tripled the revenue from the commutation of labour services.[25] But at the core of her ancestral lands in East Anglia her treatment of tenants was notably harsh. Understandably, she was very unpopular. There was a series of commissions of special inquiry (commissions of oyer and terminer) into poaching raids on her properties and other attacks on them between 1373 and 1385.[26]

The oppressiveness of her lordship was losing her income, as her serfs were trying to withdraw elsewhere. The sullen connivance of other peasants at these breaches of manorial regulations went hand in hand with much inefficiency on the part of her officials. It produced situations like the cases discovered at her manor of Walton (Suffolk) after the Great Revolt of 1381. Two of her servile tenants from here were found at Manningtree in Essex where they had set themselves up as leading townsmen. One had accumulated 63½ acres of freehold land, while the other owned 21 acres, eleven messuages, shops and cottages.[27]

From Countess Margaret's manor of Forncett, about twelve miles south-west of Norwich, we possess two bailiffs' account rolls for 1376–8 and nine court rolls from between 1373 and 1394.[28] The rents owed by the mainly modest servile holdings, averaging 5 acres, were heavy (on average 10¾d per acre), while labour services and taxes came to a further 2s per acre. It is not surprising that servile peasants, who were expected to pay over 9s for holdings of 5 acres, were abandoning them. In 1378, shortly before the Great Revolt of 1381, some 76 per cent of the area of servile tenements was in the hands of Countess Margaret's officials, or, if one prefers to count the villein holdings, eighteen out of twenty-five had escheated. It should be added that at Forncett the rule was rigorously enforced requiring any freehold land acquired by the serfs of the countess to be surrendered to her in order to be regranted to the same tenants as servile land, charged with higher rents and taxes. Between 1358 and 1376 some 50 acres, with ten-and-a-half messuages, had been degraded into this more heavily burdened servile tenure ('*terra soliata*', as it was called).[29]

A number of holdings had been abandoned by tenants who did not wish to bear any more the burden of labour services and heavy money charges. Others had belonged to men and women who had fled. One of the court rolls for 1373 names eight bondmen and bondwomen who had withdrawn from the manor without permission. An inquiry was ordered into whether a further serf had withdrawn his chattels from Forncett. Yet another fugitive is named in one of the rolls for 1374. The roll for 1394 names a serf who was leaving the manor at the time of harvest 'for greater gain', in breach of the Statute of Labourers. It is interesting to note that between a fifth and a quarter of the area once forming part of the holdings of free sokemen was also in the hands of the officials of the countess, though it is possible that some of this land had passed earlier into the hands of serfs. The manorial officials at Forncett leased the abandoned holdings to the remaining tenants, largely servile. But these leases yielded smaller rents and were free from labour services and a part, at least, of servile renders.

In 1400, when Margaret's great-grandson entered upon the countess's Norfolk estates, nineteen families of servile status held land at Forncett. For a century-and-a-half the ducal administration tried tenaciously to control their descendants. 'The consistency of this policy is remarkable when one considers the various changes in ownership during the fifteenth century,'[30] including two periods of disinheritance and confiscation of the Norfolk estates (1405–13, 1485–9). The explanation must lie largely in the fair degree of continuity in the personnel of officials. 'The conservative attitude of estate administrators was as important as that of the lord.' In trying to preserve serfdom these officials had only a partial success. Flights of bondmen continued. At least six fugitives can be identified in such fifteenth-century court rolls as survive. There were also more refusals by members of servile families to take up servile holdings. The ducal officials tried to levy annual chevage from bondmen who resided outside the lordship of the dukes, but in some cases this was difficult to enforce after a few years's absence. In 1500 not more than eight bond families were tenants, though some of them were now very prosperous people, who held considerable amounts of land and, in some cases also held leases of manorial demesnes. A member of the Bolitout family held four messuages and 78 acres in 1410, and even bigger accumulations of land by serfs occurred later. The wealthier they were the greater was the incentive to enforce their servile status in order to mulct them repeatedly. By 1525, however, only five bond families remained, and three of these were collectively freed in 1556. One of the freed men, John Dosy, surrendered his lands (86 acres with seven messuages and two half-messuages) to two tenants on condition that they paid for him the huge sum of £120 to the then Duke!

The long-drawn-out attempt of the Dukes of Norfolk to preserve and exploit bondmen at Forncett was parallel by similar policies on their other estates in East Anglia. In the sixteenth century the Howards, by then Dukes of Norfolk, were extremely conservative landlords, like their Mowbray predecessors. Of the then Norfolk manors on which bondmen are known to have existed in 1549, four were Howard estates (Forncett, Earsham, Kenninghall and Bressingham). Of the six Suffolk manors which definitely still had serfs in the 1540s, five belonged to the Howards (Framlingham, Kelsale, Earl Soham, Peasenhall and Walton). After the forfeiture in 1547 to Henry VIII of the properties of Thomas Howard, Duke of Norfolk, a collective petition was presented to Lord Protector Somerset by 26 bondmen from seven different families resident on Howard manors, asking to be manumitted for 'the charitee of Christ'. This may be the main origin of one of the articles of Ket's followers in 1549: 'We pray that all bondmen be made fre for god made all free with his precious blode sheddyng.' Certainly the East Anglian rebels in that year were very hostile to anything connected with the Duke of Norfolk. The manumissions by the royal Privy Council of forty-six former Howard bondmen from East Anglia followed between 1550 and 1553.[31]

In his edition of the valor of most of the English estates of the Lords Grey of Ruthin in

1467/8, Professor Ian Jack explained that the purpose of his study was to show that 'an able lord, who ordered his expenditure wisely, could enjoy real prosperity from his landed income in the fifteenth century'.[32] His comment refers primarily to Edmund, owner of the Grey estates from 1440 to 1490. For the estates of the last Hastings Earl of Pembroke (killed in 1389), which were partly inhertited by Edmund's grandfather, Reginald, we have a valuation made in 1392,[33] which can be compared with the valor of 1467/8. An unpublished account made by Reginald's receiver general in 1393/4,[34] which has not been used hitherto by students of their estates, can be referred to for a fuller comparison with the figures for 1467/8. For reasons that I shall explain, it is impossible to compare all of it meaningfully with the valor for 1467/8, but it does show that at both dates the Greys of Ruthin had in England alone (that is, exclusive of the Welsh properties) revenues surpassing £1,000. There exists also a more recent, detailed study of Blunham in Bedfordshire, one of the estates derived by the Greys from the Hastings inheritance.[35]

The Greys were long-lived and hard men.[36] Edmund was a violent, brutal, treacherous magnate. On 23 September 1450 his men murdered, presumably on his orders, William Tresham, Speaker for the Commons in four parliaments between 1439 and 1450. At this stage Edmund Grey was a partisan of King Henry VI and was killing a councillor of Richard, Duke of York, though he may also have had some private motive for this crime. No one was punished for it.[37] But on 10 July 1460 Edmund Grey, who commanded the right wing of Henry VI's army at Northampton, while facing the Yorkist rebels, betrayed his master. His treachery led to the sudden collapse of the royal army, the murder of its leaders and the capture of Henry VI.[38] In 1463/4 he served as the royal Treasurer, which confirms that he was regarded as a competent administrator. He was rewarded with the Earldom of Kent in 1465 and managed to survive unscathed through the political upheavals of the years 1469–85. One is not surprised that this intelligent and vigorous ruffian should have preserved the stability of his income and, indeed, increased it. He made sure that his tenants remained under his lordly control. He also appears to have been fairly successful in preventing his servants from defrauding him. Thus, in 1443–7 the accounts of his receiver general balanced very well. This was a period when the finances of many landlords were beginning to deteriorate and it is noteworthy that this was not happening seriously on the Grey estates. In 1443/4 expenditure slightly exceeded income, but only by £9. In 1446/7 Edmund's receiver general had a surplus of income over expenditure amounting to £91.[39]

Professor R.I. Jack has compared the royal valuation in 1392 of seven estates of the Hastings inheritance with the gross value of the same properties in the Grey valor of 1467/8. I prefer to compare, instead, the valor of 1467/8 with the account of Reginald Grey's receiver general in 1393/4.[40] A record of actual receipts is always superior to a mere valuation. As many as fourteen estates can be compared, including some ancestral Grey properties.

The valor of 1467/8, like other rentals and estate documents from the properties of the Greys, seems to have been a realistic document. But it is a record of *gross* income. To arrive at *net* income one has to deduct various fees charged on the revenue, other routine allowances and the cost of repairs of buildings and other items. But the valor does provide the information for calculating these necessary deductions. Thus the Grey portion of the village of Blunham in Bedfordshire, consisting of some 1,100 acres, was farmed in 1467/8 for an annual rent of £38. Its net value to Edmund Grey was £36 16s 10d, and £24 0s 2d was delivered to his receiver general.[41] Or, to cite another pair of figures, the royal valuation of seven estates of the Hastings inheritance in 1392 amounted to £315 11s 7½d. The gross value in the valor of 1467/8 came to £332 1s 4¼d, but Professor Jack was able to calculate the net value, amounting to only £295 5s 4d (a diminution of 12 per cent).[42] I shall apply the same percentage to the scaling down of the 1467/8 figure for fourteen estates compared with the account of 1393/4.

Some other facts must be reviewed before a realistic comparison can be made between the account of 1393/4 and the valor of 1467/8. Reginald Grey was challenged by several opponents who tried to deny his claim to the Hastings inheritance. He resisted them fairly successfully, but the litigation was costly. He was forced to raise quickly large sums from some of the Hastings estates. The account for 1393/4 reveals some of his expedients. Sales of timber that year yielded £113 13s 4d. Sales of wool may also have been extraordinarily large, amounting to £105 11s 4d. Much of this money came from the two Hastings properties at Burbage in Leicestershire and Foxley in Norfolk.[43] This is one reason why the receiver's income in 1393/4 is not easily comparable with revenues in more normal years.

The account for 1393/4 covers thirty-six English properties. Many of these no longer belonged to the Greys in 1467/8. Reginald Grey had had to sell a number to his most dangerous opponent, Sir William Beauchamp of Abergavenny. Altogether he had alienated some thirty manors.[44] Of the thirty-six estates named in the receiver's account for 1393/4 only fourteen can be effectively compared with the estates listed in the valor of 1467/8. In 1393/4 the cash receipts from all the thirty-six manors amounted to £981 17s 8d (including the extraordinary items mentioned above). The cash deliveries by the receiver to Lord Reginald Grey, together with expenses, were larger, amounting to £1,120 8s, and exceeding his income. Borrowing filled some of this gap: the receiver's account expressly mentions one loan of £40.[45]

The receipts in 1393/4 from the fourteen manors comparable with the list of 1467/8[46] amounted to £751 2s. If the special items like the sales of timber and wool are deducted, one is left with £531 17s 4d. In the valor of 1467/8 the total *gross* valuation of the same estates amounted to £610 10s 5½d.[47] Scaled down by 12 per cent this gives an approximate *net* value of about £537. This suggests the maintenance of a fairly stable level of normal revenues from estates.

Edmund Grey (1440–90) had already by 1467/8 increased further the properties of his family. His most important acquisition was the lordship of Ampthill in Bedfordshire, purchased in 1454 from the trustees of Ralph, Lord Cromwell.[48] Even before its purchase Grey had been the largest landowner in Bedfordshire and this acquisition of Lord Fanhope's former lordship (Cromwell was Fanhope's executor) reaffirmed the predominance of the Greys in that prosperous county. For Ampthill Edmund paid £4,333 6s 8d (6,500 marks). He clearly disposed of considerable surplus resources. His period of office as the royal Treasurer from June 1463 to November 1464 presumably enhanced still further his opportunities for procuring large funds. Edmund had to pay for the Fanhope estates by sixteen annual instalments, with the last payment completed in 1473,[49] but he controlled these properties from an earlier date, as indicated by the fact that they are included in the Grey valor of 1467/8. If the Fanhope properties are left out, the remaining thirty-three English estates (exclusive of Cheshire) can be shown to have yielded Edmund a fairly stable income. His receiver general in 1444/5 delivered £706 in cash. The figure for 1446/7 was somewhat smaller, amounting to only £650.[50] The same thirty-three properties were estimated in the valor of 1467/8 to have a gross value of between £730 and £740.[51] If my tentative deduction of 12 per cent is applied again, this would yield a net value of about £652, virtually identical with the receipts in 1446/7.

Edmund, Lord Grey of Ruthin (later Earl of Kent, d. 1490), and his wife Katherine, kneeling in prayer (The Trustees of the National Library of Scotland: Advocates MS. 18.1.7, f. 12v)

Between 1467/8 and 1498 the net value of the Bedfordshire estates appears to have increased somewhat. Their clear value in 1467/8 amounted to £339, but in 1498 it was estimated at £362.[52] One of the ways in which this increase had been achieved lay in the efficient control which the Greys managed to maintain over their customary tenants. The effective quality of their lordship can be illustrated to some extent from their manor of Blunham in Bedfordshire, for which there survive unusually plentiful and informative records.[53] The village lies 7 miles east of Bedford, on fertile land. There were other large estates there and the Greys controlled only between a third and two-fifths of the parish. A mid-sixteenth century source for this estimate shows that the share of the Greys consisted probably of 1,110 acres, comprising 680 acres of arable land held by their tenants, 225 of former demesne arable and between 100 and 150 acres of meadow and pasture, besides 66 acres belonging to the rector of the parish church.

Because we have detailed records of Edmund Grey's successive administrative arrangements at Blunham, it is essential to provide information about his tenants there. Leaving aside some twenty freeholders, he had in 1457 as many as forty-one tenants of customary land, some of whom also held portions of demesne on lease. An additional four tenants held only leases of demesne lands. Customary tenements numbered thirty-two, with half-virgates predominating (23, each of 14 acres of arable). Three of the largest landholders had between 40 and 49 acres, including one man who farmed the biggest block of demesne (41 acres). In the valor of 1467/8 the manor was estimated to have a clear value of £36 16s 10d, an increase of £10 6s 8d on the revenue received from it in 1393/4.

In the case of Blunham there is very important evidence for Edmund Grey's dealings with his customary tenants. The most informative item, a charter conceded by him in 1471 to his servile 'homage' there, has no known parallel from other Grey estates. Perhaps similar records still await discovery.

There were two successive reforms at Blunham. A new rental in 1457 appears to have raised rents of customary holdings, but also made them uniform. It fixed rents of a half-virgate and a quarterland as 8s 4d and 4s 2d respectively. These rates were repeated in the rental of 1498 and continued to operate through much of the sixteenth century. Then, in 1471, Edmund granted his charter to the customary tenants of Blunham. If we are to believe its preamble, it was as desired by them as by their lord. The charter recognized the growth in demand for land among the peasants of this prosperous village and it therefore gave customary tenants complete freedom of alienation, so long as they observed certain conditions. Entire tenements could be sold or leased freely but if a tenant wished to alienate a part of his holding he could not henceforth alienate more than 8 acres out of the 14 acres of a half-virgate and no more than 4 acres out of a quarterland of 7 acres. Earl Edmund was trying to check an excessive fragmentation of holdings which threatened to interfere with the efficient collection of rents and fines for entry. The rate for the latter was fully regulated, being fixed at 6d for an acre of arable and 20d for an acre of meadow. From later evidence we learn that a fine for entry for an entire standard tenement came to be fixed at Blunham at one year's rent (8s 4d for a half-virgate). This would suggest that such a holding was assumed to contain, besides 14 acres of arable, about 1 acre of pasture. It was a very reasonable level of fine. The charter of 1471 also stipulated that a customary tenant who sold a house (not the buyer) had to pay a fine of two years' rent, which was still not excessive. The whole arrangement reveals the interest which Earl Edmund took in the management of his estates, but at the same time it recognized the free market which had developed among the tenants. A rental of 1498 shows that there had resulted considerable amount of dealings in land. The charter of 1471 was still observed, but there was now a greater concentration of land in the hands of fewer tenants.

The story of the lordship of Dunster in Somerset under the Yorkist kings has been told by me in section IV of chapter 14. Its Luttrell lords had exploited it effectively until their temporary downfall in 1461. Professor J.M.W. Bean has cited them as an example of a family of richer gentry managing their farming successfully in the first half of the fifteenth century and enjoying 'the benefits of comparatively stable rents and farms'.[54] Its most valuable manor was Carhampton, east of Dunster. In 1461/2, out of the total revenues from Dunster of £252 8s 8¼d received by its new Yorkist lord, William, Lord Herbert,[55] £101 5s came from Carhampton (cash payments and allowances of expenses).[56] As on many estates of the south-west, the peasantry of Carhampton and of other manors pertaining to Dunster were treated harshly. I have described in section II of chapter 13 the practice of leasing the 155 acres of demesne arable at Carhampton for only one year at a time. It was divided between tenants and they had to raise crops prescribed for them, paying heavy rents.

The Herberts did this in 1461/2, 1465/6 and 1478/9, presumably merely following the previous practice of the Luttrells. At Carhampton the Herberts continued to exploit directly 37 acres of meadow. Herbage of 31 acres was sold in 1461/2 at 5s per acre, while 6 acres were

William, Lord Herbert (d. 1460) and his wife before King Edward IV (By permission of The British Library: Royal MS. 18.D.II, f. 6)

reserved for the harvesting of the lord's own hay. Seven mills were farmed in that year for £15 3s 8d, consisting of three mills for the fulling of cloth and four corn mills.

Piecemeal leasing of demesne arable was not the only oppressive and conservative practice in the Dunster estate. No doubt, in all this, the Herberts merely followed in the footsteps of the Luttrells. The rents of assize were very large. Out of £41 19s 3¼d demanded in 1461/2, everything, save 10s, was collected. Labour services continued to be commuted annually for money payments. Fines for entry of new tenants were heavy. In 1461/2 at Carhampton one amounted to 30s and one to 20s, though unfortunately the size of these tenements is not stated. In 1459/60, the last full year of tenure by the Luttrells, fourteen sessions of the Hundred Court had been held at Carhampton, yielding £2 14s in fines and amercements.[57] In the first year of the Herbert lordship these rose to £3 2s.[58]

The manor of Minehead yielded in 1461/2 in cash deliveries and allowances £86 5s 4d (out of £96 19s 2¼d charged).[59] The rents of assize were even heavier than at Carhampton, amounting to £67 3s 1¼d. Only £1 4s 0½d was not collected. For commutation of labour services £3 17 3d was charged and there is mention of 12s 4d being levied from an archaic render of *capitatio garcionum* (presumably a poll tax on adolescent boys). Another ancient render levied at Minehead from nineteen customary tenants, each paying annually 1s, was called 'lordesylver'. Some fines for entry of new tenants were again quite heavy, the largest amounting to £3 6s 8d.

At Quantoxhead, one of the most easterly Dunster manors, quite near the coast, the total amount charged to the reeve in 1461/2 came to £43 14s 3½d.[60] One of the most distinctive features was the presence of thirteen enclosed holdings of meadow and pasture, containing altogether 328 acres. The rents charged for them in that year amounted to £8 2s. In addition, there was a large area of pasture in the lord's park, farmed for £1 18s 6d.

The two later Herbert accounts, for 1465/6 and 1478/9, reveal the same pattern of revenues. There may have been an increase of resistance among officials and tenants to an absentee landlord who was also a Welsh stranger. This is suggested by a mounting burden of arrears, the nature of which is not explained in the surviving accounts. At Carhampton William Lovelace, who had served as the bailiff of the Luttrells in 1459/60, owed in 1465/6 arrears of £83 9s 4d.[61] He was still alive in 1478/9, though an amercement of 1s imposed on him was excused, as he was sick and in utter poverty.[62] As I have mentioned elsewhere,[63] the 1478/9 account includes a payment of £1 5s 6d for expenses incurred by the chief steward of the Herberts. Sir Giles Daubeny, coming to Dunster 'in the time of disturbance between the tenants, for the safe custody and government of it'.[64] One wonders whether this disturbance was some eruption of discontent among its heavily exploited peasants.

CHAPTER 17
Towards Economic Revival,
c. 1470–*c.* 1525

It is very difficult to make generally valid statements about population and economy in the fifty years after the re-establishment of more effective kingship by Edward IV in 1471.[1] Except for the years 1483–7, it was a time of more assured political regimes. The popular uprisings of 1489 in Yorkshire and of 1497 in the south-west were peripheral affairs, due to special regional circumstances.[2] The muster rolls and loan of 1522 and the subsidy of 1524/5 provide some fairly credible statistics from which we can calculate approximately the English population and the wealth of the minority which had some measurable income. Dating from a time when population was clearly rising, and the economy of some parts of England was reviving, these years 1522–25 constitute a reasonable final term to this book.

There is a Venetian account of England, written in the last years of the fifteenth century, which is in many ways a superficial and misleading description of this country. Its author underrated the amount of arable cultivation and does not seem to have known the corn-growing areas of the Midlands or East Anglia. But his picture of a delightful countryside, still well wooded, with an abundance of water and teeming with wildlife seems substantially correct. So is the impression of a basically underdeveloped and empty country when compared with our observer's northern Italy.[3]

Population seems to have been growing again in the last quarter of the fifteenth century, but slowly, in marked contrast to the much faster expansion elsewhere in north-western Europe, notably in parts of France and Germany. Julian Cornwall has suggested, though his is no more than a general impression, that in much of England growth of population might have been delayed to the 1480s and accelerated only around the turn of the century.[4] However, most scholars are in agreement that the population was again increasing by the beginning of the sixteenth century. Two dissentients of note, however, are Ian Blanchard and B.M.S. Campbell, who do not believe that there was an appreciable increase of population before the 1520s. Dr Campbell's critical scrutiny of the muster rolls of 1522 and of the records of the subsidy of 1524/5 make him doubt whether the population in 1525 surpassed two million and may have even been lower than that. He does admit, however, that 'the evidence of the lay subsidies is too equivocal to be conclusive', and Dr Miller's estimate of between 2½ and 2¾ million around 1520 (cited by me in chapter 1) does seem more probable. Dr Campbell's much lower figures seem to conflict with the probable estimates of population in the later Tudor period, as he himself recognizes.[5]

This book is not intended as a general study of the English economy, but some general comments are necessary as an introduction to developments in the countryside which will be illustrated in this chapter from a selection of examples. Two generalizations can be made safely: 'we know very little of the speed at which the sixteenth-century economy revived'[6] while the uneven rate of economic progress certainly accentuated the contrasts between different regions.

One of the well-attested features of the English economy in the late fifteenth and early sixteenth centuries was the decline of many of the English towns.[7] It seems to have been intensified by the tendency of the richer townsmen to leave the towns where they had prospered after two or three generations and to buy instead properties in the countryside. A striking instance is provided by the Springs of Lavenham in Suffolk. Thomas Spring III was the last clothier of his family to reside there. At the time of his death in 1523 he was one of the richest men, 'other than some of the peerage', to be found outside London. He was then lord of twenty-six manors in eastern England and landowner in many others. His widow and daughter were assessed for the subsidy of 1524/5 on goods valued at £1,333 6s 8d, while his son, John, who lived on an estate at Bures in Suffolk was assessed at £200 from land.[8] By contrast, leading merchants appear to have displayed only moderate interest in investing in city properties. With population stagnant, or often declining, in many towns, there was no incentive for speculating in a possible expansion of urban property values.[9] The stagnation or decline of towns meant a lack of expansion in the principal group of consumers depending for their foodstuffs on the surpluses produced in the countryside. By contrast, estates near London were profiting from the capital's steady growth.[10]

I shall be looking at several regions, like the area around London, which were experiencing particularly notable economic progress because of exceptional advantages. But there were also improvements in other areas, well-favoured admittedly by climate and well-balanced economic opportunities, where no special factors can be singled out. It was true, for example, of the estates of the Bishops of Worcester.[11] This points to widespread, though modest, progress.

The cloth industry of Suffolk and the adjoining areas of Essex is supposed to have been at the peak of its prosperity in the period that lasted into the 1520s, though, as R.H. Britnell has wisely cautioned us, 'some scepticism is in order in the absence of any figures relating to output or sales'. Lavenham in Suffolk and Coggeshall in Essex seem to have been two of the most flourishing centres, with the Springs at Lavenham and the Paycockes at Coggeshall as the two outstandingly successful clothiers.[12] The expanding flocks of sheep in East Anglia were providing wool for this industry.[13] Dr John Hatcher has suggested that a modest rise in profits of certain of the Yorkshire estates of the Percys between 1478 and 1525 may have been due to the growth of the West Riding cloth industry in the later fifteenth century, requiring increasing supplies of foodstuffs.[14]

Sir Henry Willoughby's gross income in 1524 amounted probably to about £1,400. Much of it was inherited wealth, supported by the royal favour to one of the most influential men in Nottinghamshire and a Master of Royal Ordnance. But the source of his revenue which was growing at the fastest rate were the profits from his coal-mines at Wollaton in Nottinghamshire. In the financial year 1497/8 they produced a net cash profit of £182 9s. Thereafter extraction of coal continued to increase and by 1526 this mining complex was one of the most productive in the country. Coal was not only sold locally but was also shipped by Willoughby down the River Trent as far as the Humber. Willoughby could afford to finance repeatedly expensive improvements to his mines.[15]

In the last decades of the fifteenth century parts of Cornwall and Devon were areas of exceptionally buoyant economic activity. Cornish tin production, after a decline over much of the fifteenth century, was again at its peak in the early sixteenth century, averaging after 1490 almost 500 tons. In Devon output roughly doubled between *c.* 1450 and 1500.[16] Very substantial numbers of miners were involved in the Cornish tin stannaries. Over 3,000 tinners were employed in west Cornwall in the early fifteenth century and the same was presumably true around 1500, when the level of tin production was roughly the same. There was also a host of ancillary workers.[17] All this stimulated considerable output of foodstuffs in the surrounding countryside. Devon and Cornwall profited from a revival of trade with France after the ending of warfare in 1475. Exeter experienced exceptional prosperity between 1497 and around 1510, through large imports of Gascon wine and the expanding exports of West Country woollens and tin. At the turn of the century shipments of Devon cloths from Exeter and other neighbouring harbours averaged some 10 per cent of the total exports of English woollens. According to Hoskins' calculations, Exeter's taxable wealth in 1524/5 may have placed it third or fourth among English provincial towns.[18] This vigorous economic activity provided much stimulus for the agriculture of the adjoining villages, as has been illustrated, for example, by Professor Finberg from the estates of Tavistock Abbey, north of Plymouth.[19]

In section VIII of chapter 10 I have pondered the chances of a minority of richer peasants of establishing permanently the fortunes of their families. In the depressed period of the middle and the third quarter of the fifteenth century their long-term prospects of doing this were not good. They became somewhat better towards the end of the century as I shall try to illustrate from the two well-documented examples of Roger Heritage in south-eastern Warwickshire and the Spencers in Northamptonshire, both initially owning no lands of their own and exploiting only leased properties.

The penultimate section of this chapter will attempt a summary of the tenurial position of the peasantry in the first quarter of the sixteenth century. Most English peasants were in a securer position at that time and paid less to their landlords than they had been doing at the time of the Great Revolt of 1381. Personal serfdom had greatly dwindled. No 'tidy' summary is possible. Each village was unique in its history, in its pattern of getting its livelihood and in the tenurial position of the peasantry. As Dr Joan Thirsk has pointed out, even in open-field villages, which formed one recognizable type of community, closer study often reveals all sorts of 'irregularities'.[20] All my generalizations about the tenurial situation merely aim at formulating a common framework for this very varied tenurial landscape.

II

No marked economic progress can be found on the estates of the Bishopric of Worcester under John Carpenter's immediate successor, John Alcock (1476–86). For modest improvement here we have to wait until *c.* 1500. Thereafter, however, under a succession of absentee Italian bishops, there was an increase of serious corruption by estate officials and of disaffection among the excessively pressurized tenants, leading to a recurrence of rent strikes (cf. section VI, below).

We have a roll of arrears due to Bishop Alcock at Michaelmas 1482.[21] There is no mention in it of the 'recognition' due at his accession. The demand for it had presumably been given up. But the other renders, mostly servile, which tenants on several manors had been refusing to pay to Bishop Carpenter, were still being demanded, and equally resolutely withheld. The arrears since the start of Alcock's episcopate included common fine and worksilver at Bredon. They totalled £11 7s 6d. The accumulated arrears of servile tallage at Withington amounted to £9. The arrears of common fine came to £1 15s 11½d at Bibury and to £1 4s at Bishop's Cleeve. The campaign of passive resistance clearly continued unabated on those Gloucestershire manors. The only other comparable item was £4 3s accumulated at Whitstones, by Worcester, arising out of a

Membrane of the arrears roll of the estates of Bishop John Alcock of Worcester, Michaelmas 1482 (Reproduced by permission of the Bishop of Worcester: Worcester Record Office: BA 2636, pcl 176, no. 92489) refusal to pay an additional rent imposed by a new rental. The total thus withheld (£27 9s 5½d) amounted to about 7 per cent of arrears due at that date, after six years of Alcock's episcopate (£377 18s 7¼d). Unlike Carpenter, Alcock was an important politician, serving as the acting Lord Chancellor in England during Edward IV's invasion of France in 1475 and as President of the Council for the March of Wales since 1478.[22] But even he was unable to overcome such stubborn passive resistance of his customary tenants.

As had been normal for over a century, the farmers of the tithes at Blockley owed large arrears, in some cases as many as three years old. That item (£42 18s 8d) formed about 11 per cent of the total arrears due to Bishop Alcock at Michaelmas 1482. Only £15 19s had been paid in 1481/2 by these farmers, which points to continued difficulties over raising money quickly from sales of agricultural products.

The account of the receiver general for 1499/1500,[23] for some unexplained reason, was not cited by Professor Dyer in his study of the Worcester estates. Perhaps he regarded the large cash payments to the receiver, amounting to £1,364 8s 6d,[24] as untypical. The actual receipts from estates in that year were £881 13s 11d, but the total payments by the receiver were increased through his virtual discharge of his arrears of £445 18s 1d, left over from his previous account. There is no evidence about how he managed to do this, but his large payments in that year suggest that the episcopal estates could be made to yield more than they had done under Bishop Carpenter. The last extant account of Carpenter's receiver general, for 1470/1, had put his receipts at £928 5s. His expenses and cash disbursements had amounted to £1,072 3s, as he had been able to refund some of the arrears (totalling £503) from his previous account. The receiver's performance in 1499/1500 was clearly much better.

The average receipts from the estates, listed by Professor Dyer, ranged in 1497–1505 between £945 and £994.[25] However, as he does not mention what additional amounts of arrears were paid off each year, these figures do not tell us the whole story.

If payments received from particular estates by the receiver in 1499/1500 are compared with the sums collected in 1470/1, they reveal a very similar pattern of revenues. In both cases Blockley came first (£91 in 1499/1500), as it had normally done since, at least, the 1380s. The ranking in 1499/1500 of Whitstones, just outside the walls of Worcester, and of Henbury Saltmarsh, very near Bristol, tying for second place (each with £72) was again quite typical. Nine estates with contributions of over £49 figure as leaders on both lists,[26] with the addition of Stratford-upon-Avon (£50) in 1499/1500.

Professor Dyer has noted that in the early decades of the sixteenth century large arrears ceased to accumulate. That points to a modest improvement in the economy. In his words, 'In the mid-fifteenth century about a third of the money received each year came from arrears. . . . By the early sixteenth century less than a tenth of money collected by the receiver came from arrears, so that most rents were paid in the year they were due. This reflects less reluctance on the tenants' part to pay rents, and greater ease for them in obtaining cash.'[27]

III

Outside the specially advantaged regions mentioned in the first section of this chapter it is difficult to find in existing publications evidence of economic and especially agricultural improvements in England in the last quarter of the fifteenth century and the early decades of the sixteenth. Even within the privileged regions, like the counties adjoining London, concrete information has to be ferreted out with much effort and disappointingly meagre results. Dr Joan Thirsk's fascinating survey of the 'farming regions of England'[28] cites illustrative examples almost always from later periods of the sixteenth and seventeenth centuries. She is fully assured about the importance of the growing demands of London on the agricultural production of Essex, Hertfordshire, Kent and Sussex,[29] but offers no details relevant for the early Tudor period.

More concrete evidence is available in Professor Du Boulay's studies of the estates of the Archbishops of Canterbury. There was a marked upward trend in revenues on the majority of the Kentish estates after about 1490, especially in the rich lands of east Kent, particularly the Isle of Thanet and the newly drained and exploited marshland belonging to the manor of Aldington.[30] The best evidence comes from the records of leases of the manorial demesnes. From *c.* 1480 to *c.* 1525 the rents from these leases accounted for about 40 per cent of the archbishop's revenue from land, a much higher proportion than the comparable income of the Bishops of Worcester.[31] We know most about the leases granted by Archbishop Thomas Warham (1502–32), because a register has been preserved containing the records of 156 leases conceded by him.[32] The terms for which they were granted tended to lengthen after about 1510. 'What was being leased for ten or fifteen years up to about 1500 was by the 1520s passing into the hands of farmers for twenty, thirty or forty years.' Clearly they were regarded as becoming more valuable. Some of these leases were sold or sublet to others before they had run their full course, and this could be a profitable transaction for the original lessee.[33] A similar traffic in domanial leases developed on the manors of Westminster Abbey near London.[34] We know very little about the entry fines offered for the leases of the Canterbury estates, but by the early sixteenth century they were, apparently, rising again. Some time before 1518 for a lease at Sudbury near Harrow (Middlesex), that was to be held for an annual rent of £22, a man offered a fine of £50 and also some supplementary annual payments during the duration of the lease.[35]

Professor Du Boulay has also noted that during the last twenty years of the fifteenth century there was a marked improvement in the archbishop's income from his properties. 'The arrears at the head of the accounts dwindle away as farmers and reeves paid in nearly all that they should have done. There was a positive increase in revenue on the estates as a whole, not only from better collection, but from expanding rent-rolls on the manors nearest to London . . . and from the higher-yielding leases of the east Kent demesne properties. . . . In this recovery a prominent part was played by the demesnes in the hands of farmers.'[36]

Rearing of sheep and cattle was prospering anew in parts of Kent and Sussex in the late fifteenth and early sixteenth centuries. Calais was a subsidiary destination for exports of meat. Some of the evidence for the revival of pastoral economy comes again from the leases of Canterbury demesnes. The Knatchbulls, the wealthiest of the archbishop's farmers, holding some 2,000 acres around 1500, had a fresh option for the reclamation of further areas of Romney Marsh in Kent, used for pasturing sheep.[37] To the traditional large flocks of sheep were now being added larger herds of cattle. This was happening at Alciston, the model estate of the Abbey of Battle in Sussex, and at the Pelhams' park of Loughton in Sussex, where revenues more than doubled in the last two decades of the fifteenth century, from £7 to between £14 and £16, mainly from providing pastures for horses.[38]

Margaret Beaufort, the mother of King Henry VII, was a ruthlessly efficient old lady.[39] She was particularly so in her lordship of Kendal in Westmorland, which was her dower land from the first of her many marriages. In 1453/4 it had yielded about £200 to her first husband, Edmund Tudor, Earl of Richmond. As a member of a leading Lancastrian family, she had experienced dramatic changes of fortune and she regained Kendal only between 1485 and 1487. After her son, Henry VII, had become king she was one of the most influential people in the country. Her management of Kendal showed what an intelligent and determined owner of a lordship could achieve. Cloth was woven in all the valleys radiating from the town of Kendal, with their fast-flowing rivers. In Grasmere, to the north-west of Kendal, there were eighteen fulling mills in the 1490s and early in the next century Kendal cloth was being carried to Southampton for shipment to Italy and to Bristol for transport to Spain.[40] Margaret was responsible for the erection of some of the mills and carefully supervised their maintenance, as they were increasing her income. But more profit 'was to be derived from the growing pressure on cultivable land as the population rose. There was a steady increase in rents accruing from new holdings.' Low-lying woodlands were cleared under close supervision of Margaret's officials. New rentals were negotiated with tenants to cover intakes from freshly reclaimed land and standardized rents were introduced. However, 'ruthless exploitation of lordship' caused resentment. Fines imposed by Margaret's court for illegal encroachments on her lands 'were unpopular and in one case led to a violent affray'. 'The financial yield from Kendal rose steadily under Margaret's administration, reaching an annual figure of around £380, a sum further swollen by efficient collection of long-standing arrears of rent.'[41] It was the same on most of her other huge properties, as her unscrupulous ruthlessness was combined with limitless greed.

IV

I have selected three examples of men whose careers benefited from the improved economic opportunities of the late fifteenth and early sixteenth centuries. Their descendants went on to greater successes. The Temples of Stowe, the Spencers of Althorp and the Townshends all rose to affluence and peerages. All three families produced statesmen of outstanding importance. Each of my chosen examples may have had exceptional features. They are adduced here merely to show what was possible for some men at this time in the Midlands and East Anglia.

Roger Heritage's daughter, Alice, married Thomas Temple and it is through their son, Peter, that the Temples first rose to considerable prosperity.[42] Roger may have been born in the 1440s and died in 1495. He would have been called a yeoman in his time. He does not seem to have owned much, or indeed, any land, but he farmed some 500 acres of the manorial demesne at Burton Dassett in south-eastern Warwickshire. He held that farm from at least 1480, and probably earlier, and kept it until his death, when his son, John, took it over. In 1541 it passed to John's nephew, Peter Temple.

In Roger's time the manor belonged first to Sir John Norbury and then to Norbury's heirs, the Belknaps. Roger's last Belknap lord, Sir Edward, became an important financial agent of Henry VII as Surveyor of the King's Prerogative[43] and, like other members of Henry's team of oppressive servants, may have been a harsh master. Roger paid him an annual rent of £20 and must have been an efficient man to survive as Sir Edward's farmer.

Burton Dassett lies in the Feldon area of Warwickshire, suited equally well to arable as to pastoral exploitation. Sir Edward Belknap came to own about 80 per cent of the village and Roger Heritage's son, John, enclosed most of this in 1497 with the active collaboration of Sir Edward. Presented as an encloser to Wolsey's commission of inquiry in 1517, Belknap was accused of having converted 360 acres of arable to pasture, though actually he had enclosed much more. He was also accused of evicting twelve peasant households, though he tried to defend himself by alleging that he was compelled to abandon the growing of corn because it was hard to find 'tenants to occupie their landes'.[44] He also blamed Roger Heritage for the change, which was plainly untrue, as Roger owned at his death in 1495 two teams of oxen and two ploughs, enough to exploit at least 150 acres of arable, though he may have cultivated less as prices of corn were low at that period.

Roger was farming the demesne of Burton Dassett at a time when agrarian prospects were still precarious and opportunities for profit more limited than they later became. He may have also been a more cautious man than his son and clearly preferred to depend on mixed farming, part corn-growing and part pasture. Besides cultivating crops himself, he must also have hired his plough-teams to other landholders, as they owed money to him for this in 1495. While he pastured 860 sheep, he also owned then 40 head of cattle and 12 horses. He also possessed a profitable warren for rabbits. His farm-stock and equipment were valued in that year at £109.

The enclosures carried out in 1497 by John Heritage and Sir Edward Belknap were the most extensive of all the Warwickshire enclosures presented to the commission of 1517. In 1541 Peter Temple took over at Burton Dassett a vast ranch filled with sheep and cattle and unencumbered by any peasants. He ultimately acquired the freehold of much of the village. His descendants became the Earls Temple in the eighteenth century. William Pitt, Earl of Chatham, married a sister of one of them, who became the mother of the younger William Pitt, the prime minister to George III.

The first John Spencer came from Radbourne in the same south-eastern region of Warwickshire as Roger Heritage and, like him, he appears to have owned initially little, or no land.[45] In a debate in the House of Lords in 1621, the Earl of Arundel, of the proud Howard family (dukes since 1483), thought fit to remind the first ennobled descendant of John that, while his ancestors were rendering eminent service to English kings, Spencer's forebears were mere shepherds.[46] John Spencer I did marry a co-heiress of a propertied family at Snitterfield, slightly to the north of Stratford-upon-Avon. When we first hear of him in 1497, he farmed the manor there. On the death of his uncle, John, whose executor he was, he moved to Hodnell, very near Burton Dassett, to run a grazing farm there during the minority of his cousin. In the early years of the next century he leased considerable properties in this corner of Warwickshire or just over the border into Northamptonshire. The owners were a number of both ecclesiastical and lay landlords, including the Catesbys.

Purchases of estates began in 1506 with the acquisition of Wormleighton in south-eastern Warwickshire, where Spencer created one of the two main blocks of his properties. He bought it from William Cope, son-in-law of his uncle, whose pastures at Hodnell he had been farming since 1497. Wormleighton and the adjoining manor of Fenny Compton had belonged to Sir Simon Montfort. He was an associate of Sir William Stanley, whom Henry VII was determined to destroy in 1495, and Montfort perished with him.[47] Cope, who was the Cofferer of the Royal Household under Henry VII, was granted these properties in 1498. Next year he enclosed much of Wormleighton, turning sixty people adrift and increasing its annual value by £20. In 1499 Wormleighton was already a declining village, where there had been earlier evictions. But Fenny Compton was a flourishing community, too populous to enclose. It remained an agricultural estate and in 1559 most of its peasants were customary tenants 'at will'.[48]

Purchases by John Spencer I of which the cost is known involved payments of £3,100 between 1506 and 1518,[49] but he bought also some other estates for an unknown price. Most of his purchases were of choice grassland in places which had already been depopulated and

Wormleighton manor-house, Warks., residence of the Spencers (Oxfordshire Photographic Archive, DLA, OCC)

enclosed by others. An eighteenth-century agricultural writer described them as scarcely capable of further improvement as pastures[50] and they were presumably almost as good when Spencer first acquired them. Apart from some Northamptonshire properties, most of his acquisitions lay in two compact blocks, one around Wormleighton in south-eastern Warwickshire and the other at Althorp, six miles north-west from Northampton, bought in 1508 for £800 from the Catesbys.[51] The concentration of his properties was one of the chief features of his successful sheep-farming. The Wormleighton complex was his chief sheep-ranch. Out of some 14,000 sheep his descendants owned in 1568, some 10,500 were concentrated here.[52] Another secret of John I's success was his creation of a superior variety of sheep by selective breeding. He avoided buying animals elsewhere, but kept thousands of his own ewes.[53] Later the quality of the Spencer sheep became so famous that sales of breeding stocks to others became a valuable source of income.

Wormleighton became Spencer's main residence. In 1517, at the enquiry by Wolsey's commission into depopulating enclosures, John was able to prove, with much truth, that he had acquired already depopulated localities. He could also show that he had built a new manor-house at Wormleighton and that he had created a fresh settlement there on higher and less wet ground. By the time he died in 1522 some sixty people may have been living there: his servants, shepherds, cowherds, drovers and diverse labourers. Wolsey's commission allowed him to keep all his pastures.[54]

John Spencer I served as sheriff of Northamptonshire in 1511 and was knighted shortly before his death. His heir, Sir William (d. 1532), married into one of the oldest and richest families of Northamptonshire gentry, the Knightleys. When William's heir came of age in 1545, the lands he held of the king were valued at £454 13*s* 4*d*, which was undoubtedly a serious underassessment.[55] The fortune of the Spencers comprised, in any case, huge numbers of sheep, as well as cattle, and they were famous for their hoard of ready money. They continued through the second half of the sixteenth century to buy more properties, chiefly around Wormleighton and Althorp. The latter became their chief residence, with an extensive park. At the accession of James I Sir Robert Spencer (1570–1627) was reputed to be one of the richest royal subjects, entirely from his estates and animals. In the first year of his reign James I raised him to the peerage as Lord Spencer of Wormleighton. In 1722 his descendant became Duke of Marlborough and he is, thus, an ancestor of Sir Winston Churchill.

The story of the Townshends of north-western Norfolk[56] is somewhat different from that of the Spencers. John, who died in 1466, was a prosperous yeoman, but the fortune of the family was really founded by his son, Roger I (d. 1493), a very successful lawyer, who in the last eight years of his life was one of the Justices of the Common Pleas. The surplus capital which allowed him to acquire numerous properties, chiefly in Norfolk, appears to have come from his legal income, and his legal activities created the opportunities for many of his purchases. At the end of his life he recorded that he had invested since 1468 the large sum of £3,800 in acquisitions of landed property.[57] His estates were mainly concentrated in north-western Norfolk, especially around Raynham, from where his family originated. This area of Norfolk, with lighter soils than the more fertile eastern regions of the county, could only yield reasonable crops if it were heavily manured. Hence the indispensable combination of arable cultivation with large flocks of sheep. The Townshends came to be numbered among the owners of the largest flocks in the county, with 18,468 sheep in twenty-six flocks owned by them in 1516.[58]

As was the case with John Spencer I, Sir Roger Townshend I and his heir, Sir Roger II (1478–1551), aimed at creating a very compact group of properties. Any outlying acquisitions tended to be sold after a while, or exchanged for estates in north-western Norfolk. This was one of the secrets of their success as sheep-farmers, just as in the case of the Spencers. The different flocks could be treated as effectively one unit, with much interchange of animals between different manors. Just as the Spencers, they tried, as far as possible, to rely on their own breeding of sheep. 'During 1495/6, for example, nearly 50 per cent of their sheep were ewes.'[59]

Apart from the importance of manure for arable cultivation, sheep were kept chiefly for wool, though there were also profitable sales of animals to other landowners. Production of mutton was of very subsidiary importance here in the years between *c.* 1480 and *c.* 1520.[60] Because in the 1480s Sir Roger I sold considerable quantities of wool to merchants of Lynn, to the west of the Townshend properties, it was assumed by K.J. Allison that it was destined for export abroad.[61] Since he wrote, it has become clear that there were in fact no shipments of wool to foreign countries from Lynn during the period.[62] The buyers at Lynn must have merely transported these wools by sea to the cloth-manufacturing centures further south, presumably mainly in Suffolk and Essex. The relatively low prices of the wool from the flocks of the Townshends also point to exclusive use by native textile industries. In 1494/5 Sir Roger I's widow was selling wool to clothiers at Hadleigh and Lavenham in Suffolk, but also to London merchants.[63]

Sheep-farming could be a precarious business. In 1480/1 Sir Roger Townshend I lost over 2,000 sheep through epidemic mortality and the severe winter badly affected lambing. The following summer the fleece weights were so low that his sheep-reeve called it 'an evell yere for wull'. That year a further 1,700 sheep were lost through disease.[64] There were also sharp fluctuations in the prices of wool, so that in certain years, like 1479–81, it was preferable to store most of it, awaiting better times.[65] Prices in 1497/8, 1502/3 and 1505/6 were half of what Townshend's wools fetched between 1514 and 1518.[66] Only in that second decade of the sixteenth century did there begin a sustained boom, as English cloth exports began to expand spectacularly.[67] Sir Roger II reacted by increasing the number of his flocks and rearing vastly increased numbers of sheep. While in 1507 he kept nine flocks, comprising 8,418 sheep, this jumped in 1510 to twenty flocks, containing 17,104 animals. Recurrence of epidemics led to losses of several thousands and checked expansion between 1511 and 1515, but in 1516, as mentioned before, there were 18,468 animals in twenty-six flocks. Unfortunately there are no accounts between 1519 and 1522, the evidence for 1523/4 is incomplete, and thereafter occurs another unfortunate gap until 1534.[68]

The Townshends, like other major Norfolk landowners, controlled 'foldcourses', entitling them to pasture sheep on stretches of land which in part did not actually belong to them.[69] As flocks increased, this created increasing tensions between the gentry and lesser men, though the existing evidence points to more conflicts with substantial freeholders than with poorer peasants, who could only keep few animals.[70] The control of fold-courses by major landlords also obstructed innovations in crop rotations by other landholders and this appears to have been another major reason for the hostility to the gentry who controlled them. I have mentioned in section IV of chapter 15 the abortive anti-landlord conspiracy in Norfolk in 1537. The men involved in it were substantial peasants, not poor men[71] and Sir Roger II took a leading part in arresting the plotters. He was an unpopular notable. Some of his tenants joined in the East Anglian rising of 1549, during which his house at Norwich was sacked, with a loss allegedly of goods worth £40, and he himself sought shelter at Lynn.[72] He behaved like most of his fellow justices of the peace, who likewise fled.[73]

When Sir Roger II succeeded to his estates at the very end of the fifteenth century, their annual value was estimated at about £290.[74] By 1525, through further purchases, largely financed out of the profits of his sheep-farming, he had accumulated properties valued by him in that year at £510.[75] For the subsidy of 1524/5 his movables were valued at £600, making him the second highest assessed Norfolk gentleman.[76] Sheep formed a major item in this valuation. In 1515/16, when his flocks attained their maximum recorded size, they were valued by Sir Roger II himself at £353.[77]

The Townshends became peers under Charles II. Charles Townshend, the second viscount, between 1721 and 1730 shared the effective headship of the royal government with Sir Robert Walpole, his brother-in-law.

V

Professor P.D.A. Harvey, in his excellent survey of the varieties of peasant tenure found in England towards the end of the fifteenth century,[78] describes the overall picture as 'an extraordinary muddle'. Because, as yet, customary tenures had not come within the purview of the royal courts, they had escaped the tendency of lawyers to define and standardize. Differences of substance, even on the estates of the same landowners, were matched by the absence of any consistent nomenclature.

Descriptions of various types of peasant tenure and details of their operation did not have 'any sort of technical meaning or connotation outside the manor where they were used [as] the local interpretation was all that mattered'.[79]

The slow appearance of mentions of copyhold is a part of this situation. Professor Harvey confirms what I have discussed at length in chapter 15: there was in effect, as yet, no 'copyhold tenure', though Common Law lawyers were beginning to imagine its uniform existence. Where tenants were given copies of entries on the manorial court rolls recording their admission to their holdings, this might be for customary hereditary tenements, or for life, or for varying terms of years. Mentions of people holding '*per copiam*' rarely appear in the records of the Abbey of Westminster before the end of the fifteenth century. The first mention of it at Edington Priory's estate of Coleshill in Berkshire occurs in 1528/9. 'It is in no way surprising, and may not even be significant that the fifteenth-century records of south-east Durham do not refer to tenure by copy.'[80]

I am going to draw my detailed examples largely from the two best known great estates, the properties of the Bishops of Worcester and of the Abbey of Westminster. They seem fairly representative of what was happening.

While land was plentiful, and tenants willing to accept customary tenements were often becoming scarce, the actual details of their tenure, however different, were of no great significance. Landlords wanted to retain tenants at all costs and tolerated much misbehaviour that in earlier times would have led to instant evictions. Virtual heredity of succession to their ancestral holdings was, in practice, assured for most tenants, or, at least, it was almost certain that the nearest relatives of the previous tenants would have the first refusal. Quite often they were not interested in exercising the option because they already had as much land as they could afford to exploit. The prospective heirs of tenants could often secure adequate holdings in their parents' lifetime on terms more advantageous than the tenure of their ancestral lands and were not, thefore, always interested in taking up the latter when their parents died. Other children, not entitled to step into ancestral holdings, had also fair chances of acquiring some land. The position of women improved. A more considerate set of usages often emerged, where widows of deceased tenants could retain for the rest of their lives their husbands' holdings through the operation of something similar to the jointures enjoyed by the widows of many fifteenth-century freeholders, unchallenged by their children, who had already been able to secure other tenements. Dr Barbara Harvey has amply documented these developments on some of the estates of the Abbey of Westminster.[81] This situation slowly changed in the sixteenth century, as the rural population began to grow again. It gradually became once again a matter of considerable importance to a peasant family whether their customary holding was hereditary, or for life (or a number of lives), or merely for a term of years. But their predecessors, especially in the middle decades of the fifteenth century, did not have to lose much sleep over such distinctions.

The customary wording of admissions of new tenants in some Shropshire lordships bordering on Wales reveals the contradictions between conservative usages and the realities of the situation in the fifteenth century. Tenants were admitted to hold their tenements until somebody came forward who was prepared to offer more for them. This formula is found on the Arundel lordship of Oswestry and the Corbet lordship of Caus belonging to the Staffords. At Caus, in the course of the fifteenth century, while the temporary, conditional nature of the concessions continued to be spelt out, this was contradicted by wording which referred to the grants being for 'term of life' or to a tenant with 'his heirs and assigns'.[82]

By the late fifteenth century the bulk of the English peasantry had achieved some permanent improvements. Regular, weekly labour services had virtually gone. Even on estates where they were still due theoretically, they were unlikely to be exacted. Lessees of seignorial demesnes might still be entitled to them, as was the case on some leased demesnes of the Abbey of Westminster. In practice the farmers of demesne may have preferred to let them 'fall into disuse, rather than expose their crops to the mercy of impressed labourers'.[83] Boon labour services on special occasions, like harvest time, lingered longer, but they, too, were not generally exacted.

There had been a widespread decline in regular rents, the 'assized rents' as they were usually called. Once reduced, they could not be easily raised again. Speaking of the estates of the Bishops of Worcester, Professor Dyer has noted that such abatements reached their culmination there by the middle or the later decades of the fifteenth century and that there was no attempt henceforth to reverse this.[84] On the properties of the Abbey of Westminster, while the full rents due from tenants continued to be recorded in annual accounts, 'by c. 1450 the customary land of the abbey's estate was studded with tenants who were not expected actually to pay the rent that they in theory owed'. The manorial accounts came to record regularly the rebates that had been conceded permanently. By the late fifteenth century the distinction is recorded each year between rent that was expected to be levied and the portions of rents that were withheld ('redditus retractus' and 'non levabilis').[85]

Serfdom largely ceased to be of economic significance. Landlords might still keep lists of servile families remembered to be 'serfs by blood' in order to mulct periodically wealthier members of this dwindling group. But, when we come to tenure of land, the distinctions between servile and non-servile customary holdings tend to become blurred. As Dr Barbara Harvey remarked of Westminster estates, 'in most places where the matter can be put to the test, words with a servile meaning or implication fell out of use in the context of the tenure of land between c. 1430 and c. 1470'.[86]

Accumulations by the same people of both customary and free land ceased to be unusual, though even by the late fifteenth century they were still not very common on isolated rural manors, in contrast to semi-urbanized localities. Various obstacles can be noted. One was the reluctance of some lords to permit the disintegration of the units of customary tenure, the virgates or half-virgates that on many manors constituted the base for the payments of assized rents, heriots and fines for entry. Thus, over much of the fifteenth century, the Abbey of Westminster was willing to sanction the alienations by tenants of the standard holdings, but it did its best to check piecemeal dealings in fractions of them. Another obstacle was the insistence of many landlords that the holders of customary land should continue to reside in the localities where it lay, or at least within the landlord's franchisal liberty. Absence would result in neglect of buildings. Besides, an absentee tenant was likely to sublet much of his holding without his lord's licence and this was something that landowners tried to prevent.[87] While forfeiture of customary holdings became very rare on the estates of the Bishops of Worcester, we still find a tenant at Kempsey suffering confiscation in 1529 for subletting almost all of his customary holding without permission.[88] Thus, absentee ownership of land was a privilege of freeholders and a good deal of freehold land by c. 1500 was owned by people who were not peasants.

A process of polarization between landless or virtually landless men and richer peasants, who had accumulated property, can be illustrated from many fifteenth-century villages. However, in that age of depressed agrarian economy and uncertain long-term prospects such accumulations often proved temporary and unstable (see above, chapter 10, section VIII). Their fate is a reminder of how extraordinarily difficult it was even by then for peasant families to amass the capital for relatively large enterprises. On Westminster estates, at least, the contrast is with peasant lessees of the abbey's demesnes, 'whom the monks provided initially with basic livestock and equipment'. Those families had a much better chance of holding 'their ground from generation to generation'.[89]

The gradual revival of the agrarian economy in the sixteenth century helped to make accumulations of land by peasants more numerous and potentially stabler. The rental drawn up in 1544 at Chippenham in Cambridgeshire is instructive.[90] Half the tenants held a house only, or a house and a couple of acres. But while in the Hundred Rolls of 1279 out of the 143 tenants only two had held 30 acres or more, no less than a third had farms of this size in 1544. In that year a sixth of the tenants farmed over 50 acres and the richest copyholder had acquired 101 acres. To judge by houses attached to this assemblage of copyholds, it consisted of what had been once seven separate holdings.

Various survivals of servile tenure and status fared diversely. Specifically servile taxes had been merged with assized rents, were tacitly abandoned or ran into stubborn opposition from customary tenants, who, by withholding payments, effectively killed them. I have traced this story on some of the estates of the Bishop of Worcester in chapter 11 and in section II of this chapter.

Other legacies of serfdom had still a long life in front of them and evolved further in the later fifteenth and the sixteenth centuries in ways that hampered or even completely dispossessed the successors of medieval servile tenants. Heriots did survive, though often in a modified form, adapted to new tenurial arrangements. There was such a variety of customs that it is impossible to summarize them neatly. One concrete example might illustrate this growing diversity. It describes usages on the estates of the Bishops of Worcester. Evasion of heriots became common from the late fifteenth century onwards in the case of freeholders. This happened partly through the enfeoffments to use, as heriots were only due on the death of a tenant and the tenure of lands by trustees frustrated this. Customary tenants who did not own freeholds could not create such trusts and could escape their liability to heriot only by fleeing the manor with all their animals and chattels. But gradually the manner of rendering heriots came to be regulated by agreements between the bishops and their tenants. A customary tenant who had accumulated multiple holdings, as was becoming more frequent, made an agreement that the constitutent parts should be regarded as one tenement for the purpose of rendering heriots. An alternative development, particularly after 1460 at Whitstones and Kempsey (both near Worcester), was the conclusion of agreements that on a multiple accumulation of holdings only the tenement attached to the house where the tenant continued to live should deliver the best beast as heriot. Other holdings were allowed to pay cash according to their size. Small-holders also secured agreements that they were liable only to a cash heriot. The sums demanded for cash heriots were generally not large. Yet another alternative was to include heriots in cash inside entry fines. That, too, increasingly, came to favour tenants. The consequence of these new arrangements was a substantial reduction in the number of heriots, and, in particular of heriots rendered in live animals.[91]

Arbitrary entry fines for new tenants remained potentially the most menacing feature of customary tenure. In the fifteenth century, especially in its middle decades, they tended to be light or even ceased to be exacted. But in the next century they began to increase again and could be used as a landlord's chief weapon for forcing unwelcome alterations of terms of tenure on the majority of the tenantry, for, as I have explained in section IV of chapter 15, on very many manors local customs did not regulate them. I shall illustrate in the last section of this book the pressures exerted by heavy entry fines from some examples drawn mainly from the early decades of the sixteenth century. The problem became much graver for much of the customary peasantry after about the middle of that century.[92]

By about 1500 much of the peasantry enjoyed an effective heredity of succession to their holdings, but this concealed differences of customs that became increasingly important thereafter. In Kent, for example, heredity went predominantly with partible inheritance between all the heirs under, a very ancient custom ('gavelkind'), the origins of which remain mysterious.[93] At the other end of the country, in the north of England, short-term leases appear to have been the norm in the fifteenth century. This was changing around 1500, but the peasantry gained a sort of heredity as part of unusually onerous customs that I shall be examining in more detail in the next section. As customary tenure came to be described by lawyers as copyhold tenure, we find distinctions between fully hereditary copyholds and copyholds for life, or a number of lives (normally not more than three), of a man and wife, with one of their children specifically named in the record of their admittance to the holding. Tenure for life or a few lives appears to have been especially typical of the more conservative and backward region of south-western England. It was one of the features of harsh treatment of the peasantry on many estates in this part of the country, which I have discussed in chapter 13. Unlimited copyholds of inheritance were more prevalent in the rest of southern and central England, though less so in the western Midlands.[94] In the reign of Charles I we find that some lawyers were postulating material distinctions between these two modes of tenure. Copyholders for life were not supposed, for example, to cut down timber 'for it is the destruction of [lord's] inheritance', but copyholders of inheritance were allowed to do so.[95]

To return to the fifteenth century, Barbara Harvey has illustrated from numerous examples that on the estates of the Abbey of Westminster customs varied from manor to manor as to whether people held tenements for life or in full heredity. Introduction of tenure for a number of lives was an innovation, more frequent on some manors than on others. Such innovations seem to have been more common on the abbot's portion than on that of the prior and convent.[96] Special needs of particular tenants may have led to the creation of some joint tenancies. At Launton, in Oxfordshire, Richard Bygge entered in 1409 into a combination of a virgate and a quarter-virgate inherited by his wife, Katherine Hebbe. Two years later they were re-admitted with explicit mention of a right to pass these holdings to heirs and assigns. Presumably they paid an additional fine for this. But, in 1421, having once again surrendered their lands, they were re-admitted with their two sons, both of whom were likely to have been under twelve years of age. The creation of this new, joint tenancy may have been motivated by a desire that both their sons should have a right to succession. Otherwise the custom of the manor would have given the whole of it to the younger son.[97] On the estates of the Bishops of Worcester, Professor Dyer has noted the appearance of similar multiple rights to succession in order to assure reversions of inheritance to other persons, often relatives of the sitting tenants. This became more frequent in the late fifteenth and early sixteenth centuries, reflecting the increased demand for land.[98] The beneficiary of a reversion would pay a fine when this arrangement was first made and he might be expected to agree to a higher rent when he eventually succeeded to the holding. Thus, in 1478, on the Westminster manor of Sutton-under-Brailes (Gloucestershire), Thomas Eddon

A sower, followed by a horse dragging a harrow; a misericord in Ripple Church, Worcs.; Ripple was a manor of the Bishops of Worcester (Courtauld Institute of Art: Conway Library)

claimed the reversion of 2 virgates under an arrangement made ten years earlier and recorded in a copy of the court roll. He was to pay an annual increment of rent of 7*s* 4*d*, 'but not, it appears an entry fine'. Presumably he had already paid this in 1468.[99]

In the late fifteenth century Bedfordshire was a prosperous, predominantly agrarian county, as it had been throughout the earlier Middle Ages. It is a good region for a study of the stratification of the peasantry and the prevailing tenurial arrangements.[100] My additional reason for looking at it is my personal familiarity with parts of it, as I lived for some years in the southern part of that region.

Most of its settlements lived by mixed farming, though waterways are not abundant and few localities had plentiful meadows. Hence arable cultivation was usually more important than pastoral farming, with barley as the most commonly grown corn, and wheat as the chief source of cash. Paucity of sufficient pastures determined that it was a region of fairly strictly regulated open-field agriculture. Forcible, depopulating enclosure of entire localities was very rare here in the later Middle Ages. Such settlements as disappeared then had been small and, mostly, on heavy claylands, difficult to drain and involving exceptional effort.

In the northern part of Bedfordshire there was a considerable number of freeholders, as was the case in neighbouring Buckinghamshire. In the rest of the county customary tenure of land predominated. Many people held both customary tenements and freeholds. At the prosperous complex of villages constituting the Ancient Demesne manor of Leighton Buzzard, in the extreme south-western corner of the shire, copyholds of inheritance, but with variable fines for entry, were the prevalent tenements.

Landless men, sustained mainly or entirely by wages, chiefly as agricultural labourers, formed in some parts as much as one-half of the rural population. This was so at Leighton Buzzard (63 out of the 131 taxpayers listed for the subsidy of 1524/5), and the proportion of wage-earners was even higher in the settlements surrounding that rural town.

In some Bedfordshire villages there had developed a brisk market in land. This was so at Blunham, belonging to the Greys, Earls of Kent (discussed in the preceding chapter). It was also very markedly the case at Leighton Buzzard, where in the late fifteenth century a group of between ninety and a hundred prosperous peasants controlled much of the dealings in land, often clearly speculative, and the local office-holders were predominantly drawn from this group.

Much of the land changing hands repeatedly in Bedfordshire villages was copyhold. This confirms that around 1500 in that county people did not regard customary copyhold tenure as insecure. Furthermore, prosperous merchants, including quite a number of Londoners, took the same view. The important fact is that in the last two or three decades of the fifteenth century the Bedfordshire land market in customary copyholders was invaded on a notable scale by men of superior social status to the peasants. This was particularly true of Leighton Buzzard, only 30 miles from London.

One incentive for acquiring copyholds was the freedom of their holders to devise these tenements by will, in contrast to freeholds. Copyholds were regarded as legally the property of their lords and not of the tenants. The tenants were deemed to possess only a variety of movables, like their animals and other chattels, and movables could be devised by will. To cite a specific example, in the reign of Henry VII, tenants of the Howard manor of Forncett in Norfolk, expressly described as of 'servile blood' ('*nativi de sanguine*'), are known to have been freely bequeathing to their widows, or leaving to the executors of their wills, their entire copyhold tenements.[101] Freeholders could achieve this only by the much more complicated and costly device of creating trusts to use.

Although the copyholder may always have had less security at law than the freeholder, around 1500, in Bedfordshire, not far from London, this was not regarded in practice as a serious hazard. Besides, 'merchants and gentry were probably at an advantage in acquiring copyhold land; their security and interests were protected in some measure by their social status'.[102]

VI

The changes undergone by most manors during the later Middle Ages meant a relaxation of customary tenurial arrangements. This made the future of many peasant communities very precarious. Already in the later fifteenth and early sixteenth centuries there were considerable conversions of arable into pasture in parts of the Midlands, where economic, geological and tenurial conditions were particularly propitious. That meant evictions of individual peasants or, sometimes, of entire communities of customary tenants. Later, the pressures on the peasantry extended to much of the country. When in the course of the sixteenth century population and prices rose, when land became ever more scarce and expensive, and real wages fell, those tenants, not protected any more by ancient custom, became acutely vulnerable to eviction and rack-renting. The demise of custom gave a freer rein to market forces. 'In the fifteenth century this was beneficial,' but it was only a short-term benefit, followed for a sizeable proportion of the peasantry by long-term harm.[103]

Customary tenure for life or lives, or as a hereditary arrangement, was in the sixteenth century regarded by many lords as less satisfactory than leases for terms of years. Landlords increasingly tried to transform the one into the other. Such a transformation meant the immediate levy of a fresh fine for entry. It was thus a way of deriving more speedy income from one's assets of tenant land in times of need. It also increased the chances of long-term pressure on one's tenants. I shall illustrate this later from an early example of the extortionate measures of the last Stafford Duke of Buckingham (d. 1521). But the frequency with which landlords persuaded or pressurized their tenants into this type of change increased greatly only in the second half of the sixteenth century,[104] ushering in a new wave of enclosures and evictions as well as facilitating increases in rents and fines for entry.

A ruthless, unscrupulous lord or corrupt seignorial officials could usually override manorial customs and break agreements with tenants to enforce their will on nearly helpless peasants. However badly they might be treated, most tenants tried to cling to their lands. Even if effective legal challenges were possible, and they seldom were, the cost of this was apt to be prohibitive.

The Hammonds were a long-established family farming some of the customary lands around the Abbey of Battle in Sussex. In 1488 John Hammond was conceded the family holdings together with his infant son Richard. When John died, in 1498, the abbey's treasurer proceeded to exact both heriot and fine for entry from Richard and his mother in breach of the earlier agreement. Furthermore, these dues were exacted at a punitive rate: 11*s* 4*d* entry fine (compared with 10*d* exacted from Richard's grandfather in the 1460s) and four animals for heriots due from a number of what were deemed to be separate tenements. 'One of the family holdings was a single tenement consisting of two separate *parcelle* that totalled eight acres; for the first and the only time in the extant records two animals were taken from such a tenurial unit.' The treasurer 'was exploiting the situation of an orphan and widow who had little choice but to accept the family lands on almost any terms'.[105]

The Bishopric of Worcester passed through a bad phase between 1497 and 1533. Its successive Italian bishops were absentees. The leading estate officials enjoyed long spells of office and corruptly exploited the estates, besides feuding with each other. Three generations of the knightly Poyntz family, two of whom were sheriffs of Gloucestershire, acted almost without interruption as stewards of the episcopal properties in Gloucestershire (1488–1539). John Hornyhold, an unscrupulous and corrupt man, was receiver general between 1505 and 1535. There is no evidence that he had any lands of his own, but he farmed a number of episcopal demesnes on unusually favourable terms (especially Bredon and Withington) and accumulated various other revenues. He thus 'gained a considerable income entirely from the exploitation of his official position'.[106] It is not surprising that under such officials the income of the bishopric remained fairly stagnant and that the bishopric showed little sign of sharing in the economic revival of its region.[107] Furthermore, this corrupt and greedy staff provoked a number of serious conflicts with the tenants of several estates.

The worst troubles arose partly over the one arbitrary feature of the manorial customs, the unregulated level of fines for entry. It is this part of the Worcester evidence that I wish to illustrate. Fines had been generally low on the Worcester estates between 1430 and 1470. In a substantial number of cases no fines at all were exacted, or only nominal fines. Such fines as were paid were normally less than a year's rent and usually below £1 per virgate.[108] Very different rates were being exacted in the 1530s. The most considerable rises were occurring by then on estates nearest to large towns, where demand for land was obviously rising most briskly. The highest were at Henbury Saltmarsh near Bristol, averaging now £8 per virgate. The next highest group was on manors adjoining Worcester or fairly near to it. Fines per virgate came to average £4 at Whitstones and Wick and £3 at Kempsey.[109]

The exceptionally high sums demanded at Henbury Saltmarsh account for the troubles that occurred there. In 1525 Robert Pers, brother of the Prior of Worcester Cathedral, who acted as surveyor of the bishop's estates, was allowed to have a holding of half a virgate with an addition of 5 acres for an untypically low fine of only £1 10*s*. The concession to Pers overrode the claims of members of a local family related to the previous tenant. Two of those men forcibly ejected Pers, who complained to the Star Chamber. One feature of this affair was the open support for the wronged relatives shown by Sir Anthony Poyntz, the episcopal steward in Gloucestershire, in opposition to the bishop's surveyor. This incident provoked a petition of the Henbury tenants restating the custom of their manor and demanding its observance in the future. It stressed the overriding claim of a tenant's children or relatives to his holding on payment of a reasonable fine. It also claimed that any new tenants should be approved by the remaining suitors to the manorial court.[110]

More outrageous exactions followed. In October 1530 a tenant was made to pay at Henbury Saltmarsh a fine of £13 6s 8d for a half-virgate. This would be equivalent to about twenty years' normal rent. It was abuses of this sort which probably led in 1533 to the refusal of the tenantry at Henbury to pay any rents.[111] The immediate occasion of this 'rent strike' was an action of Sir Nicholas Poyntz, Sir Anthony's son, who had succeeded his father as Gloucestershire steward. He had prohibited Henbury tenants from appearing before any of the other bishop's officers, presumably to stop complaints against his high-handed actions. The bishopric was then in royal custody. According to a report to Thomas Cromwell by John Hornyhold, the receiver general, Poyntz was letting lands and taking fines 'at his pleasure' without the assent of other officers. The tenants of Henbury refused to pay any money, so that payments of £60 due in the spring of 1533 were withheld. By the autumn of that year Hornyhold estimated his losses of revenue at £200.[112] I would conjecture that this must probably have included income from the adjoining manor of Stoke, to produce a debt of this magnitude. He was, however, an unscrupulous crook and one would dearly like to have some other versions of what really happened.

By the second quarter of the sixteenth century the northern counties of England, 'roughly north of a line drawn from Lancaster to Scarborough',[113] had peculiar, and onerous, tenurial customs (see below for details). Because of the very uneven preservation of manorial records, we cannot be sure how generalized this was. The new pattern of customs did become prevalent in Cumberland, Westmorland and, to a lesser extent, in Northumberland and County Durham, but it was also to be found in northern Lancashire and large areas of highland Yorkshire.[114] It was a recent innovation, though the exact chronology of change demands more research in each area. Earlier, in the fifteenth century, the two prevalent modes of tenure had been tenancies at will[115] and leases for fairly short terms. It was a military society, where the peasants' obligation to serve their lords, especially against the Scots, formed a prominent feature. In the 1530s the Percys could normally assemble in Northumberland a force of some two thousand well-armed men.[116] A strong personal link between the lords and their followers was highly regarded. This meant that the peasants, who were legally mere tenants at will, enjoyed as a rule an effective security of tenure and their able-bodied sons were likely to succeed them without hindrance. On the accession of a new lord a small recognition, 'a God's penny', was levied from each tenant. During the risings in 1537 in Cumberland and Westmorland, forming the local offshoots of the main Pilgrimage of Grace, the assembled peasant malcontents claimed that this was all that they had owed in the past to a new lord.[117]

The development of these essentially personal rather than contractual arrangements into more complex tenurial customs, known collectively as 'Tenant Right' is still an obscure process. These customs differed in detail from one estate to another. They were basically the outcome of bargains by which lords guaranteed to tenants security of tenure for life in return for more substantial financial returns. The recognition of 'a God's penny' on the installation of a new lord was transformed into a fine at the lord's discretion. This differed from customs in the rest of England, where a fine was normally due only from a new tenant, but not on the change of a lord. In fact this northern custom resembled more the law of leases, where a change of lordship was regarded as terminating existing leases and necessitating their renewal, involving, of course, payments of fresh fines. But rents usually remained fixed.

The men who held land by Tenant Right could alienate their holdings. The formula on the Percy estates in 1570 was of a grant to a tenant and his assigns ('*habendum sibi et assignatis suis*'). There was never any mention of heirs.[118] As for leases, in the first third of the sixteenth century, the Percy Earls of Northumberland never granted leases for more than twenty-one years. On some other northern estates lords were granting leases for only five or seven years and were renewing them only on a payment of a fresh, general fine called 'the town term'. These exactions were common in northern Lancashire and were found on some Yorkshire manors.[119]

While in the rest of England manorial customs sometimes included an expectation that fines for entry might be fixed, or at least ought to be 'reasonable', the new northern customs never set any limits on the size of fines and these went on growing through the sixteenth century. There were also fines levied both on changes of tenants and of lords. 'While there were wide differences in the rates of fines applicable on different manors of the northern counties, many of them reveal quite spectacular advances in the profits taken as fines over the course of the sixteenth century, advances which are hard to parallel elsewhere in the English experience.'[120] The early sixteenth century seems to have been a decisive period in the introduction and then escalation of these arbitrary fines, though this happened only on the estates of certain lords.[121]

General fines on the installation of a new Earl of Northumberland had been taken as early as 1498/9 on some of the Percy estates, when Henry Percy succeeded to his inheritance as the fifth earl of his family. By the 1520s the Percys were using the fully evolved formula of the northern Tenant Right in accepting a new tenant 'for the term of his life and the life of the Earl' ('*ad terminum vite sue et vite ipsius Comitis*'). There was a general fining on the estate of the tenth Lord Clifford following his death in 1523.[122]

Gradual increases of the fines exacted from new tenants holding by Tenant Right, or accepting new leases, produced large sums. Between 1520 and 1525, Henry Percy, Earl of Northumberland, received £718 from this source.[123] The growing resentment of the northern peasants at what they regarded (often, it seems, justifiably) as new exactions was one of the important causes of the adherence of thousands of them in 1536/7 to the series of risings and armed demonstration known as the Pilgrimage of Grace.[124] The rural discontents behind these movements are revealed most clearly in the records of the risings in Cumberland and Westmorland. In contrast to the Yorkshire movements, led by some peers and gentry, the troubles in the north-western counties threw up a purely peasant leadership. The principal landowners of this region, headed by Henry Clifford, Earl of Cumberland, and Sir Thomas Wharton, remained loyal royalists, though Wharton vanished for some months into hiding. These two magnates were particularly harsh landlords. Some enclosures of the Cliffords were destroyed in the second, purely peasant rising, in Westmorland, in February 1537. Wharton 'was particularly notorious for the greatly enhanced entrance fines he exacted from his tenants. There is reason to believe that the Percy tenants in Cumberland had also been immoderately squeezed in the matter of fines.'[125] Thomas, Duke of Norfolk, who commanded the royal army trying to repress these risings, wrote on 4 February 1537 that 'never were people so set against the nobles as in these parts' of the western March (Cumberland and Westmorland).[126] Hence we get the clearest expressions of what the peasantry wanted from these north-western risings. The Westmorland rebels talked of fines as an innovation and spoke of the old custom being that a God's penny, alone, was paid on the tenant's entry: 'claim your old customs and tenant right to take your farms by a God's penny, all gressums [fines for entry] and high tenings [presumably of rents] to be laid down'.[127]

One of the best-documented examples of that 'modern' phenomenon, a rack-renting 'improving' landlord,[128] is provided by Edward, the last Stafford Duke of Buckingham.[129] His extortionate proceedings were investigated by Cardinal Wolsey's agents in preparing a criminal case against him, ending in his trial and execution on charges of treason on 17 May 1521. His real offences were his boasting about descent from King Edward III, foolish comments about Henry VIII's reliance on upstart councillors like Cardinal Wolsey, and criticisms of Wolsey's policies. Buckingham was an over-ambitious, arrogant, suspicious and harsh man, with no political sense to warn him of the dangers surrounding him. He was also one of the richest landowners in the country. In the fiscal year 1514/15 the chief receiver (cofferer) of his household received £5,053 from revenues of estates.[130] But there were large uncollected arrears, particularly on the Welsh lordships, and considerable debts were owed by Duke Edward, partly to Henry VIII. From about 1519 onwards his indebtedness grew stupendously and the pressures on his tenants, always considerable, became desperately harsh.

Duke Edward's serious financial problems had been partly caused by the loss of many of the estate records after the execution for treason, in 1483, of his father, Duke Henry. More vanished during his own minority (1483–98). His officials were constantly having to seek out concealed revenues, as discussed further below. Revenues from the duke's estates did increase, though not through any marked improvements in productivity, but rather through the pressure put on his tenants, both free and customary. As I mentioned in section IV of chapter 15, when discussing the creation of an extensive park at Thornbury in Gloucestershire, his evictions of tenants, including freeholders, were actions of a magnate convinced that he was above the law and could do as he liked.

Duke Edward personally scrutinized and annotated the reports of estate officials and the efficiently arranged accounts for particular groups of properties, designed to reveal at a glance profits and arrears over extended periods. He was frequently prosecuting his officials as a method of making them completely dependent on his wishes and then continuing to maintain those harassed men in his service. In turn they were sure to pressurize the peasantry on his properties, enforcing systematically policies devised by him.

Tenancies at will were being converted into short-term copyholds at higher rents and frequent fines for entry. Customary tenants were threatened in a variety of ways in order to compel them to change their tenure into leases. Those were never to be granted for more than twenty-one years. Pressure was put on leasehold tenants whose tenancies had still some years to run to force them into surrendering those leases earlier, in order to extract fresh fines for entry. The duke's officials mostly got their way, as few tenants were prepared to offer prolonged resistance. His agents usually managed to negotiate fresh terms 'which would have satisfied all but the most rapacious landlords'. For example, in 1519 entry fines worth £167 were imposed upon sixty-eight Staffordshire copyholders. A large number of customary holdings across the Midlands were converted into leases.[131]

Some tenants did, however, refuse to give way and, despairing of future renewals of their tenure, began to neglect their lands and cease carrying out any further repairs to buildings. Some decided to quit altogether, like a miller at Navisby in Northamptonshire, who in the second decade of the fifteenth century abandoned his farm of the mill and went 'owt off towne and . . . toke another farm' from someone else. Long-term prosperity was being sacrificed to immediate spoils. Not surprisingly, vacant lands became a problem, especially in Staffordshire, Shropshire, Cheshire and Yorkshire. At the time of Duke Edward's execution in 1521 lands worth £219 9s 9½d were uninhabited.[132]

The exploitation of hereditary bondmen does not appear to have been an important feature of the Stafford estates in the fifteenth century.[133] A register of their estate deeds contains only eight manumissions between 1435 and 1454.[134] Under Duke Edward, as has been mentioned, a diligent search was conducted to 'rediscover' serfs who had been lost to sight since the disappearance in 1483 and the following years of many of the estate records of the Staffords. At first the search concentrated on the Welsh lordships, but, especially after 1504, it extended to the English properties in the Midlands. Infinite patience and low cunning was displayed by Buckingham's officers in seeking out 'concealed bondmen worth squeezing'. The duke took a personal interest in this, receiving detailed reports which were followed by his personal decisions.[135] Possessions of the reputed serfs were seized in order to force them to purchase manumissions: as much as £40 or even more was extorted from some men in this way. After Duke Edward's execution the royal surveyors found 'rediscovered' serfs on several Welsh lordships and on Stafford properties in the lordship of Holderness in the East Riding of Yorkshire, in the Midlands (Rutland, Northamptonshire, Buckinghamshire), Norfolk and Gloucestershire.[136]

The well-documented evidence of legal struggles between landlords and tenants in the first half of the sixteenth century is heavily biased towards the abnormal,[137] especially where there was a lawless abuse of their superior power by over-mighty lords, such as Duke Edward of Buckingham. There had always been good and bad landlords, but the good landlords rarely recorded the smooth working of their estates.

In chapter 12 I have discussed the depopulating enclosures, which were largely restricted to the Midlands. It was important to stress that such terrible things could happen. But even in the Midlands no Hundred had more than one third of its villages depopulated.

The importance of combining several small farms into a single farming unit, 'the engrossing of farms by bigger men, was possibly a greater social problem than the . . . controversy over enclosures, if only because it was more general'. The engrossing of farms was not confined to the Midlands but 'was going on all the time all over the country'.[138]

'We obviously rarely hear of amicable settlements between landlords and tenants over the entry fines or their rents.'[139] But it is pleasant to know that some landlords behaved differently from Duke Edward over these matters. One piece of evidence has been published by Professor A.G. Dickens.[140] His article is typical of his continuous quest for producing a balanced picture of Tudor England and to document the presence in it, also, of some socially constructive forces.[141]

Sir John Gostwick (d. 1545) descended from a long line of freeholders in the Bedfordshire village of Willington. He rose to affluence in the service of Cardinal Wolsey and was able to buy in 1529 from its lord, Thomas, Duke of Norfolk, the whole of his native manor, paying for it £1,300. He then entered into the service of Thomas Cromwell. On the creation of a special department for the collection of the First Fruits and Tenths from all ecclesiastical benefices he became in 1535 its first treasurer, retaining this office until his death. Henry VIII knighted him late in 1540, as a way of assuring him of the king's continued high regard after the execution of Thomas Cromwell. At his death in 1545 he owned some 15,000 acres at Willington and neighbouring localities.

Gostwick was a shrewd and acquisitive man of business and it is all the more revealing to find in the instructions for his son moderate and humane advice about how he should behave towards his neighbours and his own tenants. He was not to take above one year's rent for a fine of entry to a new tenant and he was not to raise the rents of men farming his lands, unless those farmers were known to have increased the rents of their undertenants. In Gostwick's eyes this was conducive to acceptance of his newly risen family as part of Bedfordshire's upper society. The instructions about fines and rents are followed immediately by an injunction 'to gett the good will and favor of all your neighbours, as well in Willington as in all the holl shere, and to doo for them and helpe them in all other causes according to your power. And in your so doing you shall please God and also have the love of them.'[142]

NOTES

ABBREVIATIONS

Add.	MS British Library, Additional Manuscript
ADP	Archivio di Stato di Prato (Italy)
AgHR	*Agricultural History Review*
BA	Bulk Accession (in Worcester Record Office references)
BL	British Library (London)
Bul. IHR	*Bulletin of the Institute of Historical Research* (subsequently *Historical Research*)
CPR	*Calendar of Patent Rolls*
EcHR	*Economic History Review*
EHR	*English Historical Review*
Foedera	*Foedera*, ed. Thomas Rymer, Record Commission edn (4 vols, 1816–69)
JHG	*Journal of Historical Geography*
LQR	*Law Quarterly Review*
Miller	Edward Miller (ed.), *Agrarian History of England and Wales*, vol. III: *1348–1500* (Cambridge, 1991)
NLW	National Library of Wales (Aberystwyth)
ns	new series
PRO	Public Record Office (London)
Rec Comm.	Record Commission
RS	Roll Series
Rot. Parl.	*Rotuli Parliamentorum*, 6 vols (1783)
Trans.	*Transactions of Bristol and Gloucester Archaeological Society*
TRHS	*Transactions of the Royal Historical Society*
VCH	*Victoria County History*
Worcester RO	Hereford and Worcester County Record Office (at Worcester)

CHAPTER 1

1   Chapter 8, pp. 744–819.
2   Ibid., pp. 1–33. Dr Miller owes much to the admirable study by John Hatcher, *Plague, Population and the English Economy, 1348–1530* (London, 1977). These are the two main sources for the rest of section I, and much of section II.
3   Miller, p. 4.
4   D.L. Farmer in Miller, Appendix D, on pp. 502–3.
5   Hatcher, *Plague* p. 43.
6   Miller, p. 6.

7   A useful account of the epidemic of 1348/9 (which actually first reached western Europe in 1347) is in P. Ziegler, *The Black Death* (Pelican Books edn, London, 1970).

8   Miller, p. 7; Hatcher, *Plague*, pp. 58–62.

9   Hatcher, ibid., pp. 21–6; Miller, pp. 4–5.

10   E.B. Fryde, *The Great Revolt of 1381*, The Historical Association, General, Series, No. 100 (London, 1981), p. 9. Though an overestimate of the decline of population in the country as a whole, it may have been near the truth for certain areas. Before 1348 East Norfolk was possibly the most densely populated region of England. One of its villages, Coltishall, seven miles north of Norwich, may have lost some 60 per cent of its population in 1349. Between 1349 and 1369 'this manor's population appears to have been reduced by 80 per cent'. Cf. Bruce M.S. Campbell, 'Agricultural progress in medieval England: some evidence from eastern Norfolk', *EcHR*, 2nd ser., 36 (1983), pp. 27–8, and Campbell, 'Population pressure, inheritance and the land market in a fourteenth-century peasant community', *Land, Kinship and Life-Cycle*, ed. R.M. Smith (Cambridge, 1984), pp. 96–7.

11   C. Oman, *The Great Revolt of 1381*, second edn, rev. by E.B. Fryde (Oxford, 1969), p. 27.

12   Miller, p. 6; J. Cornwall, 'English population in the early sixteenth century', *EcHR*, 2nd ser., 23 (1970), p. 44.

13   Especially in his *Economic Growth: England in the Later Middle Ages* (London, 1962).

14   Miller, p. 32.

15   Cf. Hatcher, *Plague*, p. 63.

16   Miller, p. 32.

17   Hatcher, *Plague*, p. 73.

18   A note of caution is needed about this evidence. It is based upon the impressive researches of E.H. Phelps Brown and S.V. Hopkins, published originally in the *Economica* for 1955–6 and reprinted in E.M. Carus-Wilson (ed.), *Essays in Economic History*, vol. II (London, 1962). But for our period their only long series of statistics of wages concerns builders' labourers in southern England. Series of agricultural wages available to them cover only a limited range of agricultural operations (winnowers and threshers).

19   Barbara Harvey, *Westminster Abbey and its Estates in the Middle Ages* (Oxford, 1977), p. 269; Hyams, *EHR*, 87 (1972), p. 611.

20   Hyams, ibid.

21   There is a good survey of the evidence from all parts of England in Hatcher, *Plague*, pp. 37–42.

22   Harvey, *Westminster Abbey*, p. 269.

23   Cited in Oman, *Great Revolt* (1969 edn), p. 152.

24   Worcester RO, 165/92225⅜, m. 1r. and 1v.

25   This is the main argument of his article, 'Deserted medieval villages in the West Midlands', *EcHR*, 2nd ser., 35 (1982).

26   Fryde in Miller, pp. 810–11.

27   Dyer, 'Deserted medieval villages', p. 89.

28   V.H. Galbraith, 'Thoughts about the Peasants' Revolt', *The Reign of Richard II: Essays in Honour of May McKisack*, ed., F.R.H. du Boulay and C.M. Barron (London, 1971), pp. 55–6.

29   *Rot. Parl.*, vol. III, p. 21 (no. 88).

30   I.J.N. Palmer, *England, France and Christendom, 1377–99* (London, 1972), pp. 10–11.

31 Fryde, *Great Revolt*, pp. 22, 29.

32 Barbara Harvey, 'Draft letters patent of manumission and pardon for the men of Somerset in 1381', *EHR* 80 (1965), pp. 89–91. The draft is printed on p. 91. Its contents are the same as those of the document included in his historical writings by Thomas Walsingham, regarded by him as the charter granted to the men of Hertfordshire (ibid., p. 89).

33 *Rot. Parl.*, vol. III, pp. 99 (no. 8) and 100 (nos. 12–13).

34 *Foedera*, vol. IV, p. 126: '*quod nulla acra terrae . . . quae in bondagio vel in servitio tenetur*'.

35 Fryde, *Great Revolt*, p. 29.

36 Ibid.

37 Palmer, *England, France and Christendom*, p. 136, n. 36, and pp. 237–8; J.A. Tuck, 'Nobles, Commons and the Great Revolt', *The English Rising of 1381*, ed. R.H. Hilton and T.H. Aston (Cambridge, 1984), pp. 209–10.

38 Fryde, *Great Revolt*, p. 34.

39 Galbraith, 'Thoughts about the Peasants' Revolt', p. 56.

40 *King, Lords and Peasants in Medieval England: The Common Law of Villeinage in the Twelfth and Thirteenth Centuries* (Oxford, 1980).

41 *EHR*, 87 (1972), p. 611.

42 Cf. L. Musset, 'Réflexions autour du problème de l'esclavage et du servage en Normandie ducale (Xᵉ–XIIᵉ siècles)' in his *Aspects de la Société et de l'Économie dans la Normandie Médiévale (Xᵉ–XIIIᵉ siècles)*, Cahier des *Annales de Normandie*, no. 22 (Caen, 1988), pp. 5–24.

CHAPTER 2

1 See F.W. Maitland's introduction to the edition by W.J. Whittaker of the *Mirror of Justices*, Selden Society, vol. VII (1893), p. XLII and n. 5. The most significant passages are on pp. 81 and 165 (no. 93), but the topic of serfdom and of the position of villeins reappears frequently. Horn shows very good acquaintance with some of the technicalities of the law of serfdom.

2 Sir Frederick Pollock and F.W. Maitland, *The History of English Law before the Time of Edward I* (Cambridge, 1895), vol. I, p. 341. The account of the 'Unfree Tenure' is by Maitland.

3 London, British Library, Harleian MS 445, f. 1r.

4 C. Dyer, 'The social and economic background to the rural revolt of 1381', *The English Rising*, ed. Hilton and Aston, p. 41.

5 An excellent recent discussion of these developments is in P. Bonnassie's collected papers. I am using the English translation by Jean Birrell, *From Slavery to Feudalism in South-Western Europe*, (Cambridge, 1991). See especially articles nos 1, 7, 9 and 10.

6 Ibid., pp. 321–3.

7 Ibid., pp. 339–40.

8 L. Musset, 'Réflexions autour du problème de l'esclavage et du servage', pp. 10–12, 18–24.

9 The citations from Stenton are from his *First Century of English Feudalism, 1066–1166* (Oxford, 2nd edn, 1961), p. 115. The best detailed accounts of the situation of the peasantry after the Norman Conquest are in R. Lennard, *Rural England 1086–1135* (Oxford, 1959), and in Sally Harvey, 'Domesday England', *The Agrarian History of England and Wales*, vol. II: *1042–1350*, ed. H.E. Hallam (Cambridge, 1988), chapter 2. See also

Helen Cam, 'The evolution of the medieval English franchise' in her *Law-Finders and Law-Makers in Medieval England* (London, 1962), pp. 23–9.

10 Cam, ibid., p. 26.

11 Bonnassie, *From Slavery to Feudalism* p. 326.

12 The account that follows in this section is based chiefly on P. Hyams's fascinating book (*King, Lords and Peasants in Medieval England*) and on Professor Hyams's other publications.

13 After 1294 whenever a double rate of taxes on movables was imposed, the Ancient Demesne and towns paid at a higher rate. Cf. J.F. Willard, *Parliamentary Taxes on Personal Property, 1290 to 1334* (Cambridge, Mass., 1934), p. 9.

14 See below, chapter 3, section IV.

15 J. Hatcher, 'English serfdom and villeinage: towards a reassessment', *Past and Present*, 90 (1981), p. 34.

16 Quoted by Sally Harvey, 'Domesday England', p. 50.

17 Bonnassie, *From Slavery to Feudalism*, pp. 330–2, 336 and n. 105.

18 Hyams, *King, Lords and Peasants*, pp. 249–50. For Gilbert Foliot see D. Knowles, *The Episcopal Colleagues of Archbishop Thomas Becket* (Cambridge, 1951), pp. 37–49.

19 A.L. Poole, *Obligations of Society in the XII and XIII Centuries* (Oxford, 1946), p. 13.

20 E. Miller, 'The English economy in the thirteenth century: implications of recent research', *Past and Present*, 28 (July 1964), pp. 21–40. The passages cited here are on pp. 21–2.

21 Hatcher, 'English serfdom and villeinage', pp. 6–7. Christopher Dyer's estimate is lower: 'at the end of the process [of legal definition of the status and tenure of the peasantry] about a half of the rural population had been classified as unfree'. Cf. his *Standards of Living in the Later Middle Ages: Social Change in England, c. 1200–1520* (Cambridge, 1989), p. 137. Because the Hundred Rolls of 1279, on which these estimates are largely based, do not survive for the areas of particularly widespread serfdom in parts of the west Midlands and in south-western England, it is probable that both these estimates are too low.

22 R.H. Hilton, *The English Peasantry in the Later Middle Ages* (Oxford, 1975), p. 140.

23 Cf. below, chapter 4.

24 R.H. Hilton, *The Decline of Serfdom in Medieval England* (London, 1969), p. 20. On pp. 18–24 Hilton provides a survey of the distribution of servile and free tenantry in different parts of England.

25 R. Lennard, 'The economic position of the Domesday *villani*', *Economic Journal*, 56 (1946), pp. 244–64.

26 Miller, 'The English economy in the thirteenth century' p. 26; Hilton, *Decline of Serfdom*, p. 20, and Hilton, *English Peasantry* p. 139.

27 E.B. Fryde, *William de la Pole, Merchant and King's Banker, (d. 1366)*, (London, 1988), pp. 109–10.

28 R. Lennard, 'The economic position of the bordars and cottars of Domesday Book', *Economic Journal*, 61 (1951), p. 342.

29 I. Kershaw, 'The great famine and agrarian crisis in England, 1315–22', *Past and Present*, 59 (1973). The quotation in the text is from p. 29.

30 Edited with other similar records in M. Hollings, *The Red Book of Worcester*, Worcestershire Historical Society (4 pts, 1934–50).

31 R.H. Hilton, *A Medieval Society: The West Midlands at the End of the Thirteenth Century* (Cambridge, 1966, repr. 1983), pp. 122–3; Christopher Dyer, *Lords and Peasants in a*

Changing Society: The Estates of the Bishopric of Worcester, 680–1540 (Cambridge, 1980), pp. 108, 110.

32 For the topography of Kempsey see Helen E. O'Neil, 'Court House excavations, Kempsey, Worcestershire, January, 1956', *Transactions of the Worcestershire Archaeological Society*, 33 (1956), pp. 33–9.

33 Hilton, *A Medieval Society*, p. 123.

34 Dyer, *Lords and Peasants*, p. 79.

35 See below, chapter 6.

36 R.E. Glasscock, *The Lay Subsidy of 1334* (London, 1975), pp. 350–5. Kempsey is on p. 350.

37 Dyer, *Lords and Peasants*, p. 110.

38 Ibid.

39 C. Dyer, *Standards of Living in the Later Middle Ages: Social Change in England, c. 1200–1520* (Cambridge, 1989), pp. 110–17.

40 Hyams, *King, Lords and Peasants*, pp. 49–50.

41 E.g., the Abbey of Halesowen (Staffordshire) between 1252 and 1285 (a badly governed house according to a visitation of 1311) and the Abbey of Vale Royal (Cheshire) between 1326 and 1336. For Halesowen see G.C. Homans, *English Villagers of the Thirteenth Century* (1941, repr. New York, 1960), pp. 276–84, and Z. Razi, 'The struggles between the abbots of Halesowen and their tenants in the thirteenth and fourteenth centuries', *Social Relations and Ideas: Essays in Honour of R.H. Hilton* ed. T.H. Aston *et alii* (Oxford, 1983). For Vale Royal see G.C. Coulton, *The Medieval Village* (Cambridge, 1925), pp. 131–5.

42 For some examples see below in this section.

43 G.C. Homans, *English Villagers of the Thirteenth Century* (1941, repr. New York, 1960); J. Hatcher, 'English serfdom and villeinage: towards a reassessment', *Past and Present*, 90 1981), pp. 3–39.

44 Hatcher, ibid., pp. 15, 22.

45 R.M. Smith, 'Some thoughts on "hereditary" and proprietary rights in land under customary law in thirteenth and early fourteenth century England' in *Law and History Review*, 1 (1983), p. 98.

46 Ibid., p. 122.

47 Ibid., p. 106.

48 See below, chapter 3.

49 Cf. M.M. Postan, *The Famulus: the Estate Labourer in the Twelfth and Thirteenth Centuries* (London, 1954).

50 Smith, 'Some thoughts on "hereditary" and proprietary rights', pp. 120–2.

51 See below, chapters 4 and 5.

52 Worcester RO, 166/92230.

53 C. Dyer in *The English Rising*, ed. Hilton and Aston, p. 33.

54 R.M. Smith, *loc. cit.* (1983), pp. 124–6.

55 J.A. Raftis, *The Estates of Ramsey Abbey: A Study in Economic Growth and Organization* (Toronto, 1957), p. 238.

56 Smith, 'Some thoughts on "hereditary" and proprietary rights', p. 117.

57 R.H. Hilton, 'Building accounts of Elmley Castle, Worcestershire, 1345–6', *Birmingham Historical Journal*, 10 (1965), pp. 78–87. I visited Elmley in 1991.

58   E.B. Fryde in Miller, p. 762.

59   Hyams, *King, Lords and Peasants*, p. 268.

60   Bonnassie, *From Slavery to Feudalism*, p. 326 and n. 63.

61   Henry de Bracton, *De Legibus et Consuetudinibus Angliae*, (ed.) S.E. Thorne (4 vols, Cambridge, Mass., 1968–77); F.W. Maitland (ed.), *Bracton's Note Book* (3 vols, London, 1887). See also S.E. Thorne, *Henry de Bracton, 1268–1968* (Exeter, 1970).

62   P. Vinogradoff, *Villainage in England* (Oxford, 1892); F.W. Maitland in Sir Frederick Pollock and F.W. Maitland, *The History of English Law before the Time of Edward I* (Cambridge, 1895), vol. 1.

63   'The origins of a peasant land market in England', *EcHR*, 2nd ser., 23 (1970); 'The action of Naifty in the early Common Law', *LQR*, 90 (1974), pp. 326–50; 'The proof of villein status in the Common Law', *EHR*, 89 (1974), pp. 721–49; *King, Lords and Peasants in Medieval England: The Common Law of Villeinage in the Twelfth and Thirteenth Centuries* (Oxford, 1980).

64   E. Davenport, *The Economic Development of a Norfolk Manor, 1086–1565* (Cambridge, 1906), appendix X, p. lxxii.

65   Ibid., p. 70. I return to this evidence in section III of chapter 16.

66   E.B. Fryde in Miller, p. 764.

67   C.N.L. Brooke and M.M. Postan (eds), *Carte Nativorum: A Peterborough Abbey Cartulary of the Fourteenth Century*, Northamptonshire Record Society, XX (Oxford, 1960), pp. xi–xxviii ('The Manuscript', by C.N.L. Brooke); E. King, *Peterborough Abbey, 1086–1310: A Study in the Land Market* (Cambridge, 1973), chapter 6 ('*Carte Nativorum*'), pp. 99–125.

68   On the origins and procedure of this see Hyams, 'Action of Naifty'; on types of proof used in this and other actions dealing with status see Hyams, 'Proof of villein status'. There is a more summary account in chapter 10 of Hyams, *King, Lords and Peasants*. For the text of the writ of Naifty see G.D.G. Hall (ed.), *The Treatise on the Laws and Customs of the Realm of England commonly called Glanvill* (c. 1187–9). The writ is on pp. 141–2 (Glanvill, XII, 11).

69   Hyams, 'Action of Naifty', p. 335.

70   Hyams, *King, Lords and Peasants*, pp. 263–4. The writ is in Glanvill, XII, 10 (Hall, *Glanvill*, p. 141).

71   Glanvill, V, 1–2 (ibid., pp. 53–6).

72   Hyams, 'Action of Naifty', pp. 328–30. See also Hyams, *Kings, Lords and Peasants*, index on p. 295 (under *De libertate probanda*).

73   Hyams, *King, Lords and Peasants*, p. 166 and n. 18.

74   Ibid., p. 342.

75   Ibid., pp. 328–32.

76   Ibid., pp. 337–8.

77   Hyams 'Proof of villein status', p. 727, and *King, Lords and Peasants*, p. 215.

78   This is stressed by Hyams in 'Action of Naifty', p. 331, n. 31.

79   Ibid. and E.B. Fryde in Miller, p. 767.

80   Though regular civil litigation by means of this assize may have developed only in the last years of Henry II. Cf. Hall, *Glanvill*, p. 167, n. 1. The writ is edited *Glanvill*, XIII, 32–3, 38, on pp. 167–70.

81   The writ is edited *Glanvill*, XIII, 3, 7–13 (ibid, pp. 150, 151–7).

82   D.M. Stenton, *English Justice between the Norman Conquest and the Great Charter, 1066–1215* (London, 1965), p. 43.

83 An example is a case in Devon in 1238 cited in Hyams, 'Action of Naifty', p. 335, n. 56.

84 Hyams, *King, Lords and Peasants*, pp. 97–102 and n. 78, on p. 102.

85 Hyams, 'Action of Naifty', p. 340. See also R.H. Hilton, 'Freedom and villeinage in England', *Past and Present* 31 (1965), p. 15 and examples there cited, pp. 17–19.

86 Hyams, *King, Lords and Peasants*, pp. 250–1.

87 Ibid., p. 250.

88 Hyams, 'Proof of villein status', p. 730.

89 Ibid., 734–41.

90 Ibid., p. 742 and n. 2.

91 Ibid., p. 746.

92 Hyams, *King, Lords and Peasants*, pp. 54–5.

93 Ibid., pp. 56–63.

94 Ibid., p. 55. The same chapter 6 ends with the conclusion (ibid., p. 65) that 'servile tenure almost never received any protection in the royal courts'.

95 Ibid., pp. 114–15.

96 Ibid., p. 115 and n. 133.

97 Ibid. See also below, section VII, for a monstrously unjust case of this in 1356 at the Earl of Warwick's manor of Elmley Castle.

98 Smith, 'Some thoughts on "hereditary" and proprietary rights': pp. 115–19 (Bury St Edmund's); pp. 119–20 (Peterborough). See also King, *Peterborough Abbey*, pp. 99–125.

99 Oxford, Balliol College, Bursary Muniments, collection A.19.

100 Ibid., nos 3b and 3c.

101 For example, ibid., no. 2a (2½ acres of arable held for 2s a year), a deed probably of c. 1200–30.

102 Hyams, *King, Lords and Peasants*, p. 186.

103 Ibid, p. 118.

104 F.W. Maitland in Pollock and Maitland, *History of English Law*, vol. I, p. 357.

105 Hyams, *King, Lords and Peasants*, p. 197.

106 Ibid., p. 186.

107 Ibid., p. 184.

108 Ibid., p. 187. Merchet is discussed by Hyams on pp. 187–91.

109 Ibid., p. 189.

110 Ibid., p. 193. Tallage is discussed by Hyams on pp. 191–3.

111 Ibid., p. 267.

112 Smith, 'Some thoughts on "hereditary" and proprietary rights', p. 98.

113 A book of excerpts from the manorial court rolls compiled at the Abbey of St Albans in 1354/5 contains the earliest entries for seven different manors dated 1237, 1238, 1240, 1244 and 1247. Cf. A.E. Levett, *Studies in Manorial History*, ed. H.M. Cam, M. Coate, L.S. Sutherland (Oxford, 1938), pp. 80–1. A similar collection of excerpts for one of the manors of the Abbey of Bury St Edmunds starts in 1259 (ibid., p. 81, n. 1). The earliest manorial court rolls from the estates of the Abbey of Ramsey survive for 1239/40. Cf. Raftis, *The Estates of Ramsey Abbey*, p. 107. See also Smith, 'Some thoughts on "hereditary" and proprietary rights', pp. 98–100.

114 Brooke and Postan (eds), *Carte Nativorum*, p. xxxviii (court rolls of the Abbey of Ramsey, 1239) and p. xlvi (Chalgrave, Beds., 1294). On Chalgrave see also P. Hyams 'The origins of a peasant land market in England', *EcHR*, 2nd ser., 23 (1970), p. 27 and n. 2.

115 E.B. Fryde, 'The tenants of the bishops of Coventry and Lichfield and of Worcester after the plague of 1348–9', *Medieval Legal Records edited in memory of C.A.F. Meekings* (London, 1978), p. 252.

116 Worcester RO, 193/92627, $^{11}/_{12}$.

117 Ibid., 158/92014.

118 Hyams, *King, Lords and Peasants*, p. 198.

119 Ibid., p. 187.

120 Ibid., p. 268

121 Miller, 'The English economy in the thirteenth century', p. 25; E. Miller, 'England in the twelfth and thirteenth centuries: an economic contrast?', *EcHR*, 2nd ser., 24 (1971), pp. 10–12; P.D.A. Harvey, 'The Pipe Rolls and the adoption of demesne farming in England', *EcHR*, 27 (1974), pp. 345, 353–8.

122 D.A. Carpenter, 'English peasants in politics, 1258–1267', *Past and Present*, 136 (1992), pp. 19–27, cites several examples from the middle years of the reign of Henry III.

123 Ibid., pp. 19–20.

124 Cf. R.E. Archer, 'The estates and finances of Margaret of Brotherton, *c.* 1320–99', *Historical Research*, 60 (1987), pp. 264–79.

125 C. Dyer in *The English Rising*, ed. Hilton and Aston pp. 31–2.

126 Worcester RO, BA 989, ref. 899:95, box 1, no 2.

127 Harvey, *Westminster Abbey*, p. 245.

128 E. Miller, *The Abbey and Bishopric of Ely* (Cambridge, 1951), p. 109.

129 Ibid., p. 110.

130 R.H. Hilton, 'Gloucester Abbey leases of the late thirteenth century'. I am using the text reprinted in his *English Peasantry in the Later Middle Ages* (Oxford, 1975), pp. 148–60.

131 Ibid., pp. 150 and 158–9 (text of deed).

132 Ibid., p. 150, n. 35: '*Ita tamen quod sanguis eorum nullatenus immutetur sed ipsi et eorum successio nostri servi et servilis condicionis existunt.*'

133 E. Mason (ed.), *The Beauchamp Cartulary Charters, 1100–1268*, Pipe Roll Society, ns, 43 (1980), no. 265 on p. 151.

134 Barbara Harvey, 'The "crisis" of the early fourteenth century', *Before the Black Death: Studies in the 'crisis' of the early fourteenth century*, ed. B.M.S. Campbell (Manchester, 1990), p. 17.

135 The account of Langenhoe that follows is based on R.H. Britnell, 'Production for the market on a small fourteenth-century estate', *EcHR*, 2nd ser. 19 (1966), pp. 380–7. See also R.H. Britnell, 'Minor landlords in England and medieval agrarian capitalism', *Past and Present*, 89 (1980), pp. 6–7, 13, 16–17.

CHAPTER 3

1 R.H. Hilton and T.H. Aston (eds), *The English Rising of 1381* (Cambridge, 1984).

2 I owe thanks to Miss Faith for giving me the first, original version of her paper, which I shall be using here (1981).

3 I shall be using both of Dyer's versions (1981 and 1984), but mainly the 1984 one.

4 In H. Mayr-Harting and R.I. Moore (eds), *Studies in Medieval History presented to R.H.C. Davis* (London, 1985), pp. 247–70.

5   Brooks, ibid., p. 265.

6   Ibid., p. 266.

7   J. Hatcher, 'England in the aftermath of the Black Death', *Past and Present*, 144 (1994), p. 34.

8   G.C. Macaulay (ed.), *The Complete Works of John Gower*, vol. I (Oxford, 1899), pp. 293–4; *Rot. Parl.*, vol. III, p. 21 (no. 88).

9   Introduction and appendix II to Oman, *Great Revolt* (1969 edn); Fryde, *Great Revolt*, pp. 13–15; E.B. Fryde, 'Parliament and the Peasants' Revolt to 1381', reprinted as no. XIII in my *Studies in Medieval Trade and Finance* (London, 1983).

10   J. Taylor, *English Historical Literature in the Fourteenth Century* (Oxford, 1987), p. 42.

11   Translated in R.B. Dobson (ed.), *The Peasants' Revolt of 1381* (London, 1970), p. 63.

12   K.G. Feiling, 'An Essex manor in the fourteenth century', *EHR*, 26 (1911); J.A. Brent, 'Alciston manor in the later Middle Ages', *Sussex Archaeological Collections*, 106 (1968); P.F. Brandon, 'Demesne arable farming in coastal Sussex during the later Middle Ages', *AgHR*, 19 (1971).

13   R.H. Britnell, 'Feudal reaction after the Black Death in the Palatinate of Durham', *Past and Present*, 128 (1990), pp. 28–47.

14   J. Hatcher, *Rural Economy and Society in the Duchy of Cornwall, 1300–1500* (Cambridge, 1970), p. 104. For details of tenures in Cornwall see below, chapter 13, section III.

15   Translated in Dobson (ed.), *Peasants' Revolt*, p. 63.

16   See below, chapter 4, section IV.

17   Hatcher, 'England in the aftermath of the Black Death', p. 31.

18   Britnell, 'Feudal reaction' pp. 28–47.

19   Raftis, *The Estates of Ramsey Abbey*, p. 257, n. 15.

20   D.L. Farmer in Miller, p. 483.

21   B.H. Putnam, *The Enforcement of the Statutes of Labourers during the first Decade after the Black Death, 1349–59* (New York, 1908) remains the most important publication on the first period of this legislation. D.L. Farmer's account (1991), cited in the preceding note, is the most up-to-date, brief, but useful, account for the whole period 1349–1500 (Miller, pp. 483–90). See also my own account, ibid., pp. 753–60. These are the three principal sources for this section, citing the most important other publications. The text of the ordinance of June 1349 is in *Statutes of the Realm*, vol. I, pp. 307–8.

22   E.B. Fryde, in Miller, p. 754.

23   S.B. Chrimes, *English Constitutional Ideas in the XV Century* (Cambridge, 1936), p. 235, n. 4. The statute of 1378 is in *Statutes of the Realm*, vol. II, p. 11 (2 Richard II, c.8).

24   Britnell, 'Feudal reaction', p. 29.

25   The most important figures are listed by Farmer in Miller, p. 484.

26   W.O. Ault, 'Open-field husbandry and the village community: a study of agrarian by-laws in medieval England', *Transactions of the American Philosophical Society*, ns, 55 (7), (Philadelphia, 1965).

27   J.A. Raftis, *Tenure and Mobility: Studies in the Social History of the Medieval English Village* (Toronto, 1964), pp. 112, 126.

28   E.M. Thompson, 'Offenders against the Statute of Labourers in Wiltshire, A.D. 1349', *The Wiltshire Archaeological and Natural History Magazine*, 33 (1904), pp. 384–409. The title is misleading as the roll of the justices really dates from 1352.

29   Dyer in *The English Rising*, Hilton and Aston, p. 25.

30   B.H. Putnam, 'The Justices of Labourers in the fourteenth century', *EHR* 21 (1906), p. 527 and n. 75.

31   Ibid., pp. 517–38; B.H. Putnam, 'The transformation of the Keepers of the Peace into the Justices of the Peace, 1327–80', *TRHS*, 4th ser., 12 (1929), pp. 19–48; A. Harding, 'The revolt against the justices', *The English Rising*, ed. Hilton and Aston, pp. 165–93.

32   *Rot. Parl.*, vol. II, p. 296 (no. 15).

33   Britnell, 'Production for the market', p. 385. For his farming see above, chapter 2, section VII.

34   E. Chapin-Furber (ed.), *Essex Sessions of the Peace, 1351, 1377–79,* Essex Archaeological Society (Colchester, 1953), pp. 51, 68–9.

35   Hatcher, 'England in the aftermath of the Black Death', pp. 19–20.

36   C. Dyer in *The English Rising*, ed. Hilton and Aston, p. 25.

37   E.A. Bond (ed.), *Chronica Monasterii de Melsa (1180–1506)*, RS, vol. III (1868), p. 128.

38   A. Harding, in *The English Rising*, ed. Hilton and Aston, pp. 185–6.

39   B.H. Putnam, 'Chief Justice Shareshull and the economic and legal code of 1351–52', *University of Toronto Law Journal*, 5 (1944), pp. 281–2.

40   For the operation of this scheme in Worcestershire see below, chapter 4, section II.

41   Figures based upon Putnam, *Enforcement of the Statutes of Labourers*, supplemented by my own additions from various classes of exchequer records.

42   Putnam, *Enforcement of the Statutes of Labourers*, p. 221; D.L. Farmer in Miller, pp. 484–5.

43   Hatcher, 'England in the aftermath of the Black Death', pp. 23–5.

44   Brent, 'Alciston manor', p. 95. I will return to the later history of Alciston in chapter 8, sections I and III.

45   E.B. Fryde, 'The financial policies of the royal governments and popular resistance to them in France and England, *c.* 1270–*c.* 1420' (originally published in 1979), reprinted as no. I in my *Studies in Medieval Trade and Finance* (London, 1983), p. 847 (of the original 1979 pagination). For fees and annuities paid out of the customs see W.M. Ormrod in *EcHR*, 2nd ser., 40 (1987), p. 35 and n. 49.

46   Putnam 'Transformation of Keepers of the Peace', pp. 45–7.

47   *Statutes of the Realm*, vol. I, p. 367.

48   D.L. Farmer in Miller, pp. 485–6.

49   In Hilton and Aston (eds), *The English Rising* pp. 9–42.

50   These are discussed in part IV of A.E. Levett, *Studies in Manorial History* (Oxford, 1938).

51   Hilton and Aston (eds), *The English Rising*, pp. 10–11.

52   N. Brooks in *Studies in Medieval History*, ed. Mayr-Harting and Moore, pp. 268–70.

53   In the papers of the Past and Present Society's conference of 1981 and in Hilton and Aston (eds), *The English Rising*, p. 43ff.

54   C. Dyer in *The English Rising*, ed. Hilton and Aston, p. 34.

55   *Rot. Parl.*, vol. III, p. 103 (no. 30).

56   See the preface to Gower's *Vox Clamantis* in G.C. Macaulay, *The Complete Works of John Gower*, (4 vols, Oxford, 1899–1902), vol. IV, p. xxxi.

57   Dyer in Hilton and Aston (eds), *The English Rising*, p. 15.

58   Galbraith, 'Thoughts about the Peasants' Revolt', p. 53. Professor Galbraith suggests that

the author may have been William Pakington, Keeper of the King's Wardrobe (ibid., pp. 48–51). I find this probable. This suggestion is doubted by J. Taylor (*English Historical Literature*, p. 319), but I find his comments unconvincing.

59 T. Wright (ed.), *Political Poems and Songs Relating to English History*, RS (1859), p. 225.

60 R.H. Hilton, *Bond Men Made Free* (London, 1973, repr. 1988), p. 224.

61 G.A. Holmes, *The Estates of the Higher Nobility in Fourteenth-Century England* (Cambridge, 1957), pp. 51–2. I owe thanks to Professor Holmes for giving me a copy of his book.

62 The account that follows is based chiefly on the excellent monograph by K.C. Newton, *Thaxted in the Fourteenth Century* (Chelmsford, 1960).

63 Ibid., p. 31.

64 Harding in *The English Rising*, ed. Hilton and Aston, p. 186, n. 90. For the widespread hostility to John of Gaunt, Duke of Lancaster, see Fryde, *Great Revolt*, pp. 13–14, 19–23.

65 Newton, *Thaxted*, p. 31 and n. 99, p. 58.

66 E.B. Dewindt, *Land and People in Holywell-cum-Needingworth* (Toronto, 1972), pp. 268–9.

67 See above, chapter 2, section IV; Razi, 'Abbots of Halesowen and their tenants'.

68 The best account is R. Faith, 'The *Great Rumour* of 1377 and peasant ideology', reprinted in *The English Rising*, ed. Hilton and Aston. There is an earlier study by J.H. Tillotson, 'Peasant unrest in the England of Richard II: some evidence from royal records', *Historical Studies* (Canberra), 16 (1974), pp. 1–16.

69 R. Faith in *The English Rising*, ed Hilton and Aston, p. 43.

70 There is an excellent study of one such manor by M.K. McIntosh, *Autonomy and Community: The Royal Manor of Havering 1200–1500* (Cambridge, 1986).

71 Ibid., p. 164.

72 There is much evidence about this in M.A. Barg, 'The villeins of the ancient demesne', *Studi in Memoria di Federigo Melis* (Naples, 1978), vol. I, especially in table I, pp. 224–7.

73 R. Faith, '*Great Rumour*', appendix, pp. 36–9.

74 Ibid., pp. 3–5.

75 Ibid., pp. 4–5.

76 Ibid., pp. 15, 36.

77 *Rot. Parl.*, vol. III, pp. 21–2. Translated in Dobson (ed.), *Peasants' Revolt*, pp. 76–8.

78 Faith, 'Great Rumour', p. 4 and n. 8 (on p. 30).

79 *Rot. Parl.*, vol. III, p. 17 (no. 54).

80 D.L. Farmer in Miller, p. 485.

81 Chapin-Furber (ed.), *Essex Sessions*, p. 69.

82 Fryde, *Great Revolt*, p. 26.

83 E.B. Fryde in Miller, pp. 758–9. For the harsh lordship over her tenants of Countess Margaret of Norfolk see below, chapter 16, section III.

84 *Rot. Parl.*, vol. II, pp. 340–1 (no. 116).

85 B.H. Putnam (ed.), *Proceedings before the Justices of the Peace in the Fourteenth and the Fifteenth Centuries* (London, Ames Foundation, 1938), p. cxxiii.

86 W.W. Skeat (ed.), *The Vision of William concerning Piers the Plowman* (Oxford, 1886), vol. I, pp. 222–3.

87 Macaulay, *Works of John Gower*, vol. I, pp. lxviii, 277.

88 Cf. J.A. Tuck in *The English Rising*, ed. Hilton and Aston, pp. 208–9.

89 This section is based mainly on my two articles, both reprinted in *Studies in Medieval Trade*.

They are: no. I, 'The financial policies of the royal governments and popular resistance to them in France and England, *c.* 1270–*c.* 1420' (originally published in 1979) and no. XIII, 'Parliament and the Peasants' Revolt of 1381' (originally published in 1970). See also my revised edition of Oman, *Great Revolt*, introduction, pp. xii–xxii, and appendix II, pp. 164–6.

90 Fryde, *Studies in Medieval Trade and Finance*, no. I, p. 852.

91 D.L. Farmer in Miller, p. 484.

92 Ibid.

93 Fryde, *Great Revolt*, pp. 11–12.

94 J.A. Tuck in *The English Rising*, ed. Hilton and Aston, p. 204.

95 Fryde, *Great Revolt*, pp. 14–15.

96 Taylor, *English Historical Literature*, appendix V: 'Chronicle accounts of the Peasants' Revolt'. See especially p. 321.

97 Translated in Dobson (ed.), *Peasants' Revolt*, pp. 134–7.

98 There is a critical scrutiny of the information provided in it by N. Brooks in *Studies in Medieval History*, ed. Mayr-Harting and Moore, pp. 250–2.

99 V.H. Galbraith (ed.), *The Anonimalle Chronicle 1333–1381* (Manchester, 1927), pp. 134–5. The late Professor Galbraith very kindly gave me a copy of his edition.

100 Fryde, *Great Revolt*, pp. 30–1.

101 N. Brooks in *Studies in Medieval History*, ed. Mayr-Harting and Moore, pp. 262–6; Chapin-Furber (ed.), *Essex Sessions*, pp. 8–25, *passim*.

102 M. Rampton, 'The Peasants' Revolt of 1381 and the written word', *Comitatus* (Los Angeles), 24 (1993), p. 51; M.M. Taylor (ed.), *Some Sessions of the Peace in Cambridgeshire in the Fourteenth Century, 1340, 1380–83* (Cambridge, 1942), pp. xliii, 50.

103 N. Brooks in *Studies in Medieval History*, ed. Mayr-Harting and Moore. pp. 262–6.

104 Taylor, *English Historical Literature*, p. 320.

105 *Foedera*, vol. IV, p. 126.

106 Ibid., '*quod nulla acra terrae . . . quae in bondagio vel in servitio tenetur*'.

107 E.B. Fryde in Miller, p. 779.

108 Ibid., pp. 779–80.

109 Galbraith (ed.), *Anonimalle Chronicle*, pp. 144–5.

110 E.B. Fryde in Miller, p. 780. The passage in Froissart is cited in Dobson (ed.), *Peasants' Revolt*, p. 370.

111 E.B. Fryde in Miller, pp. 780–1, summarizing the *Anonimalle Chronicle*, p. 147, in Galbraith's edition.

112 Translated in Dobson (ed.), *Peasant's Revolt*, p. 186.

113 T. Stemmler, 'The Peasants' Revolt of 1381 in Contemporary Literature', *Functions of Literature: Essays Presented to Erwin Wolff* (Tübingen, 1984), pp. 36–7. I owe thanks to Dr Stemmler for giving me a copy of his article.

114 J.A. Tuck in *The English Rising*, ed. Hilton and Aston, pp. 194–5; Fryde, *Great Revolt*, p. 31.

115 Hilton and Aston (eds), *The English Rising*, pp. 11–12.

116 A. Réville et C. Petit-Dutaillis, *Le Soulèvement des Travailleurs d'Angleterre en 1381* (Paris, 1898), pp. 213–14, 220.

117 E.B. Fryde, *William de la Pole, Merchant and King's Banker (d. 1366)* (London, 1988), Preface, p. i.

118 G.A. Holmes, *The Later Middle Ages, 1272–1485* (Edinburgh, 1962), photostat facing p. 132. For the ownership of Moze see S. Walker, *The Lancastrian Affinity, 1361–99* (Oxford, 1990), p. 194, n. 72, and *Calendar of Inquisitions Post Mortem*, 17, nos 58–9 (16 August, 15 Rich. II).

119 Levett, *Studies in Manorial History*, pp. 89–90, 179, 191–2, 204.

120 Powell, *The Rising in East Anglia*, pp. 14–21.

121 Oman, *Great Revolt* (1969 edn), p. 128. Henry Knighton's chronicle is the primary source for these events. Cf. Taylor, *English Historical Literature*, p. 320 and n. 21.

122 Oman, *Great Revolt* (1969 edn), p. 118.

123 Ibid., pp. 133–4; Hilton, *Bond Men Made Free*, pp. 172–4, 177.

124 C. Dyer, in *The English Rising*, ed. Hilton and Aston, pp. 33–7.

125 Réville et Petit-Dutaillis, *Soulèvement des Travailleurs*, pp. 216–17; Hilton, *Bond Men Made Free*, p. 217.

126 C. Dyer in *The English Rising*, ed. Hilton and Aston, p. 36.

127 J.S. Roskell, 'Sir Richard de Waldegrave of Bures St. Mary, Speaker in the parliament of 1381–2', *Proceedings of the Suffolk Institute of Archaeology*, 27 (1957), pp. 154–75. See also on Waldegrave Fryde in Miller, pp. 782–3.

128 *Rot. Parl.*, vol. III, p. 100 (no. 17), translated in Dobson (ed.), *Peasants' Revolt*, pp. 330–1.

129 Cf. J.S. Roskell, *The Impeachment of Michael de la Pole, Earl of Suffolk, in 1386, in the Context of the Reign of Richard II* (Manchester, 1984).

130 *Rot. Parl.*, vol, III, p. 150 (no. 6), translated in Dobson (ed.), *Peasants' Revolt*, p. 362.

131 *Rot. Parl.*, vol. III, p. 100 (no. 17).

132 *Vox Clamantis* in *Works of John Gower*, ed. Macaulay, vol. IV, pp. 79–80.

133 J.G. Bellamy, 'The northern rebellions in the later years of Richard II', *Bulletin of the John Rylands Library* (Manchester), 47 (1965), p. 264.

CHAPTER 4

1 His principal publication is *Lords and Peasants in a Changing Society: The Estates of the Bishopric of Worcester, 680–1540* (Cambridge, 1980).

2 Sally Harvey in *Agrarian History*, vol. II, ed. Hallam, p. 106.

3 The most recent critical review of the evidence is in the fascinating book by P. Sims-Williams, *Religion and Literature in Western England, 600–800* (Cambridge, 1990). See especially chapters 5, 6 and 12. See also Delia Hooke, 'Village development in the West Midlands', *Medieval Villages*, ed. D. Hooke (Oxford, 1985), pp. 125–54. On pp. 127–31 and 135 there is a valuable reconstruction of the origins and settlement pattern of the episcopal estate of Tredington (in Worcestershire until 1931, when transferred to Warwickshire).

4 Dyer, *Standard of Living* (1989), p. 136.

5 Sims-Williams, *Religion and Literature*, pp. 122–4. The abbey was founded by the Hwiccan dynasty and continued to be intimately associated with its members until the early eighth century.

6 R.H. Hilton, 'Gloucester Abbey leases of the late thirteenth century' (originally published in 1956). I am citing the reprinted text in Hilton's *The English Peasantry in the Later Middle Ages* (Oxford, 1975), pp. 142–5.

7   M. Hollings (ed.), *The Red Book of Worcester* (4 pts, Worcestershire Historical Society. 1934–50).

8   They were Withington, Cleeve, Bibury and Henbury in Gloucestershire, and Blockley, Bredon, Kempsey, Whitstones and Hartlebury in Worcestershire. These five were in the eastern group of estates, particularly fractious in the middle decades of the fifteenth century. For more details see below, chapter 9.

9   C. Dyer, 'A redistribution of incomes in fifteenth-century England?', *Past and Present*, 39 (1968), p. 14.

10 Dyer, *Lords and Peasants*, pp. 236–8.

11 E.B. Fryde, 'The tenants of the bishops of Coventry and Lichfield and Worcester after the plague of 1348–49' *Medieval Legal Records Edited in Memory of C.A.F. Meekings*, ed. R.F. Hunnisett and J.B. Post (London, 1978), p. 230.

12 Some of the early leases are discussed in chapter 5.

13 For the history of the episcopal properties in the fifteenth century see chapters 6, 9, 11 and 17.

14 Fryde, 'Tenants of the bishops', pp. 228–32 and the tables on pp. 242–57. Some of the texts are published on pp. 258–66.

15 *Rot. Parl.*, vol. II, p. 238 (no. 10).

16 PRO, K.R. Subsidies, E179/200/15. A few excerpts from it are printed in Putnam, *Enforcement of the Statutes of Labourers* pp. 357–8. See also the proceedings brought against the tax collectors of the levy in Worcestershire of the second year of the triennial grant (in 1353) for alleged fraudulent appropriation of the money (£55 7s 10d) intended for distribution among the impoverished localities, Exchequer Plea Roll, E13/82B, m. 32v. (1360). The enrolled account for the second year of the triennial grant is in L.T.R. Enrolled Accts. E359/14, m. 45v.

17 For details see below, section III of this chapter.

18 PRO, K.R. Escheators' Accts (E136), 12/20, 13/28 and 28A, 14/13 (the vacancy of 1361/2); ibid., 13/30 and 14/16 (the vacancy of 1364), from which there also survives an elaborate extent of the bishopric, PRO Ancient Extents, SC11 (Roll 724); Foreign Acct Rolls, E364/3., m. G (the vacancy of 1369).

19 Fryde, 'Tenants of the bishops', p. 235.

20 Ibid., pp. 232–5, 256–7 (tables F–G, covering some Warwickshire and Staffordshire estates). For details see below, section III of this chapter.

21 There survives also an isolated but very detailed account for the valuable estate of Blockley, then in north-eastern Worcestershire, for 1383/4 (Worcester RO, 157/92007).

22 For the dates of medieval accounts and court rolls surviving for these estates see Dyer, *Lords and Peasants*, pp. 392–4.

23 Stay of the auditors for two days and three nights at Bredon in April 1394 'pro compillacione unius novi rotuli facti de annuis redditibus et firmis pertinentibus sedi episcopali episcopatus Wygornie'. Cf. Worcester RO, BA 2636 (as are all subsequent references to Worcester documents, unless otherwise indicated), 157/92012⅛.

24 Cf. the record for Wick Episcopi, ibid., BA 2636, 9 (IV) f. 33r., where pannage of pigs is excluded because treated as 'casualis' income.

25 Not 1393/4, as in Dyer, *Lords and Peasants*, p. 119.

26 Worcester RO, BA 2636/9 (IV), ff. 33–8.

27 For details see below in this chapter, *passim*.

28 This section is mainly based on the sources discussed above, in section II of this chapter.

29 See below, section IV.

30 Dyer, *Lords and Peasants*, p. 238–40.

31 Worcester RO, 159/92049. See also below, section VI.

32 C. Dyer, *Hanbury: Settlement and Society in a Woodland Landscape* (Leicester, 1991), p. 52.

33 Worcester RO, BA 57, 705/7.

34 Ibid., BA 2636/165/92229.

35 The amounts of the normal assessment in Worcestershire are tabulated in R.E. Glasscock, *The Lay Subsidy of 1334* (London, 1975), pp. 349–55.

36 L.F. Simmonds, 'Some remnants of the medieval landscape in South Worcestershire', *Transactions of the Worcestershire Archaeological Society*, 37 (1961), pp. 7, 9–10.

37 See below, section VII.

38 *CPR, 1348–50*, p. 245–6.

39 Fryde, 'Tenants of the bishops', p. 229, citing Thoresby's episcopal register (Worcester RO, BA 2648, 3 (II), pp. 11, 49, 51).

40 R.H. Hilton and P.A. Rahtz, 'Upton, Gloucestershire, 1959–1964', *Trans. BGAS* 85 (1966), p. 83. Worcester RO, 157, no. 92007 (account for Blockley).

41 See below, section V.

42 This section is based mainly on Fryde, 'Tenants of the bishops', pp. 231–5 and the tables on pp. 242–57.

43 D.L. Farmer in Miller, p. 450; J. Titov, 'Lost rents, vacant holdings and the contraction of peasant cultivation after the Black Death', *AgHR*, 42 (1994), p. 112.

44 See below, sections V–VII.

45 *CPR, 1350–54*, p. 275.

46 Fryde, 'Tenants of the bishops', p. 231 and n. 67.

47 Ibid., p. 232.

48 Ibid., p. 231.

49 Worcester RO, 166/92230.

50 Ibid., 158/92014.

51 The 1392/3 estimates of revenue are to be found in Worcester RO, BA 2636/9 (IV), ff. 33–8.

52 Figures for twelves estates come from the record cited in the preceding note. They are: Fladbury with Throckmorton, Ripple, Hartlebury, Wick, Whiston, Bredon and Kempsey in Worcestershire; Bishop's Cleeve, Withington, Henbury and Stoke in Gloucestershire. The thirteenth was Blockley (now Glos.), for which I use the figure in the account for 1383/4 (157/92007). The income from customary renders in 1392/3 (and Blockley in 1383/4), amounted to £22 5s 3½d, as compared with £37 2s 11½d due from the same estates in the survey of 1299.

53 See below, chapters 9 and 11.

54 The account that follows of the estates of the see of Coventry and Lichfield in 1349 is based on Fryde, 'Tenants of the bishops', pp. 232–5, 256–7.

55 Jean Birrell in *VCH Staffs.*, vol. VI (1982), pp. 3, 8–9, 20.

56 For agrarian difficulties in Staffordshire in the first half of the fourteenth century and the labour services on the episcopal estates see ibid., pp. 28, 35–7.

57 Hilton, *English Peasantry*, p. 230.

58 Fryde, 'Tenants of the bishops', p. 233 and n. 83, p. 234 and n. 84.

59 Ibid., p. 233 and n. 82.

60 C. Dyer, *Warwickshire Farming, 1349–c. 1520* (Oxford, 1981), p. 6 and n. 20 on p. 37.

61 Jean Birrell in *VCH Staffs.*, vol. VI, pp. 38–9.

62 The account of what happened on the properties of the Bishops of Worcester in and after 1361 is based on Fryde, 'Tenants of the bishops', p. 235.

63 *VCH Worcs.*, vol. III, (1913), p. 254.

64 Dyer, *Lords and Peasants*, p. 146.

65 Ibid., pp. 119, 146.

66 Ibid., p. 120.

67 Worcester RO, 163/92160.

68 Ibid., 160/92050.

69 The most recent, excellent summary of this legislation is by Professor Farmer in Miller, pp. 483–90. See also above, chapter 3, section III.

70 What follows is based on Fryde, 'Tenants of the bishops', p. 239.

71 Worcester RO, 160/92052.

72 Ibid., 160/92051.

73 PRO, K.R. Subsidies, E179/113/35A.

74 Dyer, *Lords and Peasants*, p. 245; *VCH Glos.*, vol. VIII, (1968), map on p. 5 and p. 6.

75 Sims-Williams, *Religion and Literature*, p. 382.

76 Fryde, 'Tenants of the bishops', p. 237.

77 Worcester RO, 161/92113$\frac{5}{6}$.

78 PRO, SC6/1143, no. 18. This is also the source for the figures of income during the same vacancy from other episcopal manors mentioned below.

79 Dyer, *Lords and Peasants*, p. 123; Worcester RO, 160/92050.

80 Ibid., 160/92050.

81 Ibid., 159/92049$\frac{3}{7}$ and 159/92049$\frac{4}{7}$.

82 See below, chapter 6.

83 Worcester RO, 160/92050.

84 Ibid., 193/92628$\frac{4}{9}$ (dorse).

85 See below, chapter 6, section VI.

86 Worcester RO, 192/92626$\frac{10}{12}$.

87 See below, chapter 5, section III.

88 There is an excellent account of these two manors in the fourteenth century in C. Dyer, 'Population and agriculture on a Warwickshire manor in the later Middle Ages', *University of Birmingham Historical Journal*, 11 (1968), pp. 113–27. This is my principal source.

89 Ibid., p. 114. Sims-Williams, *Religion and Literature*, pp. 371–373.

90 Worcester RO, 163/92160.

91 *Lords and Peasants*, chapter 5, pp. 113–49.

92 In Miller, pp. 443–51, 503 (prices of grains); see also Dyer, *Lords and Peasants*, pp. 130–1 (prices of crops on the estates of Worcester).

93 For a more detailed discussion of the vacant holdings on the Worcester estates see below, chapter 9, section III. But see also the end of this section.

94 Harvey, *Westminster Abbey*, p. 245.

95 R.H. Hilton, 'A rare Evesham Abbey estate document', in his *Class Conflict and the Crisis of Capitalism* (London, 1985), pp. 102–7.

96 W.P. Marett (ed.), *A Calendar of the Register of Henry Wakefield, Bishop of Worcester, 1375–95*, Worcestershire Historical Society, ns, no. 7, (Worcester, 1972), p. xlv.

97 D.L. Farmer in Miller, p. 452.

98 Dyer, 'Population and agriculture', pp. 117–18; Worcester RO, 163/92158½ (1375/6); 163/92161 (1376/7); 163/92162 (1377/8); 163/92163 (1380/1), including a rent collector's account alongside a reeve's.

99 W.A. Pantin (ed.), *Documents Illustrating the Activities of the General and Provincial Monks, 1215–1540*, vol. III, Camden Society, 3rd ser., no. 54 (1957); Hilton, *English Peasantry*, pp. 61–2.

100 Fryde, 'Tenants of the Bishops', p. 239.

101 Dyer, *Lords and Peasants*, p. 142.

102 D.L. Farmer in Miller, p. 503.

103 Dyer, *Lords and Peasants*, p. 142

104 D.L. Farmer in Miller, p. 487.

105 Dyer, *Lords and Peasants*, p. 142.

106 D.L. Farmer in Miller, p. 487.

107 Dyer, *Lords and Peasants*, pp. 142–3.

108 Ibid., p. 142.

109 E. Searle, *Lordship and Community, Battle Abbey and its Banlieu, 1066–1538* (Toronto, 1974), pp. 304–8.

110 M. Mate, 'Agrarian economy after the Black Death: the manors of Canterbury Cathedral Priory, 1348–91', *EcHR*, 37 (1984), p. 353.

111 Dyer, *Lords and Peasants*, pp. 275, 283.

112 Ibid., p. 274.

113 *Westminster Abbey*, chapter IX. See also her account of the Oxfordshire manor of Islip in *VCH Oxon*, vol. VI (1959), p. 214. For a discussion of Westminster estates see below, chapter 8, sections IV and VI.

114 Harvey, *Westminster Abbey*, p. 246.

115 Worcester RO, 157/92007.

116 Ibid., 165/92226½.

117 Ibid., 165/92225½ and box 166, nos 92230, 92240, 92246, 92261.

118 Ibid., 158/92016.

119 Thus, the same commutation was operating in 1393/4, described in the account for that year as 'at the lord's will'. Ibid., 157/92012½.

120 Ibid., 193/92628½.

121 Ibid., BA 2636/9 (IV), f. 37v.

122 Ibid., f. 33v.

123 D.L. Farmer in Miller, p. 503; Dyer, *Lords and Peasants*, p. 131.

124 Dyer, ibid., p. 146.

125 Hollings (ed.), *Red Book of Worcester*, vol. IV, p. 401.

126 PRO, SC6/1143/18.

127 The account for the vacancy of 1302/3 may not have included sales of wool as the executors of the deceased Bishop Godfrey Giffard would have removed the sheep and the keeper of the bishopric may have restocked estates with only the essential minimum number of animals.

128 Worcester RO, BA 2636/9 (IV), ff. 33–8. See above, section II, for this record.
129 Dyer, *Lords and Peasants*, p. 119.
130 Worcester RO, 157/92007.
131 Dyer, *Lords and Peasants*, p. 194.
132 Ibid., p. 122.
133 The eight estates were Hampton Lucy, Blockley, Bredon, Hanbury, Hartlebury, Kempsey, Whitstones and Wick. The figures for the loss of revenue are derived from the survey by the episcopal officials in 1392/3, preserved in Worcester RO, BA2639/9, (IV) ff. 33–8.
134 Dyer, 'Population and agriculture', p. 119 and n. 26. Part of the loss was offset by leasing the vacant 8 virgates for pasture at an annual rent of £3 15s, reducing the net loss to £2 2s.
135 See below, chapter 6, section III.
136 Dyer, 'Population and agriculture', p. 118.
137 Worcester RO, 166/92260.
138 Ibid., 166/92240.
139 For details about the topography and history of this estate see below, chapter 6.
140 Worcester RO, 157/92007.
141 Ibid., 157/92008.
142 See below, chapter 6.
143 Ibid.
144 This does not include deliveries to them in kind and other perquisites.
145 Fryde, 'Tenants of the bishops', p. 239.
146 The relevant entries on the dorse of Worcester RO, 157/92007, are partly damaged, but the full figures can be reconstructed from ibid., 157/92008.
147 Fryde, 'Tenants of the bishops', pp. 237–8.
148 Worcester RO, 193/92627¹¹⁄₁₂.
149 Ibid., 161/92113⅜.
150 Fryde, 'Tenants of the bishops', p. 252.
151 Worcester RO, 158/92015.
152 Ibid., 157/92012⅙.
153 Ibid., 158/92014.
154 Ibid., BA 2639/9(IV), f. 34.
155 Ibid., f. 16r.
156 Ibid., 158/92014.
157 See above, section VI.
158 Worcester RO, 158/92015.
159 Ibid., 193/92628⅜.
160 See above, section II. This record is preserved today in a register of miscellaneous evidences (Worcester RO, BA 2639/9(IV), ff. 33–8).
161 Dyer, *Lords and Peasants*, p. 147.
162 Worcester RO, 193/92627¹¹⁄₁₂.
163 Ibid., 157/92012⅙.
164 Ibid., 166/92262.
165 Ibid., 160/92063.
166 See below, chapter 5, section III.
167 See below, chapter 9.

CHAPTER 5

1   Hilton, *English Peasantry*, p. 66: 'when the world recovers better'.

2   See, for example, above, chapter 3, section IV, for the tenants of Thaxted in Essex.

3   Barbara Harvey, 'The leasing of the Abbot of Westminster's demesnes in the later Middle Ages', *EcHR*, 2nd ser., 22 (1969), pp. 21–2.

4   Ibid., pp. 20–1.

5   For more evidence, chiefly from the period 1390–1430, see below, chapter 8.

6   E. Power, *The Wool Trade in English Medieval History* (Oxford, 1941), pp. 38–9.

7   For example, on the estates of *Westminster Abbey*, p. 279.

8   Power, *Wool Trade*, p. 38, n. 1.

9   See especially below, chapters 8–11.

10 Published in Holmes, *Estates of the Higher Nobility*, pp. 126–8. Holmes's commentary on it is on pp. 117–19.

11 Ibid., p. 118, n. 2.

12 Ibid., p. 118.

13 Compare R.A.L. Smith, *Canterbury Cathedral Priory* (Cambridge, 1943), p. 193 and n. 1: 'the first were for short terms varying from 3 to 10 years. The period of from 5 to 7 years seems to have been the most common.'

14 Holmes, *Estates of the Higher Nobility*, pp. 127–8.

15 Ibid., p. 119.

16 The court rolls had been destroyed on 16 June 1381 by a deliberate raiding party which broke into the duke's manor-house. Cf. Powell, *The Rising in East Anglia*, pp. 27–8.

17 Harvey, 'Westminster's demesnes', pp. 24–5.

18 Holmes, *Estates of the Higher Nobility*, p. 119; S. Walker, *The Lancastrian Affinity, 1361–1399* (Oxford, 1990), p. 183, n. 5.

19 See N.S.B. Gras, *The Evolution of the English Corn Market* (Cambridge, Mass., 1926), p. 490 (index under Lynn).

20 Harvey, 'Westminster's demesnes', pp. 19, 21, 23–4.

21 Add. MS 28,024 [Earl Thomas's cartulary], f. 189v.

22 Harvey, 'Westminster's demesnes', pp. 20–1, 24.

23 Ibid., p. 25. Referring to Westminster properties she remarks: 'there is no reason to think that these officials have been any less regular and successful in their deceits than was the habit of their kind elsewhere'.

24 Cited by J.S. Drew, 'Manorial accounts of St Swithun's Priory, Wincheter' (originally published in 1947), reprinted by E.M. Carus-Wilson in *Essays in Economic History*, vol. II (London, 1962), p. 29.

25 See especially H.S. Bennett, 'The reeve and the manor in the fourteenth century', *EHR*, 41 (1926), pp. 358–63.

26 M. Morgan, *The English Lands of the Abbey of Bec* (Oxford, 1946), pp. 112, 132.

27 Cf. D.L. Farmer in Miller, p. 444.

28 For the earlier history of these estates in the second half of the fourteenth century, see above, chapter 4. For the evidence of leases after 1395 see below, chapter 9.

29 Dyer, *Lords and Peasants*, p. 148.

30 See above, chapter 4.

31   Worcester RO, 160/92060. The narrative that follows is based on the manorial accounts, ibid., box 160, nos 92060–4 (1388/9–1406/7).

32   Ibid., no. 92062.

33   Ibid., no. 92063.

34   Ibid., no. 92061.

35   Ibid., no. 92063.

36   Ibid., 193/92626%2.

37   Ibid., no. 92063.

38   Ibid., no. 92064.

39   Harvey, 'Westminster's demesnes', p. 24; 'the saving in costs which a landlord operating on the scale of the abbot of Westminster might . . . anticipate from leasing his new demesnes'.

40   The evidence is set out in F.R.H. du Boulay, 'Late continued demesne farming at Otford', Archaeologial Cantiana, 73 (1959) and idem, The Lordship of Canterbury: An Essay on Medieval Society, (London, 1966), p. 226.

41   Dyer, Lords and Peasants, p. 239.

42   See above chapter 4, for the details of its history in the second half of the fourteenth century.

43   Dyer, Lords and Peasants, p. 123.

44   Worcester RO, 165/92225%.

45   Ibid., no. 92226½.

46   Ibid., 166/92262.

47   Ibid.

48   Ibid., nos 92260, 92262.

49   Ibid., 163/92169.

50   See above, chapter 4, for the details of their history in the second half of the fourteenth century. See also C. Dyer, 'Population and agriculture on a Warwickshire manor'.

51   Worcester RO, 163/92169.

52   Ibid.

53   Ibid., BA 2639/9(IV), 43696, (a collection of records and rentals of various dates) known as the Peverel Register), ff. 144v.–145r. I have assigned this part of the records in it to 1419 (from internal evidence).

54   The writ is appended to 163/92169.

55   Ibid. 164/92178A (court roll, 4 October 1453) and 193/92627¹¹⁄₂ (roll of enquiries about which the bishop and his council should be consulted, 1452).

56   See below, chapter 11.

57   Worcester RO, 163/92168.

58   Ibid., 192/92627/%2.

59   Ibid., 163/92169.

60   Ibid., and Dyer, 'Redistribution of incomes', p. 122.

61   Harvey, 'Westminster's demesnes', pp. 21–2.

62   There is much information about their careers in J.T. Driver, 'The knights of the shire for Worcestershire during the reigns of Richard II, Henry IV and Henry V', Transactions of the Worcestershire Archaeological Society, 40 (1963), pp. 42–64. The account that follows is partly based on this article.

63   See below, chapter 11.

64   Dyer, *Lords and Peasants*, pp. 156–7.

65   K.B. McFarlane, *The Nobility of Later Medieval England* (Oxford, 1973), p. 140.

66   T.R. Nash, *Collections for the History of Worcestershire*, 2nd edn. (London, 1799), vol. I, p. xvii, and Driver, 'Knights of the shire for Worcestershire'.

67   Dyer, *Lords and Peasants*, p. 379.

68   N. Denholm-Young, *Seignorial Administration in England* (Oxford, 1937), p. 26, n. 5; C. Ross, *The Estates and Finances of Richard Beauchamp, Earl of Warwick* (Oxford, Dugdale Society, 1956), p. 12. The fee of 20 marks was partly secured on the revenue of the earl's estate of Elmley Castle. Cf. Worcester RO, BA 989/899.95, parcel 6, no. 98 (1427/8).

69   Ross, *Estates of Richard Beauchamp*, pp. 11–12.

70   A. Steel, *The Receipt of the Exchequer 1377–1485* (Cambridge, 1954), p. 424 (the chamberlainship); J.L. Kirby, 'The rise of the Under-Treasurer of the Exchequer', *EHR*, 72 (1957), p. 673.

71   See below, section V of this chapter.

72   Harvey, 'Westminster's demesnes', pp. 21, 26; Dyer, *Lords and Peasants*, p. 384.

73   Dyer, ibid., p. 380.

74   Ibid.

75   C. Dyer, 'The deserted medieval village of Woollashill', *Transactions of the Worcestershire Archaeological Society*, 3rd ser., I (1965–7).

76   The account is enrolled on PRO Foreign Roll, E374/71 (15 Hen. VI), m. 3 (or C), continued on Pipe Rolls, E372/282, *Wygornia*, dorse (15 Hen. VI), and E372/283, *Wygornia*, dorse (16 Hen. VI). A copy (but without the evidence on Pipe Roll 16 Hen. VI) was preserved among the records of the bishopric, Worcester RO, 193/92628⅝.

77   Worcester RO, BA/2639, 9 (IV), 43696 (Peverel Register), f. 55v. [a charter of Bishop Mauger (1200–12) concerning 1½ hides held by John Throckmorton at Fladbury, Hull and Upton in Blockley].

78   Caughton in west Warwickshire, acquired by John Throckmorton through marriage to its heiress, became the main residence of Robert Throckmorton after *c.* 1474. Cf. C. Carpenter, 'The English gentry and their estates', *Gentry and Nobility in Late Medieval Europe*, ed. M. Jones (Gloucester, 1986), pp. 42–3.

79   Worcester RO, BA 2639, 9 (IV), 43696 (Peverel Register), f.20v.

80   C. Dyer, 'A redistribution of incomes in fifteenth-century England', *Past and Present*, 39 (1968), p. 27; Peverel register, *cit. supra*, f. 128v.

81   PRO, Foreign Roll, E374/71, m. 3.

82   Worcester RO, 193/92628⅝.

83   PRO, K.R. Memoranda Roll, E159/215 (17 Hen. VI), '*brevia directa baronibus*', Hilary t., m. 2 (a petition of the custodians for allowances). See also Dyer, *Lords and Peasants*, p. 160.

84   Worcester RO, 193/92628⅝.

85   PRO, Foreign Roll, E374/71, m. 3.

86   Worcester RO, 193/92628⅝.

87   Ibid., and PRO, Ministers' Accts., SC6/1143, no. 21.

88   Worcester RO, 193/92628⅝, and PRO, Pipe Roll, E372/283, *Wygornia*, dorse (16 Hen. VI).

89   Ibid.

90   Worcester RO, Register of Bishop John Carpenter (BA 2648, b.716:093), vol. I, f. 42r. and II. (pp. 91–2).

91   Ibid., under 1449: '*pro maiori agestamento et commodo tenentium*'.

92   Worcester RO, 193/92627¹⁹⁄₂. Cited by Dyer, *Lords and Peasants*, p. 214.

93   Dyer, ibid., p. 384.

94   Worcester RO, 175/92475.

95   Ibid., 37, vol. III, f. 242r. and v. (no. 43806).

96   *Nobility of Later Medieval England*, p. 223.

97   Dyer, 'Redistribution of incomes', p. 27.

98   In 1459–60 Thomas Throckmorton was the earl's steward at the most important of the earl's Cotswold manors, Elmley Castle, Worcester RO, Elmley Accts, parcel 6, no. 113.

99   Dyer, *Lords and Peasants*, p. 380.

100   Ibid., p. 186.

101   Worcester RO, 37, vol. III, f. 243r. and v. (no. 43806).

102   Dyer, *Lords and Peasants*, p. 380. He was acting as steward in 1473.

103   Christine Carpenter, *Locality and Polity: A Study of Warwickshire Landed Society, 1401–1499* (Cambridge, 1992), pp. 118–19.

CHAPTER 6

1   There is a useful discussion of the medieval breeds of English sheep in M.L. Ryder, 'Medieval sheep and wool types', *AgHR*, 31 (1984). See also A. Hanham, *The Celys and their World* (Cambridge, 1985), p. 113.

2   Letter of 21 June 1403 from the Cambini in London to Francesco Datini at Florence. See below, in this section, for a discussion of the Datini records I have used.

3   H. Hoshino, *L'Arte della Lana in Firenze nel Basso Medioevo* (Firenze, 1980), p. 225.

4   For the importance earlier in the fourteenth century of wools from northern England and the north-eastern Midlands see my booklet, *The Wool Accounts of William de la Pole*, St Anthony's Hall Publications, no. 25 (York, 1964), reprinted as no. IX in my *Studies in Medieval Trade and Finance* (London, 1983).

5   My figures for wool exports are derived chiefly from E.M. Carus-Wilson and O. Coleman, *England's Export Trade, 1275–1547* (Oxford, 1963).

6   Ibid., pp. 59, 61, and G.L. Harriss, *Cardinal Beaufort: A Study of Lancastrian Ascendancy and Decline* (Oxford, 1988), pp. 412–13.

7   The best recent account of the trade of the English merchants of the Staple is in Hanham, *The Celys*.

8   See below, section IV of this chapter.

9   See especially *Aspetti della vita economica medievale; Studi nell'archivio Datini di Prato* (Siena, 1962) and *Documenti per la storia economica dei secoli XIII–XVI* (Firenze, 1972, with assistance of Elena Cecchi).

10   Especially 'Werner Sombart e i problemi della navigazione nel medio evo', in *L'Opera di Werner Sombart nel Centenario della Nascita* (Milano, 1964), pp. 87–149.

11   ADP, Fondaco di Firenze, Carteggio da Londra, no. 664. Their firm went bankrupt after the death of Giovanni Orlandini in 1422. Cf. R. de Roover, *The Bruges Money Market around 1400* (Brussels, 1968), pp. 18–19.

12   ADP, Fondaco di Firenze, Carteggio da Londra, no. 664.

13   Fryde, *Studies in Medieval Trade,* no. XIV, pp. 306–7 and n. 66 on p. 307.

14   Ibid., no. XIV, and Carus-Wilson and Coleman, *England's Export Trade*, pp. 51–5.

15   A.A. Ruddock, *Italian Merchants and Shipping in Southampton, 1270–1600* (Southampton, 1951), pp. 49–50.

16   Fryde, *Studies in Medieval Trade*, no. XV, p. 347.

17   Ibid., no. XV, pp. 347–8.

18   Melis, 'Werner Sombart', pp. 93–9.

19   Ibid., p. 101: '*sono castella*'.

20   ADP, Fondaco di Firenze, Carteggio da Londra, no. 664, *passim*.

21   Melis, 'Werner Sombart', pp. 112–13.

22   ADP, Fondaco di Firenze, Carteggio da Londra, no. 664.

23   Fryde, *Studies in Medieval Trade*, no. XV, pp. 347–8.

24   Ibid., no. XIV, p. 310, and no. XV, p. 348; A. Tenenti et C. Vivanti, 'Les grands traffics d'état à Venise: les galères "da mercato" (1332–1534)', supplement, 'Le film d'un grand système de navigation; les galères marchandes vénitiennes, XIV-XVI siècles', *Annales: Économies, Sociétés, Civilisations*, 16 (1961).

25   ADP, Fondaco di Firenze, Carteggio da Londra, no. 664, letter of the Orlandini of 14 May 1403.

26   Ibid: '*ognuno, melanesi e altri, che soleano fornissi in Lindisea, tutti si rivolgono in Chodisgualdo*'.

27   Carus-Wilson and Coleman, *England's Export Trade*, pp. 54–5.

28   See the maps in R.H. Hilton, 'Winchcombe Abbey and the Manor of Sherborne', reprinted in his *Class Conflict and the Crisis of Feudalism: Essays in Medieval Social History* (London, 1985), p. 18 (400 ft contour of the Cotswolds), and in Dyer, *Lords and Peasants*, p. 10 (200 ft contour). I have visited on many occasions much of this area and have been to many of the localities mentioned in this chapter.

29   Hilton, *A Medieval Society*, pp. 12–13; Sims–Williams, *Religion and Literature*, p. 377.

30   The same thing happened also at Henbury Saltmarsh (adjoining Bristol), but no sheep were kept there.

31   Worcester RO, 160 (no. 92061); N. Saul, *Knights and Esquires: The Gloucestershire Gentry in the Fourteenth Century* (Oxford, 1981), p. 230 (appointment of Cassy as chief baron of the exchequer in 1389). For a descendant a century later, the all-powerful farmer of the Abbey of Westminster's estate of Deerhurst see above, chapter 4, section III, and Harvey, 'Westminster demesnes', p. 21.

32   Hilton, *Class Conflict*, p. 34.

33   See below, section VI of this chapter, and chapter 11.

34   Harriss, *Cardinal Beaufort*, p. 412.

35   Worcester RO, 154/52586¼.

36   Ibid., 193/92628⅝ (dorse). See also the excellent account in Dyer, *Lords and Peasants*, pp. 136–9.

37   Dyer, ibid., p. 136.

38   For the topography of Blockley and the origins of the estate see H.P.R. Finberg, *Gloucestershire Studies* (Leicester, 1957), pp. 5–11 (map on p. 6). See also the map on p. 74 of Hilton and Rahtz, 'Upton, Gloucestershire'.

39   Worcester RO, 157/92007 (account for Blockley, 1383/4).

40   Ibid., 193/92628⅝ (roll of arrears, 1389).

41   ADP, Fondaco di Firenze, Carteggio da Londra, No. 664, *passim*.

42   A practice resorted to by the Orlandini. Cf. ibid., letter of 31 January 1403.

43   For his effigy see Hilton, *English Peasantry* pp. 88–9.

44   For the year of his death see J.J. Simpson, 'The wool trade and the woolmen of Gloucestershire', *Trans. BGAS*, 53 (1931), p. 89.

45   Dyer, *Warwickshire Farming*, p. 16.

46   Simpson, 'Wool trade of Gloucestershire', p. 89, and Saul, *Knights and Esquires*, p. 231.

47   *Lords and Peasants*, p. 139, n. 29 and p. 140.

48   My total is based on Worcester RO, 157/92007.

49   Ibid., and Dyer, *Lords and Peasants*, p. 138.

50   *Wool Trade*, p. 40. See also below, section VI of this chapter.

51   Hilton, *Medieval Society*, p. 83.

52   PRO, K.R. Exch. Acc. Var., E101/128/30, m. 10.

53   ADP, Fondaco di Firenze, Carteggio da Londra, no. 664.

54   PRO, E101/128/30, m. 10 (London Hosting Account, 1442/3).

55   C.D. Ross (ed.), *Cartulary of Cirencester Abbey, Gloucestershire* (London, 1964), vol. I, p. xxii.

56   This account of Winchcombe's wool husbandry, with its centre at Sherborne, is based on Hilton, *Class Conflict*, pp. 18–35.

57   A sheep farm was maintained here until *c.* 1450. Cf. Harvey, *Westminster Abbey*, pp. 150–1.

58   This is my suggestion. For the wool fairs at Burford and Northleach see below, section IV of this chapter.

59   See below, in this section.

60   *ADP*, Fondaco di Firenze, Carteggio da Londra, 25 April 1401.

61   PRO, K.R. Customs Accts., E122/139 nos 4 and 11.

62   This section is based almost entirely on ADP, Fondaco di Firenze, Carteggio da Londra, no. 664. Individual items are identifiable by their dates.

63   'Dicievisi pregi sechondo la valuta di Borifortte alla Fiera che danno il suono a tutto Chontisgualdo'.

64   Letters of 13 April and 13 June 1402.

65   Letter of 4 January 1403.

66   For the importance of the right length of fleeces see Hanham, *The Celys*, p. 113.

67   Letter of 2 July 1403.

68   Letter of the Cambini of 11 March 1402.

69   Hanham, *The Celys* p. 115–16.

70   Letter of the Cambini of 29 July 1402.

71   See below, chapter 10, for a fuller discussion of the economic crisis after 1449.

72   G.A. Holmes, 'The "Libel of English Policy"', *EHR*, 76 (1961), pp. 199–200.

73   J. Heers, 'Les Gènois en Angleterre: la crise de 1458–60', *Studi in Onore di Armando Sapori*, vol. II (Milan, 1957), pp. 809–32.

74   E.B. Fryde, 'Anglo-Italian commerce in the fifteenth century: some evidence about profits and the balance of trade', *Revue Belge de Philologie et d'Histoire*, 50 (1972), pp. 345–55, reprinted as no. XVI in Fryde, *Studies in Medieval Trade*.

75   E.B. Fryde, 'Italian merchants in medieval England, *c.* 1270–*c.* 1500', *Aspetti della vita medievale, Atti del Convegno di Studi nel X Anniversario della morte di Federigo Melis* (Firenze, 1985), p. 217.

76   This was the justified complaint against the Italians of the author of the 'Libel of English Policy'. Cf. Holmes, 'The "Libel of English Policy"', pp. 201–2.

77 R.A. Goldthwaite, 'The Renaissance economy: the precondition for luxury consumption' *Aspetti della vita medievale.*

78 M. Mallett, 'Anglo-Florentine commercial relations, 1465–1491', *EcHR*, 2nd ser., 15 (1962), p. 257.

79 Cf. Fryde, *op. cit.* (1983), XV, pp. 343, 363.

80 G.A. Holmes 'Anglo-Florentine trade in 1451', *EHR*, 108 (1993), pp. 380–1; R. de Roover, *The Rise and Decline of the Medici Bank, 1397–1494* (Cambridge, Mass., 1963), pp. 321–7.

81 O. Coleman, 'Trade and prosperity in the fifteenth century: some aspects of the trade of Southampton', *EcHR*, 2nd ser., 16 (1963), pp. 13–14.

82 Carus-Wilson and Coleman, *England's Export Trade*, pp. 60–1.

83 Fryde, *Studies in Medieval Trade*, no. XIV, pp. 312–14; W.B. Watson, 'The structure of the Florentine galley trade with Flanders and England in the fifteenth century', *Revue Belge de Philologie et d'Histoire*, 39/40 (1961/2). For the information about 1443/4 see ibid., 1962, pp. 338–9.

84 J.L. Kirby, 'The Issues of the Lancastrian Exchequer and Lord Cromwell's estimates of 1433', *Bull. IHR*, 24 (1951), p. 133.

85 M.E. Mallett, *The Florentine Galleys in the Fifteenth Century* (Oxford, 1962).

86 PRO, K.R. Customs Accts., E122/140/62, mm. 67–8.

87 The story of William Cantelowe's wool that follows is based mainly on the article by George Holmes, 'An Anglo-Florentine partnership in 1451', *EHR*, 108 (1993), pp. 380–6.

88 Cf. W.I. Haward, 'The financial transactions between the Lancastrian government and the merchants of the Staple from 1449 to 1461', *Studies in English Trade in the Fifteenth Century*, ed. E. Power and M. Postan (London, 1993), pp. 295–8.

89 Ruddock *Italian Merchants*, p. 82.

90 This is a draft of Balmayn's letter preserved in the Salviati archive at Pisa (Holmes, 'Anglo-Florentine trade', p. 385).

91 This and other statistics of wool prices are based on D.L. Farmer in Miller, pp. 513–15.

92 The evidence about the sailings of the Venetian galley fleets is derived from the chart in A. Tenenti and C. Vivanti, 'Les grands trafics d'état à Venise, les galères *da mercato*, 1322–1534', *Annales: Économies, Societé, Civilisations*, 16, no. 1 (1961).

93 R. de Roover, *The Rise and Decline of the Medici Bank, 1397–1494*, (Cambridge, Mass., 1963), p. 328.

94 In Miller, p. 515.

95 PRO, E101/128, no. 36 and K.R. Memoranda Rolls, E159/235 and 236. See also W. Childs, 'To oure losse and hindraunce': English credit to alien merchants in the mid-fifteenth century', *Enterprise and Individuals in Fifteenth-Century England*, ed. J. Kermode (Stroud, 1991), pp. 68–98.

96 Childs, ibid., p. 89.

97 Worcester R.O., 193/92627½ (account of Richard Harris, master shepherd, 23 November 1448 to 23 November 1449) and ibid., 192/92626½ (account of the same, 23 November 1449 to 23 November 1450). They were used in Dyer, *Lords and Peasants* pp. 150–1.

98 This debt was discharged during the following period of account (November 1448 to November 1449).

99 See above, section III of this chapter, for the wool clip of 1384 and the sale of this wool.

100 Worcester RO, 193/92627¹⁰/₁₂.

101 Dyer, *Lords and Peasants*, p. 151 and n. 8.

102 Worcester RO, 175/92429.

103 Ibid., 157/92008: '*De 26 li. 13s. 4d. receptis de firma 2500 Multonum de Stauro domini, nuper dimissorum Thome Bleke ad firmam per indenturam, nihil . . . hoc anno, quia dicti multones vendi prefato Thome Bleke in grosso, nec nulli multones domini fuerunt super manerium ibidem.*'

104 See below, chapter 10.

105 For example, in the list of arrears at Michaelmas 1412 (Worcester RO, 192/92687⁸/₁₂) appear a sale of '1 sack 3 tods 1½ stones of wool' to John Banham of Worcester from the flock at Withington, sales at Blockley of 7 sacks of wool and 139 woolfells to William Collyng and of 2 sacks to John Banham. I conjecture that such piecemeal sales were made for local cloth-making.

106 T.H. Lloyd, *The Movement of Wool Prices in Medieval England* (Cambridge, 1973), p. 3.

107 Dyer, *op. cit.*, pp. 328–9.

108 Ibid., p. 329.

109 R.H. Britnell, *The Commercialisation of English Society 1000–1500* (Cambridge, 1993), p. 201.

110 See below, chapter 11, section V (Hampton Lucy and Hatton).

CHAPTER 7

1 For sources see below, section II.

2 S.F. Hockey, *Quarr Abbey and its Lands 1132–1631* (Leicester, 1970), pp. 194–7.

3 Cf. F. Melis, 'La formazione dei costi nell' industria laniera alla fine del Trecento', *Economia e Storia*, I (1954).

4 See below, section III.

5 Cf., E.B. Fryde, 'The English cloth industry and the trade with the Mediterranean, *c.* 1370–*c.* 1480' (originally published in 1976), *Studies in Medieval Trade*, no. XV, pp. 350–4.

6 E.M. Carus-Wilson, 'The woollen industry before 1550', *VCH: Wilts.*, vol. 4 (1959), p. 124.

7 Fryde, *Studies in Medieval Trade*, no. XV, pp. 351–2. Leonardo Contarini had purchased in 1440–2 'Cotswold' cloths for £248, priced at £2 13s 4d each (ibid., p. 351).

8 Cf. E.M. Carus-Wilson, 'Evidences of industrial growth on some fifteenth-century manors', cited from the reprint in *Essays in Economic History*, ed. Carus-Wilson, vol. II (1962), pp. 154–9.

9 J. Thirsk, 'Industries in the countryside', *Essays in the Economic and Social History of Tudor and Stuart England in Honour of R.H. Tawney*, ed. F.J. Fisher (Cambridge, 1961), p. 71.

10 J.F. Willard, 'Inland transportation in England during the fourteenth century', *Speculum*, 1 (1926); Fryde, 'The Wool Accounts of William de la Pole', *Studies in Medieval Trade*, no. IX, p. 10.

11 I am using here and in the rest of this chapter the valuable doctoral thesis of J.N. Hare, 'Lord and tenant in Wiltshire, *c.* 1380–*c.* 1520' (University of London, 1975). I am very grateful to Dr Hare for the loan of his thesis. See also R. Faith, 'Berkshire: fourteenth and fifteenth centuries', *The Peasant Land Market in Medieval England*, ed. P.D.A. Harvey (Oxford, 1984).

12   *VCH: Wilts.*, vol. 4, p. 20.

13   Ibid., p. 2.

14   For the revival of the Norman economy after 1420 see M. Mollat, *Le Commerce Maritime Normand à la Fin du Moyen Age* (Paris, 1952), p. 25ff. For the products of the Norman woollen industries see P. Wolff, *Commerces et Marchands de Toulouse, vers 1350–vers 1450* (Paris, 1954), pp. 240–1, 263–4.

15   Harriss, *Cardinal Beaufort*, pp. 412–13.

16   Ibid., pp. 407–10 (a list of Beaufort's lands).

17   *VCH: Wilts.*, vol. 4, pp. 20, 22 and n. 5 (article of R. Scott).

18   Ibid., pp. 134–5 (article of E.M. Carus-Wilson).

19   D.L. Farmer, 'Two Wiltshire manors and their markets', *AgHR* 37 (1989), pp. 10–11.

20   PRO, Ministers' Accts, SC6, 1131/9 (stock account).

21   J.S. Drew, 'Manorial accounts of St. Swithun's Priory, Winchester' (originally published in 1947), reprinted in *Essays in Economic History*, ed. Carus-Wilson, II, pp. 12–30; J.N. Hare, 'The monks as landlords: the leasing of the monastic demesnes in southern England', *The Church in Pre-Reformation Society. Essays in Honour of F.R.H. Du Boulay*, ed. C.M. Barron and C. Harper-Bill (Woodbridge, 1985), p. 85.

22   Hare, 'Lord and tenant in Wiltshire', pp. 54–65.

23   M.J. Stephenson, 'Wool yields in the medieval economy', *EcHR*, 41 (1988), p. 385.

24   Ibid., pp. 382–4.

25   N.S.B. Gras and E.C. Gras, *The Economic and Social History of an English Village (Crawley, Hampshire), A.D. 909–1928* (Cambridge, Mass., 1930). I am citing pp. 81–2, 307, 423–5.

26   Ibid., p. 62, and Harriss, *Cardinal Beaufort*, pp. 412–13.

27   Hare, 'Lord and tenant in Wiltshire', pp. 54–64.

28   Ibid., pp. 62–4, 66–71. I prefer Dr Hare's treatment of this evidence to that in Lloyd, *Movement of Wool Prices*, pp. 25–6. Lloyd carelessly ascribes the Wiltshire manors of Aldbourne and Berwick to Berkshire (p. 25) and his views about profits of wool-farming on these estates seem to be unjustifiably pessimistic (cf. Hare's thesis, pp. 67–71). Lloyd's insertion of the modern accounting category of capital depreciation (pp. 26–7) is purely theoretical.

29   PRO, Ministers' Accts (Duchy of Lancaster), DL29, 684/11081–3 (20–1 Hen. VI), 684/11084–6 (21–2 Hen. VI), 685/11087 (22–3 Hen. VI).

30   Hare, 'Lord and tenant in Wiltshire', p. 62.

31   The amount in the duchy accounts is 17 sacks, 4 tods, 1 clove, 4½lb. Each sack contained 364 lb, each tod 28 lb, with 13 tods making 1 sack. Each clove contained 7 lb, with 4 cloves making 1 tod.

32   Each sack again of 364 lb. Each stone contained 14 lb, with 26 stones making up a sack.

33   See above, chapter 6, section VI.

34   PRO, DL29/684/11081.

35   Hare, 'Lord and tenant in Wiltshire, pp. 67–9.

36   PRO, DL29/684/11081.

37   Lloyd, *Movement of Wool Prices*, p. 25; Hare, 'Lord and tenant in Wiltshire', pp. 68–9.

38   For the disasters of 1438–40 see below, chapter 10, section II.

39   For these wool prices see above, section I.

40   PRO, DL29/685/11087.

41 'Lord and tenant in Wiltshire', pp. 70–1.

42 PRO, DL29/684/11081–6 and 685/11087; J.N. Hare, 'The demesne lessees of fifteenth-century Wiltshire', *AgHR*, 29 (1981), pp. 8–9.

43 Richard Goddard had held before 1431 a virgate at Aldbourne for rent and labour services (Hare, ibid., p. 10). Thomas Goddard had been reeve of Aldbourne in 1441–3 (DL29/684/11081 and 684/11085).

44 Hare, 'Demesne lessees of fifteenth century Wiltshire', pp. 9–11, and PRO, DL29/685/11087; M. Morgan, *The English Lands of the Abbey of Bec* (Oxford, 1946), pp. 121, 131–2.

45 PRO, DL29/685/11087.

46 R. Faith in *Peasant Land Market in Medieval England*, ed. Harvey, p. 171. See below, chapter 10, section VIII, for a more detailed use of Dr Faith's study of Berkshire estates.

47 J.N. Hare, 'The monks as landlords: the leasing of the monastic demesnes in southern England', in *The Church and Pre-Reformation Society*, ed. Barron and Harper-Bill (Woodbridge, 1985), pp. 85–6.

48 Gras and Gras, *Economic and Social History of an English Village* p. 82.

49 Hare in Barron and Harper-Bill (eds), *Church and Pre-Reformation Society*, p. 86.

CHAPTER 8

1 C. Richmond, *John Hopton: A Fifteenth Century Suffolk Gentleman* (Cambridge, 1981), pp. 30, 78–80.

2 Miller, pp. 573–6.

3 Harvey, 'Westminster's demesnes', pp. 21, 25–7.

4 See above, chapters 4 and 5.

5 See below, section III of this chapter, for some detailed examples.

6 D.L. Farmer in Miller, p. 450.

7 V.M. Shillington in *VCH: Hants*, vol. V (1912), p. 421.

8 Harvey, 'Westminster's demenes', pp. 19–20; Harvey, *Westminster Abbey*, p. 150.

9 J. Saltmarsh, 'A college home-farm in the fifteenth century', *Economic History*, III (1936), pp. 155–72.

10 J.A. Brent, 'Alciston manor in the later Middle Ages', *Sussex Archaeological Collections*, 106 (1968), pp. 89–102.

11 V.M. Shillington in *VCH: Hants*, vol. V, pp. 421–2. For it earlier history see E. Robo, 'The Black Death in the Hundred of Farnham', *EHR*, 44 (1929), pp. 560–71. See also Titov *loc. cit.* (1994), p. 106.

12 See above, chapter 7, section III.

13 Farmer in Miller, p. 503.

14 Brent, 'Alciston manor', p. 95.

15 In Miller, p. 451.

16 Dyer, *Estates of the Bishops of Worcester*, pp. 148–9.

17 See above, chapter 4, section VIII.

18 See below, section IV of this chapter.

19 See below, section III of this chapter.

20 See above, chapters 6 and 7 (wool), and below, chapters 10 and 11.

21 A.J. Pollard, *North-Eastern England during the Wars of the Roses: Lay Society, War and Politics, 1450–1500* (Oxford, 1990), pp. 43, 49–50.

22 J.M.W. Bean, 'Plague, population and economic decline in the later Middle Ages', *EcHR*, 2nd ser. 15 (1963), pp. 432, 435.

23 Ibid., pp. 428–9; A.J. Pollard, 'The North-Eastern Economy and the Agrarian Crisis of 1438–1440', *Northern History*, 25 (1989), pp. 93–104.

24 This was regarded by the Common Law lawyers as the correct form by the time Sir Thomas Littleton wrote his *Tenures* (by 1481). Cited in E. Kerridge, *Agrarian Problems in the Sixteenth Century and After* (London, 1969), p. 139.

25 There is a good discussion in Z. Razi, 'The myth of the immutable English family', *Past and Present*, 140 (1993), pp. 37–42. For a more detailed discussion see below, section V of this chapter.

26 Cf. F.M. Page, *The Estates of Crowland Abbey: A Study in Manorial Organization* (Cambridge, 1934), p. 149.

27 *Statutes of the Realm*, vol. II, pp. 233–5 (6 Hen. VI).

28 See below, section V of this chapter.

29 See below, chapter 11, for some evidence from the estates of the Bishops of Worcester.

30 Raftis, *Tenure and Mobility*, p. 189.

31 See the perceptive remarks of M. Rubin, 'The poor', *Fifteenth-Century Attitudes: Perceptions of Society in Late Medieval England*, ed. R. Horrox (Cambridge, 1994), pp. 169, 182.

32 In Miller, p. 621.

33 See below, section V of this chapter.

34 A private manorial court exercising criminal jurisdiction.

35 A.J. Pollard, 'Estate management in the later Middle Ages', *EcHR*, 2nd ser., 25 (1972), pp. 560–1. Talbot was then in serious financial difficulties, having been a prisoner in France from 1429 to 1433 and needing to pay an exorbitant ransom. Cf. *idem, John Talbot and the War in France, 1427–1453* (London, 1983), pp. 113–16.

36 N. Kenyon, 'Labour conditions in Essex in the reign of Richard II' (originally published in 1934), reprinted in Carus-Wilson (ed), *Essays in Economic History*, vol. II, pp. 91–103.

37 D.L. Farmer in Miller, p. 487.

38 Cf. above, chapter 4, section VI.

39 D.L. Farmer in Miller, pp. 487, 489.

40 Ibid., p. 487.

41 Ibid.

42 B.H. Putnam, introduction to H.E. Salter (ed.), *Medieval Archives of the University of Oxford*, vol. II, Oxford Historical Society, vol. 73, pp. ix–xv.

43 D.L. Farmer in Miller, pp. 489–90.

44 Page, *The Estates of Crowland Abbey*, pp. 315–16.

45 Raftis, *The Estates of Ramsey Abbey*, p. 201.

46 F.R.H. Du Boulay, 'Late-continued demesne farming at Otford', *Archaeologia Cantiana*, 73 (1959), p. 123, n. 3.

47 Brent, 'Alciston manor', pp. 89–102. See also P.F. Brandon, 'Demesne arable farming in coastal Sussex during the later Middle Ages', *AgHR*, 19 (1971), pp. 113–34, and E. Searle, *Lordship and Community: Battle Abbey and its Banlieu, 1066–1538* (Toronto, 1974), index, p. 473, under Alciston.

48   D.L. Farmer, in Miller, p. 489.

49   The subsequent fortunes of direct farming at Alciston are traced below, in chapters 10 and 16.

50   Du Boulay, 'Demesne farming at Otford', pp. 116–24.

51   Ibid., p. 121.

52   Ibid., pp. 120–1.

53   E.B. Fryde in Miller, pp. 748–9.

54   Du Boulay, 'Demesne farming at Otford', p. 121, n. 3 and p. 124.

55   Ibid., pp. 122–3.

56   Ibid., p. 124, and Du Boulay, Lordship of Canterbury, p. 226.

57   Introduction to Edition of Custumal and Bye-laws of the Manor of Islip, Oxfordshire, Oxfordshire Record Society, vol. 40 (Oxford, 1959), pp. 80–1; VCH: Oxon, vol. VI (1959), accounts of Islip, pp. 210–15, and of Launton, pp. 235–9; 'The leasing of the Abbot of Westminster's demesnes in the later Middle Ages', EcHR, 2nd ser., 22 (1969), pp. 17–27; Westminster Abbey and its Estates in the Middle Ages (Oxford, 1977), pp. 148–63. Much of my account of the Westminster estates is based on a combination of most of these sources.

58   Harvey, 'Westminster's demesnes', p. 19, and the last account of the receiver of Walter de Wenlok in 1307 in Harvey (ed.), Documents illustrating the Rule of Walter de Wenlok, Abbot of Westminster, 1283–1307, Camden Society, 4th ser., (1965), pp. 209–10.

59   Harvey (ed.), Custumal of Islip, p. 81.

60   D.L. Farmer in Miller, p. 503.

61   Harvey, Westminster Abbey, p. 156.

62   Harvey, 'Westminster's demesnes', p. 23.

63   Ibid., pp. 21–3.

64   Harvey, Westminster Abbey, pp. 159–60.

65   Ibid., pp. 128–9.

66   Harvey, 'Westminster's demesnes', p. 23.

67   See below, chapter 9.

68   Harvey, 'Westminster's demesnes', p. 24, and see also her Westminster Abbey, pp. 160–1.

69   Harvey, Westminster Abbey, p. 163.

70   R.H. Hilton, The Economic Development of some Leicestershire Estates in the Fourteenth and Fifteenth Centuries (London, 1947), pp. 158–9.

71   The following paragraph is partly based (with some additions) on C. Dyer, 'English peasant buildings in the Middle Ages (1200–1500), Medieval Archaeology, 30 (1986), pp. 22–3.

72   Ibid., p. 29.

73   There is a good survey of some of the problems in P. McClure, 'Patterns of migration in the late Middle Ages: the evidence of English place-name surnames', EcHR, 32 (1979), pp. 167–82. He cites the pessimistic conclusion of Eilert Ekwall that 'surname evidence does not lend itself to being exploited statistically', (p. 171). I fully agree.

74   Harvey, Westminster Abbey, p. 262.

75   M. Spufford, A Cambridgeshire Community: Chippenham from Settlement to Enclosure (Leicester, 1965), pp. 31–2.

76   B.M.S. Campbell, 'Population pressure, inheritance and the land market in a fourteenth-century peasant community', Land, Kinship and Life-Cycle, ed. R.M. Smith (Cambridge, 1984), pp. 96–7.

77   F.W. Maitland, 'The history of a Cambridgeshire manor' (originally published 1894), reprinted in *Selected Essays of F.W. Maitland*, ed H.M. Cam (Cambridge, 1957), pp. 24, 38.

78   Page, *The Estates of Crowland Abbey*, pp. 146–53.

79   Ibid., pp. 146–9.

80   Ibid., pp. 156, 438–40, 442–4.

81   Ibid., p. 149.

82   The evidence is in the various court rolls: ibid., pp. 418, 426, 428–9, 435.

83   Ibid., pp. 428, 430.

84   Ibid., p. 153.

85   Ibid., pp. 441–2.

86   Ibid., pp. 150–1.

87   E. King in Miller, p. 627.

88   J.A. Raftis, *Warboys* (Toronto, 1974), p. 265; C. Howell, *Land, Family and Inheritance in Transition: Kibworth Harcourt, 1280–1700* (Cambridge, 1983), p. 45.

89   Raftis, *The Estates of Ramsey Abbey*, pp. 293–4, 296–300.

90   Ibid., pp. 294, 298.

91   Ibid., p. 294.

92   Ibid., p. 298.

93   J.A. Raftis, 'Changes in an English village after the Black Death', *Medieval Studies* (Toronto), 29 (1967), p. 175.

94   E. King in Miller, pp. 628–30, and E.B. Fryde, ibid., pp. 789–90. The evidence comes from the publications of J.A. Raftis and his various collaborators at Toronto.

95   King, ibid., pp. 625–6.

96   T.H. Lloyd, 'Some documentary sidelights on the deserted Oxfordshire village of Brookend', *Oxoniensia*, (1964/5), pp. 123–8.

97   Cf. Dyer, 'Deserted medieval villages', pp. 24–5, and *idem* in Miller, pp. 86–7.

98   C. Dyer, 'The deserted medieval village of Woollashill', pp. 55–61. See also above, chapter 5, section IV.

99   The following two paragraphs are based chiefly on S. Raban, *Mortmain Legislation and the English Church, 1279–1500* (Cambridge, 1982), pp. 33–4.

100 Hilton, *English Peasantry*, pp. 64, 69.

101 Howell, *Land, Family and Inheritance,* pp. 48–50.

102 Harvey, *Westminster Abbey*, p. 269, n. 1, and p. 305.

103 E. Powell, *The Rising in East Anglia in 1381* (Cambridge, 1896), p. 35; E.B. Borstall in *Norfolk Archaeology*, 31 (1955), p. 211.

104 Borstall, ibid., pp. 211, 215.

105 On the Bishop of Ely's manor of Wilburton see Cam (ed.), *Essays of F.W. Maitland*, pp. 16–40.

106 Ibid., pp. 17–20, 32; E. Miller, *The Abbey and Bishopric of Ely* (Cambridge, 1951), p. 17 and n. 5.

107 Cam (ed.), *Essays of F.W. Maitland*, p. 28.

108 Ibid., pp. 26–7.

109 Lancashire RO, DDK 1746/14.

110 Cam (ed.), *Essays of F.W. Maitland*, pp. 28, 32–3.

111 See below, chapter 9, section IV.

112 P.D.A. Harvey (ed.), *The Peasant Land Market in Medieval England* (Oxford, 1984), pp. 332–7.

113 Ibid., pp. 335–7.

114 J.A. Tuck in Miller, p. 588.

115 Harvey (ed.), *Peasant Land Market*, p. 311 (article of T. Lomas).

116 R.A. Lomas, 'Developments in land tenure on the Prior of Durham's estate in the later Middle Ages', *Northern History*, 13 (1977), p. 39.

117 See below, chapter 10, section III.

118 The account that follows is based on R.H. Hilton, 'Kibworth Harcourt: a Merton College manor in the thirteenth and fourteenth centuries', *Studies in Leicestershire Agrarian History*, ed. W.G. Hoskins (Leicester, 1949), and on Howell, *Land, Family and Inheritance*, chapter 4.

119 Hilton in *Leicestershire Agrarian History*, ed. Hoskins, p. 32 and p. 34, n. 70.

120 Ibid., pp. 39–40.

121 Howell, *Land, Family and Inheritance*, pp. 48–9.

122 E. King in Miller, p. 626.

123 Howell, *Land, Family and Inheritance*, p. 50.

124 Ibid., p. 50.

125 Ibid., pp. 44, 50.

126 Ibid., p. 50.

127 Ibid., p. 53.

128 Ibid., p. 50.

129 C.M. Gray, *Copyhold, Equity and the Common Law* (Cambridge, Mass., 1963), pp. 9–10.

130 Howell, *Land, Family and Inheritance*, pp. 50–1.

131 Ibid., pp. 51, 54.

132 Ibid., pp. 52–3.

133 Harvey, *Westminster Abbey* p. 265.

134 Ibid., p. 245.

135 Ibid., p. 263.

136 Ibid., pp. 257–9.

137 Ibid., pp. 262–3.

138 Ibid., p. 269, and n. 1.

139 Ibid., p. 268.

140 Ibid., p. 269.

141 Ibid., p. 261 and n. 4; p. 270.

142 '*Quia tenuit ad firmam et non pro serviciis et consuetudinibus*', ibid., p. 251.

143 Ibid., pp. 245, 254–5 (my italics).

144 Ibid., p. 256.

145 B. Harvey in *VCH: Oxon.*, vol. VI, pp. 237–8.

146 Ibid., pp. 213–15, and her *Westminster Abbey*, p. 270.

147 For some examples see below, chapter 13.

148 K.B. McFarlane, *The Nobility of Later Medieval England* (Oxford, 1973), p. 221.

149 J.N. Hare, 'The lords and their tenants: conflict and stability in fifteenth-century Wiltshire', *Conflict and Community in Southern England*, ed. B. Stapleton (Stroud, 1992), pp. 20–1.

150 Hilton, *Decline of Serfdom*, pp. 51–2.

CHAPTER 9

1   For details see below, section V.

2   The eleven estates are: Abberley, Beoley, Comberton, Elmley Castle, Elmley Lovett, Fickenappletree, Grafton Flyford, Ribbesford, Salwarpe, Shrawley, and Wadborough. They are the only ones for which comparison is possible. They represented two-thirds of the value of the earl's properties in Worcestershire in 1397 (£351 out of £529). For the latter figure see A. Goodman, *The Loyal Conspiracy: The Lords Appellant under Richard II* (London, 1971), p. 142.

3   *Calendar of Inquisitions Miscellaneous, 1392–99*, no. 302, pp. 159–62.

4   PRO, Rentals and Surveys SC12/8/45. C. Ross in *The Estates and Finances of Richard Beauchamp, Earl of Warwick* (Oxford, Dugdale Society, 1956) mentioned it (p. 4, n. 2), but was unable to date it. My date is based on comparison with the reeve's account for Elmley Castle of 1434/5 (Worcester RO, BA 989, ref. 899: 95, box 6, no. 103).

5   Worcester RO 192/92627½. For more details see below, section V.

6   See below, section III.

7   Worcester RO, 9 (IV), 43696, ff. 30v.–32r.

8   For the sources of this evidence see below, section II. The ten estates are Blockley, Bredon, Hartlebury, Kempsey, Whitstones, Wick and Wichenford (only taxes) in Worcestershire, and Bibury, Cleeve, Henbury Saltmarsh and Withington in Gloucestershire. They include a number of the most valuable episcopal properties.

9   See below in this chapter and in chapter 11.

10   Dyer, *Lords and Peasants*, p. 194. I have deducted from Professor Dyer's figure £32 for Peter's Pence, as I have included it instead under servile taxes.

11   Worcester RO, 9(IV), 43696, ff. 29r–30r. There is mention of such a new rental dating from 1410/11 in a list of arrears of 1453 (ibid. 193/92627¹¹⁄₂).

12   Ibid., 9(IV), ff. 27r.–27v.

13   Ibid., f. 163r.

14   Worcester RO, 174/92465. See also below, section VI of this chapter.

15   Dyer, *Lords and Peasants*, pp. 154, 188, 200.

16   E.F. Jacob, *The Fifteenth Century, 1399–1485* (Oxford, 1961), pp. 431–3.

17   L.R. Betcherman, 'The making of bishops in the Lancastrian period', *Speculum*, 41 (1966), pp. 404–12. For Pope Martin's veto over the recommendation of Polton for London see ibid., p. 406, n. 52.

18   Worcester RO, 175/92475: '*Et de DCCC libris receptis de executoribus Domini Thome Polton . . . tam pro Reparacionibus Castrorum, Maneriorum et aliarum domorum quam pro aliis superoneribus et reprisis . . . per quandam concordiam . . . ad instanciam Domini Henrici Cardinalis et Episcopi Wyntonie . . . .*' For Bourchier's acquisition of the bishopric see Harriss, *Cardinal Beaufort*, pp. 239–40.

19   Dyer, *Lords and Peasants* pp. 188, 203. For Polton's patronage of Wode see also above chapter 5, section IV.

20   This is my impression from Carpenter's voluminous register in two volumes (Worcester RO, b.716:093, BA 2648, no. 6, pts 2 and 3). See also R.M. Haines, 'Aspects of the episcopate of John Carpenter, Bishop of Worcester, 1444–76', *Journal of Ecclesiastical History*, 19 (1968) and Dyer, *Lords and Peasants* pp. 154–5.

21 Worcester RO, 9(IV), 43696, ff. 30v.–32r.

22 London, Brit. Libr. Add. MS 6165, p. 169.

23 Worcester RO, 9(IV), 43696, ff. 14r.–21v.

24 Ibid., 192/92627⁹⁄₁₂.

25 Ibid., 9(IV), 43696, ff. 116r.–151r. It is not dated but the internal evidence of the taxes collected during the vacancy by the royal officials points to 1418/19.

26 Much of this evidence was used in Dyer, 'Redistribution of incomes', pp. 19–20. But Professor Dyer used only the records in the Worcester archive and did not combine them with the records of accounting at the exchequer, which provide some further information and help to clarify more fully what happened.

27 Worcester RO, 192/92627/⁹⁄₁₂.

28 Ibid., 193/92628⁹⁄₁₀.

29 PRO, Foreign Roll, E364/71, m. 3; L.T.R. Memoranda Rolls, 14 Hen. VI, E368/208, *Recorda,* Michaelmas, m. 22, and 16 Hen. VI, E368/210, *Visus et Status Compotorum,* Hilary, mm. 1–2; Pipe Rolls, 15 Hen. VI, E372/282, and 16 Hen. VI, E372/283, *Wygornia* membranes (dorses).

30 The two drafts of their petition used in Dyer, 'Redistribution of incomes' are Worcester RO, 174/92471 and 92465. The petition finally presented to the exchequer had a slightly different wording (PRO, K.R. Memoranda Roll, 17 Hen. VI, E159/215, *Brevia Directa Baronibus,* Hilary, m. 2r., and 2v. Dyer was mistaken ('Redistribution of incomes', p. 20 and n. 46) in assuming that there exist three drafts of this petition. Another petition, concerning one particular item, is in PRO, Ministers' Accts, SC6/1143, no. 21.

31 Worcester RO, 175/92475.

32 See above, chapter 5, section III.

33 Worcester RO, 162/92114 (1394/5); 9(IV) 43696, f. 16v. (Michaelmas 1408).

34 Wick and Wichenford, ibid., f. 14r.; Kempsey, ibid., f. 15r. (1408) and f. 27v. (?1411/12); Fladbury, ibid., f. 18v.; Stoke, ibid., f. 17r.; Withington, ibid., f. 17v.

35 Worcester RO, 158, nos 92013⅜ and 92028; 159/92030.

36 Dyer, *Lords and Peasants,* 152.

37 See above, section II, for the sources used here.

38 Worcester RO, 9(IV), 43696, f. 150; 175/92475. For the difficulties under Bishop Carpenter see below, chapter 10, section IV, and chapter 11.

39 At Henbury Saltmarsh £1 17s 2d was lost between 1395 and 1419. At Hampton Lucy and Hatton the losses amounted to at least £5 16s 8d between 1392 and 1419, with a further loss of £3 by 1427/8. At Wick and Wichenford there was a decline of £5 10s 8d between 1408/9 and 1419, with a further loss of 6s on a lease of a meadow. At Aston £2 had been lost by 1419 and there were losses of less than £1 each on farms of three other properties. The sources for Henbury Saltmarsh and Hampton are cited in section III of chapter 5. See also Worcester RO, 9(IV), 43696, f. 141r. (Henbury), f. 144r. (Hampton and also 164/92171), ff. 14r. and 125r. (Wick and Wichenford), f. 129v. (Aston), ff. 16v. and 134v. (Cleeve), ff. 15v. and 152v.–153r. (Ripple) and f. 130v. (the saltworks at Droitwich).

40 Ibid., ff. 28v. and 146v.; 167/92726; C. Dyer, *Hanbury: Settlement and Society in a Woodland Landscape* (Leicester, 1991), p. 56.

41 For evidence about most of the notables discussed in this and the next paragraphs see above, sections IV and V of chapter 5. See also below, section V of this chapter.

42 Carpenter, *Locality and Polity*, p. 169.

43 Worcester RO, 167/92276.

44 Dyer, *Lords and Peasants*, p. 380.

45 See above, chapter 8, sections V and VI.

46 Some evidence is listed in the R.K. Field, 'Worcestershire peasant buildings, household goods and farming equipment in the later Middle Ages', *Medieval Archaeology*, 9 (1965). See especially the appendices on pp. 125–45.

47 Dyer, *Hanbury*, p. 53. This was a localized meaning for 'toft'.

48 Field, 'Worcestershire peasant buildings', no. 1 on p. 133 and no. 6 on p. 134.

49 Ibid., no. 24 on p. 130.

50 Dyer, *Hanbury*, p. 55. In 1410/11 John Elvyn was holding 3 half-virgates, including one called by his family name [Worcester RO, 9(IV), 43696, f. 29r.].

51 Worcester RO, 9(IV), ff. 28–30. A rental of that date is cited in 193/92627¹⁰/₂ (1453).

52 Dyer, *Hanbury*, pp. 4–11.

53 Ibid., p. 54. See also above, chapter 4, section III.

54 Fryde, 'Tenants of the bishops', p. 248.

55 Dyer, *Hanbury*, p. 55.

56 Worcester RO, 9(IV), 43696, ff. 28–30.

57 See above, chapter 8, section VI, and Gray, *Copyhold*, pp. 9–10.

58 Worcester RO, 165/92227⅞.

59 Ibid., 9(IV), 43696, f. 27r. and v.

60 Ibid., f. 163r. and v.

61 For evidence from 1381/2 see Fryde, *Records in Memory of Meekings*, p. 244.

62 Worcester RO, 192/92627⅝₂.

63 Ibid., 193/92628⅞ (the custodians' copy of their account).

64 Dyer, 'Redistribution of incomes', p. 19, n. 39.

65 See above, section I.

66 Worcester RO, 174/92465. The same words are repeated in the audit of the custodians' account, PRO, LTR Memoranda Roll, 16 Henry VI. *Visus et Status Compotorum*, Hilary, mm. 1–2. Cited from the petition by Dyer, 'Redistribution of incomes', p. 20.

67 Dyer, ibid., p. 21. For the epidemic of 1434 see also below, chapter 10, section II.

68 Worcester RO, 174/92465.

69 Ibid. Professor Dyer ('Redistribution of incomes', pp. 19–22) gives an account of this demand of the custodians and of its consequences. He uses only the records in the Worcester archive and does not supplement them by the records of accounting at the exchequer, which help to clarify further what had happened.

70 PRO, Ministers' Accts, SC6/1143/18.

71 Ibid., Foreign Roll, E364/71, m. 3, (enrolled account of the custodians).

72 Fryde, *Records in Memory of Meekings*, p. 232.

73 Ibid., p. 253; Worcester RO, 166/92230.

74 Dyer, 'Redistribution of incomes', p. 20.

75 Hilton, *English Peasantry* pp. 66–7.

76 Dyer, 'Redistribution of incomes', pp. 21–2.

77 The doubt is mine.

78 Dyer, 'Redistribution of incomes', p. 22.

79 Bishop Bourchier's first account for 1435/6 makes no mention of the recognition (cf. Worcester RO, 175/92475).

80 The custodians' account, Worcester RO, 192/92627/⁵⁄₁₂ (the account of their receiver) and PRO, Foreign Roll, E364/71, m. 3; Bourchier's first account, Worcester RO, 175/92475.

CHAPTER 10

1 M. Bailey, 'Rural society', ed. Horrox, p. 153. This is a very balanced and wise survey. I owe thanks to my friend, Colin Richmond, for giving me a copy of it.

2 Hatcher, *Plague*, pp. 35, 37. On pp. 37–9 Dr Hatcher provides references to the principal regional studies sustaining this general conclusion. See also his important article in *Essays in Honour of Edward Miller* (Cambridge, 1996), pp. 237–72.

3 R.B. Dobson, 'Urban decline in late medieval England', *TRHS*, 5th ser., 27 (1977), p. 20.

4 Ibid., p. 11; W.G. Hoskins, *The Midland Peasant: The Economic and Social History of a Leicestershire Village* (London, 1957), p. 83.

5 See below, sections II and III.

6 Hatcher, *Plague*, p. 51.

7 B.M.S. Campbell in *AgHR*, 41 (1993), p. 64.

8 For the start of the conflict with the Hanse see M. Postan in Power and Postan, *Studies in English Trade*, pp. 127–9. The figures for exports in 1448/9 are based on Carus-Wilson and Coleman, *England's Export Trade*, pp. 61–2, 96–7. A good recent survey of the economic consequences of the revival of the French war and the popular disturbances in 1450 is in I. Harvey, *Jack Cade's Rebellion of 1450* (Oxford, 1991). For the decline in the prices of wool see above, chapter 6, section VI. See also below, sections V and VI in this chapter, for more evidence about the economy after 1448.

9 Cf. R.A. Griffiths in *Speculum*, 43 (1968), pp. 625–6, 631; below, chapter 12, section III (Devon).

10 See for these more fortunate areas Britnell, *Commercialisation of English Society*, p. 193. The evidence for Devon and Cornwall is based mainly on Hatcher, *Rural Economy and Society in the Duchy of Cornwall, 1300–1500* (Cambridge, 1970) However, J.M.W. Bean's review of this in *Speculum*, 47 (1972), pp. 766–69, suggests a need for more complex explanations.

11 Britnell, *Commercialisation of English Society*, p. 191.

12 H.E. Hallam, 'The agrarian economy of South Lincolnshire in the mid-fifteenth century', *Nottingham Medieval Studies*, 11 (1967), pp. 94–5.

13 Cf. the suggestive remarks of A.J. Pollard in *North-Eastern England during the Wars of the Roses*, p. 254 (the share of financial difficulties in contributing to the outbreak of fighting in 1453 in Yorkshire between the Percys and the Nevilles).

14 See below, chapter 11, for detailed evidence.

15 See below, section III.

16 J.M.W. Bean, 'Plague, population and economic decline in the later Middle Ages', *EcHR*, 2nd ser., 15 (1963), p. 429; Hatcher, *Plague*, p. 57.

17 See above, chapter 8, section V.

18 P. Heath, 'North Sea fishing in the fifteenth century: the Scarborough fleet', *Northern History*, 3 (1968), pp. 62, 65–8.

19 Pollard, 'North-eastern economy', p. 93; Dobson, *Durham Priory, 1400–1450*, p. 266.

20 Farmer, 'Grain yields on the Winchester manors', pp. 557–8, and, using the same evidence, in Miller, pp. 444, 504, 507.

21   D.L. Farmer, in Miller, p. 445.

22   C. Dyer in *EcHR*, 44 (1991), p. 139.

23   Bean, 'Plague, population and economic decline', p. 429; Hatcher, *Plague*, p. 58.

24   A full collection of relevant citations from chroniclers is in P.J.P. Goldberg, 'Mortality and economic changes in the diocese of York, 1390–1514', *Northern History*, 24 (1988), pp. 45–6.

25   Heath, 'North Sea fishing', pp. 65–8.

26   Goldberg, 'Mortality and economic changes in York', p. 45.

27   Pollard, 'North-eastern economy', and *idem, North-Eastern England during the Wars of the Roses* pp. 51–2. This summarizes (pp. 50–2) the evidence and conclusions of his more detailed study of 1989 (*Northern History*, 25), cited at the start of this note.

28   Lloyd, *Movement of Wool Prices*, p. 27.

29   M. Mate, 'Pastoral farming in south-east England in the fifteenth century', *EcHR*, 2nd ser., 40 (1987), p. 526.

30   Ibid., pp. 525–6; Brent, 'Alciston manor', p. 97.

31   Mate, 'Pastoral farming', p. 525.

32   See above, chapter 7.

33   Hatcher, *Plague*, pp. 38–40.

34   Ibid., p. 41.

35   R.A.L. Smith, *Canterbury Cathedral Priory: A Study in Monastic Administration* (Cambridge, 1943), p. 197, and Hatcher, *Plague*, p. 40.

36   A. Savine, 'English monasteries on the eve of the dissolution' in *Oxford Studies in Social and Legal History*, ed. P. Vinogradoff (Oxford, 1909), pp. 283–4.

37   P.F. Brandon's study of Alciston in 'Arable farming in a Sussex scarp-foot parish during the late Middle Ages', *Sussex Archaeological Collections*, 100 (1962), p. 71; Brent, 'Alciston manor'; P.F. Brandon, 'Cereal yields on the Sussex estates of Battle Abbey during the later Middle Ages', *EcHR*, 2nd ser., 25 (1972), 403–20, cited on p. 420; J.N. Hare, 'The monks as landlords: the leasing of the monastic demesnes in Southern England', *The Church in Pre-Reformation Society*, ed. Barron and Harper-Bill, pp. 85, 87, 89.

38   Brandon, 'Arable farming in a Sussex scarp-foot parish', p. 62.

39   Brent, 'Alciston manor', p. 97; Mate, 'Pastoral farming in south-east England', (1987), p. 526 and n. 22.

40   Cf. E. Searle, *Lordship and Community: Battle Abbey and its Banlieu, 1066–1538* (Toronto, 1974), map facing p. 10 and review of her book by F. Hockey in *Speculum*, 52 (1977), pp. 430–5.

41   Searle, *Lordship and Community*, pp. 368–9.

42   E. Searle and Barbara Ross (eds), *Accounts of the Cellarers of Battle Abbey, 1275–1513* (Sydney, 1967), pp. 30–1.

43   See above, chapter 8, section V.

44   Raftis, *The Estates of Ramsey Abbey*, p. 293.

45   Ibid., pp. 296–9, and below, section V.

46   Above, chapter 8, section V. The comment about 'economic confusion' occurs in Hatcher, *Plague*, (1977), p. 38.

47   Page, *The Estates of Crowland Abbey*, p. 154.

48   The best account is in A.J. Pollard's article in *Northern History* for 1989 ('North-eastern

economy'), with a briefer summary in his book, *North-Eastern England during the Wars of the Roses*.

49 Pollard, 'North-eastern economy', p. 94.

50 Ibid., pp. 94, 99.

51 Dobson, *Durham Priory*, p. 253.

52 Ibid., p. 271, and J.A. Tuck, 'War and society in the medieval north', *Northern History*, 21 (1985), p. 33.

53 Dobson, *Durham Priory*, p. 270.

54 See above, chapter 8, section VI.

55 Tuck, 'War and Society', pp. 41–2.

56 Dobson, *Durham Priory*, pp. 284–85.

57 Pollard, 'North-eastern economy', p. 100.

58 Dobson, *Durham Priory*, pp. 285–6.

59 Ibid., pp. 286–90.

60 Ibid., pp. 288–9.

61 Ibid., p. 284.

62 Ibid., p. 253.

63 Pollard, *North-eastern England during the Wars of the Roses*, p. 53.

64 Storey, *Thomas Langley*, p. 68.

65 Pollard, 'North-eastern economy', pp. 94, 98.

66 Pollard, '*North-eastern England during the Wars of the Roses*, p. 54.

67 J.M.W. Bean, *The Estates of the Percy Family, 1416–1537* (Oxford, 1958), pp. 29–31.

68 Pollard, 'North-eastern economy' pp. 94–7, 101–2.

69 See above, chapter 8, section V.

70 An article originally published in 1957, reprinted in *English Peasantry*, pp. 161–73.

71 See below, chapter 12.

72 Dyer, *Hanbury*, p. 56.

73 Dyer, *Warwickshire Farming*, p. 11.

74 C. Dyer, 'A small landowner in the fifteenth century', *Midland History*, 1 (1972), pp. 1–14; Carpenter, *Warwickshire 1401–99*, pp. 127–8, 458; E.B. Fryde in Miller, p. 807.

75 Hilton, *English Peasantry* pp. 168–70; Carpenter, *Warwickshire 1401–99*, pp. 128, 130 and n. 127 on p. 130.

76 A. Watkins, 'Cattle grazing in the Forest of Arden in the later Middle Ages', *AgHR*, 37 (1989), p. 16 and n. 16.

77 J.R. Birrell in *VCH: Staffs*, vol. VI (1979), especially pp. 45–7 and 'The forest economy of the Honour of Tutbury in the fourteenth and the fifteenth centuries', *University of Birmingham Historical Journal*, 8 (1962), pp. 114–34.

78 Birrell, 'Tutbury', p. 121.

79 Pollard, *North-Eastern England during the Wars of the Roses*, pp. 61–2.

80 Richmond, *John Hopton*, p. 99.

81 Cf. my brief summary in Miller, pp. 804–7, and Isobel Harvey, *Jack Cade's Rebellion of 1450* (Oxford, 1991).

82 See for these documents E.B. Fryde in Miller, p. 804, n. 144.

83 Ibid., p. 804.

84 Carus-Wilson and Coleman, *England's Export Trade*, pp. 61–3, 96–7.

85 H.P.R. Finberg and W.G. Hoskins, *Devonshire Studies* (London, 1952), pp. 241–5; Hatcher, *Rural Economy and Society in Cornwall,* p. 289.

86 Cited by M. Keen in *Essays in Honour of P. Chaplais* (London, 1989), p. 297.

87 P. Wolff, *Commerce et Marchands de Toulouse, vers 1350–vers 1450* (Paris, 1954), pp. 236–40.

88 See above, chapter 7 (especially section III).

89 M. Mate, 'Pastoral farming in south-east England', p. 527.

90 Stephenson in *EcHR*, 41 (1988), p. 387.

91 The discussion of the Wiltshire and Hampshire risings that follows is based chiefly on J.N. Hare, 'The lords and their tenants: conflict and stability in fifteenth-century Wiltshire', *Conflict and Community in Southern England*, ed. B. Stapleton (Stroud, 1992), pp. 16–17. Detailed evidence is set out in chapter VI of his Ph.D. thesis, 'Lord and Tenant in Wiltshire, c. 1380–c.1520's' (London, 1975).

92 Harvey, *Jack Cade's Rebellion*, p. 126.

93 PRO, Ancient Indictments, KB9/133, nos 23, 33–5.

94 Cf. above, section I of this chapter.

95 See, for example, M. Mate on the manors of the Pelhams and of the Duchy of Lancaster in Sussex, in Miller, pp. 684–5.

96 Ibid., p. 685.

97 Harvey, *Jack Cade's Rebellion*, pp. 82, 167, 169.

98 M. Mate in Miller, p. 625 and n. 240.

99 Smith, *Canterbury Cathedral Priory*, p. 197; Hatcher, *Plague*, pp. 40–1; J.M.W. Bean in Miller, p. 546.

100 F.R.H. Du Boulay, *The Lordship of Canterbury* (1966), pp. 225–6.

101 Ibid., and Hatcher, *Plague*, p. 41.

102 M. Mate, 'Pastoral farming in south-east England', pp. 531–2.

103 M. Mate in Miller, p. 123; Searle, *Lordship and Community*, p. 253.

104 Ibid.

105 M. Mate, 'The economic and social roots of medieval popular rebellion: Sussex in 1450–1', *EcHR*, 45 (1992), p. 672; Searle, *Lordship and Community*, p. 455.

106 Cf. the remarks of Du Boulay, *Lordship of Canterbury* pp. 225–6.

107 Cited by Hatcher, *Plague*, p. 38.

108 Raftis, *The Estates of Ramsey Abbey*, pp. 292–3.

109 Ibid., p. 300.

110 Ibid., pp. 296–99.

111 In addition to his *The Estates of Ramsey Abbey*, see especially *Tenure and Mobility* and *Warboys*.

112 Raftis, *The Estates of Ramsey Abbey*, p. 266.

113 Ibid., p. 301.

114 Raftis, *Tenure and Mobility*, p. 173.

115 Raftis, *The Estates of Ramsey Abbey*, p. 301.

116 Raftis, *Tenure and Mobility*, pp. 198–9.

117 Ibid., pp. 191–6.

118 BL, Harleian MS 445, ff. 231r., 246v.

119 Ibid., f. 255r.

120 Raftis, *Tenure and Mobility*, pp. 183–9.

121 Raftis, *The Estates of Ramsey Abbey*, pp. 296–9. The list of abbots is on p. xx.

122 Pollard, *North-Eastern England during the Wars of the Roses*, p. 78. This is the principal source for the account of the north-east that follows (especially part I, chapter 3).

123 Ibid., p. 78.

124 See above, section III, and Pollard, *North-Eastern England during the Wars of the Roses*, p. 53.

125 Ibid.

126 Pollard, ibid., p. 56.

127 See below, chapter 12.

128 Ibid., and Pollard, *North-Eastern England during the Wars of the Roses*, pp. 56–7.

129 Pollard, ibid., p. 58.

130 Ibid., pp. 67–8.

131 R.H. Britnell, 'The Pastons and their Norfolk', *AgHR*, 36 (1988), p. 133.

132 Richmond, *John Hopton*. My account of Hopton's properties is based on Richmond's chapter 2 ('The Estates').

133 Ibid., pp. 39–40.

134 Edward Miller's phrase in Miller, p. 32.

135 Richmond, *John Hopton*, pp. 66–9.

136 Ibid., p. 99.

137 Ibid., p. 98.

138 Britnell, 'The Pastons and their Norfolk', p. 134; K.J. Allison, 'Flock management in the sixteenth and seventeenth centuries', *EcHR*, 2nd ser., 11 (1958), p. 107.

139 Richmond, *John Hopton*, pp. 47, 55, 59–60.

140 The most recent, and much improved, edition of the correspondence of the Pastons is by Norman Davis: *Paston Letters and Papers of the Fifteenth Century* (2 vols, London, 1971–6). Davis also published a useful selection in *Paston Letters* (Oxford, 1976). My principal sources for the account that follows are: H.S. Bennett, *The Pastons and their England*, (Cambridge, 1951); R.H. Britnell, 'The Pastons and their Norfolk', *AgHR*, 36 (1988), pp. 132–44; C. Richmond, *The Paston Family in the Fifteenth Century: The First Phase* (Cambridge, 1990) and 'Landlord and tenant: the Paston evidence', Kermode (ed.) *Enterprise and Individuals in Fifteenth-Century England*, ed. J. Kermode (Stroud, 1991) pp. 25–42.

141 Britnell, '*The Pastons and their Norfolk*', p. 133.

142 In H.S. Bennett's phrase (*The Pastons and their England*, p. 4).

143 Richmond, *The Paston Family*, chapter 1, pp. 1–22.

144 Ibid., chapters 7 and 8 (pp. 206–61).

145 Britnell, 'The Pastons and their Norfolk', p. 134.

146 *Paston Letters*, ed. Davis, p. x.

147 A list of the Pastons' properties, with dates when they held them, is in Britnell, 'The Pastons and their Norfolk', p. 133 and n. 10. See also Richmond in *Enterprise and Individuals*, ed. Kermode, pp. 25–6.

148 Britnell, ibid., pp. 136–7.

149 Richmond in *Enterprise and Individuals*, ed. Kermode (1991), pp. 31–3.

150 Britnell, 'The Pastons and their Norfolk', p. 142.

151 Ibid., pp. 137, 140; Richmond in *Enterprise and Individuals*, ed. Kermode, pp. 25–7, 36–7.

152 Britnell, 'The Pastons and their Norfolk', pp. 140–2, and Richmond in *Enterprise and Individuals*, ed. Kermode, pp. 34–7.

153 R. Faith, 'Berkshire: fourteenth and fifteenth centuries', *Peasant Land Market,* ed. Harvey, pp. 157–8.

154 See also above, chapter 7, sections III and IV, for some further examples from the southern estates of the Duchy of Lancaster, and Hatcher, *loc. cit.* (1996), pp. 261–2.

155 R. Faith in *Peasant Land Market,* ed. Harvey, pp. 157–8.

156 Ibid., pp. 116–18.

157 Ibid., pp. 173–4, and Dyer, 'Were there any capitalists in fifteenth-century England?', *Enterprise and Individuals,* ed. Kermode, p. 18.

158 Faith in *Peasant Land Market,* ed. Harvey, pp. 167, 171.

159 Ibid., pp. 110, 166–7.

160 J.N. Hare, 'Durrington: a chalkland village in the later Middle Ages', *Wiltshire Archaeological Magazine,* 74 (1981). For the farmers of the demesne see pp. 142–5 and also J.N. Hare in *AgHR,* 29 (1981), p. 12.

161 R.H. Hilton in *University of Birmingham Historical Journal,* 10 (1965), p. 78.

162 Worcester RO, BA989 (ref. 899.95), box 1, no. 3a.

163 Ibid., box 4, nos 73a, 74.

164 Ibid., box 6, nos. 95, 103–5.

165 Ibid., box 6, no. 113.

166 The narrative that follows is based on accounts and court rolls for Hampton (Worcester RO, BA 2636). See also Dyer, *Lords and Peasants,* pp. 157–8.

167 Worcester RO, 57/92007.

168 Ibid., 164/92172.

169 Ibid., 9(IV), 43696, f. 145r.

170 Ibid., 164/92171.

171 Ibid. 164/92176.

172 Ibid., 176/92489.

173 Ibid. 193/92627^{10}/₁₂.

174 Ibid. 165/92225¾.

175 Ibid.

176 Ibid., Register of Bishop John Carpenter, (BA 2648, b.716:093, vol. 6, pt 3), vol. II, 32.

CHAPTER 11

1 Worcester RO, BA 2636, 190/92614.

2 It consists only of payments to the bishop by his receiver general recorded in his account ibid, 175/92480. Direct payments to Bishop Carpenter from particular estates are not included.

3 Ibid., 168/92313 (account of receiver general) and 175/92477 (valor for Michaelmas 1454).

4 Ibid., 174/92470/¾ (account of receiver general) and 175/92479 (valor for Michaelmas 1457).

5 This is the main conclusion of R.M. Haines ('Aspects of the Epicopate of John Carpenter, Bishop of Worcester, 1444–1476', *Journal of Ecclesiastical History,* 19 (1968), pp. 11–12, 40. The biographical information on Carpenter in this paragraph is based on his article. Haines also published Carpenter's injunctions to the diocese of Worcester in 1451 in the *Bulletin of the Institute of Historical Research,* 40 (1967), pp. 203–7.

6   Accounts of receiver general for 1453/4 (Worcester RO, 168/92313) and 1456/7 (ibid., 174/92470/⅜) and Dyer, *Lords and Peasants*, p. 204.

7   Hilton, *English Peasantry*, pp. 70–1.

8   See also his article, 'A redistribution of incomes in fifteenth-century England', *Past and Present*, 39 (1968), pp. 11–33.

9   He lists them on pp. 392–4.

10 Worcester RO, 175/92475, 175/92480, 168/92313, 174/92470⅜, 175/92483, 175/92484, 176/92493–4, 175/92485, 176/92487, 174/92473.

11 For example, the list of arrears at Michaelmas 1462 lists such claims under a large number of estates (ibid., 176/92488, *passim*).

12 Ibid., 175/92477, 175/92479, 174/92472, 176/92486.

13 Ibid., 175/92477.

14 For example, the huge account for Blockley in 1458/9, ibid., 157/92008.

15 Ibid., 191/92625⅔/₂; 176/92488; 176/92490.

16 *Lords and Peasants*, pp. 180, 185.

17 Dyer, 'Redistribution of incomes', p. 31.

18 Dyer, *Lords and Peasants*, p. 284.

19 Ibid., p. 383–4.

20 Power and Postan (eds), *Studies in English Trade*, p. 53.

21 Dyer, *Lords and Peasants*, pp. 180–2.

22 Ibid., pp. 279, 380.

23 Ibid., pp. 277–9.

24 Worcester RO, 193/92627¹⁰/₁₂.

25 Ibid., 164/92177.

26 Dyer, *Lords and Peasants*, p. 165.

27 For Westbury collegiate church see above, section I. For palaces at Worcester and Hartlebury see Dyer, *Lords and Peasants*, p. 202; Haines, 'Episcopate of John Carpenter': Worcester RO, 174/92473 (account of receiver general, 1470/1).

28 Dyer, *Lords and Peasants*, pp. 172–3, 207; Worcester RO, 193/92627/¹⁰/₁₂ (under Hampton); 175/92483 (account of receiver general, 1460/1).

29 Dyer, *Lords and Peasants*, p. 166.

30 See above, chapter 5, section V.

31 Dyer, *Lords and Peasants*, p. 176.

32 Hilton, *English Peasantry*, pp. 67–8.

33 For defaults to pay taxes see Dyer, 'Redistribution of incomes', pp. 22–3, and E.B. Fryde in Miller, pp. 794–5.

34 Worceser RO, 158/92015.

35 Ibid., 158/92016 (court roll); 157/92012/⅛ (account roll, 1393–4).

36 Ibid., 193/92627/¹⁰/₁₂.

37 Ibid., 191/92625/⅔/₂, 176/92488, 176/92490 (arrears rolls); E.B. Fryde in Miller, p. 795.

38 Dyer, 'Redistribution of incomes', pp. 25–6.

39 Worcester RO, 193/92627/¹⁰/₁₂.

40 See Dyer, 'Redistribution of incomes', and E.B. Fryde in Miller, as well as the three arrears rolls cited in note 37.

41 Dyer, *Lords and Peasants*, pp. 286–7.

42 Ibid., p. 274.

43 Ibid., p. 285.

44 Ibid., pp. 270–2. Many manumissions are recorded in the two volumes of Bishop Carpenter's episcopal register (Worcester RO, BA 2648, b. 716:093, no. 6, pts 2 and 3).

45 Worcester RO, 193/92627/¹⁹⁄₁₂; Dyer, 'Redistribution of incomes', p. 24, and *Lords and Peasants*, pp. 213, 272.

46 Worcester RO, 157/92008.

47 Ibid., 157/92007.

48 Ibid., 157/92008.

49 Ibid., 174/92472 and 176/92486 (valors).

50 Dyer, *Lords and Peasants*, p. 183.

51 Ibid., pp. 184, 214; list of arrears in 1462 from Worcester RO, 176/92488.

52 Dyer, *Lords and Peasants*, pp. 167, 183–4.

53 Ibid., pp. 173, 182–3; arrears rolls, 176/92488 and 176/92490; 193/92627/¹⁹⁄₁₂.

54 For the earlier history of these estates see above, chapter 4, sections V and VI, and chapter 5, section III.

55 See above, chapter 5, section III.

56 Worcester RO, 163/92168.

57 See above, chapter 5, section III. A later Thomas Rowes was described as *nativus domini* in the court roll for 20 January 1453 (Worcester RO, 164/92177).

58 Worcester RO, court rolls, 164/92178A and 164/92182.

59 Ibid., 9(IV), 43696, ff. 144v.–145r.

60 Ibid., 164/92171 and 92173.

61 Ibid., 164/92171 and 92172. For the history of the Kynne family see above, chapter 10, section VIII.

62 Ibid., 175/92480 (account of the receiver general for 1447/8).

63 See above, chapter 10, section VIII.

64 Ibid.

65 Worcester RO, 164/92183.

66 Ibid., 164/92177.

67 In *Land, Kinship and Life-Cycle*, ed. Smith, pp. 307–8.

68 Worcester RO, 164/92174 and 92177.

69 Ibid., 164/92178A (court roll for October 1453) and 164/92179 (Hampton account for 1454/5). For William Bernard as reeve see ibid., 164/92174 (court roll for October 1449). Pathelowe was Bernard's predecessor as reeve (ibid., 164/92176). For his tenure of 1 virgate see ibid., 164/92185.

70 Ibid., 164/92174 (court roll for April 1450).

71 Ibid., 191/92625/³⁄₁₂ (list of arrears for 1459/60); 163/92159/³⁄₄ (Hampton account, 1461/2); Dyer, *Lords and Peasants*, p. 185.

72 Worcester RO, 64/92175.

73 Ibid., 164/92175 and 164/92181.

74 Ibid., 193/92627¹⁹⁄₁₂.

75 Ibid., 164/92181.

76 For the disturbed political and military situation of 1456/7 see R.L. Storey, *The End of the House of Lancaster* (London, 1966), pp. 179–84.

77 Worcester RO, 164/92187.

78 Dyer, *Lords and Peasants*, p. 268.

79 J. Kail (ed.), *Twenty-Six Political and other Poems*, Early English Texts Society, no. CXXIV (1904), pp. ix–xi and no. III, lines 101–2. The two paragraphs that follow are mainly based on E.B. Fryde in Miller, pp. 795–6.

80 Hilton, *English Peasantry*, p. 65.

81 John Vampage was withholding each year a rent of 16*s* 9*d* which he owed at Ripple. Cf. Dyer, 'Redistribution of incomes', pp. 27–8.

82 See, for example, ibid., pp. 22–3. This very well-documented example actually refers to the non-payment of local seignorial taxes.

83 Dyer, *Lords and Peasants*, pp. 166–7.

84 Worcester RO, 191/926265/³⁄₂ and 176/92490.

85 Ibid., 157/92008r. (section of *allocatio redditus*). For the lost labour services see dorse.

86 Dyer, 'Redistribution of incomes', pp. 27–8, 30.

87 Dyer, *Lords and Peasants*, p. 284.

88 E.B. Fryde in Miller, pp. 796–7.

89 See, for example, D.L. Farmer's table of corn prices in Miller, pp. 504–5.

90 Ross, *Edward IV*, pp. 42, 45, 395.

91 Hilton, *English Peasantry*, pp. 71–3. For the sources see C.L. Kingsford, *English Historical Literature in the Fifteenth Century* (Oxford, 1913), pp. 356–7.

92 Dyer, *Lords and Peasants*, p. 383. For Salwey as Arnold's deputy see Worcester RO, 174/92470/⅜ (Arnold's account, 1456/7, last section).

93 Dyer, ibid., pp. 184–5, 189.

94 Worcester RO, 157/92008 and 176/92488.

95 Ibid., 191/92625/³⁄₂, 176/92488 and 176/92490.

CHAPTER 12

1 My deep interest in this subject goes back to reading, as a student, R.H. Tawney, *The Agrarian Problem in the Sixteenth Century* (London, 1912). This chapter is based, above all, on the various publications of Tawney, M. Beresford and J.G. Hurst, W.G. Hoskins, R.H. Hilton and Joan Thirsk. I have known all these scholars and have learnt much from conversations with some of them.

2 M. Beresford and J.G. Hurst, *Deserted Medieval Villages: Studies* (London, 1971; new edn., Gloucester, 1989), pp. 34–5.

3 Some of Dugdale's notes on the operation of the 1518 commission in Warwickshire, of which John Hales was a member, are preserved, as are also the notes, from evidences compiled by John Hales in 1549, about the inquiries of 1517/18. The latter were preserved in 1656 by another John Hales of Coventry. They are printed in I.S. Leadam (ed.), *The Domesday of Inclosures*, vol. II (London, 1897), pp. 647–66.

4 For his membership of the commission of 1518 see E. Kerridge, *EHR*, 70 (1955), p. 214 and n. 3. See also the preceding note. On Hales's activities in 1548/9 see E. Lamond (ed.), *A Discourse of the Common Weal of this Realm of England* (Cambridge, 1893), pp. xxv–xxviii, xxxix–xli; Tawney, *Agrarian Problem* (new edn, New York, 1967), p. 385.

5 Lamond, (ed.), *Common Weal*, p. lxiii.

6   Beresford and Hurst, *Deserted Medieval Villages*, p. 16.

7   Ibid., p. 11.

8   Lawrence Stone in the introduction to the 1967 edition of Tawney, *Agrarian Problem*, p. xii.

9   H. Thorpe, 'The lord and the landscape' (first published in 1965), *English Rural Communities*, ed. D.R. Mills (London, 1973), p. 44.

10   This is one of the implications of Dyer, *Warwickshire Farming*.

11   Joan Thirsk (ed.), *The Agrarian History of England and Wales*, vol. IV (1967), pp. 248–9.

12   Joan Thirsk, *Tudor Enclosures*, Historical Association, general ser., no. 41 (London, 1959), pp. 14, 16.

13   There is an admirable discussion of the probable origins of the Midland open fields and of other English field systems in G.C. Homans, 'The explanation of English regional differences', *Past and Present*, 42 (1969). See particularly pp. 27–8. The best technical account of the fully developed open field is in C.S. and C.S. Orwin, *The Open Fields* (2nd edn, Oxford, 1954). Mr Orwin was the estates bursar of Balliol College, Oxford. There is a valuable collection of articles in Trevor Rowley (ed.), *The Origins of Open-Field Agriculture* (London, 1981). Dr. Thirsk's view that open field developed late for agricultural and demographic reasons are disproved by evidence from archaeology, air photography and place-name studies pointing to its existence in some English localities already in the Anglo-Saxon period. She is right, however, in stressing that it was more tightly enforced in periods of rising population.

14   K.J. Allison, 'The lost villages of Norfolk', *Norfolk Archaeology*, 31 (1955), pp. 132–3 and the map facing p. 133; B.M.S. Campbell, 'The regional uniqueness of English Field Systems? Some evidence from eastern Norfolk', *AgHR*, 29 (1981), pp. 16–28.

15   Cited in I. Blanchard, 'Population change, enclosure and the early Tudor economy', *EcHR*, 2nd ser., 23 (1970), p. 436.

16   Thirsk, *Tudor Enclosures*, p. 7.

17   M. Beresford, *The Lost Villages of England* (London, 1954), pp. 103–4.

18   R.B. Manning, *Village Revolts: Social Protests and Popular Disturbances in England, 1509–1640* (Oxford, 1988), pp. 3–4.

19   L.A. Parker, 'Agrarian revolution at Cotesbach, 1501–1612', *Studies in Leicestershire Agrarian History*, ed. W.G. Hoskins (Leicester, 1949), pp. 43–8.

20   R.H. Hilton, in *VCH: Leics.*, vol. III (1955), pp. 192–3. He believes that only the demesne was enclosed, but W.G. Hoskins, who seems to be right, expands this to the whole village ('Seven deserted villages in Leicestershire', *Transactions of the Leicestershire Archaeological and Historical Society*, 33 (1956), pp. 46–7.

21   Cited in Thirsk, *Tudor Enclosures*, p. 4, n. 1.

22   Dyer, *Warwickshire Farming*, pp. 26–7.

23   Cited in Lamond (ed.), *Common Weal*, p. 149.

24   Cited in M. Beresford, 'Habitation versus improvement', *Essays in the Economic and Social History of Tudor and Stuart England in Honour of R.H. Tawney*, ed. F.J. Fisher (Cambridge, 1961), p. 43.

25   There is a good summary in Thirsk (ed.), *Agrarian History*, vol. IV, pp. 214–37.

26   Tawney, *Agrarian Problem*, p. 385.

27   Ibid., pp. 387–8, and Historical Manuscripts Commission, *Calendar of the Manuscripts of . . . the Marquis of Salisbury preserved at Hatfield House, Hertfordshire*, pt 14 (1923), pp. 27–8.

28 Thirsk, *Tudor Enclosures*, p. 11.

29 Ibid., p. 20.

30 See below, section V.

31 Thirsk, *Tudor Enclosures*, pp. 20–1.

32 See the fascinating paper of H.S.A. Fox, 'The people of the Wolds in English settlement history', *The Rural Settlements of Medieval England: Studies Dedicated to Maurice Beresford and John Hurst*, ed. M. Aston, D. Austin and C. Dyer (Oxford, 1989), pp. 77–101.

33 Cf. J. Gould, 'Mr Beresford and the lost villages', *AgHR*, 3 (1955), p. 112 (with special reference to Leicestershire); Manning, *Village Revolts*, p. 14.

34 Beresford and Hurst, *Deserted Medieval Villages*, p. 19.

35 Thirsk, *Tudor Enclosures*, p. 19; Mary E. Finch, *The Wealth of Five Northamptonshire Families, 1540–1640* (Oxford, 1956), p. 89.

36 Beresford, *Lost Villages of England*, p. 247.

37 Leadam (ed.), *The Domesday of Inclosures*, vol. I, pp. 162–3.

38 J.E. Martin, *Feudalism to Capitalism: Peasant and Landlord in English Agrarian Development* (London, 1983), pp. 126–7. 204–5. See also Hilton, *Decline of Serfdom*, p. 45.

39 M. Cherry, 'The struggle for power in Mid-fifteenth-century Devonshire', *Patronage, the Crown and the Provinces,* ed. R.A. Griffiths (Gloucester, 1981), pp. 121, 131, 135–7; H.S.A. Fox in Miller, pp. 730–1; *Rot. Parl.*, vol. V, pp. 284–5.

40 C. Richmond, 'The transition from feudalism to capitalism in the archives of Magdalen College, Oxford: a note', *History Workshop Journal*, 37 (1994), p. 167.

41 See below, chapter 16, for the granges of the Spencers, one of the richest sheep-farming families of Tudor England, sited in previously depopulated villages.

42 J.S. Roskell, 'William Catesby, counsellor to Richard III', *Bulletin of the John Rylands Library, Manchester*, 42 (1959), pp. 150–2; Jean R. Birrell, 'The *Status Maneriorum* of John Catesby, 1385 and 1386', *The Dugdale Society: Miscellany I*, ed. R. Bearman (Oxford, 1977), pp. 23–8.

43 Beresford, 'Deserted villages of Warwickshire', p. 94; Thorpe, 'Lord and landscape', pp. 41–3; Dyer, *Warwickshire Farming* pp. 18–21; Dyer, 'Deserted medieval villages', pp. 24, 30.

44 Jean R. Birrell, 'The forest economy of the Honour of Tutbury in the fourteenth and fifteenth centuries', *University of Birmingham Historical Journal*, 8 (1962), pp. 121–2, 124–6.

45 Pollard, *North-Eastern England during the Wars of the Roses*, p. 62.

46 Ibid., p. 60.

47 Cited in Tawney, *Agrarian Problem*, p. 6, n. 4.

48 Cited in Beresford, 'Deserted villages of Warwickshire', p. 57.

49 P. Ramsey, *Tudor Economic Problems* (1963), p. 48; Carus-Wilson and Coleman, *England's Export Trade*, pp. 109–14 (cloth exports, 1485–1516).

50 W.G. Hoskins, 'The deserted villages of Leicestershire', in his *Essays in Leicestershire History* (Liverpool, 1950), p. 86.

51 See below, section IV.

52 W.J. Ford, 'Some settlement patterns in the central region of the Warwickshire Avon', *Medieval Settlement: Continuity and Change*, ed. P.H. Sawyer (London, 1976), pp. 274–94.

53 This paragraph is chiefly based on G.E. Fussell, 'Four centuries of Leicestershire farming', *Studies in Leicestershire Agrarian History*, ed. W.G. Hoskins (Leicester, 1949), pp. 154–76, and on W.G. Hoskins, 'The Leicestershire farmer in the sixteenth century', in his *Essays in Leicestershire History* (Liverpool, 1950), pp. 123–83.

54 G.E. Fussell in *Leicestershire Agrarian History*, ed. Hoskins, p. 154.

55 Hoskins, *Essays in Leicestershire History*, p. 164.

56 See in W.G. Hoskins, *The Making of the English Landscape* (London, 1955), p. 94, a map of 'Deserted Villages in Leicestershire', indicating the western boundary of heavy clay soils.

57 Thirsk, *Tudor Enclosures*, p. 20.

58 Cited by T.S. Ashton in a memoir of 'Richard Henry Tawney, 1880–1962', *Proceedings of the British Academy*, 48 (1962), p. 464. For more details see below, chapter 15, sections I and VI, and chapter 17, section II.

59 W.G. Hoskins, *The Midland Peasant: The Economic and Social History of a Leicestershire Village* (London, 1957).

60 R.H. Hilton in VCH: Leics., vol. III, pp. 194–5; Hoskins, 'Deserted villages of Leicestershire', *Essays in Leicestershire History* p. 86; *idem, Midland Peasant*, p. 28.

61 Hoskins, 'Deserted villages of Leicestershire', *Essays in Leicestershire History*, p. 93 and n. 2. For further details see below, section V.

62 I am using T. Hearne (ed.), *Joannis Rossi Antiquarii Warwicensis Historia Regum Angliae*, 2nd ed (Oxford, 1745), pp. 120–4, and a partial translation, with identification of most of the localities, in W.E. Tate, 'Enclosure acts and awards relating to Warwickshire', *Transactions and Proceedings of the Birmingham Archaeological Society*, 65 (for 1943/4, published 1949), pp. 57–63. The best account of Rous is in T.D. Kendrick, *British Antiquity* (London, 1950), pp. 19–29.

63 Hearne (ed.), *Historia*, pp. 120–1.

64 Ibid., p. 121.

65 Left unpublished at Rous's death in 1491. It does not appear to have been known to John Hales, but Dugdale consulted one of the extant copies. It was first published by Hearne in 1716 and republished in 1745 (in the edition used here).

66 Hearne (ed.), *Historia*, p. 124, and Tate, 'Enclosure acts', p. 60 (English translation) and p. 61, n. 1 (Latin text).

67 See above, chapter 5, section III.

68 M. Beresford, 'The lost villages of medieval England', *The Geographical Journal*, 117 (1951), p. 133.

69 Beresford, *Lost Villages of England*, pp. 147–8.

70 Tate, 'Enclosure acts', p. 59 (English translation), and p. 60, n. 1 (Latin text).

71 C. Dyer, 'Deserted medieval villages', p. 25.

72 See above, chapter 10, section IV; Hilton, *English Peasantry*, pp. 163–71; Dyer, 'Deserted medieval villages', p. 26; Rous in Tate, 'Enclosure acts', p. 58 and p. 60, n. 1 (referred to as Murdak).

73 Beresford, 'Deserted villages of Warwickshire', p. 106.

74 Dyer, 'Deserted medieval villages', p. 26; Rous in Tate, 'Enclosure acts', p. 58 (Caldcote) and p. 60, n. 1.

75 Hilton, *English Peasantry*, pp. 171–2; Dyer, 'Deserted medieval villages', p. 26; Rous in Tate, 'Enclosure acts', p. 59 and p. 60, n. 1.

76 See above, section II and III.

77 Rous in Tate, 'Enclosure acts', p. 58 and p. 60, n. 1; Dyer 'Deserted medieval villages', pp. 24–5; S.L. Thrupp, *The Merchant Class of Medieval London, 1300–1500* (Chicago and London, 1948), p. 373; Beresford, 'Deserted villages of Warwickshire', p. 89.

78 Beresford, ibid., p. 54 and n. 4; Rous in Tate, 'Enclosure acts', p. 59 and p. 60, n. 1.

79 Hearne (ed.), *Historia*, pp. 121–2.

80 Rous in Tate, 'Enclosure acts', pp. 59–60 and pp. 60–1, n. 1.

81 C. Phytian-Adams, *Desolation of a City: Coventry and the Urban Crisis of the Late Middle Ages* (Cambridge, 1979), pp. 58–61.

82 The main sources used are: Hoskins, *Essays in Leicestershire History*, pp. 67–107; *idem* 'Seven deserted village sites', pp. 36–51 and a table (appendix I) by J. Thirsk in *VCH Leics.*, vol. III, pp. 254–9.

83 See above, section II; Hoskins, *Essays in Leicestershire History*, pp. 75–9; *idem*, 'Seven deserted village sites', pp. 46–7; J. Thirsk in *VCH: Leics.*, vol. III, p. 257.

84 Hoskins, 'Essays in Leicestershire History', pp. 74–5; *idem*, 'Seven deserted village sites', pp. 44–5; J. Thirsk in *VCH: Leics.*, vol. III, p. 256.

85 Hoskins, 'Essays in Leicestershire History', pp. 85–6; J. Thirsk in *VCH: Leics.*, vol. III, p. 257.

86 Hoskins, 'Essays in Leicestershire History', pp. 79, 83–4; J. Thirsk in *VCH: Leics.*, vol. III, p. 257.

87 Hoskins, 'Essays in Leicestershire History', p. 105 and n. 1; J. Thirsk in *VCH Leics.*, vol. III, p. 259.

88 J. Thirsk in *VCH: Leics*, vol. III, p. 255.

89 E.B. Fryde in Miller, p. 813.

90 Dyer, *Warwickshire Farming*, p. 22.

91 Magdalen College, MS Quinton 56. I owe grateful thanks to my friend, Colin Richmond, for giving me a transcript of this petition.

92 Richmond, 'Transition from feudalism', pp. 167–9. I once again owe Professor Richmond thanks for giving me a copy of this article. Elys's letter was originally published in W. Denton, *England in the Fifteenth Century* (London, 1888), pp. 318–20.

93 Dyer, 'Deserted medieval villages', p. 29.

94 'The returns of the Inquisitions of Depopulation', *EHR*, 70 (1955), pp. 212–28. Kerridge reiterates these views in his *Agrarian Problems in the Sixteenth Century and After* (London, 1969). As an example of his one-sided viewpoint one may cite the attack in his Introduction on R.H. Tawney's 'wholly untrue picture of early capitalism as cruel and greedy, destructive alike of social welfare and true spiritual values'.

95 J. Martin, 'Enclosure and the Inquisitions of 1607: an examination of Dr Kerridge's article "The returns of the Inquisition of Depopulation"', *AgHR*, 30 (1982), pp. 41–8.

96 Ibid., pp. 42–4.

97 Ibid., p. 42.

98 Kerridge, 'Returns of the Inquisitions of Depopulation', p. 212.

99 Ibid., p. 228.

100 E.F. Gay, 'The Midland Revolt and the Inquisitions of Depopulation of 1607', *TRHS*, ns, no. 18 (1904), pp. 224–5.

101 Ibid., p. 225.

102 See below, in this section.

103 K.J. Allison, M.W. Beresford and J.G. Hurst, *The Deserted Villages of Northamptonshire* (Leicester, 1966), p. 46.

104 E.B. Fryde in Miller, p. 813, and below, section VI.

105 J. Thirsk in *Agrarian History*, vol. IV, p. 254.

106 C.J. Bond in P.J. Jarvis and T.R. Slater (eds), *Field and Forest: An Historical Geography of Worcestershire and Warwickshire* (Cambridge, 1982), pp. 152–4; Hoskins, 'The deserted villages of Leicestershire', *Essays in Leicestershire History*, pp. 99–100.

107 Leadam, *Domesday of Inclosures*, vol. I, p. 222.

108 Ibid.; Hoskins, *Essays in Leicestershire History*, p. 81.

109 The fullest study is in the unpublished Ph.D. thesis (University of London) of L.A. Parker, 'Enclosure in Leicestershire, 1485–1607', used by W.G. Hoskins and Joan Thirsk. For other sources see above, section IV (the enclosures in Leicestershire, *c.* 1450–85).

110 J. Walter and K. Wrightson, 'Dearth and the social order in early modern England', *Past and Present*, 71 (1976), p. 30; Manning, *Village Revolts* p. 220.

111 Hoskins, *Essays in Leicestershire History*, p. 79; *idem, Making of the English Landscape,* p. 94.

112 See above, section IV.

113 Hoskins, *Essays in Leicestershire History*, pp. 79–85, 94–8; *idem*, 'Seven deserted village sites', pp. 38–9 (Baggrave), 40–1 (Cold Newton), 48–51 (Lowesby and Quenby); *idem, The Making of the English Landscape: Leicestershire* (London, 1953), p. 27–8.

114 Leadam, *Domesday of Inclosures*, vol. I, p. 237; Hoskins, *Essays in Leicestershire History*, pp. 98–9.

115 Leadam, ibid., p. 234; Hoskins. ibid., p. 100.

116 Hoskins, ibid., p. 86; Mary E. Finch, *The Wealth of Five Northamptonshire Families*, Northamptonshire Record Society, no. 19(1956), pp. 135–6 (Brudenell of Deene); E.B. Fryde in Miller, pp. 810–11.

117 Leadam, *Domesday of Inclosures*, vol. I, p. 238; Hoskins, *Essays in Leicestershire History*, p. 86.

118 Leadam, ibid., pp. 234–6, 241–2; Hoskins, ibid., pp. 94–5; J. Thirsk (using Dr Parker's thesis) in *VCH: Leics.*, vol. III, pp. 255, 257.

119 Leadam, ibid., pp. 234–6, 240–2.

120 Hoskins, *Essays in Leicestershire History*, p. 93 and n. 2; Beresford and Hurst in *Transactions of Leicestershire Archaeological and Historical Society*, 39 (1963/4), no. 8, on p. 28.

121 G.W. Bernard, *The Power of the Early Tudor Nobility* [the fourth, fifth and sixth Talbot Earls of Shrewsbury] (Brighton, 1985), pp. 143, 149–50.

122 Hoskins, *Essays in Leicestershire History*, pp. 89–92; Beresford and Hurst in *Transactions of Leicestershire Archaeological and Historical Society*, 39, no. 49, on p. 32.

123 Hoskins, *ibid.*, pp. 88–9 and p. 89, n. 1.

124 Ibid., p. 86 and n. 1.

125 Leadam, *Domesday of Inclosures*, vol. I, p. 152.

126 Ibid., pp. 571–9. The Buckinghamshire presentments are printed in ibid., pp. 158–214.

127 Ibid., pp. 161–4, 209–10.

128 Hoskins, *Essays in Leicestershire History*, pp. 100–1.

129 Historical Manuscripts Commission, *Salisbury [Cecil] Manuscripts*, vol. XIX (for 1607) (1965), p. 150.

130 Cited from F.J. Furnivall, *Ballads from Manuscripts,* Ballad Society, no. I (1868), p. 37. This reference to the famine in Edward II's reign is to the events of 1315–17.

131 Cited, in modernized spelling, from Hoskins, *Essays in Leicestershire History*, p. 100.

CHAPTER 13

1   J. Hatcher, *Rural Economy and Society in the Duchy of Cornwall, 1300–1500* (Cambridge, 1970) and *idem*, 'A diversified economy: later medieval Cornwall', *EcHR*, 2nd ser., 22 (1969), pp. 208–27; J.N. Hare's doctoral thesis and various publications cited above, in chapter 7; Edward Miller and H.S.A. Fox in Miller.

2   H.P.R. Finberg and W.G. Hoskins, 'The wealth of medieval Devon', *Devonshire Studies* (London, 1952), pp. 219, 221, 227; W.G. Hoskins, *Devon* (London, 1954), p. 62.

3   Sally Harvey in *Agrarian History*, vol. II, *1042–1350*, ed. H.E. Hallam (Cambridge, 1988), pp. 68–9.

4   Sally Harvey, 'The extent and profitability of demesne agriculture in England in the later eleventh century', *Social Relations and Ideas, Essays in Honour of R.H. Hilton*, ed. T.H. Aston et al. (Oxford, 1983), pp. 58–60.

5   Miller, pp. 710–11; Hoskins, *Devon*, p. 90.

6   R.W. Hoyle, 'Tenure and the land market in early modern England . . .', *EcHR*, 43 (1990), p. 6.

7   Finberg and Hoskins, *Devonshire Studies*, p. 219; J. Hatcher in *Agrarian History*, vol. II, ed. Hallam, pp. 676, 680; J.H. Tillotson in [Australian] *Historical Studies*, 16 (1974), pp. 5–6.

8   W.G. Hoskins, *The Age of Plunder: The England of Henry VIII, 1500–1547* (London, 1976), p. 61; Hatcher, *Rural Economy*, p. 79.

9   PRO, DL29/684, nos 11081–2.

10 There is a useful account of these episcopal estates in P.M. Hembry, *Bishops of Bath and Wells, 1540–1640: Social and Economic Problems* (London, 1967), chapter I.

11 PRO, SC 6/1131/9.

12 Worcester RO, BA 2636, 162/92125.

13 Bean, *Estates of the Percy Family*, pp. 51–64. A table of entry fines in Somerset and Dorset is on p. 59.

14 H.S.A. Fox in Miller, pp. 736–7.

15 Miller, p. 710.

16 E.B. Fryde in Miller, p. 764.

17 Aberystwyth, NLW, Badminton Collection, nos 1556–8.

18 H.P.R. Finberg, *Tavistock Abbey: A Study in the Social and Economic History of Devon* (Cambridge, 1951), pp. 76–7.

19 J. Hatcher, 'Non-manorialism in medieval Cornwall', *AgHR*, 18 (1970), pp. 8, 10–11; E.B. Fryde in Miller, pp. 874–5.

20 J. Hare in Stapleton (ed.), *Conflict and Community*, pp. 24–5,

21 The best account is in J. Hatcher, 'Non-manorialism in medieval Cornwall'. This is the main source of this section.

22 Ibid., p. 9.

23 Ibid., p. 2.

24 Ibid., p. 10.

25 The following paragraph is based on Dr Hatcher's article, 'Non-manorialism in medieval Cornwall', and a much fuller account in his book, *Rural Economy*, especially chapters 7 and 8.

26 Hatcher, *Rural Economy*, p. 199.

27   PRO, Chancery Warrants (C81), Privy Seal, no. 10.237.

28   This is one of the important conclusions of the article by Dr Rosamund J. Faith, 'Peasant families and inheritance customs in medieval England', *AgHR*, 14 (1966), pp. 91–2.

29   F.N. Robinson (ed.), *The Works of Geoffrey Chaucer*, 2nd edn (Oxford, 1957), pp. 252, 766.

30   'The lords and their tenants: conflict and stability in fifteenth-century Wiltshire', *Conflict and Community*, ed. Stapleton, pp. 16–34.

31   Ibid., p. 20.

32   Ibid., p. 21, and Miller, p. 711.

33   Hare, ibid., p. 21; M.A. Hicks in *Journal of Legal History*, 4 (1983), pp. 64–5.

34   Miller, pp. 709–10.

35   E.M. Carus-Wilson in *VCH: Wilts.*, vol. IV, pp. 130–1.

36   Ibid., pp. 129–32; E.B. Fryde in Miller, p. 765; J. Hare in Stapleton (ed.), *Conflict and Community*, pp. 21–2.

37   See above, chapter 3, section IV.

CHAPTER 14

1   See above, chapter 10, section I (Yorkshire), and chapter 12, section III (Devon).

2   *CPR, 1467–77*, p. 522.

3   K.B. McFarlane, *The Nobility of Later Medieval England* (Oxford, 1973), p. 58.

4   Worcester RO, BA 989, ref. 899:95, parcel 6, no. 113.

5   For a general account see J.E. Lloyd, *Owen Glendower* (Oxford, 1931). For the Mortimer lordship of Denbigh see G.A. Holmes, *The Estates of the Higher Nobility in Fourteenth-Century England* (Cambridge, 1957), pp. 101, 160. For the Talbot lordship of Whitchurch see A.J. Pollard, 'Estate management in the later Middle Ages; the Talbots and Whitchurch, 1383–1525', *EcHR*, 25 (1972), pp. 553–66. R. Ian Jack has provided a more up-to-date reconsideration of what happened in the Grey lordship of Ruthin in 'Owain Glyn Dŵr and the lordship of Ruthin', *Welsh History Review*, 2 (1965), pp. 303–22. There is a short account of the destruction in Shropshire by Ann J. Kettle in *VCH: Salop*, vol. IV (Oxford, 1989), pp. 76–7, and a much fuller account of what happened on the Arundel properties in the lordships of Chirk and Oswestry in the doctoral thesis of Llinos O.W. Smith, 'The lordships of Chirk and Oswestry, 1282–1415' (University of London, 1970). For Oswestry she uses accounts and court rolls at the National Library of Wales at Aberystwyth seen by me, from which I have added some details.

6   Smith, 'Lordships of Chirk and Oswestry', p. 400.

7   Aberystwyth, NLW, Aston Hall [Lordship of Oswestry] MS, no. 5788 (account for Sandford).

8   Lloyd, *Owen Glendower*, p. 86, and Ann J. Kettle in *VCH: Salop*, vol. IV, pp. 76–7.

9   PRO, KR Subsidies, E179/166/48, cited by Ann J. Kettle in *VCH: Salop*, vol. IV, p. 77.

10   Smith, 'Lordships of Chirk and Oswestry, p. 408, n. 1.

11   Jack, 'Owen Glyn Dŵr and the Lordship of Ruthin'.

12   Holmes, *Estates of the Higher Nobility*, pp. 101, 160.

13   Pollard, 'Estate management', pp. 560–1; Ann J. Kettle in *VCH: Salop*, vol. IV, p. 77 (using Pollard's doctoral thesis).

14   Smith, 'Lordships of Chirk and Oswestry', p. 391, 393.

15 Cf. court rolls at the National Library of Wales (Aston Hall MSS, nos 5352 (October 1400) and 5353 (June 1403)).

16 NLW, Aston Hall MSS, nos 5787 (1402/3), 5788 (1403/6), 5789 (1408/9), 5790 (1410/11).

17 Smith, 'Lordships of Chirk and Oswestry', p. 403.

18 Ibid., pp. 393–9.

19 Ibid., pp. 408–11.

20 There are short but good accounts in J.J. Bagley, *Margaret of Anjou, Queen of England* (London, 1948), pp. 113–16, and P.M. Kendall, *Warwick, the Kingmaker* (London, 1957), pp. 79–87. For the ravaging by armies during the Wars of the Roses see A. Goodman, *Military Activity and English Society, 1452–1497* (London, 1981), pp. 214–18 (The plundering by Queen Margaret's army on its march southwards early in 1461 is discussed briefly on p. 215).

21 Cited in A.J. Pollard, *North-Eastern England during the Wars of the Roses*, p. 282. For this portion of the chronicle see Kingsford, *English Historical Literature*, pp. 128–9.

22 Ibid., p. 152; Jacob, *The Fifteenth Century*, p. 524; A. Rogers (ed.), *The Making of Stamford* (Leicester, 1965), p. 39.

23 Kingsford, *English Historical Literature*, p. 247.

24 Ross, *Edward IV*, pp. 167–8, 401.

25 See, for example, S.J. Payling, 'The Ampthill Dispute: a study in aristocratic lawlessness [Exeter's] and the breakdown of Lancastrian government', *EHR*, 104 (1989), pp. 881–907.

26 Kendall, *Warwick*, p. 305, where there is a brief sketch of his earlier career.

27 Ross, *Edward IV*, p. 156.

28 Ross, ibid., p. 184, 336.

29 For Exeter's presence in the Lancastrian army at Barnet see Ross, *Edward IV*, p. 167. For his flight to sanctuary and his removal from there in May see ibid., p. 184. Duchess Anne was allowed by her brother, Edward IV, to divorce Henry and marry her lover, Thomas St Leger (ibid.).

30 Preston, Lancashire RO, DOK 1746/14. I owe the discovery of this account to my friend, Professor Colin Richmond.

31 For those estates see Payling, *Ampthill Dispute*, p. 884.

32 H.C. Maxwell-Lyte, *Dunster and its Lords, 1066–1881* (1882), pp. 61–2.

33 *CPR, 1467–77*, p. 522.

34 *CPR, 1461–67*, p. 286.

35 The fullest study is by G.H.R. Kent, 'The Estates of the Herbert family in the mid-fifteenth century' (unpublished Ph.D. thesis, University of Keele, 1973). I wish to thank Dr Kent and Professor Colin Richmond for lending me a copy of it.

36 *CPR, 1461–67*, p. 286.

37 NLW, Badminton Collection, roll 1556. For further evidence about the estates of the lordship of Dunster see above, chapter 13, section II, and below chapter 16, section III.

38 J.A.F. Thomson, 'The Courtenay family in the Yorkist period', *Bull. IHR*, 45 (1972), pp. 236–46; M.A. Hicks in *Journal of Legal History*, 4 (1983), p. 60.

39 *CPR, 1461–67*, p. 231 (22 September 1462).

40 NLW, Badminton Collection, rolls 1556 and 1557. This is the source for the account of the Luttrell estates in 1461–66 that follows. I shall cite particular entries only for matters of special interest.

41 Ibid., roll 1556, m. 2v.

42 R.W. Dunning, 'East Quantoxhead', *VCH: Som.*, vol. V (1985), p. 122.

43 NLW, Badminton Collection, rolls 1556, m. 4r., and 1557, m. 4v.

44 Ibid., rolls 1556, m. 5r., and 1557, m. 6r.

45 Thomson, 'Courtenay family', pp. 234, 237; Ross, *Edward IV*, p. 141, n. 1.

46 Thomson, ibid., pp. 236–42.

47 *CPR, 1467–77*, p. 330.

48 Ibid., p. 364 (1 December 1472).

49 Left out of the restoration of Dunster to Anne, the widowed Countess of Pembroke (ibid.).

50 NLW, Badminton Collection, roll 1558.

51 Ibid., m. 3r.: '*tempore perurbacionis inter tenentes ibidem*'.

52 Ibid., m. 4r.

53 *Calendar of Inquisitions Post Mortem, Henry VII*, vol. III, no. 582, on p. 349.

CHAPTER 15

1 Chapters 4 and 9 (on the estates of the Bishops of Worcester), and chapter 8, section VI.

2 The whole passage on copyholds is cited in E. Kerridge, *Agrarian Problems*, pp. 138–40. For the importance of Littleton's treatise see T.F.T. Plucknett, *Early English Legal Literature* (Cambridge, 1958), p. 113.

3 Harvey, *Westminster Abbey*, p. 285.

4 BL, Harley MS 445, calendared in E.B. Dewindt, *The 'Liber Gersumarum' of Ramsey Abbey* (Toronto, 1976). The calendar is inadequate, as words which had special technical meaning are not cited precisely (e.g. '*sequela*') and significant legal details are partly left out. Whenever possible I shall cite the original manuscript.

5 Worcester RO, BA 2636, 193/92627¹¹⁄₁₂.

6 Harvey, *Westminster Abbey*, p. 285.

7 Ibid.

8 The paragraph that follows is based on A.B. Simpson, *An Introduction to the History of the Land Law* (Oxford, 1961), pp. 69–74, 87–9; S.F.C. Milsom, *Historical Foundations of the Common Law* (London, 1969), pp. 127–32.

9 Common Law did provide remedies against such collusion, but they were inadequate. Cf. Simpson, *Land Law*, p. 71, n. 2.

10 Titow, 'Lost rents', p. 105, n. 26; at Marvell (Berkshire) in 1372/3 Stephen Smyth took the tenement once of Richard atte Moore for 4s, '*ultra certum redditum sic sibi dimisse quousque aliquis venerit ad finiendum et tenendum secundum antiquam consuetudinem*'.

11 Ibid., p. 103.

12 Harvey, *Westminster Abbey*, p. 279, and above, chapter 8, section VI. See also below, chapter 17, for the situation around 1500.

13 Dyer, *Estates of Worcester*, pp. 293–4.

14 M. Spufford, *A Cambridgeshire Community: Chippenham from Settlement to Enclosure* (Leicester, 1965), pp. 35–7.

15 Worcester RO, BA 1592, box 2, no. 31.

16 Ibid., BA 2636, 165/92225⅚ (Henbury Saltmarsh, probably in 1435); 164/92177 (Hatton,

part of Hampton Lucy, October 1452); 164/92178A (Hampton, April 1454) and 164/92185 (Hampton, May 1460).

17   F.W. Maitland, *Collected Papers*, ed. H.A.L. Fisher (Cambridge, 1911), vol. II, pp. 400–2.

18   Harvey, *Westminster Abbey*, p. 278.

19   Ibid., p. 279.

20   Tawney, *Agrarian Problem*, pp. 289, 293–4.

21   Worcester RO, BA 2636, 193/92627$^{11}\!/_{12}$.

22   Ibid.

23   Dewindt, '*Liber Gersumarum*', pp. 8–11.

24   BL, Harley MS 445, f.1r. It is no. 1 in Dewindt's calendar.

25   Raftis, *Tenure and Mobility*, p. 202, n. 86.

26   For example: BL, Harley MS 445, f. 225v. (Dewindt, no. 3961), December 1449; ibid., f. 246v. (Dewindt, no. 4248), December 1454.

27   Raftis, *Tenure and Mobility*, p. 203, n. 87.

28   Ibid., p. 200.

29   Ibid., p. 202, n. 86.

30   Ibid., continued on p. 203; Harley MS 445, f. 231r. (Dewindt, no. 4031), August 1451.

31   That such distrust was in some cases well justified is shown by events on Ramsey's manor of Shillington in Bedfordshire. The abbey had seized land acquired by its bondmen outside its own jurisdiction. The tenants appear to have informed the royal escheator of this, and he then sequestrated these properties on the grounds that Ramsey had broken the Statute of Mortmain in not applying for a royal licence and not paying the fine due for this. The abbey had to give up this land. Cf. Harvey (ed.), *Peasant Land Market* p. 213–15.

32   BL, Harley MS f. 255r. (Dewindt, no. 4354).

33   Raftis, *Tenure and Mobility*, pp. 198–9.

34   Harvey, *Westminster Abbey*, p. 285; Dyer, *Estates of Worcester*, p. 294; Raftis, *Tenure and Mobility*, p. 200.

35   See, for example, Harvey, ibid., p. 284.

36   Dyer, *Estates of Worcester*, p. 294–5.

37   L.A. Parker, 'The Agrarian Revolution at Cotesbach' in *Studies in Leicestershire Agrarian History*, ed. Hoskins, pp. 57–71. The three evicted leaseholders were penalized for 'their clamorous courses held agaynst' Quarles. See also Manning, *Village Revolts*, pp. 244–5.

38   Manning, *Village Revolts*, pp. 237–41; Finch, *Wealth of Five Northamptonshire Families*, 'Tresham of Lamport', pp. 72–8, 87–93.

39   Tawney, *Agrarian Problem*, pp. 294–301.

40   Richmond, 'Transition from feudalism', p. 166.

41   I.S. Leadam in *TRHS*, ns, vol. 6 (1892), pp. 188–90; C. Rawcliffe, *The Staffords, Earls of Stafford and Dukes of Buckingham, 1394–1521* (Cambridge, 1978), pp. 64–5.

42   C.E. Moreton, *The Townshends and their World: Gentry, Law and Land in Norfolk, c. 1450–1551* (Oxford, 1992), pp. 32–8, 185–7.

43   Aberystwyth, NLW, Peniarth MS 280. D., pp. 16–17, 25. There are eight manumissions in this record.

44   For example: Worcester RO, Register of Bishop Carpenter, BA 2648, b.716:093, no. 6, pt 2, vol. I, f. 38v. (manumission of John Hervy of Fladbury, 27 June 1446). There are numerous deeds of manumission in the two volumes of this register.

45   Ibid., vol. I, f. 81v.: '*Noverint me [in] prefati Thome totum ius meum, titulum et clameum, que habeo in prefato Thoma ratione alicuius servitutis de cetero exigere vel vendicare poterimus, sed per presentes sumus exclusi imperpetuum*.' The grammar is imperfect, but the meaning is quite clear.

46   Ibid., vol. I, p. 55 (pencil numeration).

47   NLW, Peniarth MS 280. D, p. 19.

48   Dewindt, '*Liber Gersumarum*', no. 191 and n. 13.

49   See above, chapter 10, section VI; Raftis, *Tenure and Mobility*, pp. 183–9, 276–7.

50   Worcester RO, Register of Bishop Carpenter, BA 2648, b.716:093, no. 6, pt 2, vol. I, f. 52r, and v.

51   Bailey, 'Rural society', *Fifteenth-Century Attitudes*, ed. Horrox, p. 158.

52   I.S. Leadam, *Select Cases before . . . the Court of the Star Chamber*, Selden Society Series, vol. 16 (1902), pp. cxxvi–xxix.

53   J.H. Baker (ed.), *The Reports of Sir John Spelman*, vol. II, Selden Society Series, vol. 94 (for 1977, published 1978), p. 192.

54   A. Savine, 'Copyhold cases in the early Chancery proceedings', *EHR*, 17 (1902), pp. 296–303; Gray, *Copyhold, Equity and the Common Law*, pp. 24–31. I have summarized some of them in Miller, pp. 808, 814–17.

55   Gray, ibid., chapter I. See also M.E. Avery, 'The history of the equitable jurisdiction of Chancery before 1460', *Bull. IHR*, 42 (1969), pp. 129–44.

56   Gray, ibid., p. 34.

57   Avery, 'Equitable jurisdiction', p. 134.

58   PRO, Early Chancery Proceedings, C1/9/139, a and b; Savine, 'Copyhold cases', no. 1, on pp. 298–9; Gray, *Copyhold Equity and the Common Law*, pp. 28–9.

59   PRO, C1/19/237; Savine, ibid., no. 5, on p. 300; Gray, ibid., p. 25.

60   PRO, C1/9/353; Savine, ibid., no. 2, on p. 299; Gray, ibid., p. 31.

61   PRO, C1/31/342–5; Savine, ibid., no. 7, on pp. 301–2; Gray, ibid., pp. 29–31.

62   PRO, C1/19/162; Savine, ibid., no. 4, on pp. 299–300; Gray, ibid., pp. 25–7.

63   Gray, ibid., pp. 157 (n. 22, a), 158–9 (no. 3).

64   Ibid., p. 159, no. 4.

65   Ibid., pp. 31–3, 54–8.

66   Ibid., pp. 58–9.

67   Ibid., p. 59.

68   See ibid., chapters II ('The acquisition of Common Law remedies') and III ('The Elizabethan courts and the Common Law of copyhold'). For chronology see also Baker, *English Legal History*, pp. 171–2; Milsom, *Historical Foundations of the Common Law*, pp. 136–7. See also Baker (ed.), *Spelman's Reports*, vol. II, pp. 179–82.

CHAPTER 16

1   J.S. Roskell, 'Sir Richard de Waldegrave of Bures St. Mary, Speaker in the Parliament of 1381/2', *Proceedings of the Suffolk Institute of Archaeology*, 27 (1957), pp. 154–75. I owe thanks to Professor Roskell for giving me copies of many of his articles on various medieval Speakers.

2   *Rot. Parl.*, vol. III, p. 100 (no. 17), translated in Dobson (ed.), *Peasants' Revolt*, pp. 330–1. I have cited this speech once before, at the end of my account of the revolts of 1381 (chapter 3, section VI).

3   McFarlane, *Nobility of Later Medieval England*, p. 49.

4   Ibid., pp. 48–9.

5   Ibid., pp. 123–5.

6   Bailey, 'Rural society', *Fifteenth-Century Attitudes*, ed. Horrox, p. 157; J.A. Tuck in Hilton and Aston (eds), *The English Rising*, pp. 201–2.

7   E.B. Fryde in Miller, p. 766.

8   Du Boulay, *Lordship of Canterbury*, p. 189 and frontispiece (London, 1966).

9   R.H. Hilton, *Decline of Serfdom*, p. 50.

10 *Rot. Parl.*, vol. III, pp. 273, 294; Hatcher, 'England in the aftermath of the Black Death', p. 18.

11 A. Savine, 'Bondmen under the Tudors, *TRHS*, ns, 17 (1903), pp. 261, 448–9.

12 Richmond, *Paston Family in the Fifteenth Century*, p. 55, and above, chapter 10, section VII (Norfolk); above, chapter 10, section I (Devon and Yorkshire), and chapter 12, section III (Devon).

13 J. Blow, 'Nibley Green, 1470: The last private battle fought in England'. I am using the revised version reprinted in C.D.D. Crowder, *English Society and Government in the Fifteenth Century* (Edinburgh and London, 1967), p. 97.

14 S.M. Wright, *The Derbyshire Gentry in the Fifteenth Century*, Derbyshire Record Society series, no. 8 (Chesterfield, 1983), pp. 10, 22–3, 141.

15 McFarlane, *Nobility of Later Medieval England*, p. 213.

16 Ibid., pp. 50, 183, 222–3.

17 Jones and Underwood, *The King's Mother*, pp. 107–8.

18 McFarlane, *Nobility of Later Medieval England*, p. 49.

19 See especially J.L. Kirby, 'The issues of the Lancastrian Exchequer and Lord Cromwell's estimates of 1433', *Bull. IHR*, 24 (1951). I wish to thank Dr Kirby for a copy of this article.

20 See S.J. Payling in *Nottingham Medieval Studies*, 30 (1986), pp. 67–96.

21 K.B. McFarlane, *England in the Fifteenth Century* (London, 1983), p. 240, n. 21.

22 McFarlane, *Nobility of Later Medieval England*, p. 49.

23 Archer, 'The estates and finances of Margaret of Brotherton', pp. 264–79. This is a useful collection of evidence; the harsh image of Margaret's personality is mainly my own deduction from it.

24 Archer, ibid., p. 272.

25 Ibid., pp. 272–5. For the Sussex properties of Battle Abbey see above, chapter 10, section III.

26 R. Faith in Hilton and Aston (eds), *The English Rising*, p. 35, n. 55.

27 Dyer, 'The social and economic background to the rural revolt of 1381', *The English Rising*, ed. Hilton and Aston, pp. 24–5, 40.

28 F.G. Davenport, *The Economic Development of a Norfolk Manor, 1086–1565* (Cambridge, 1906), p. 70, n. 1. The account of Forncett that follows is based on Davenport's book and on her earlier article, 'The decay of villeinage in East Anglia' (1900), reprinted, with some corrections, in E.M. Carus-Wilson, *Essays in Economic History*, vol. II (London, 1962), pp. 112–24. See also Hilton, *Bond Men Made Free*, p. 169.

29 This practice at Forncett and on estates of other landlords is also discussed above, in section V of chapter 2.

30 Bailey, 'Rural society', *Fifteenth-Century Attitudes*, ed. Horrox, p. 157.

31 D. MacCulloch, 'Kett's Rebellion in context', *Past and Present*, 84 (1979), pp. 55–7.

32 R.I. Jack, *The Grey of Ruthin Valor: The Valor of the English Lands of Edmund Grey, Earl of Kent, drawn up from the Ministers' Accounts of 1467/8* (Sydney, 1965), p. 7. This is the chief source for my account of the Grey estates.

33 Ibid., p. 28.

34 Aberystwyth, NLW, Badminton Collection, roll 1559.

35 A. Jones in Harvey (ed.), *Peasant Land Market*, pp. 194–202.

36 For Reginald Grey see R.I. Jack, 'Entail and inheritance: the Hastings inheritance, 1370 to 1436', *Bull. IHR* 38 (1965) and R.I. Jack, 'Owain Glyn Dŵr and the lordship of Ruthin', *Welsh History Review*, 2 (1965).

37 Jack, *Grey of Ruthin Valor*, p. 36, p. 74, n. 4; J.S. Roskell, *The Commons and their Speakers in English Parliaments 1376–1523* (Manchester, 1965), p. 240 and n. 2.

38 P.M. Kendall, *Warwick the Kingmaker* (London, 1957), pp. 64–5; R.I. Jack, 'A quincentenary: the battle of Northampton, July 10th 1460', *Northamptonshire Past and Present*, 3 (1960), pp. 21–5.

39 Jack, *Grey of Ruthin Valor*, pp. 42–3.

40 NLW, Badminton Collection, roll 1559.

41 Jack, *Grey of Ruthin Valor*, pp. 30, 91.

42 Ibid., p. 28.

43 NLW, Badminton Collection, roll 1559.

44 Jack, *Bull IHR*, 38 (1965), pp. 5–6, 11 (and n. 8), 12.

45 NLW, Badminton Collection, roll 1559.

46 The manors are (in the order in NLW, Badminton Collection, roll 1559): Ashill (Norfolk); Great Braxtead (Bucks., Hastings estate); Badmondisfield (Suffolk, Hastings estate); Reydon (Suffolk, Hastings estate); Yardley Hastings (Northants.); Wootton (Northants., Hastings estate); Brampton (Hunts.); Burbage (Leics., Hasting estate); Blunham (Beds., Hastings estate); Foxley (Norfolk, Hastings estate); Hemingford Grey (Hunts.); Harrold (Beds., Hastings estate); Podington (Beds., Hastings estate); Stoke Hammond (Bucks.).

47 Jack, *Grey of Ruthin Valor*, pp. 13–6.

48 Ibid., pp. 34–5.

49 Ibid.

50 Ibid., pp. 37, 42.

51 Ibid., p. 37.

52 Jones, 'Bedfordshire: fifteenth century', *Peasant Land Market*, ed. Harvey, p. 183.

53 Ibid., p. 196. The account that follows is based on this article.

54 In Miller, p. 584. The account that follows is based on three rolls at the National Library of Wales, Aberystwyth: Badminton Collection, rolls 1556 (1461/2), 1557 (1465/6), 1558 (1477–9).

55 NLW, Badminton Collection, roll 1556, m. 7.

56 Ibid., mm. 1v., 2r. and v.

57 Sir H.C. Maxwell-Lyte (ed.), *Documents and Extracts Illustrating the History of the Honour of Dunster*, Somerset Record Society Publications, vol. 33 (1918), no. 211, on p. 229.

58 Ibid., no. 213, on p. 230.

59 Aberystwyth, NLW, Badminton Collection, roll 1556, m. 3r. and v.

60 Ibid., m. 4r.

61   NLW, Badminton Collection, roll 1557, mm. 3r., 5v., 6r. For his previous service to the Luttrells see Maxwell-Lyte (ed.), *Documents Illustrating the History of Dunster*, no. 211 on p. 229.

62   NLW, Badminton Collection, roll 1558, m. 1v.

63   See above, chapter 14, section IV.

64   NLW, Badminton Collection, roll 1558, m. 3r.: '*tempore perturbacionis inter tenentes . . . pro salva custodia et bona gubernacione habenda*'.

CHAPTER 17

1   I am indebted most of all to the remarkable survey of England at the start of the Tudor age in the introductory chapters of W.G. Hoskins, *The Age of Plunder: The England of Henry VIII, 1500–1547* (London, 1976).

2   Cf. E.B. Fryde in Miller, pp. 808–9.

3   Edited in R.H. Tawney and E. Power (eds), *Tudor Economic Documents* (London, 1924), vol. III, pp. 1–11. I am using mainly the summary in Hoskins, *Age of Plunder*, p. 4.

4   J. Cornwall, 'English population in the early sixteenth century', *EcHR*, 2nd ser., 23 (1970), p. 44.

5   I. Blanchard, 'Population change, enclosure and the early Tudor Economy', *EcHR*, 23 (1970), pp. 427–45; B.M.S. Campbell, 'The population of early Tudor England: a revaluation of the 1522 muster rolls and 1524 and 1525 lay subsidies', *Journal of Historical Geography*, 7 (1981), pp. 145–54. See especially his conclusions on p. 154.

6   R.W. Hoyle, 'Tenure and land market in early modern England . . .' *EcHR*, 2nd ser., 43 (1990), p. 18.

7   W.G. Hoskins, 'English provincial towns in the early sixteenth century', *TRHS*, 4th ser., 6 (1956), pp. 1–19; C. Phytian-Adams, *Desolation of a City: Coventry and the Urban Crisis of the Late Middle Ages* (Cambridge, 1979), especially pp. 281–90; R.H. Britnell, *Growth and Decline in Colchester, 1300–1525* (Cambridge, 1986), p. 193 and the sources there cited.

8   Hoskins, 'English provincial towns', p. 7.

9   Ibid., pp. 8–12.

10   See below, section III. One indication of the expansion of London's population are the civic authorities' efforts to expand the imports of corn and improve arrangements for its storage. Cf. N.S.B. Gras, *The Evolution of the English Corn Market from the Twelfth to the Eighteenth Century* (Cambridge, Mass., 1926), pp. 77–81.

11   See below, section II.

12   Britnell, *Colchester*, pp. 190–2.

13   See above, chapter 10, section VII, and below, section IV.

14   Bean, *Estates of the Percy Family*, pp. 47–8; J. Hatcher, 'A diversified economy: later medieval Cornwall', *EcHR*, 2nd ser., 22 (1969), p. 227.

15   A. Cameron, 'Sir Henry Willoughby of Wollaton', *Transactions of the Thoroton Society of Nottinghamshire*, 74 (1970), pp. 10–21. For his gross revenue in 1524 see p. 11. For the coal mines see pp. 11–13.

16   J. Hatcher, 'Myths, miners and agricultural communities', *AgHR*, 22 (1974), p. 55.

17   Ibid., pp. 57–8.

18   E.M. Carus-Wilson, *The Expansion of Exeter at the Close of the Middle Ages* (Exeter, 1963), *passim*.

19   H.P.R. Finberg, *Tavistock Abbey* . . . (Cambridge, 1951), especially chapter VIII and chapter IX, section III.

20   J. Thirsk, 'The common fields', *Past and Present*, 29 (1964), pp. 5–7.

21   Worcester RO, 176/92489.

22   B. Putnam (ed.), *Proceedings before the Justices of the Peace in the Fourteenth and Fifteenth Centuries, Edward III to Richard III* (London, 1938), p. 432; Ross, *Edward IV*, pp. 222, 321–2.

23   Worcester RO, 176/92625¾.

24   The main group of cash payments by the receiver totals £964 8s. 1d. But there was a further payment of £400 after the completion of the audit of the receiver's account.

25   Dyer, *Lords and Peasants*, p. 177.

26   They were (with deliveries in 1499/1500 in brackets): Bredon (£66 10s), Alvechurch (£66 5s), Bishop's Cleeve (£65 17s), Ripple (£60 2s), Stoke by Henbury (£57 11s), Fladbury (£56 13s), Wick and Wichenford (£50 3s), Kempsey, (£49 6s).

27   Dyer, *Lords and Peasants*, p. 185.

28   J. Thirsk in chapter I of *Agrarian History*, vol. IV.

29   Ibid., pp. 49–50, 53, 55.

30   F.R.H. Du Boulay, 'A rentier economy in the later Middle Ages: the Archbishopric of Canterbury', *EcHR*, 2nd ser., 16 (1964), pp. 434–5.

31   Du Boulay, *Lordship of Canterbury*, p. 244. For the demesnes of the Bishops of Worcester earlier in the fifteenth century see above, chapter 9, section III.

32   Du Boulay, *Lordship of Canterbury*, pp. 226–7.

33   Ibid., pp. 230–1.

34   Harvey, *Westminster Abbey*, p. 161.

35   Du Boulay, *Lordship of Canterbury*, p. 231.

36   Ibid., p. 226.

37   Ibid., pp. 236–7. Their descendants became peers in 1880 as the Lords Brabourne (ibid., p. 235).

38   M. Mate, 'Pastoral farming in south-east England in the fifteenth century', *EcHR*, 40 (1987), pp. 534–5.

39   The account that follows is based mainly on chapter 4 of Jones and Underwood, *The King's Mother*.

40   Thirsk (ed.), *Agrarian History*, vol. IV, pp. 20–1.

41   Jones and Underwood, *The King's Mother*, pp. 123–4.

42   The account that follows is based mainly on N.W. Alcock (ed.), *Warwickshire Grazier and London Skinner, 1532–1555: The Account Book of Peter Temple and Thomas Heritage*, British Academy Records of Social and Economic History, ns, no. 4 (London, 1981), introductory chapter, pp. 1–38; Dyer, 'Were there any capitalists in fifteenth-century England?', *Enterprise and Individuals*, ed. Kermode pp. 10–16.

43   For this office, discontinued by Henry VIII, see W.C. Richardson, 'The Surveyor of the King's Prerogative', *EHR*, 56 (1941), pp. 52–75.

44   For a succession of royal pardons secured by the Belknaps to protect them from prosecution for their illegal enclosures and evictions of tenants see Beresford, *Lost Villages of England*, pp. 131–2. For Belknap's defence of his action see N.W. Alcock, 'Enclosure and depopulation in Burton Dassett: a 16th century view', *Warwickshire History*, 3 (1977), p. 182.

45 My account of the Spencers that follows is based chiefly on chapter III ('Spencer of Althorp') in Mary E. Finch, *The Wealth of Five Northamptonshire Families, 1540–1640*, Northamptonshire Record Society Series, vol. 19 (for 1955; published Oxford, 1956) and H. Thorpe, 'The Lord and the landscape, illustrated through the changing fortunes of a Warwickshire parish, Wormleighton' (originally published in 1965), cited here from a reprint in D.R. Mills (ed.), *English Rural Communities* (London, 1973), pp. 31–82.

46 Finch, *Five Northamptonshire Families*, p. 38.

47 See above, chapter 12, section IV.

48 Finch, *Five Northamptonshire Families*, p. 49, n. 2.

49 Ibid., p. 39.

50 Ibid., p. 43.

51 Thorpe, 'Lord and landscape', p. 55.

52 Ibid., p. 61.

53 Finch, *Five Northamptonshire Families*, p. 40.

54 Thorpe, 'Lord and landscape', pp. 56, 59–60. For other improvements claimed by John Spencer I see R. Millward and A. Robinson, *Landscape of Britain: the West Midlands* (London, 1971), pp. 158–9.

55 Finch, *Five Northamptonshire Families*, pp. 39–40.

56 The account of the Townshends that follows is based on Moreton, *The Townshends and their World*. It incorporates the evidence in K.J. Allison, 'Flock management in the sixteenth and seventeenth centuries', *EcHR*, 2nd ser., 11 (1958), pp. 98–112.

57 We have Roger I's memorandum, written shortly before his death, enumerating his purchases and the prices he paid. Roger II continued this practice. Cf. Moreton, *The Townshends and their World*, pp. 116, 129. For a list of their acquisitions, with dates and prices, see Appendix 6, pp. 212–20.

58 Ibid., Appendix 9, pp. 225–6.

59 Ibid., p. 171.

60 Ibid., pp. 169–70.

61 Allison, 'Flock Management', p. 107. Moreton *The Townshends and their World*, p. 173 unfortunately accepted this view.

62 Carus-Wilson and Coleman, *England's Export Trade*, pp. 66–8.

63 Moreton, *The Townshends and their World*, p. 173.

64 Ibid., pp. 167–8.

65 Ibid., p. 174.

66 Ibid., Appendix 11, pp. 243–4.

67 Carus-Wilson and Coleman, *England's Export Trade*, pp. 113–15.

68 Moreton, *The Townshends and their World*, Appendix 9, p. 226.

69 Ibid., pp. 183–4; A. Simpson, 'The East Anglian foldcourse: some queries', *AgHR*, 6 (1958).

70 Moreton, *The Townshends and their World*, p. 184–5. For the fold-courses, and the conflicts they caused, see also MacCulloch, 'Kett's Rebellion in context', pp. 51–3.

71 Moreton, ibid., p. 184, n. 135.

72 See above, chapter 15, section IV; Moreton, *The Townshends and their World* p. 137.

73 Bindoff, *Kett's Rebellion 1549*, Historical Association, general ser., G.12 (London 1949), pp. 16–17.

74 Moreton, *The Townshends and their World*, p. 131.

75 Ibid., pp. 131–2.

76 Ibid., p. 134.

77 Ibid., Appendix 13, p. 247.

78 Harvey (ed.), *Peasant Land Market*, pp. 328–38 ('Conclusion').

79 Ibid., p. 329.

80 Ibid., pp. 329–30, 337–8.

81 Harvey, *Westminster Abbey*, pp. 296–9.

82 NLW, court rolls in the Arundel Collection of Aston Hall, *passim*; Ann J. Kettle in *VCH: Salop.*, vol. IV, p. 111.

83 Harvey, *Westminster Abbey*, p. 271.

84 Dyer, *Lords and Peasants*, p. 287.

85 Harvey, *Westminster Abbey*, pp. 292–3.

86 Ibid., p. 275.

87 Ibid., pp. 301–11, 275–6.

88 Dyer, *Lords and Peasants*, p. 295.

89 Harvey, *Westminster Abbey*, p. 290.

90 M. Spufford, *Cambridgeshire Community*, pp. 38–41. For some details of its earlier history see above, chapter 15, section II.

91 Dyer, *Lords and Peasants*, pp. 285–7.

92 Hoyle, 'Tenure and the land market', p. 10.

93 See the sensible remarks in A. Everitt, *Continuity and Colonization: The Evolution of Kentish Settlement* (Leicester, 1986).

94 Tawney, *Agrarian Problem*, p. 298; Hoyle, 'Tenure and the land market', p. 8.

95 Tawney, ibid., p. 296 and n. 2.

96 Harvey, *Westminster Abbey*, pp. 280–4.

97 Ibid., pp. 281–2.

98 Dyer, *Lords and Peasants*, p. 294.

99 Harvey, *Westminster Abbey*, p. 280.

100 The account that follows is based mainly on A. Jones, 'Bedfordshire: Fifteenth Century', *Peasant Land Market*, ed. Harvey, pp. 179–251.

101 Davenport, *Economic Development of a Norfolk Manor*, pp. lxxviii–lxxx.

102 Jones, 'Bedfordshire', *Peasant Land Market*, ed. Harvey, p. 251.

103 Hatcher, 'English serfdom and villeinage', pp. 38–9.

104 A recent study, for example, estimates that large quantities of customary land were converted to leasehold in Yorkshire in the century before 1640. Cf. R.W. Hoyle 'An ancient and laudable custom: the definition and development of Tenant Right in north-western England in the sixteenth century', *Past and Present*, 116 (1987), p. 54.

105 Searle, *Lordship and Community*, pp. 374–5.

106 Dyer, *Lords and Peasants*, pp. 160–2.

107 Ibid., pp. 177, 190.

108 Ibid., pp. 287–8.

109 Ibid., pp. 288–92.

110 Ibid., pp. 161, 296.

111 Ibid., p. 280.

112 Ibid., p. 279.

113 Hoyle, 'An ancient and laudable custom', p. 24.

114 R.W. Hoyle, 'Lords, tenants and Tenant Right in the sixteenth century: four studies', *Northern History*, 20 (1984), p. 39. This is one of my main sources (ibid., pp. 38–63). See also *idem*, 'An ancient and laudable custom', pp. 24–55; *idem*, 'Tenure and the land market', pp. 1–20; and a series of remarkable publications by M.E. James. The most relevant here are *Change and Continuity in the Tudor North: The Rise of Thomas, First Lord Wharton*, Borthwick Papers, no. 27 (York, 1965) and 'The concept of order and the Northern Rising of 1569', *Past and Present*, 60 (1973), pp. 49–83.

115 James, 'Concept of order', pp. 53, 63–4.

116 Ibid., pp. 63, 71.

117 See below, in this section.

118 James, 'Concept of order', p. 63 and n. 69.

119 Hoyle, 'An ancient and laudable custom', p. 33.

120 Ibid., p. 42.

121 Ibid., pp. 42–3.

122 Ibid., p. 28.

123 Bean, *Estates of the Percy Family*, pp. 52–3.

124 The fullest collection of materials about these peasant movements and of statements of peasant grievances is in M. and R. Dodds, *The Pilgrimage of Grace and the Exeter Conspiracy* (2 vols, Cambridge, 1915). See especially vol. I, pp. 192, 225–6, 370–2, and also in *EHR*, 5 (1890), pp. 72–3. See also A.G. Dickens, 'Secular and religious motivation in the Pilgrimage of Grace' (originally published in 1967), reprinted in *idem, Reformation Studies* (London, 1982). My friend, Professor Dickens, generously gave me a copy.

125 James, *The Rise of Thomas, First Lord Wharton*, pp. 24–5.

126 Ibid., p. 24.

127 Hoyle, 'An ancient and laudable custom', p. 31 and n. 28.

128 K.B. McFarlane's comments in *The Nobility of Later Medieval England* (p. 206).

129 The chief publications besides McFarlane's book cited in the preceding note are: C. Rawcliffe, 'Henry VII and Edward, Duke of Buckingham: the repression of an over-mighty subject', *Bull. IHR*, 53 (1960), pp. 114–18; B.J. Harris, 'The Buckingham estates', *Past and Present,* 43 (1969), pp. 146–50; A. Levine, 'The fall of Edward, Duke of Buckingham', *Tudor Men and Institutions*, ed. A.J. Flavin (Baton Rouge, 1972), pp. 31–48; C. Rawcliffe, *The Staffords, Earls of Stafford and Dukes of Buckingham, 1394–1521* (Cambridge, 1978), especially pp. 54–65.

130 Rawcliffe, *Staffords*, p. 133.

131 Ibid., p. 63.

132 Harris, 'Buckingham estates' p. 148.

133 Rawcliffe, *Staffords*, p. 60.

134 NLW, Peniarth MS 280 D.

135 McFarlane, *Nobility of Later Medieval England*, pp. 224–5, and Rawcliffe, *Staffords*, p. 60–1.

136 Rawcliffe, ibid., p. 61.

137 This last section of my book owes much to various publications of the late Prof. W.G. Hoskins, especially to *The Age of Plunder. The England of Henry VIII, 1500–1547* (London, 1976), pp. 62–70.

138 Ibid., pp. 67–8.

139 Ibid., p. 66.

140 'Estate and household management in Bedfordshire, *c.* 1540', *Bedfordshire Historical Record Society*, 36 (1956), pp. 38–45. H.P.R. Finberg has published in the same volume (pp. 48–131) a more general account of 'The Gastwicks of Willington', of whom the man discussed by Dickens was the most eminent member. For Professor Dickens's article I am using the text reprinted in his *Reformation Studies*.

141 Dickens, ibid., p. 421.

142 Ibid., pp. 425–6.

SELECT BIBLIOGRAPHY

The bibliography consists mainly, but not entirely, of a selection of publications cited in this book. I have usually omitted works used for only a single topic, unless they are important. I have included also some publications not cited here but which I regard as particularly valuable and which have influenced my judgement. The works cited for the period before the fourteenth century are mainly connected with chapter 2, on serfdom.

I have not given a list of unpublished sources used. They consist mainly of manuscripts in the Public Record Office in London and the County Archive at Worcester. There is a valuable list of the latter in Christopher Dyer, *Lords and Peasants in the Changing Society: The Estates of the Bishopric of Worcester 680–1540* (Cambridge, 1980), pp. 391–4, though he has consulted more manuscripts than I have been able to see. I have used also some manuscripts at the National Library of Wales at Aberystwyth, at the British Library in London and at the Bursary Archive of Balliol College, Oxford. Lastly, there are materials on the wool trade from the Datini archive at Prato.

The bibliography of publications is divided as follows:

I   General (numbered consecutively for purposes of reference)
II   Legal
III   Demography and Economy
IV   Rural Society
V   Agriculture and Patterns of Settlement
VI   Depopulation and Enclosures
VII   Popular Revolts
VIII   Particular Regions
IX   Particular Estates and Landlords

I GENERAL

1   Aston, M., Austin, D., Dyer, C. (eds). *The Rural Settlement of Medieval England: Studies Dedicated to M. Beresford and J. Hurst* (Oxford, 1989)

2   Aston, T.H. et al. (eds). *Social Relations and Ideas: Essays in Honour of R. H. Hilton* (Oxford, 1983)

3   Bonnassie, P. *From Slavery to Feudalism in South-western Europe*, tr. Jean Birrell (Cambridge, 1991)

4   *[Cambridge] Agrarian History of England and Wales, The* vol. II: *1042–1350*, ed. H.E. Hallam (Cambridge, 1988)

5   *[Cambridge] Agrarian History of England and Wales, The* vol. III: *1348–1500*, ed. Edward Miller (Cambridge, 1991)

6   *[Cambridge] Agrarian History of England and Wales, The* vol. IV: *1500–1640*, ed. Joan Thirsk (Cambridge, 1967)

7 Carus-Wilson, E.M. *Essays in Economic History*, vol. I (London, 1954) and vol. II (London, 1962)

8 Coulton, G.C. *Medieval Village* (Cambridge, 1925)

9 Dickens, A.G. *Reformation Studies* (London, 1982)

10 Du Boulay F.R.H. and Barron C.M. (eds.) *The Reign of Richard II: Essays in Honour of May McKisack* (London, 1971)

11 Fryde, E.B. *Studies in Medieval Trade and Finance* (London, 1983)

12 Glasscock, R.E. *The Lay Subsidy of 1334* (London, 1975)

13 Goodman, A. *Military Activity and English Society, 1452–97* (London, 1981)

14 Griffiths, R.A. *The Reign of King Henry VI: The Exercise of Royal Authority, 1422–1461* (London, 1985)

15 Harvey P.D.A. (ed.). *The Peasant Land Market in Fifteenth-Century England* (Oxford, 1984) [See especially his 'Introduction' and 'Conclusion'.]

16 Harvey, Sally. 'The extent and profitability of demesne agriculture in England in the later eleventh century' in Aston (ed.), *Social Relations and Ideas* [item I.2, above]

17 —. 'Domesday England' in *[Cambridge] Agrarian History*, vol. II [item I.4, above]

18 Hilton, R.H. *The English Peasantry in the Later Middle Ages* (Oxford, 1975)

19 —. *Class Conflict and the Crisis of Feudalism: Essays in Medieval Social History* (London, 1985)

20 Holmes, George A. *The Estates of the Higher Nobility in the Fourteenth Century* (Cambridge, 1957)

21 Homans, G.C. *The English Villagers of the Thirteenth Century* (Cambridge, Mass., 1941)

22 Hoskins, W.G. *The Age of Plunder: The England of Henry VIII, 1500–1547* (London, 1976)

23 Kingsford, C.L. *English Historical Literature in the Fifteenth Century* (Oxford, 1913)

24 Lennard, R. *Rural England, 1086–1135: A Study of Social and Agrarian Conditions* (Oxford, 1959)

25 Lloyd, J.E.L. *Owen Glendower* (Oxford, 1931)

26 McFarlane, K.B. *The Nobility of Later Medieval England* (Oxford, 1973)

27 — *England in the Fifteenth Century, Collected Essays* (London, 1981)

28 McKisack, May. *The Fourteenth Century, 1307–1399* (Oxford History of England, vol. 4, Oxford, 1959)

29 Miller, E. and Hatcher, J. *Medieval England: Rural Society and Economic Change, 1086–1348* (London, 1978)

30 Poole, A.L. *Obligations of Society in XII and XIII Centuries* (Oxford, 1946)

31 Ross, C. *Edward IV* (London, 1974)

32 Savine, A. 'English monasteries on the eve of the Dissolution' in *Oxford Studies in Social and Legal History*, vol. I, ed. P. Vinogradoff (Oxford, 1909)

33 Storey, R.L. *The End of the House of Lancaster* (London, 1966)

II LEGAL

Ault, W.O. *Open-field Husbandry and the Village Community: A Study of Agrarian By-laws in Medieval England*, American Philosophical Society, ns, 55, no. 7 (Philadelphia, 1965)

Brooke, C.N.L. and Postan, M.M. (eds.). *Carte Nativorum: A Peterborough Abbey Cartulary of the Fourteenth Century*, Northamptonshire Record Society, 20 (Oxford, 1960)

Chrimes, S.B. *English Constitutional Ideas in the Fifteenth Century* (Cambridge, 1936)

Chapin-Furber, E. (ed.). *Essex Sessions of the Peace, 1351, 1377–79* (Essex Archaeological Society, Colchester, 1953)

Gray, C.M. *Copyhold, Equity and the Common Law* (Cambridge, Mass., 1963)

Hyams, P.R. 'The origins of a peasant land market in England', *EcHR*, 2nd ser., 23 (1970)

—. 'The action of Naifty in the early Common Law', *LQR*, 90 (1974)

—. 'The proof of villein status in the Common Law', *EHR*, 89 (1974)

—. *King, Lords and Peasants in Medieval England: The Common Law of Villeinage in the Twelfth and Thirteenth Centuries* (Oxford, 1980)

Kenyon, N. 'Labour conditions in Essex in the reign of Richard II', *EcHR*, 1st ser., 4 (1934), reprinted in Carus-Wison, (ed.), *Essays in Economic History*, vol. II [item I.7, above]

Milsom, S.F.C. *Historical Foundations of the Common Law* (London, 1969)

Maitland F.W. [Introduction to] *'The Mirror of Justices'* ed. W.J. Whittaker, Selden Society, 7 (London, 1893)

Plucknett, T.F.T. *Early English Legal Literature* (Cambridge, 1958)

Pollock, Sir Frederick and Maitland, F.W. *The History of English Law before the Time of Edward I*, 2 vols (2nd edn., Cambridge, 1897) [The section on the law of serfdom by F.W. Maitland.]

Putnam, B.H. 'The justices of labourers in the fourteenth century', *EHR*, 21 (1906)

—. *The Enforcement of the Statutes of Labourers during the First Decade after the Black Death, 1349–59* (New York, 1908)

—. 'The transformation of the keepers of the peace into the justices of the peace, 1327–1380', *TRHS*, 4th ser., 12 (1929)

— (ed.). *Proceedings before the Justices of the Peace in the Fourteenth and the Fifteenth Centuries* (Ames Foundation, London, 1938)

—. 'Chief Justice Shareshull and the economic and legal codes of 1351–52', *University of Toronto Law Journal*, 5 (1944)

Savine, A. 'Copyhold cases in the early chancery proceedings', *EHR*, 17 (1902)

Simpson, A.W.B. *An Introduction to the History of the Land Law* (Oxford, 1961)

Van Caenegem, R.C. *English Lawsuits from William I to Richard I*, 2 vols, Selden Society, 106–7 (London, 1990–1)

III DEMOGRAPHY AND ECONOMY

Bernard, G.W. *War, Taxation and Rebellion in Tudor England: Henry VIII, Wolsey and the Amicable Grant of 1525* (Brighton, 1986)

Blanchard, I. 'Population change, enclosure and early Tudor economy', *EcHR*, 2nd ser., 23 (1970)

Britnell, R.H. *The Commercialisation of English Society, 1000–1500* (Cambridge, 1993)

Campbell, B.M.S. 'The population of early Tudor England: a revaluation of the 1522 muster rolls and 1524–25 lay subsidies', *JHG*, 7 (1981)

—. 'Population pressure, inheritance and the land market in fourteenth-century England' in R.M. Smith (ed.), *Land, Kinship and Life-Cycle* (Cambridge, 1984)

— (ed.), *Before the Black Death: Studies in the Crisis of the Early Fourteenth Century* (Manchester, 1991) [See especially the introduction by Barbara Harvey.]

Carus-Wilson, E.M. 'Evidences of industrial growth on some fifteenth-century manors', *EcHR*, 2nd ser., 12 (1959), reprinted in Carus-Wilson (ed.), *Essays in Economic History*, vol. II [item I.7, above]

—. *The Expansion of Exeter at the Close of the Middle Ages* (Exeter, 1963)

— and Coleman, O. *England's Export Trade, 1275–1547* (Oxford, 1963)

Cornwall, J. 'English population in the early sixteenth century', *EcHR*, 2nd ser., 23 (1970)

Dobson, R.B. 'Urban decline in late medieval England', *TRHS*, 5th ser., 27 (1977)

Goring, J.J. 'The general proscription of 1522', *EHR*, 86 (1971)

Harvey, Barbara 'The population trend in England between 1300 and 1348', *TRHS*, 5th ser., 16 (1966)

Hatcher, J. *English Tin Production and Trade before 1550* (Oxford, 1973)

—. *Plague, Population and the English Economy, 1348–1500* (London, 1977)

—. 'Mortality in the fifteenth century: some new evidence', *EcHR*, 2nd ser., 39 (1986)

—. 'England in the aftermath of the Black Death', *Past and Present*, 144 (1994)

Heath, P. 'North Sea fishing in the fifteenth century: the Scarborough fleet', *Northern History*, 3 (1968)

Hoskins, W.G. 'English Provincial Towns in the early sixteenth century', *TRHS*, 5th ser., 6 (1956)

Kershaw, I. 'The great famine and agrarian crisis in England, 1315–22', *Past and Present*, 59 (1973)

Lloyd, T.H. *The Movement of Wool Prices in Medieval England*, Economic History Society, Supplementary Paper no. 6 (London, 1973)

Perroy, E. 'À l'origine d'une économie contractée: les crises du XIVᵉ siècle', *Annales, Économies, Sociétiés, Civilisations*, 4 (1949)

Phelps-Brown H. and Hopkins, Sheila V. *A Perspective of Wages and Prices* (London, 1981)

Phytian-Adams, C. *Desolation of a City: Coventry and the Urban Crisis of the Late Middle Ages* (Cambridge, 1979)

Pollard, A.J. 'The north-eastern economy and the agrarian crisis of 1438–40', *Northern History*, 25 (1989)

Postan, M.M. 'Some economic evidence of the declining population in the later Middle Ages', *EcHR*, 2nd ser., 2 (1950)

Power E. and Postan, M.M. (eds). *Studies in English Trade in the Fifteenth Century* (London, 1933)

Power, E. *The Wool Trade in English Medieval History* (Oxford, 1941)

Titow, J. 'Lost rents, vacant holdings and the contraction of peasant cultivation after the Black Death', *AgHR*, 42 (1994)

IV RURAL SOCIETY

Bailey, M. 'Rural society' in R. Horrox (ed.), *Fifteenth-Century Attitudes: Perceptions of Society in Late Medieval England* (Cambridge, 1994)

Dyer, C. 'Power and conflict in the medieval village' in Hooke (ed.), *Medieval Villages* [below]

—. 'English peasant buildings in the later Middle Ages', *Medieval Archaeology*, 30 (1986)

—. *Standards of Living in the later Middle Ages. Social Change in England, c. 1200–1500* (Cambridge, 1989)

Faith, R. 'Peasant families and inheritance customs in medieval England', *AgHR*, 14 (1966)

Field, R.K. 'Worcestershire peasant buildings, household goods and farming equipment in the later Middle Ages', *Medieval Archaeology*, 9 (1965)

Hatcher, J. 'English serfdom and villeinage: towards a reassessment', *Past and Present*, 90 (1981)

Hilton, R.H. 'Freedom and villeinage in England', *Past and Present*, 31 (1965)

—. *The Decline of Serfdom in Medieval England* (London, 1969)

Hooke, D. (ed.). *Medieval Villages* (Oxford, 1985)

Leadam, I.S. 'The last days of bondage in England', *LQR*, 9 (1893)

Razi, Z. 'Family, land and the village community in later medieval England', *Past and Present*, 93 (1981)

Rubin, R. 'The poor' in R. Horrox (ed.), *Fifteenth-Century Attitudes: Perceptions of Society in Late Medieval England* (Cambridge, 1994)

Savine, A. 'Bondmen under the Tudors', *TRHS*, ns, 17 (1903)

Smith, R.M. (ed.). *Land, Kinship and Life-Cycle* (Cambridge, 1984)

V AGRICULTURE AND PATTERNS OF SETTLEMENT

Bennett, H.S. 'The reeve and the manor in the fourteenth century', *EHR*, 41 (1926)

Brandon, P.F. 'Arable-farming in a Sussex scarp-foot parish during the late Middle Ages', *Sussex Archaeological Collections*, 100 (1962)

—. 'Demesne arable farming in coastal Sussex during the later Middle Ages', *AgHR*, 19 (1971)

—. 'Cereal yields on the Sussex estates of Battle Abbey during the later Middle Ages', *EcHR*, 2nd ser., 25 (1972)

Campbell, B.M.S. 'The regional uniqueness of English field systems? Some evidence from eastern Norfolk', *AgHR*, 29 (1981)

—. 'Agricultural progress in medieval England: some evidence from eastern Norfolk', *EcHR*, 2nd ser., 36 (1983)

Farmer, D.L. 'Grain yields on the Winchester manors in the later Middle Ages', *EcHR*, 2nd ser., 30 (1977)

Ford, W.J. 'Some settlement patterns in the central region of the Warwickshire Avon' in Sawyer (ed.), *Medieval Settlement* [below]

Fox, H.S.A. 'The people of the Wolds in early settlement history' in Aston, Austin, Dyer (eds), *Rural Settlement* [item I.1, above]

Fussell, G.E. 'Four centuries of Leicestershire farming' in W.G. Hoskins (ed.), *Studies in Leicestershire Agrarian History* (Leicester, 1949)

Homans, G.C. 'The explanation of English regional differences', *Past and Present*, 42 (1969)

Hooke, D. 'Preconquest estates in the West Midlands: preliminary thoughts', *JHG*, 8 (1982)

Hoskins, W.G. *The Making of the English Landscape: Leicestershire* (London, 1953)

—. *The Making of the English Landscape* (London, 1955)

Mate, M. 'Pastoral farming in south-east England in the fifteenth century', *EcHR*, 2nd ser., 40 (1987)

Millward R. and Robinson, A. *Landscapes of Britain: the West Midlands* (London, 1971)

Orwin, C.S. and C.S. *The Open Fields* (2nd edn., Oxford, 1954)

Plucknett, T.F.T. *The Medieval Bailiff* (London, 1954)

Rowley, Trevor (ed.). *The Origins of Open-Field Agriculture* (London, 1981)

Sawyer, P.H. (ed.). *Medieval Settlement, Continuity and Change* (London, 1976)

Thirsk, Joan. 'Industries in the countryside' in F.J. Fisher (ed.), *Essays in the Economic and Social History of Tudor and Stuart England in Honour of R.H. Tawney* (Cambridge, 1961)

—. 'The Common Fields', *Past and Present*, 29 (1964)

Sims-Williams, P. *Religion and Literature in Western England, 600–800* (Cambridge, 1990) [For patterns of early settlement.]

VI DEPOPULATION AND ENCLOSURES

Beresford, M.W. 'The deserted villages of Warwickshire', *Transactions of the Birmingham and Midlands Archaeological Society*, 66 (for 1945, published 1950)

—. *The Lost Villages of England* (London, 1954)

—, Allison, K.J. and Hurst, J.G. *The Deserted Villages of Northamptonshire* (Leicester, 1966)

Beresford M.W. and Hurst, J.G. *Deserted Medieval Villages: Studies* (London, 1971; new edn, Gloucester, 1989)

Dyer, C. 'The deserted medieval village of Woollashill', *Worcestershire Archaeological Society*, 3rd ser., I (1965–7)

—. 'Deserted medieval villages in the West Midlands, *EcHR*, 2nd ser., 35 (1982)

Gould, J. 'Mr. Beresford and the lost villages', *AgHR*, 3 (1955).

Hearne, T. (ed.). *Joannis Rossi* [John Rous's] *Antiquarii Warvicensis Historia Regum Angliae* (2nd edn, Oxford, 1745)

Hilton, R.H. 'A study in the pre-history of English enclosure in the fifteenth century' (1957), reprinted in *idem, English Peasantry*. [Item I.18, above]

Hoskins, W.G. (ed.). *Studies in Leicestershire Agrarian History* (Leicester, 1949) [introduction by Hoskins]

—. 'Galby and Frisby' and 'The deserted villages of Leicestershire' in *Essays in Leicestershire History* (Liverpool, 1950)

—. 'Seven deserted villages in Leicestershire', *Transactions of the Leicestershire Archaeological and Historical Society*, 33 (1956)

—. *The Midland Peasant: The Economic and Social History of a Leicestershire Village* [Wigston Magna] (London, 1957)

Kendrick, T.D. *British Antiquity* (London, 1950) [account of John Rous]

Kerridge, E. 'The returns of the inquisitions of depopulation', *EHR*, 70 (1955)

—. *Agrarian Problems in the Sixteenth Century and After* (London, 1966)

Lamond, E. (ed.). *A Discourse of the Common Weal of this Realm of England* (Cambridge, 1893) [Written probably in 1549, published in 1581]

Leadam, I.S. 'The inquisition of 1517: inclosures and evictions', *TRHS*, ns, 6–8 (1892–4), 14 (1900)

— (ed.). *The Domesday of Inclosures, 1517–18*, 2 vols (Royal Historical Society, London, 1897)

Lloyd, T.H. 'Some documentary sidelights on the deserted Oxfordshire village of Brookend', *Oxoniensia*, 29–30 (1964–5)

Martin, J. 'Enclosure and the inquisitions of depopulation of 1607: an examination of Dr. Kerridge's article . . .' *AgHR*, 30 (1982) [concerning Kerridge, 1955 [above])

Parker, L.A. 'The agrarian revolution at Cotesbach, 1501–1612' in Hoskins, *Studies in Leicestershire Agrarian History* [above]

Richmond, C. 'The transition from feudalism to capitalism in the archives of Magdalen College, Oxford: a note', *History Workshop Journal*, 37 (1994)

Tate, W.E. 'Enclosure acts and awards relating to Warwickshire', *Transactions and Proceedings of Birmingham Archaeological Society*, 65 (for 1943/4, published 1949)

Tawney, R.H. *The Agrarian Problem in the Sixteenth Century* (London, 1912; new edn, New York, 1967, with an introduction by L. Stone) [See also T.S. Ashton, 'R.H. Tawney, 1880–1962', *Proceedings of the British Academy*, 48 (1962)]

Thirsk, Joan. 'Agrarian History, 1540–1950' in *VCH: Leics.*, vol. II (1954)

—. *Tudor Enclosures*, Historical Association, general ser., 41 (London, 1959)

Thorpe, H. 'The lord and the landscape', *Birmingham Archaeological Society*, 80 (1965), reprinted in D.R. Mills (ed.), *English Rural Communities: The Impact of a Specialized Economy* (London, 1973)

Villages Désertés et Histoire Economique, XIᵉ–XVIIIᵉ Siècle (S.E.V.P.E.N., Paris, 1965)

VII POPULAR REVOLTS

'Anonimalle Chronicle', 1333–1381, The, ed. V.H. Galbraith (Manchester, 1927)

Aston, M.E. 'Lollardy and sedition, 1381–1431', *Past and Present*, 57 (1960)

Bindoff, S.T. *Ket's Rebellion*, Historical Association, general ser., 12 (London, 1949)

Brooks, N. 'The organization and achievements of the peasants in Kent and Essex in 1381' in H. Mayr-Harting and R.I. Moore (eds), *Studies in Medieval History presented to R.H.C. Davis* (London, 1985)

Dickens, A.G. 'Secular and religious motivation in the Pilgrimage of Grace' (1967) reprinted in Dickens, *Reformation Studies* [item I.9, above]

Dobson, R.B. (ed.). *The Peasants' Revolt of 1381* (London, 1970)

Dodds, M.H. and R. *The Pilgrimage of Grace, 1536–37 and the Exeter Conspiracy, 1538*, 2 vols (Cambridge, 1915)

Dyer, C. 'A redistribution of incomes in fifteenth-century England', *Past and Present*, 39 (1968)

—. 'The social and economic background to the rural revolt of 1381' in Hilton and Aston (eds), *The English Rising* [below]

Faith, R. 'The "Great Rumour" of 1377 and peasant ideology', in Hilton and Aston (eds), *The English Rising* [below]

Fryde, E.B. *The Great Revolt of 1381*, Historical Association, general ser., 100 (London, 1981)

—. 'Peasant rebellion and peasant discontents' in *[Cambridge] Agrarian History*, vol. III [item I.5, above]

Galbraith, V.H. 'Thoughts about the Peasants' Revolt' in Du Boulay and Barron (eds), *Reign of Richard II* [item I.10, above]

Gay, E.F. 'The Midland Revolt and the inquisitions of depopulation, 1607', *TRHS*, ns, 18 (1904)

Harding, A. 'The revolt against the justices' in Hilton and Aston (eds), *The English Rising* [below]

Hare, J.N. 'The Wiltshire rising of 1450: political and economic discontent in fifteenth-century England', *Southern History*, 4 (1982)

Harvey, Barbara. 'Draft letters of manumission and pardon for the men of Somerset in 1381', *EHR*, 80 (1965)

Harvey, Isobel *Jack Cade's Rebellion of 1450* (Oxford, 1991)

Hilton, R.H. 'Peasant movements in England before 1381', *EcHR*, 2nd ser., 2 (1949), reprinted in Carus-Wilson, (ed.), *Essays in Economic History*, vol. II (item I.7, above]

—. *Bond Men Made Free: Medieval Peasant Movements and the English Rising of 1381* (London, 1973)

— and Aston, T.H. (eds). *The English Rising of 1381* (Cambridge, 1984)

Macaulay, G.C. (ed.). *The Complete Works of John Gower*, 4 vols (Oxford, 1899–1902)

MacCulloch, D. 'Ket's Rebellion in context', *Past and Present*, 84 (1979)

Manning, R.B. *Village Revolts, Social Protest and Popular Disturbances in England, 1509–1640* (Oxford, 1988)

Mate, M. 'The economic and social roots of medieval popular rebellion in Sussex in 1450–51', *EcHR*, 2nd ser., 45 (1992)

Oman, C. *The Great Revolt of 1381* (2nd edn., revised by E.B. Fryde, Oxford, 1969)

Powell, E. *The Rising in East Anglia in 1381* (Cambridge, 1896)

Razi, Z. 'The struggles between the Abbot of Halesowen and his tenants' in Aston et al. (eds), *Social Relations* [item I.2, above]

Réville A. *Le Soulèvement des Travailleurs d'Angleterre en 1381*, ed. C. Petit-Dutaillis (Paris, 1898)

Roskell, J.S. 'Sir Richard Waldegrave of Bures St. Mary, Speaker in the Parliament of 1381–82', *Proceedings of the Suffolk Institute of Archaeology*, 27 (1957)

Taylor, J. *English Historical Literature in the Fourteenth Century* (Oxford, 1987) [Appendix V, 'Chronicle accounts of the Peasants' Revolt']

Tuck, J.A. 'Nobles, Commons and the Great Revolt of 1381' in Hilton and Aston (eds), *The English Rising* [above]

Wilkinson, B. 'The Peasants' Revolt in 1381', *Speculum*, 15 (1940)

VIII PARTICULAR REGIONS

Birrell, Jean R. 'The forest economy of the Honour of Tutbury in the fourteenth and fifteenth centuries', *University of Birmingham Historical Journal*, 8 (1962)

—. 'Medieval agriculture' in *VCH: Staffs.*, vol. VI (1979)

Dyer, C. *Warwickshire Farming, c. 1349–1520*: Preparations for Agricultural Revolution, *Dugdale Society Occasional Paper*, 27 (Oxford, 1981)

Faith, R. 'Berkshire: fourteenth and fifteenth centuries' in Harvey (ed.) *Peasant Land Market* [item I.15 above]

Finberg, H.P.R. and Hoskins, W.G. *Devonshire Studies* (London, 1952)

Hare, J.N. 'Lord and Tenant in Wiltshire, c. 1380–c. 1520' (Unpublished Ph.D. thesis, University of London, 1975)

—. 'The demesne lessees of fifteenth-century Wiltshire', *AgHR*, 29 (1981)

—. 'Change and continuity in Wiltshire agriculture in the late Middle Ages' in W. Minchinton (ed.), *Agricultural Improvement, Medieval and Modern* (Exeter, 1981)

—. 'The monks as landlords: the leasing of the monastic demesnes in southern England' in C.M. Barron and C. Harper-Bill (eds), *The Church in Pre-Reformation Society: Essays in Honour of F.R.H. Du Boulay* (Woodbridge, 1985)

—. 'The lords and their tenants. Conflict and stability in fifteenth-century Wiltshire' in B. Stapleton (ed.), *Conflict and Community in Southern England* (Stroud, 1992)

Hilton, R.H. *The Economic Development of Some Leicestershire Estates in the Fourteenth and Fifteenth Centuries* (London, 1947)

—. 'Medieval Agrarian History' in *VCH: Leics.*, vol. II (London, 1954)

—. *A Medieval Society: The West Midlands at the End of the Thirteenth Century* (London, 1966)

Hoyle, R.W. 'Lords, tenants and Tenant Right in the sixteenth century: four studies', *Northern History*, 20 (1984)

—. 'An ancient and laudable custom: the definition and development of Tenant Right in north-western England in the sixteenth century', *Past and Present*, 116 (1987)

James, M.E. *Change and Continuity in the Tudor North: The Rise of Thomas, First Lord Wharton*, Borthwick Institute Paper, 27 (York, 1965)

—. 'The concept of order and the Northern Rising of 1569', *Past and Present*, 60 (1973)

Jones, Andrew 'Bedfordshire: fifteenth century' in Harvey (ed.), *Peasant Land Market* [item I.15, above]

Kettle, Ann J. 'Agriculture, 1300–1540' in *VCH: Salop*, vol. IV (London, 1989)

Lomas, T. 'South-east Durham: late fourteenth and fifteenth centuries' in Harvey (ed.), *Peasant Land Market* [item I.15 above]

Pollard, A.J. *North-Eastern England during the Wars of the Roses: Lay Society, War and Politics, 1450–1500* (Oxford, 1990)

Wright, S.M. *The Derbyshire Gentry in the Fifteenth Century*, Derbyshire Record Society, 8 (Chesterfield, 1983)

IX PARTICULAR ESTATES AND LANDLORDS

Alcock, N.W. (ed.). *Warwickshire Grazier and London Skinner, 1532–1555: The Account Book of Peter Temple and Thomas Heritage*, British Academy Records of Social and Economic History, ns, IV, (London, 1981)

Archer, R.E. 'The estates and finances of Margaret of Brotherton, *c.* 1320–1399' [Countess and later Duchess of Norfolk], *Historical Research*, 60 (1987)

Bannister, A.T. 'Manorial customs on the Hereford bishopric estates', *EHR*, 43 (1928)

Bean, J.M.W. *The Estates of the Percy Family, 1417–1537* (Oxford, 1958)

Bennett, H.S. *The Pastons and their England* (Cambridge, 1951)

Brent, J.A. 'Alciston manor in the later Middle Ages' [estate of Battle Abbey], *Sussex Archaeological Collections*, 106 (1968)

Britnell, R.H. 'Production for the market on a small fourteenth-century estate' [Langenhoe, Essex], *EcHR*, 2nd ser., 19 (1966)

—. 'The Pastons and their Norfolk', *AgHR*, 36 (1988)

—. 'Feudal reaction after the Black Death in the Palatinate of Durham', *Past and Present*, 128 (1990)

Davenport, F.G. 'The decay of villeinage in East Anglia' *(1900)*, reprinted in *Carus-Wilson (ed.), Essays in Economic History*, vol. II [item I.7, above]

—. *The Economic Development of a Norfolk Manor [Forncett]: 1086–1565* (Cambridge, 1906)

Davis, N. (ed.). *The Paston Letters and other Letters and Papers of the Fifteenth Century*, 2 vols (Oxford, 1971–6)

Dewindt, E.B. (ed.). *The 'Liber Gersumarum' of Ramsey Abbey: A Calendar and Index* (Toronto, 1976)

Dickens, A.G. 'Estate and household management in Bedfordshire, *c. 1540*' *(1956)*, reprinted in idem, *Reformation Studies* [item I.9, above]

Dobson, R.B. *Durham Priory, 1400–1450* (Cambridge, 1973)

Du Boulay, F.R.H. 'Late continued demesne farming at Otford', *Archaeologia Cantiana*, 73 (1959)

—. 'A rentier economy in the later Middle Ages: The Archbishopric of Canterbury', *EcHR*, 2nd ser., 16 (1964)

—. 'Who were farming the English demesnes at the end of the Middle Ages?', *EcHR*, 2nd ser., 17(1965)

—. *The Lordship of Canterbury: An Essay on Medieval Society* (London, 1966)

Dyer, C. 'Population and agriculture on a Warwickshire manor in the later Middle Ages' [Hampton Lucy and Hatton], *University of Birmingham Historical Journal*, 11 (1968)

—. 'A small landowner in the fifteenth century' [John Brome of Warwickshire], *Midland History*, 1 (1972)

—. *Lords and Peasants in a Changing Society: The Estates of the Bishopric of Worcester, 680–1540* (Cambridge, 1980)

—. *Hanbury: Settlement and Society in a Woodland Landscape* (Leicester, 1991)

—. 'Were there any capitalists in fifteenth-century England?' *[Roger Heritage] in J. Kermode (ed.), Enterprise and Individuals in Fifteenth-Century England* (Stroud, 1991)

Finberg, H.P.R. *Tavistock Abbey: A Study in the Social and Economic History of Devon* (Cambridge, 1951)

Finch, M.E. *The Wealth of Five Northamptonshire Families, 1540–1640, Northamptonshire Record Society, 19* (for 1955, published Oxford, 1956)

Fryde, E.B. 'The tenants of the Bishops of Coventry and Lichfield and of Worcester after the plague of 1348–49' in *R.F. Hunnisett and J.B. Post (eds.), Medieval Legal Records edited in Memory of C.A.F. Meekings* (London, 1978)

Gras N.S.B. and Gras, E.C. *The Economic and Social History of an English Village: Crawley, Hampshire, AD 909–1928* (Cambridge, Mass., 1930)

Halcrow, E.M. 'The decline of demesne farming on the estates of Durham Cathedral Priory', *EcHR*, 2nd ser., 7 (1955)

Harris, B.J. 'The Buckingham estates', *Past and Present*, 43 (1969)

Harvey, Barbara. *[Histories of Islip and of Launton in] VCH: Oxon*, vol. VI (Oxford, 1959)

— (ed.). *The Custumal and the Bye-Laws of the Manor of Islip* [Oxon.], Oxfordshire Record Society, 40 (1959)

—. 'The leasing of the Abbot of Westminter's demesnes in the later Middle Ages', *EcHR*, 2nd ser., 22 (1969)

—. *Westminster Abbey and its Estates in the Middle Ages* (Oxford, 1977)

Hatcher, J. 'A diversified economy: later medieval Cornwall', *EcHR*, 2nd ser., 22 (1969)

—. *Rural Economy and Society in the Duchy of Cornwall, 1300–1500* (Cambridge, 1970)

—. 'Non-manorialism in medieval Cornwall', *AgHR*, 18 (1970)

—. 'Myths, miners and agricultural communities', *AgHR*, 18 (1970)

Hollings, M. (ed.). *The Red Book of Worcester* [Bishopric], 1 vol. in 4 parts (Worcestershire Historical Soc., Worcester, 1934–50)

Howell, C. *Land, Family and Inheritance in Transition: Kibworth Harcourt* [Leic.] *1260–1700* (Cambridge, 1983)

Jack, R.I. (ed.). *The Grey of Ruthin Valor: The Valor of the English Lands of Edmund Grey, Earl of Kent, drawn up from the Ministers' Accounts of 1467–68*, (Sydney, 1965)

Jones, M.K. and Underwood, M.G. *The King's Mother: Lady Margaret Beaufort, Countess of Richmond and Derby* (Cambridge, 1992)

King, E. *Peterborough Abbey, 1086–1310* (Cambridge, 1973)

Levett, A.E. *Studies in Manorial History* [estates of the Abbey of St Albans] (Oxford, 1938)

Lomas, R.A. 'Developments in land tenure on the Prior of Durham's estate in the later Middle Ages', *Northern History*, 13 (1977)

—. 'The Priory of Durham and its demesnes in the fourteenth and fifteenth centuries', *EcHR*, 2nd ser., 31 (1978)

McIntosh, M.K. *Autonomy and Community: The Royal Manor of Havering, 1200–1500* (Cambridge, 1986)

Maitland, F.W. 'The history of a Cambridgeshire manor' [Wilburton, Ely's property], *EHR*, 9 (1894), reprinted in H.M. Cam (ed.), *Selected Historical Essays of F.W. Maitland* (Cambridge, 1957)

Miller, E. *The Abbey and Bishopric of Ely* (Cambridge, 1951)

Moreton, C.E. *The Townshends and their World: Gentry, Law and Land in Norfolk, c. 1450–1551* (Oxford, 1992)

Newton, K.C. *Thaxted in the Fourteenth Century* (Chelmsford, 1960)

Page, F.M. *The Estates of Crowland Abbey* (Cambridge, 1934)

Pollard, A.J. 'Estate management in the later Middle Ages: the Talbots and Whitchurch, 1383–1525', *EcHR*, 2nd ser., 25 (1972)

Raftis, J.A. *The Estates of Ramsey Abbey* (Toronto, 1957)

—. *Tenure and Mobility: Studies in the Social History of the Mediaeval English Village* [estates of Ramsey] (Toronto, 1964)

—. 'Changes in an English village after the Black Death' [Upwood, Hunts.], *Mediaeval Studies* (Toronto), 29 (1967)

—. *Warboys: Two Hundred Years in the Life of an English Mediaeval Village* (Toronto, 1974)

Rawcliffe, C. *The Staffords, Earls of Stafford and Dukes of Buckingham, 1394–1521* (Cambridge, 1978)

Richmond, C. *John Hopton: A Fifteenth-Century Suffolk Gentleman* (Cambridge, 1981)

—. *The Paston Family in the Fifteenth Century: The First Phase* (Cambridge, 1990)

—. 'Landlord and tenant: the Paston evidence' in J. Kermode (ed.), *Enterprise and Individuals in Fifteenth-Century England* (Stroud, 1991)

Searle, E. and Ross, Barbara (eds), *Accounts of the Cellarers of Battle Abbey, 1275–1513* (Sydney, 1967)

Searle, E. *Lordship and Community: Battle Abbey and its Banlieu* (Toronto, 1974)

Smith, Llinos O.W. 'The Lordships of Chirk and Oswestry, 1281–1415' (Unpublished Ph.D. thesis, University of London, 1970)

Smith, R.A.L. *Canterbury Cathedral Priory* (Cambridge, 1943)

Spufford, Margaret. *A Cambridgeshire Community: Chippenham from Settlement to Enclosure* (Leicester, 1965)

Storey, R.L. *Thomas Langley and the Bishopric of Durham, 1405–1437* (London, 1961)

INDEX OF PEOPLE AND PLACES

SUBJECT INDEX